ARIOSTO IN THE MACHINE AGE

Ariosto in the Machine Age

ALESSANDRO GIAMMEI

UNIVERSITY OF TORONTO PRESS
Toronto Buffalo London

Toronto Buffalo London
utorontopress.com

ISBN 978-1-4875-4679-3 (cloth)
ISBN 978-1-4875-4680-9 (EPUB)
ISBN 978-1-4875-4681-6 (PDF)

Toronto Italian Studies

Library and Archives Canada Cataloguing in Publication

Title: Ariosto in the machine age / Alessandro Giammei.
Names: Giammei, Alessandro, 1988– author.
Series: Toronto Italian studies.
Description: Series statement: Toronto Italian studies | Includes bibliographical references and index.
Identifiers: Canadiana (print) 20230444431 | Canadiana (ebook) 20230444571 | ISBN 9781487546793 (cloth) | ISBN 9781487546816 (PDF) | ISBN 9781487546809 (EPUB)
Subjects: LCSH: Ariosto, Lodovico, 1474–1533 – Influence. | LCSH: Ariosto, Lodovico, 1474–1533 – Criticism and interpretation. | LCSH: Art and literature – Italy – History – 20th century. | LCSH: Motion pictures and literature – Italy – History – 20th century.
Classification: LCC PQ4598.A2 G53 2024 | DDC 851/.3 – dc23

Cover design: Val Cooke
Cover image: Giorgio de Chirico, *Il grande metafisico*, 1917, oil on canvas, photo © Christie's Images / Bridgeman Images

We wish to acknowledge the land on which the University of Toronto Press operates. This land is the traditional territory of the Wendat, the Anishnaabeg, the Haudenosaunee, the Métis, and the Mississaugas of the Credit First Nation.

This book has been published with the assistance of the Department of Italian Studies at Yale University and the Frederick W. Hilles Publication Fund of Yale University.

University of Toronto Press acknowledges the financial support of the Government of Canada, the Canada Council for the Arts, and the Ontario Arts Council, an agency of the Government of Ontario, for its publishing activities.

Canada Council for the Arts
Conseil des Arts du Canada

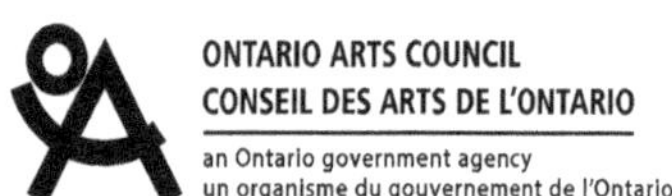

Funded by the Government of Canada
Financé par le gouvernement du Canada

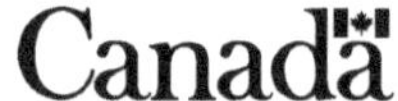

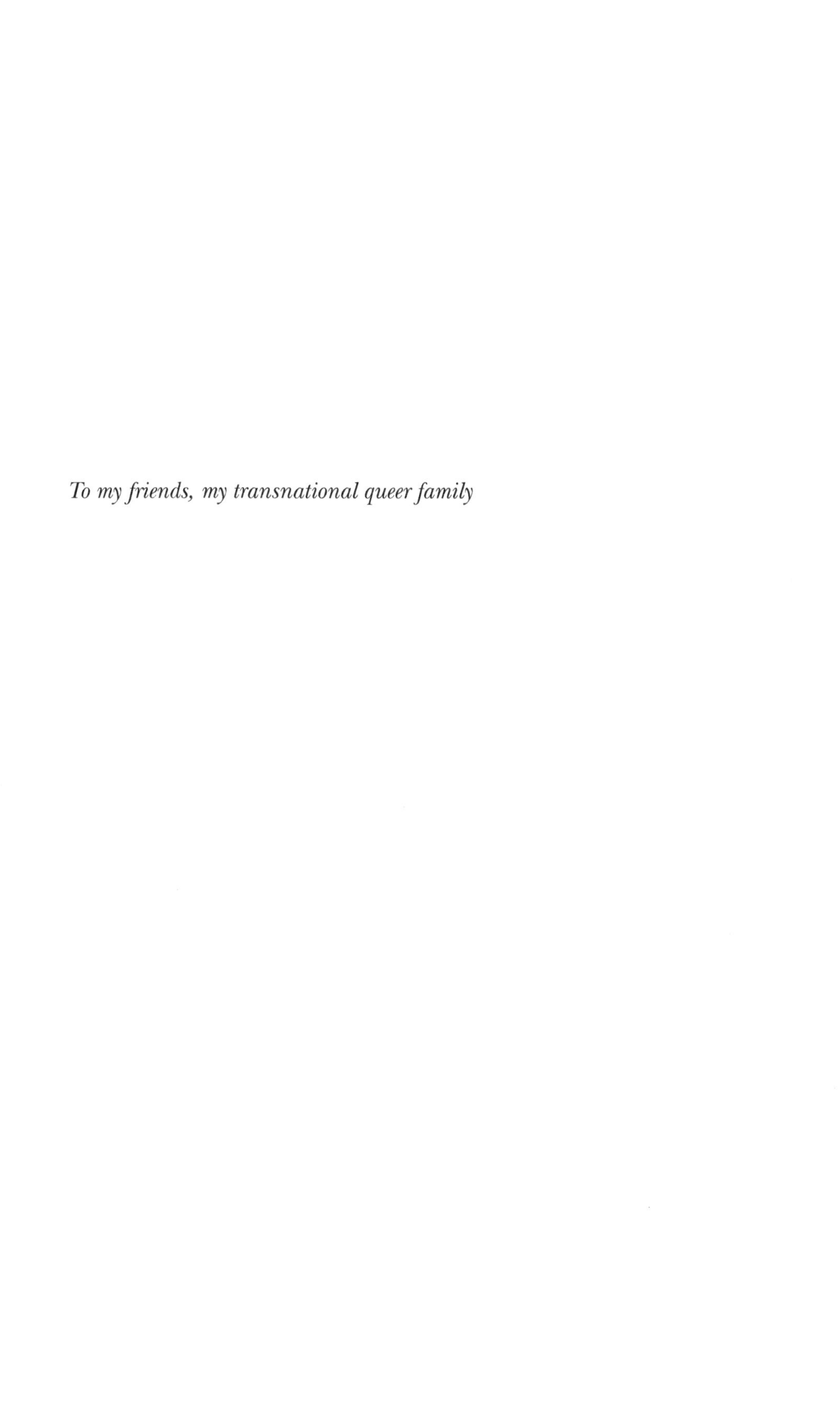

To my friends, my transnational queer family

Contents

Illustrations

Preface

Before this book begins, I shall offer a brief explanation of what I mean by its title. I owe this explanation, in particular, to my fellow "Ariosto scholars," so to speak, and to those who study the arts, literatures, and histories of Italophone modernisms. I wrote *Ariosto in the Machine Age* imagining an interlocutor beyond my own linguistic, cultural, and disciplinary background, so the Introduction that follows these few pages should serve as the primary point of access for most readers. This Preface, on the other hand, is a threshold that I am offering specifically to those who share my supposed field of inquiry: what we call "Italian Studies."

I should start by saying that this is not a study of Ludovico Ariosto as a biographical, historical figure. When I say "Ariosto" here, I am not really making claims about a sixteenth-century man. On the contrary, I am convoking a cultural myth generated by the disparate symbolic needs of five centuries of European reception of the Italian Renaissance. As a matter of fact, this book intends to challenge the passive, automatic undertones of these very words, "re-ception" and "Re-naissance." It proposes an alternative perspective (and methodology) to look at the prismatic modern afterlives of authors considered, like Ariosto, classical, canonical, foundational. That is why most of the stories collected in its four chapters are not examples of direct intertextuality, citation, and visualization. Rather than focusing on more traditional instances of genealogical reception of Ariosto's work in twentieth-century culture (such as Italo Calvino's rewritings of, and essays on, the *Orlando Furioso*, Fabrizio Clerici's illustrations, Odilon Redon's iconographies based on its most famous episodes, or Luca Ronconi's theatrical and cinematic adaptations of its plots), this book reveals the repressed presence – or the forced revival – of Ariosto's ghost in the most significant phenomena of late modern Italophone culture.

The first chapter shows that Ariosto's monument in Ferrara, as a marmoreal spectre with its own necromantic agency, had a spiritual and aesthetic influence over avant-garde artists and writers – and shaped, in particular, the destiny of Metaphysical painting. The second chapter reconstructs the rich trans-historical dialogue between Ariosto's "spirit" and Massimo Bontempelli, the author who coined the term "Magical Realism" in literature. The third chapter reveals the appropriations and abuses of Ariosto's words, bones, physical features, places, biological descendants, and cultural legacies perpetrated by fascist intellectuals – and it advocates for a rethinking of how we still celebrate mythologized pasts and their iconic figures. The fourth and last chapter tells the story of how the *Orlando Furioso*, despite attempts by Luchino Visconti, Alessandro Blasetti, and Federico Fellini, was never adapted for the stage or the screen before Ronconi's and Sanguineti's experimental theatrical rewriting (or *travestimento*) in 1969.

It is crucial to underline that, even for cultivated readers such as modern poets, painters, politicians, and filmmakers, Ariosto's intermedia and trans-historical afterlife may have been more familiar, more meaningful and generative, than the letter of his actual texts. As I will illustrate more thoroughly in the Introduction, derivative works of art and literature have been diffracting the posthumous diffusion of the *Orlando Furioso* in particular, making it possible (if not typical) to love and appreciate Ariosto's work without ever having read his poem cover to cover. Ariosto's posthumous life has been a vital polyphony, largely independent from the discernible intentions of any single author – especially those of Ariosto himself. Its irreducible plurality and vastness mirrors that of the plot of the *Furioso*. This book may be read as a chapter in a ghost story: the story of how Ariosto acclimated in all the ages and arts of the past five centuries. For reasons that have to do with conventional disciplinary and historical boundaries, it is a chapter that was never written before.

Because of its richness and fractal articulation, Ariosto's reception (what Italianists call *fortuna*, what I am describing as an afterlife) has progressively informed an autonomous node of research across academic fields, languages, and historical periods. Studies abound around various combinations of such variables: Ariosto in early modern French art, Ariosto in Elizabethan England, Ariosto in German philosophy, Ariosto in modern Latin American fiction, Ariosto in Anglophone popular culture, and so on. These studies, when looked at synoptically, form a line of constantly generative influence, especially in Europe. However, the line fades between chronological limits that one may define as the end of Romanticism and the beginning of postmodernity. Between Delacroix and Calvino, Lord Byron and Salman Rushdie, Ingres and Borges, Ariosto's afterlife appears to be relegated, for the most part, to the erudition of modern scholars such as Ida Wyss, Benedetto Croce, Edmund Gardner, and Henri Hauvette. Filling this chronological gap across media and arts is a collateral result of the methodological approach that this book adopts.

In order to see Ariosto's ghost between the end of the nineteenth century and the end of the Second World War, one needs to renounce traditional definitions of the zeitgeist of that era in Europe. I decided to call that age, retrieving an out-of-fashion term rooted in cultural and economic history, the Machine Age. I wanted to allude to a specific chronological span, centred in the interwar period. I wanted to do so through a term that was intuitively understandable but somewhat unfamiliar. I wanted to link Ariosto's presence in late modernity with technological innovations that have to do with the industrial reproducibility of art and literature, with warfare, and with the dissemination of political ideas. Similar innovations characterized Ariosto's own age, and are featured in his works. Machines, from arquebuses to printing presses, were crucial for the political and editorial context in which he operated too. That may be part of the reason why the protagonists of this book, in different ways, all considered Ariosto their contemporary in the Machine Age.

I adopted this formula, "the Machine Age," also because I did not want to frame my object of study into a terminology that would intrinsically marginalize it. This book about modernism does not reclaim the role of Ariosto in the development of modernism. Nor does it simply extend what has been done for other centuries, in the study of Ariosto's reception within specific disciplines, to the first half of the twentieth. On the contrary, this is a book that challenges traditional accounts of modernism, and uses the early twentieth century to propose a different posthumous approach to the intermedia afterlife of canonical literary myths.

Ariosto, after all, is not a myth of modernism per se, if by this term we mean a Franco- and Anglo-centric movement primarily concerned with disruption. Ariosto was not an idol of the avant-gardes if we buy into their rhetoric of uncompromising absolutes, nor was he particularly dear to modern academic artists who resisted change and advocated for a return to order. Yet, in the Machine Age, Ariosto provided a model for putting into practice key modernist paradigms: montage, meta-narration, mythopoeia. And Virginia Woolf chose Orlando to name her most haunted and metamorphic character: the protagonist of a satire suspended between high literature and popular success, an irreducibly double novel.

Because of its doubleness and diffracted evolution (what in the Introduction I will frame as Ariosto's amphibology, proposing to queer our understanding of his unsolvable contradictions), vanguardists and traditionalists were able to simultaneously mirror themselves in Ariosto's afterlife. The late modern Italy that emerges from this book, torn between cosmopolitan Paris and fascist Rome, can only be invoked as a collage to be philologically interpreted. It requires a gaze directed on the unlikely intersections of movements and trends. And directed, as I mentioned, beyond direct cases of literary tribute, visualization, and citation.

All the conjurings of Ariosto's ghost reconstructed in this book were, in fact, creatively imprecise: out of focus in the lens of a traditional study of reception. It is not surprising that, in the indexes of books that discuss the artists and movements featured here, Ariosto's name is consistently absent or marginal. Metaphysical artists encountered Ariosto almost by chance, and painted or described him without tapping into the *Furioso*'s iconography. Famously inspired by Metaphysical art, Bontempelli founded Magical Realism by asking Ariosto for literary gifts and by imitating his style and structures. He directly cited him only when he had to defend his own poetics from the criticism of fellow fascist intellectuals. Ferrarese fascists, in 1933, intended to make Ariosto present in their city, adopting a rhetoric and a philosophy of history disturbingly similar to those that inform current centennial celebrations, re-enactments, and exhibitions of the past. The only direct exercise of literal reception explored in this book is that of adaptation, attempted between experimental theatre and commercial cinema in the era of neorealism. It is no coincidence that such exercises invariably failed throughout the Machine Age.

Some of the ideas, techniques, and stylistic choices that the protagonists of this book attributed to Ariosto's influence were arguably conceived by other, earlier authors such as Matteo Maria Boiardo, or were already present in classical and medieval epic, from the *Aeneid* to the *Chanson de Roland.* However, my goal here is not that of correcting a literary genealogy, or establishing a chronological primacy. Rather than unearthing a pristine, original Ariosto, I am looking holistically (simultaneously, synoptically) at the constitutively unoriginal Ariosto that results from a stratigraphy of appropriations. While Ariosto's case is particularly conducive to such an approach, I believe that the same methodology would prove revealing if applied to other figures whose afterlives produced a similarly powerful and consequential mythology.

This is, I hope, a book about how to deal with any monumental, impervious, or elusive legacy from the past. I wrote it in search of a dialogue with anyone who thinks critically about how we simplify or fetishize, appropriate or venerate, those texts and images that, we are told, built our identity – be it a national, ethnic, aesthetic, or poetic declension of what we call "identity." It is also to decolonize my mind from such concepts that I decided to publish *Ariosto in the Machine* in English, an acquired language that, admittedly, I do not fully govern.

In the following pages, quotes from the *Orlando Furioso* come from Cesare Segre's edition (Milan: Mondadori, 1964) and Barbara Reynolds' translation (London: Penguin Classics, 1975). When not specified otherwise, all translations are my own.

Acknowledgments

In my favourite line from the *Orlando Furioso*, Ariosto reminds us that "Chi va lontan da la sua patria, vede." At the end of this journey, started in Italy and in Italian and concluded in English on the other side of the Atlantic, I am not sure where my "patria" is anymore. If anywhere, it must be in what I learned from the incredible women who have mentored me across the transformations that this book went through over the years. Lina Bolzoni, in Pisa, initiated me into early modern studies and invited me to be more ambitious, more curious, and happier when it comes to my work as a scholar. I am grateful for her guidance and her friendship. Jane Tylus, first in Pisa and then in New York (and now in New Haven!), was the first to show me how to make this book – and myself – a pilgrim between different academic cultures, in a permanent state of translation. In Princeton, Susan Stewart and Mary Harper empowered me to make my work on Ariosto's afterlife more transnational, trans-historical, and trans-disciplinary, while Gaetana Marrone kept it in dialogue with the field of Italian Studies. Roberta Ricci, in and around Philadelphia (and in the intangible land of countless phone calls and Zoom meetings), gave me the material, intellectual, and emotional support that I needed to keep on writing while learning, through her model, how to be a professor – even in the midst of a global pandemic. Without these generous *maestre*, I would not be in the number of those who went *lontano* – and this book would not exist.

Nicholas Terpstra, Lindsay Waters, and Luca Somigli believed in my manuscript and helped me find a home for it. I am grateful to the University of Toronto Press for their excellent work, and in particular to my editors, Mark Thompson and Janice Evans, and the three anonymous referees whose generous reviews greatly encouraged me and improved the book. I am also grateful to Tere Claire Mullin and Judy Williams for their editorial help. Part of Chapter 1 was published in "Ariosto, the Great

Metaphysician," *Modern Language Notes* 132.1 (2017): 135–62. Some ideas in Chapter 2 were already explored in "Prime note su una genealogia: Ariosto & Galileo in Pirandello, Bontempelli, Calvino," *il verri* 57 (2015): 57–77. I thank the journals' editors and reviewers for their feedback.

Several fellowships and grants supported the research that informs *Ariosto in the Machine Age*, as well as its material realization: a Borsa di perfezionamento and a Borsa di scambio from Scuola Normale Superiore, and a Cotsen Postdoctoral Fellowship and a William Hallum Tuck '12 Memorial Fund Award from Princeton University, as well as a start-up fund from Bryn Mawr College. I thank Kathryn Lofton, the Office of the Dean of the Humanities, and the Frederick W. Hilles Publication Fund at Yale University for providing me with crucial subventions for the iconographic apparatus and production costs. I am also grateful to the institutions that gave me access to their collections and archives: the Archivio Storico Comunale di Ferrara, Palazzo Schifanoia and Casa di Ludovico Ariosto (Musei Civici di Arte Antica), the emeroteca and special collections funds at the Biblioteca Comunale Ariostea, the Archivio Storico della Regione Emilia Romagna, the Archivio Alinari in Florence, the Archivio Alessandro Blasetti at the Cineteca di Bologna, the Archivio Luchino Visconti at the Fondazione Gramsci in Rome, the Fondazione Primo Conti in Fiesole, the Associazione per Filippo de Pisis in Milan, Simone Quilici and the Archivio Mimì Quilici Buzzacchi, Massimo Carpi and the Futur-ism collection in Rome, the Archivio Achille Funi in the Studio d'arte Nicoletta Colombo in Milan, the Sturla family (in particular Paolo Sturla Avogadri), and Dr. Arianna Fornasari in Ferrara. My sincerest thanks go to the librarians who made my work possible at the Biblioteca della Scuola Normale Superiore in Pisa, the Biblioteca Nazionale Centrale and Biblioteca Angelo Monteverdi in Rome, the Biblioteca Comunale Ariostea in Ferrara, Bobst Library in New York, the Firestone and Marquand libraries in Princeton, the Canaday and Carpenter libraries in Bryn Mawr, Knight Library in Eugene, and the Sterling and Beinecke libraries at Yale University. I could not have retrieved many of the images included in this book without the generous help of Paolo Baldacci.

Working side by side with extraordinary colleagues nourished my intellect and my spirit throughout this endeavour. I wrote the entire first draft of this book, in Italian, sharing a library table with a bosom friend, Ida Campeggiani, whose understanding of both Ariosto and modern Italian literature never ceases to inspire me. Luca D'Onghia, who met us for lunch, coffee, and dinner almost every day, showed me that it is possible to be at the same time the most rigorous and the most hilarious of philologists. My endless chats, laughs, nocturnal walks, espressos at *i signori*'s, horoscope readings from *La gazzetta dello sport*, pizzas at *il mio capriccio*, and cigarette breaks with Ida and Luca are the bedrock of this book. In New York, where I spent a semester at NYU and decided to devote my perfezionamento studies to Ariosto, I was welcomed by new friends at Casa Italiana Zerilli-Marimò who made me want to move continents. Among them, I want to thank Nicola Lucchi, Nicola Cipani, Stefano Albertini, Elena Visconti, Anna Wainwright, and Valeria Castelli for their patience, hospitality, and help. In Princeton, where I started turning my work into a monograph in English, I shared an office with Maria Paula Saffon Sanin and Bernadette Pérez, two remarkable scholars and friends. Stefan Eich and Monica Huerta shared the office next to ours, completing the team known as "the Scheide diaspora." Along with honorary members from Joseph Henry House Ava Shirazi, Justin Perez, and Nijah Cunningham, this team – now scattered throughout the continent but still close knit – always makes me feel at home.

I am grateful for the wonderful community that Susan Stewart and Mary Harper – and then Michael Gordin and Beate Witzler – fostered at the Society of Fellows in the Liberal Arts at Princeton University, where I spent three joyful and transformational years working on this book. I thank all the Postdoctoral and Faculty Fellows for their advice, feedback, and collegiality. At Princeton I also benefited from the presence of encouraging and generous colleagues in many branches of the humanities. I thank Christy Wampole, Maria DiBattista, Tom Hare, Wendy Heller, Leonard Barkan, Tony Grafton, Eileen Reeves, Federico Marcon, Veronica White, Carol Chiodo, Sara Teardo, Michael Wachtel, Effie Rentzou, Guangchen Chen, David Minto, Alberto Rigolio, Janet Kay, Susanna Berger, Andrew Hamilton, Tineke D'Haeseleer, Cristophe Litwin, Jonny Thakkar, Elena Fratto, and Pietro Frassica. For the many *crostate* and their family-style mentorship, I am particularly grateful to Simone and Ilaria Marchesi, and to Anna Cellinese.

I was able to write most of this book thanks to a full year of Junior Research Leave from Bryn Mawr College, which I spent at the University of Oregon. I am grateful to both institutions for their support. At Bryn Mawr I also had the good fortune of meeting inspiring colleagues who were excited about my manuscript. I am particularly thankful to Azade Seyhan, Homay King, Matt Feliz, Rad Edmonds, David Cast, Shiamin Kwa, and Madhavi Kale for caring about my scholarship and encouraging me to write. I thank Chiara Benetollo, Daria Bozzato, Luca Zipoli, and Giulio Genovese for reviving the zestful and collegial atmosphere established in the Department of Transnational Italian Studies by Nicholas Patruno and Roberta Ricci, and I thank our outstanding students (both at Bryn Mawr and Haverford College) for their curiosity and passion. I finished this book at Yale University, as I was starting a new exciting journey. For their warming welcome I thank Millicent Marcus, Serena Bassi, Christiana Purdy, Simona Lorenzini, Deborah Pellegrino, Anna Iacovella, and Michael Farina, as well as a thriving community of graduate students across disciplines – in particular Taylor Yoonji Kang, who generously read my Introduction, Costanza Barchiesi, Francesca Beretta, Francesca Leonardi, Federica Parodi, and Nicholas Berrettini.

Vital to this project were many conversations with colleagues both in Europe and the United States. For their intellectual generosity I thank Martina Piperno, Jo Ann Cavallo, Domenico Starnone, Stefano Jossa, Stephanie Lanfranchi-Guilloux, Daniel Javitch, Eugenio Refini, Mario Telò, Matteo Residori, Barry McCrea, Michele Matteini, Tommaso Pomilio/Ottonieri, Gian Maria Annovi, Nicola Gardini, Francesco Casetti, Armando Maggi, Jennifer Scappettone, Stefania Benini, Giusi Russo, the researchers at the CTL laboratory in Pisa (2011–17), and the Cosmopolitan Italies Collective (in particular Kenyse Lyons, Alessia Valfredini, Catherine Adoyo, Laura Ingallinella, and Anthony Tamburri). Teaching Ariosto within the seminar "Black Queer Jewish Italy" at Princeton, at Bryn Mawr, and at Yale was essential to frame the Introduction of this book, and I thank my students for teaching me how to look at the *Orlando Furioso* from without. I would also like to thank the institutions that invited me to lecture about the ideas at the root of this book: the Taylorian Institute at the University of Oxford, the Center for the Humanities at CUNY's Graduate Center (in particular Monica Calabritto), the Department of Transnational Italian Studies at Bryn Mawr College, the Department of Romance Languages at the University of Oregon (in particular Gina Psaki and Nathalie Hester), the Center for Italian Modern Art in New York (in particular Laura Mattioli, Chiara Trebaoicchi, and Carlotta Castellani), the MDRN lecture series at the Katholieke Universiteit in Leuven, the Sotheby's Institute of Art in London, the Department of Italian Studies at Yale University, and the Italian Modernities Lecture Series at Stanford University (in particular Andrea Capra, Laura Wittman, and Griseldo Dule). Thanks to a grant from the Humanities Council and the Program in Italian Studies, in 2017 I was able to organize the conference Chivalric Imageries at Princeton University, and I thank all the participants for their insights on my Ariostean work – Nora Stoppino, Francesco Erspamer, Geoff Klock, and others mentioned elsewhere in these acknowledgments.

I am grateful to Giulio Ferroni for his jovial and generous support over the years, and for commissioning me two essays (about chivalric culture and Italian Surrealism) that were crucial to reconfiguring my trans-historical research into a monograph. Keala Jewell always offered me encouragement and help: assisting her in her research as a *laureando* changed the way I look at Italian modernism. Ara Merjian, a volcanic mentor and dear friend, read my "Ariosto manuscript" in its initial Italian form and then again in English, years later, right before I submitted it for peer review. I treasure his advice and honesty, the sincere and practical quality of his support, and his sense of humour. Flavio Fergonzi, who taught me how to look at paintings as a literary critic and how to read texts as an art historian, made me feel authorized to work on modern artists. Without him, I would have never written the first chapter of this book.

Jhumpa Lahiri, *mia prima amica*, turned Piazza Nassau into San Cosimato square, and gently guides me through the many metamorphoses of my amphibian life. We seldom speak in English, and yet my English owes her a great debt of gratitude. Chiara Valerio understood this book before I finished writing it, and Michela Murgia commanded me also to write other things. My family of origin, my parents Antonio and Simonetta, and especially my sister Giorgia, never stopped cheering me on. Neither did some special friends and mentors who helped me finish my first book but could not see this one in print: Bianca Antonelli, Lorenzo Antonioli, Biancamaria Frabotta, Giulia Niccolai, and Milli Graffi. I did not know Daniel T. Grimes when I started working on this book but, if I hadn't met him halfway through, I could not have finished it. His support, complicity, and quiet enthusiasm are essential ingredients of my life. To Dan goes my strongest thank you.

ARIOSTO IN THE MACHINE AGE

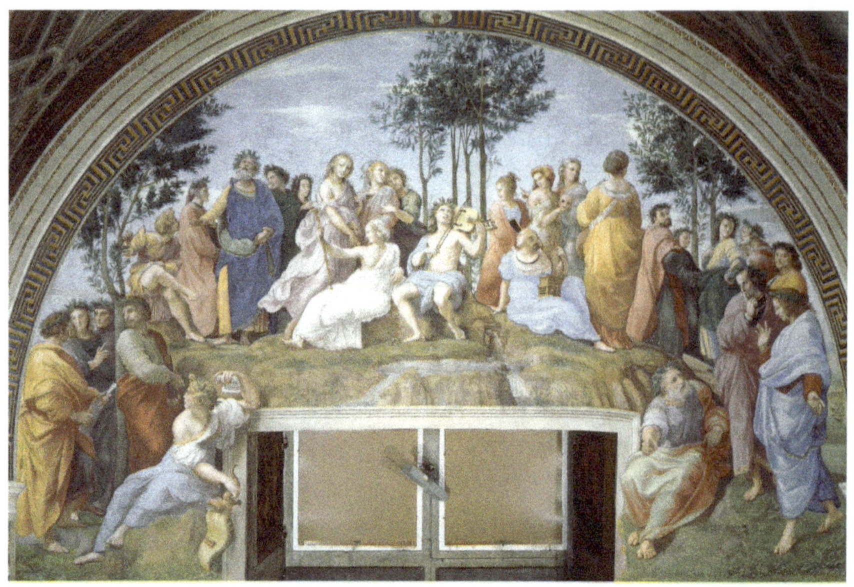

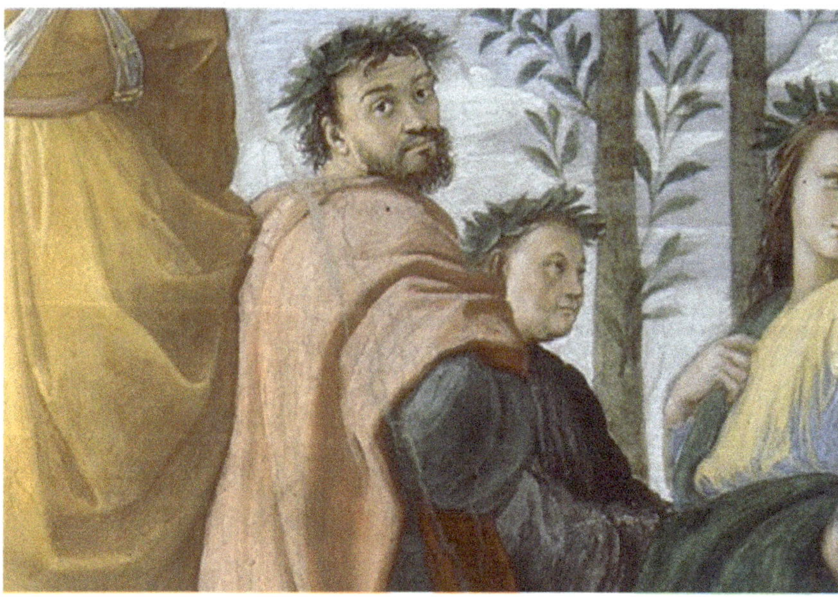

Figures 0.1 (top) and 0.2 (bottom, detail). Raffaello Sanzio, *Parnassus*, 1509–11, fresco, base 670 cm, Apostolic Palace, Vatican City. Image in the public domain, courtesy of user: Erzalibillas/Wikimedia Commons.

Introduction

Peeking from Parnassus – Ariosto the Amphibian

As to every poet what may chance –
Or fate allot as a private doom –
He traveled the roads of Ferrara
And, at the same time, walked the moon.

The dross of dreams that have no shape –
The mud that the Nile of sleep leaves by –
With the stuff of these for skein, he'd move
Through that gleaming labyrinth and escape

Jorge Luis Borges, *Ariosto and the Arabs,* 1960

If you enter the most important room that Raphael frescoed in the Vatican and look up to its depiction of Mount Parnassus, one pair of painted eyes will look directly back at you (figure 0.1). Nine muses, a god, and eighteen poets populate that wall in the room of the Segnatura, and a few of them seem to gaze beyond the painted surface, into various angles of the room where you stand. But only one appears to have just turned his head in order to reciprocate your stare – in order to greet you, one could say, or at least acknowledge your presence (figure 0.2). It is almost as if, even from the remote altitudes of the most detached and unperturbed otherworld of mythology, he could notice that you entered that room in the Vatican Museums; as if you distracted him, for an eternal moment, from his eternal conversation with the other laurelled dead masters of classical poetry. The lines across his forehead express a mild surprise, a disquieting sense of calm awareness. One could swear that he knows he is in a painting.

Unlike anyone else in the room (including you), that poet seems to know exactly what is going on, on each side of the flat fictional image that he inhabits. He can hear both Apollo's divine music and your squeaking steps on the marble floors, the chatter of living tourists around you and the debate among immortal poets in Parnassus. He is simultaneously on top of that timeless hill and in Rome, right now, with you.

Historians of art and literature do not believe anymore that that young bearded man, in Raphael's intentions, could really represent the protagonist of the book that you are reading, Ludovico Ariosto.[1] When Raphael painted the room, Ariosto was still only a local playwright and diplomat from the refined but small northern dukedom of Ferrara, not famous enough to share eternity with Sappho and Homer, Petrarch and Dante, in the Pope's favourite room. After all, when Ariosto visited his court as an ambassador in 1510, the Pope himself had threatened to feed that Ferrarese writer to the fish.[2] Nonetheless, the immense international influence that, only a few years later, Ariosto started to cast all over Europe with his new epic poem, the *Orlando Furioso,* convinced many observers, throughout the past five centuries, that he had to be among the great poets immortalized by Raphael in his pictorial microcosm of humanism, and most of them recognized him in the fixed, alert, but unconcerned gaze of the bearded poet on the right.[3]

They were wrong, of course. But it remains true that, if the history of Western literature was a narrative film, Ludovico Ariosto would be the first major player to transgress the main interdiction of traditional realistic fiction and look into the camera.[4]

Hither and Thither

To be sure, today, any serious expert in Renaissance iconography will tell you that that face actually belonged to some erudite sixteenth-century Italian humanist, someone whose name does not mean anything to almost anyone anymore. Still, the way the bearded poet keeps on welcoming the fresco's audience (the way he looks back at you) does have something to do with Ariosto; with how Ariosto eventually earned his spot in Parnassus, just not in time for his friend Raphael to paint him there. Yes, that staring man was not supposed to portray Ariosto. Yet, to our posthumous eyes, he uncannily does. His posture in between worlds (his ability to make you consider, for a split second, that maybe you are the one trapped in a fresco) represents what Ariosto came to mean for modernity: an inextricable amalgam of Olympian detachment and quotidian awareness, classical untimeliness and immediate presence.

Jorge Luis Borges summarized this foundational duality in a fulminating literary portrait of Ariosto: "He traveled the roads of Ferrara / and, at the same time, walked the moon."[5] When fiction is at the same time worldly and lunar, when it reminds you of the room where you are but takes you a million miles from there, is it evasion, daydream, fable? Or are the terrestrial roads of Ferrara (and rooms of Rome) more clearly visible from the aerial perspective of the moon (and of Parnassus)? Does realism make it easier to lose yourself and drown in a fantastic world, or does it keep you more firmly anchored to this one? And is storytelling even allowed to speculate about itself this way, without becoming a brainy, self-conscious postmodern game? Can one wholeheartedly climb to the top of Parnassus but still know that classical poetry is an evolving illusion, and keep an eye out for what happens beyond the waving veil of that illusion?

Published in 1516, reforged in a longer version in 1521, and finally perfected in its definitive 1532 edition, Ariosto's *Orlando Furioso* was received as an instant classic. However, as commentators started to notice later in the century, it defied the classical unities established by Aristotle. The literary debate that, after Ariosto's death in 1533, arguably initiated what we call literary theory was strongly influenced by the *Furioso*: both a model for and a disruption of poetic traditions.[6] This means that critics have been discussing this unorthodox but canonical poem for five hundred years. Throughout this time, the main questions remained the same, all centred on the dichotomies between classicism and innovation, fabulation and realism, pure poetry and the crises of history. On the divide, in sum, between the room and Parnassus.

It is easy to agree, now that so much time has passed, on the fact that modern fiction is singularly indebted to Ariosto's legacy, from the wilful folly of Cervantes' *Quixote* to the trans-historical and transsexual social satire of Woolf's *Orlando*. What remains difficult is to univocally describe the substance of that legacy: to choose between the opposing terms that polarize any fundamental question about Ariosto. Duality has always been the defining feature of this poet: the most influential literary voice of the high Renaissance but also, at least in the so-called canon, the hardest to fully fit into the norms and values of that age. After all he selected, as his personal emblem, a figure of ambiguity: the Latin motto *pro bono malum*, with the image of bees smoked out of their hive (figure 0.3). He chose it to open the first edition of the *Orlando Furioso*, consecrating his legacy to the most fundamental of tangled binaries: that of good and evil. Again, however, it is difficult to choose. Did he mean that anything good (the bees' work) is destined to be unjustly compensated with evil (the beekeeper's fire)? Or that, in order to get to something good, like honey, one must endure some evil? To blend the two opposites, readers came up with opposing unifying principles, interpreting Ariosto's emblem as

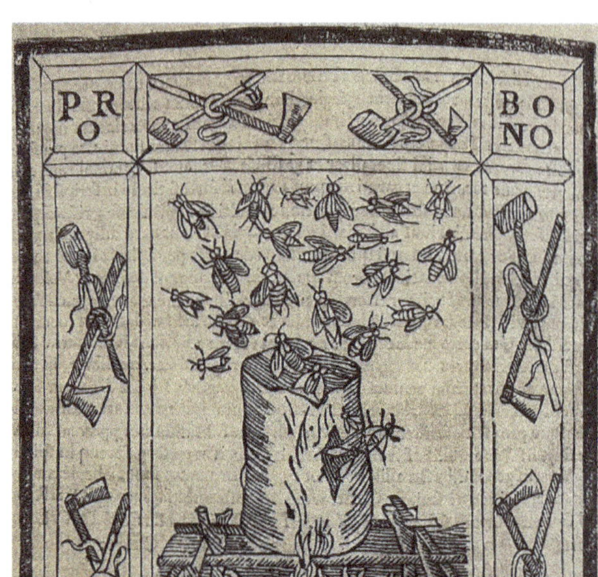

Figure 0.3. Woodcut of Ariosto's personal impresa in Ludovico Ariosto, *Orlando Furioso* (Ferrara: Giovanni Mazzocchi, 1516), dol. a2 *verso*. Biblioteca Comunale Ariostea, Ferrara.

a symbol of either ingratitude or grace.[7] Even synthesis leads back to the middle of a crossroads when reading Ariosto.

After Hegel, who saw in the *Furioso* the birth of a self-determining subjectivity in literature through irony,[8] modern criticism coalesced around an idealistic keyword to solve the endless bifurcations of Ariosto's historical figure and literary legacy: harmony.[9] His defining quality was a superior ability to harmonize, like a divine musician: to blend the dissonant elements of a poem as vast as the cosmos in a resolved symphony of sublime balance. This serene image, which recalls Apollo's ecstasy in Raphael's *Parnassus*, has then been progressively dragged down to earth by philology and historicism. Postwar readers rooted Ariosto's work in the frustrating chaos of his life as a courtier, diplomat, and governor: a poet who had to deal with demanding dukes and protesting peasants, the need to earn a living and the dream to endlessly write.[10]

At the end of the millennium, that dream inspired influential interpretations of Ariosto as a master of serious lightness, able to swiftly glide over a world on fire, sitting in his library in Ferrara but also on the back of a moon-landing Hippogriff in his poem.[11] Structuralism and narratology revealed the geometrical modernity of his fiction, which used the same chess set of medieval chivalric stories and classical myths but played unprecedented games, invariably checkmating the reader. Ariosto's proverbial harmony became bitter,[12] it morphed into the steady hum of a perfect machine,[13] and eventually turned into its opposite: contradiction.[14] Binary oppositions (and opposing syntheses of them) kept on dominating our understanding of the *Orlando Furioso.* The potentially infinite crossed destinies generated by binary logic informed the latest products of its reception in literary and cinematic narratives.[15] Quite a curious afterlife for a sardonic stoic who insisted on the opportunity of always seeking out "the middle path."

The thing is that, as the intersectional position of the gazing poet in (and out of) Raphael's fresco shows, not all crossroads demand a choice. Borges loved Dante as much as he loved Ariosto, and Dante famously despised uncommitted people, placing them in a vestibule because they do not belong anywhere, not even in Hell. However, rejecting binary choices (or better, contemplating unsynthesized polar opposites at once, like the dual citizen of two countries at war with each other) turns out to be the most honest option once one understands that, depending on the context, divides may dwindle, and choices themselves turn into caprice. This might be what Borges really meant when he described Ariosto roaming terrestrial roads and lunar valleys "at the same time." Inhabiting the boundary that appears to separate the most fundamental things (fantasy and reality, comedy and tragedy, tradition and disruption, duty and desire, harmony and contradiction) is like keeping a finger in a wound, ironically stopping both bleeding and healing. There's no more elegant way to reveal the existence, exact position, and permeability of a fence than to sit on it.[16]

Any complex epic poem should be read ambiguously, and even Virgil's *Aeneid* is arguably both a celebration and a critique of the empire prophesied in its stanzas. In fact, counter-readings of that quintessential Roman model may have jumpstarted the reception of Ariosto's *Orlando Furioso* as an ambivalent, sardonic work. However, unlike Ariosto's emblem, classic epic always presupposes the existence of a straight, correct alternative between good and evil, even when its protagonists end up not choosing it. As a genre, epic is based on a series of only apparently forking paths. The *Orlando Furioso*, instead, queers epic duty with the centrifugal diversions of individual desires. It does so by drawing on its Italian predecessors (chiefly, Boiardo) who had combined the Carolingian and Arthurian narrative traditions of northern Europe with the Mediterranean arabesque of chivalric romance.[17]

In the *Furioso*, to our posthumous eyes, quests are not just heroic deeds to be completed or wondrous adventures of errant knights. As it has been recently argued, they represent a new cognitive instrument, a learning device: a tool to know the world and evolve.[18] From the point of view of later ages, Ariosto seems to look at familiar figments as if they were unexplored lands, making the junctures of his epos truly twofold for the first time. He sits on the divide between the enchanting appeal of popular stories and a disenchanted understanding of their mechanics, between euphoric exploitation and dysphoric deconstruction. Think of the relationship, today, between superhero comic books and what we call, to mark a difference that is hard to define, graphic novels.[19]

In the eyes of late modernity, which elected him as an ancestor, Ariosto contributed to the invention of modern storytelling precisely by turning a fictional world of old refrains and tropes, with its recognizable automatons destined to endlessly recombine the same narrative options, into a credible, knowable, explorable universe of moral ambiguity and untapped simultaneous options. A world that appreciates its own fictionality, and therefore appears to trespass into reality, like the poet in the room of the Segnatura. To talk about this poetics of happily unresolved chasms in terms of harmony, one shouldn't think of Apollo, but of some Dionysian musician: a modern composer who faced the exhaustion of classical forms but still made use of them. Alas, just as Raphael painted *Parnassus* too early to include Ariosto in it, Ariostean criticism came up with the idea of harmony too early to conceive it through the revealing lens of, say, the classical experimentalism of a Stravinsky. For the first time, this book entertains such an anachronic possibility, fundamentally altering a five-hundred-year-old debate on the origin of modern fiction and, at the same time, reconfiguring the genealogy of a certain Dionysian brand of modernity itself – one that, directly inspired by Ariosto four centuries after his death, sat on the fence that only apparently divides old from new, artifice from reality, rational from irrational.

What I propose is rather simple. Looking at the *Furioso* from the vantage point of its modern afterlife makes it possible to confirm, and to move a step forward, the interpretations of its text that dominated the past quarter of a century. The point of Ariosto's poetry is indeed to blur the very binaries that we came up with to explain it. Not to fill the gulf that separates classicism and novelty, realism and magic, epic and romance, academic appreciation and commercial success. Not to cross the distance between Earth and the moon, or to arrange the contradictions of world and fiction into a single harmonized chord. On the contrary, Ariosto manages to be on both the edges of his dualities at once, "hither and thither" as Osip Mandelstam put it in his 1933 poem about him, "forever breaking / the music of narration."[20]

It has never been productive to try and reduce those dualities to unities, but it is also imprecise (and, ultimately, less exciting) to resolve them into harmonic or oxymoronic syntheses, like the competing genes of two parents of the same species that either love or hate one another. Ariosto resists both disentanglement and blending, boundaries and the opposition of regions that they demarcate. In this, he is similar to his Hippogriff, fruit of the union of a griffin and a mare from a remote Asian mountain where such crossings, if rarely, occur.

Governor *and* poet, bitter *and* serene, lunar *and* mundane, five centuries after he took Parnassus (*and* an unprecedentedly wide audience) by storm with his *Orlando Furioso*, Ariosto invites our age of virtual realities and serious ironies to read him as an amphibian, simultaneously in and out of the illusions that he conjured: humanism, classicism, originality, chivalry, magic, epos, realism, and the Renaissance itself.

The Swan and the Otter

Simultaneity is a term that sounds more relevant for avant-garde, rather than Renaissance, poetics and aesthetics. In fact, after Impressionism, it defined the visual and textual experiments of artists that aimed to subvert the norms established by Renaissance art and literature: Orphists, Cubists, Futurists, and Surrealists, inspired by new physical and metaphysical conceptions of time and space. Yet, if we adopt this term as a keyword for Ariosto, we can disrupt the centennial tailspin of critical paradigms that expected readers to choose one way in his poetic crossroads, or to integrate them into a synthesis. Ultimately, in Borges' poem, what matters is not the historical concreteness of the roads of Ferrara, nor is it the daring fantasy of moonwalking in the sixteenth century. What matters is the locution that connects the two poles: "at the same time."

Ariosto, like the gazing poet in Raphael's fresco, is at the same time with you and with Apollo, hither and thither, current and classical. But simultaneity also characterizes his narrative strategies and contents, beyond the binaries of traditional epos and romance. The most revealing recent readings of the *Furioso* insist on the fact that its entangled storylines take place, at the same time, in all the continents of early modern geography (not to mention the gates of Hell, the earthly paradise, and of course the moon),[21] and that some of its heroes are, at the same time, male and female, queer and straight, normative and boldly deviant.[22] Ariosto wrote plots and characters with a double-edged pen, tying the knots of narrative fabric and human experience.[23]

You can find his Angelica, the princess of Cathay, running in the halls of an enchanted castle and, at the same time, right outside at the entrance. The paladin Bradamante, when she falls in Merlin's cave in Canto III, remains in the world of the living but, at the same time, has a chance to meet both the dead and those who are yet to be born, including some early readers of the book that tells her story. Orlando himself is the quintessential wise paladin and, at the same time, a new standard model for irrational brutality, the one that Quixote will deliberately imitate in the wilderness of La Mancha.[24] In the *Furioso,* anyone can be at the same time valorous and opportunistic, the breaker and maker of codes, an old witch and a young maiden.

Predicated on simultaneity in its structure, moral texture, and cast of characters, the *Furioso* was also simultaneously addressed to humanists and commoners alike: devotees of Ovid's *Metamorphoses* and fans of titillating battle stories. Keeping a lucid eye on both the room and Parnassus, Ariosto wrote for one of the most refined courts of Renaissance Europe and, at the same time, for a nascent industrial mass market of narrative consumption. That is why his book was, at the same time, the first popular bestseller of the age of print and the first benchmark of literary quality for early modern criticism. When, in the spring of 1516, he received the first copies from the press, Ariosto destined some for monarchs and fellow intellectuals, some for direct sale.[25] He was both author and editor, product and investor. He expected to make an immediate profit and, at the same time, to be recognized as a great poet, worthy of a pension that would have allowed him to concentrate exclusively on intellectual work.

Ariosto was among the first to realize that the only way left to join the company of Apollo with the revered humanists of the past was to contemplate the fact that humanism itself is a fantasy (if not a fraud), one that demands some healthy scepticism in order to be fully embraced – and exploited. After all, he is credited with coining the very term "humanist," but one shouldn't forget that he did so in one of his satirical letters, celebrating and deriding humanism, in theory and practice, at the same time.[26] He was also the last to retell the stories of Charlemagne's paladins and Camelot's knights without being considered a mere continuator, adaptor, or epigone.[27] His poem, simultaneously derivative and original, marks the beginning of modern narrative but represents, at the

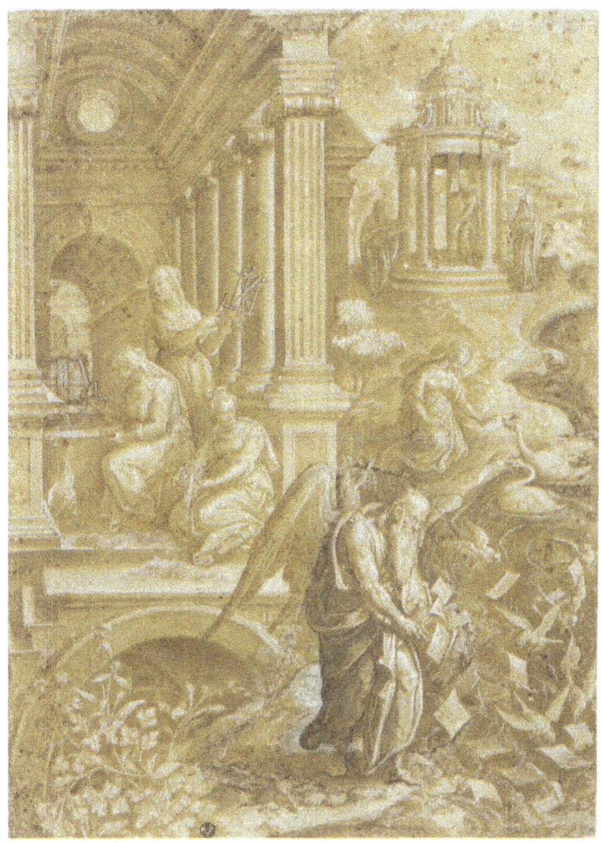

Figure 0.4. Jan van der Straet, *Allegorical Subject: Virtue and Time* (*Soggetto allegorico: la Virtù e il Tempo*), 1581, bistre and whiting on paper, 4.69 × 3.44 cm, Uffizi Galleries, Florence. © Gabinetto Disegni e Stampe della Galleria degli Uffizi.

same time, the last grandiose revival of a long literary age and its fading social, military, and philosophical myths. A swan song but, as in one of Aesop's most ambiguous fables, one that saves the swan's life rather than ending it.[28]

Swans, elegant birds able to glide as swiftly through air as they do on the surface of the water, provided Ariosto with the perfect allegory for creativity itself: for what it means to be a poet (figure 0.4). In the *Furioso,* when the English knight Astolfo flies up to the moon on the back of the Hippogriff, he sees two magnificent swans swimming on the river Lethe. He learns that Time, a hasty old man, endlessly throws the names of all mortals in the current, delivering them into oblivion, and that a flock of clumsy birds of prey dive above the water to save a few. However, these greedy and exclusively aerial birds cannot really distinguish the deserving names from those that should be forgotten, and are too weak to hold on to them anyway. Lunar images of mediocre poets, they soon have to drop the legacy of those that they write about back into the waves. Only the rare swans, aquatic and aerial at the same time, are able to both save the right names from the water and raise them up to the temple of immortality. One's afterlife is safe in their beaks (XXXV, 10–16).

Not that Ariosto had any illusions about what the endurance of high art really entails. A swan himself, acclimated to both the river of chaotic contingencies and the calm skies of eternity, he commented on his own allegorical fable with a note of disenchanted realism. Even the greatest heroes of literature were surpassed, in human history, by thousands of braver, more compassionate, or stronger women and men, but we remember only the winners, the ancestors of rich families: those who could orient the attention of storytellers towards their deeds. In fact, astute powerful people pay artists to colonize the future, making their nefarious actions disappear from the memory of readers. "If for truth you are particular," Ariosto reveals, you should know that "like this, quite in reverse, the story goes": Dido is remembered as "a whore" only because the author of the *Aeneid* "was not her friend," Trojans were much more successful than they appear in the *Iliad*, Penelope was not as chaste as the *Odyssey* pretends, and so on (XXXV, 25–7).

Again, in order to get on Parnassus with Homer, Virgil, and their greatest literary successors, one has to be honest and deceitful at the same time – another undecidable bifurcation that divided Ariosto's most authoritative readers.[29] It is not the apparent candour of the swans that makes them a symbol for true poets, nor is it just their supposed nobility, beautiful voice, and rarity. Their amphibology is a crucial feature. In fact, it is their defining quality.

Right after describing the lunar swans and their allegorical role in the economics of fame and memory, Ariosto abruptly moves his narrative, in the same canto, back on Earth. There, a damsel destined to inspire one of Mozart's most bifurcated characters, Fiordiligi, is looking for a knight willing to save her beloved Brandimarte from Rodomonte, the arrogant king of Algiers. Since Rodomonte fights on a narrow bridge over a river, Fiordiligi needs an amphibian champion, able "to fight as well in water as on land" simultaneously: "as though an otter, not a knight, he were" (XXXV, 34).

Fiordiligi finds this otter-knight in a she, not a he: the paladin Bradamante, whom she addresses as a man before realizing that she is a maiden too (though armoured), herself in search of her own kidnapped lover. It is this simultaneous co-presence of two roles and perspectives, rather than the mere ability to fight on land and in water, that makes Bradamante the right champion for the mission: she agrees to fight Rodomonte because Fiordiligi's earnest story shakes off her jealous belief that all men must be unfaithful. As a woman warrior, invincible and in love, Bradamante directly understands Fiordiligi's predicament and, at the same time, has the power to do something about it.

To describe her unique amphibious profile, Ariosto uses a set of three rhyming words that he has already employed to talk about Orlando's descent from wisdom to madness, the central simultaneity of contraries that gives the whole poem its very title (XXX, 5). The first is of course *lontra*, "otter." The other two are two meaningfully opposite interpretations of the same word, *incontra*: "meeting," or "encountering," and "against," or "in opposition." This two-faced word also reads like a combination of the three Italian prepositions for "in" or "at" (*in*), "with" (*con*), and "between" or "among" (*tra*). It could be read as a formula for the amphibology that I have been describing: "in with between." Its very morphological substance alludes to the cohabitation and cooperation of distinct features in the same physical or conceptual space; at the same time.

Ariosto borrowed this exact scheme of two words in threefold rhyme from Dante's *Inferno*. There, in Canto XXII, Dante encounters the souls of the grafters, condemned to be eternally immersed in a pit of boiling tar. In a formidable chain of similes, he compares these submerged sinners not only with the otter ("lontra," 36), but also with a small bestiary of other animals that simultaneously belong to two worlds: dolphins ("dalfini," 19), toads ("ranocchi," 26), and frogs ("rana," 33). Dante was accused of the very same malfeasance that led these sinners to damnation, and he was exiled from his beloved Florence because of it. However, with his medieval moral compass and Virgilian approach to epic, he rejected the amphibian nature that, according to Ariosto, informs even the greatest acts of poetry. To write fiction and lucidly deal with reality at the same time (to be a maiden and a warrior, a wise madman, a poet in a political world) ultimately means to be a grafter: a swan, an otter. Only poetasters, like birds of prey, cannot swim at all.

Though painfully familiar with ingratitude and committed to seek grace, Dante could never have chosen Ariosto's motto, *pro bono malum*, for his emblem. In Raphael's *Parnassus*, he is clearly recognizable on the opposite side to our bearded amphibious poet, and looks directly to his guide and model Virgil, fully immersed in the illusion of the fresco. The allegory on the moon in the *Orlando Furioso* reveals to us that he was a swan too. However, unlike Ariosto, he did not know – or, at least, he did not say.

Magician's Toolkit

The potential hypocrisy of Ariosto's amphibian position, at the same time in and in between worlds and beliefs, is abolished by his forthcoming awareness, by his look into the camera. Simultaneously addressing both his audiences (the patron and the public, the court and the world) in the first person, as himself, from the pages of the *Furioso*, he candidly admits more than once not to entirely believe in his own second-hand fables. After all, while he promised from the very beginning to tell "things unattempted yet in prose or rhyme" (I, 2), his book is what one would today call a sequel: an immediate continuation of the last, unfinished masterpiece of chivalric romance: Matteo Maria Boiardo's *Orlando Innamorato* (1495).

Following an established convention of the chivalric genre, the *Furioso* pretends to draw on the same given fictional source from which Boiardo had supposedly obtained his stories: the first-hand chronicles of Turpin, a legendary medieval archbishop. It treats its antecedent as an *objet trouvé*: a readymade, to use another keyword more suited to avant-garde poetics. This way, Ariosto can claim not to be responsible for either the initial setting of his narrative chessboard or the patent absurdity of many of the moves that he makes on it. He "gave himself," to quote Borges' poem one last time, "to the slow pleasure [...] of dreaming again on dreams already dreamed."

At the same time, Ariosto's omnipresent authorial voice frequently reassures readers about the originality of his declaredly derivative material, and confirms its plausibility even in the most impossibly magic passages. When he describes Ruggiero's flights across Europe, for instance, he lets you know that the knight did not sleep on the back of the flying Hippogriff at night, as this would have been impractical. Of course, more reasonably and comfortably, Ruggiero landed every evening and looked for a decent inn, where he could eat well and rest (X, 73). Such a detail has the sole function of forcing you to fully entertain the plausibility of an impossible situation: to take seriously what you know is preposterous – just as, conversely, you should take the *Iliad*, the *Aeneid*, and the *Odyssey* with a grain of salt. Ariosto's literary grafting is painstakingly honest, his dreams prodigiously lucid. The best magical acts, after all, remain spectacular even if the magician is confident enough to explain the trick while performing it.

Rather than intermixing illusions and pragmatism in an idyllic or contradictory harmony, torn between sour disappointment and the deceitful lightness of evasion, Ariosto keeps opposites separate and simultaneously valid. He makes them share the same non-binary human and animal bodies, narrative structures and events, as well as poetic ideas. His storytelling allows one to remain sceptical while enjoying fantasy, to speak truth to power in the very act of celebrating it, to feel entertained and frustrated, at the same time, by an unusually long, complicated cluster of storylines played out by dozens of characters. Consider, again, the emblematic example of the Hippogriff: a plot device that allows those characters to be quickly disseminated all over the known world and beyond, suddenly expanding a familiar setting to the edges of the universe.

In the *Furioso,* this utterly fantastic beast paradoxically enhances the verisimilitude of a global, even cosmic narrative matter, just as the impossible physics of faster-than-light travel makes science fiction possible at a galactic scale. The description of this animal reveals the radicalness of Ariosto's amphibology, which can't be brushed off as a lighthearted or impish joke. The Hippogriff is "not a fiction," he guarantees (IV, 18), but rather one of the many uncommon, unfamiliar, or still unknown potential products of Nature herself, the most daringly inventive of creative forces. It is as natural as it is speculative. It reminds us that, if anything, Nature is more inexhaustible than imagination.

Like swans and otters, like dolphins, toads, and frogs, like storytellers and their most fully human characters, like the bearded poet in Raphael's fresco, the Hippogriff belongs to two worlds and two species (horses and gryphons: one real, one fictional) at the same time. That's why it can take you to the moon and to the inn. Borges, in his *Book of Imaginary Beings,* praised the credible plausibility, not the imaginativeness, of this quintessentially amphibious Ariostean invention.[30] Alberto Manguel, who as a teenager used to read aloud for Borges when he went blind, attributes to "imaginary verisimilitude" its viral success in narratives set at the crossroads of world and fantasy, from Calderón de la Barca's *Life Is a Dream* to J.K. Rowling's *Harry Potter.*[31]

Most of the critical categories that we have been using so far to interpret the amphibology of Ariosto's poetry have something to do with simultaneity, but none of them embraces the concept to its full extent: to the point of considering the reality, rather than just the realism, of a Hippogriff – and the inherent disruptiveness of classicism, unoriginality of novelty, sophistication of universal appeal, and so on. It is necessary to adopt an amphibious perspective in order to sustain Ariosto's gaze across ages; in order to read him like a Hippogriff, instead of the sum, clash, or harmonic blending of two mortal enemies like a griffin and a mare.

Borges read Ariosto from that perspective. It is no surprise that the amphibian nature of the *Furioso,* at the juncture of mere reality and mesmerizing realism, old and new, erudite and popular, entertainment and frustration, logic and folly, is revealed so immediately by the words of a creative reader who, like Borges, was himself obsessed with mirrored duplicities, co-presence, and dreams. Indeed, the simple connecting formula that keeps together the *Furioso*'s forking paths, "at the same time," frames Ariosto as a technical and ideal model for an entire toolkit of "simultaneity tricks" that are familiar to Borges' readers. They constitute his poetics, along with that of other Ariostean narrators of the recent past who quoted the *Furioso* or wrote about it in their work, from Alejo Carpentier and Italo Calvino to Salman Rushdie and Jim Jarmusch.

The toolset that I am referring to is varied, but held together by the same uncanny synchronism that connects Parnassus with the room through the gaze of Raphael's bearded poet. It includes the montage of simultaneous actions in a fractal but single arc: the mechanisms of suspense and world building that inform serial novels, cohesive episodic films or short-story books, and expanded universes.[32] It also includes metafiction, of course, a form of radical irony that intersects experienced and imagined worlds, questioning the boundary between them. It provides experimental narrators and rational surrealists with the right credentials to reclaim a canonical genealogy: roots in the most glorified genre of the most glorified age of what we call Western civilization. It models a form of trans-historical classicism that seeks to radically renovate genres and forms while continuing their traditions – and to do so not only for an ivory tower of literati, but also for the masses that art can reach through its industrial reproducibility.

Montage, metafiction, surreal irony, and mainstream high art, along with the acclimation of classical tropes in the quotidian anonymity of modern life, informed the postwar global poetics of Magical Realism. Arguably, the same toolkit even generated the postmodernist styles that David Foster Wallace famously combined into the term "Lynchian."[33] Ariosto put this toolkit together. After all, Wallace's *Infinite Jest* may be thematically modelled after *Hamlet,* the *Odyssey,* and Joyce's *Ulysses,* but its defining structural strategies of diversion and distraction, which make it frustrating and entertaining at the same time, imitate the narrative montage of the *Orlando Furioso.*[34] In Jarmusch's 2013 film *Only Lovers Left Alive,* Wallace's novel and Ariosto's poem appear together in the suitcase of an ageless and androgynous hipster vampire who, like Woolf's Orlando, spent centuries reading "great books" and mingling with their authors.

As Jarmusch had noticed since his early experiments with narrative montage,[35] towards the end of the twentieth century Ariosto's poetics of simultaneity nourished the crisis and reconfiguration of the novel as a form. According to Goethe and Walter Scott, it had informed the development of that same form in the nineteenth century. However, all its technical and theoretical components sound particularly relevant for the temporal spell that, in the history of fiction, separates those two ages. Like the very term "simultaneity," which fastens the two ages conceptually, they informed the age of avant-garde experimentalism, and the so-called return to order that followed it. The age of Einstein's relativity and Stravinsky's dissonance, the age in which the embryos of ideas like symbiogenesis and parallel universes were first conceived. An amphibian age.

Now, in the realm of aesthetics, one of the most consequential phenomena of that age had its epicentre in Ariosto's city, Ferrara. From there, it expanded north to modernist Paris and south to Mussolini's Rome, eventually reaching Borges' Argentina and the rest of Latin America before the end of the Second World War. It was a crucial point of origin for all the modern realisms that found themselves unsatisfied with reality but not ready to get rid of it: not only Magical Realism, but also Surrealism and neorealism. The artists and writers who animated it intended to do exactly what Ariosto did. They claimed to reforge classicism, figuration, and realism itself by continuing and disrupting, embracing and debunking, practising and overcoming them all *at the same time*. To do so, they looked to Ariosto as a lively totem, a model, and an interlocutor.

Armed with Ariosto's toolkit of rational magic, between the birth of Futurism and the end of fascism this amphibian avant-garde claimed to bring forth a new Renaissance, alternative to both the novelty for novelty's sake of coeval experimental movements and the pedantic passéism of sclerotic conventions. Not an imitation or presentification of the Renaissance, like the one orchestrated, in the interwar period, by fascist public art and propaganda to colonize Italy's past: not just the revival or re-enactment of a supposedly golden age.

The amphibian perspective that these artists and writers adopted to look back into Ariosto's eyes, as equals across the screen of time, was also at odds with the declared genealogy that, in the same years, linked Eliot and Pound with Dante, or Brecht and Pirandello with Galileo. In fact, the history of Ariosto's extraordinary multimedia legacy has ignored them entirely, and no study of their work has mentioned Ariosto's name if not in passing. Until now.

Amphibious Avant-Garde

You are reading an amphibian book, a book that looks simultaneously at Ariosto's Renaissance and at the new Renaissance conceived by his avant-garde interlocutors. This book is about the origin of some of the most ubiquitous poetic facets of our time: metafiction, speculative realism, serial narrative, intermedia world building, and the moral paradoxes of irony. But it is also about the gateway through which these Ariostean tricks of simultaneity reached us. It looks into the workshop of modernists who, in turn, were looking into the workshop of Ariosto's *Orlando Furioso.*

All the ages and all the arts of the past five centuries have looked into that early modern workshop. Ariosto's very dual nature (his entertaining complexity, his modern classicism, his mastery of both courtly sophistications and printing machines) made him singularly influential. Canonized into Parnassus by critics and scholars,[36] he also remained consistently present in the imagery, narratives, and melodies of highbrow and popular creators across media.

One could say that, to understand Ariosto's function in the history of culture, his afterlife in operas, paintings, plays, and books by others is more important than the letter of his own text. After all, the gargantuan mass and structural maze of that text generated its own incredibly varied reception and, at the same time, make it almost impossible for a reader to simply cross it, cover to cover, without getting lost. It counts more lines than the *Odyssey*, the *Divine Comedy*, and *Paradise Lost* combined, and its resistance to synthesis extends to the deceitfully simple art of summary. According to lore, when Elizabeth I grew tired of Sir John Harington (her godson and, incidentally, the inventor of the flush toilet), she ordered him to complete a full translation of the *Furioso.* The deed appeared to be so immense that the queen expected never to see him again.[37]

Luckily, Sir John did translate a vast portion of Ariosto's poem, or we probably wouldn't have had Shakespeare's *Much Ado about Nothing*, Spenser's *Faerie Queene*, and Byron's *Don Juan.* Many others followed his lead. By the end of the sixteenth century, the *Orlando Furioso* had already been reprinted by more than two hundred presses in seven languages.

The vastness of its plot and the intricacies of its narrative montage challenged the very format of printed books, pushing typographers to provide readers with inventive orienting tools: outlines of cantos, rubrics, moral allegories, and, most importantly, illustrations.[38] Transcending the boundaries of language, this generative kaleidoscope of printed images quickly turned the poem into an iconographic basin for both high and applied arts all over Europe, in public and private spaces.[39] Episodes and characters popularized by these visual excerpts gained their own artistic life, becoming the centre of derivative works of music and theatre from the Baroque age on. And of course, from Laura Terracina's 1550 feminist commentary to the puppet theatre of Sicilian folklore, the text of the *Furioso* was creatively recombined and rewritten by countless writers and translators, including some of the protagonists of this book.

The mapping of half a millennium of Ariosto's reception has generated, in the recent past, grandiose exhibitions and encyclopedic works of research across disciplines. However, you are not reading just a missing chapter of this international and trans-historical story of literary influence. By looking at his acclimation in the age of the avant-garde, this book directly changes our understanding of Ariosto's original diffractive enigma. It reclaims him as an ancestor not of the triumph of humanism and Renaissance Italianate classicism, nor of tragic scepticism and resentful disillusion towards the inescapable realities of a nascent modernity. Ariosto, the swan and the otter, the Hippogriff, the amphibian, is not just the poet of harmony and ingratitude. He is the literary ancestor of simultaneous, non-binary approaches to identity, fiction, and Nature, to the relationship between past and future, good and evil, and to the very function of art.

Ariosto broke with the system of moral, stylistic, and human binary oppositions that Fredric Jameson placed at the core of his genre and age.[40] Feminist criticism has showed, in the past few decades, how that framework does not apply to gendered relations of power in the *Orlando Furioso*.[41] Now, the hermaphrodites, living objects, talking statues, sailing rooms, Nicodemite politics, and alternative realities that Ariosto inspired in the work of twentieth-century vanguardists urge us to extend the non-binary amphibology that he pioneered beyond gender and power, queering the whole cosmos of the *Furioso*.

The Francocentric and mostly Anglophone history of modernism and interwar European culture tends to call the modern phenomenon at the centre of this book "Italian Surrealism." It is not, however, as that term suggests, a regional variety of a quintessentially international movement. In fact, its development pre-dates that of Surrealism, and its protagonists inspired Surrealists in the first place.[42] After the First World War, this so called Italian Surrealism actually opposed the defining irrationality of its supposed French counterpart, simultaneously advocating for a more lucid take on contemporary reality and a return to pre-modern Mediterranean myths and tropes. This amphibious avant-garde, which morphed into an equally amphibious neoclassicism, might be called, more fruitfully, Ariostean Surrealism. Its most impactful ideas were all directly inspired, as this book reveals, by dialogues with Ariosto.

When Giorgio de Chirico conceived Metaphysical art between Florence and Paris, he dreamed of Ariosto's knights. Then, when he moved to Ferrara and definitely divorced his artistic destiny from that of French Surrealists, he encountered Ariosto's statue, and learned from it how to become himself a monument. His brother, Alberto Savinio, described this encounter in one of the most amphibious books of post-Futurist experimentalism, *Hermaphrodito,* and populated his novels with timeless but ordinary figures inspired by both Ariosto's characters and their sources in classical literature. Both the brothers' iconic experiments with geography, navigable interiors, and the infinite stratigraphy of references of mythology directly stemmed from Ariosto's poetry.

When Massimo Bontempelli, inspired by de Chirico's Ferrarese painting, coined the term Magical Realism in literature, he directly invoked Ariosto's name, asking him for the gift to see, at the same time, the material reality of his own century and what lies just beyond its boundaries. He then wrote metaphysical fables that prefigured Borges' and Calvino's inventions, imagining impossibly plausible lunar worlds based on the *Furioso.* Along with Savinio, he looked at Ariosto's storytelling in order to apply the novelty of cinematic montage to serial novels.

Towards the end of the Second World War, at the sunset of Ariostean Surrealism, two of the founders of neorealism tried to directly adapt Ariosto for cinema and theatre. They failed, but their attempts to reduce the *Orlando Furioso* into a script revealed how illusory were the paradigms that coeval criticism adopted to synthesize its amphibology. In the 1930s, the same paradigms had dominated, though often in a twisted way, attempts to co-opt Ariosto into the propaganda of the fascist regime. Fascist intellectuals, grafters devoid of any Ariostean amphibology, fundamentally misunderstood the *Orlando Furioso.* They tried to homologate it into the unities and syntheses demanded by their regime's aesthetics. Instead of encountering Ariosto as a living monument, a ruin that belongs to the remote as much as the recent past,[43] they mobilized his bones, descendants, face, and papers, turning him into an idol, a relic, a zombie, and a revenant.

This modern story, which stretches across the first half of the twentieth century, fills the gap that separates Romanticism and Postmodernism in the history of Ariosto's afterlife. At the same time, as I said, it allows us to finally shutter the crystallized critical dead ends that, for five hundred years, have forced Ariosto's early modern poetry either hither or thither, in or out of the binary divides that it reveals and questions.

One important way in which this book, like Ariosto's poem, is amphibious is that it deals with images and texts at the same time, at the crossroads of the disciplinary boundary that divides art history and literary criticism. That is why I started with Raphael's fresco, and why the protagonists of the first chapter are going to be artists who wrote and painted at the same time. The most famous of them, de Chirico, one of the most influential figures of modernism, certainly entered the room of the Segnatura, and was greeted by the bearded poet's Ariostean gaze. We know that because, right after he spent the war years in Ferrara, revolutionizing his Metaphysical School through Ariosto's lesson, he started visiting museums to directly imitate their Renaissance masterpieces, and Raphael's *Parnassus* was one of them. Alas, de Chirico's unfinished copy, painted in 1920, is now lost.[44] However, its traces remain in his later work.

Decades after his famous Metaphysical phase, when even the vanguardist classicism of his Ariostean painting was exhausted, de Chirico started to do something that, in the years of his most fruitful dialogue with Ariosto, he never did. He painted scenes from the *Orlando Furioso*. One in particular obsessed him since the 1940s: Ruggiero saving Angelica, on the back of the Hippogriff, from a sea monster. Playing with chronologies and styles, de Chirico always composed this scene so that it could be read, simultaneously, also as a depiction of Perseus rescuing Andromeda in Ovid's *Metamorphoses*, and of the medieval legend of Saint George liberating Princess Silene from a dragon. These paintings, in which the rescued damsel is always modelled after his wife, are so amphibian that de Chirico exhibited them under different titles. After all, as he wrote in his last, unfinished novel, "the most implausible things" are all around us at all times, "within reach," and even a garden lizard is also, at the same time, "the dragon grounded by Saint George who defeated the spirit of evil, it is the dragon pierced by the spear of Perseus to save Andromeda, the one beheaded by Ruggiero's sword to save Angelica."[45]

The last Angelica that he painted, probably in 1950 (figure 0.5), is cheered by a cherub like the Andromeda in Rubens' Baroque painting from Ovid. Her saviour wears sixteenth-century armour, which Ariosto himself (but not his medieval paladins) could have worn in battle. The Hippogriff is not even a Pegasus, just a simple horse. There is no monster. The Chinese Angelica, who is also the Libyan Silene, who is also the Ethiopian Andromeda, looks, with the blue eyes of the artist's wife and muse, outside of the canvas, directly at you. She is both an

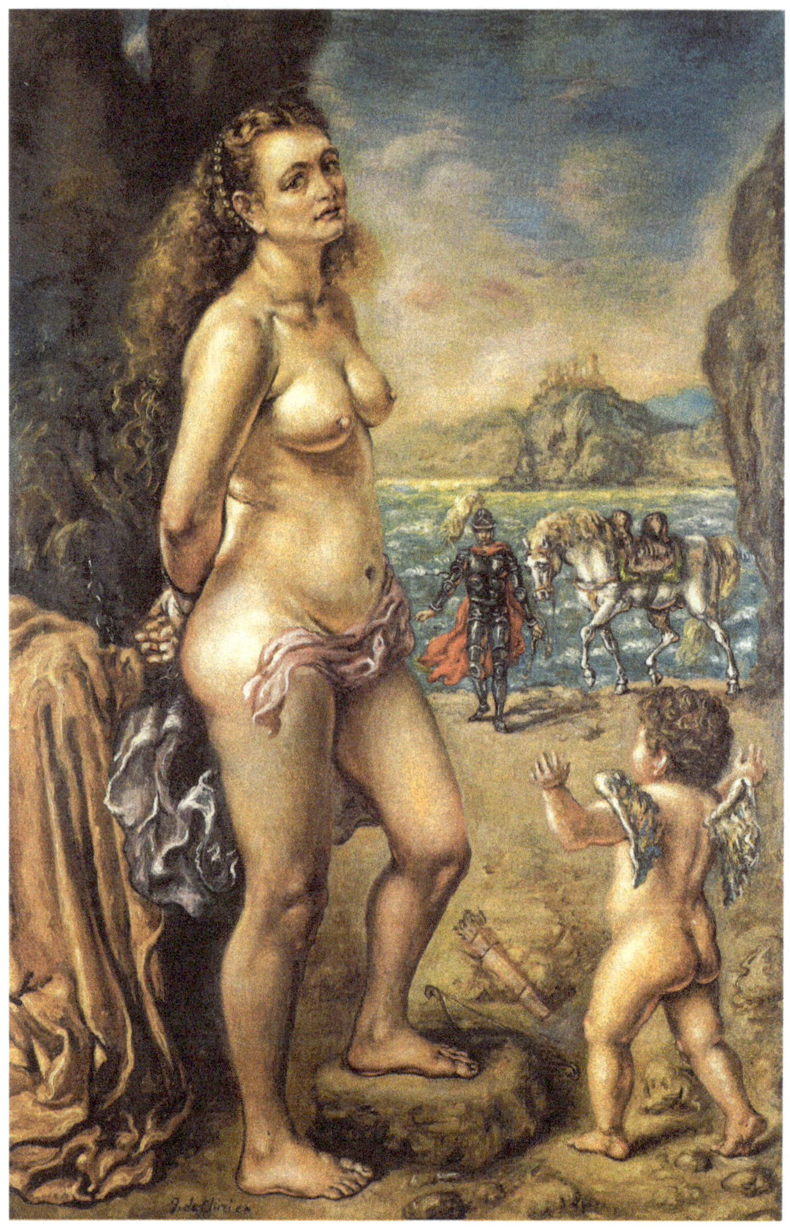

Figure 0.5. Giorgio de Chirico, *Ruggiero and Angelica* (*Ruggiero e Angelica*), 1946–50, oil on canvas, 152 × 103 cm, Collezione Giorgio e Isa de Chirico, Rome.

invention and an incarnation of the poet whom de Chirico read in Athens as a child, then dreamed about in Munich and in Paris, then encountered in Ferrara, and finally joined in Rome and on Parnassus. The poet who taught us how magic is really at our fingertips, that "the most implausible things are here, within reach," that forking paths don't always demand a choice.

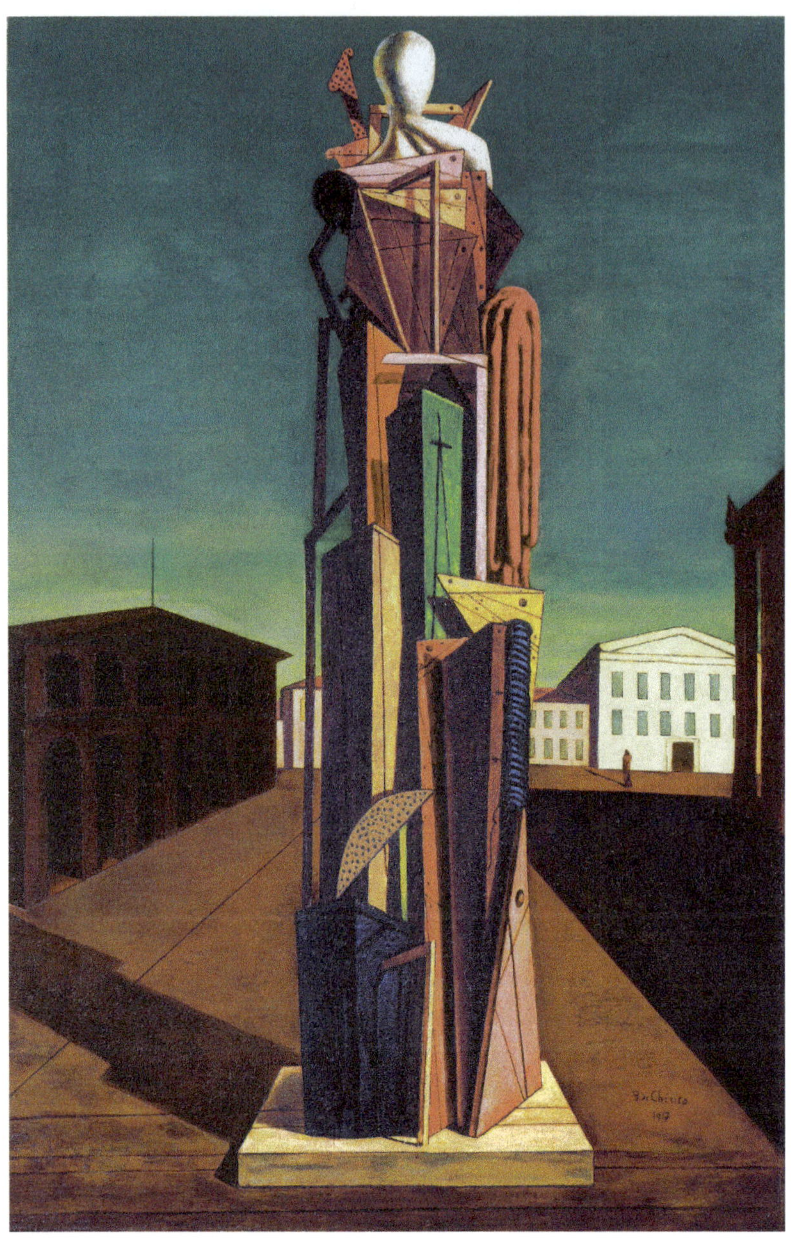

Figure 1.1. Giorgio de Chirico, *The Great Metaphysician* (*Il grande metafisico*), 1917, oil on canvas, 104.5 × 69.8 cm, private collection. © 2022 Artists Rights Society (ARS), New York/SIAE, Rome.

Chapter One

The Great Metaphysician: Ariosto's Encounters with Ferrara's Avant-Garde

This is what makes that smile of Ariosto's so true and so justly celebrated: "Natura lo fece e poi ruppe lo stampo." After Nature stamps a man of genius, she breaks the die.

Arthur Schopenhauer, *On Genius*, 1844

Against a viridian sky made agleam by varnish, in the centre of a square cut by incongruous shadow lines, a cluster of elongated objects stands still, shored up by slender wooden beams (figure 1.1). Drawing stencils, set squares, a piece of cloth, a number of rigid pencil cases: the vertical assemblage in the foreground, taller than the deserted architecture, could come from an artist's workshop, from the colossal desk of a Titan painter. It occupies the entire height of the canvas. There is no sky above, only behind. Atop, white and faceless as a humble sewing mannequin carved out of pure marble, an anthropomorphic bust dominates the surrounding cityscape, looking even taller because of the uncanny perspective. This painting, signed "G. de Chirico 1917," is an icon of European modernism, arguably the most influential piece of art painted in Italy in the twentieth century. It inspired Surrealist painting, Dadaist sculpture, and Cubist scenography.[1] It is a final synthesis of the visual tropes and intellectual revelations that informed Metaphysical art, the most significant Italian contribution to modernism along with Futurism. And it secretly is, as I will show in this chapter, a portrait of Ludovico Ariosto.

Ariosto is hardly mentioned in the indexes of monographs and catalogues about Metaphysical art. Yet, his name appears in one of the earliest written meditations about this movement, *Que purrait être la peinture de l'avenir*,[2] possibly the most quoted page in the legendary Parisian notes that Giorgio de Chirico left behind when he and his brother moved to Italy to join the army and become citizens. When they arrived, in the summer of 1915, their military barracks were on the same street where Ariosto's house had been standing for four centuries. Their first Italian city, after shorter pre-war interludes in Florence, Turin, and Milan, was Ferrara, where Ariosto lived most of his life under the Este dukes, and where his monument, in 1915, was among the tallest structures of the cityscape. It is there that, during the war, Ludovico Ariosto became a totem, a ghostly sculptural idol for the de Chiricos. Other avant-garde artists and poets, between 1915 and 1917, initiated them into the mysteries of the Renaissance city. On the shared experience of those mysteries, suspended between ages, urban objects, literary memories, and spectral apparitions, the brothers founded their Metaphysical school.

In order to understand how Ariosto climbed on top of de Chirico's modernist column of scraps and became the Great Metaphysician, I will start from an earlier apparition of his ghost in Ferrara. The story of Ariosto's dialogue with Metaphysical experimentalists is one of visual and textual revelations at the crossroads of modern and Renaissance Ferrara, and starts with the wanderings of a local Futurist, Corrado Govoni, with a disoriented visitor from Florence. Govoni was the first friend of the de Chiricos in Ferrara. His rather un-Futurist rapport with Ariosto's mystical presence in his city sets the stage for the enigmatic encounters described in this chapter.

A Futurist Stroll in the Past

After a precocious literary debut torn between Japonesque sophistries and modernist objectivity, in 1910 Corrado Govoni invited Italy's most groundbreaking group of artists and writers to his hometown. Their Futurist Manifesto had been published in the Parisian newspaper *Le Figaro* a year before. Govoni, then twenty-six years old, organized a mesmerizing soirée for the Futurists in Ferrara's eighteenth-century theatre of Via del Turco. During that evening of real-time painting, literary performance, and taunting of the bourgeois audience, his poems were recited on the stage by Filippo Tommaso Marinetti, the founder of the movement.

From that night, Govoni playfully adhered to Futurism and became its most illustrious Ferrarese proponent, inaugurating a phase of his work that remains the most famous and celebrated. He is especially remembered for the enchanted and surreal quality of the handwritten *parolibere* (words-in-freedom) that he published in 1915 with the title *Rarefazioni e parole in libertà.* He was completing this book of visual poems, signed "Corrado Govoni Futurista," when he received the visit of another Futurist,

Fernando Agnoletti, who was passing through Ferrara to join Mussolini's Fascio d'azione rivoluzionaria in Milan with Marinetti.

Interventionism was escalating in Italy in the early months of 1915, and Agnoletti had acquired fame for a military fanfare, *Trento e Trieste.* This warmongering anthem, published the year before in Ardengo Soffici's and Giuseppe Papini's journal *Lacerba,* was about to be printed as a stand-alone booklet by *La Voce.* It was through these two flagship literary periodicals of Florence's avant-garde, *Lacerba* and *La Voce,* that Agnoletti and Govoni had come to know each other. The chronicle of their Ferrarese meeting was published in the latter, with the title *I poeti di Ferrara,* in May 1915. Two years later, it became a chapter in Agnoletti's most acclaimed book.[3]

In *I poeti di Ferrara,* Agnoletti recounted his day in Ferrara with Govoni. The story starts from the green ramparts of the old city: the "route of the knights" on top of Ferrara's walls where, in the early twentieth century, horses still passed by "with muffled steps"[4] in the effluvia of the hemp that, according to an old legend, drove the Ferrarese mad. From there, Agnoletti and Govoni descended into Contrada Mirasole to visit Ludovico Ariosto's sixteenth-century house. Hardly a Futurist itinerary, especially considering the exchange that preceded it.

> Over the walls, the houses, and the fields, he pointed at a bleary figure suspended in the sky.
>
> – It's Ariosto, he said.
>
> – Where did they put him?
>
> – Down under there's a square. The gardens of Ferrara are so many and so wide that the squares remain unknown. The city is full of airy clearings filled with flowered trees. If you could see how big was his. Not anymore.
>
> – Let's go see him.
>
> – Let's go. I like Ariosto.
>
> – Me too!
>
> – There are sunny, melodious stanzas with a broad horizon.
>
> – There is that joy of galloping on virgin meadows, riding in the company of wonder.[5]

In fairness, Govoni's love for the Renaissance legacy of his hometown was not entirely disavowed as he embraced modernist poetics. When he collected his lyrical and Futurist texts in a 1920 anthology, he chose a curious frontispiece: a picture of himself, at eighteen, dressed in a sixteenth-century Estense costume (figure 1.2).[6] Still, his 1915 conversation about Ariosto with Agnoletti was quite unorthodox. Or rather, it was a bit too orthodox, so to speak, for a couple of Futurists on the eve of

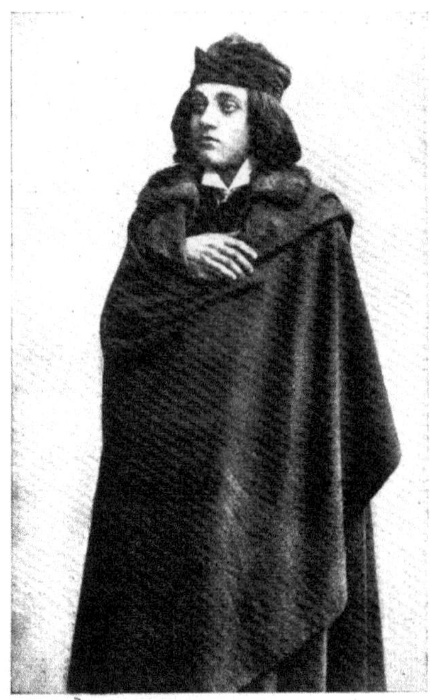

Figure 1.2. Govoni at eighteen, photograph on the frontispiece of Corrado Govoni, *Poesie scelte* (Ferrara: Taddei & Figli, 1920). Biblioteca Comunale Ariostea, Ferrara.

the Great War. Wasn't the plan of their movement "to destroy museums, libraries, and academies of every sort"?[7] Both Govoni and Agnoletti must have been aware of this contradiction. In fact, their dialogue continued with an alarmed expression of guilt ("What would Soffici say?") followed by a second one ("What would Papini say?").[8] Their concerns, however, were baseless.

Ardengo Soffici, a forceful leader of Florence's avant-garde, was the editor of *La Voce* and founder of *Lacerba.* He had famously got into a fist fight with Marinetti's Futurist group at the Giubbe Rosse café in Florence over an exhibition review. In pre-war Italy, he was a champion of anti-traditional radicalism. Yet, probably unbeknownst to Govoni and Agnoletti, he was not immune to Ariosto's charms. In 1911, the year in which he brought Parisian Cubism to the attention of Italian artists through his seminal article *Picasso e Braque,* Soffici was editing a collection of Ariosto's minor poems. In the long preface, he described Ariosto not as a dusty old master to be replaced by new voices, but as a herald of modernity. According to Soffici, "the same language and rhythm of our century's passion is almost forewarned and foreseen" in Ariosto's Renaissance elegies.[9] Two years later, Giovanni Papini, the other modernist eminence in the circle of *La Voce* and co-founder of *Lacerba*, used a line from Ariosto's *Furioso* as the opening epigraph of his most successful book, the autobiographical novel *Un uomo finito*.

In sum, neither Soffici nor Papini could scold younger Futurists for liking Ariosto. However, when they followed the "bleary figure" of Ariosto to his house, Govoni and Agnoletti did something more than pay a cheeky tribute to a classic poet. Their stroll to Contrada Mirasole became a disorienting crossing of memories, both personal and literary.

The first strange symptom of this sudden blending of literature and experience, past and present, was the overlapping of Ariosto's house with another spectral landmark: Dante's tomb in Ravenna, which Agnoletti had just visited in his trip, via Ferrara, to Milan. The two sites (arguably the least Futurist places that one could write about in 1915 Italy) were connected, in Agnoletti's meaningfully deceptive recollection, by a mysterious laurel oak.

As soon as they reached Ariosto's house, Agnoletti asked Govoni about the tree. For unexplained reasons, he expected to find it in the courtyard: "Where did I see it? They cut Astolfo's laurel!" Then, he realized that he had seen it elsewhere, in the city where Dante was buried, along with "marble, sepulchres, white virgins on the golden nave."[10] But, since Astolfo is Ariosto's character and not Dante's, why would his laurel be in Ravenna? Agnoletti's ruse of memory alluded to one of the many cases of intertextuality between Ariosto and Dante, the great poets of Ferrara and Florence, noble ancestral mirrors of the two modern protagonists of the story: the Ferrarese Govoni and the Florentine Agnoletti. In the *Orlando Furioso*, before riding the Hippogriff through the skies to recover Orlando's wits from the moon, the paladin Astolfo is transformed into a tree by Alcina, a malicious sorceress. The scene in which an arboreal Astolfo speaks to the pagan warrior Ruggiero, hissing through his own bleeding branches (VI, 26–9), echoes an iconic passage of Dante's *Inferno*, in which the damned soul of Pier delle Vigne, turned into a tree, addresses Dante as he enters the Woods of Self-Murderers in Hell (*If*, XIII, 31–7). Virgil, who guides Dante in the fiction, was famously the literary father of these arboreal episodes: his Polydorus, also turned into a tree in the *Aeneid* (III, 13–68),[11] has an identical dramatic conversation with Aeneas.[12]

A stratigraphy of cities, poets, and poems, between fiction and reality, encompassed medieval, Renaissance, and modern references in the old streets of 1915 Ferrara. The memory of a real tree at Dante's tomb was connected to Dante's fictional tree in *Inferno*, which inspired Ariosto's fictional tree in the story of Astolfo, which Agnoletti expected to find in Ariosto's real house. It is no surprise that Agnoletti could competently play, in his story, with these echoes between the *Orlando Furioso* and the *Divine Comedy*. Before turning into an habitué of the most vanguardist venue in Florence, the Caffè delle Giubbe Rosse, he had been a Dante scholar at the University of Glasgow. But what matters is that Ferrara's Ariostean landmarks (the statue in the sky, the house with no laurel) were the catalysts of a momentary lapse in his new literary life as an Italian vanguardist. He and Govoni bonded by reciprocally confessing a love for the *Orlando Furioso*, not knowing that it was shared by their avant-garde leaders. When, in Agnoletti's story, they finally entered Ariosto's home, their excitement was ebullient. Agnoletti's geographical and temporal disorientation, ignited by the misremembered laurel, bordered on fantasies of reincarnation.

> I was keeping my ear open, in vain, for the nightingale who used to speak to me, in the fresh evenings, from Astolfo's laurel. I had inhabited those rooms and the gardens, but in a different city, in a different age.
>
> We went up to the study. The good man had looked here for quiet peace. At this table he had tidied the rhymes, concluded the great joyful cycle, hosted the toilsome paladins among the colonnades of the last great poem. Here! this table! him! The only living men are those who love the dead.
>
> I signed, in the album, the last signature. With my heart I blew the kiss of those who love and leave.[13]

As Ariosto's Astolfo is a literary memory of Dante's Pier Delle Vigne, Agnoletti experienced Dantesque memories in Ariosto's house. He had already been in that house, but in a different city (Ravenna? Florence?), in a different age (earlier in his life? in Ariosto's Renaissance? in Dante's Middle Ages?), recalling symbolic emblems of poetic prowess and glory (the nightingale, the laurel). A direct filiation of literary metempsychosis links the Florentine Dante to the Ferrarese Ariosto to the Florentine Agnoletti and the Ferrarese Govoni. These are "the poets of Ferrara" in the title: a genealogy of writers possessed by each other in a sixteenth-century building on the eve of the First World War. No Futurist imperative could hide the fact that literature, at its core, is a form of necromancy: that "the only living men are those who love the dead."

In the varied history of the avant-garde network of pre-war Italy, this strange Ferrarese episode may not be as singular as it looks. Agnoletti was

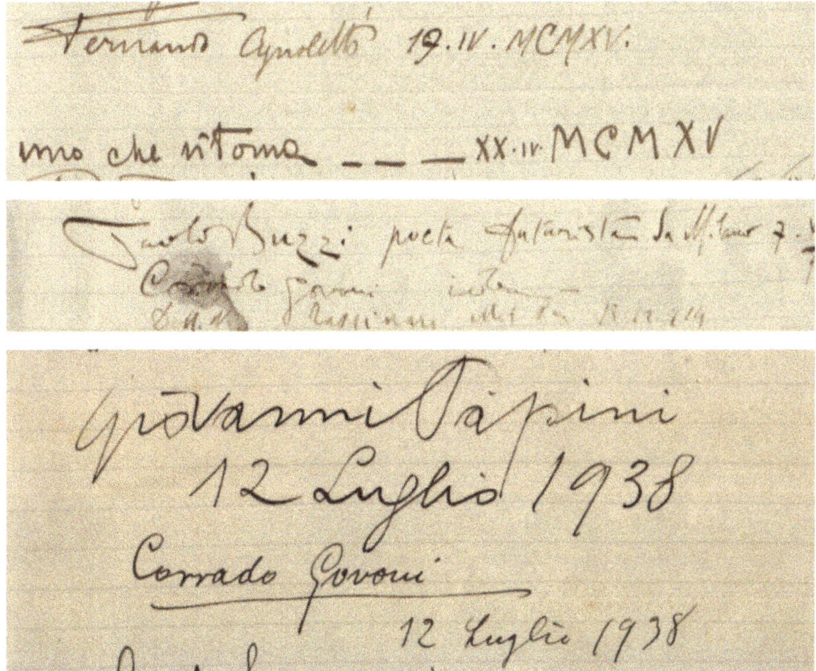
Fernando Agnoletti 19.IV.MCMXV.
uno che ritorna – – – XX.IV.MCMXV
Paolo Buzzi poeta futurista da Milano
Giovanni Papini
12 Luglio 1938
Corrado Govoni
12 Luglio 1938

Figure 1.3. Signatures of Fernando Agnoletti, Corrado Govoni, Paolo Buzzi, and Giovanni Papini in the visitors' register of Ariosto's house in Ferrara. Courtesy Musei Civici di Arte Antica, Ferrara.

the only Futurist who published a chronicle of a tour of Ariosto's house, but not the only one who was guided there by Govoni, whose signature, as recounted in *I poeti di Ferrara*, is in the "album" of Ariosto's house: the visitors' register. To be precise, Govoni did not sign his name, but wrote, under Agnoletti's, the enigmatic alias "one who comes back …" (figure 1.3). He did so because, four months before, he had already guided another fellow Futurist to Ariosto's house. There is no chronicle of this 1914 visit in *La Voce* or any avant-garde journal, but the register shows both signatures: "Paolo Buzzi, Futurist Poet from Milan," along with a more laconic "Corrado Govoni, idem." And many pages later, in 1938, Govoni's signature appears again, this time with that of Giovanni Papini himself – who, by then, had become a fascist professor of literary history.

After the Futurists, between 1915 and 1918, it was the turn of Metaphysical painters and writers to experience a transformational love for the dead through Ariosto's mysterious local aura in "the first really modern city in Europe."[14]

Schopenhauer's Advice

The "bleary figure" that Govoni and Agnoletti spotted in the sky from the walls of Ferrara was a statue, a nineteenth-century sculpture of Ludovico Ariosto. It stood, and still stands, on top of a marble column in the centre of the largest piazza of the *addizione erculea*, an area of Ferrara developed by Duke Ercole I d'Este in the Renaissance (figure 1.4). Ercole I bought that column at the end of the fifteenth century, but it was erected only a century later by the papal administrators of the Baroque age. Throughout the centuries, the column hosted a Pope, an allegory of Liberty, and Napoleon. Ariosto was finally installed on it in 1833, and the square was named after him as Piazza Ariostea. The sight of this marmoreal ghost lured Govoni and Agnoletti to Ariosto's house in April 1915, but it was the monument itself, in the centre of the piazza, that captivated de Chirico's Metaphysical imagination in the following two years – and beyond. A series of surreal experiences of temporal simultaneity and visual revelation, similar to that recounted by Agnoletti, took place in Piazza Ariostea between 1915 and 1917. The de Chirico brothers, along with other acolytes of their Metaphysical School, chronicled or depicted these experiences in literary and pictorial works. In the following pages, I am going to reconstruct this cluster of Metaphysical revelations around Ariosto's monument, which culminated with de Chirico's painting *The Great Metaphysician*. But let me start from the beginning.

Agnoletti's *I poeti di Ferrara* was published, in 1915, on May 15. A week and a day later, Italy declared war on Austria. A week and a day later than that, Giorgio de Chirico and his brother Andrea (by then already known by his nom de plume, Alberto Savinio) arrived in Ferrara, via Turin, from Paris, where they had been gaining fame in Montparnasse: Savinio as Guillaume Apollinaire's favourite musician, de Chirico as the painter that Surrealists would later champion as their precursor. Govoni, as I mentioned, was their first friend. Before finding their own apartment, the de Chiricos lived in Govoni's house in Via Centoversuri, as his guests.

At Govoni's, the brothers browsed the issues of *La Voce* that, as a contributor, he received by mail.[15] Likely, they read Agnoletti's Ariostean story there. In 1916, they would co-sign their own publication in *La Voce*: an imaginative piece of creative prose about Ferrara by Savinio, titled *"Frara" città del Worbas*, accompanied by a poem by de Chirico titled *Mister Govoni Sleeps*. This poem, dedicated to Govoni's dreams, was originally written in the first months of their sojourn in Ferrara, in the summer of 1915.

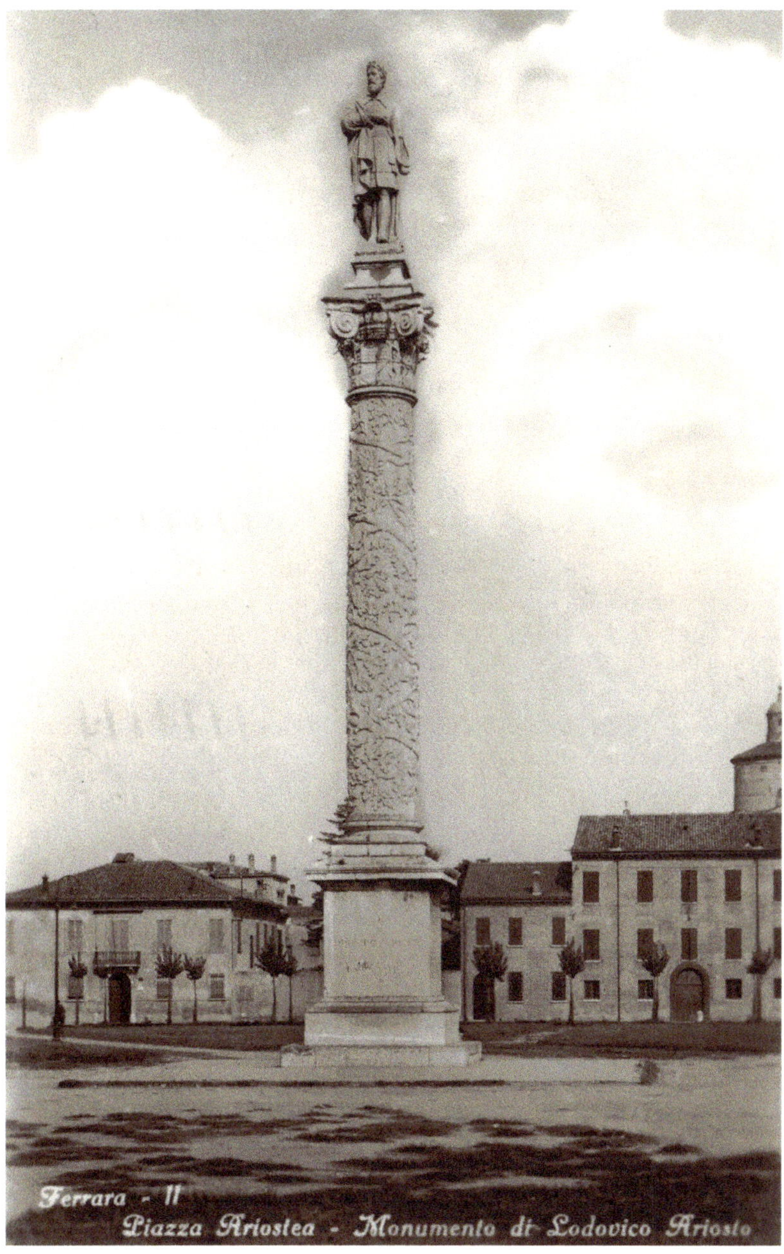

Figure 1.4. Postcard of Piazza Ariostea, 1934. Postcard owned by the author, image in the public domain.

Mister Govoni Sleeps

In the city where they hail him among a thousand statues on pedestals
so low it seems they are walking along with the hurried citizens.
On the stage everything is a mystery …
The mirror on the easel. The painting is not yet finished.
The philosopher sleeps. Someone knocks at the door.
It is his friends; because the sun already descends, and shadows
already long get longer, and invite
peripatetic friendship.
… Someone knocks at the door. In vain! in vain! …
The obscene maid shouts from the window:
All night he has been wakeful, watching
the piazza, and the red castle, and the clear river …
and now he sleeps, sleeps, sleeps, … and one must not,
must not wake him![16]

Mister Govoni Sleeps includes an inventory of the visual themes that dominate Metaphysical painting. Some of these themes were entirely developed in Ferrara: the looming presence of the Estense red castle, for instance, as well as the idea of the cityscape as a well-lit (and yet mysterious) theatrical stage. These pictorial ideas are at the core of one of the most quintessentially Ferrarese paintings by de Chirico, *The Disquieting Muses* of 1918 (figure 1.5). Other elements, like the canvas as mirror, the painting-within-the-painting, or the geometry of lengthening shadows, had been de Chirico's visual obsessions for years. In particular, the theme of Italian squares with statues on low pedestals was foundational for Metaphysical aesthetics.

De Chirico developed these tropes as pictorial refrains in Paris, before the war, in the most iconic period of his artistic research. He was inspired by his contemporary artists as well as some carefully selected Romantic models, such as Max Klinger and Arnold Böcklin. But, most of all, he was inspired by philosophers, Friedrich Nietzsche and Arthur Schopenhauer in particular.[17] The latter was especially important for the development of his conceptual investment in the aesthetics of squares and monuments, which recur in both the de Chiricos' writings and visual works.

As I said, the ideal Italian piazza with a low monument was an essential visual paradigm of de Chirico's early painting. In fact, according to his recollection, Metaphysical art started in 1909, during an autumnal afternoon, with a vision of Piazza Santa Croce in Florence (figure 1.6).[18] This vision resulted in a painting in which de Chirico represented Dante's statue (the geometrical centre of the Florentine piazza until 1966, when it was relocated because of a devastating flood) as a beheaded ruin (figure 1.7).

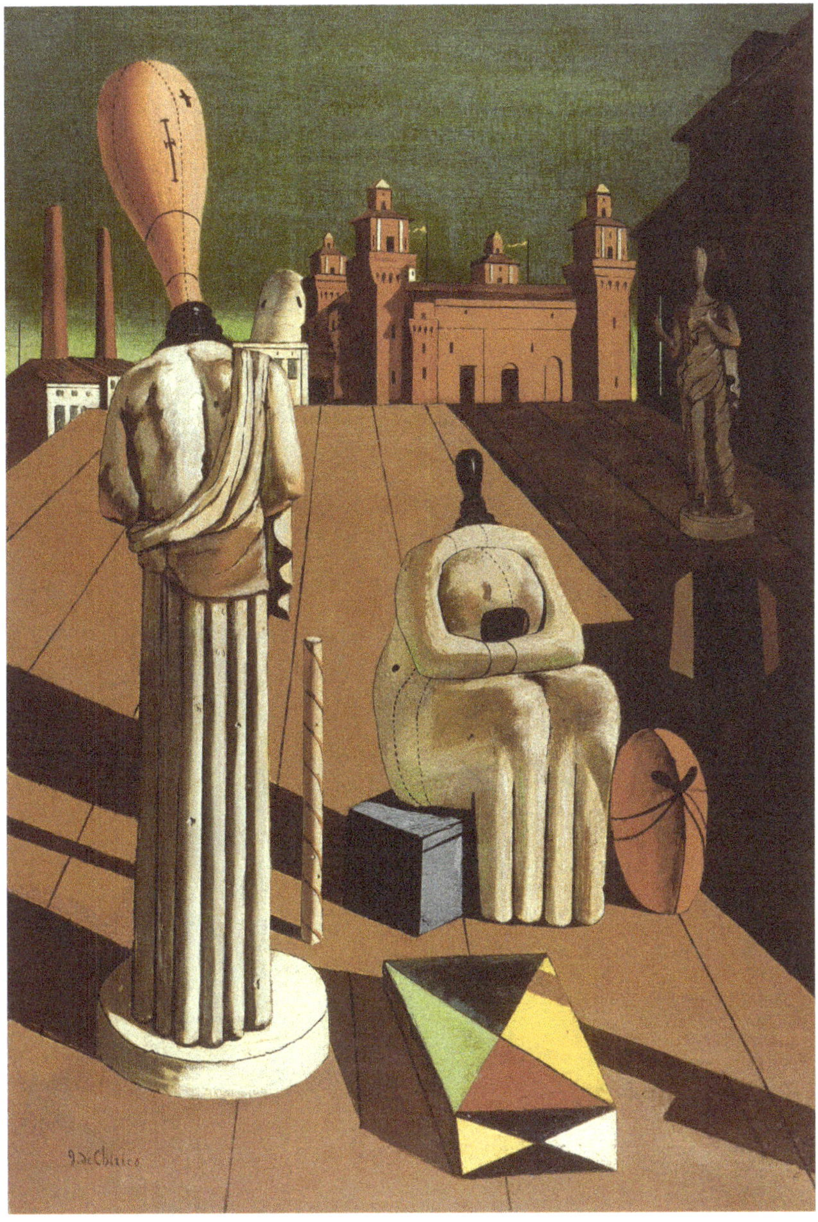

Figure 1.5. Giorgio de Chirico, *The Disquieting Muses* (*Le muse inquietanti*), 1918, oil on canvas, 97 × 66 cm, Collezione Mattioli, Milan. © 2022 Artists Rights Society (ARS), New York/SIAE, Rome.

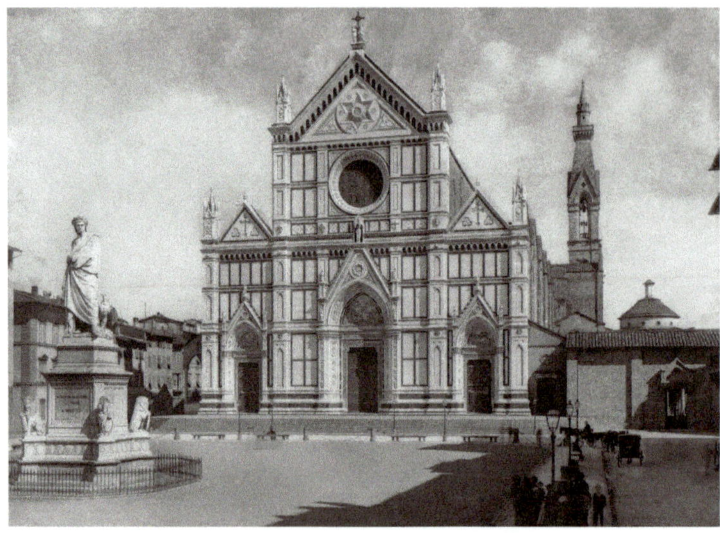

Figure 1.6. Piazza Santa Croce in Florence with Dante's monument in the middle before the flood (Facciata della Basilica di Santa Croce a Firenze). Photograph by Anchise Mannelli, ca. 1905. © Archivi Alinari-archivio Mannelli, Florence.

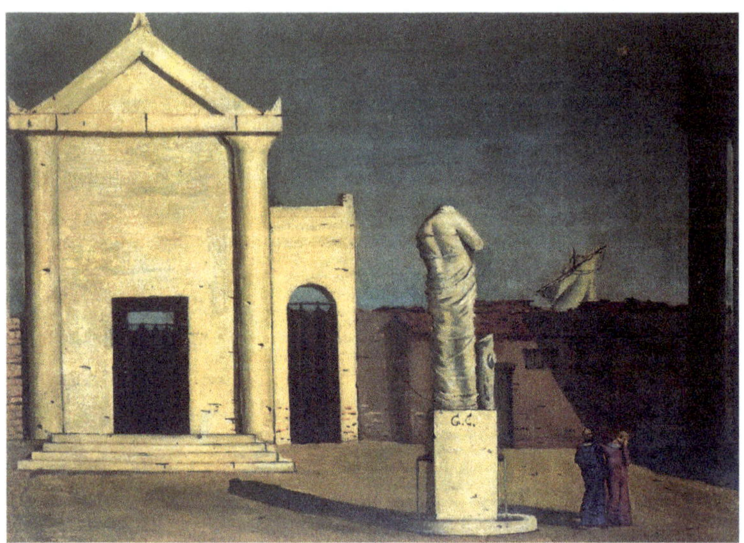

Figure 1.7. Giorgio de Chirico, *Enigma of an Autumn Afternoon* (*L'énigme d'un après-midi d'automne*), 1909, oil on canvas, 45 × 60 cm, private collection, Zurich. © 2022 Artists Rights Society (ARS), New York/SIAE, Rome.

Between 1912 and 1913, a sleeping marmoreal Ariadne appeared in eight different paintings by de Chirico, including *The Soothsayer's Recompense* (figure 1.8). Each of these obsessive repetitions of the same subject represented a different square.[19] The recurring monument in the squares was a famous classical statue (figure 1.9) whose copies, at the time, could be admired in the Vatican museums and in Villa Corsini in Florence, or in the illustrations of Solomon Reinach's *Rèpertoire de la statuaire grecque et romaine*, a central visual source for de Chirico and Savinio. In a surreal "Canto" of Savinio's first book, *Hermaphrodito* (1918), several public statues of nineteenth-century politicians die, falling on their pedestals, "like abandoned Ariadnes." A few lines below, in the same text, a bald woman climbs "like a tin lizard / on the plinth / of Emanuele Filiberto in the pure Turin."[20] These visions evoke Turinese monuments, and in particular a famous equestrian statue of the ancestor of Italy's royal family, Emmanuel Philibert of Savoy (figure 1.10). The same statue appears in some of de Chirico's Parisian works, for instance *The Pink Tower* of 1913 (figure 1.11).

Dante, Ariadne, the politicians, and Emmanuel Philibert have one thing in common. Their statues are mounted on low plinths. Transfigured into essential monuments in de Chirico's paintings, they almost share the same geometrical plane with the people at their feet. To quote from *Mister Govoni Sleeps*, they are "on a pedestal so low it seems they are walking along with the hurried citizens." In terms of pictorial composition, a significant amount of empty space separates them from the top of the canvas: precisely the opposite of what happens in the astonishingly vertical painting from which this chapter started, *The Great Metaphysician* (figure 1.12). This ideal relation between people in marble and human bystanders in de Chirico's early paintings and Savinio's early writings comes directly from *On the Metaphysics of the Beautiful*, the nineteenth chapter of the second volume of Schopenhauer's *Parerga and Paralipomena*:

> [I]t is an obvious lack of taste, in fact an absurdity, to put a statue on a pedestal ten to twenty feet high where no one can ever see it clearly [...]. Seen from a distance, it is not clear; but when we approach it, it is so high up that it has a clear sky as its background, which dazzles the eyes. In Italian cities, especially in Florence and Rome, the statues stand in large numbers in the squares and streets, but are all on quite low pedestals so that they can be clearly seen. [...] Thus, even here we see the good taste of the Italians. The Germans, on the other hand, are fond of a tall confectioner's stand with reliefs to illustrate the exhibited hero.[21]

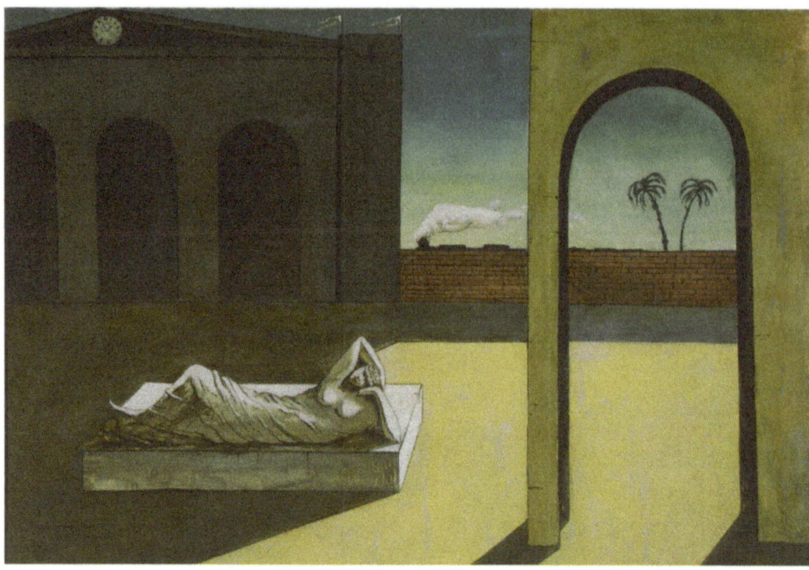

Figure 1.8. Giorgio de Chirico, *The Soothsayer's Recompense* (*La ricompensa dell'indovino*), 1913, oil on canvas, 135.6 × 180 cm, Philadelphia Museum of Art, Philadelphia. © 2022 Artists Rights Society (ARS), New York/SIAE, Rome.

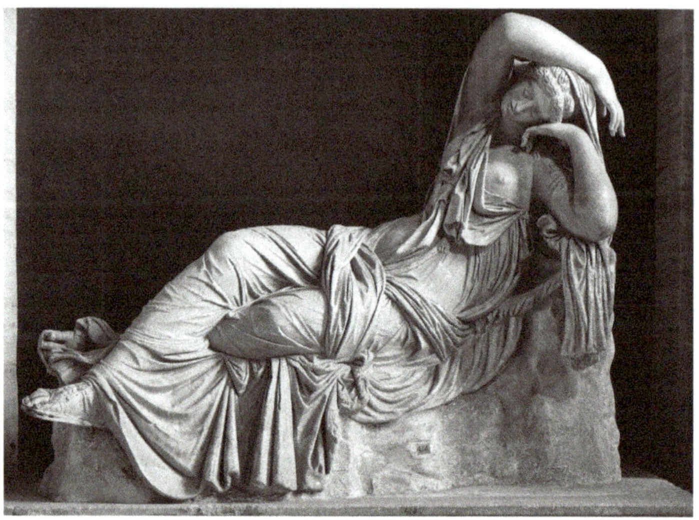

Figure 1.9. Sleeping Ariadne, second century BCE, marble, 226 × 129 × 103 cm, Vatican Museums, Vatican City. Photograph Fratelli Alinari, ca. 1890. © Archivi Alinari, Florence.

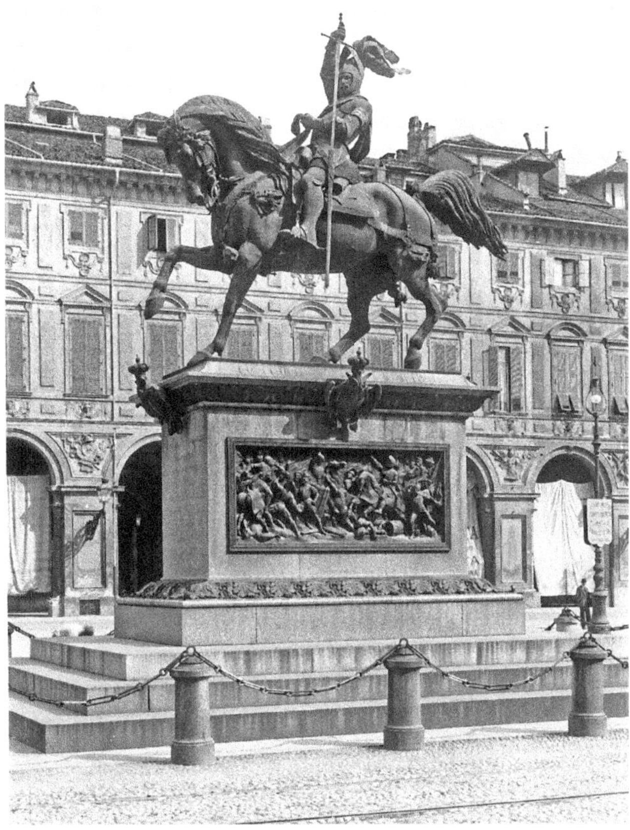

Figure 1.10. Monument to Emmanuel Philibert of Savoy in Piazza San Carlo in Turin. Photograph Fratelli Alinari, ca. 1915–20. © Archivi Alinari, Florence.

De Chirico believed firmly in this Italianate imperative, and echoed it in his theoretical writings. In the section titled "Metaphysical Aesthetics" of his longest essay on Metaphysical art, he paraphrased Schopenhauer in order to explain the main concern of his painting from 1910 to 1914: the "problem of Italian architectural Metaphysics."

> Schopenhauer, who knew a thing or two on such matters, advised his fellow countrymen not to place the statues of their famous men on columns or too high pedestals, but rather to put them on low plinths, "as they do in Italy, he said, where some marble men seem to be on the same level of the passersby and to walk with them."[22]

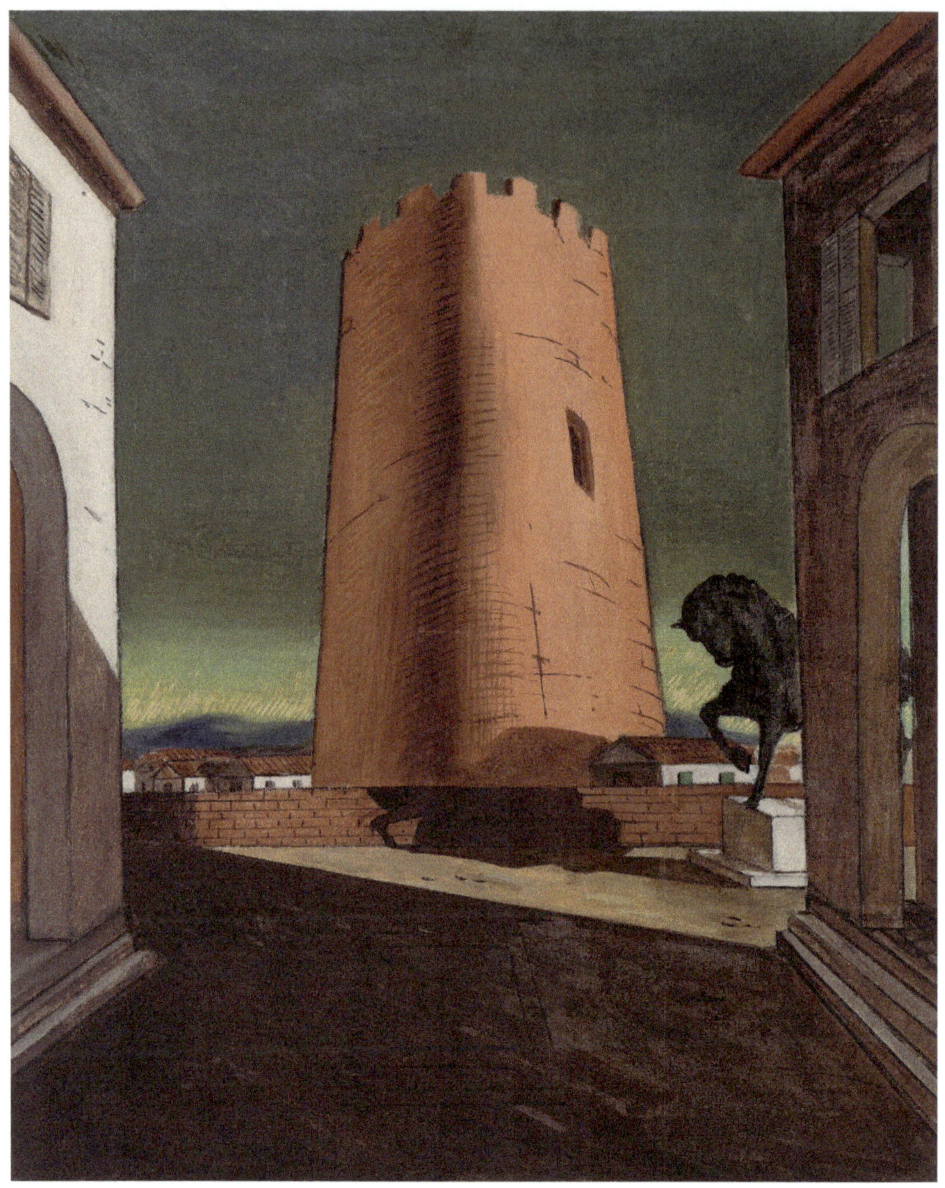

Figure 1.11. Giorgio de Chirico, *The Pink Tower* (*La tour rose*), 1913, oil on canvas, 73.5 × 60.5 cm, Barnes Foundation, Philadelphia. © 2022 Artists Rights Society (ARS), New York/SIAE, Rome.

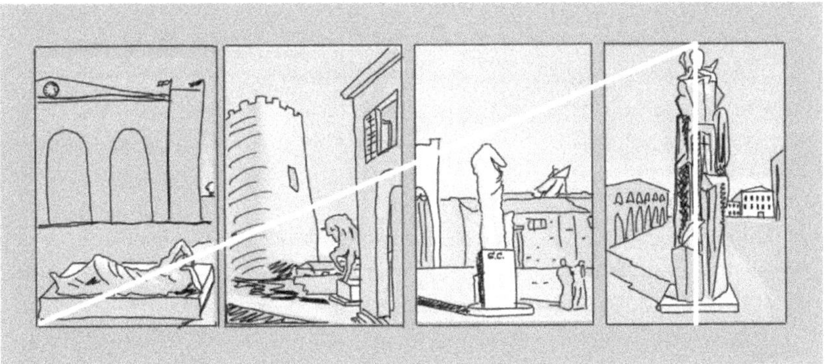

Figure 1.12. Scale comparison of the monuments represented in de Chirico's *The Soothsayer's Recompense, The Pink Tower, Enigma of an Autumn Afternoon,* and *The Great Metaphysician.*

Later, in an article written in French to present his 1935 exhibition in Prague, he insisted on the same point, alluding to the same passage.

> When they mingle with men, the gods just become more divine. I felt this in Olympia, on a moonlit night, looking, from outside, through the windows of the museum built among pines and ruins, on the banks of the river Alpheus with its muddy water, at Hermes, a masterpiece by Praxiteles. This statue rests on a very low plinth so that, when there are visitors, it seems to be alive like them. One could say it is going to move, to talk, and even to walk, to leave the room, to disappear. It is indeed a serious aesthetic and, I would add, metaphysical error to place the statues on too high pedestals, and especially to install them on top of columns. Schopenhauer has stigmatized such a heresy, which is particularly spread in Germany.[23]

Considering the consistency of this Metaphysical motif, rooted in a passage from Schopenhauer that clearly left a strong mark in de Chirico's aesthetics, one can't help but wonder: how did he react to Ariosto's monument? When he arrived in Ferrara with his brother, to reclaim the Italianness of their family and of their aesthetic inspiration (but not – yet – their passports, since they were Greek-born stateless Europeans educated in Germany), that monument was one of the most striking urban landmarks they encountered. The "bleary figure" that their friend and host Govoni identified for Agnoletti, with its very tall pedestal, was in stark contradiction with Schopenhauer's advice. And it was so in the middle of a "sorely metaphysical city,"[24] as de Chirico described Ferrara.

An autobiographical short story by Savinio and a cryptic essay on vision by de Chirico show the brothers' respective Metaphysical reactions to Ariosto's anti-Metaphysical monument. Both were written in Ferrara, the first while de Chirico was painting *The Great Metaphysician*, the second while its photographic reproduction was about to be released in the opening issue of the journal *Valori plastici*. The publication of these two texts also roughly coincided with the brothers' respective departures from Ferrara (Savinio's in 1917, de Chirico's the following year). It was at the end of their Ferrarese experience that, in retrospect, both the de Chiricos were able to make sense of their meetings with Ariosto's marble ghost, and to start encoding what they learned from him in the enigmatic cyphers of their prose and painting.

The Poet in Marble

Savinio left Ferrara in the summer of 1917. Summoned to his native Greece as a translator for Italy's royal army, he travelled by train to the port of Brindisi and then crossed the Ionian sea on a steamboat, like a modern Jason. In Ferrara he had become an avant-garde writer, publishing the first fragments that would form, a year later, his unclassifiable multilingual book *Hermaphrodito*. He wrote one of these fragments while leaving, as a farewell to the disquieting city. It was published in July, in the avant-garde journal *La Brigata*, with the simple title *Ferrara … Partenza*. The setting of this brief, ironic story of wry but tranquil absurdity is Piazza Ariostea.

> I looked at it again, as a usual phenomenon: in the middle of that square sliced like a solar quadrant, I saw the very tall marble column; on top of the stem there was the adventurous poet, who lived and died smacking of bourgeoisie.[25]

Starting on a note of dreamy familiarity, Savinio presents the only two characters of the story. One is the departing author, the other is an element of the landscape. Not the statue of the poet but, according to the letter of the text, "the adventurous poet" himself, standing, as usual, on his column. The "usual phenomenon" of the first line takes place immediately, in the following paragraph, and evokes visual tropes of Metaphysical art.

> As if a sapper wind was blowing – but it was not – I looked at the enormous tubular shaft: it was swashing … washing … washing, and it bent. It traced

> the fourth part of an ideal circle in the sky. It descended, like a benevolent white finger that intended to indicate, on the horizon: all clear, en avant, route!
>
> Phlegmatically, without any noise, it tamely lay down on the grass, where it broke and loosened into a number of tambours that slowly rolled. They stood there for a bit; then they liquefied like snowy drifts in the hollows of little valleys.[26]

Fragments of marble columns would recur, after the end of the decade, in de Chirico's painting and in Savinio's own visual art. There is, however, at least one interesting precedent. In *The Serenity of the Scholar* (figure 1.13), one of the Paris masterpieces that de Chirico painted on unusually shaped canvases, a white gentleman (a ghost? a statue?) leans on the segment of a fluted round column. In front of him, only visible through its shadow on a wall, a tall campanile bends and breaks, like Ariosto's column in Savinio's text. Despite the unconcerned vertical levitation of a puff of vapour from a locomotive, two yellow flags are flying in the wind, which is and is not blowing – again as in Savinio's text. And, in that text, the image of a benevolent white finger indicating the way on the horizon recalls another 1914 painting by de Chirico: *Still Life: Turin, Spring* (figure 1.14). A giant black pointing hand on a vertical white background dominates the left portion of this Nietzschean enigma, which also evokes the Turinese equestrian monument that I mentioned before.

In any event, what really connects Savinio's vision to Metaphysical aesthetics, solving the unacceptable verticality of Ariosto's monument, is Ariosto's behaviour right after the impossible bending and vanishing of his too tall pedestal.

> The poet in marble jumped off the pedestal on which the boredom of centuries had detained him for much too long, with the gliding pirouette of a telegraph deliverer bolting from a moving tram.
>
> ("LA PATRIA," written in black, stayed there, for the order of the peoples.)
>
> First of all he scratched his left buttock; then he whipped the theorbo, which was slung around his neck by a knotted twine, over his shoulder, and he walked with saccadés and shaky steps towards Palazzo Massari, pulling some of his robe over the eyes to protect them from the blazing sun.[27]

Ariosto's jump, as I will show, was a turning point in Metaphysical aesthetics. In Savinio's surreal recollection, the poet in marble dismounted his pedestal to join our company: to mingle with humans. And, as de

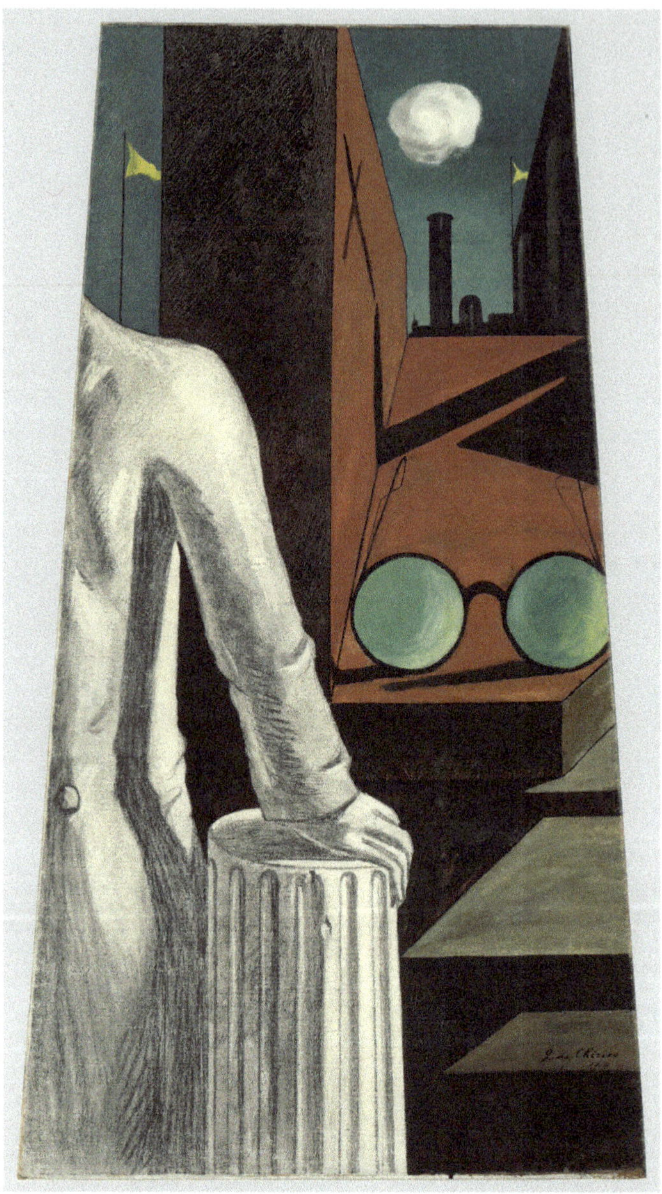

Figure 1.13. Giorgio de Chirico, *The Serenity of the Scholar* (*La serenité du savant*), 1914, oil on canvas, 130.1 × 72.4 (54.9), Museum of Modern Art, New York. © 2022 Artists Rights Society (ARS), New York/SIAE, Rome. Photograph © 2003 MoMA New York.

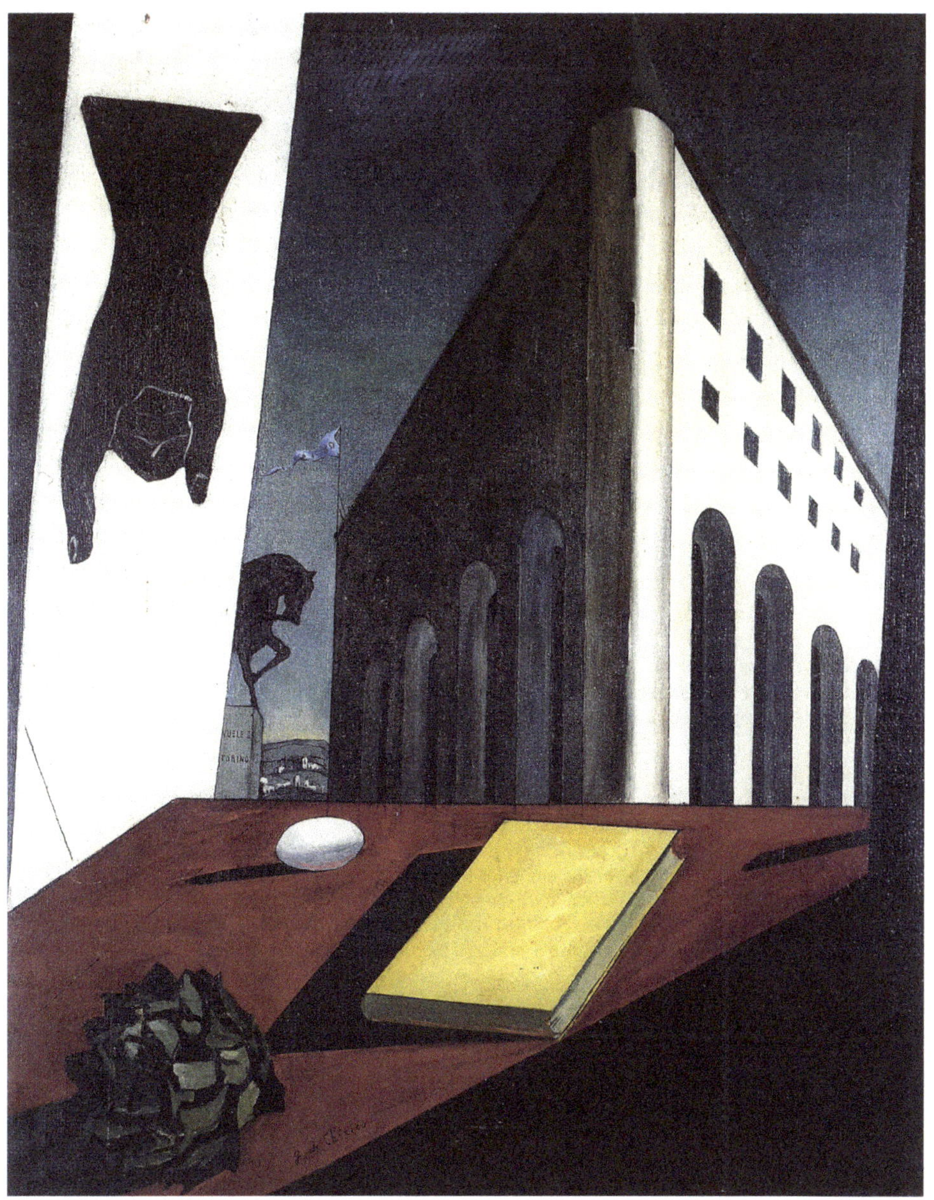

Figure 1. 14. Giorgio de Chirico, *Still Life: Turin, Spring* (*Nature morte, Torino printanière*), 1914, oil on canvas, 125 × 102 cm, private collection. © 2022 Artists Rights Society (ARS), New York/SIAE, Rome.

Chirico put it in his description of Hermes' low statue in Olympia, "when they mingle with humans, the gods just become more divine." Ariosto, however, was not a god, and he came to life like the ordinary, claustrophilic brilliant poet that he was as a man. The nonchalant realism of such an extraordinary, fantastic event is striking and hilarious at the same time in Savinio's text. The living statue acts clumsily – as anyone would after centuries of standing sleep – and walks away, just as Praxiteles' Hermes couldn't do in the archaeological museum that de Chirico wrote about in 1935. Unlike Hermes, however, Ariosto needed his pedestal to bend and break. It was not his monument that suggested, per se, a Metaphysical vision: Savinio's imagination needed to alter the architectural reality of Ferrara to make him join his company in the twentieth century.

Once Ariosto is free from the tall pedestal, he (it?) scratches, shuffles, and shades the marble eyes with marble cloth. Then, he deserts the square just as he deserted his own collapsed monument, and starts meandering in the city. His motivations remain mysterious: does he just happen to come to life on the day of Savinio's farewell? Is he paying homage to the departing argonaut by bending the column and abjuring its heretical verticality? Is the observer actually witnessing a fictional phenomenon? Is he intellectually triggering one? The poet's name on the other hand, is no enigma, even if it is never mentioned in the story (or in the whole of *Hermaphrodito*).[28] Savinio chose to quote just half of his monument's engraving, putting it between the only pair of brackets in the whole text. However, the entire revealing inscription ("A LODOVICO ARIOSTO, LA PATRIA," "To Ludovico Ariosto, by his homeland") is still visible, a century later, in the centre of Piazza Ariostea (figure 1.15). And Piazza Ariostea is certainly the setting of this vision: only one square, in Ferrara, has a lawn with radial walkways converging on a column. Palazzo Massari is really close to it (just a few feet along Corso Porta a Mare). And the tramway, a Ferrarese motif of de Chirico's drawing (figure 1.16) and Savinio's writing,[29] used to run along its perimeter, which connects the castle and Porta a Mare.

In sum, in a lucid reverie filled with Metaphysical visual tropes, Savinio exorcised the shocking verticality of the monument in Piazza Ariostea by demolishing its "enormous tubular shaft" and giving realistic life to the "adventurous poet" on top of it. Awakenings of marble and bronze men would take place in many later writings by de Chirico and Savinio: from the marmoreal Ovid that guides the protagonist in Savinio's *Speaking to Clio* (1939) to the nameless moving statue that, according to de Chirico, haunted Achille Funi's pictorial dreams.[30] However, in all the writings by the brothers, the "poet in marble," with its incongruously tall column, was the very first to actually animate and jump off its pedestal to mingle

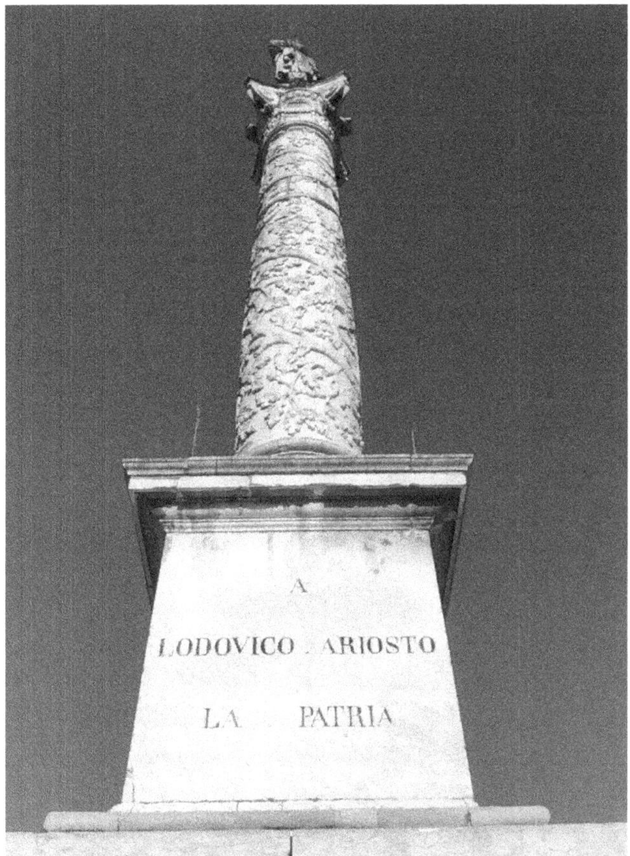

Figure 1.15. Ariosto's monument in Piazza Ariostea, Ferrara, in 2017. Photograph Alessandro Giammei.

with living people. Ariosto's statue in *Ferrara … Partenza* started a Metaphysical genealogy of moving statues, despite, to quote de Chirico once again, its inherent "metaphysical error."

A question, however, remains. Why did Savinio set his pivotal departure scene in such an incongruous square in the first place, when Ferrara is so full of perfectly "Italian" cityscapes (figure 1.17)? An ominous Savonarola in marble animatedly preaches on a low pedestal in the homonymous piazza, vividly recalled by de Chirico in a 1920 article.[31] A Garibaldi in bronze seems to be on the verge of falling from his low plinth, almost like a sleeping Ariadne, in the Giardini Margherita. Pope

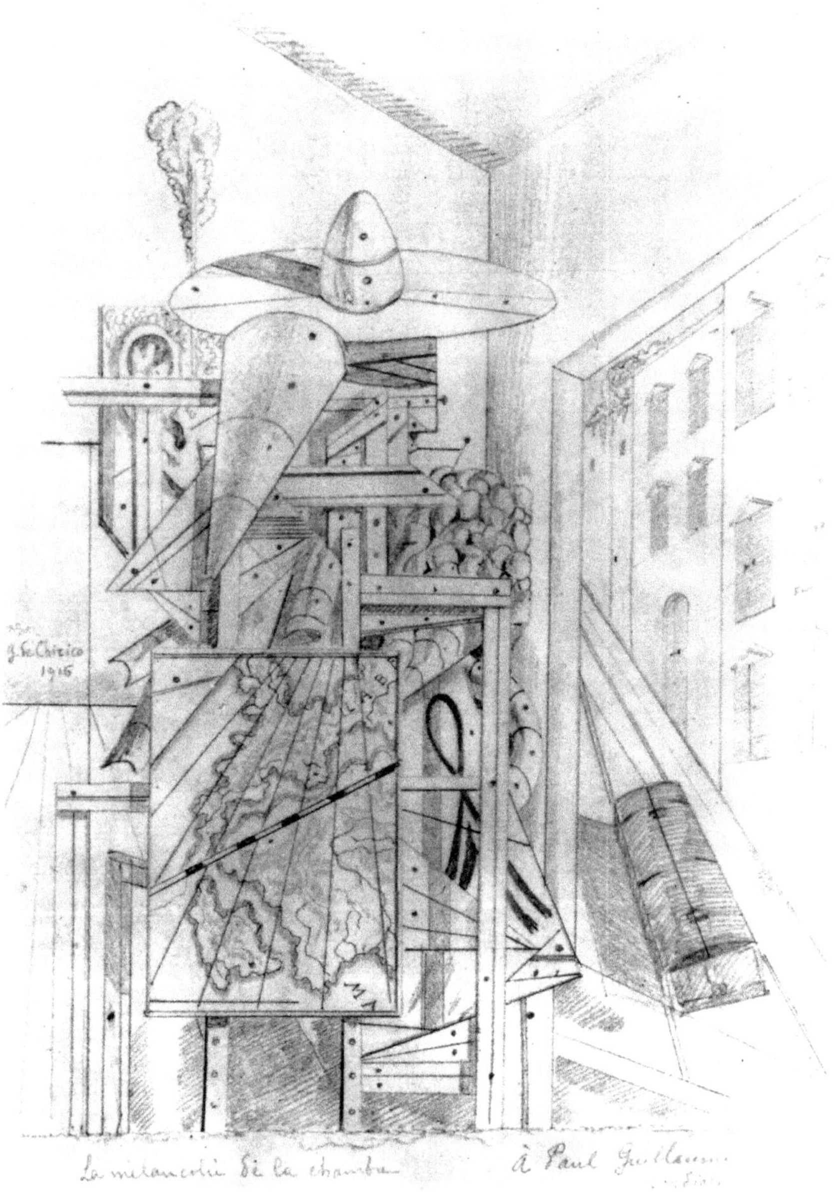

Figure 1.16. Giorgio de Chirico, *Melancholy of the Room* (*La mélancholie de la chambre*), 1916, pencil on paper, 31 × 20.5 cm, private collection. © 2022 Artists Rights Society (ARS), New York/SIAE, Rome.

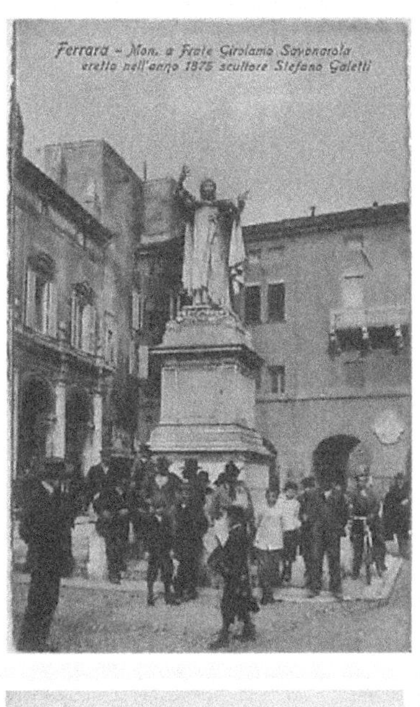

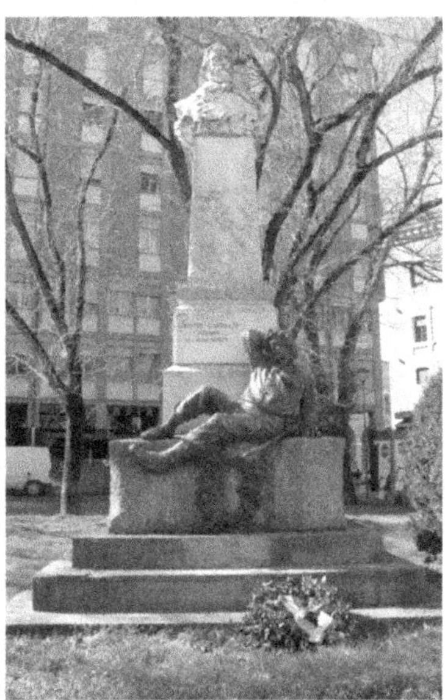

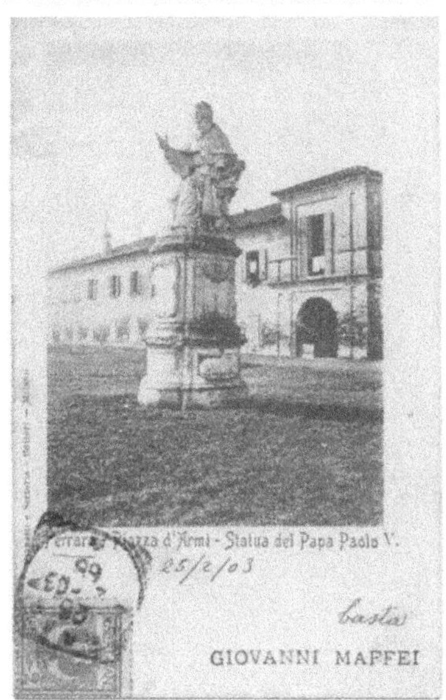

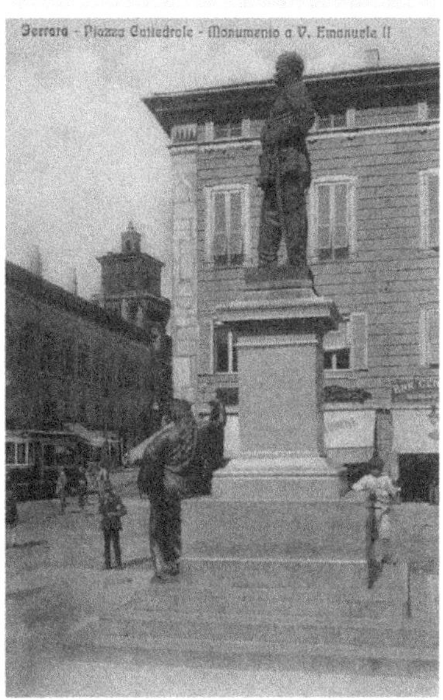

Figure 1.17. Four Ferrarese monuments: Girolamo Savonarola, Giuseppe Garibaldi, Pope Paul V, and Vittorio Emanuele. Postcards and pictures owned by the author, images in the public domain.

Paul V, sitting on his marble throne, used to bless the passersby from a low plinth in Piazza d'armi, before they moved him to the courtyard of the Chiesa dell'Addolorata. Even King Vittorio Emanuele himself, back in the first decades of the twentieth century, used to inhabit a low pedestal in Piazza della Cattedrale. An allegory of Ferrara, sculpted by Giulio Monteverdi, was leaning on his basement with a hand on her hip, literally sharing the same ground with bystanders.[32] Aren't these the low statues of *Il signor Govoni dorme*? Aren't these the protagonists of the last poem written by de Chirico in Ferrara, *L'ora inquietante*, so intertextually linked with *Ferrara … Partenza*?[33]

> All the houses are empty
> Sucked up by the aspirator sky.
> All the piazzas deserted.
> All the pedestals widows.
> The statues – migrated in long
> Stone caravans
> Toward faraway ports. […][34]

To understand why Ariosto's monument was so significant for Savinio, we need to move to the other Ferrarese text that engages it from a Metaphysical perspective: de Chirico's essay *Arte metafisica e scienze occulte.* In the summer of 1918, a few months before the end of the war, de Chirico wrote this piece to clarify the difference between the mysteries of his art and those of occultism. His pictorial visions, he explained, are much more interesting than the results of séances or psychic photography: "as far as I am concerned," he stated, "I believe that there is much more mystery in a square fossilized in the flare of meridian light than in a dark room, in the middle of the night, during a session of spiritism."[35]

The comparison between the clarity of metaphysics and the liquefying vagueness of occult practices led de Chirico to reconstruct a small gallery of examples of what one can see through the "beautiful dream dreamt with open eyes, at the height of noon, in the face of inexorable reality"[36] that is modern art in the Anthropocene:

> The sky has to be enclosed in rectangular windows and in the arches of urban porticos if we want to deftly milk the vast breasts of its treacherous dome. The earth itself, hard and compact, that we feel under the soles of our boots, is defeated today by the metaphysicality of human constructions, despite the chains of its granite mountains, the night of its centenarian woods, and the agitation of its sterile, tormenting seas. And so today you see a suburban factory watched over by the solemn lookout of the chimneys;

> you see a train station, a piazza surrounded by cubes of coloured stones and adorned with *squares* and statues wearing coats, they spring high spurts, real geysers of metaphysical lyricism that you wouldn't receive from any natural landscape, lovely or lugubrious, on our planet.[37]

Maurizio Fagiolo suggested linking each of these visions to specific canvases of de Chirico's Ferrarese period: works that depict the structures and chimneys of the factories on the Po River, and clothed statues sharing a square stage with colourful polyhedrons. These Metaphysical cityscapes, such as those in *The Disquieting Muses* or *Metaphysical Interior with Large Factory* (1916), were inspired, according to de Chirico, by "that joy, that serenity that, in art, is provoked by the apparition of a metaphysical image."[38] As an emblematic example of such superior images, de Chirico added one last Metaphysical revelation. This time he did not just rapidly mention it: he described it in detail, narrating its genesis in his own eye and mind.

> Yesterday, in the afternoon, passing through a street that stretches between tall and dark houses, I saw a column appear at the end, surmounted by a statue. I would later learn that it was Ariosto's. Seen this way, between those two walls of blackened stone that looked like the walls of an ancient sanctuary, the monument got something mysterious and solemn, and the rather metaphysicizing passer-by could expect to hear the voice of a god prophesying from the square.[39]

This apparition – an echo of Govoni and Agnoletti's sighting, and of Savinio's "usual phenomenon" in *Ferrara … Partenza* – completed the gallery of Ferrarese views of *Arte metafisica e scienze occulte* with a last, powerful image presented as a mental event or, to use de Chirico's words, a metaphysical fact: *un fatto metafisico*, resulting from the marriage of sight and thought. This last, more thoroughly described revelation should be connected, just like those of factories and squares and coated statues, to a specific painting of the period. That painting, the one from which this chapter started, might very well be the most important of de Chirico's Ferrarese years if its title, *The Great Metaphysician*, is to be taken seriously.

High Degree of Metaphysicality

In *Arte Metafisica e scienze occulte*, de Chirico explains that Metaphysical revelations are triggered by inherently Metaphysical objects. Metaphysical objects need to be recognized, isolated, and graded by a Metaphysical intelligence. Such objects respond to a concrete hierarchy: a scale of metaphysicality ("metafisicità") that is both discovered and imposed by the observer.

In the layout of *Ars Nova*, the journal of modernist music in which *Arte metafisica e scienze occulte* was printed, the apparition of Ariosto's monument opens, after a blank space with three asterisks, the second of the essay's three parts. After the distinction between occultism and Metaphysics in the first part, this central section focuses on how a Metaphysical painter "Metaphysicizes" objects. The "primitive peoples," explains de Chirico, used to unconsciously separate some special things from ordinary objects through their "vague mystical instinct." A modern "artefice" (a material creator of art, an intellectual artisan) can instead consciously, willingly distinguish "such things" from the chaotic mass of visible matter, and then measure and assign them their natural "grade" of significance.[40]

This theory of vision was evidently indebted to Schopenhauer's *Wille und Vorstellung*. It was also influenced by the fascinating measuring instruments in the laboratory of a legendary Italian physicist and astronomer, Giuseppe Bongiovanni, whom de Chirico and Savinio befriended in Ferrara. The main logical result of the theory is that, according to de Chirico, vision itself is not passive reception, but a form of active analysis and election. The seer manipulates the power of visible things by "guiding, or better increasing, fixing or shrewdly exploiting the metaphysicality revealed in the objects": their "metaphysical state."

> Such a metaphysical state is represented, in those objects that are endowed with it, by a badge that determines its grade. No need to say that the graded object is intrinsically worth as much as a non-graduated one. Objects that are garnished and given a chevron in such a way acquire a special value and significance in the crowd of polymorphic and monomorphic volumes that encumber our planet.[41]

The idea of measuring the degree of Metaphysicality of objects to assign them a grade or rank is not just theoretical. De Chirico depicted the "gallone," the badge or measure that determines such grades, in several ways during the Ferrarese years. A literal military chevron (figure 1.18) appears in a number of drawings of the period, as well as in canvases such as *The Revelation of the Solitary* (figure 1.19). In other works, objects are "graded" in the painting by actual linear devices. A striking example is offered by the measuring sticks and thermometers in the preparatory study for *The Toys of the Sage* (figure 1.20), which were then turned into set-squares in the painted version. Carlo Carrà, the other master of Metaphysical painting, who shared a room with de

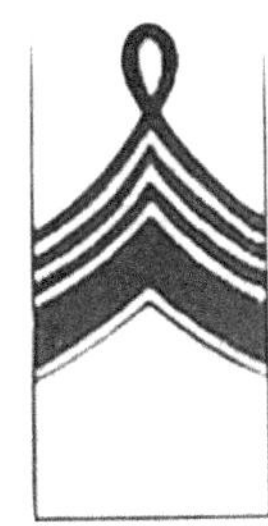

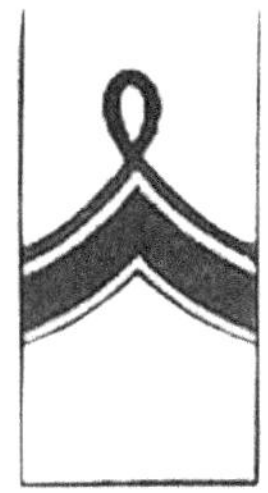

Figure 1.18. Military chevrons on the sleeves of enlisted soldiers (ranks of Sergente Maggiore and Sergente) of the Italian Royal Army. The two insignia on the left are as they appeared from December 1915 to March 1917, on the right as they appeared after March 1917.

Chirico in Ferrara's psychiatric clinic, included measuring instruments in his coeval compositions inspired by de Chirico's theories: a giant ruler, compasses, and oddly marked mercury columns (figures 1.21 and 1.22).

The most eloquent and, at the same time, indecipherable declension of this motif is a painting that de Chirico composed around the time of Savinio's departure, *Tobias' Dream* (figure 1.23). The vertical organization of this Ferrarese interior is slightly less pronounced but similar to the striking one of *The Great Metaphysician*, which was painted in the same months. The foreground is occupied by a measuring object that looks like a thermometer, or a giant marble metronome; a stele divided into seven degrees. Each interval of this graduated scale, except the first and the last, corresponds to a letter, forming the cryptic cypher A I D E L. A blend of biblical and hermetic imageries, Greek lexicon and family symbology, may lie behind the letters, and the object has been interpreted in various ways. However, the obsession for measurement and grading expressed in *Arte metafisica e scienze occulte* is definitely at the core of this impenetrable masterpiece. And I believe that its imagery, like all the Metaphysical visions discussed above, should be linked to a specific Ferrarese urban object.

I am alluding to one of Ferrara's most curious landmarks: the linear water gauge in marble that marks out one of the columns of the portico in Piazza Savonarola (figure 1.24). This object, called the *Padimetro*, is a monumental hydrometer that has been registering the water levels of the Po River since 1705. As its vertical quadrant still shows today, it was

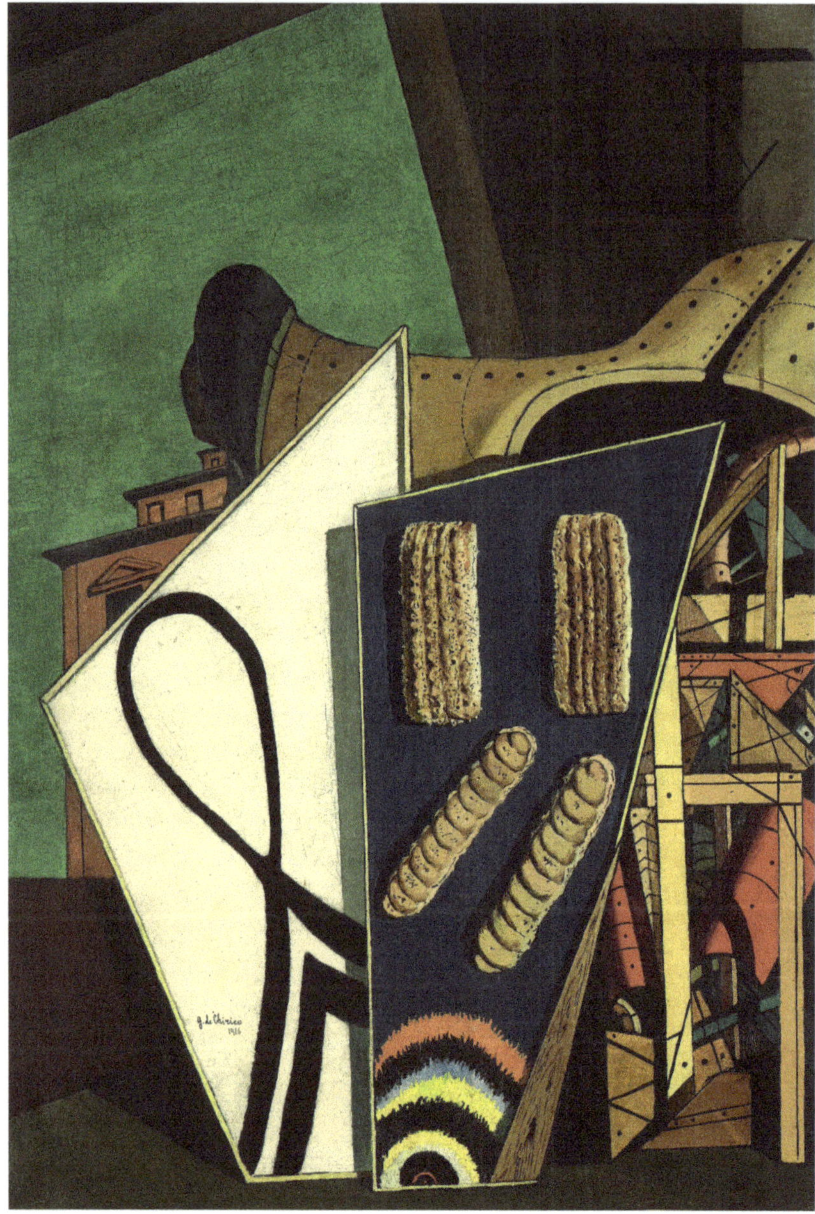

Figure 1.19. Giorgio de Chirico, *The Revelation of the Solitary* (*La révélation du solitaire*), 1916, oil on canvas, 76.8 × 53 cm, private collection. © 2022 Artists Rights Society (ARS), New York/SIAE, Rome.

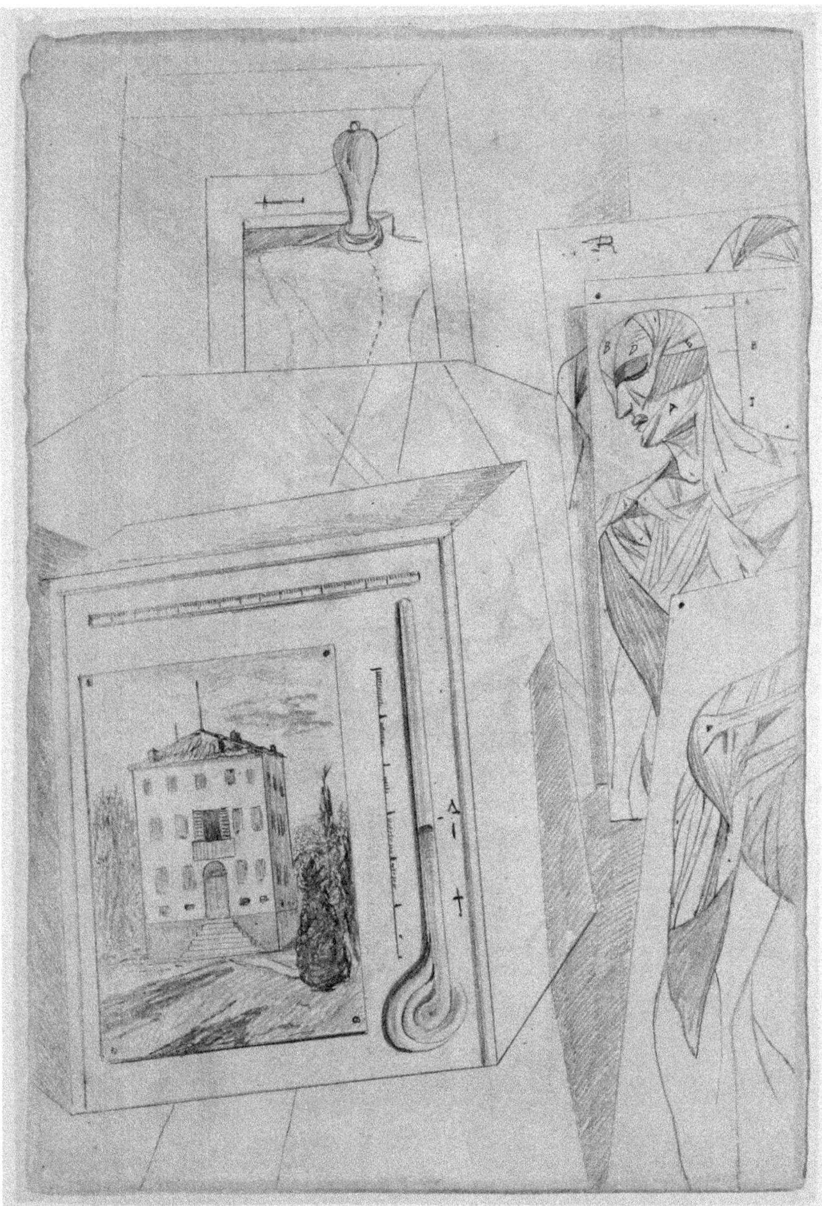

Figure 1.20. Giorgio de Chirico, preparatory drawing for *The Toys of the Sage* (Studio per *Les Jeux du Savant*), 1917, pencil on paper, 32 × 22 cm, private collection.© 2022 Artists Rights Society (ARS), New York/SIAE, Rome. Courtesy Galerie Natalie Seroussi.

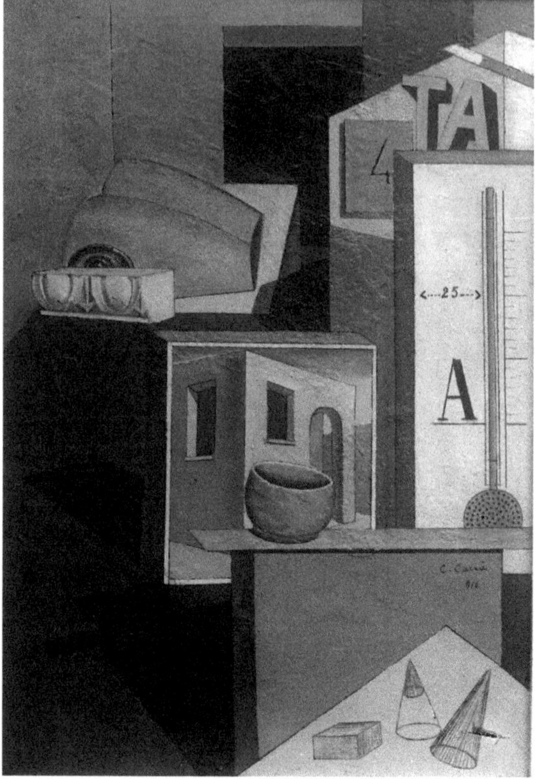

Figure 1.21. Carlo Carrà, *TA Composition* – first version (*Composizione TA* – prima versione), oil on canvas, 1916 (reworked in 1918), 70.5 × 54.5 cm, Museo di arte moderna e contemporanea di Trento e Rovereto, Rovereto. © 2022 Artists Rights Society (ARS), New York/SIAE, Rome. Photograph Archivio Carlo Carrà.

marked with a new record exactly in 1917, in the middle of de Chirico's work on *Tobias' Dream* and *The Great Metaphysician*. Its flat white scale marks the sharp corner of a colonnade that could be the physical echo of the Metaphysical structure that is represented in the painting within the painting, on the right of the A I D E L stele.

Considering the agency of the artist as observer, and the place of honour that Ariosto's prophesying statue takes, in de Chirico's essay, as the culmination of a gallery of urban revelations, one might ultimately suppose that not only is the choice of the marble poet meaningful, but also

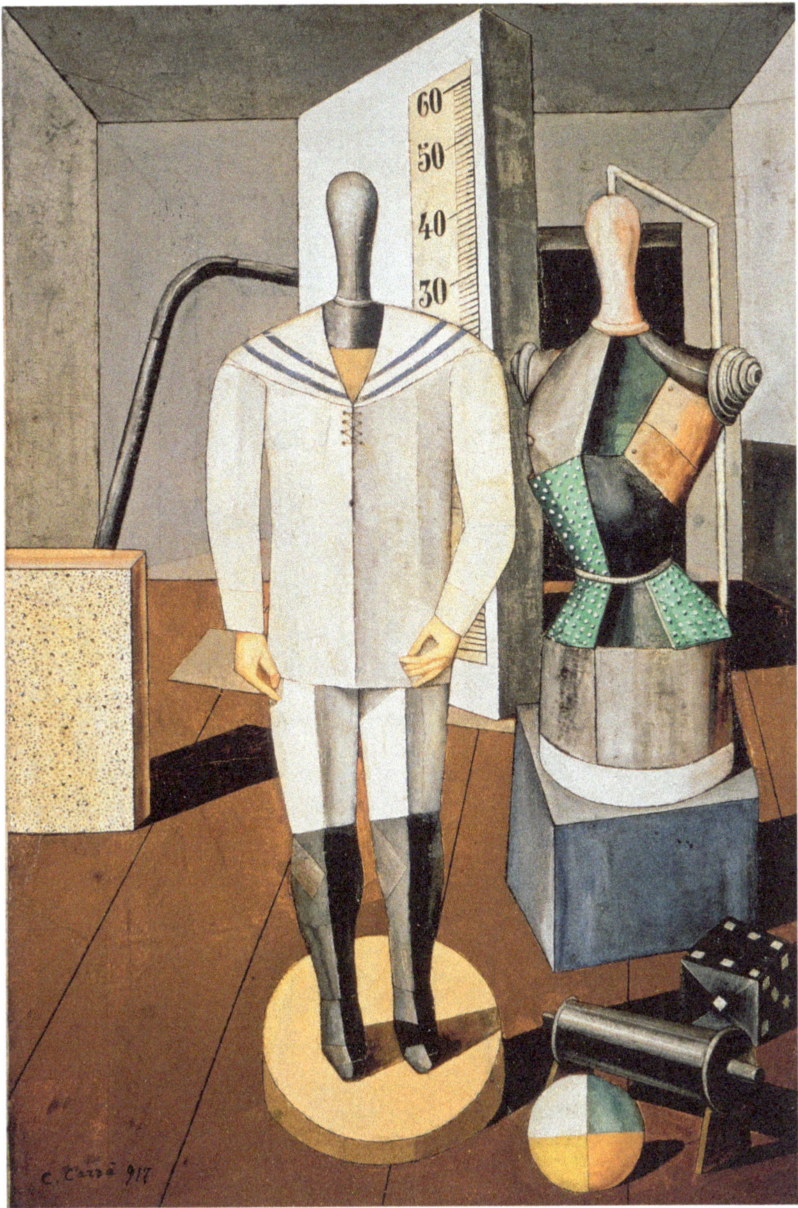

Figure 1.22. Carlo Carrà, *Mother and Son* (*Madre e figlio*), 1917, oil on canvas, 90 × 59.5 cm, Pinacoteca di Brera, Milan. © 2022 Artists Rights Society (ARS), New York/SIAE, Rome. Photograph © Luca Carrà.

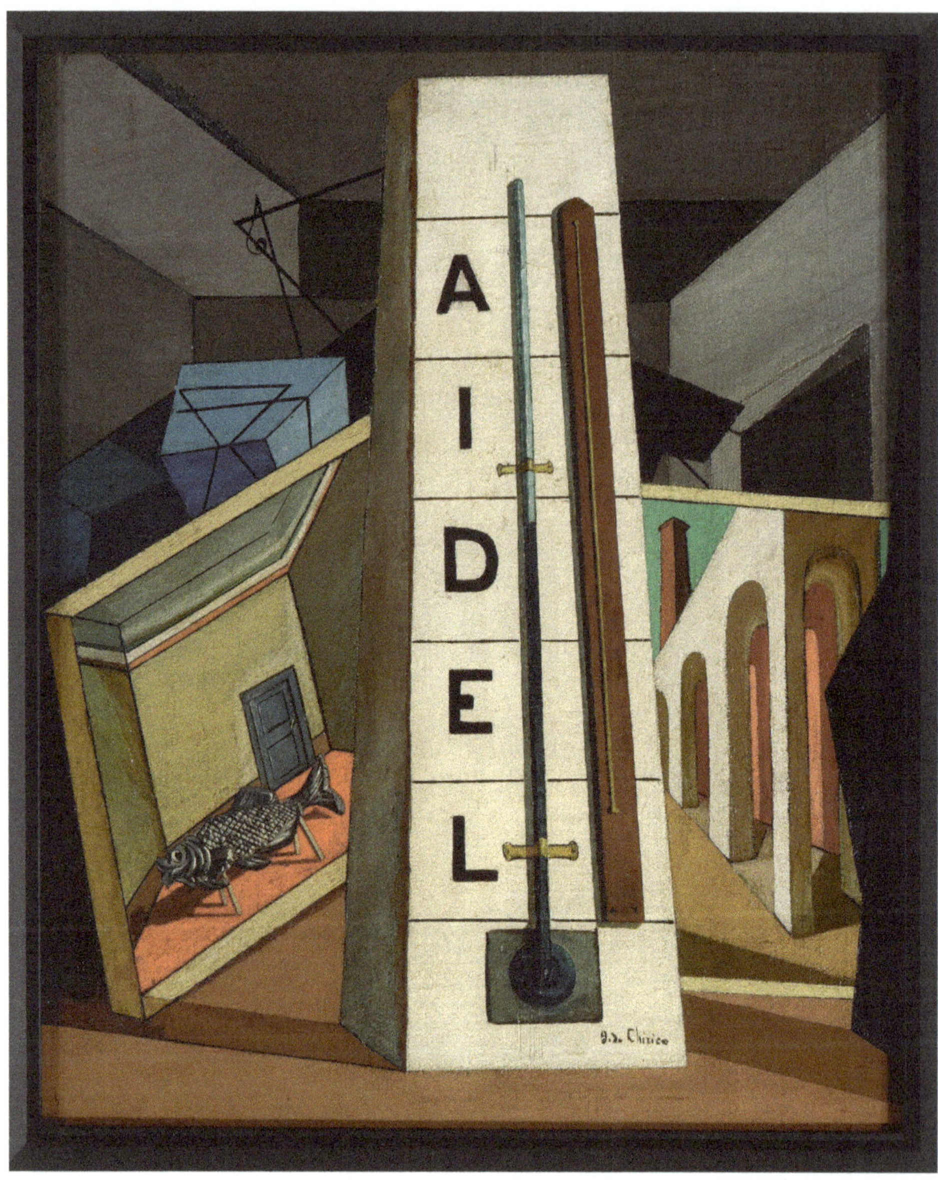

Figure 1.23. Giorgio de Chirico, *Tobias' Dream* (*La rêve de Tobie*), 1917, oil on canvas, 59 × 48.9 cm, The Bluff collection, USA. © 2022 Artists Rights Society (ARS), New York/SIAE, Rome.

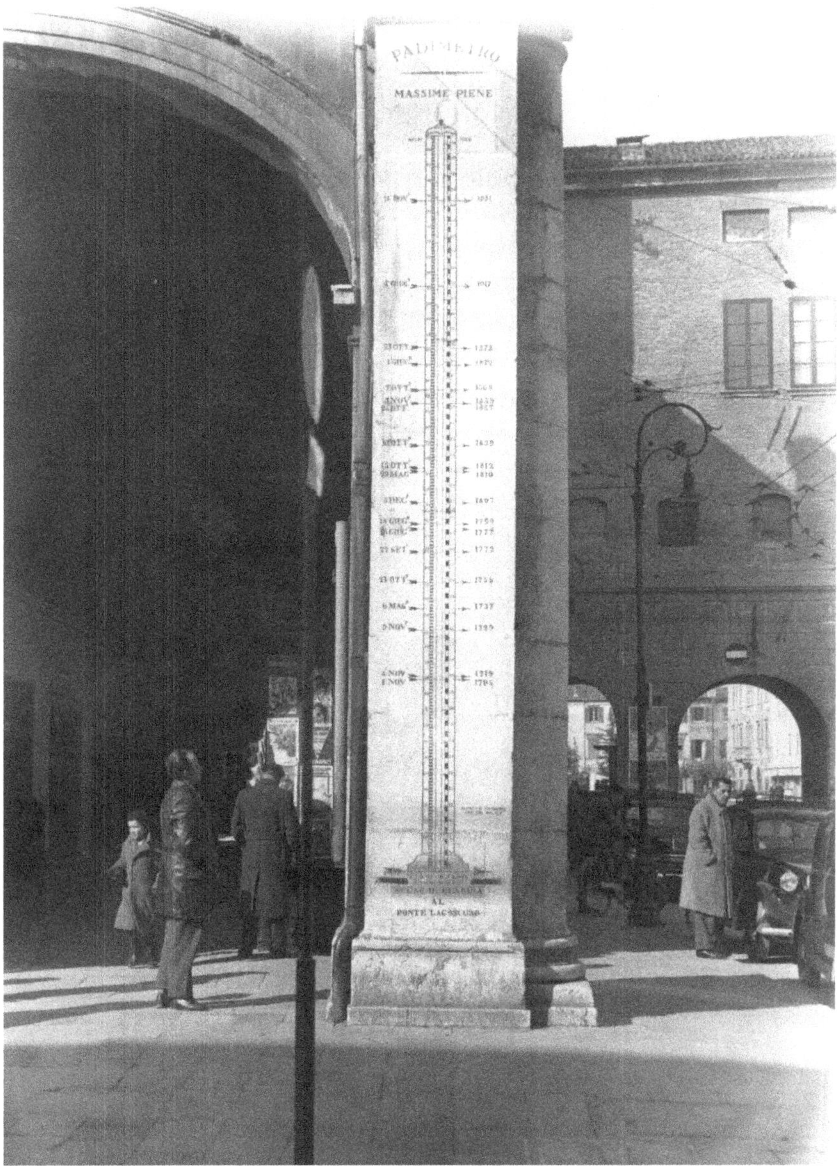

Figure 1.24. Photograph of the marble *Padimetro* (hydrometer) in Piazza Savonarola, Ferrara, early 1950s, 23.5 × 17.5 cm. Provveditorato regionale alle opere pubbliche, Series 5, Ufficio del Genio Civile di Ferrara, Album 3, Photograph 51/127. Courtesy Archivio Storico della Regione Emilia Romagna.

such an object – the petrified poet on his pedestal in that specific square – is graced, to use de Chirico's words, by a high "degree" of "metaphysicality." After all, de Chirico himself "graduated" it – not by placing a mercury column or a military chevron on it, but by titling the painting that represents its apparition with a self-explanatory qualification. Indeed, while many things are "metaphysical" in de Chirico's titles, he painted only one "Metaphysician" during the Metaphysical period of his painting. He also "graduated" him with an eloquent rank: "the Great." On the A I D E L scale of *Tobias' Dream*, the marmoreal ghost spotted by Govoni, met by Savinio as it jumped off its pedestal, and seen by de Chirico at the end of a narrow street in Ferrara would reach the top grade: the A of Ariosto.

All the clues gathered so far point to one solution of the enigma that informs *The Great Metaphysician.* In Schopenhauerian terms, the square is "absurd," and the column is a "heresy," but the statue on top of it can awaken and solve the "metaphysical error" of its plinth because it is special. De Chirico gave to Ariosto an ideal badge, favouring him over Ferrara's other more Schopenhauerian men in marble and bronze. In *Arte metafisica e scienze occulte*, he transfigured the incongruous monument into an emblem of the cerebral visions of Metaphysical aesthetics. Then, he turned it into the subject of a pivotal painting, revolutionizing the aesthetics of the Metaphysical square.

In 1920, already in a different phase of his artistic life and far away from Ariosto's city, de Chirico meaningfully placed the "ineffable Piazza Ariostea" at the epicentre of the "wonderful apparitions of spectrality and subtle beauty that stop and stun the astute passerby, educated in the mysteries of intelligence," in the "city of surprises," the "sorely metaphysical city."[42] No other square with a monument that tall appeared in de Chirico's iconography, not even in the late pastiches inspired by his own early work, the so called Neo-Metaphysical paintings. Verticality, in his landscapes, remained a prerogative of landmarks of the Machine Age (chimney stacks, skyscrapers) or vestiges of bygone ages (castellated towers, lighthouses). *The Great Metaphysician* is the one exception, and that is why it is so iconic. It was elaborated in a version dated 1925 and titled *The Great Machine*, today housed in the Honolulu Museum of Art (figure 1.25). It was painted again, in the mid-1920s, by de Chirico himself – in a new, darker version that he misleadingly dated to 1916 and sold to his tailor and friend, the great collector Adriano Pallini (figure 1.26). It was then re-envisioned as a statue (figure 1.27), and finally repainted, again and again, in a number of self-plagiaristic late compositions that are hard to attribute, with certainty, to de Chirico's own hand.

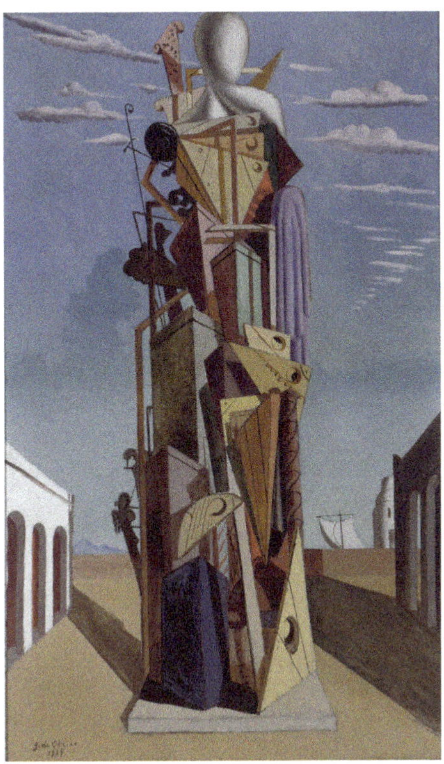

Figure 1.25. Attributed to Giorgio de Chirico (probably painted by Oscar Dominguez), *The Great Machine* (*La grande macchina*), 1925, oil on canvas, 156.2 x 93.3 cm, Honolulu Museum of Art, Honolulu. Photo credit: Collection of the Honolulu Museum of Art; gift of the Friends of the Academy, 1945 [309.1]). © 2022 Artists Rights Society (ARS), New York/SIAE, Rome.

The high "grade of metaphysicality" of the painting (and, therefore, of its subject) is confirmed in other ways. As mentioned, it was the first painting by de Chirico to appear in the journal *Valori Plastici*, the most official platform of de Chirico's and Savinio's ideas after the Ferrarese years. It also became the flagship piece of de Chirico's personal exhibition at the Casa d'Arte Bragaglia, the swan song of Metaphysical art. The event, organized in Rome at the beginning of 1919, turned out to be a fiasco, and triggered a dramatic turn in de Chirico's painting after the Ferrarese years – a turn that, as I will discuss towards the end of this chapter, should be linked to the encounter with Ariosto as well. However, de Chirico invested a lot in the exhibition, and *The Great Metaphysician* was its emblem. On the first page of the newspaper *L'Ora*, an ironic review of the exhibition was accompanied by a cartoon with a caricature of *The Great Metaphysician* (figure 1.28). The painting's towering faceless protagonist is, in all probability, the "Orthopedic God" mocked in the most famous review of the exhibition: Roberto Longhi's fierce and ideological

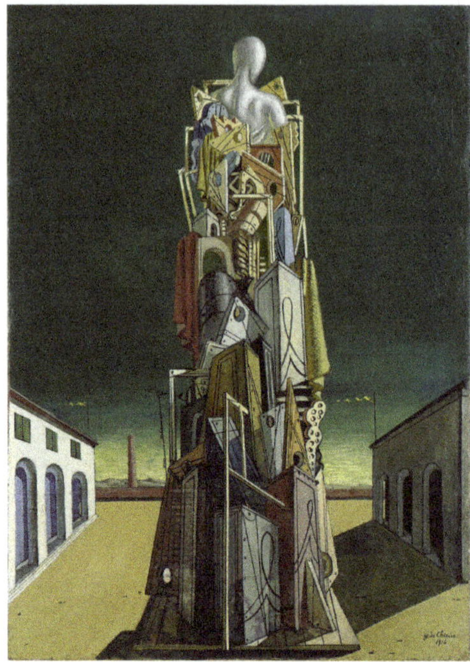

Figure 1.26. Giorgio de Chirico, *The Great Metaphysician* (*Le grand métaphysique*), 1945 (dated 1916 by the artist), oil on canvas, 110 × 80 cm, Staatliche Museen zu Berlin, Berlin. © 2022 Artists Rights Society (ARS), New York/SIAE, Rome. Photo Credit: bpk Bildagentur/Nationalgalerie/ Jörg P. Anders/Art Resource, NY.

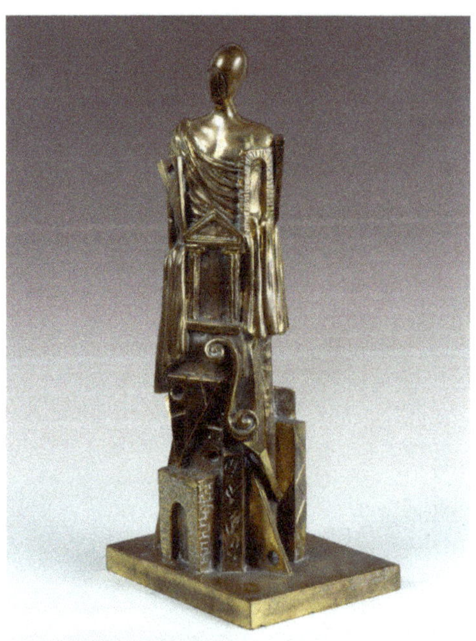

Figure 1.27. Giorgio de Chirico, *The Great Metaphysician* (*Il grande metafisico*), 1970, golden bronze, 17.5 × 23 × 52 cm, Casa Museo Giorgio de Chirico, Rome. © 2022 Artists Rights Society (ARS), New York/SIAE, Rome. Photo Credit: Mondadori Portfolio/Alessandro Vasari/Art Resource, NY.

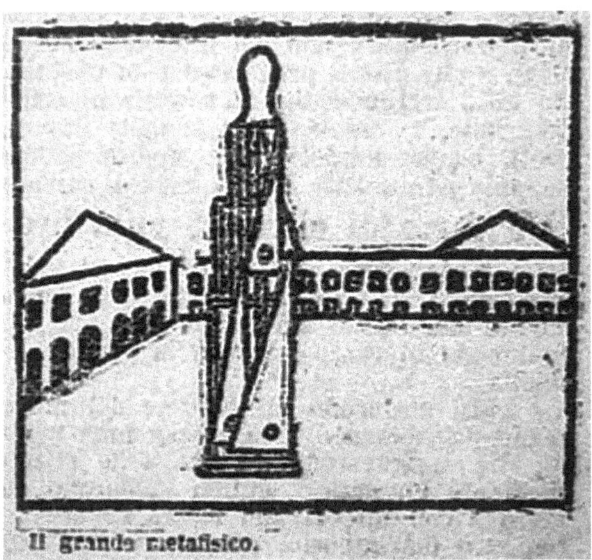

Figure 1.28. *Il grande metafisico,* Anonymous cartoon in *L'ora,* 20.56, February 25–6, 1919.

slating of Metaphysical painting titled *Al dio ortopedico.* And de Chirico himself resorted to the iconography of the Piazza Ariostea vision for a cartoon, which he sent to Soffici's military comic journal *La Ghirba* (figure 1.29). He drew it, right before the exhibition, as a self-parody. The pun is frankly atrocious, but the image is intriguing: a corporal in uniform – a disproportionately tall caricature of de Chirico himself – stands where Ariosto should stand, in the centre of the piazza where *The Great Metaphysician* is set.

The importance of Ariosto, poet in marble and great Metaphysician, for de Chirico and Savinio became less cryptic in some creative ideas conceived in Ferrara after the visionary encounters with his statue. Besides shocking them as a sculptural totem who prophesies and comes to life, Ariosto turned into a source of imagery, technical ideas, and aesthetic paradigms. In the second half of this chapter I will argue that de Chirico's Metaphysical interiors, along with the literary and pictorial expressions of their "geographical fatality," were inspired by Ariosto's poetry. I will also show that Ariosto's *Orlando Furioso,* in its content and narrative style, was at the core of the developments of Metaphysical art and literature after the war, up until some very overt tributes in the 1930s

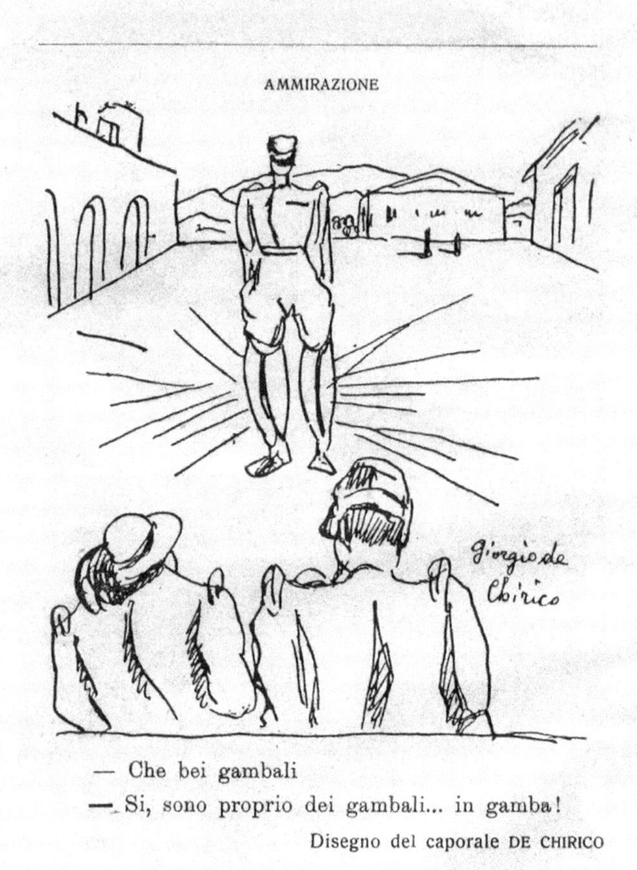

Figure 1.29. Giorgio de Chirico, *Ammirazione*, cartoon in *La Ghirba*, 3, April 21, 1918.

and 1940s. However, before discussing the consequences of the revelatory shocks reconstructed so far, one last metaphysical stroll needs to be recalled. The flâneur this time was Filippo de Pisis, a Ferrarese writer and artist who considered himself "a profound reader and adorer of Ariosto." De Pisis was, like Govoni, a guide for the de Chiricos in Ferrara. He initiated the brothers into the delight of localness, showing them the oddly shaped breads, the mysterious battle cry of "Worbas" engraved on the old castle, and, more importantly, Ariosto's square. His Metaphysical literature helps us to understand more clearly how Piazza Ariostea turned into an epicentre of avant-garde revelations during the First World War.

Peripatetic Friendship

Filippo de Pisis was the first to realize and publicize the fact that *The Great Metaphysician,* just like Savinio's *Ferrara … Partenza,* is a vision of Piazza Ariostea. In the summer of 1918, while the photograph of that painting was starting to circulate in *Valori Plastici* as an emblem of de Chirico's idiosyncratic avant-garde, de Pisis was invited to give a talk on modern art at the Teatro del Casino in Viareggio. A twenty-two-year-old Bohemian marquis, unwilling to conceal his extravagance and queer mannerisms, this younger adherent of the Metaphysical School addressed his Tuscan audience with the earliest recorded description of de Chirico's painting. He revealed its urban inspiration, and reclaimed it as an experience that he personally shared with de Chirico and his brother.

> If you want to feel the same great thrill that the background of De Chirico's *The Great Metaphysician* arouses in me, you should stand, some day, in the high, meridian quiet of Piazza Ariostea in Ferrara, where it was painted.
>
> The square is deserted; at the deep end, on the right, there is the red house, cubical like a psychic castle in a text by Alberto Savinio; in front of it, further down, the yellowish house with its tympanum, and its line of light and empty Paolo-Veronese-green windows. In the background, a tall man awaits, all wrapped up in a black robe. The long shadows take shape very quietly, while the tangled knot of the triangular, shiny geometrized objects of the centre, which towers like a huge column, seems to sing again *absurd declinations and problems that are unusual to our spirit.*
>
> Here! To our weary eyes, the squared plane of the square, in the lambency of the solar beams, seems to start twisting, slowly, "just like the *roulette* when it is about to stop."[43]

Savinio and de Chirico met de Pisis when they moved into a small apartment in Via Montebello, the same street, in all probability, from which de Chirico saw, at the corner with Via Cortile, the apparition of the marble Ariosto described in *Arte metafisica e scienze occulte.* Luigi Filippo de Pisis (whose real name was Tibertelli, an old cognomen of the papal aristocracy) grew up in the city. He lived in Palazzo Calcagnini, a few feet from the de Chiricos' doorstep. He was a writer, but he was also destined to become a rather *sui generis* painter. His legendary room, a real cabinet of curiosities, was a material counterpart of the obsession for inanimate objects that pervaded Metaphysical art. He was the perfect companion for the "peripatetic friendship" encouraged, in de Chirico's poem about Govoni's sleep, by the extending shadows of Ferrara's evenings.

While the First World War was raging in Europe, de Pisis spent many nights wandering through Ferrara with the de Chiricos. The urban excursions of this small crew of Metaphysicians are the theme of his surreal and fragmentary writings of the period. The first booklet in which he collected these narrative experiments was frantically completed in a couple of months after Savinio's departure from Ferrara. Its title is a rather Futurist formula: the bare date, *Mercoledì 14 novembre 1917.* However, according to de Pisis, *Mercoledì* "had nothing to do with [Futurism]," and pioneered, instead, "a new kind of prose that we could call, just to be clear, Metaphysical prose."[44] Though never identified by name, Piazza Ariostea is prominently featured in this text.

Writing exclusively in the first person, de Pisis starts *Mercoledì* by confessing an initial passéist spleen. He compares himself to the aristocratic eighteenth-century humanist Gasparo Gozzi, and admits an eagerness for new, greater ways to express his talent. The first section ends with a climax of heroic aspirations. These wishes are accompanied by visionary, self-assigned horoscopes, such as "I will fly on the airplanes and the unreachable zeppelins of Metaphysics," or even "all the future men will hail me as their Lord." However, the delirium is abruptly disrupted by a mysterious, and almost untranslatable, statement: "One night, the one who is buried alive rose from his sleep like a fakir and divinized himself."[45] The meaning of this line is revealed in the third section of the booklet, the longest one, in which a revelation dissolves the plaintive inertia of the beginning. It was de Pisis himself who used to be "buried alive" in his sleep. "Now," he states, "I rise, I divinize myself."[46] Piazza Ariostea is the setting of this rebirth.

> ... Lost on Earth, but also for us *the fatal hour* came!
>
> The barriers were broken! I could finally see clear! Oh my cowardice, my misery thus far!
>
> The squared square, after much wandering, was the theatre of our joy and our elevation. Almost everything disappeared in the divine instant! Trepidation, as well as an indescribable pain, are still with me because I fear that the moment will vanish, leaving no trace, like many others.[47]

The "fatal hour," italicized in de Pisis' prose, is the title of one of his early visual works, a 1919 composition that combines collage and tempera on mounted paper (figure 1.30). In it, objects are approached with a Metaphysical fascination for their enigmatic intransitivity, and illogically juxtaposed with Dadaist playfulness. The playing card in the lower

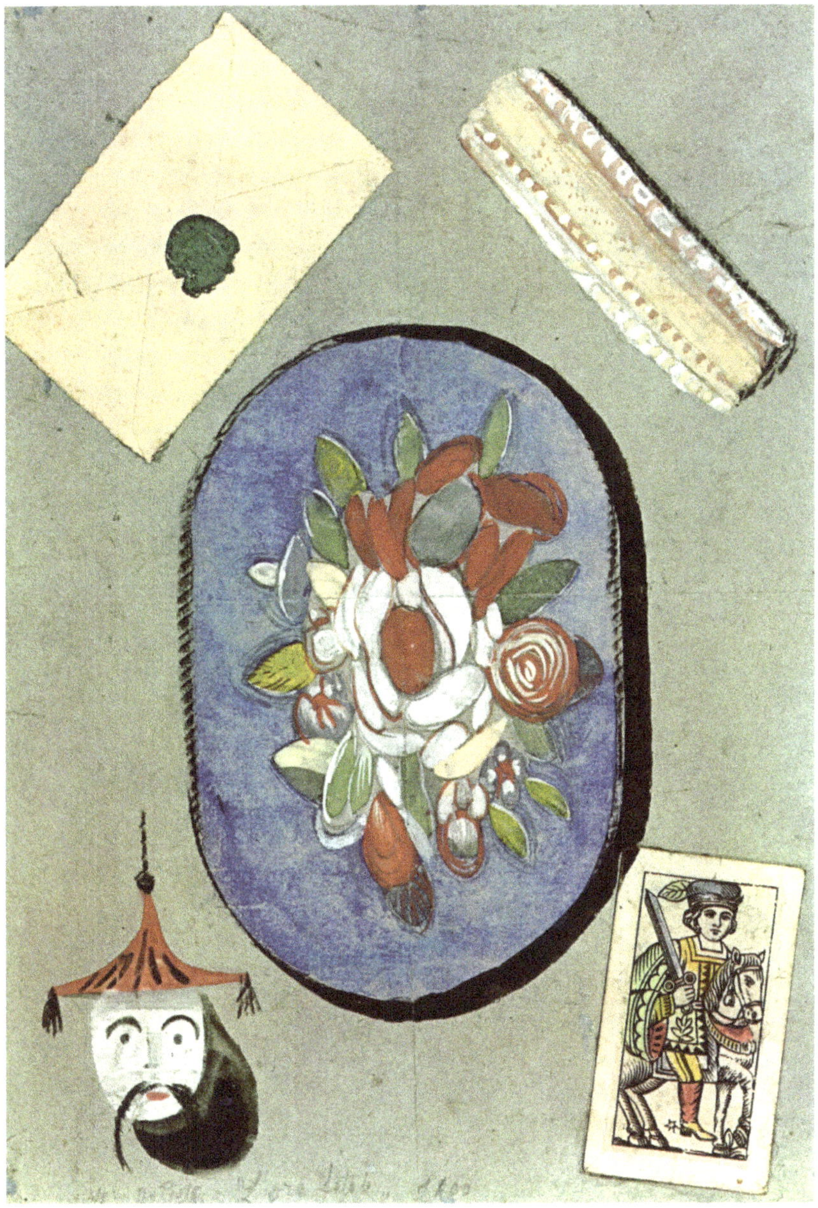

Figure 1.30. Filippo de Pisis, *The Fatal Hour* (*L'ora fatale*), 1919, tempera-collage on paper, 32 × 23 cm, private collection. Courtesy Associazione per Filippo de Pisis, Milan.

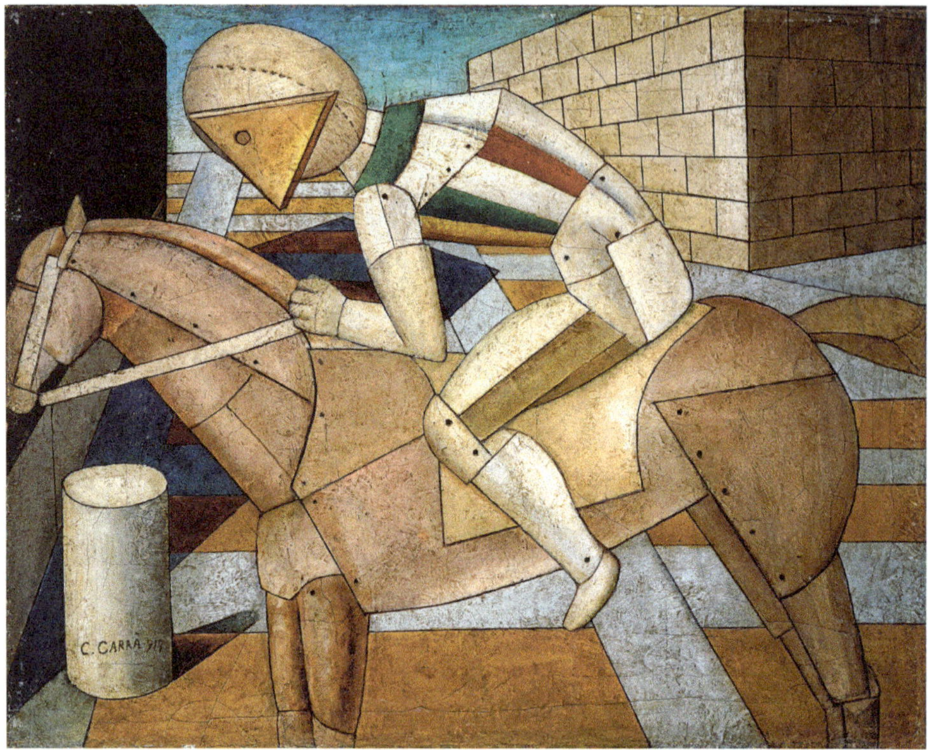

Figure 1.31. Carlo Carrà, *Western Knight* (*Cavaliere occidentale*), 1917, oil on canvas, 52 × 67 cm, Collezione Mattioli, Milan. © 2022 Artists Rights Society (ARS), New York/SIAE, Rome.

right corner, under the Ferrarese biscuit, is particularly interesting. It connects the painting with the Ariostean prose of *Mercoledì*, from which it takes its title. Cards appear in other works of the same period (a time in which de Pisis was creating his own entire deck of *carte romagnole*),[48] but, for this composition, he chose the nine of swords, a knight, alluding to the chivalric imagery of his inspiration. Ariosto, after all, was the poet of knights. The card hints at the fascination for knights and riding horsemen that heavily inspired Metaphysical paintings like Carlo Carrà's *Western Knight* (figure 1.31) and *Chase* (1915), or Savinio's later *Pompeian Promenade* (figure 1.32) – one of his earliest visual exercises after the Ferrarese years. However, the passage from *Mercoledì* insists on nocturnal wanderings in the open rather than on the sentimental enchantments of de Pisis' later pictorial interiors. Ariosto's square, as I said, is

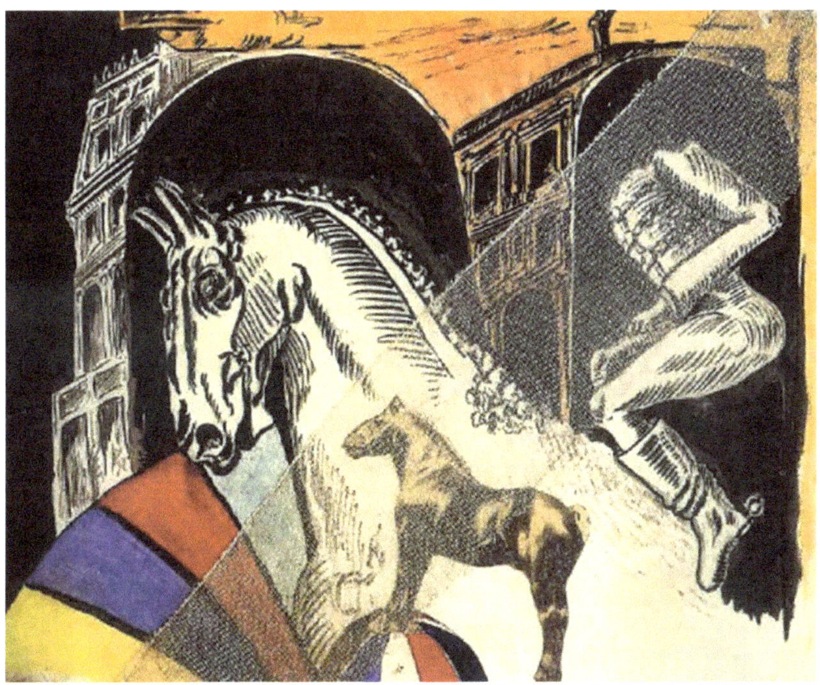

Figure 1.32. Alberto Savinio, *Pompeian Promenade* (*Promenade Pompéienne*), 1925–6, mixed media and collage on canvas, 21.5 × 27.5 cm, private collection.

never mentioned by name, but de Pisis' description of its monument is unequivocal.

> The squared square with the high column at its centre! We went around it thoroughly, and then we stopped under the column, looking up. The footprints of our steps did not mark the ground, the air did not solidify our forms into a number of moulds, nothing changed, but we were two very powerful dominators of the passing and of the staying matter.[49]

In this passage, Ariosto's monument becomes a totem again, a revealing idol. No actual magic happens (no "occultism," to use de Chirico's categories) and yet the Metaphysical wanderers change while looking up at Ariosto's statue. Finally, what Savinio called a "usual phenomenon" is re-enacted in de Pisis' narration: the verticality of the column is broken, and its marmoreal inhabitant becomes a living co-protagonist of the text.

> At some point I wanted to raise my arms and stand like that, paralysed in the *moment dream, aggressive vision* of a primordial essence. And I desperately recalled, with no tears, without even a sigh (my god, my god! ...) other nights!
>
> Us, standing still under the column, the pedestal, white parallelepiped with sharpened corners, right angles, the lips of the sguscio as sharp as razors, and then the white cylinder of the column that bends backwards, little by little, and then tears, and the fatuous statue, heroic lookout, chalky-suit, olympic, eyes-blind, marmoreal, static, *mannequin* that is just about to fall down like a rigid skittle, fasten to a hinge, like the white Roman, magnetized by the floury-faced actress or by a CIRCUS clown.[50]

A few lines after this surreal event, de Pisis envisions again the square as a gigantic wheel, with Ariosto's column as its linchpin: "Ecco che il piano (piazza) quadro forse incomincia lentamente a girare come la roulette che sta per fermarsi." It is hard to translate this passage. De Pisis defines Piazza Ariostea a "piano (piazza) quadro," which might mean "the squared plane of the square" or, more literally, "the plane (square) painting." The relation between this mental chronicle from the piazza and *The Great Metaphysician*, in any event, is certain. De Pisis self-quoted this very sentence in his lecture in Viareggio, the description of *The Great Metaphysician* from which this section started. In that lecture he described the painting's subject, Piazza Ariostea, as a roulette, with exactly the same formula. He himself established a connection between this literary vision and de Chirico's painting. And, by describing the bending and breaking of the column, he linked *The Great Metaphysician* with Savinio's *Ferrara ... Partenza.* Through de Pisis' testimony, Ariosto's Metaphysical apparitions coalesce into one single enigmatic revelation shared by different artists.

Ariosto Smoking a Tuscan Cigar

I believe that the point of *Mercoledì* was to mythologize an intellectual baptism. De Pisis guided his older friends, the two Metaphysicians, to Ariosto's monument – which is, per se, not just a postcard landmark, but a crossroads of times and meanings, with its nineteenth-century statue on a sixteenth-century column surrounded by medieval buildings and modern tramways. However, it was the de Chiricos' metaphysical synthesis of it (a new, uncanny gaze over a familiar subject) that initiated de Pisis to modernism: to the "new sentiment" that he described in his text.

In *Mercoledì*, the encounter with the marble Ariosto is represented as a foundational divide. It is the "fatal" moment at the centre of the book, and it recurs again and again in the following pages, like a Nietzschean untimely loop.

It recurs in the paragraph that follows the vision of the bending column and the animation of the statue ("Let's recall, let's recall again the other nights in this squared square!")[51] and then, again, in the following one ("that night, we were once again in the squared square: we went around it. The porticos saw us, we enjoyed their airiness, we did not number the columns").[52] The reiterated evocation of Piazza Ariostea finally overlaps with de Chirico's pictorial vision of it. In the text, de Pisis sees de Chirico in the act of measuring and grading the metaphysicality of the square, and mentally turning Ariosto's monument into the Great Metaphysician. The column, previously compared to a roulette, becomes a die, maybe as a tribute to "Le Hasard" of Mallarmé's seminal avant-garde poem. The "you" to whom de Pisis' prose is addressed is de Chirico.

> I saw you as the constructor on the free ground (the roundness of the globe was defeated, your space was truly *being* in the *non-being*!) I saw you constructing your architectural world of pleasure, and you were not the happy creator anymore but the world was you and you were him. Your happy, trembling corner flags waved on the highest pinnacles! Crazed, I would have wanted to cling to the marble jambs with my teeth to devour them. [...] The column looked like a die. If raised, it would have taken the slightly pyramided sidewalk with it, stuck like a mould. The porticos were well built, the ceiling of the sky was almost poky (only a strange nebula like an aborted moon, high up, very high, still imprisoned the spirit, which was now walking forward with mammoth feet).
>
> And yet, the spirit stretched out, he set himself free, he experienced the rapid joy of invention. That's it, done! ...[53]

De Pisis' impervious, allusive discourse includes motifs of Metaphysical imagery (corner flags, architecture, perspectival flat grounds) along with specific details from *The Great Metaphysician* – not just the porticos and the monument itself, but also the low sky, the crepuscular and cloudy light, the tension of the vertical element enclosed between two ideal parallel planes. These lines of prose simultaneously offer a chronicle of de Chirico's conception of *The Great Metaphysician* and a vision of the painting itself.

The following section of *Mercoledì* is titled after Archimedes' proverbial exclamation: "Eypeka!!!" In it, de Pisis seems to finally acknowledge bare reality: the physical appearance of a scene that the Metaphysicians had

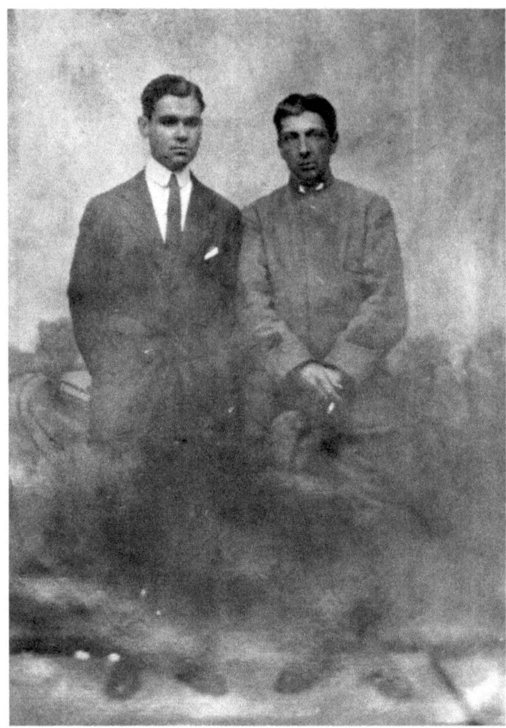

Figure 1.33. Filippo de Pisis and Giorgio de Chirico in Ferrara, 1917, photograph. Courtesy Associazione per Filippo de Pisis, Milan.

just transcended. The passage simply describes the actual square with two young men in it. One of them looks like a "shabby corporal," the other like a "plainclothes seminarist," just as de Chirico and de Pisis looked in a 1917 photo (figure 1.33). More revelations, more visions crowd the following lines, but one fact is clear: "The column, for now, will not fall, it will not bury us." Playing again with the word "quadro," which means both painting and square, de Pisis seems to take note of the completion of de Chirico's painting, setting the date on which the vision of Ariosto's monument definitively became *The Great Metaphysician*: "On Saturday, December 22, 1917, the painting square" (or "the squared square") "was not anymore; it had been, it was, and it would be in the future."[54]

Finally, in the last section of *Mercoledì*, a few lines from the end, a brief scene in a café ends with a sudden apparition of the marble man. During the mental transfiguration of the squared square in earlier passages, Ariosto was just about to fall down his bent column. Now, he travels incognito through the city, entering a café in a military uniform that shows his rank and grade. "On my right," writes de Pisis, "Lodovico Ariosto, smoking a Tuscan cigar: a sublieutenant uniform, black flashes, silver stars."[55]

At last, in the final stretch of the text, the mysterious interlocutor of the crew of Metaphysicians is named (and "graduated"). Did his "fatuous statue" manage to escape from his pedestal, as in Savinio's *Ferrara … Partenza*, to blend in with the Ferrarese bourgeoisie? Did Ariosto come back to life after de Chirico finished his *Great Metaphysician*? And why is he wearing a military uniform? Are the "black flashes" and "silver stars" the badges of his "degree of metaphysicality"? Or does he finally coincide with de Chirico, the "shabby corporal," almost as in a spectral possession? To shed some light on these mysteries one has to read the concluding lines of the book, in which the interlocutor of de Pisis' narrating voice becomes the other protagonist of Ferrara's metaphysical painting, Carlo Carrà.

> The solitude was immense: on the blackboard, the half lines and segments of the most undetermined indeterminability.
>
> A great joust of extrasensory values.
>
> *The metaphysical chambers* were about to animate, O CARRÁ, and De Chirico (our common friend!) to transfigure into a white Fantômas, romanic statue, pleated folds, ogival-smooth head, a tennis racket, a square ball in his hand, he was witnessing the *marvel of marvels*.[56]

Two crucial Ferrarese canvases by Carrà are clearly conjured here, both of which were painted between 1917 and 1918 and then reworked in the following years, to erase the most evident influence of de Chirico's coeval painting. The first, *Solitude* (figure 1.34), is dominated by the geometrical blackboard evoked at the beginning of de Pisis' passage. The second, *Oval of the Apparitions* (figure 1.35), includes the marble mannequin with a tennis racket described in the text: a recurring Metaphysical trope for Carrà. In the *Oval*, this faceless white subject stands in front of an equally white monolith. By featuring it in his text, de Pisis invites us to read that vertical block of marble as a column: a pedestal that has just been dismounted.

In the text, before turning into the statue with a tennis racket of Carrà's painting, de Chirico "transfigure[s] into a white Fantômas." This beloved character of French popular fiction, an often faceless or masked criminal and master of disguise, was an inspiration for some of the least decipherable of de Chirico's early works in Paris.[57] Among these, the most famous and influential is *The Brain of the Child* (figure 1.36). As de Pisis seems to suggest, among the many visual sources of the white figure that stares at the closed book with closed eyes there is a film adaptation of the Fantômas novels, shot by Louis Feuillade in the early 1910s (figure 1.37).

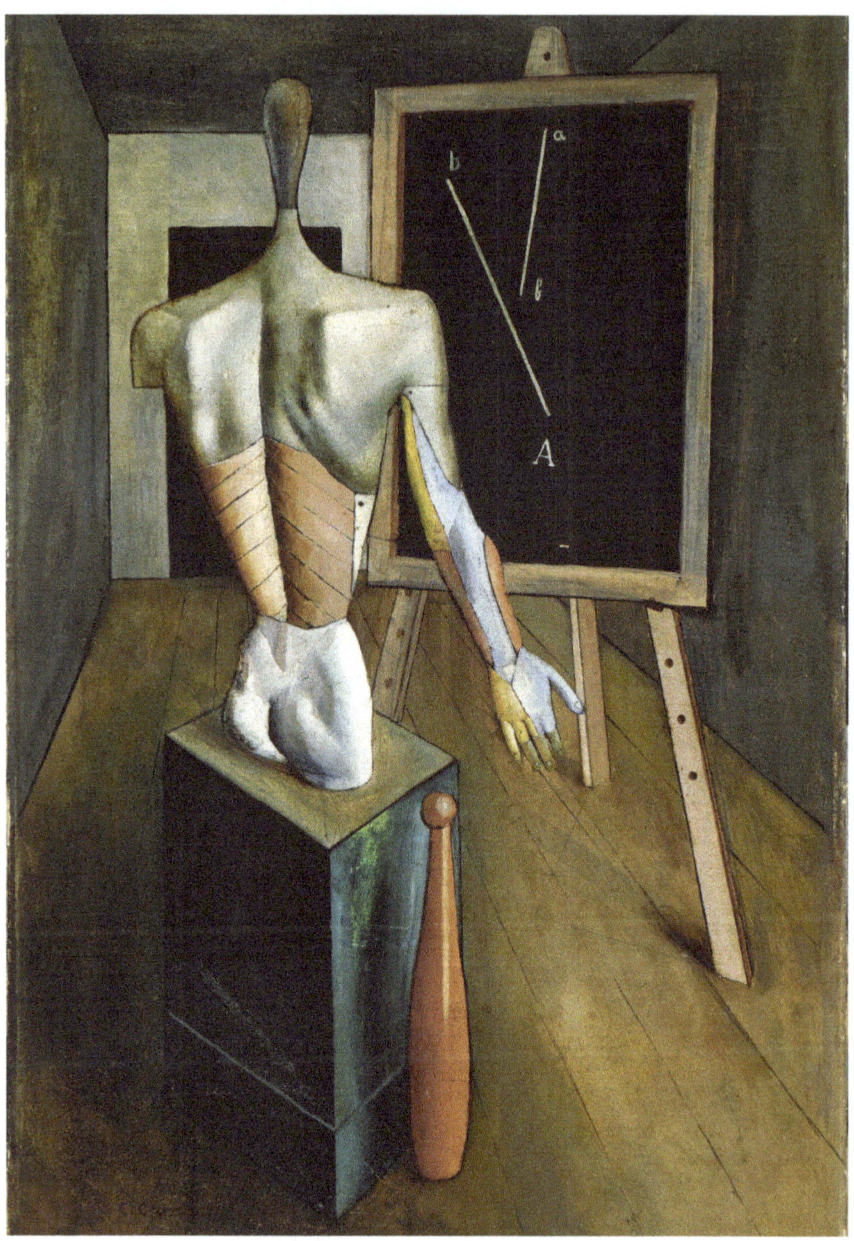

Figure 1.34. Carlo Carrà, *Solitude* (*Solitudine*), 1917–26, oil on canvas, 91.5 × 55.5 cm, Private collection. © 2022 Artists Rights Society (ARS), New York/SIAE, Rome. Photograph © Luca Carrà.

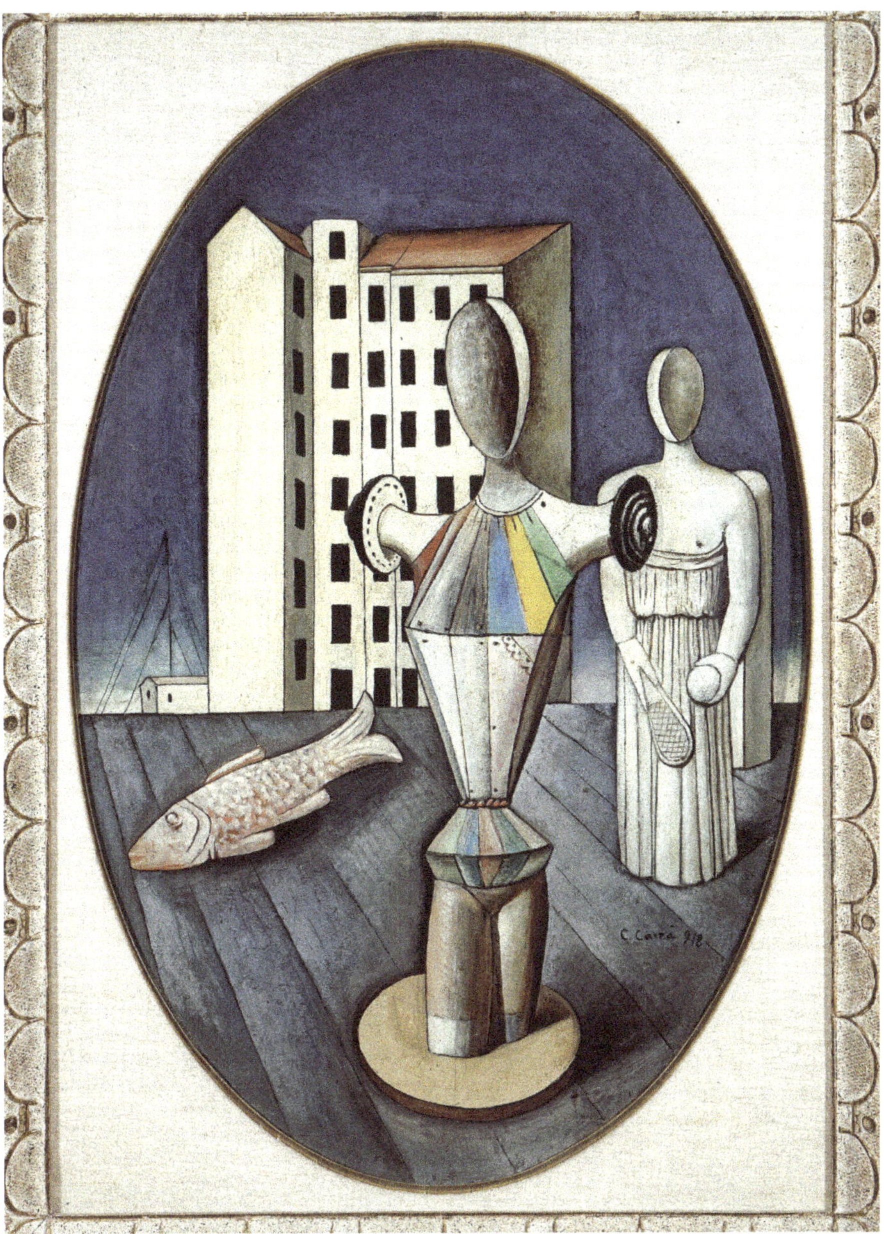

Figure 1.35. Carlo Carrà, *Oval of the Apparitions* (*Ovale delle apparizioni*), 1918, oil on canvas, 92 × 60 cm, Galleria Nazionale d'Arte Moderna, Rome. © 2022 Artists Rights Society (ARS), New York/SIAE, Rome. Photograph © Luca Carrà.

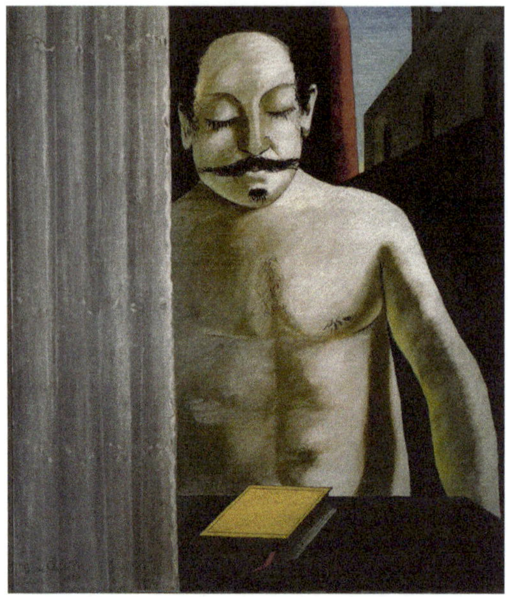

Figure 1.36. Giorgio de Chirico, *The Brain of the Child* (*Le cerveau de l'enfant*), 1914, oil on canvas, 80 × 65 cm, Moderna Museet, Stockholm. © 2022 Artists Rights Society (ARS), New York/SIAE, Rome. Photo Credit: Cameraphoto Arte, Venice/Art Resource, NY.

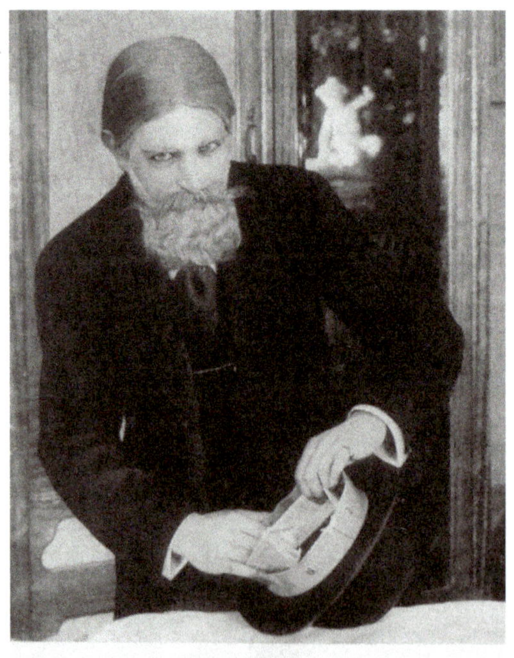

Figure 1.37. Victor Michel, *Fantomas. Feuillade. 1913*, photographic plate based on original film still, representing René Navarre as Fantômas, wearing one of his many disguises, in *Fantômas* by Louis Feuillade, 1912–13, 10 × 8.75 cm. From Nicole Vedrès, *Images du Cinéma Français* (Paris: Chêne, 1945) n. 99, p. 58. © Les Éditions du Chêne, Paris.

De Chirico kept the exaggerated mustache of Fantômas' disguise, but his protagonist is more similar to a statue than a living person. And the vertical element on the left looks like a fluted column. De Pisis may have considered this pivotal painting, which strongly impacted the development of Surrealism in France, as a prophecy of the Ferrarese motif of Ariosto jumping off his tall column.

Ariosto's statue, the white Fantômas, de Chirico's body, and the marmoreal tennis player of Carrà's *Oval* are overlapped in de Pisis' prose. And, through this ekphrastic chronicle, a number of other Metaphysical paintings could be linked to the shocking encounter with Ariosto's statue in Piazza Ariostea. The iconography of Carrà's *Oval* is famously repeated, without the column, in his *The Metaphysical Muse* (figure 1.38), which includes geographical tropes that, as I will argue below, are also related to Ariosto's influence. The same white character of *The Brain of the Child* encounters a headless dummy in de Chirico's *The Revenant* (figure 1.39). This 1918 painting is genetically linked to a series of drawings depicting similar scenes, including *The Apparition* (figure 1.40). In it, the standing protagonist rests his arm in the folds of his tunic just as Ariosto's statue in Ferrara does (figure 1.41),[58] while a kneeling mannequin venerates him. It is interesting that de Pisis, in his *Confessioni*, directly connected de Chirico's *Il ritornante* to Piazza Ariostea, strangely switching *The Great Metaphysician* with the 1918 dreamlike interior: "the deserted square of *Il ritornante* (one of the de Chirico's most beautiful paintings)," he wrote, "is Piazza Ariostea."[59] But the most direct visualization of the encounter, described in *Mercoledì*, between Ariosto's monument and Ferrara's Metaphysicians comes from de Pisis' own atelier.

In 1922, de Pisis sent a photograph of his latest work to Primo Conti, a young Futurist writer and artist who was then experimenting with Metaphysical aesthetics. The picture is titled *Study for the Painting "The First Apparition"* and depicts the drawing of a man in a sculptural pose with a leaning, stylized column falling down behind him (figure 1.42). There is no trace, today, of a painting by de Pisis titled *The First Apparition*, and the drawing is lost, but the photo of this project survived in Conti's archive. It now confirms how impactful the lucid dream of Ariosto jumping off his tall marble pedestal was for Ferrara's Metaphysical art.

Ancient Ghosts, Eternal Truths

It should be noted that Ariosto's local aura struck de Pisis' imagination years before he met de Chirico, Savinio, Carrà, and the other vanguardists who worked in Ferrara during the war years. Just like Govoni, he

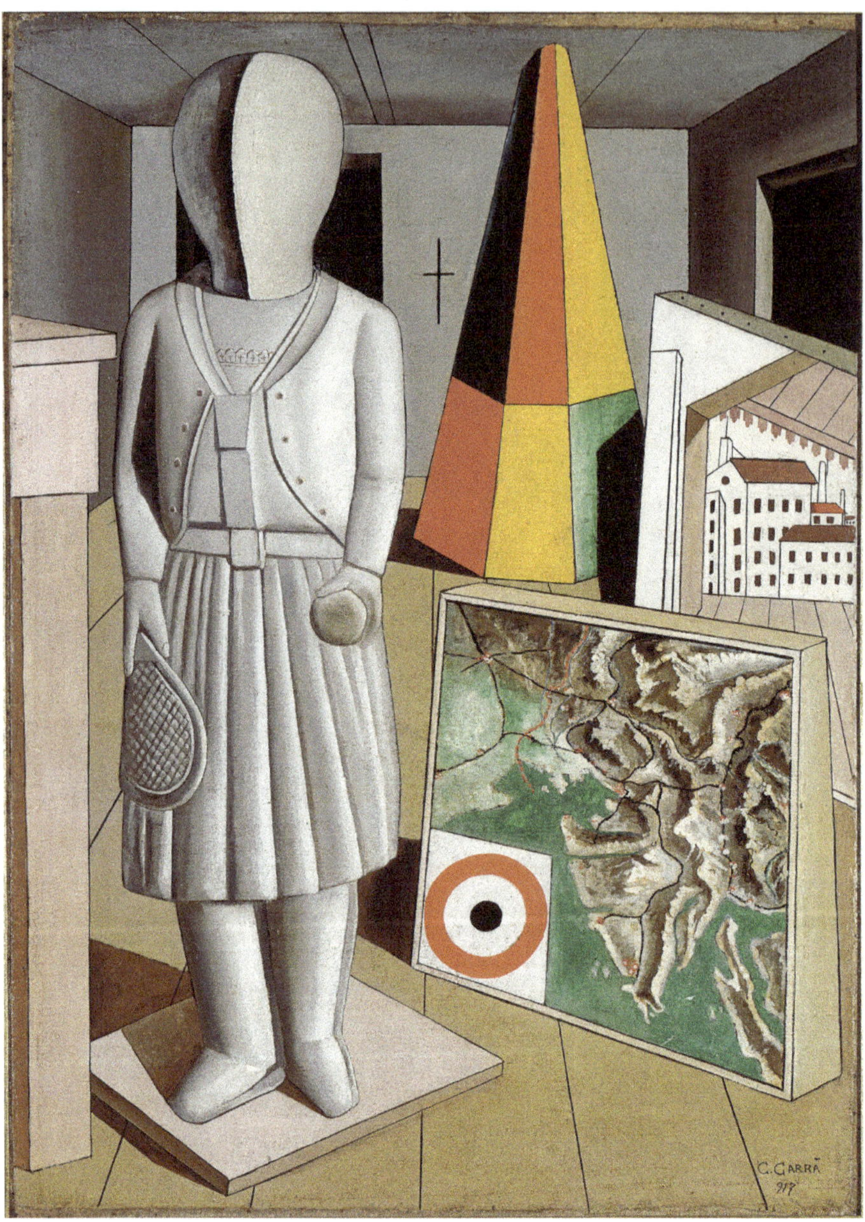

Figure 1.38. Carlo Carrà, *The Metaphysical Muse* (*La musa metafisica*), 1917, oil on canvas, 90 × 66 cm, Pinacoteca di Brera, Milan. © 2022 Artists Rights Society (ARS), New York/SIAE, Rome. Photograph © Luca Carrà.

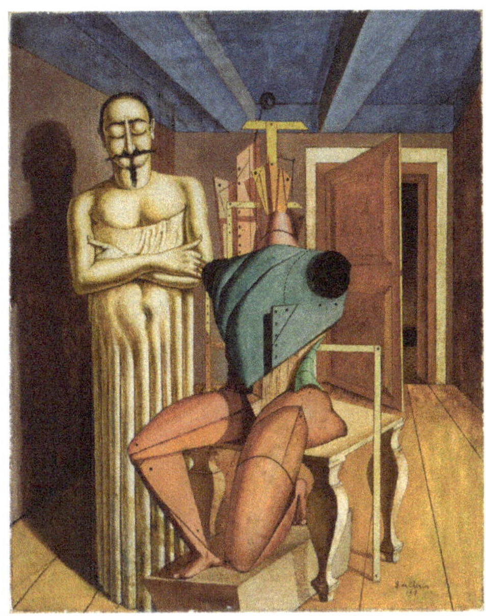

Figure 1.39. Giorgio de Chirico, *The Revenant* (*Il ritornante*), 1917–18, oil on canvas, 94 × 77.9 cm, Centre Pompidou, Paris. © 2022 Artists Rights Society (ARS), New York/SIAE, Rome. Digital Image © CNAC/MNAM, Dist. RMN-Grand Palais/Art Resource, NY.

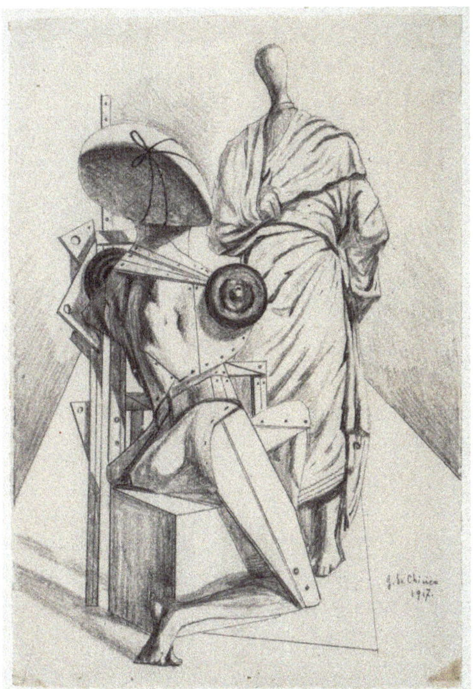

Figure 1.40. Giorgio de Chirico, *The Apparition* (*L'apparizione*), 1917, pencil on paper, 32 × 22.5, Galleria Nazionale d'Arte Moderna, Rome. © 2022 Artists Rights Society (ARS), New York/SIAE, Rome.

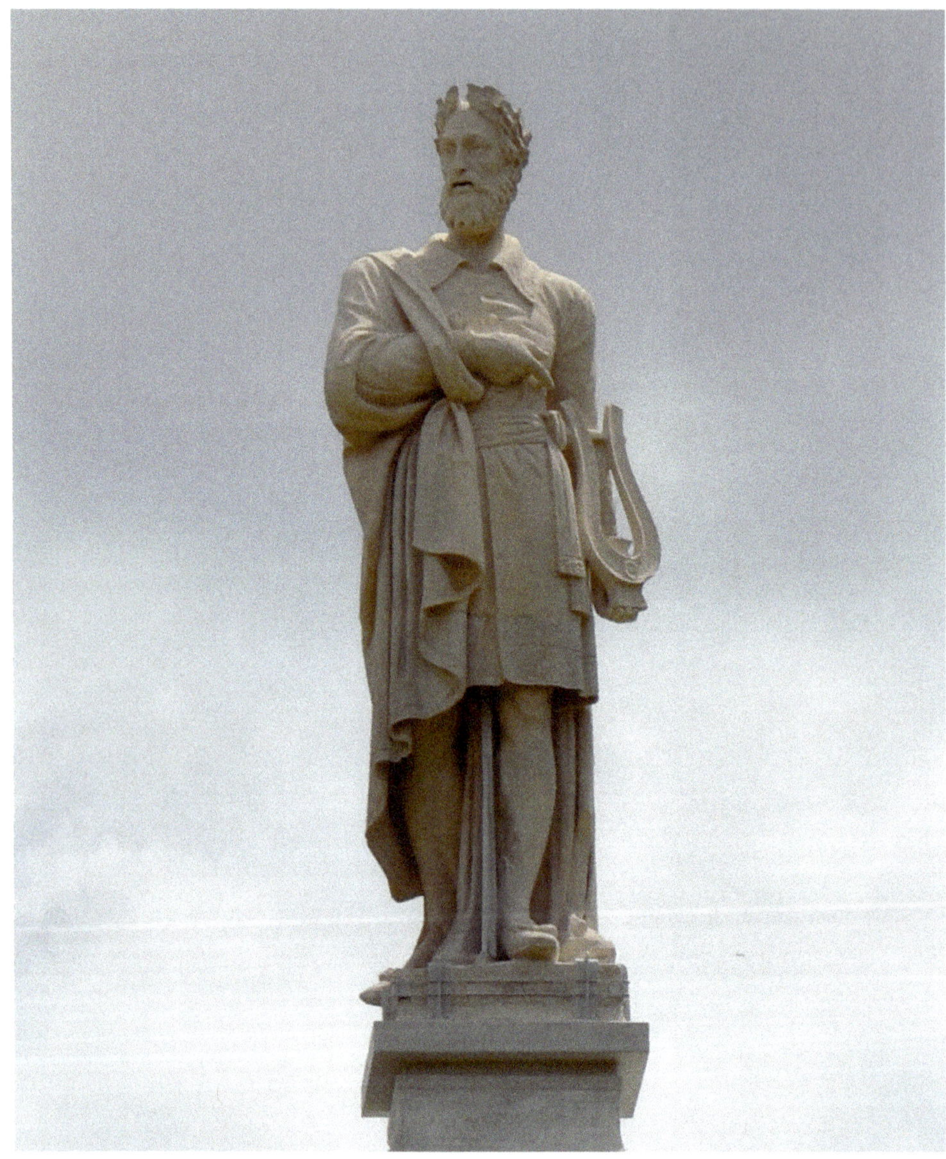

Figure 1.41. Ariosto's monument, sculpted by Francesco and Mansueto Vidoni and erected in 1833 in Piazza Ariostea, after the 2018–19 cleaning and restoration. Digital photograph © 2019 Benedetta Caglioti.

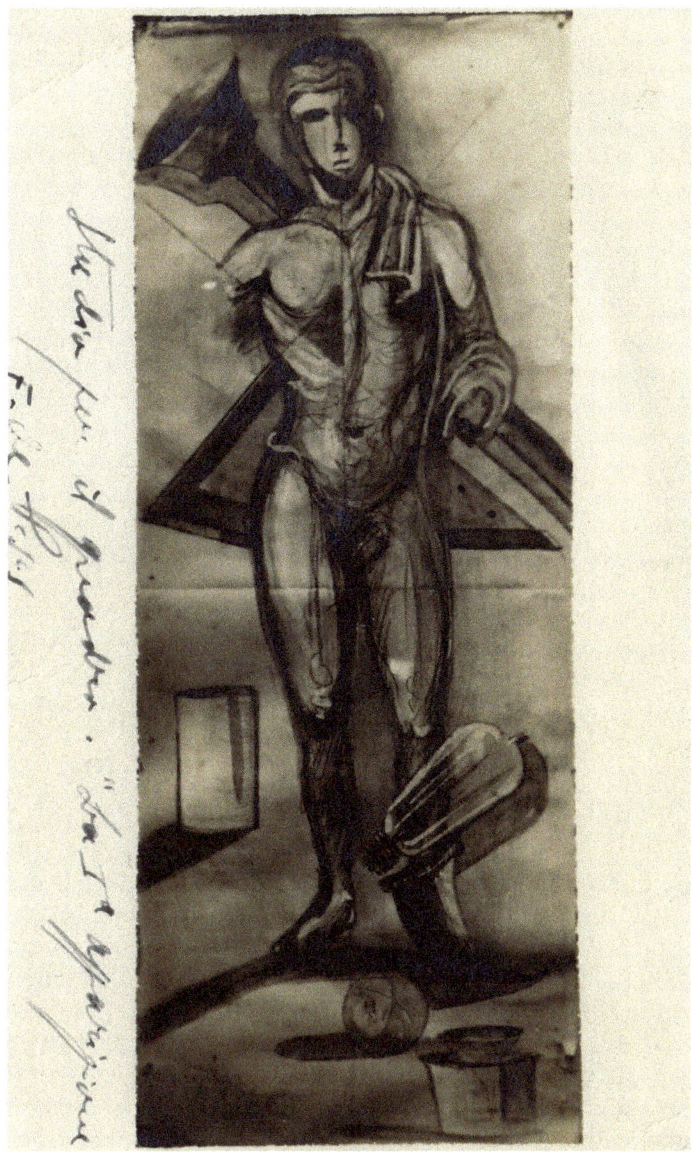

Figure 1.42. Signed photograph of Filippo de Pisis, study for the painting *The First Apparition* (Studio per il quadro *La 1a apparizione*), lost original pencil drawing on paper, 1922, Archivio Primo Conti, Corrispondenza F. De Pisis-P. Conti, Fiesole. Courtesy Fondazione Primo Conti.

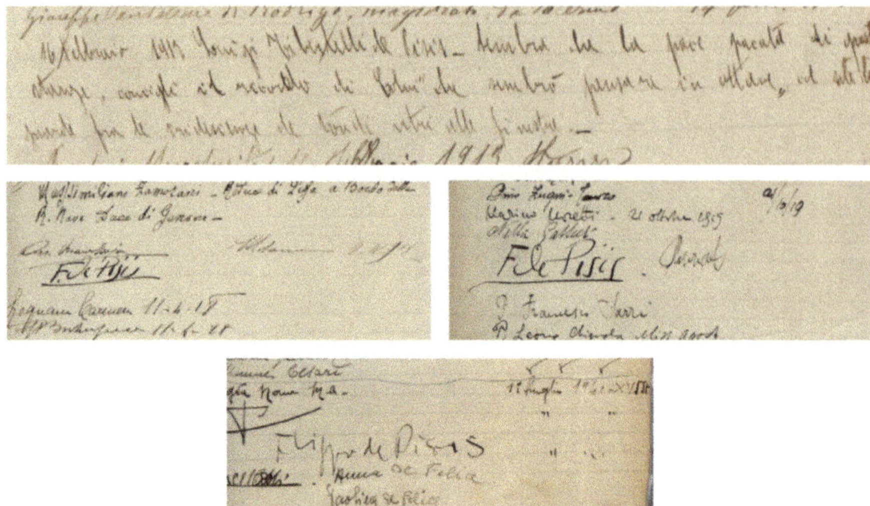

Figure 1.43. Filippo de Pisis' note and signatures in the visitors' register of Ariosto's house in Ferrara. Courtesy Musei Civici di Arte Antica, Ferrara.

was familiar with Ariosto's house. And, just like Agnoletti and the other Futurists that Govoni brought there, he signed the visitors' register. He was sixteen, a student of Ferrara's Liceo Ariosto, when he left his first signature. Among the many names of tourists and literary pilgrims on the register's page, "Luigi Tibertelli de Pisis" stands out because of the long message that accompanies it (figure 1.43). This message, dated February 16, 1913, praises the "peaceful peace" ("la pace pacata") of Ariosto's room, and calls him "the One who seemed to think in octaves" ("Colui che sembrò pensare in ottave"). When de Pisis visited the house again, in the spring of 1918, he used the same iconic signature that appears on all his paintings: "F. de Pisis." In the visitors' register of Ariosto's house, the same signature appears again in 1919 and, a bit more trembling, in 1940. By then, de Pisis was a celebrated modern artist, and had moved away from the enigmas of his Metaphysical years. Not from the obsession for Piazza Ariostea though, since the fatal place would appear again in his mature paintings – and in particular in an eponymous urban landscape dated 1935.

A personal intimacy with Ariosto, his fellow Ferrarese poet, accompanied de Pisis through his life. However, it was the experience of the "peripatetic friendship" with the de Chiricos that uprooted Ariosto from a bookish, scholastic, and traditional knowledge for him. A Metaphysical approach to urban visions made it possible, for de Pisis, to meet Ariosto in a café, to identify with him or overlap him with de Chirico, and to guess or actively conjure the presence of his deconstructed monument in some crucial works by de Chirico and Carrà. With his literary recollection of nocturnal strolls in Piazza Ariostea, de Pisis confirmed from a third angle what de Chirico's and Savinio's paintings and texts suggested: despite its anti-Metaphysical verticality, Ariosto's monument was chosen as one of the most Metaphysical objects in Ferrara, and the poet in marble on it was given the chevron of a Great Metaphysician. As de Pisis' *Mercoledì* cryptically shows, Ariosto's encounter with the de Chiricos in Ferrara was a turning point in the relationship between the avant-garde and the past, on the model of Govoni's and Agnoletti's simultaneous experience of Futurism and memory after sighting Ariosto in Ferrara's sky.

What did these unexpected venerations and transfigurations of Ariosto's monument mean for the development of Metaphysical art and literature in Italy? What were the effects of the encounter that turned Ariosto's statue into the faceless protagonist of the most iconic canvas of de Chirico's Ferrarese years? In the rest of this chapter, I am going to discuss the consequences of Ariosto's secret, totemic influence in the de Chirico brothers' work. However, before I do that, let me show how Ariosto's myth kept on informing de Pisis' "Metaphysical prose."

An interesting trans-historical reverie related to Ariosto's influence appeared in the most ambitious literary work by de Pisis: *La città dalle cento meraviglie.* This book, published in 1920, was a fragmented autobiographical novel dedicated to Ferrara. Before publishing it, de Pisis had mentioned the "squared square" of *Mercoledì,* with its "white column, very high, in the middle," in *Il verbo di Bodhisattva,* a mysterious Nietzschean text that he wrote at the end of 1917 under the pseudonym Maurice Barthelou.[60] He had also described Piazza Ariostea as a place of errant meditation and spiritual elevation in *Grilli in piazza Ariostea,* one of the *Prose* that he collected and published three years later.[61] In the same miscellaneous book, he mentioned the erotic love of Angelica and Medoro from the *Orlando Furioso* in a brief ekphrastic passage of the text titled *Museo*:

> Angelica and Medoro, under the laurel thicket and among the bushes of myrtle, beautiful, half-naked; him, strong shepherd with golden locks and alabaster white flesh, her, perfect and delirious with passion; they consumed each other in long and repeated embraces.[62]

The most significant later echo of the Piazza Ariostea epiphany of 1917 is in the chapter *Spiriti ariosteschi* (Ariostean Spirits), the most overt tribute to Ariosto in *La città dalle cento meraviglie.* At the beginning of the book, de Pisis had placed himself in direct genealogical descent (both in a literary and, possibly, a biological sense) from Ariosto.

> The land from which my *being* has drawn its vital juices is rather rich with poets and poetasters. However, I feel that only very few among them are worthy of me. [...] I bow before Ariosto, the dear Messer Lodovico. In fact, I can consider him my ancestor. (My elders maybe were his friends, and they saw him passing by on the honest walkways of the old city.)[63]

Several pages after this preamble, *Spiriti ariosteschi* opens with an invitation to walk in a specific place in the old city. It is the same walkway, on top of Ferrara's walls, from which Agnoletti's story started in 1915. In the text, de Pisis promises that, when the bells of the cathedral chime the hour, any pilgrim walking on "the ancient wall of the pentagonal city" will feel Ariosto's octaves flying around like birds. The lines from the *Orlando Furioso* that he quotes[64] are those about the impossible magnificence of Alcina's city, as it appears to Ruggiero (VI, 59):

> A line of bastions has caught his eye
> Which rings the mighty citadel around.
> They are so tall they almost touch the sky,
> And from their topmost height down to the ground
> They seem to be of solid gold (and I
> Am told by some that evidence was found
> Of alchemy): however that may be,
> They glitter so, they look like gold to me.

According to de Pisis, a similar urban magic can be contemplated from the ramparts, looking down at Ferrara's cityscape.

> [B]y the power of those lines you will think of a cyclopic city all encircled in a long, pink wall, with scary windows. A city so tall that it reaches the sky, and all made of gold. A city that might have risen thanks to an alchemic spell (as Messer Ludovico says [...]), a city in which all men walk lightly and are obsessed with the demon of mystery and do not care about anything else than the contemplation of the "Eternal Truths."[65]

Here, de Pisis is paraphrasing Ariosto's octave, which is closed by the ironic doubt about the architecture of Alcina's city (is it made of actual gold or is it a product of alchemy?). The interplay of literary memory, reality, and fantasy continues in the following lines with an alternative suggestion stemming from the same octave: a vision of a room with frescoed walls. The room to which de Pisis alludes is certainly the Hall of the Months in the Schifanoia Palace, a masterpiece of Renaissance symbology to which I will come back several times in the rest of this book. Like Alcina's kingdom, the splendid painted room helps the pilgrim to lose, in de Pisis' words, "adherence with this 'basso loco,' and to live totally in the grip of ancient ghosts and eternal truths."[66] In the iconographical system of Schifanoia, the supernatural realm of symbolic pagan gods is linked to human history through the celestial mediation of astrology. The different overlapping worlds of Schifanoia's hermetic cosmology invite to transcendence. Fantasy, in de Pisis' text, is welcomed as a way to evade a despised reality. To describe material reality, de Pisis uses the locution "basso loco," a formula that Dante used to describe both the allegorical wood and Lucifer's seat: the lowest point in the protagonist's life and the lowest circle of Hell (*If* I, 61; IX, 28).

The urban pilgrim imagined by de Pisis (like de Pisis himself, evidently) does not want to be rescued from the spells of alchemy and Alcina's magic. On the contrary, they both enjoy the company of the "ancient ghosts." Reality, for them, is like Hell, artistic hallucinations are a kind of mendacious but desirable sorcery, the pentagonal city is ancient and modern at once, real and fantastic, physical and Metaphysical. While for Govoni and Agnoletti the only living men are "those who love the dead," for de Pisis the only reality worth inhabiting is a fantastical one. In both cases, Ariosto is the key to connect past and present, physics and Metaphysics. His manifestations in the modern cityscape as a revealing apparition, a walking man in marble, a smoking soldier, or a literary ghost, allow modern wanderers to contemplate the "eternal truths" without travelling through time: nostalgia is abolished by the living presence of an immortal, friendly past.

Chamber Navigations

The epiphany shared with de Pisis in Piazza Ariostea, and then mythologized in texts and paintings by all three, suggested new themes and perspectives to de Chirico and Savinio. These motifs and ideas differentiated the Ferrarese phase of their Metaphysical art and literature from the Parisian one, which is more studied and canonized in the history of European modernism. One of the most intriguing consequences of their encounter with Ariosto's marble ghost is related to geography, and in particular to cartography. Maps appear prominently in de Chirico's paintings and Savinio's writings in the Ferrarese years. But they were also a quintessential Renaissance preoccupation in Ferrara, where some of the most famous fifteenth-century *mappamondi*, including the legendary Cantino planisphere, were collected by the Este dukes.

Geographical accuracy and the representation of the world are aspects of the *Orlando Furioso* that have intrigued scholars for centuries.[67] Ariosto was able to experiment with geography thanks to a simple but game-changing plot device: the Hippogriff, a fantastic mount that, ironically, is described in a credible way.[68] This flying beast allows knights to explore the entire known world and even to visit other worlds, including the earthly paradise. Thanks to the Hippogriff, the setting of the poem shifts continuously, revealing the vastness and relative precision of Ariosto's geographical awareness. Adventures lead the protagonists of the *Furioso* way beyond the shores of Europe, putting them in touch with otherness in terms of environment, race, and culture.[69]

Such an enthusiasm for the modern cultural value of intercontinental journeys in the age of early colonialism is an enhanced echo of the classical epic trope of geographic curiosity, from the *Odyssey* to Dante. It is evident not just in the plot of the poem but also in the extra-diegetic moments in which the voice of the poet himself intervenes to disrupt the narrative. An emblematic case is at the beginning of Canto VII, where Ariosto summarizes the cognitive dilemmas of the modern traveller. Those who travel far and then come back to narrate their experience, explains Ariosto, directly compete with fiction in the minds of listeners (VII, 1).

> He who has left his native country sees
> – As further off he goes – things far removed
> From what he thought to find; and when he is
> Recounting them at home may be reproved
> For telling lies, since ignoramuses,
> Unless with touch and sight they've plainly proved
> A thing, will not believe it; thus it comes,
> This Canto will seem strange to stay-at-homes.

This prologue to Canto VII is an example of Ariosto's literary irony, of his playful mastery of the paradoxes of realism. The comedic effect is of course related to the fact that the following canto features, among a number of magicians and sorceresses, a warrior giantess riding a werewolf from a faraway land. However, the irony is also rooted in Ariosto's own reputation for being the most proud of "stay-at-homes." He never left his native country, not even to follow his patron, Ippolito d'Este, to Hungary, when he was appointed Archibishop of Esztergom. When Ariosto was forced to travel to become governor in Garfagnana, he did so reluctantly. At least, that is how he described himself in the the *Satires*, the autobiographical letters in verse to which he entrusted his own self-fashioning. The emblematic passage about geography is in the third *Satira*, tercets 55 to 65:

> I am more pleased to rest my idle limbs than to boast that they have been to Scythia, India, Ethiopia, and beyond. Men's appetites are various [...] Some love their homeland, while others delight in foreign shores. Let him wander who desires to wander. Let him see England, Hungary, France, and Spain. I am content to live in my native land. I have seen Tuscany, Lombardy, and the Romagna, and the mountain range that divides Italy, and the one that locks her in, and both the seas that wash her. And that is quite enough for me.

In the Dantesque stanzas of this *Satira*, Ariosto fabricated his intellectual identity as a stoic, dignified poet, devoted to Horatian and Petrarchan *otium*. His self-fashioned rejection of active life influenced the reception of his literature and of his figure in general, making generations of critics forget that, despite his many attempts to get a pension and focus exclusively on writing, he was a diplomat, an effective political advisor, and even an authoritative administrator. He dealt with the complaints of peasants and the strategies of politicians as much as he dealt with flying Hippogriffs and magical cities, if not more.

It is important to notice that, even in the sardonic *Satires*, Ariosto never claimed indifference for the world. Rather than provincialism or cultural introversion, his idleness was the necessary condition to experience the world in a different, Metaphysical way, transcending the material drags of travelling while embracing its imaginative dimension. The third *Satira* continues:

> Without ever paying an innkeeper, I will go exploring the rest of the Earth with Ptolemy, whether the world be at peace or else at war. Without ever making vows when the heavens flash with lightning, I will go bounding over all the seas, more secure aboard my maps than aboard ships.

In the original text, Ariosto did not directly use the Italian words for "maps" and "ships" but rather two synecdoches, which allude to charts and vessels through the material that they are made of: *carte* (papers) and *legni* (woods). Such a rhetorical trick makes room for a fruitful ambiguity, since the "papers" can also be the pages on which poems are written, and "wood" is also the material of Ariosto's legendary armchair, a relic that attracted many visitors to his house in Ferrara throughout the centuries. At the end of the *Furioso*, in the meta-narrative prologue of the last canto

(XLVI, 1), Ariosto represents himself on a wooden ship (*legno*), and realizes that the conclusion of his work, the harbour of his poetic journey, is close. He does so by consulting a chart (*carta*) that is both a metaphorical map and the concrete piece of paper on which he is writing: a page that is about to run out of space. The poem itself is, of course, the *legno* on which he is travelling, a metaphorical ship. But it is written on *carta*, from a still chair made of *legno*.

Paper and wood, map and ship, poetry and geography, Ariosto's room and the entire world end up coinciding in the intertextual dialogue between the *Furioso* and the *Satires*. The lexicon of the poem's ending is the same as that used in the third *Satira*, at the intersection of cartography and literature as forms of metaphysical navigation represented through their most material, physical reality. The powerful Ariostean idea of immobile journeys, of adventurously travelling the world while sitting in a room, is clearly echoed in what Savinio wrote right after describing his meeting with Ariosto's monument in Piazza Ariostea. It informs, in particular, *La partenza dell'Argonauta*, the longest section of *Hermaphrodito*.

La partenza dell'Argonauta is a literary chronicle of Savinio's military journey from Ferrara to Thessaloniki in 1917, following the surreal farewell to the Metaphysical city narrated in *Ferrara … Partenza*. It tells, in sum, what happened after Savinio saw Ariosto's statue coming to life and jumping off its pedestal. The adventurous tone of the narration justifies the title, which alludes to Apollonius of Rhodes' *Argonautica*. Both the de Chiricos were inspired by the epic tale of Jason and his Argonauts – and also by Homer's *Odyssey*, which is clearly evoked throughout the seven parts of Savinio's text.

True to the poetics of Metaphysical art, Savinio's narrative in *La partenza dell'Argonauta* combines realistic details and mythological apparitions, delirious visions and war news, quotations in French, Latin, Italian, and Greek. Besides the allusions to classical epic poems, Savinio openly evoked chivalric adventures as well. For instance, in his text, he mentally transfigured a game of cards among his fellow soldiers into a chivalric tournament, and used Luigi Pulci's *Morgante Maggiore*, one of the most influential precedents of Ariosto's *Furioso*, to back up an invented etymology of the Italian word for gambling.[70] At the end of the journey, Savinio's narrator claims "a brotherly familiarity with errant knights,"[71] and looks for Don Quixote on his military ship. He also directly evokes the *Orlando Furioso*, overlapping the political fury of the new prime minister of Italy (whose surname was Orlando) with the literary one of Ariosto's protagonist.[72] However, the main connection between *La partenza dell'Argonauta* and Ariosto's poetry goes beyond puns and quotations, and it is not merely thematic.

The passage in which Savinio most clearly reveals the influence of Ariosto's geographical poetics is at the beginning of the voyage. In it, the narrator describes his train trip from Ferrara to the south. The route is the opposite of the one that Agnoletti took in 1915, and in fact Ravenna, the city where Dante was buried, is the first stop. In Savinio's compartment, there is a comrade in arms who wears a large "pezzuola geografica," a scarf with a geographical chart on it. The scarf captivates Savinio, who focuses on it and forgets the smells, the noises, and the jolts of the train. After an ekphrastic description of this scarf, which is "embroidered with a beautiful representation of Italy [...] leaning steadily on Europe's heart with its large stirrups," Savinio looks closely at the cartographical details.

> I bring my attention to the geographical part of the scarf, where the figure of the boot is broken by the waviness of the creases. On the humps of the fabric, I find the Lazio region and Rome, marked by a disk circled in black. Above it, the Tyrrhenian sea washes the shores of the Ligurian gulf. On the right, I find Ferrara, marked by a small asterisk, and I follow the trace of my own journey along the red line that represents the railway network.[73]

The route that Savinio, both as narrator and character, is about to take physically is travelled on a map first, mentally and visually. The virtual space of the *carta* (which here is not paper, but rather silk) progressively adheres to the real one crossed by the train (a room of steel, rather than an armchair of wood). Then, Savinio realizes a disquieting simultaneity: when his eyes reach the city of Ravenna on the map, the real city begins to appear outside the train's window. The moving room represented by the train's compartment, with its comfortable seat and its embroidered map, allows for a paradoxical elaboration of Ariosto's self-fashioning as an adventurous stay-at-home. Just like Ariosto, Savinio travels the world both physically and Metaphysically. His train wagon is a ship and a room, his fellow soldier's scarf is a map: steel and silk replace wood and paper in his Ariostean immobile journey.

Becoming a Statue

In his most ambitious literary work, the 1929 novel *Hebdomeros*, de Chirico would explore the same textual clash between interior and exterior, stillness and adventure, that Savinio experimented with through Ariosto's model. In a famous passage, the protagonist (a Metaphysical alter-ego of the artist himself) navigates around his own room.

> Hebdomeros had to flee. He went all around his room in a boat, continually forced into a corner by the undercurrent and, at last, abandoning his frail craft and gathering all his strength and skill as a former gymnast, he hoisted himself up to the window which was placed very high, like the window of a prison.[74]

Hebdomeros, like Ariosto, enjoys adventures but, at the same time, prefers to be indoors, even when he travels. "He liked nothing but rooms, good rooms where one could shut oneself up, with the curtain drawn and the doors closed."[75] De Chirico represented his chamber navigations in an Ariostean and Homeric late painting: *The Return of Ulysses* (figure 1.44). However, Ariosto's idea of sailing aboard maps while sitting in a room influenced de Chirico much earlier. As I mentioned, Ariosto's Metaphysical take on indoor travelling offers a key to read the most quintessentially Italian themes of de Chirico's work: worlds framed in paintings, maps as windows, and visualized geographical itineraries within rooms. Ara Merjian, in an essay about Metaphysical interiors, clustered these themes in a formula that encapsulates the dominating sentiment of de Chirico's Ferrarese period: "willful claustrophilia."[76]

De Chirico's textual self-representation as a modern artist, between 1916 and 1918, was often based on an association between his room and a sailing ship. In a 1916 poem he wrote: "My window is a ship's porthole. / My easel is a mast without its sail."[77] A year later, in a fragment titled *Promontorio*, he described the hardwood floor of his studio as "similar to the painted deck of a long-distance packet boat."[78] In 1918, he repeated and clarified the same metaphor: "My room is a beautiful vessel where I can take adventurous voyages worthy of a headstrong explorer."[79] And, in a poem dedicated to Carlo Carrà, he used the title *Journey* to define a series of purely mental peregrinations: journeys that were taken without leaving home.

> I think of a city in Alaska on a winter
> morning, white below the white
> mountains, near the dark
> sea.
> I think about a packet boat that bunkers in Tenerife
> on a warm September afternoon and then sets sail
> toward the ports of old Europe.[80]

In sum, after seeing his statue "prophesying," de Chirico must have read Ariosto, and appreciated the hybridization of poetry and geographical fantasy in the *Satires* and the *Furioso*, as Savinio did. De Chirico's

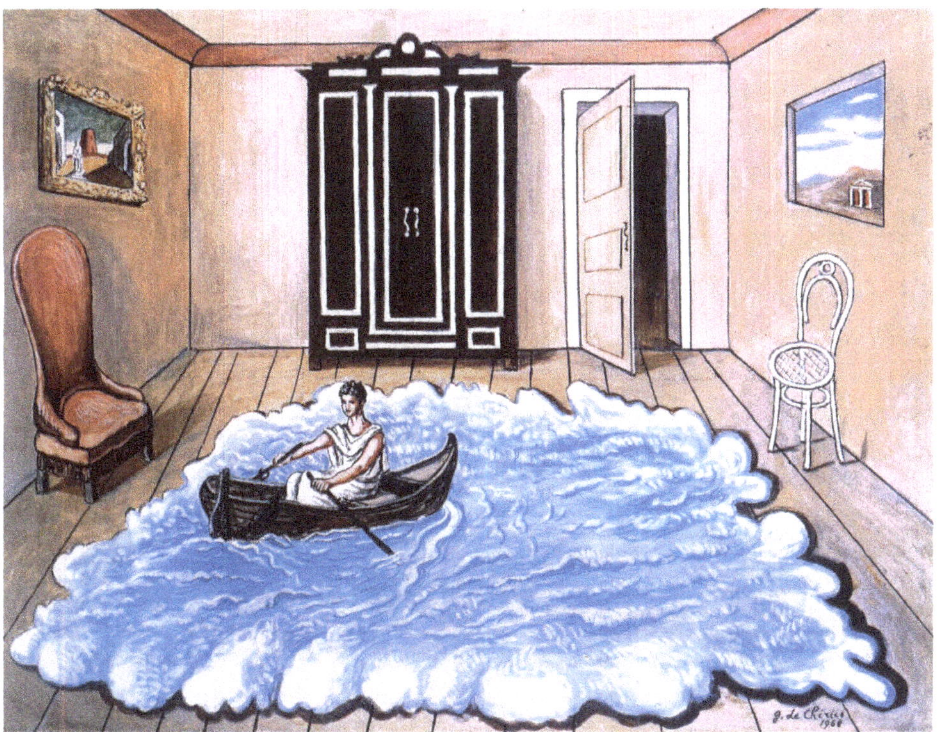

Figure 1.44. Giorgio de Chirico, *The Return of Ulysses* (*Il ritorno di Ulisse*), 1968, oil on canvas, 59.5 × 80 cm, Fondazione Giorgio e Isa de Chirico, Rome, © 2022 Artists Rights Society (ARS), New York/SIAE, Rome.

self-fashioning as a claustrophilic mental traveller in his poems is a form of identification with the proud "stay-at-home" of the *Satires*. In his paintings of the same years recurs the Ferrarese theme of Metaphysical interiors. Thoroughly explored, in its philosophical and iconographic sources, by Merjian (who also acknowledged the role of Ariosto's *Satires* in its development), this theme is based on a puzzling overlapping of domestic scenes and landscapes: the room and the world again, the window and the canvas, the chair and the Hippogriff. Similar visual ideas were explored by de Chirico's acolytes: Carrà of course, and de Pisis with his later series of still lives all set in his room, but also Govoni, who dedicated an entire page of *Rarefazioni e parole in libertà* to the theme of the "Sentimental Room" (figure 1.45).

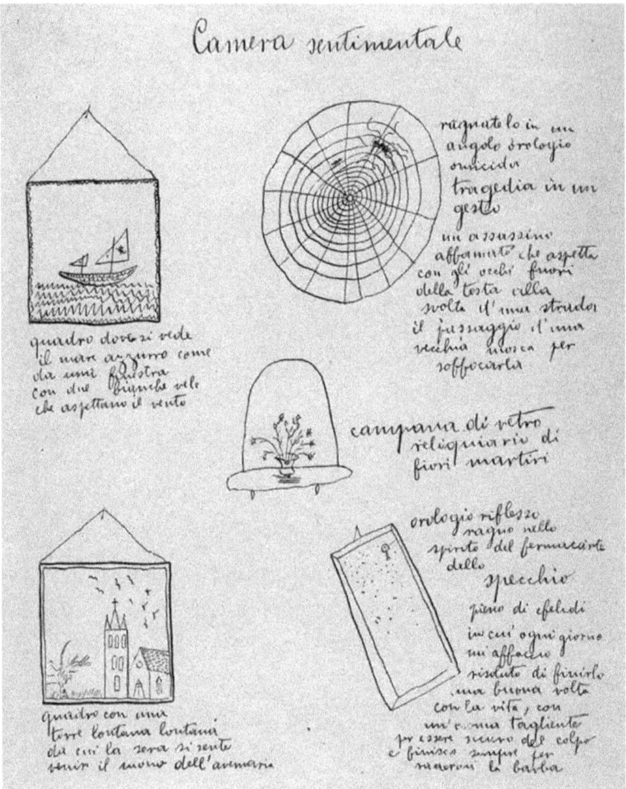

Figure 1.45. Corrado Govoni, “Sentimental Room” (“Camera sentimentale”), in *Rarefazioni e parole in libertà* (Milan: Edizione Futuriste di “Poesia,” 1915), p. 13. Biblioteca Comunale Ariostea, Ferrara.

Interestingly, de Chirico’s Metaphysical interiors are often characterized by a visual obsession with actual cartography. Maps appear, for instance, in *The Melancholy of Departure* (figure 1.46), in coeval paintings (such as *Politics*, realized in the same year), and in the elaborate drawings that de Chirico sent to Paul Guillaume, from Ferrara, in 1916: *The Melancholy of the Room* (reproduced earlier) and *Geographic Spring*. Ariosto’s Ptolemaic “carte,” emblematically theorized in the *Satires* and visualized so often and so astutely in the early illustrated editions of his poem (figures 1.47 and 1.48), are to be included in the rhizome of genetic inspirations of this essential group of paintings.[81]

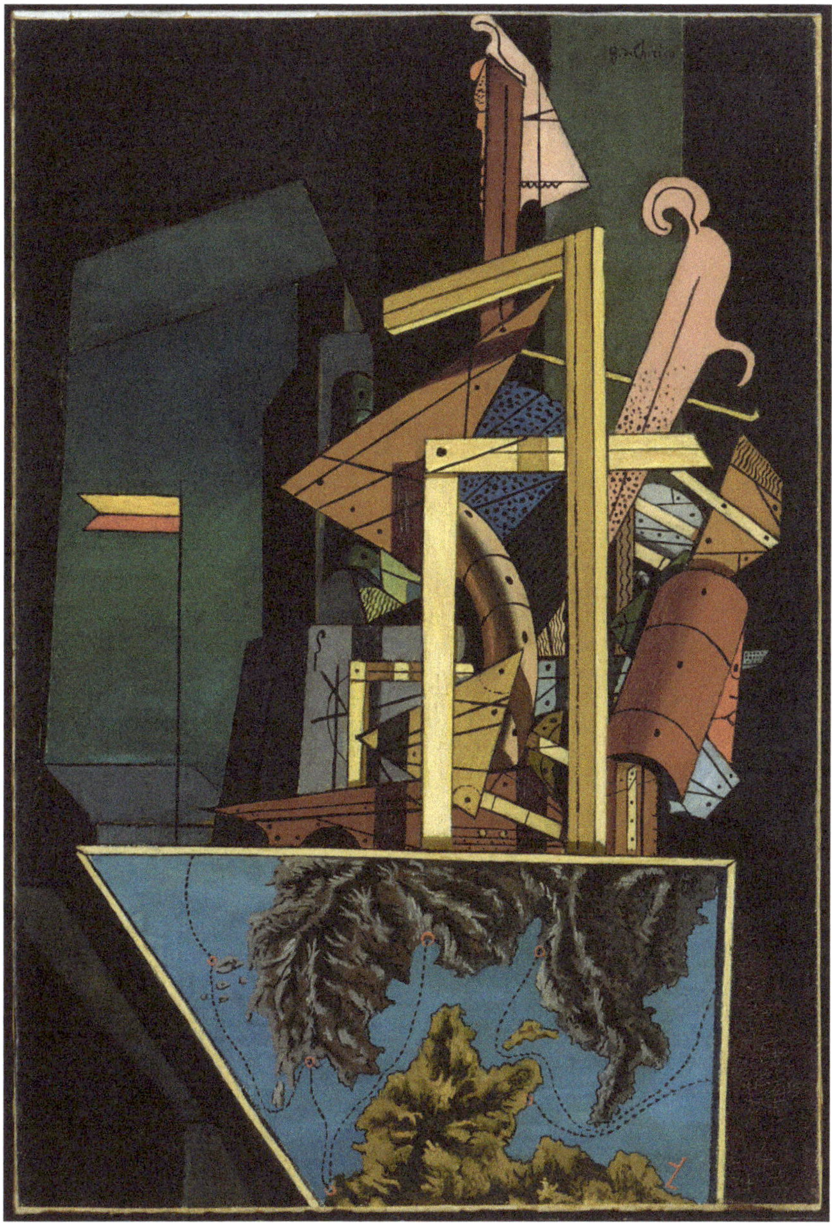

Figure 1.46. Giorgio de Chirico, *The Melancholy of Departure* (*La mélancolie du départ*), 1916, oil on canvas, 51.8 × 35.9 cm, Tate Gallery, London. © 2022 Artists Rights Society (ARS), New York/SIAE, Rome.

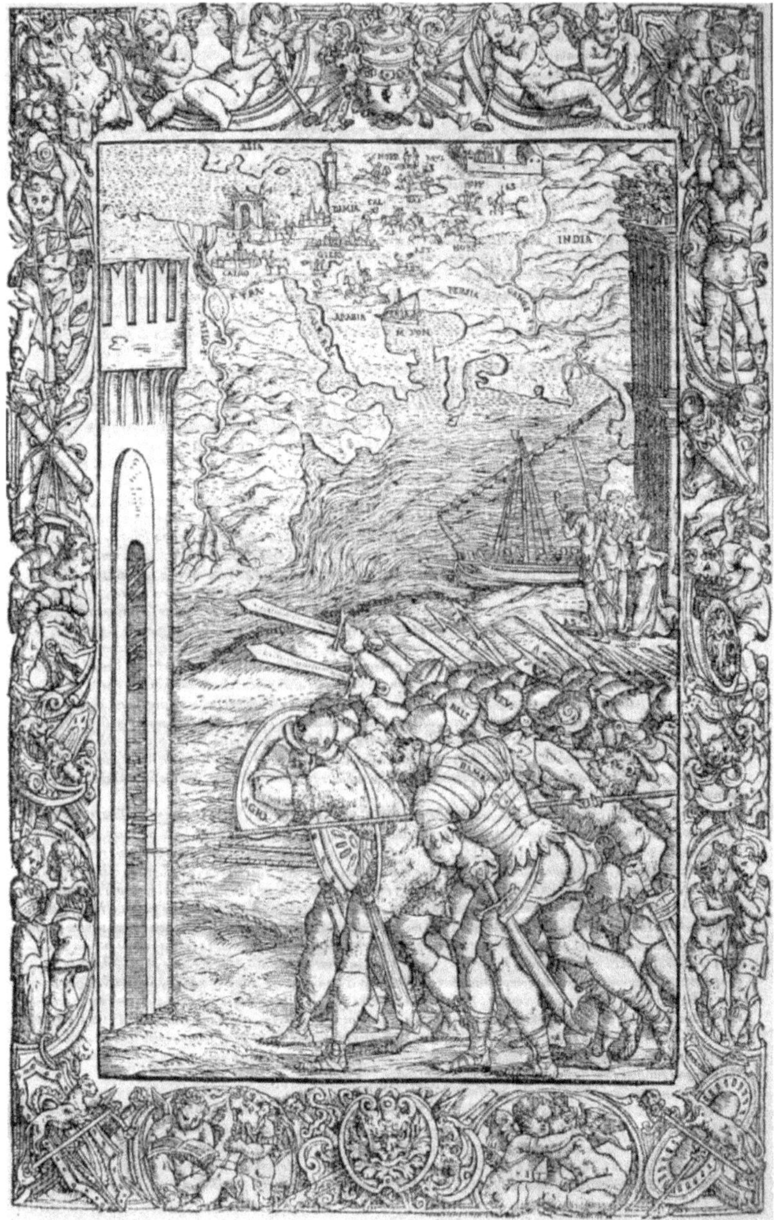

Figure 1.47. Illustration of Canto XV from Ludovico Ariosto, *Orlando Furioso* (Venice: Vincenzo Valgrisi, 1556). Biblioteca Comunale Ariostea, Ferrara.

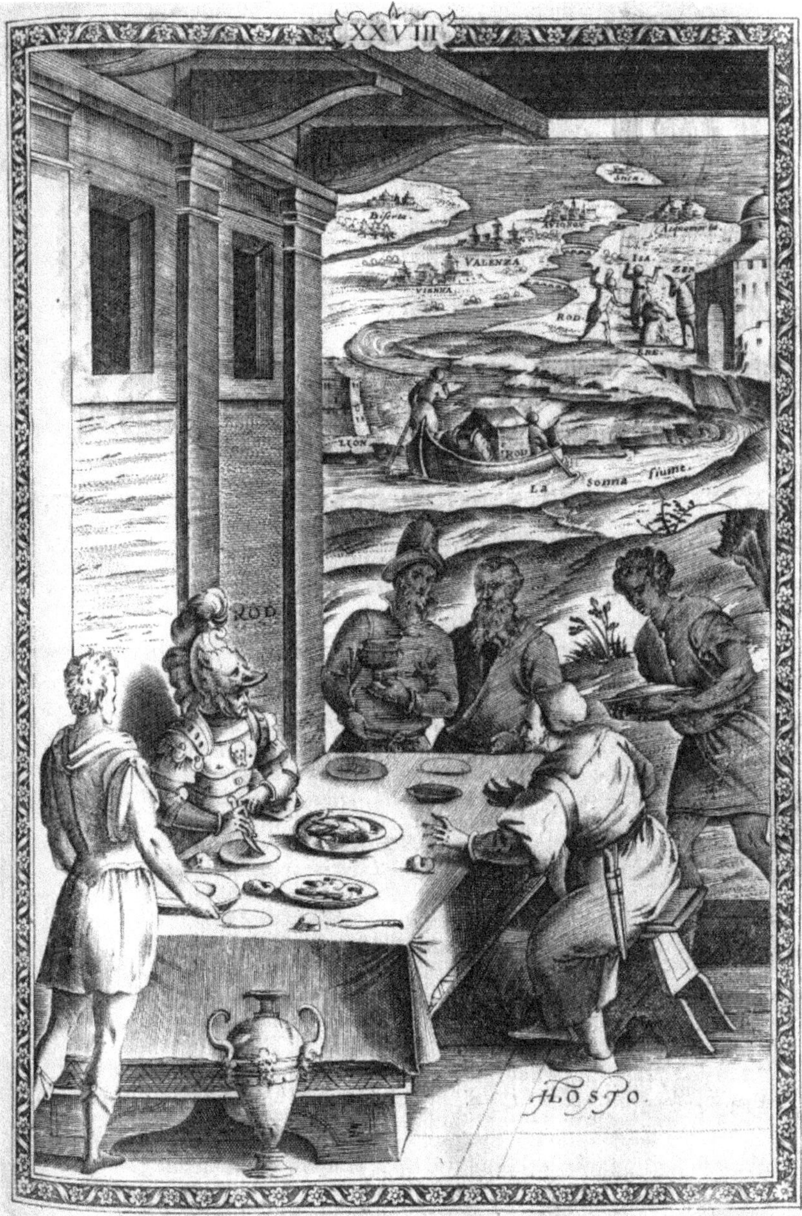

Figure 1.48. Girolamo Porro, copperplate illustration of Canto XXVIII from Ludovico Ariosto, *Orlando Furioso* (Venice: Francesco de' Franceschi, 1584). Biblioteca Panizzi, Reggio Emilia.

Admittedly, the *Satires* is not the most popular of Ariosto's works. While we know that Evaristo de Chirico, an engineer who built the railway networks of Pelion and Thessaly, made his sons acquainted with the *Orlando Furioso* in their childhood,[82] the *Satires* were probably not among de Chirico's and Savinio's formative readings. However, exactly when the trope of cartographic explorations and introverted adventurousness started appearing in the brothers' visual and literary works, a new edition of Ariosto's *Satires* was published in Italy by Massimo Bontempelli. And Bontempelli, the founder of Magical Realism, was one of de Chirico's and Savinio's closest artistic comrades in Italy. His edition of the *Satires* was printed in 1916 by Milan's Istituto Editoriale italiano. It was the first twentieth-century edition of Ariosto's so-called minor works, and had quite a resonance in Ferrara, where the previous edition of the *Satires* was published in 1874 for the anniversary of Ariosto's birth. It is likely that de Chirico and Savinio read this new edition in Ferrara, in the months when they were wandering in Piazza Ariostea with de Pisis.

The frontispiece of Bontempelli's edition shows a cropped, black and white reproduction of Titian's *Portrait of a Man*. For centuries, this sixteenth-century masterpiece has been wrongly considered to be a portrait of Ludovico Ariosto. The identification of the bearded man portrayed by Titian with the author of the *Orlando Furioso* was so prevalent and popular that the painting is still used today as a cover image for Ariosto's books. His distinctive oblique gaze became a looking-glass for de Chirico, who mirrored himself not only in the literary image of the *Satires*, a self-portrait in verse, but also in Ariosto's iconography.

De Chirico's 1924 *Autoritratto* is a crowning achievement of his long pictorial research on his own image (figure 1.49). Comparing this self-portrait with Titian's painting (figure 1.50), Mario Ursino insisted on the similarities between de Chirico's swelling jacket and the exquisite quilted doublet that is, essentially, the protagonist of Titian's portrait.[83] I do not find such a formal, plastic parallel particularly cogent. In fact, I believe that the two portraits are, as far as pictorial values are concerned, antithetical. The two sleeves in the foreground – one chalky, stuffed, and heavy, the other satiny, airy, and calligraphic – are poles apart. Yet, the position of the busts in relation with the horizontal plane of the sills, developed from the portraits of Giorgione's Venetian school, is comparable. Furthermore, the very distinctive psychological attitude of the faces (the lines of the lips and of the eyebrows, the direction of the eyes, the balance between light and shadow) suggests a kinship.

However, what really pushes me to underline a relation between de Chirico's *Autoritratto* and Titian's painting is the simple fact that the latter was thought to represent Ariosto. Bontempelli's 1916 edition of

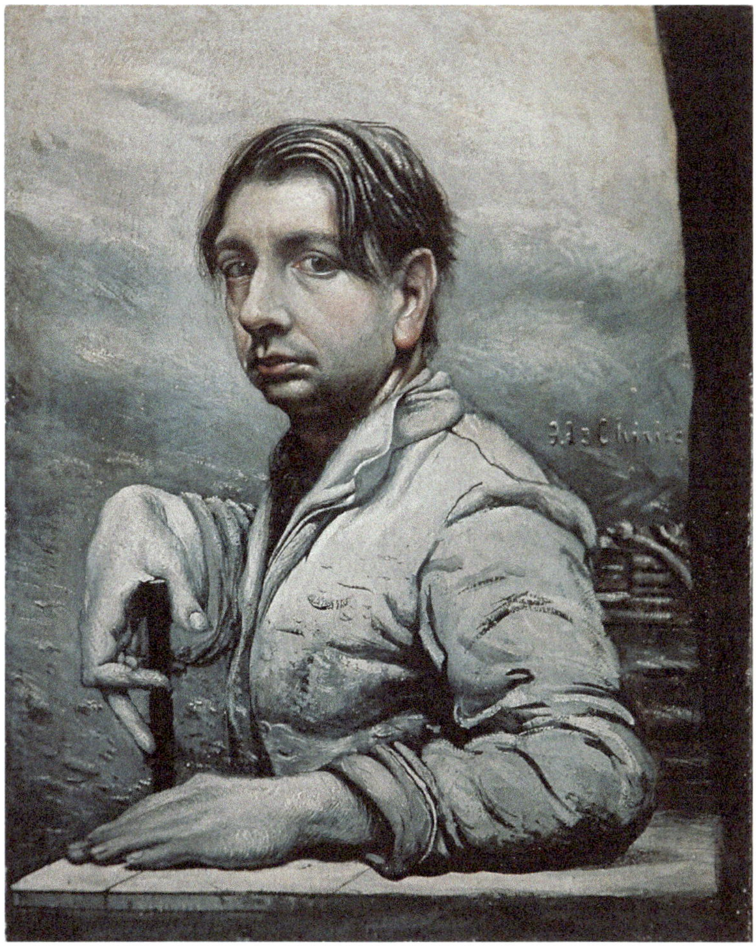

Figure 1.49. Giorgio de Chirico, *Self-Portrait* (*Autoritratto*), 1924, tempera on canvas, 75 × 62 cm, private collection. © 2022 Artists Rights Society (ARS), New York/SIAE, Rome.

the *Satires*, with its black and white reproduction at the very beginning, offered de Chirico a reminder of this fact. Clearly, like most of de Chirico's self-portraits, the 1924 *Autoritratto* is influenced by Poussin's and Böcklin's models, as critics have noticed.[84] Still, the posture and expression of Titian's *Portrait* have a role in my reading of the *Autoritratto* because they are features of the poet in marble, as he verbally depicted himself in the

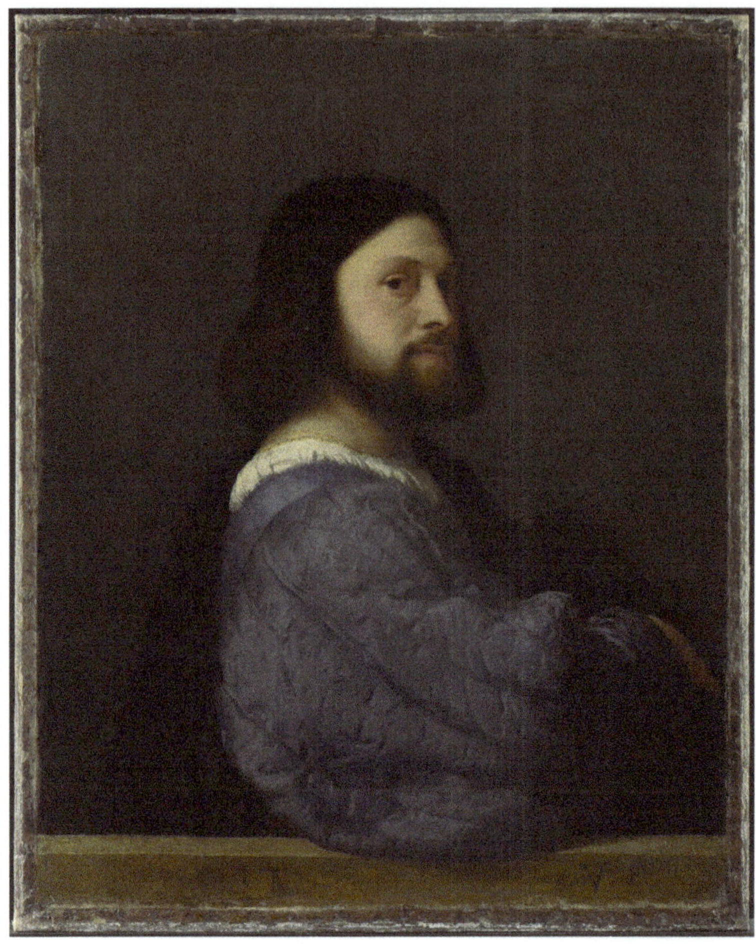

Figure 1.50. Tiziano Vecellio, *Portrait of Gerolamo (?) Barbarigo*, ca. 1509, oil on canvas, 81.2 × 66.3 cm, National Gallery, London. Photograph © The National Gallery, London.

Satires: a serene, inactive, visionary Metaphysician in de Chirico's eyes. And, more importantly, in the *Autoritratto* de Chirico turned himself into a statue. In a symmetrical subversion of what happened in Savinio's and de Pisis' literary animations of Ariosto's monument in Piazza Ariostea, de Chirico petrified his own body and became a monument himself.

A hint that connects Savinio's "poet in marble" with this monumentalized de Chirico is the detail of the fossilized lyre in the background, on the right, which alludes to the "theorbo" in Savinio's *Ferrara ... Partenza* and, of course, to Ariosto's marble lyre in the Piazza Ariostea monument. And the game of mirrors that interlaces portraits and self-portraits, men in flesh and men in marble, comes full circle with the idea, proposed by Maurizio Fagiolo, that *The Great Metaphysician* should be read as a self-portrait too.[85]

The Ariostean Period

Raymond Queneau famously joked that de Chirico's work is divided into two parts: "the early and the bad."[86] In between these two phases (the celebrated original Metaphysical production, in Paris and Ferrara, and the later, despised Roman baroqueries and neo-Metaphysical self-plagiarisms) there is a parenthesis that has been called, quoting a passage from de Chirico's memoirs, "the Romantic period."[87] This period of technical experimentation with tempera painting on neo-classical subjects and Magical Realism started at the end of the war and continued through the early years of fascism. Critics have associated de Chirico's repudiation of his own iconic aesthetics after leaving Ferrara with many factors. In 1919, his first major Italian exhibition of Metaphysical paintings was, as I mentioned, a failure. In the 1920s, as Queneau's comment shows, his relationship with French Surrealists became belligerent. Former companions, such as Carlo Carrà, appropriated his visual themes, and imitators plagiarized his Metaphysical works, saturating the European market with fakes. In addition, after the end of the war, fascist totalitarianism started changing Italy's cultural landscape.

I would argue that de Chirico's transition between Metaphysics and what came after was watched by the same untimely ghost that inspired, at the cusp between the two periods, *The Great Metaphysician.* Rather than "Romantic," this phase of de Chirico's painting (and of Savinio's writing, as I will discuss below) could be called the Ariostean Period. The rest of this chapter will show why. However, first of all, it is important to remember that de Chirico's Ariostean turn at the end of the second decade of the century was the visible outlet of a much earlier subterranean river of influence. As I mentioned at the beginning of this chapter, de Chirico developed a fascination with Ariosto's poem since before Ferrara, from the very beginning of his creative life.

Some of de Chirico's earliest theoretical and autobiographical writings were composed in Paris between 1911 and 1915, and remained unpublished for seventy years. De Chirico left some of these manuscripts in his studio in Montparnasse, where they were collected by Jean Paulhan along with drawings, paintings, and other objects. The rest of the papers, though, almost fifty pages, travelled with him to Italy. There, they were acquired by Paul Eluard, who in turn gave them as a present to Pablo Picasso in 1937. The file, now preserved in the Musée Picasso in Paris, includes a 1912 meditation that provides one of the very few possible glimpses into de Chirico's mental laboratory before the most celebrated phase of his work. In this text, he mentioned only two literary sources for his juvenile inspiration.

The first is the *Odyssey*, and in particular the episode of Ogygia: "a passage from Homer captivates me – Ulysses on Calypso's island."[88] De Chirico famously quoted this passage in *Enigma of the Oracle* (1910) through the Romantic filter of Arnold Böcklin's *Odysseus und Kalypso* (1882). The figure of Ulysses from Böcklin's painting and from de Chirico's elaboration is the same that appears in the background of *The Great Metaphysician*, and inspired Savinio's early lost drawing *The Oracle*.[89] The second literary source mentioned by de Chirico in the 1912 text is Ariosto's *Orlando Furioso*.

> [...] or rather while reading Ariosto: Ruggiero, that kind of errant knight resting under a tree, falling asleep while the horse grazes around him; everything is solitary and silent, one would expect to see a dragon passing by in the skies; the scene enthralls me, I imagine the knight, the horse, the landscape, all at once, it's almost a revelation but this is not yet enough for me.[90]

The absence, in de Chirico's early production, of any painting comparable to this Ariostean meditation is suspicious. Böcklin, explicitly mentioned a few lines below in the same text, was profoundly inspired by the *Furioso*. De Chirico had plenty of Ariostean paintings by Böcklin to elaborate on, as he did on the Homeric scene. "From Ariosto," Savinio would indeed note in his most famous book, "Böcklin drew inspiration for some of his finest paintings."[91]

Gerd Roos conjectured that de Chirico may actually have painted a series of very early chivalric works based on Ariosto and on Böcklin's Ariostean iconographies. In his hypothesis, these works could have been completed before 1910, but then destroyed by de Chirico himself after the beginning of his fully Metaphysical phase.[92] What is certain is that, after the encounter that resulted in *The Great Metaphysician*, de Chirico, in his Ariostean Period, did finally resort to Böcklin's visualizations of the *Orlando Furioso* to exit the impasse of his post-war pictorial research.

With the Ariostean *Autoritratto* still on his easel, de Chirico sent two large canvases to the 1924 Biennale in Venice, the first major international exhibition to welcome his work and to confirm the rise of his fame in Italy. Both paintings, dramatically different from any of his famous

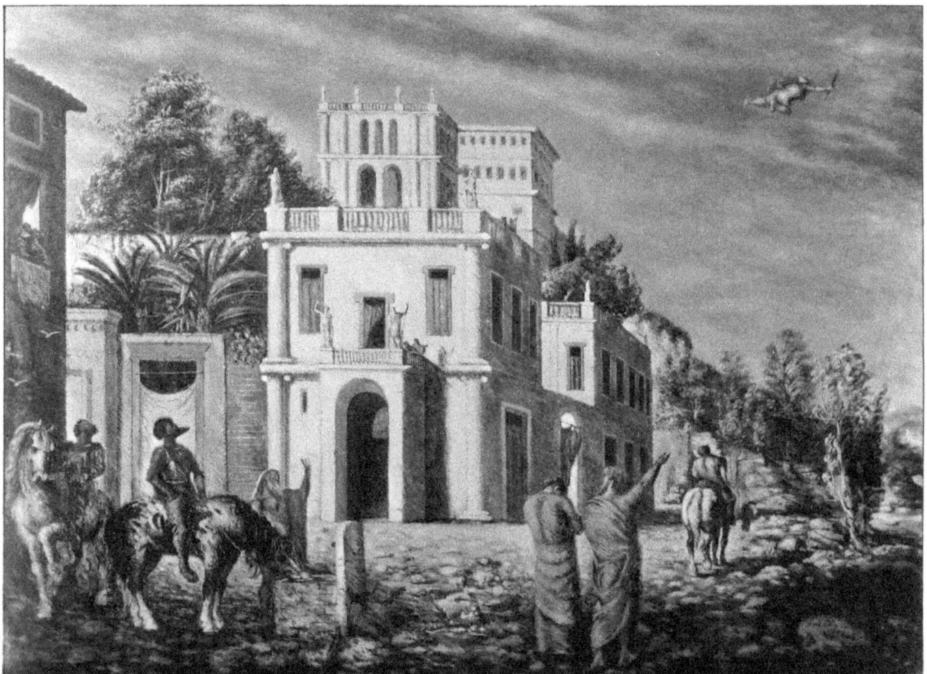

Figure 1.51. Giorgio de Chirico, *Ottobrata*, 1924, tempera on canvas, 135 × 183 cm, Galleria dello scudo, Verona.

early works, were based on chivalric imagery. *Ottobrata* represented the departure of an errant knight from an enchanted villa (figure 1.51), while *Duels to Death* depicted a battle, with horses, armoured knights, swords, waving standards, and pikes (figure 1.52). I believe that these two emblematic compositions of de Chirico's post-Ferrara years perfectly show the consequences of the revelation triggered by the encounter with Ariosto that I reconstructed.[93]

What informed de Chirico's enigmatic chivalric scenes throughout the 1920s – and his brother's experimental narrative of the period – is the *Furioso*'s magical but realistic atmosphere, its ironic disenchantment, its inextricable tangle of plots and characters, its ability to overlap classical

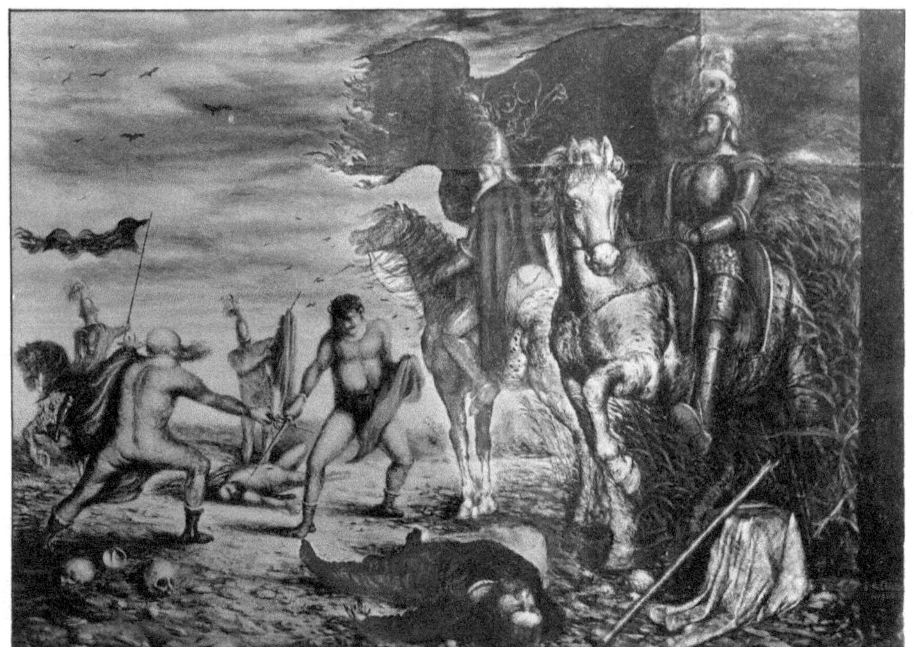

Figure 1.52. Giorgio de Chirico, *The Duels to Death* (*I duelli a morte – Les duels à la mort*), 1924, tempera on canvas, 131 × 188 cm, private collection. © 2022 Artists Rights Society (ARS), New York/SIAE, Rome. Photograph © La Biennale di Venezia, ASAC (Archivio Storico delle Arti Contemporanee).

myths, medieval plots, and Renaissance reality in a way that inspired Romantic painters and philosophers. Some of de Chirico's still lives of the period drew inspiration from the same imagery. This is the case, for instance, with the 1924 composition *Cuirass and Watermelons,* with its armour and swords abandoned in a valley (figure 1.53), which de Chirico painted again almost forty years later, in Baroque style, with the overtly Ariostean title *Ariostean Still-Life* (figure 1.54). Along these lines, *Duels to Death* is finally, more than ten years after the Homeric *Enigma of the Oracle,* the Ariostean painting based on Böcklin that one could have expected to see after reading de Chirico's 1912 Parisian text. Its iconography is based on an assemblage of Böcklin's works inspired by the *Furioso.* The armoured body of the knight in the foreground, on the right, is essentially a copy of Böcklin's *The Adventurer* (figure 1.55), a serene tempera

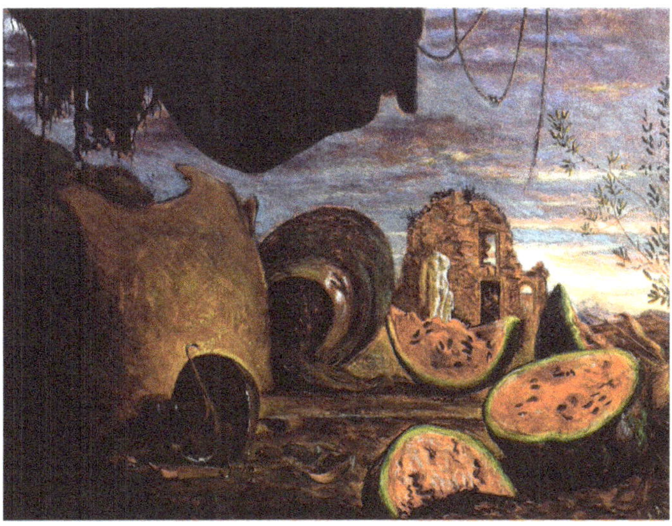

Figure 1.53. Giorgio de Chirico, *Cuirass and Watermelons* (*Corazza e cocomeri*), 1924, oil on canvas, 74 × 100 cm, private collection. © 2022 Artists Rights Society (ARS), New York/SIAE, Rome. Photo Credit: HIP/Art Resource, NY.

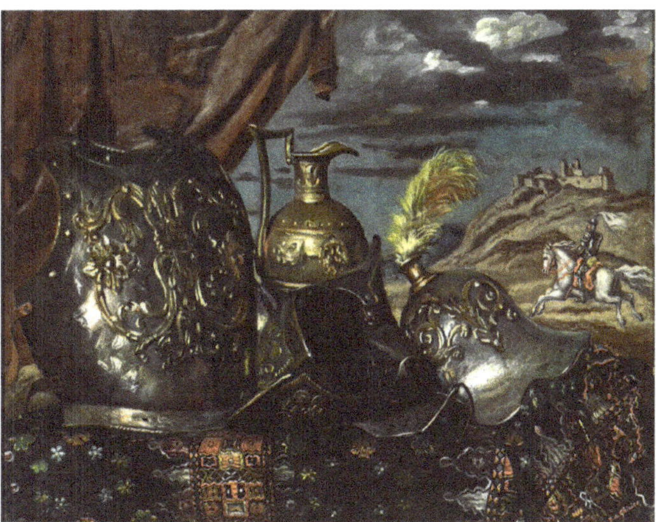

Figure 1.54. Giorgio de Chirico, *Cuirasses with Knight* or *Ariostean Still-Life* (*Corazze con cavaliere* o *Natura morta ariostesca*), 1940, oil on canvas, 87 × 112 cm, Galleria Tornabuoni, Fiesole. © 2022 Artists Rights Society (ARS), New York/SIAE, Rome. Courtesy Tornabuoni Art.

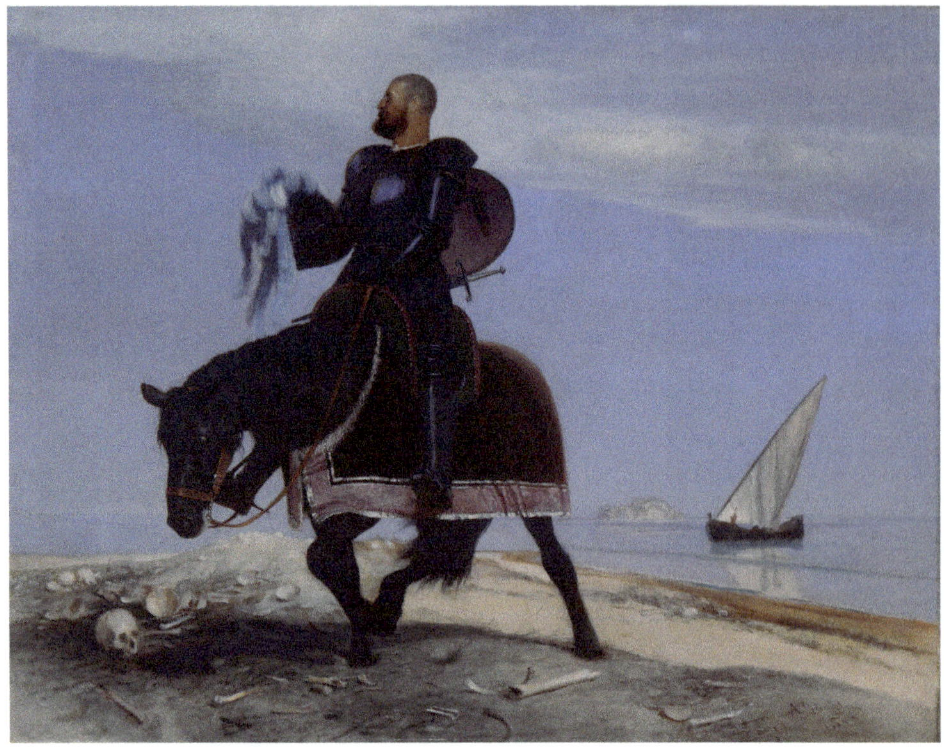

Figure 1.55. Arnold Böcklin, *The Adventurer* (*Der Abenteurer*), 1882, tempera on canvas, 116 × 150.5 cm, Kunsthalle Bremen, Bremen. Photograph © Kunsthalle Bremen.

that almost looks like a collage. In it, Böcklin depicted Astolfo in search of the giant Caligorant at the mouth of the Nile (XV, 42). The detail of the skulls, in the lower left corner of de Chirico's painting, is retraced from *The Adventurer* as well (figure 1.56). On the other hand, the warrior in the background, with the spear, the helmet, and the cloak, looks like a combination of the two Ruggieros that Böcklin painted in his "rescues of Angelica" of 1873 and 1880 (figures 1.57 and 1.58).

The same iconography is also at the core of one of Savinio's earliest known visual experiments, *The Birth of Venus* (figure 1.59). This collage, which Pia Vivarelli dated between 1925 and 1926,[94] shows a faceless version of Böcklin's Angelica, emerging from a marmoreal sprawl of collapsed columns and ruins. To make it, Savinio glued a blank piece of paper on a larger sheet of cardboard. On the bottom

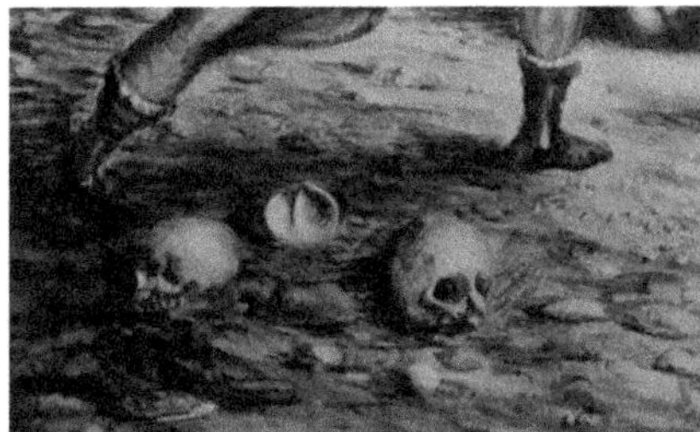
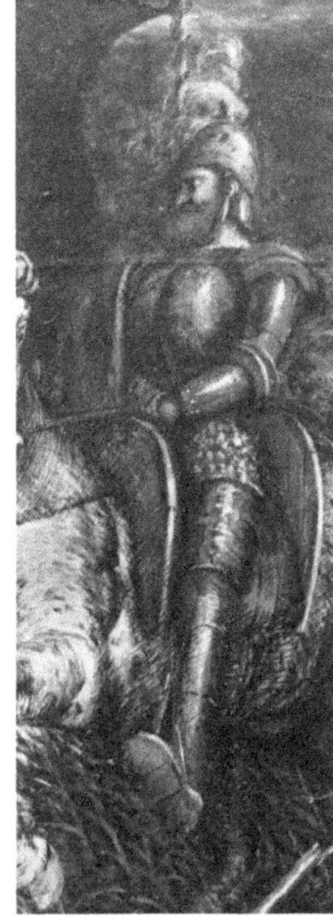

Figure 1.56. Details from de Chirico's *The Duels to Death* that directly quote Böcklin's *The Adventurer* (knight, skulls).

of that piece of paper, he glued a postcard from his native Greece: a colourized view of the excavation of Demeter's Sanctuary in Eleusis, printed in Zurich (figure 1.60). For the last layer, he traced over Böcklin's painting: he cut out the feminine figure, anonymized her, and glued her body over the composition. The final effect gives the impression of a faceless Renaissance idol rising from ancient ruins to reach the void of a proverbial white page. In a 1919 essay that bears a Greek version of the same title, *Anadioménon*, Savinio had used the myth of Venus rising from the ocean to describe the evolution of art. He compared the peak of modern aesthetics, Metaphysical painting, to the last phase of Greek sculpture, in which statues detach their limbs from their body and start to move.[95] The connection with Ariosto's animated statue in Ferrara is flagrant.

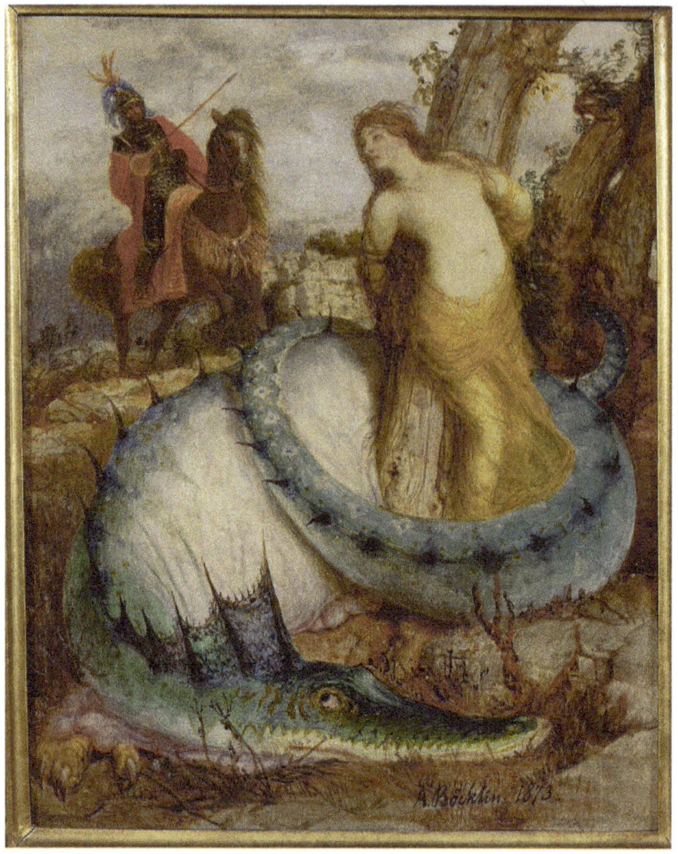

Figure 1.57. Arnold Böcklin, *Angelica Guarded by the Dragon* (*Angelica ven einem Drachen bewacht*),1837, tempera on wood, 46 × 37 cm, Nationalgalerie – Staatliche Museen, Berlin. Photograph © Erich Lessing/Art Resource, NY.

Interestingly, Savinio's 1919 essay concludes with a reflection on irony,[96] the quintessential trait of Ariosto's style and, in Savinio's theory, a fundamental aspect of modern painting. Irony, Savinio explains, is one of those intellectual foundations of modern pictorial sensitivity that are lacking in French culture. In France, art almost reached its "spiritual fullness"[97] in the nineteenth century, but then stopped, leaving the lead to the Italian avant-garde of Metaphysical painters such as de Chirico and Carrà. In a later article, Savinio pointed at irony to distinguish the Italian intelligence of the interplanetary flights of

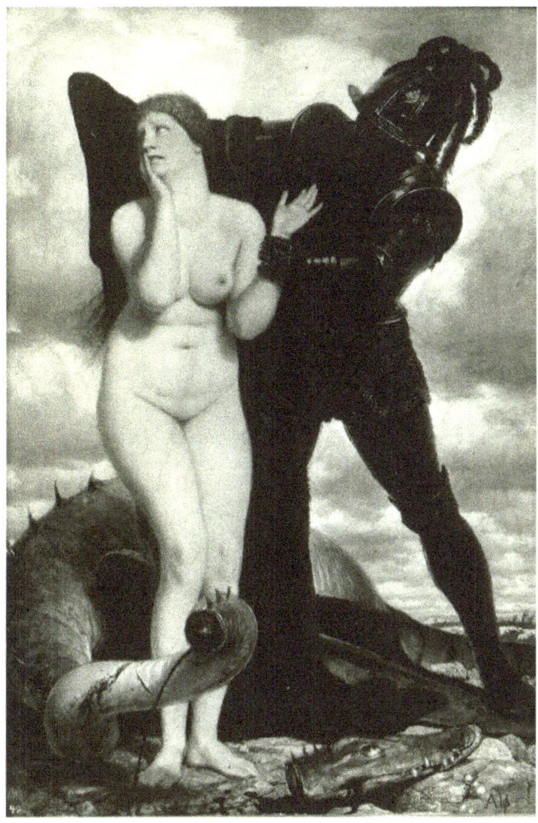

Figure 1.58. Arnold Böcklin, *Ruggiero Frees Angelica from the Claws of the Dragon* (*Ruggiero befreit Angelica aus den Klauen des Drachen*), ca. 1880, oil on wood, 82.5 × 55 cm, Museum Kunstpalast, Düsseldorf, Inv.-Nr. M 5047 (lost art work). Photograph © Museum Kunstpalast, Düsseldorf.

Ariosto's *Furioso* from the less imaginative rationality of French "astronomical fantasy."

> If Ludovico Ariosto was able to ride Hippogriffs and, without damage, send his paladins to wander through interplanetary heavens, it is because messer Ludovico never let this very useful guiding light go: irony. The opposite type of Ariosto is known as Flammarion.[98]

For Savinio, Ariosto, able to reach the moon while sitting on his chair, is a much better guide to transcend physics than the protagonist of the

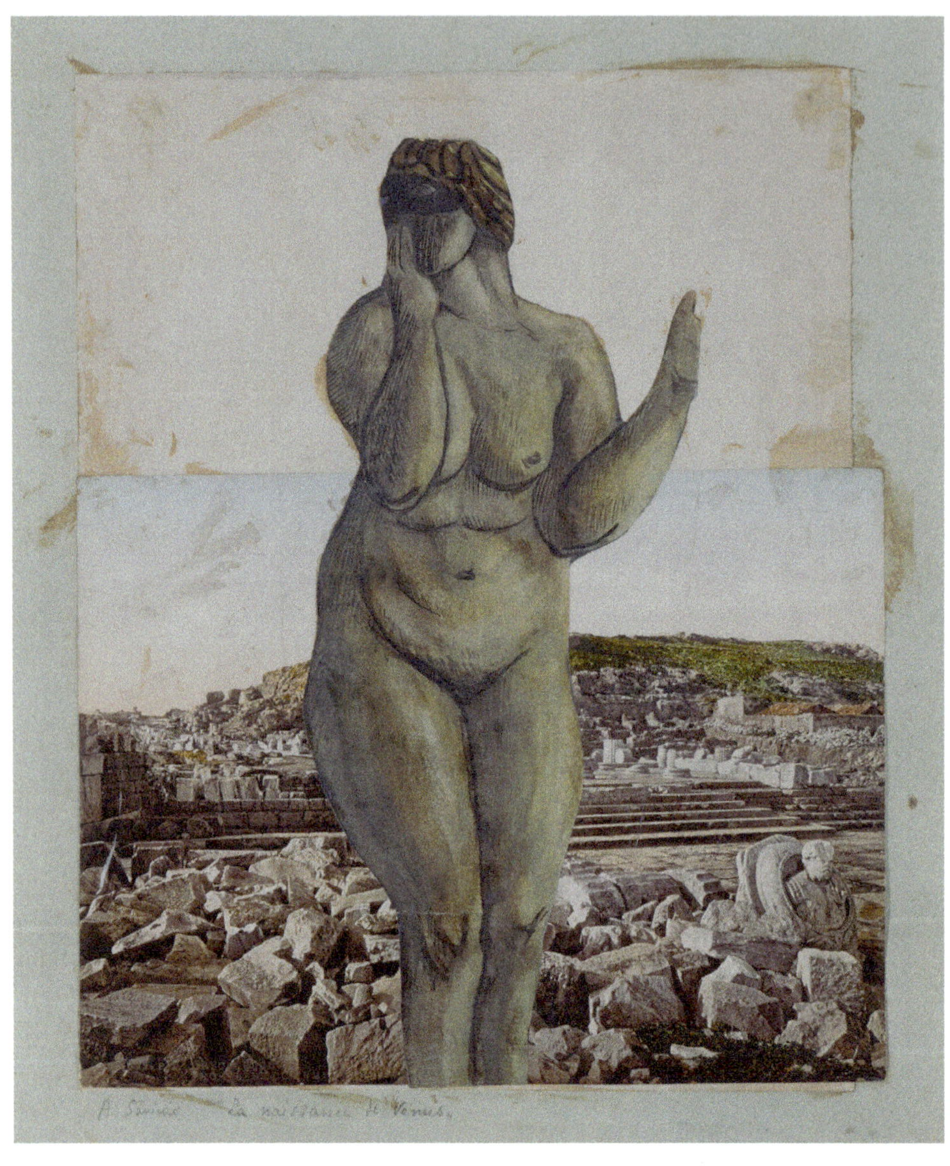

Figure 1.59. Alberto Savinio, *The Birth of Venus* (*La Naissance de Venus*), 1925–6 (?), ink, watercolour, and collage on paper, 27.5 × 22.3 cm, private collection, Rome. © 2022 Artists Rights Society (ARS), New York/SIAE, Rome.

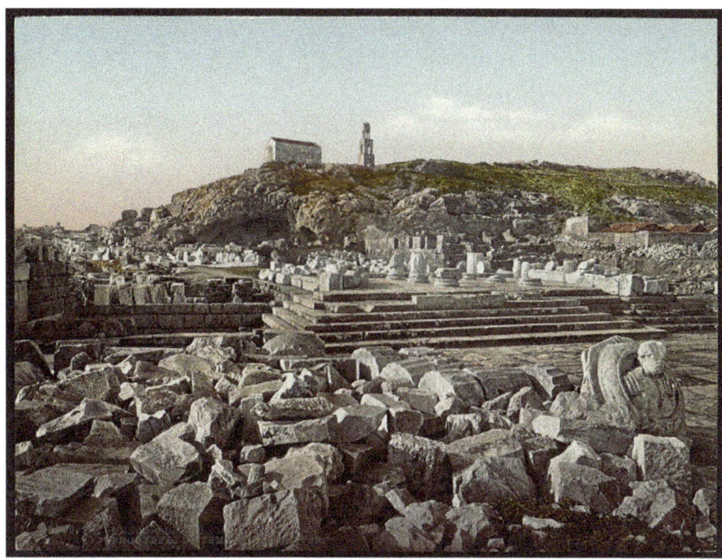

Figure 1.60. Temple of Demeter in Eleusis, Greece, Photoglob Co (Zürich), *Grèce. Eleusis. Propylees du Temple de Démètĕr,* ca. 1890, colour photochrom, 17 × 23 cm. Retrieved from the Library of Congress, image in the public domain.

famous mysterious engraving that Camille Flammarion published in his *L'atmosphère: météorologie populaire* (figure 1.61). Unlike Ariosto's immobile excursions in the tangible and consciously impossible universe of his poem, Flammarion's engraving, published on the year of de Chirico's birth, lacks irony. The same, from Savinio's point of view, could be said of French modernism. From Impressionism to Surrealism, French art lacked the "guiding light" of a Metaphysical, Ariostean, irony.

Another piece of prose by Savinio helps to decode the Roman villa surrounded by knights in de Chirico's other main chivalric painting of the Ariostean period, *Ottobrata.* In the same year in which de Chirico painted it and sent it to Venice, Savinio published an ekphrastic meditation on Italian autumns in the *Rivista di Firenze.* This rare text, which was never included in Savinio's collected works, has the same title as de Chirico's painting: "Ottobrata." Ottobrata is an untranslatable Italian word. It describes a quintessentially Mediterranean meteorological phenomenon and refers to a period, in the month of October, in which a recurring Atlantic high pressure system increases temperatures in Southern Europe. In central Italy this triggers, in particular, a brief and clear

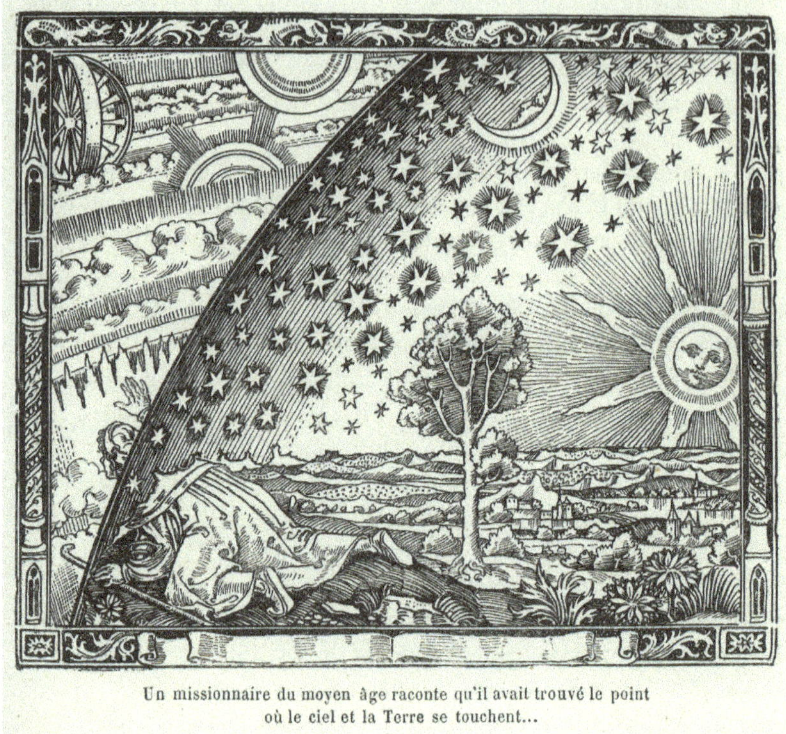

Figure 1.61. *A medieval missionary tells that he has found the point where heaven and Earth meet* (*Un missionaire du moyen âge raconte qu'il avait trouvé le point où le ciel et la Terre se touchent*), wood engraving in Camille Flammarion, *L'atmosphère: météorologie populaire* (Paris: Hachette, 1888). Image in the public domain.

second summer in the middle of autumn. Savinio's text was inspired by this phenomenon, like de Chirico's painting, and it translated de Chirico's chivalric vision into words. It openly mentioned Ariosto's poem along with Tasso's *Gerusalemme Liberata*: "The most beautiful poetry, the most profound and sumptuous art is inspired by autumn. I know entire poems, like the *Gerusalemme* or the *Orlando Furioso*, that are entirely set under an autumnal sky."[99]

The Art of Montage

Savinio's fiction, in the 1920s, was haunted by Ariosto's influence as well. His most ambitious literary project of the decade, *Angelica o la notte di maggio*, owes its title (and the name of its protagonist) to Ariosto's Angelica, the fleeing princess of the *Orlando Furioso*. Published in 1927, but elaborated between 1922 and 1925, this experimental novel was the first book by Savinio to completely abandon a first-person perspective. Instead of focusing on Savinio's own biography, it recounts the fictional story of a beautiful Greek dancer, Angelica, and her manic suitor, the Baron von Rothspeer. The plot is set in a surreal version of modern Mediterranean Europe.

In the novel, Rothspeer is obsessed with Angelica. Savinio describes her through the feminine stereotypes that Ariosto, in the adventures of his Angelica, had ironically subverted, making her able to escape the many assaults attempted by most of the male characters of the poem. A bashful and passive woman, a reluctant natural seductress, Savinio's Angelica has no interest in Rothspeer, but he loses his mind for her. He forgets about his duties to chase her, and is repeatedly ridiculed in his attempts to possess her. A kinship between this Angelica and Ariosto's Angelica has been already suggested by readers,[100] and the chivalric inspiration of the erotic dynamic is clear. Rothspeer's heinous goal, echoing that of several paladins and Saracens in the *Furioso* (I, 42–3), is to take Angelica's virginity. This febrile urgency mirrors the sexual threats that Ariosto's Angelica faces since the first canto of the *Furioso*. And, as in the *Furioso*, masculine desire is invariably frustrated in Savinio's novel. While Rothspeer manages to marry Angelica, he can never fulfil his real goal. He ends up mad and unsatisfied like Orlando, Ruggiero, the hermit, and other suitors of the runaway princess in Ariosto's poem.

In Savinio's novel, the reason why Rothspeer's desires remain unfulfilled is that Angelica is affected by a Metaphysical form of narcolepsy, which turns her into a living statue. Her unreachable, removed sleeping body fights off Rothspeer's possessive siege with an "invulnerable, remote, closed" idleness. Repeatedly frustrated, Rothspeer's disturbing attempts to take advantage of Angelica's unresponsive sleeping body recall, in particular, the episode of Angelica and the hermit in the *Furioso*. In Canto VIII (45–50), Angelica meets the old wanderer and seeks his help. The hermit, however, makes her fall asleep with a potion, revealing his malevolence. His intention is to rape her. However, the impotence of old age prevents the hermit from performing this act of violence. Tired from the unsuccessful effort, he eventually falls asleep as well. Like the hermit in the *Furioso*, Rothspeer falls asleep alongside Angelica after trying to grope her, unable to complete the compulsive erotic quest that animates him throughout the novel.[101]

The scene of Rothspeer lusting after a sleeping Angelica, unaware of his imminent failure, is a modern literary variation on a mythological

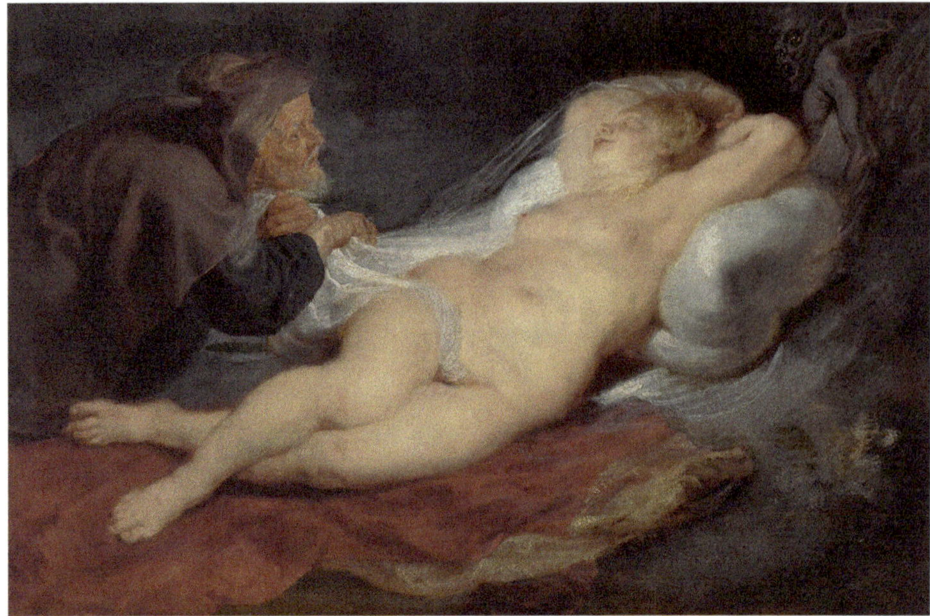

Figure 1.62. Peter Paul Rubens, *Angelica and the Hermit*, 1625–8, oil on wood, 43 × 65.5 cm, Kunsthistorisches Museum Wien, Gemäldegalerie, Vienna. © KHM-Museumsverband.

theme that was explored by several Renaissance artists. The most striking examples are Titian's *Pardo Venus* and Rubens' *The Hermit and the Sleeping Angelica* (figure 1.62), which draws on the *Furioso*. While Savinio was writing *Angelica*, de Chirico was studying these paintings to refine his technique on classical museum models. In later years, de Chirico would directly copy Rubens' depiction of Ariosto's scene. However, alluding to another mythological rape, he titled his version *Sleeping Leda* (figure 1.63).

Besides these thematic and onomastic correspondences with the *Furioso*, the most important parallel between Ariosto's poem and Savinio's novel is formal and structural. Opening *in medias res*, like an epic poem, Savinio's story interlaces episodes that take place at the same time but in different locations, creating a sense of frustrating disruption that ironically echoes, in the structure of the novel, the protagonist's inability to fulfil his goal in the plot. Changes of scene are abrupt and frequent. The author's extra-diegetic voice governs this alternation of storylines

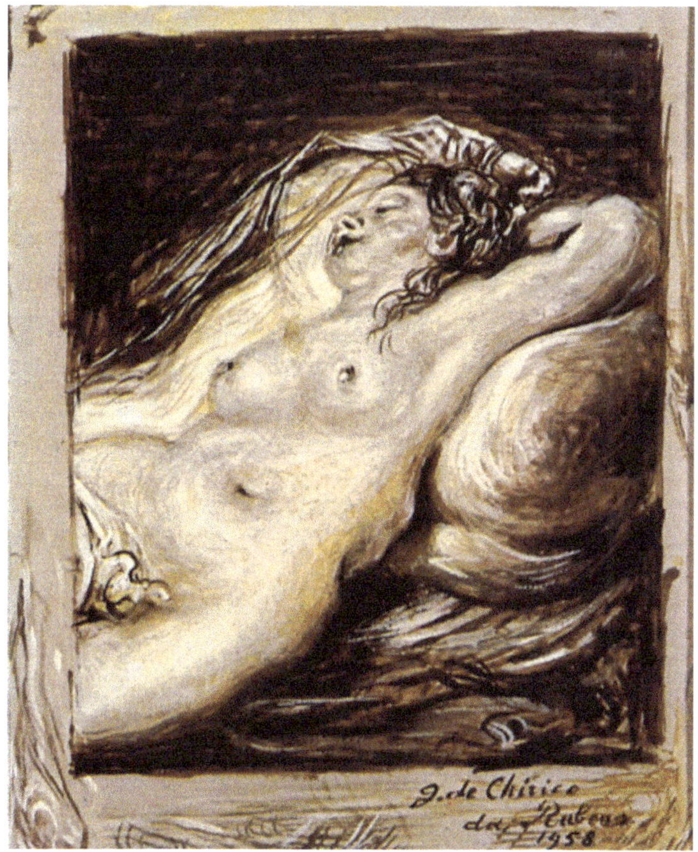

Figure 1.63. Giorgio de Chirico, *Sleeping Leda (after Rubens)* (*Leda addormentata (da Rubens)*), 1958, oil on cardboard, 39 × 29.5 cm, Fondazione Giorgio e Isa de Chirico, Rome. © 2022 Artists Rights Society (ARS), New York/SIAE, Rome.

by directly intervening in the text. Sometimes, the interruption is justified by structural necessity: for instance, when a new character needs to be introduced, or two narrative strands need to progress to the same moment in time. In other passages, a transition is called for by the narrator's simple curiosity, or a capricious desire for variety.

The second chapter, for instance, opens on the sea, in Rothspeer's stateroom.[102] However, Savinio's voice starts wondering about Angelica, and the narration suddenly moves to her bedside. Soon, the narrator intervenes again, this time invoking his muse, just as in a chivalric poem.

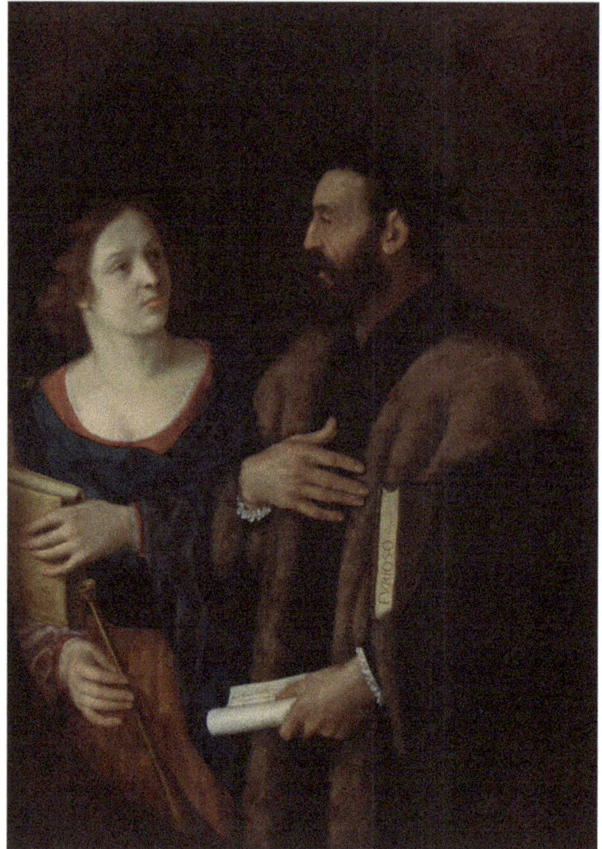

Figure 1.64. Guercino's School, *Ariosto and the Muse Clio* (*Ariosto e la musa Clio*), ca. 1650, oil on canvas, 112 × 81 cm, Ducal Palace, Sassuolo. Courtesy Gallerie Estense di Modena.

He does not call for Calliope, the muse of Epic, though, but for Clio, the muse of History. Clio would become Savinio's guide in the Etruscan wanderings of *Speaking to Clio,* a 1939 book in which Ovid's statue, like Aristo's in 1917 Ferrara, comes to life and accompanies the narrator and the readers through the mysteries of central Italy. Clio was also associated with the *Orlando Furioso,* as she ensured that the paladins who initiated the Este dynasty would be remembered long enough for Ariosto to immortalize them in his epic poem.[103] In the rare iconography of a seventeenth-century painting from Guercino's school (figure 1.64), Clio intimately converses with Ariosto, who holds the *Furioso* under his arm and a parchment with the first canto in his hand. The painting, which belonged to the Este family, is preserved in the ducal palace of Sassuolo.

In *Angelica o la notte di maggio*, after the first change of scene of Chapter 2, Savinio's narrator addresses Clio directly and asks her to leave the villa. He wants her to bring the narrative of his novel back to Rothspeer's ship, in order to make the story progress. However, this interlude is cut short (literally in the middle of the sentence) because Rothspeer, in the meantime, gets back to the villa on his own. The novel follows him again until a sudden interruption (once again in the middle of a sentence) moves the narration outdoors, where a new character is about to ring the bell of the villa. And so on.

This narrative montage represents a modern, extreme version of one of Ariosto's main structural devices. The *entrelacement*, a technique inherited from the oral tradition of chivalric fiction and reinvented for the *Orlando Furioso*, allowed Ariosto to evade Aristotelian structures and effectively blend epic and romance, the exploding desires that lead to adventure and the centripetal duties that call back to the battle ground.

Rather than being merely digressive and additive, like most previous chivalric poems until Boiardo,[104] Ariosto's labyrinthine abandonment and resumption of narrative threads structurally respond to an internal competition among the quests of his many characters in the story. The function of the *entrelacement* in the *Furioso* is not to create suspense, but to advertise the fictionality of the poem and to mirror, in the reading experience, the frustrations and missteps of the protagonists. As Sergio Zatti noted, one of the *Furioso*'s main original contributions to modern storytelling lies in this new reciprocal relationship between the classical romance features of the *entrelacement* and the element of the quest: "the play between the mode of telling and its semantic referent."[105] Savinio adopted a syncopated version of Ariosto's *entrelacement* to mirror the frustrated, stumbling erotic quest of Rothspeer. Rothspeer's mission interlaces with the competing desires of the other characters, from Angelica's own quest for transcendence to the attempts that a mysterious celestial lover makes to rescue her.[106]

In 1944, for the preface to a new edition of *Angelica o la notte di maggio* that was never printed, Savinio explained his modern *entrelacement* by writing that the novel was inspired by cinematic montage: "by the spirit and technique of the cinematograph."[107] The idea that Ariosto was an ancestor of cinema and that his *Furioso* was based on a "complex chain of [...] pictorial moving frames" thematically and technically linked together by "what filmmakers call the art of montage"[108] had already been expressed in 1930 by Anton Giulio Bragaglia. Bragaglia, a pioneer of Futurist photography and cinema, was one of the de Chiricos' closest collaborators after they left Ferrara. In 1919 he hosted de Chirico's first Roman exhibition in his gallery and, in 1938, he produced Savinio's play *Capitan Ulisse* in his theatre. His fascination with Ariosto, whom he considered "a poet forced to use words just because he couldn't use a camera,"[109] led Bragaglia to curate a monumental edition of Ariosto's comedies in 1947. His seminal Futurist film *Perfido incanto* (1917) was set in a magical palace. This spectral space, governed by the sorcerer Atanor in the film, was evidently inspired by the castle of the wizard Atlante in Canto XII of the *Furioso*, a central narrative node for the montage of many quests of the poem.

As I said, Savinio's constant disruptions of his own narration are a structural representation of Rothspeer's failures in pursuing his goal. They make the reader experience the same repeated frustration of the character's desire and, ultimately, of the illusory nature of any unrestrained obsessive quest, invariably destined to remain unsatisfied. In this, Savinio imitates one of Ariosto's most masterful uses of narrative transition: the passage between the end of Canto X and the beginning of Canto XI.

The episode is one of the most famous in the poem, and is the subject of the painting by Böcklin that inspired Savinio's *The Birth of Venus*. While flying between Scotland and Ireland, Ruggiero sees Angelica chained to the rock of Ebuda and rescues her from the monstrous Orca. However, with the naked princess on his Hippogriff, Ruggiero is suddenly overwhelmed by desire. He swiftly lands, and frantically tries to remove his armour in order to seize what he considers to be the prize for his heroic endeavour: Angelica's virginity. Ariosto's interrupting voice catches him in this clumsy attempt, which remains narratively suspended until its eventual failure at the beginning of the next canto. Angelica, as we learn after turning the page, is able to flee by using her magic ring.

Daniel Javitch used this overlapping of Ruggiero's *coitus interruptus* with what he called *cantus interruptus* as an example of Ariosto's experimental use of narrative rupture, a feature of the *Furioso* that was glossed over by late modern supporters of the poem (those contemporary with Savinio) and condemned by its early detractors (those contemporary with Ariosto) because of its anti-classical, subversive nature.[110] By reviving it within a cinematic spirit, Savinio embraced a subtle lesson of modernity from the poet in marble that he had met in Ferrara.

Stratigraphy of Angelica

The episode of Ruggiero liberating Angelica offered a fruitful theme to both de Chirico and Savinio from the 1930s on. In those years, Savinio

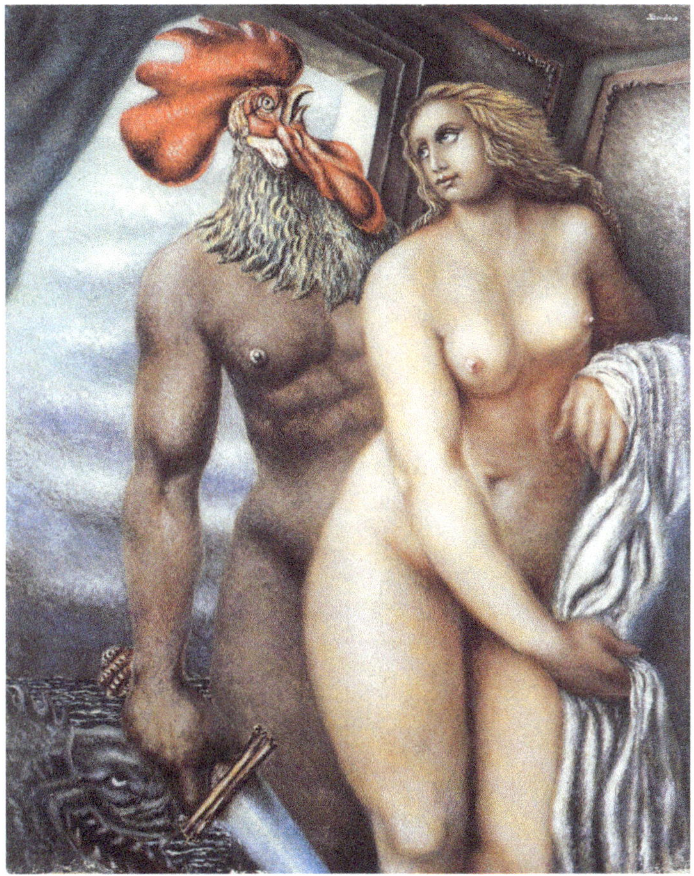

Figure 1.65. Alberto Savinio, *Ruggiero and Angelica* (*Roger et Angélique*), 1931, oil on canvas, 90 × 73 cm, private collection, Milan. © 2022 Artists Rights Society (ARS), New York/SIAE, Rome.

started his painting career and de Chirico definitively entered his "bad" period.

That of Ruggiero and Angelica is the only scene not from the Greco-Roman tradition that Savinio chose for the series *Chant d'amour*, commissioned by Léonce Rosenberg for his legendary apartment. In this 1931 oil, Ruggiero's lustful daze is alluded to by his surreal rooster's head (figure 1.65). Savinio quotes the naked Venus of Correggio's *The School of Love* (figure 1.66), but also the reptile grin of the monster in Ingres' depiction of the same scene of the *Furioso* (figure 1.67). Ingres' Ariostean

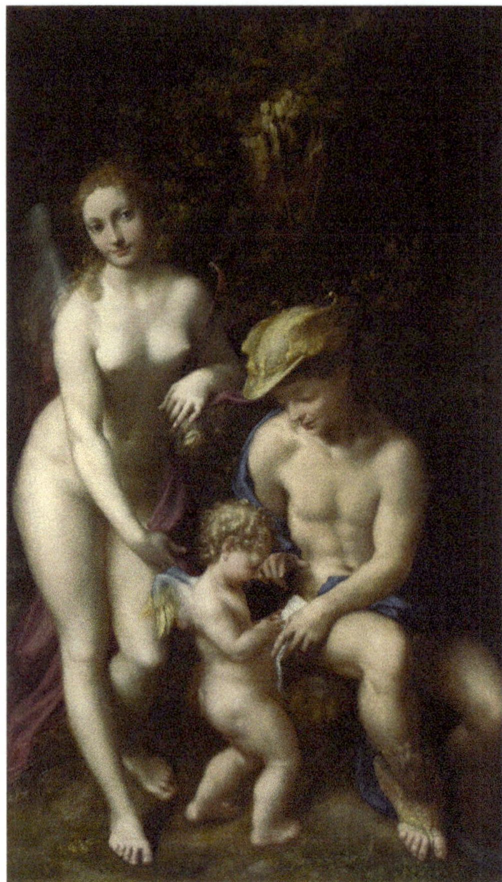

Figure 1.66. Correggio, *Venus with Mercury and Cupid ("The School of Love") (Educazione di Cupido)*, ca. 1525, oil on canvas, 155.6 × 91.4 cm, National Gallery, London. Photograph © National Gallery, London/Art Resource, NY.

iconography (the monster in particular) was also a source of inspiration for a large painting that de Chirico sent to the XXIII Venice Biennale with the title *Perseus Liberating Andromeda.* He later sold the same painting as *Ruggiero Frees Angelica* (figure 1.68).

A pastiche of visual quotations from Böcklin, Delacroix, and de Chirico's own late painting, the theatrical composition includes rocks that allude to Dalì's Surrealism, a knight armoured as in a sixteenth-century chivalric scene by Rubens, and a princess with a post-war hairdo and modern jewellery. This painting clearly understands Ariosto's material as an intersection between classicism and modernity: the ancipital gateway between antiquity and the twentieth century, origins and originality.[111] Ruggiero's rescue of Angelica, repeated, within the *Furioso,* by Orlando's

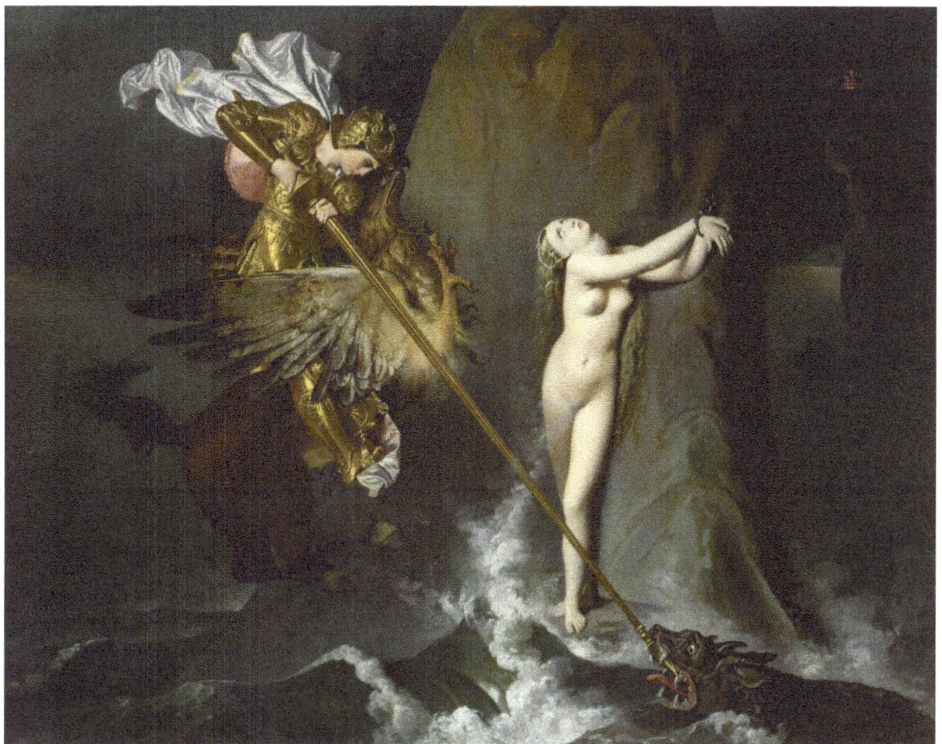

Figure 1.67. Jean Auguste Dominique Ingres, *Ruggiero and Angelica* (*Roger et Angelique*), 1819, oil on canvas, 147 × 190 cm, Musée du Louvre, Paris. Photograph © Erich Lessing/Art Resource, NY.

rescue of Olimpia, is in fact a rewriting of the episode of Perseus rescuing Andromeda in Ovid's *Metamorphoses*, which in turn elaborates on Greek mythology.

As we saw at the end of the Introduction of this book, de Chirico came back to this inherently intertextual and trans-historical subject numerous times in his late work (figures 1.69 and 1.70). He consistently used the Ariostean characters of Ruggiero and Angelica in the titles, but he incorporated elements (a Pegasus, pearls, cherubs) from Ovid's iconographic tradition. And a similar interplay of Ovidian and Ariostean memories characterized Savinio's parallel explorations of the same theme: from the ballet *Persée*,[112] written for Michel Fokine's choreography, to the chapter "The Voice of the Dragon" in

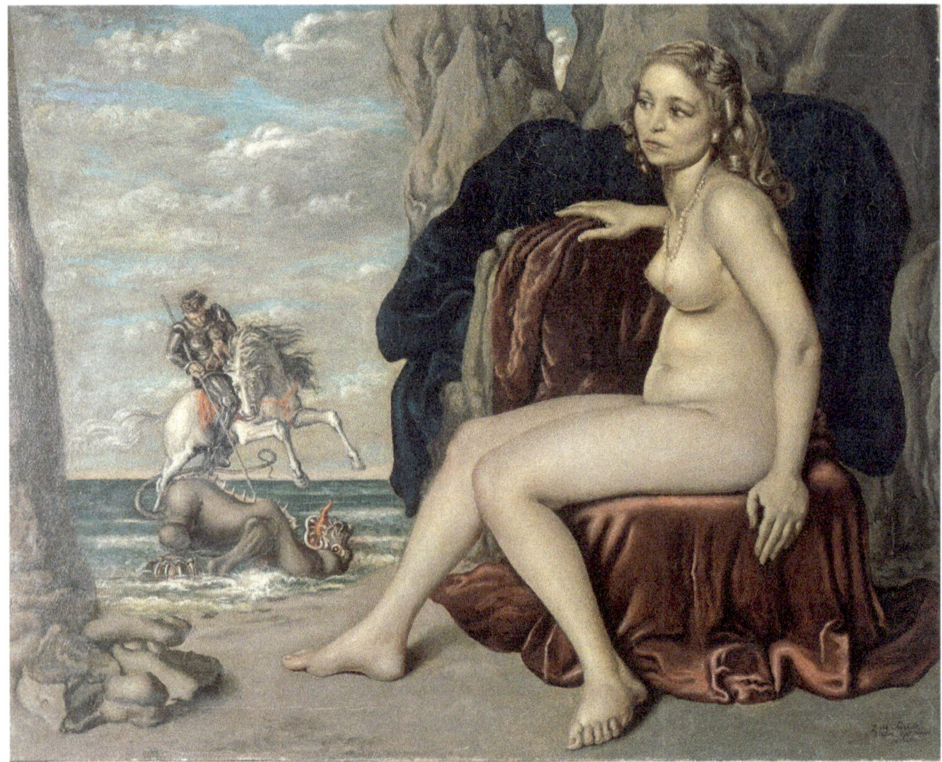

Figure 1.68. Giorgio de Chirico, *Perseus Frees Andromeda* or *Ruggiero Frees Angelica* (*Perseo libera Andromeda* o *Ruggiero libera Angelica*), 1940–1, oil on canvas, 90 × 118 cm, private collection, Rome. © 2022 Artists Rights Society (ARS), New York/SIAE, Rome. Photograph © akg-images.

his autobiographical novel *Tragedy of Childhood.* Autobiography is an essential key to read the gallery of Angelicas that appear in the brothers' post-metaphysical work. Savinio named his own children, born in 1928 and 1934, Angelica and Ruggiero. And the unconcerned naked Angelicas in Giorgio's paintings are modelled after his second wife, Isabella. After all, the iconography of Ruggiero in those paintings (his rampant horse without wings, his long spear) directly evokes another mythical slayer of dragons who shares the same name with de Chirico: Saint George.

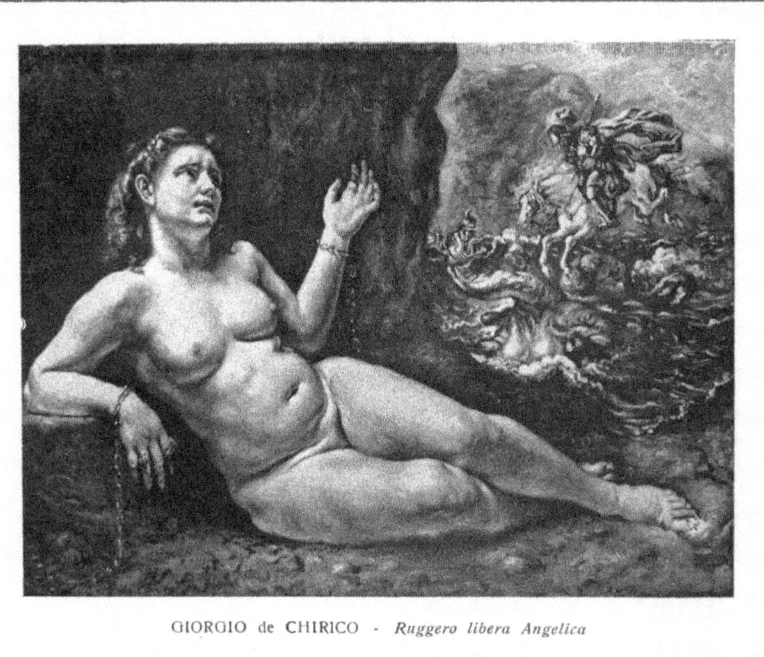

Figure 1.69. "Giorgio de Chirico, *Ruggiero libera Angelica*," photograph of a painting of unknown location attributed to Giorgio de Chirico (ca. 1950), halftone print, 9.8 × 12 cm, Federico Zeri Photo Archive, inv. 176650, Bologna. © 2022 Artists Rights Society (ARS), New York/SIAE, Rome. Courtesy Fototeca Federico Zeri, Università di Bologna.

Ariosto is the equidistant fulcrum between the de Chiricos' modern mythological stratigraphy and its classical sources. His Angelica is, at the same time, Ovid's ancient Andromeda and a twentieth-century woman, just as his *entrelacement* is both medieval and cinematic. Ariosto's Horatian, humanistic idleness is a model for experimental narrative and geographic iconography; his statue is able to desert its own marble monument to inhabit the modern city. More than a repertoire of episodes to rewrite or depict, Ariosto's legacy suggested to de Chirico and Savinio a way to be new and classical at the same time. It allowed them to go back

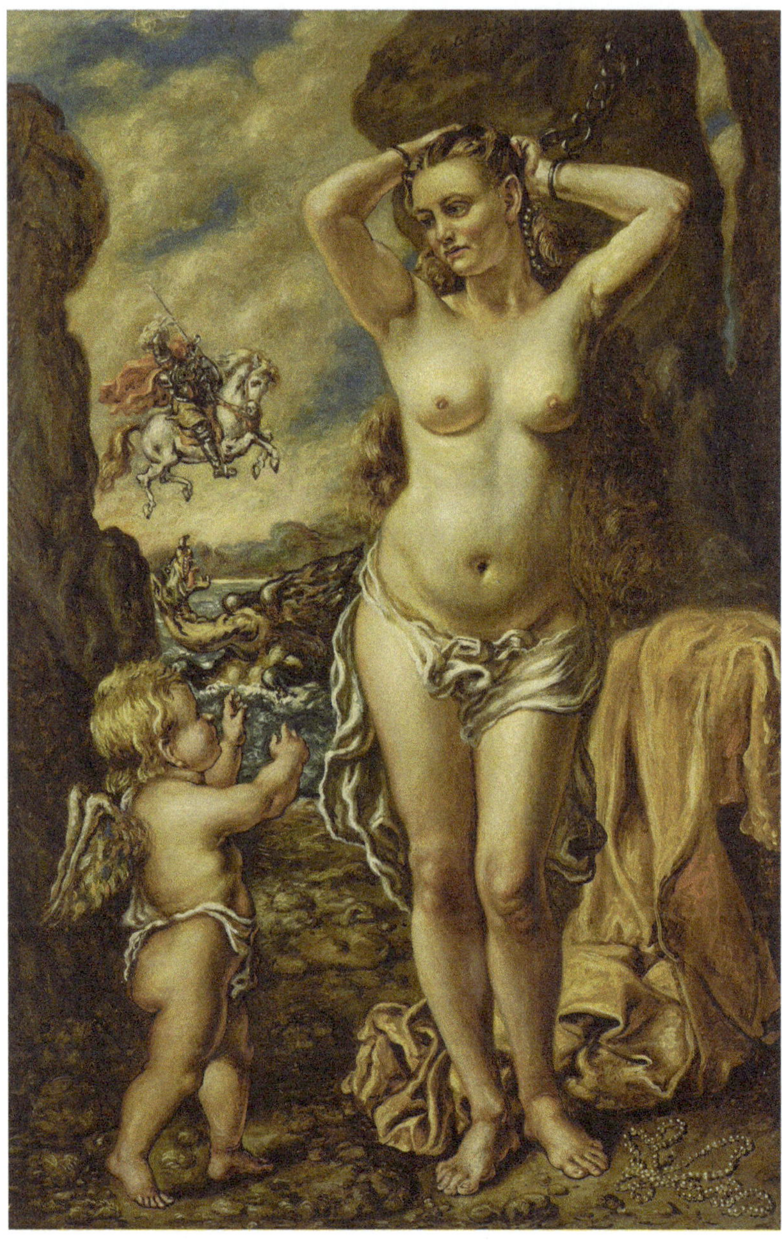

Figure 1.70. Giorgio de Chirico, *Angelica and Ruggiero* (*Angelica e Ruggiero*), 1946–50, oil on canvas, 152 × 103 cm, Galleria Nazionale d'Arte Moderna, Rome. © 2022 Artists Rights Society (ARS), New York/SIAE, Rome. Photo Credit: Mondadori Portfolio/Alessandro Vasari/Art Resource, NY.

to the origin of modernity in order to truly become untimely, like Böcklin's Angelica rising from a sea of ruins in Savinio's collage. De Chirico's aspiration to transfigure into a statue, expressed in the 1924 *Autoritratto*, was not an abjuration of modernism, but rather a Nietzschean evasion from chronology: an attempt to reach the same "eternal truth" that de Pisis attributed to Ariosto. After all, as Govoni and Agnoletti said without renouncing their Futurist poetics, "the only living men are those who love the dead."

In a lecture that he gave at the Lyceum Club in Florence, in 1942, Savinio declared that the real goal of any "authentically modern" art should be to make statues "jump off their pedestals and join our company." He concluded by explaining that "modern art, Italian art, should have the goal not just to represent this, but to actually make it happen."[113] In *Childhood of Nivasio Dolcemare*, his autobiographical protagonist had, as a child, the same modernist aspiration that de Chirico had expressed in the Ferrarese years: not just to mingle with men in marble, but to become one, rising above the mediocrity of "the Man of Flesh, the Marsupial Man, the Incurable Plebeian." To turn into "the Man of Marble,"

> He foresaw that he would someday reach this form of supreme freedom. He was already modelling himself on the image of the Hard and Solitary Man, the Man of Diamond, a fusion of Achilles and Orlando, the Man of Marble Walking.[114]

In an epode that he wrote in 1917 for de Pisis, published at the end of *Arte metafisica e scienze occulte*, de Chirico had prophesied, "One day I too will be man of marble."[115]

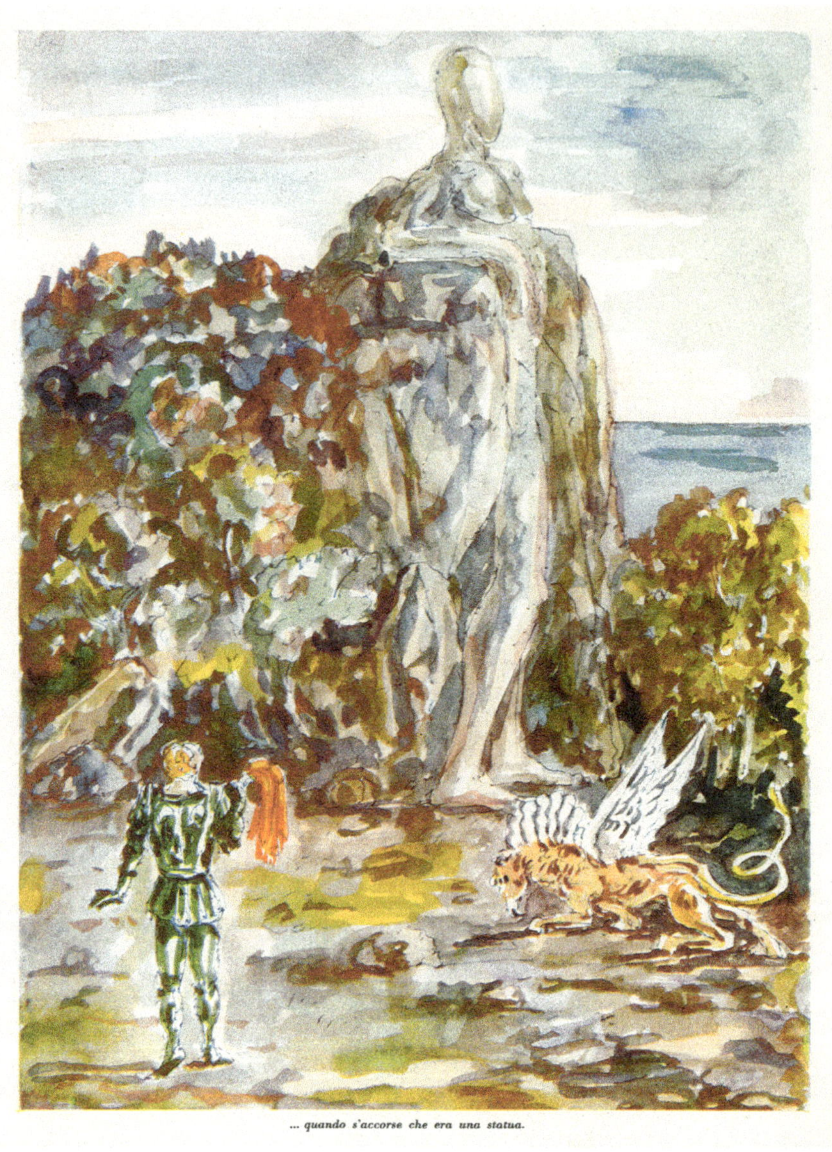

Figure 2.1. Giorgio de Chirico, … *Quando s'accorse che era una statua*, 1941, photoreproduction of watercolour on paper, from Massimo Bontempelli, "Le ali dell'ippogrifo," in *Tempo* (March 20, 1941). Biblioteca Nazionale Centrale di Roma (BNCR). No reproduction is permitted without authorization from the BNCR. © 2022 Artists Rights Society (ARS), New York/SIAE, Rome.

Chapter Two

Ludovico's Gifts: The Ariostean Spirit of Magical Realism

We laymen have always been intensely curious to know – like the Cardinal who put a similar question to Ariosto – from what sources that strange being, the creative writer, draws his material, and how he manages to make such an impression on us with it and to arouse in us emotions of which, perhaps, we had not even thought ourselves capable.

Sigmund Freud, *Creative Writers and Day-Dreaming*, 1907

A monumental man in stone contemplates the Pacific Ocean (figure 2.1). Its body is carved out of a white cliff, covered in maritime vegetation. At its feet, the Hippogriff is resting after a long flight, swirling his lion tail in the air. His rider Ruggiero, the Saracen warrior destined to convert and marry Bradamante, looks up in awe at the indifferent giant. This faceless creature is not a trick of the eye, nor is it one of the strange island's deities or exotic monsters. It is a tangible statue, both primitive and modern, sculpted by mysterious, indigenous artists of a bygone age. The medieval African prince is looking at an imaginary Polynesian idol. Or, more precisely, one of Ariosto's main characters is looking at the totemic version of one of Giorgio de Chirico's mannequins.

There is no trace of such an encounter in the octaves of Ariosto's poem. This watercolour painting of Ruggiero with a monolithic Titan is not a modern illustration of the *Orlando Furioso.* It illustrates, on the other hand, a spinoff of Ariosto's story, written in the middle of the Second World War by Massimo Bontempelli. This spinoff takes place during Ruggiero's involuntary flight from the Pyrenees to Alcina's magical island, in the Japanese archipelago.[1] In the sixteenth century, Ariosto, who could not know much about the American continent, elegantly glossed over that part of Ruggiero's world tour. In the twentieth century, Bontempelli, the author that I will discuss throughout this chapter, had a chance to fill

Ariosto's gaps, and to imagine his own episode of the *Orlando Furioso.* He titled it *The Hippogriff's Wings*, and asked de Chirico to paint its illustrations. It was one of Bontempelli's last works, the crowning achievement of a long literary career that, I believe, was consistently inspired by a protean, inexhaustible fascination with Ariosto's lucid fantasy.

Massimo Bontempelli was a protagonist of Europe's modernism, one of the most influential Italian authors of the interwar period. Italo Calvino described him as "the number 1 Italian novelist" of the early twentieth century, "the Italian writer who had the most authority as a model."[2] When he wrote *The Hippogriff's Wings*, in 1941, Bontempelli was an international literary celebrity, and he had already declared his love for the *Orlando Furioso* in crowded public lectures in two continents. However, as I will show, his devotion to Ariosto dated back to the very beginning of his creative life, three decades before. It accompanied him through many apparently radical transformations: from Neoclassicism to Futurism, from experimentalism to the Return to Order, from the presidency of the fascist writers' union to the expulsion from the party and a subsequent prohibition to publish. In this chapter I will show how Ariosto's influence shaped the various phases of Bontempelli's literature. Above all, I will argue that Ariosto offered a poetic cornerstone for Bontempelli's most important contribution to contemporary fiction: the invention of Magical Realism as a literary style in 1919, and its theorization in 1927.

"Magical Realism" is one of the most polygenetic and equivocal terms of twentieth-century criticism. According to scholarly consensus, the term was coined by German art critic Franz Roh to describe visual reactions to Expressionism in the late 1920s. Since then, it has had a wide and articulate reception in the literary world, especially among Latin American writers. Ariosto's fantasy, and in particular his ability to ironically present the most implausible events with a realistic, nonchalant tone, have inspired several authors affiliated with this modern narrative style. From Hubert Lampo's surreal take on the Arthurian cycle to Russell Hoban's *Angelica Lost and Found*, from Jorge Luis Borges' *Ariosto and the Arabs* to Salman Rushdie's *The Enchantress of Florence*, the umbrella category of Magical Realism has been particularly permeable to Ariosto's influence. I am not going to attempt a new or stricter definition of Magical Realism in general. My goal is to show that, at its conception during the fascist regime, Magical Realism was understood by Bontempelli as a way to revive Ariosto's literary style in modern narrative: to do something entirely new by imitating an old model. And, incidentally, to be a fascist writer without embracing the fascist aesthetics promoted by nationalist propaganda.

A famous explicit link between the *Furioso* and modern magical poetics was established, in 1975, by Alejo Carpentier. Carpentier explained his own *real maravilloso* style by placing it within a trans-historical and global *estilo barroco.* This Baroque style, in Carpentier's conception, was rooted in Europe's early modernity. "In Italy," he stated, "the emperor of the Baroque is Ariosto with his *Orlando Furioso.*"[3] Bontempelli is credited with applying the term Magical Realism to literature for the first time, but his role in the early transnational development of the style is minimized by critics. His real merit, I believe, was that he had understood, at the beginning of the twentieth century, what Carpentier noted in 1975. He was the first European writer to practise and theorize the re-use of the disenchantment of Renaissance fantasy in order to evade modern reality without abjuring realism altogether. Or, to quote a synthesis of his favourite passage from the *Furioso,* as he formulated it in 1930, "to rise up to the clouds on the back of the Hippogriff and then come down at night to sleep at a decent inn." To explain this archetype of Italian realistic magic, borrowed from Ruggiero's adventures in the *Furioso,* Bontempelli stated: "indeed, when years ago I pointed at an artistic paradigm and I called it 'Magical Realism,' I made sure to cite Ariosto."[4]

In the following pages, I will argue that Bontempelli's adoption of Ariosto as a model for modernity was key to hybridizing tradition and the avant-garde in the interwar period. It also offered a way to import the novelty of Metaphysical art into literature. I will start by showing that Bontempelli's Ariostean, rational narrative magic, antithetical to the delirious associative dreams of French Surrealism, started way before the official coinage of the term Magical Realism. Within the manifold literatures that that term encompasses, Bontempelli established an intertextual genealogy of lucid imagination and lunar marvel that includes later masters such as Borges and Calvino. And, as I will discuss towards the end of the chapter, he did so while negotiating, through Ariosto's Renaissance example, his relationship with fascist ideology.

Modest Beginnings

Son of a railway engineer, like de Chirico and Savinio, Massimo Bontempelli grew up moving from town to town along the unfurling train lines of the newborn Kingdom of Italy. He graduated from the University of Turin in 1902, but failed to secure a permanent position as a middle school teacher. His reluctant wanderings went on. He taught in many peripheral schools, always as a substitute, all the while trying to make a name for himself as a poet. His literary style, at the time, was deeply inspired by Giosuè Carducci's classicist barbarism.

Though ambitious and tenacious, Bontempelli had little success at first.[5] A real chance at national recognition arrived only when he was about to turn thirty. In 1907 Carducci died, just months after he had become the first Italian Nobel Laureate. Bontempelli, who considered himself Carducci's disciple, gave a eulogy for him in *L'Aquila.* It was his first public lecture.[6] The success of this event impressed one of the most prestigious periodicals in the country, *Nuova Antologia,* which agreed to publish a small selection of Bontempelli's poems. This very limited but highly visible space on the national literary stage provided Bontempelli with a chance to present himself as a credible author. He decided to approach the task in a failsafe, traditional way. He exhibited his literary ancestry.

Bontempelli sent to *Nuova Antologia* four odes addressed to four of his literary models: four lyrical portraits of beloved poets that formed his own genetic self-representation. Predictably, they were all Italian men. The first two are easy to guess: Carducci, of course, and another poet-professor, Arturo Graf, who regularly collaborated with *Nuova Antologia* and had been Bontempelli's advisor in Turin. The other two are less obvious, and remained the only early modern poets ever mentioned in Bontempelli's entire production in verse. One was Torquato Tasso, the mannerist master of Christian epic. The other was Ludovico Ariosto.

The four 1907 odes in *Nuova Antologia* represented Bontempelli's first step out of literary anonymity, his first manifesto of poetics. Yet, besides one coeval review,[7] they received virtually no attention by critics, not even in recent scholarly attempts to unearth Bontempelli's early traditionalist writings.[8] The reason is probably that Bontempelli himself, as soon as he acquired fame, systematically erased his pre-1920 publications from official bibliographies and recollections. When he did refer to anything that he had written before the age of forty, he labelled those works as spurious, rejected: "opere rifiutate."[9]

In truth, the style and content of the odes for Graf and Carducci, which open and close the small auto-anthology, betray a "shamelessly ultra-classicist"[10] sentiment that Bontempelli, in later years, wanted to brush off. Besides a religious devotion to Carducci's *Odi Barbare,*[11] these two academic poems show Bontempelli's ignorance, at the time, about what was happening in literature beyond his national horizon, and his petty preoccupation with editorial success after years of passionate study of the classics.[12] Hardly exciting material. However, the other two odes, for Tasso and Ariosto, reveal unexpected intuitions and concerns. By addressing more remote literary ancestors, Bontempelli planted the seed of his later famous ideas on the relationship between art and society, and the chaos of reality at large.

There is a clear distinction between Tasso and Ariosto in the odes. Bontempelli admired Ariosto for his art, for his lucid ability to sing an age that was as golden as it was horrific. Tasso, on the other hand, was a biographical hero for him, not a literary one. The first two lines of the ode for Tasso are unequivocal on this point: "I love, Torquato, more than your rhymes / you."[13]

This sentiment actually echoes a rich Romantic tradition, which saw Tasso as a martyr of poetry.[14] His life as a southern outsider in Ferrara, his madness, and his imprisonment in a mental hospital fascinated European artists, writers, and musicians, from Goethe to Liszt. Lord Byron, for instance, unlike Futurists and Metaphysicians, was not particularly impressed by Ariosto's landmarks when he visited Ferrara. He preferred "the cell where Tasso was confined in the hospital of St. Anna," because, he stated, "[it] attracts a more fixed attention than the residence or the monument of Ariosto – at least it had this effect on me."[15]

In the early nineteenth century, a timely French translation of Byron's *Lament for Tasso* inspired two paintings by Eugène Delacroix that offer a visual synthesis of Tasso's Romantic myth. In the earliest (1825), the poet shares his cell with a small mob – fellow imprisoned madmen, yet so different from him – that derides his bilious intellectual solitude. These madmen humiliate and, at the same time, elevate Tasso, in a kind of artistic immolation. The second painting (figure 2.2) articulates Tasso's otherness even more clearly. The poet's pose alludes to the iconography of melancholy established by Albrecht Dürer. Tasso turns his back to the three other figures that populate the scene in the background. The composition accompanies our gaze through the allegory: a curtain geometrically separates Tasso from the rest of the world, the bars of his cell seem to imprison the rest of the madhouse rather than him, and the madmen, leaning through those bars, are visually connected to him by the long seat that dominates the gloomy space. Meaningfully, they reach for the papers scattered out of his sight. Tasso is alienated from common people, and yet he works for them. His saturnine insanity, so clearly represented by the vulnerability of his bare chest and wild look, elects and curses him. His claustrophobic cell may be, paradoxically, the only space of real freedom. It is, however, the opposite of Ariosto's navigable studio, the domestic room that Ariosto declared himself content with in his *Satires*. It is the tragic antithesis of the extroverted interiors that inspired the claustrophilic geographic imagination of Metaphysical art.

Bontempelli's passion for Tasso's nineteenth-century myth was likely rooted in Italy's own Romanticism. Specifically, Bontempelli had certainly read Leopardi's *Operette morali*, in which Tasso is a character and, in

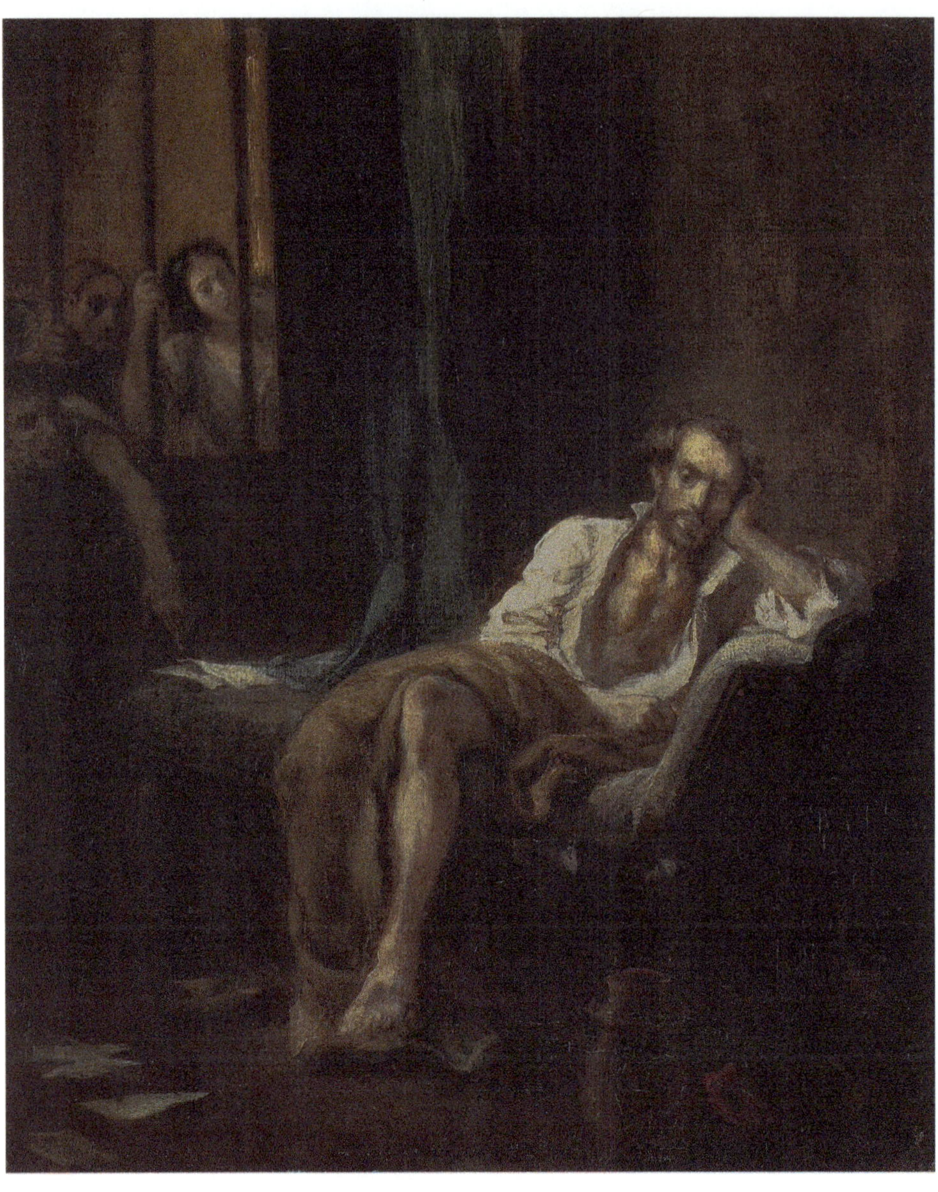

Figure 2.2. Eugène Delacroix, *Tasso in the Madhouse* (*Tasso nell'Ospedale di Sant'Anna in Ferrara*), 1839, oil on canvas, 60 × 50 cm, Inv. no.1919.1, Oskar Reinhart Collection "Am Römerholz," Winterthur. Courtesy the Oskar Reinhart Collection.

his cell, dialogues with his own personified genius. Bontempelli's ode for Tasso never mentions the *Gerusalemme liberata* or any other of his works. It discusses Tasso's brilliance in the abstract, and condemns those who ruined his life. In the poem, rather than exploring what a poet does, Bontempelli uses Tasso to describe who a poet is or should be. The ode investigates the very condition of being a poet, and the social potential of such a status.

The first nine stanzas summarize one of the most dramatized days of Tasso's life. On March 11, 1579, he went to the duke's castle and, to use Bontempelli's magniloquent words, "injured in sublime impetus / an entire Court."[16] The historical and political context is sketched rapidly but precisely ("Alfonso marries a Gonzaga; he fears / harm from Rome; the Calvinists surround him")[17] in order to give room to Tasso's psychology. His rage against the duke, which will cost him his freedom, is then expressed in direct speech. This anathema echoes Carducci's *Alla città di Ferrara,* a long poem in which the city is described as "cursed by Dante, cursed for Tasso."[18] However, Carducci blamed Tasso's imprisonment for disrupting his art, and in particular the *Liberata,* which is both openly referenced and formally evoked in his poem's intertextual fabric. Bontempelli, on the other hand, only focused on Tasso as a man, and on his abstract "Genius." This "melancholic demon," according to Bontempelli, was "so true and sweet" for Tasso but "a joke for the vulgar people."[19] From a stylistic point of view, instead of using Tasso's own Petrarchan forms, Bontempelli adopted Carducci's "barbarian" version of the Sapphic stanza. In that Neoclassical metric measure, he made Tasso pronounce a prophecy. He made him imagine a future in which poets would be liberated from the control of political and economic powers, and able to lift up the destiny of their nation.

The future imagined by Tasso in the ode was clearly not (yet) the present in which Bontempelli was living and writing in 1907. In the text, Bontempelli's own voice overlaps with Tasso's in wishing for a future Italy where "poets will become teachers / for artisans."[20] As in a Platonic republic, these new poets even rise to the role of arbitrating human judgment. In the last stanzas, Tasso's prophecy concludes by portraying the ideal citizen of this utopia. For such a superior artist, Bontempelli used the word "Poeta" with a capital P.[21]

> Man in his heart and affection, gentle
> he goes along with men and looks like a god on earth.
> He is the calm, and the laughter, and the prosperity
> after a war –[22]

A far cry from Torquato's own "melancholic demon," this serene figure is introduced, but not exemplified, by Tasso. In the ode, Tasso offers, as in all his Romantic mythologizations, a cautionary tale rather than a model. He could have been this kind of gentle and approachable human deity, but only if his harsh times had not imprisoned his body in a cell and his genius in a troubled mind. Like the Baptist for the Christ in the Gospels, or Cavalcanti's Giovanna for Dante's Beatrice in the *Vita Nuova*, for Bontempelli Tasso was a herald, a forerunner. His special status as a literary martyr allowed him to see more clearly, and to prepare the world for the arrival of the true embodiment of an ideal aesthetic future.

Such an ideal would be fulfilled by the future "Poet" that Bontempelli himself clearly aspired to become. This "Poet," in Bontempelli's odes, was modelled by a writer who actually preceded Tasso, both chronologically and in the pages of *Nuova Antologia.* It is to Ariosto that Bontempelli reserved the title of "Poet," with a capital letter. It is Ariosto whom Bontempelli asked, in the 1907 odes, to teach him how to become what Tasso prophesied.

Ludovico's Gifts

Unlike that for Tasso, the ode for Ariosto does not linger on any biographical episode. Bontempelli described Ariosto as a lucid artist, aware of both the horrors and the splendid achievements of his age. He was able, according to Bontempelli, to observe reality with a serene detachment, and to seize its most joyful fruits. In the ode, Bontempelli illustrated the main aspects of Ariosto's poetic mastery and, more importantly, asked for them as gifts.

> Give me the joy, O Ludovico, the gift
> to calmly contemplate the world
> and, reaching for the good in all the things,
> to extract a jocund juice from them.
> This is the way you understood, while loving it,
> that century of yours, drenched in gold and blood, and such a fruit
> you picked from it that, where there is grief and tears,
> there is no way you don't educe laughter.[23]

The long, passionate ode for Tasso was written by an admirer. In this shorter and more thoughtful text, on the other hand, Bontempelli positioned himself as Ariosto's reader and disciple. Tasso's life was inimitable, while Ariosto's art was to be imitated. Bontempelli composed the ode for him in faux octaves that visually mimic the stanzas of the *Orlando Furioso.*[24]

As Bontempelli noted, Ariosto was hardly a detached genius of fantasy, unconcerned with the reality of his times. In the *Furioso* he exalted the intellectual advancements of modernity while subtly criticizing its abominations. He praised the work of "Leonardo, Andrea Mantegna, Gian Bellino" (XXXIII, 2) but condemned the coeval military use of gunpowder (XI, 26) and the way in which political power forced art into complacency and adulation (XXXIV, 77). Bontempelli saw his own present, the Machine Age, through the same double lens: an age that was "evil, inside, of a hundred cruelties, / lucid, at its peaks, of beautiful brilliance," a century more "substantial and great / than the previous eras."[25] In his ode, he said to Ariosto, "I too, O Poet, love my era."[26] Then, he proceeded to describe it.

The protagonists of the twentieth century, in the ode, are Freedom and Science. Freedom, previously just abstract and theoretical, now regulates, in Bontempelli's theory of modernity, the "human competition," while the spirit of revolution is channelled by laws and ideals. Science does not try the "arcane doors" of alchemy and astrology anymore. It overcame the mere curiosity of nineteenth-century Naturalism, and impacts, instead, "the entire dominion of active forces."[27] The role of literature, in this young new world so reminiscent of Ariosto's, recalls the utopia imagined by Tasso's prophecy in the other ode.

In the ode for Tasso, Bontempelli envisioned a future in which the "Poet" would "teach, in his verses, / that man must act in harmony / with the universe." In the ode for Ariosto, he explained to "Ludovico" that Science, in the twentieth century, "wants the life of men to be / in effortless harmony with the life of the universe." He put the particularity of human experience in relation with the complexity of reality, and he did so in order to ask Ariosto, as if he were a muse, for "the gift" to be able to see and sing the same aspiration to harmony that the *Furioso* was able to express almost five hundred years before. This rhetoric has, of course, positivistic echoes, and gives an impression of outdated Enlightenment ideals. However, it is interesting that Bontempelli centred the prophecy of Tasso and the model offered by Ariosto on a modern and rational desire for harmony.

Harmony is the keyword of one of the most groundbreaking essays in the history of Ariosto's reception. It was written by Benedetto Croce, one of Italy's most influential modern thinkers, in 1917. Croce's concept of Ariostean harmony is still relevant in the current scholarly discourse on the *Furioso.* He developed it to describe precisely the "gift" that Bontempelli asked for in his poem: a form of ironic awareness that is very different from the comedic irony of other chivalric poets loved by the Romantics, such as Rabelais and Pulci.

> One could say that Ariosto's irony is like the eyes of God, who observes the movement of creating, loving it equally, in good or ill, in the greatest parts as in the smallest, in man and in the grain of sand, because He made it all, only seizing in it the movement, the eternal dialectic, the rhythm, and the harmony.[28]

Ten years before Croce's seminal essay, Bontempelli was still drawing on nineteenth-century sources, and in particular on Francesco De Sanctis' post-Hegelian reading of Ariosto's irony as "the laughter that preludes to science."[29] However, his 1907 intuition already tended towards Croce's modern synthesis, which influenced the understanding of the *Furioso* and its author throughout the twentieth century. Harmony intertextually connects the odes for Tasso and Ariosto. Its different uses confirm once again that Bontempelli used Tasso's unfortunate story to advocate for a redemption of the role of poets, destined to show humanity the way towards universal harmony. However, he looked to Ariosto as a literary model to put such aspirations into practice. Besides anticipating Croce's ideas, by assuming this position Bontempelli surprisingly challenged Carducci's authority.

Twenty years before Bontempelli's odes, Carducci had established a literary dialogue with, among others, Tasso and Ariosto. He did so in one of his most important books, *Rime nuove.* However, he gave Tasso and Ariosto opposite roles to those chosen by Bontempelli. Not that Carducci would have ever written anything like "I love, Ludovico, more than your rhymes, you," but, for him, Tasso was the literary example, the source of ideal keywords and formal archetypes for a new poetry. Ariosto, on the other hand, was mostly a fascinating character worthy of a psychological and biographical investigation.

In the second book of Carducci's *Rime nuove,* Tasso is one of the protagonists of two poems dedicated to the sonnet, the form that dominates the entire section. In *Il sonetto,* he follows Dante and Petrarch as the central ancestor in the history of this quintessentially Italian metrical form. The history of the sonnet, in the poem, continues with Alfieri and Foscolo, and culminates with the imitation and innovation of Carducci himself ("Not sixth but last I count me in that band").[30] Tasso is then included in the European panorama of the twin poem *Al sonetto,* in which he genealogically follows, again, Dante and Petrarch, and precedes Michelangelo, Shakespeare, Milton, and Camões. Tasso is one of Carducci's technical models because he dressed the sonnet in "epic splendour" and infused it with classical elegance. Carducci aspired to continue the line of his small multilingual canon by inheriting, from "prigion Torquato," a Latin *dulcedo* that he described as a sweet perfume.[31]

Ariosto is evoked in *Rime nuove* when Carducci, in another poem, mirrors himself in the painting by Titian that was believed to be his portrait. As I mentioned in the previous chapter of this book, Bontempelli would choose the same portrait for the frontispiece of his edition of Ariosto's minor works in 1916, to which I will return. Inspired by the painting, Carducci parallelled his sentiments for Lina, one of his lovers and muses, with those that Ariosto harboured for his paramour (and eventually secret wife) Alessandra. Envying Ariosto for the success of his clandestine relationship, Carducci described Alessandra with words that echo one of Ariosto's sonnets (*Rm*, XXX).[32] These sonnets were good models for the description of Carducci's love struggles, but evidently not good enough to grant Ariosto a place, alongside Tasso, among the masters of the genre.

Despite closing his odes in *Nuova Antologia* with a grandiose tribute to Carducci, Bontempelli engaged with Tasso and Ariosto in an anti-Carduccian, original way. He aspired to become more like the Ariosto that Carducci described in scholarly essays than the Ariosto that Carducci evoked as a poet.[33] He definitely had no interest in the classical "perfume" of Tasso's rhymes. Instead of just continuing a tradition, he wanted to directly learn from Ariosto how to write about the twentieth century. Ariosto held the literary keys to access what Bontempelli's new literature intended to represent: the anxieties, the sparkles of greatness, and the achievements towards modern harmony. "This I want, with my art, to convey / O Ludovico," he concluded, asking Ariosto for the joy and the "abandonment" (which became "courage" in the final edition of the poem) that would make his literary endeavour possible.

Opening with the plea for "the gift / to calmly contemplate the world" and extract from it a delightful lymph, Bontempelli's ode to Ariosto ends with a second request. Bontempelli asked for a more technical gift: the ability to make sense, through literature, of the ungovernable web of interlaced storylines that constitutes what happens in the world; to recognize a pattern in the fabric of reality, and turn it into narration. This Ariostean talent of "revealing the design within the tangle" clearly prefigured, in 1907, the ambition of Bontempelli's later works.

Once he abandoned Carduccian classicism, Bontempelli spent most of his career trying to remain lucidly faithful to reality while filling it with awe-inspiring miracles, new myths, and elements of rational magic. Twenty-one years after publishing the odes, he still called Ariosto "the poet who is dearest to our heart"and "the most ethereal harmonizer of fantasy and reality" in the flagship journal of Magical Realism.[34] Before I discuss that culminating phase of Bontempelli's dialogue with Ariosto, let me show how that dialogue developed in the years of the First World War and how it then influenced his most studied novels of the early 1920s.

Blossoming Irony

In 1907, Bontempelli asked "Ludovico" for the gifts of a serene vision of reality and narrative control over its chaos. Joy, abandonment, and courage were the literary qualities that he hoped to inherit from Ariosto. He would fulfil this program, as I will show, a decade later, at a pivotal point in his creative life: the moment that he chose as the official beginning of his career. In the meantime, he struggled to define his intellectual profile.

In his writings of the period, until the end of the First World War, Bontempelli eclectically explored several stylistic and ideological options. He collected satirical novellas and lyrical poems into two small books, he started working as a cultural journalist and wrote for theatre. He kept his finger on the pulse of both the new Futurist experiments and the familiar Carduccian muses of respectable academism. Appearing in *Nuova Antologia* brought about some positive changes in his career. The journal assigned him the direction of a narrative section,[35] and he was able to leave behind the frustrations of adjunct teaching. His collaborations with periodicals and newspapers became progressively more prestigious and less provincial. He eventually started writing for Italy's main national paper, *Corriere della sera.*

In the years between the ode for Ariosto and his departure for the front, Bontempelli had finally settled in Milan. Throughout the war years, and immediately after, his poetry became more and more experimental. In Milan he started promoting avant-garde books and became close with Marinetti's Futurist group. At the same time, the day job that he kept for most of the decade was very much at odds with the incendiary rhetoric of the Futurist Manifesto. He worked as a cultural editor for the Istituto Editoriale Italiano, curating, in particular, the Italian Classics section of the publishing house. This may very well have been the most anti-Futurist occupation in the whole of pre-war Milan. The double identity that Bontempelli cultivated in this period was probably the root of his later aspiration to burn bridges with the immediate literary past, while connecting modernity with its most authentic origins in the Renaissance and antiquity. This counterintuitive interpretation of both classicism and modernism would make him declare, twenty years later, that most traditionalists tend to simply "call 'tradition' the latest or penultimate trends" instead of looking at "primordial fountainheads" of modernity such as "the Ariostean spirit."[36]

The results of Bontempelli's activity in the 1910s mirror the contradictory nature of his position as an avant-garde poet editing the classics. The texts of his first (and only) Futurist book, *Il Purosangue*, were all linear. He adopted the movement's thematic enthusiasm for speed, violence, and technology, but mostly rejected Marinetti's prescriptions on syntax and visual synthesis. At the same time, for the "Classici" series that he curated, he systematically chose the most experimental and extravagant authors of Italy's Renaissance. He started with an anthology of the obscene and satirical Carnival Songs of fifteenth-century Florence, and then resuscitated controversial minor masters. He published the forgotten works of misfits and marginalized authors such as Giovan Battista Gelli, "Lorenzaccio" de' Medici, and Giuseppe Baretti. The only exception to this small anti-canon was, of course, Ariosto.

The last book that Bontempelli edited for the Istituto Editoriale was the new edition of Ariosto's *Satires* and comedies that I mentioned before. The essay that he penned to introduce that book is an important milestone in the development of Bontempelli's Ariostean modernism after the programmatic ode of 1907. Bontempelli worked on his edition of Ariosto throughout 1915, and published it in 1916. In the same period, before his enlistment, he was travelling between Milan and the front as a correspondent. In fact, he kept on writing intensively throughout the war,[37] while also serving as a field artillery officer and receiving a number of medals and military distinctions. If read in parallel with his contemporary reflection on the *Satires*, his journalistic reports from the combat line reveal an Ariostean inspiration. Soon collected in the book *Dallo Stelvio al mare* (another of his rejected works), these war writings were Bontempelli's first attempt to put into practice the 1907 Ariostean program of observing reality with detachment in order to get "a jocund juice" even from its most tragic aspects.

Among snippets of military information dressed in a para-Futurist interventionist rhetoric,[38] the most literary passages of Bontempelli's reportages often centred on the observation of odd details. These incongruous, unexpected things suddenly lightened the gravity of the military context. For instance, while exploring a temporary encampment, Bontempelli noticed a gate. This gate was the only surviving structure in the area, which had been entirely swiped by bombings. In the desolate expanse of debris and rubble, the gate still bore a plaque that said "The plants are entrusted to the care of the public."[39] The absurdity of such a polite sign in the middle of that wasteland (which probably used to be a public garden) made Bontempelli comment: "irony can blossom even in this desolation."[40] He bumped into spontaneous flowerings of irony even on the trench lines, where he found comedic warnings on the latrines' doors ("Austrians are kindly requested to make themselves known before entering").[41] Then, from the top of a hill, Bontempelli contemplated the frontline between the armies of the Austro-Hungarian Empire and the Italian Kingdom. The valley was filled with humble tents, a few horses and shining bayonets, soldiers cooking on blackened stones or washing their clothes in the river. Bontempelli expected a much different landscape for the most technologically advanced battleground of military history. The 1915 military camp on the other hand, both primitive and epic, "could be," he commented, "in the *Orlando Furioso.*"[42]

In later years, irony would become a cornerstone of Bontempelli's theorization of Magical Realism. In a 1926 essay titled *Foundations,* he described it as "a way to get out of contingencies, to free ourselves from too tight an adherence to the surface of things." Irony, he added, is "the foundation of a superior lucidity."[43] This concept of irony was already expressed quite clearly in his reports from the front. And those reports were evidently inspired by the intentions formulated, a few years before, in the ode to Ariosto: to "calmly contemplate the world" and "educe laughter" "where there is grief and tears." Ariosto's influence is even more evident if, as I proposed, one reads *Dallo Stelvio al mare* in parallel with Bontempelli's introduction to his edition of Ariosto's works. In that essay, written in the same months in which he was corresponding from the front, he drew an original intellectual portrait of Ariosto.

> [...] this resigned and clever man, Ludovico Ariosto, along with the adventures of his life as a forced courtier (endured with the spirit of one who is not at all an adventurous man, and would only love to calmly daydream within the walls of his house), this sort of intellectual Sancho Panza, is the protagonist of that juicy autobiography that is constituted by the seven so-called *Satires*: autobiographical capitoli in epistolary form, without external links that force them into unity. From this book emerges the character of the man [...].
>
> A satire, yes, but without any malice, even when it is sour. It laughs, and it even seems serene – and, indeed, it is. A serenity, to be sure, made of selfishness, of that inactive (and therefore innocuous) selfishness that is typical of imaginative temperaments. Not blind, however, not indifferent. Read, in the first *Satire,* the depiction of the Borgias' Rome: how precise, Machiavellian, well structured, and coherent it is! But Ludovico does not have an apostolic temperament: he doesn't feel like starting a crusade against evil. He prefers to dodge evil, to avoid the road in which one could encounter evil things. He looks for an alley, he goes into the bushes, he sits in a solitary

place [...] behind a little hedge, he follows the Hippogriff's flight with his eyes, he discusses with Astolfo and Alcina, he feels and lives the infinite world of his fantasy.

This reading of the *Satires* (and, obliquely, of the *Orlando Furioso*) clarifies Bontempelli's interpretation of Ariosto. Bontempelli read Ariosto's vision of the world at the intersection of political awareness and imaginative evasion, reluctant practicality and selfish serenity, reality and fantasy. His essay was not just an academic exercise: it included seminal ideas that he would later articulate to describe and theorize Magical Realism.

For instance, discussing how the aristocrats in the Estense court pretended to enjoy the erudite dramas of Ferrara's 1502 theatre season, he explained that "classical culture and classical taste were imposed and spread by what we now call snobbishness." He compared this Renaissance phenomenon with the "Wagnerism" of twentieth-century Italy.[44] Exactly the same example would return in one of Bontempelli's first official works, *La vita intensa*, an avant-garde novel published in 1919 to which I will return in the next section. In the novel, the narrator states that "for the great diffusion of artistic and practical novelties we should rely on snobbishness: the Wagnerism that dominated Europe in the last thirty years [...] is the greatest proof of this truth."[45] More importantly, Bontempelli used the same idea again, in 1932, to defend Magical Realism from fascist critics. These critics accused Bontempelli's literary style of being incapable of representing contemporary Italy. His response was that "the courtiers who listened to Ariosto reading the octaves of his *Orlando* couldn't dream that the fantasy world of that most non-adherent poet would become, for us, the most true and profound interpretation of Italy's sixteenth century."[46]

Bontempelli's 1916 portrait of Ariosto as a "sort of intellectual Sancho Panza" completed a de-Romanticization that he had started with the 1907 odes. Sancho's oppressive master, Don Quixote, was a model of imaginative power for the Romantics. A deluded traditionalist who forcefully extended the fiction of his books to embrace a decidedly unchivalric reality, Quixote was also, like Tasso, the subject of one of Delacroix's paintings. Delacroix represented him as an isolated, tragic hero, adopting the same posture and compositional relation with other figures that he had used for Tasso. Carducci was an admirer of Quixote too, and translated Heinrich Heine's preface to a German edition of Cervantes' novel. He published it in series in an Italian journal, titled *Don Chisciotte*, that he helped to start. The fact that Bontempelli, instead of Quixote, chose his comedic sidekick Sancho to describe Ariosto represented a post-Romantic turning point.

Quixote is a character who must be read ironically, but who seems to lack any ironic awareness. Bontempelli's Ariosto is more akin to a cultivated Sancho. He plays along, tongue in cheek, with fantasies that he enjoys but ultimately does not believe in. He is conscious of the absurdity of his subaltern situation, and resolute at least to make the most out of it. Luigi Pirandello, in his influential 1908 essay *L'umorismo*, had established a demarcation between Ariosto's irony and Cervantes' humour. The two were separated, from Pirandello's perspective, by the Copernican revolution: by the very possibility of wholeheartedly believing in humanism. By associating Ariosto with a learned version of Cervantes' most grounded character, Bontempelli blurred Pirandello's demarcation, subtly arguing that Ariosto's serious playfulness was already enough to unveil the false bottom of reality that Cervantes hilariously exposed decades later.

Bontempelli deviated from Pirandello's take on the evolution of ironic comedy at the dawn of early modern fiction. This slight but fundamental deviation made Bontempelli a precursor not only of Croce's harmony but also of the "bitter harmony" that Albert Ascoli and other later critics attributed to Ariosto, interlacing his two conflicting images of weaver of fables and lucid man of his century.[47] In the 1916 essay, Bontempelli looked at Ariosto's comedies as a repertoire of oblique references to problems and events of early modern Italy. He noticed that a cutting remark, evidently directed to the papal court, was omitted in the verse version of *La Cassaria* to avoid political trouble. He detected other criticisms of the Pope in *Il Negromante* and *Scolastica*.[48] He declared that Ariosto's occasional tendency to move his classical theatre "rather close to the real life of his time" was a form of "refinement," and that the filtered allusions to sixteenth-century facts were the only "truly Ariostean"[49] passages of the comedies.

It should be noted that, when writing about Ariosto's theatre, Bontempelli adopted again the rare word that he used in the ode: "intrico," which means tangle, chaotic plot, ungoverned knot of stories. By using this word, he showed himself not to be interested in the convoluted mass of entertaining events that formed Ariosto's dramas, but only in Ariosto's ability to make a "disegno" (design) emerge from the apparent disorder of those events. Once again, the program established in 1907 remained clear in Bontempelli's mind. Ariosto inspired him to talk about his own historical time, but obliquely, through irony, and to extract elegant narrative designs from the mess of reality. He fully applied this program in the novels that he wrote after the war.

Modern(ist) Adventures

In the first editorial of the journal *"900"*, a sort of manifesto of his mature poetics, Bontempelli stated that the twentieth century started in 1919.[50] That is the year in which he rejected all the works analysed so far in this chapter. It is also the year in which he started writing experimental novels that critics later considered to be the first examples of his Magical Realism,[51] despite the fact that he would only coin the term a few years later. A decorated veteran and, finally, an accomplished journalist, in 1919 Bontempelli was not a provincial writer anymore. He travelled to Paris and befriended international intellectuals such as de Chirico and Savinio. In Milan, he frequented Carlo Carrà and Mario Sironi, who had sketched his portrait in 1917. All these Metaphysical artists were mentioned in his 1921 novel *La vita operosa*, which portrays its author as a cosmopolitan modernist. However, it was in his previous novel, *La vita intensa*, that Bontempelli synthesized his experiences with Futurism and Neoclassicism for the first time. In 1919, with *La vita intensa*, Bontempelli proposed a new, more autonomous attempt at literary originality, based on the Ariostean aspirations expressed in the previous years.

La vita intensa appeared in ten issues of the illustrated journal *L'Ardita*, from March to December 1919. At first glance, it looked like a series of autonomous stories, printed in regular monthly instalments. However, Bontempelli conceived them as interconnected episodes of a "novel of novels." Indeed, "romanzo dei romanzi" was the subtitle that he chose when the publisher Vallecchi, in 1920, printed *La vita intensa* as a single volume. I believe that the conception, the structure, and the themes of this book, one of Bontempelli's most innovative and representative works, were imbued with the "Ariostean spirit" that he later acknowledged as one of the few true fountainheads of modernity.

Bontempelli defined each of the ten short stories that he published in *L'Ardita* as a novel. Specifically, an adventure novel ("romanzo d'avventure"), as each of their identical subtitles invariably said. They were, after all, properly divided into chapters, and closed by the formula "fine del romanzo" (the end of the novel). Nonetheless, each of these novels was also a chapter of *La vita intensa*, the novel of novels, and they were all preceded by an overall preface. In this humorous preface, Bontempelli mocked both Futurists and traditionalists, and declared that the goal of *La vita intensa* was "to reforge the European novel."[52] The irony of such a declaration made it even more credible. "If one writes a novel," noted Bontempelli, "and puts a preface in that novel, one absolutely cannot declare less than that."[53]

In the preface, Bontempelli articulated a very clear and modernist premise for the ten sub-novels that would form the meta-novel *La vita intensa.* He promised to tell only real facts, each worthy of an entire novel but narrated succinctly. He also stated that he would only tell facts that happened to him, in Milan, from twelve to twelve thirty, in one single morning. However, in order to "reforge the European novel," in each of the instalments he parodied a different sub-genre of nineteenth-century fiction: romance, psychological drama, bildungsroman, detective story, and so on. And, while the ten sub-novels had only him, as a character and author, in common, he promised that their disparate vicissitudes and narrative styles would eventually converge into one overall cohesive arc. All these authorial promises seem to form the recipe for an impertinent disaster, intentionally destined to dismantle the traditional novel as a form and declare its death. On the contrary, in 1919 Bontempelli was acting like a magician who is confident enough to show the nature of his own trick while performing it. Through internal references and narrative progressions that are only fully appreciable once one reads the final meta-novel as a whole, *La vita intensa* does eventually respond to a clear single design, playfully and ingeniously traced throughout the apparent chaos of the ten sub-novels. By writing it, Bontempelli expressed both scepticism and profound love for the tradition of the European novel.[54]

One element that links *La vita intensa* and Ariosto's *Orlando Furioso* is its very intention to reforge a genre through a new synthesis of disparate materials from a saturated vein. Ariosto built his originality on the intermixed re-use of popular Arthurian and Carolingian stories that, between the fifteenth and the sixteenth century, were saturating Europe's newborn editorial market. He did not invent a new narrative universe, but directly continued an existing poem that Matteo Maria Boiardo had left unfinished, the *Orlando Innamorato.* Despite using trite material, Ariosto arguably brought chivalric epic, as a genre, to its most refined and complex literary peak. He celebrated its conventional forms and ethos exactly by doubting their validity and showing their obsolescence. Bontempelli's programmatic renewal of the novel, neither iconoclastic nor imitative, was akin to Ariosto's euphoric, nostalgic disenchantment with his own genre.

From a stylistic point of view, *La vita intensa* also used the same rhetorical toolkit that allowed Ariosto to build his *Furioso* on divagation, surprise, and dispersion while still reaching a final consistency. This was the "gift" of "revealing the design within the tangle" that Bontempelli had asked for in his 1907 ode. One of the most visible devices that he adopted to remind readers of the overall structure of *La vita intensa* is the intrusion of his voice, as a narrator, in the montage of the various stories. The second sub-novel, for instance, opens with a direct address to the journal *L'Ardita* that hosted its first edition. Bontempelli personified the journal as the muse-like (or better patron-like) figure of "Miss *Ardita*."[55] In the passage, he discussed his novel with the medium on which it was printed. The narrator's voice explains to the "Gentle Miss *Ardita*," for instance, that the title of the previous sub-novel, *La vita intensa*, "remains the title of the entire series," and therefore of the resulting, comprehensive meta-novel. Bontempelli used the chivalric term "ciclo" (cycle) to define such a series. However, the examples with which he compared it, from Zola to Balzac, were nineteenth-century feuilleton novels. We will see in the next section how significant this parallel between chivalric cycles and the epic of serialized novels was for Bontempelli's conception of modern narrative fragmentation. For now, let me show how this fragmentation works.

In *La vita intensa*, the passages in which the narrator disrupts his own storytelling often play with an ironic awareness of the medium, shared by the author and his audience. For instance, Bontempelli divided the sixth sub-novel, titled *Morte e trasfigurazione*, into two instalments, and closed the first with a "promise" to the reader.

> (The continuation [...] will be narrated in the next issue [of *L'Ardita*]: this way, in this novel series of mine, in which none of the effects that the art of narration discovered through the centuries should be missing, we'll also have the splendidly suspenseful effect of a "to be continued" exactly in the most anxiously vibrating point of the tangle.)[56]

Of course "tangle" here translates the Ariostean keyword "intrico." In his entire works, Bontempelli used this word only here, in the 1907 ode to Ariosto, and in the 1916 preface to Ariosto's *Commedie e Satire*.[57] But what is important to notice is Bontempelli's display of the periodical nature of the medium for which his meta-novel was conceived. He knew that the "posterity" for whom, in the preface, he declared that he wrote *La vita intensa*[58] would read it in the final form of a single bound volume. He knew that most readers, therefore, would just need to turn a page to defuse the suspense triggered by this interruption. Still, in the final edition, he maintained the original division between the two sub-novels, along with the "promise" that bridged them for the faithful readers of *L'Ardita*. Ariosto, in his original elaboration of the technique of *entrelacement*, adopted similar forms of meta-literary (meta-editorial?) divertissement.

As a genre, the chivalric poem evolved from public narrations that maintained vestiges of their original oral format. The adventures and quests of paladins spread throughout Europe in written, and later printed, codifications, but their folkloric origins determined stylistic and structural traditions that remained active for centuries.[59] The very partition of chivalric poems into cantos made out of rhyming octaves is a result of this process.[60] When Ariosto wrote the *Furioso*, it was an established convention to close a canto with a brief anticipation of what would be narrated in the following one. These chivalric trailers and recaps had the function of generating suspense in listeners before they could autonomously pace their enjoyment of stories by silently reading them in books. Ariosto maintained the convention, even if he was the first great poet to write original chivalric content mostly for the book market, instead of addressing a popular or courtly audience of listeners. Sometimes, he brought the convention to its extreme consequences by placing the climax of the narration exactly at the juncture between two cantos. One example is the "cantus interruptus" that I have already mentioned:[61] the disruption of the narration between Cantos X and XI, when Ruggiero is about to assault Angelica after saving her from the Orca. At the height of suspense, the author intervenes, frustrating rather than arousing the excitement of readers. He does so by addressing his patron directly, as if the narration was happening in real time in the Estense castle.

> My canto is too long (I do not doubt it)
> And wearisome, my lord, perhaps has proved,
> And so this history is now postponed
> Until an hour more pleasing shall be found (X, 115)

The ironic game of mirrors is formidable: Ariosto knows that his readers know (that he knows that they know, etc.) that he did not write his poem to read it aloud in court, but rather to spread it (and sell it) through the many industrially reproduced copies of a printed book. Similarly, Bontempelli knew that most of his audience (including the editors of *L'Ardita*) would actually read his sub-novels in the bound pages of an edition. The suspense, in both cases, is openly formal, ironic, arbitrary. It justifies itself with an obviously false practical necessity, imposed by the traditional format of the genres of chivalric epic and serialized novel. Another interesting example of "cantus interruptus" in the *Furioso* is at the end of Canto XXXIII, when Ariosto interrupts Astolfo's journey to the Underworld just to resume it, a turn of page later, in the following canto:

> Let me defer the story of his deeds,
> As is my custom, till another night.
> My pages now are full, and it is best
> That I should cease my song a while and rest (XXXIII, 128)

This particular variation of the trope is reminiscent of the meta-literary conclusion of Dante's *Purgatory*: "but, since all the pages / readied for this second canticle are full, / the curb of art lets me proceed no farther" (*Pg*, XXXIII, 139–41). In both cases, the text acknowledges the material reality of the very page on which its author is writing, just as Bontempelli acknowledged the material reality of the periodical in which his stories appeared. However, unlike Dante, both Bontempelli and Ariosto knew, once again, that their texts were eventually destined to be read in a book, not in the pages of a manuscript or in an ephemeral periodical publication. And while Dante ran out of pages at the end of his canticle, Ariosto and Bontempelli interrupted their narrations "in the most anxiously vibrating point of the tangle." Rather than building suspense, their goal was to gently mock the very mechanics of suspense building. They were advertising the fictionality of their work, and highlighting the original mechanics of their genres.

The Serialized Novel as a Poem

Structural discontinuities are a defining feature of the *Orlando Furioso*. Their unorthodox use triggered a critical debate among Ariosto's contemporaries, which has been described as the birth of Narratology.[62] Another fundamental aspect of Ariosto's originality is the way in which he blended Carolingian epic and Arthurian romance, often employing the *entrelacement* exactly to shift from the centripetal stage of the siege of Paris (the epic pole of duty and military heroism) to the many fantastic adventures that knights end up chasing all over the world. In *La vita intensa*, Bontempelli imitated the well-orchestrated disorder of this dynamic as well.

Each monthly instalment of the meta-novel revolves around the modern bourgeois equivalent of an epic mission. The characters, however, for modern and bourgeois reasons, tend to be diverted or distracted from these quests, and embark instead on alternative accidental adventures. A clear example is the sub-novel *Il caso di forza maggiore* (the case of force majeure), in which Massimo, the protagonist and narrator, receives a telegram. The telegram informs him that he has to meet with his friend Piero for an important but mysterious appointment. Just like Ariosto's cantos, which are all introduced by moral narratorial addresses or proems, *Il caso di forza maggiore* begins with a philosophical reflection by the author. In it, Bontempelli determines that "the most characteristic thing of the modern world"[63] is not cinema or the automatic lighter, nor is it a Futurist myth like the train or the engine. It is the appointment: a categorical duty that did not exist in antiquity and that Massimo, as a modern character and writer, must take very seriously in the chapters of the sub-novel that he is inhabiting and writing.

Despite his initial commitment to the quintessentially modern mission of being punctual for his appointment (a "categorical, serious, ineluctable duty"),[64] a series of comically banal challenges tests Massimo's valour. From a lack of cigarettes, all sold out even at the cigar shop, to a long wait for a tramway car, he encounters many unexpected setbacks. These accidents of modern life, which end up forming the substance of the sub-novel, continuously distract Bontempelli from his quest, both as a character and a narrator. A beautiful woman on the tramway, for instance, tempts him as a narrator: "if only I could write, today, a seductive love story instead of an adventure novel."[65] At the same time, in the fiction, she also makes him miss his stop as a character. When the narrator comments on the character's mistake, he alludes to Aristotelian rhetorical rules, the same that Ariosto's sixteenth-century critics used to blame the excessive divagations of the *Orlando Furioso.* The conclusion is that both the character and the story cannot proceed, and need to go back: "Aristotle," noted Bontempelli, "says that, when one goes too far, one needs to go back a little bit."[66]

The chronicle of the failed appointment, just like all the other sub-novels of *La vita intensa,* is based on a continuous alternation between duty and desire. The characters of the meta-novel (and in particular the narrator and protagonist) are supposed to proceed along a storyline, but the line, unexpectedly, always forks. The narrator declares his moral and aesthetic ambition to follow the established path ("following a straight and well-planned line of action is what distinguishes men from beasts")[67] but playfully fails, both as a writer and as a character. He leaves the many storylines set up by each sub-novel's premise unresolved, and mostly narrates the unplanned adventures produced by their derailments instead. This mechanism often references the typical chivalric tropes of Ariosto's *Furioso.* In one sub-novel, for instance, Massimo receives his "sacrosanct mission"[68] from a proverbial damsel in distress. His jealous neighbour asks him to start a quest to restore her honour: "would you help me," she asks, "in this endeavour of justice?"[69] In this, she echoes the requests of Angelica to Sacripante in Canto I, or those of Olimpia to Orlando in Canto X. In Bontempelli's novel, however, the damsel's quest remains unsolved, at least until the finale of the entire book.

As a matter of fact, all the frustrating discontinuities in the linearity of each single sub-novel are eventually resolved in the very last of them, the conclusion of the meta-novel. In the finale of *La vita intensa,* all the ends of the entangled skein are interlaced in a longer instalment, titled "the novel of novels." In this final story, all the characters of all the previous sub-novels visit the narrator's house. The result is a phantasmagoric closing gathering: dozens of women sit on the same sofa, characters who died in previous sub-novels (or who were revealed to have never existed) walk into the living room along with the regular ones, and even the character of Massimo Bontempelli himself, in an extreme narratological play between reality and realism, shows up and dialogues with the author, as if they were two different people. One could be tempted to say that the scene is surreal, but of course Surrealism did not yet exist in 1919.

Unlike Surrealist writers, in the finale of *La vita intensa* Bontempelli, as a narrator, professes to be as shocked as his readers. He describes the impossible event with lucid surprise, perfectly aware of its absurdity, and claims to be just reporting what really happened to him in real life. The first sentence of the whole hyper-novel, after all, was "I am going to tell true facts, that happened to me,"[70] and all the other incongruities that took place in previous instalments were always scrupulously justified with realistic details. For instance, when, as a character, he said that he became a professor of Albanian without knowing Albanian, he proved to readers the realism of such an impossible deed. He recalled his friendship with a man from Molise and the two words in Albanian that that man had taught him, and chronicled the entire job interview (nonsensical but hilariously plausible) that he went through to get the position. In another sub-novel, he even told the story of how he once took his own life and, "only years later," got married, before starting to write novels. This colossal non sequitur, like the others, challenged its own absurdism by insisting on first-hand particulars that nobody else could know: the number of gun shots, the time of death, the way the corpse was found, even the "legal paperwork"[71] that was rigorously completed by the police.

This comical use of the autobiographical narrator's authority to claim the truth of preposterous events would become a crucial element of Bontempelli's later Magical Realism. His approach to the problem of merging magic and realism was different from the kind of Magical Realism described by Carpentier's *Real maravilloso*, in which fiction focuses on strange aspects of reality that appear unbelievable but are, ultimately, true. It was also different from other techniques later associated with the term, like the inclusion of fantastical elements in a realistic setting, or the narration of everyday events as extraordinary. Bontempelli's Magical Realism was a form of irony that exceeded the boundaries of the diegesis: a disenchanted use of realism in which both the author and the reader are aware of the limits of the medium that connects them. Ariosto was the original model for this kind of Magical Realism.

It is not surprising that in the 1930s, as I mentioned, Bontempelli would explain Magical Realism by recalling the episode of Ruggiero dismounting the Hippogriff to sleep at a decent inn in the *Orlando Furioso.* The very introduction and description of the Hippogriff in the *Furioso* (IV, 8) show very well how Ariosto used his authorial voice to make the magical narrative material of his poem ironically credible:

> His horse was not a fiction, but instead
> The offspring of a griffin and a mare.
> Its plumage, forefeet, muzzle, wings and head
> Like those of its paternal parent were.
> The rest was from its dam inherited.
> It's called a Hippogriff. Such beasts, though rare,
> In the Rhiphaean mountains, far beyond
> The icy waters of the north, are found.

Borges, in his *Book of Imaginary Beings,* praised the accuracy of this description.[72] It starts with a claim of truth (the impossible beast is supposed to be "naturale") similar to the one that opens Bontempelli's preface to *La vita intensa* (his absurd stories are supposed to be "fatti veri"). Ariosto specifies in detail where, and from which crossbreed, Hippogriffs are born. He also adds, to enhance the realism, that such breedings occur only rarely. Daniel Javitch, drawing on Robert Durling's seminal work on the interventions of the narrator in the *Furioso,*[73] talked about "the advertising of fictionality"[74] to describe this passage, as well as many other clashes between realism and implausibility in Ariosto's poem. These contradictory descriptions and narrations allowed Ariosto to put his own authority into question by exercising it to the extreme.

By adopting Ariosto's narrative techniques, as he planned to do since 1907, Bontempelli anticipated, in a less cinematic way, the modern *entrelacement* of Savinio's *Angelica o la notte di maggio.* More importantly, he also anticipated the rhizomatic complexity of the two most structurally Ariostean works written by Borges and Calvino: *The Garden of Forking Paths* and *The Castle of Crossed Destinies.* His following book, *La vita operosa,* relied on a similar structure. It was published in monthly instalments like *La vita intensa.* One of the instalments (the second chapter in the final edition) revolves around an authorial reflection about forking paths, and the possible realities generated by a character's choice between two directions. The section is titled "Hercules and Little Red Riding Hood," alluding to two emblematic narratives of forking paths. It insists on the same dichotomy between heroism and fable, duty and desire that nourished the apparently chaotic and accidental narrative progression of *La vita intensa.* Publishing both the works as serialized novels, in subsequent episodes each separated by an editorial hiatus, Bontempelli applied his poetics of disruption, inherited from Ariosto, to the very experience of writing and reading. His interlaced "adventure novels" (or "adventure tales" as he titled the episodes of *La vita operosa*) threaten to suddenly take a completely different turn, to collapse into chaos, or simply to stop, up until the very end. Only in the finale is their overall unity (the "design within the tangle") eventually revealed. The final product was of course planned from the beginning, but both the author and the reader had to cross the unstable path of its adventurous editorial development to be able to contemplate it in full.

In 1932, in one of his theoretical essays, Bontempelli showed himself to be aware of the direct filiation that connects chivalric fiction and the nineteenth-century practice of serialized publishing. In that essay, he established a connection between Ariosto's narrative mode and his own ironic experimentation with the medium of the serialized novel or feuilleton. Bontempelli derided those academic critics who frowned upon books made out of pieces previously published in newspapers and journals. He asserted that most of the best products of modernism "passed through periodicals, the real acid test" of literary quality. In the same essay, he argued that the entirety of Italy's greatest literature is constituted by "brief things." "Petrarch's epistles," in Bontempelli's interpretation, "are essays in journals, Aretino's letters are newspaper articles," and so on. To fit the *Furioso* into this framework, he revealed, thirteen years later, the idea that generated his two first official books, *La vita intensa* and *La vita operosa.*

> It will be easy for anyone to push my argument to its extreme consequences: What about the Orlando Furioso? Well, the Orlando is a pure and simple "serialized novel" that Ariosto used to read in episodes (each canto an instalment, with all the suspensions that are typical of a serialized novel) to the lords and ladies of the court.[75]

To "reforge the European novel," Bontempelli simply realized that the genre itself was a direct descendant of the chivalric poem. Therefore, he approached the novel in the way Ariosto approached his folkloric ancestors, with their paladins and errant knights, their adventurous and epic stories, their orally transmitted dramatic pathos. He adopted Ariosto's main techniques: irony, *entrelacement*, "cantus interruptus," the advertisement of fictionality, and the swift ability to reveal, in the end, the design within the tangle. In later works, more influenced by Metaphysical art and the nascent Surrealist movement, he would also engage more directly with Ariosto's imagery, mythologies, and magical tropes.

The Mirror and the Moon

At the dawn of fascism, between the success of his serialized novels and the definitive theorization of Magical Realism in *"900"*, Bontempelli wrote two fantastical books. These books, *The Chess-Set in the Mirror* and *Eva ultima*, were deeply influenced by the most otherworldly and magical elements of the *Orlando Furioso*. In the early 1920s, Bontempelli's intellectual friendship with de Chirico and Savinio became pivotal for his poetics, so the three artists' autonomous revivals of Ariosto's legacy converged at this juncture. In fact, when Bontempelli republished all of his official works with Mondadori twenty years later, he collected *The Chess-Set in the Mirror* and *Eva ultima* in a single volume titled "Two Metaphysical Fables."[76]

Each of these "fables" represents a tribute to one of the nineteenth-century masters that André Breton would later include in his *Anthologie de l'humour noir*, the compendium that provided Surrealism with a literary ancestry in 1940. In particular, *The Chess-Set in the Mirror* was evidently inspired by Lewis Carroll, and specifically by *Through the Looking-Glass*, the sequel to *Alice in Wonderland*, his most famous novel. *Eva ultima*, on the other hand, was a gothic and Metaphysical elaboration of Villiers de l'Isle-Adam's seminal masterpiece *L'Ève future*. In any event, the *Orlando Furioso* was, for both novels, a less immediately recognizable but more influential hypotext. In the central part of this chapter, I am going to show why.

Let me start from *The Chess-Set in the Mirror*. Bontempelli published this book in the children's literature series of the Florentine publisher Bemporad in 1922. It was then republished many times, for almost a century, oscillating between highbrow and children's series and becoming one of Bontempelli's most internationally famous texts.[77] In the novel, Bontempelli again used his authority as a witness. The story, as he stated from the beginning, happened to him when, as an eight-year-old boy, he was grounded in a room with a large mirror and a chess set in front of it. All of a sudden, the white king in that chess set (not the one in the room, but the one reflected in the mirror) started speaking. He invited Massimo to join him on the other side of the glass. When Massimo crossed the reflecting surface, he found himself in a large empty valley, and started exploring the world inside the mirror.

As in Carroll's novel, the real protagonist of *The Chess-Set in the Mirror* is its setting. The whole story is an exploration and a progressive understanding of the mirror and its inhabitants, and it ends when Massimo falls asleep only to wake up in the room from which he started (probably, but not certainly, on the original side of the mirror). Bontempelli's mirror is, nonetheless, completely different from Carroll's Looking-Glass World. To be sure, Bontempelli certainly knew *Through the Looking-Glass*, since its first Italian edition came out for the Istituto Editoriale Italiano while he was working there.[78] In fact, *The Chess-Set in the Mirror*, along with the contemporary *Sua Altezza!* by Annie Vivanti, represented one of the very few episodes of Carroll's reception in Italy before the end of fascism.[79] The beginning and the ending of Bontempelli's novel are very similar to those of Carroll's *Alice*, and both novels have the same number of chapters.[80] However, there is a philosophical difference between Carroll's mirror and Bontempelli's. Both are rooted in geometry and a paradoxical excess of rationalism, but the effects that they produce are almost opposite.

When Alice crosses through her looking-glass, she enters a mirror image of the same room that she left. The world beyond that room is based on the Victorian nonsense of logical paradoxes, literal manifestations of puns, parodies of nursery rhymes, and unreliable rules. A similar, if less inventive, inventory of absurdities animated Annie Vivanti's elaboration of Carroll's world. In *Sua Altezza!*, figurative language has real effects, and phonetic associations between words can make the objects that they identify collide.[81] Bontempelli's mirror, on the other hand, is a two-dimensional world of reflected images. It presents no magic or absurdity besides the fact that everything that has ever been reflected in it is forever duplicated in its metaphysical reality. In addition, objects, once reflected and stored in the mirror, acquire speech and agency there.

Sergio Tofano, the popular Italian illustrator of children's books who drew the images for the novel's first edition, rendered Bontempelli's vision with simple elegance. The scenes that happen before the crossing (figure 2.3) have a visible ground. The one that takes place at the end (figure 2.4) portrays Massimo at the crossing of the three lines that define the three-dimensional reality outside the mirror. Conversely, in the scenes that happen inside the mirror (figure 2.5), characters and objects float in the white void of the page. Their feet rest on nothing; their scale and relative positions are the only elements that make them legible. By crossing the glass, Massimo does not enter a fantastic land beyond the mirror, but the mirror itself. To be precise, rather than "through" the mirror, he goes inside it.

The nature of this two-dimensional reality within reality recalls Plato's Metaphysics and, of course, his myth of the cave. In Bontempelli's mirror, for instance, chess pieces believe themselves to be the true, eternal archetypes of mortal humans outside the mirror. The mirror is also reminiscent of Edwin Abbott Abbott's *Flatland*, which was translated into Italian only in 1966, when Calvino saluted it as a touchstone for

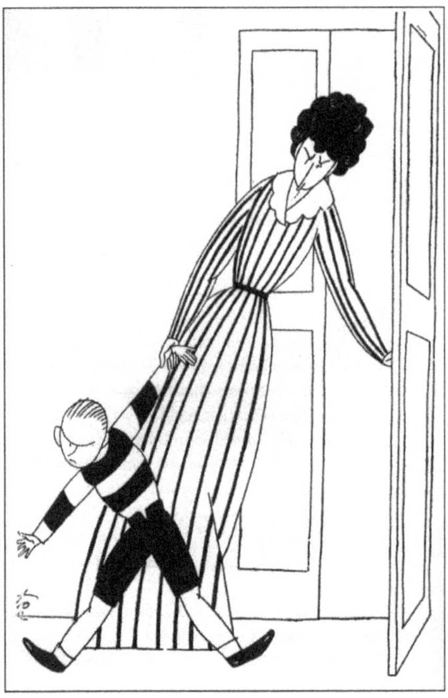

Figure 2.3. Sto (Sergio Tofano), illustration for Massimo Bontempelli, *La scacchiera davanti allo specchio* (Florence: Bemporad, 1922).

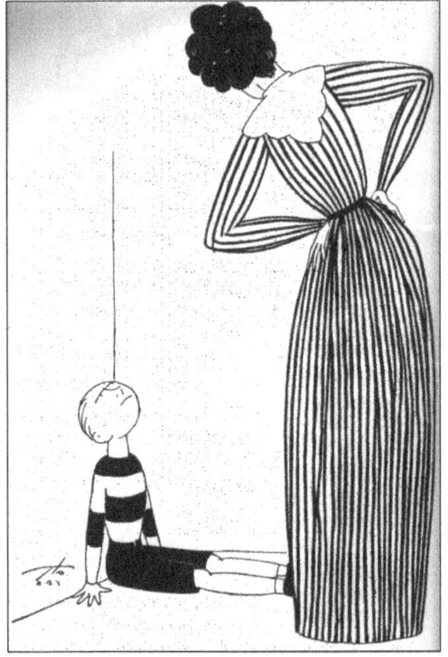

Figure 2.4. Sto (Sergio Tofano), illustration for Massimo Bontempelli, *La scacchiera davanti allo specchio* (Florence: Bemporad, 1922).

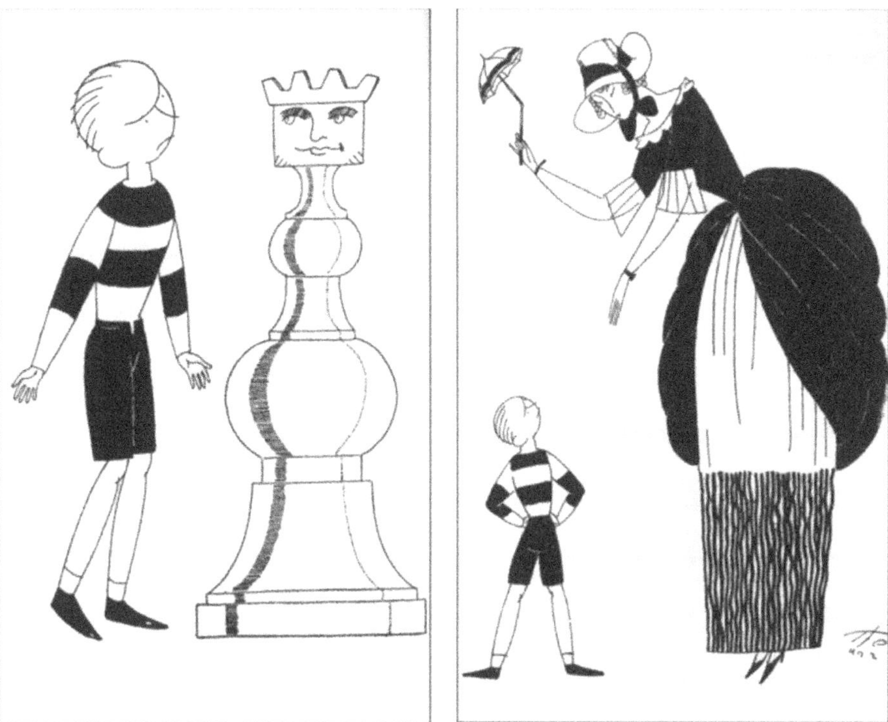

Figure 2.5. Sto (Sergio Tofano), illustrations for Massimo Bontempelli, *La scacchiera davanti allo specchio* (Florence: Bemporad, 1922).

the rational fantastic fiction that he was developing along the lines of Bontempelli's pre-war model.[82] The most compelling intertextual parallel, however, is with the mirror of the Earth that floats in the skies of the *Orlando Furioso*, the metaphysical and geographical site of all the things lost in the world and all the useless vanities that Time incessantly wears out: Ariosto's moon. We now know, thanks to the studies generated by Eugenio Garin's seminal work on Leon Battista Alberti's *Intercenales*, that the allegorical physics and metaphysics of Ariosto's moon were based on a web of sources. The most important of these sources was Alberti's *Somnium*. However, that text was only discovered in the 1960s. Throughout Bontempelli's life, critics believed that Ariosto conceived the moon as a mirror of our world for the first time, inventing a new trope.

The journey to the moon is one of the most famous elements of the *Furioso*'s plot. Astolfo flies there on Elijah's flaming chariot in order to fix the very accident that made Orlando furious. His mission is to find, on the moon, the wits that Orlando lost on Earth when he found out about Angelica's love for the young Muslim soldier Medoro. By breathing his wits back into his brain, Orlando can cure his madness and resume his duty as Charlemagne's paladin. When Astolfo approaches the moon, he finds it to be "Equal (though somewhat smaller) in their sight / To our own globe" (XXXIV, 70). It appears like a spherical mirror, "bright / As spotless steel." The metaphysical relation between our world and this reflecting globe, "the nearest of the planets" (XXXIV, 67), is explained by Saint John the Apostle in the following canto. Astolfo asks Saint John about an old man who continuously throws platelets with engraved names into the stream of the river Lethe. The saint explains that the man is the lunar double of what on Earth is Time, and the platelets represent the memory of people whose destiny is concluded.

> You must believe, my son, no frond is stirred
> On earth that is not mirrored in this sphere.
> Every result of every act and word
> Its corresponding counterpart has here. (XXXV, 18)

Bontempelli's mirror works in a similar way, at least according to the white king of the chess set, who guides Massimo for most of his journey. All the names of all the people who walked the Earth are collected on the moon, even if most are washed out in the river of oblivion. Correspondingly, as the white king explains to Massimo, "every mirror in the world" stores "all the images of all the men, women, and children who have ever seen themselves in it,"[83] even after their death. However, from the king's point of view, the world is a chaotic imitation of the Cartesian simplicity of the mirror, not the other way around.

> Everything that occurs among human beings, especially the most important things, which one studies in history, are nothing more than confused imitations and [a] hodgepodge of variants of the great games of chess we have played.[84]

Through the allegory of his moon, Ariosto showed the irrelevance of everyday earthly concerns and the pettiness of shortcuts to fame and power. These mediocre facts of our world become meaningless in the eternal scale of the moon's revealing correspondences. Similarly, through his mirror, Bontempelli argued that any form of narcissistic exceptionalism is a delusion. The explanation of the king, modelled after Saint John's description of Ariosto's moon, is in fact contradicted by another sentient object that Massimo meets in the mirror. This second inorganic guide of young Massimo is the quintessential emblem of de Chirico's Metaphysical art, a mannequin who reigns over a valley of inanimate things. Massimo finds him after a long exploratory journey that takes up the entirety of the thirteenth chapter.

Valleys of Lost Things

In the first few chapters of *The Chess-Set in the Mirror*, Massimo interacts with the chess pieces and a number of human images from different times in the past. All of them were, at some point, reflected in the mirror, and their images were stuck there: Massimo's grandmother as a young woman, a burglar who tried to rob his parents' house before Massimo was born, a couple who looked into the mirror in the eighteenth century, when it was owned by someone else, and so on. Bored with these encounters and unable to leave the mirror, Massimo tries to see if there is an end to the apparently infinite and colourless plane in which he is trapped.

At first, in his exploration, Massimo cannot see anything different. After walking for a while, he starts to perceive a difference in height. Going up, he hears the murmurs of wind shaking trees, and wonders if he has "wandered into the middle of an invisible forest."[85] As he leaves these immaterial woods behind, he starts to hear another "harmonious rushing sound, something like water, maybe a stream," which gets louder and louder until he is "struck by the strange feeling that [he] might be crossing a bridge." He keeps on going, until the sounds and the tactile sensations under his feet make him feel that he is "standing at the seacoast, on the shore of a quiet sea." Worried that he might drown, he has a moment of hesitation, but then the colourless ground itself starts guiding his steps uphill, as if he has encountered a cliff. When he reaches the top, which is immersed in mist, he looks down, expecting to see "those streams, or the woods, or the sea, whose sounds [he]'d heard."[86] Instead, the landscape that opens in front of him is made out of all the inanimate objects that were ever reflected in the mirror. Their non-verbal voices, based on the material of which they are made (wood, glass, metal, cloth), shaped the invisible geography that Massimo crossed in his exploration: faded echoes of places that exist in the world outside the mirror.

The physical conformation of Ariosto's moon is the source that inspired this idea. While it appears, like the mirror, as a spotless and uniform surface of reflecting steel, Ariosto's moon actually is a vast and varied land. Astolfo realizes this as he gets closer to it. Like Bontempelli's mirror, the moon has rivers, woods, shores, hills, and plains. This lunar geography is made out of the same elements that one can find on Earth, but their position and nature are different.

> Astolfo had two reasons for surprise:
> First, that the kingdom of the lunar sphere
> Should be so large, when such a tiny size
> Its circle seems to us when glimpsed from here;
> Next, that he had to screw up both his eyes
> To see the globe we live on plain and clear.
> Since earth and ocean have no proper light,
> Their image does not rise to a great height.
>
> There, other lakes and rivers, other rills
> From ours down here on earth are to be found,
> And other plains and valleys, other hills.
> Cities and castles on the moon abound;
> The size of houses with amazement fills
> The paladin; extending all around
> Are deep and solitary forests where
> Diana's huntress-nymphs pursue the deer. (XXXIV, 71–2)

As usual, Ariosto described something patently unreal through the ironic rigour of credible elements. From the moon, Astolfo cannot discern the details of Earth's surface, so it is reasonable that readers cannot directly see, from Earth, the luxurious lunar landscapes described in the *Furioso.* While Carroll (like his Italian imitator Vivanti in 1922) opened a door to an inexplicable upside-down world, Ariosto provided Bontempelli with a model for the creation of a fantastic space that is both impossible and explainable. Alice is as disoriented as her readers are, while Astolfo and Massimo deduce and receive plausible explanations for the absurdities that they witness. Bontempelli's mirror, like the moon, is still in our universe: it is marvellous but it still makes sense. Its geography, like that of the moon, reflects the earthly one and has a rational explanation. Dante made a similar experiment with realism when he described his own supposedly personal experience in the detailed geography of Hell, Purgatory, and Paradise. However, unlike Ariosto and Bontempelli, he firmly believed in the existence of these places, and expected his readers to grasp their factual reality beyond the veils of allegory.

Before moving on to *Eva ultima,* I would like to draw one last intertextual parallel between *The Chess-Set in the Mirror* and Canto XXXIV of Ariosto's *Furioso.* As hinted before, this parallel has to do with the coeval research of Bontempelli's friends de Chirico and Savinio. Massimo's geographical adventure culminates with the encounter with the mannequin, who governs the mass of objects that form the only visible panorama in the mirror. Bontempelli describes this special place in detail:

> The mist had disappeared completely: everything was luminous and clear. There were – in that vast depression, squared off like military parade grounds, but sunk far below the level of the ground on which I was standing – a huge number of different objects: furniture of all descriptions, chairs, tables, shelves, chests, and also draperies, bouquets of flowers in short and tall, narrow and round-bellied vases. There were cushions, and a lot of jars of all shapes, and there were books, a hammer lying near a file and other such tools, a clothes hook, brushes of all kinds, combs and vials, a retort of the type you see in chemistry laboratories, and feathery things, the ones that servants use to dust furniture.[87]

This valley gathers the images of what Francesco Orlando would call "obsolete objects."[88] Both its physical appearance and its metaphysical function recall the most important place on Ariosto's moon: the great valley where everything that is lost on Earth (including Orlando's wits) is stored.

> The duke did not delay to view each sight,
> For that was not the aim of his ascent.
> Between two mountains of prodigious height
> The travellers to a deep valley went.
> What by our fault, or Time's relentless flight,
> Or Fortune's chances, or by accident
> (Whatever be the cause) we lose down here,
> Miraculously is assembled there. (XXXIV, 73)

While Bontempelli's valley collects the images of literal objects, Ariosto's is filled with allegorical ones, of which he only describes a few. Interestingly, some coincide with those mentioned in *The Chess-Set in the Mirror*: vials, of course, which on the moon contain the wits lost on earth, but also broken jars (the servitude of courtiers), hooks (flattery), and flowers (the donation of Constantine). In any event, the miserable nature of those lost things, which reveal the vanity of our traffics on Earth, clearly inspired the melancholy of the mannequin's realm in Bontempelli's mirror. In that realm, the images of forgotten objects live in the illusion of being the true, eternal archetypes of human reality outside the mirror.

Objects have been central protagonists of Metaphysical art since its inception. In his influential pre-war Parisian paintings, such as the emblematic *Song of Love* (figure 2.6), de Chirico blurred the boundary

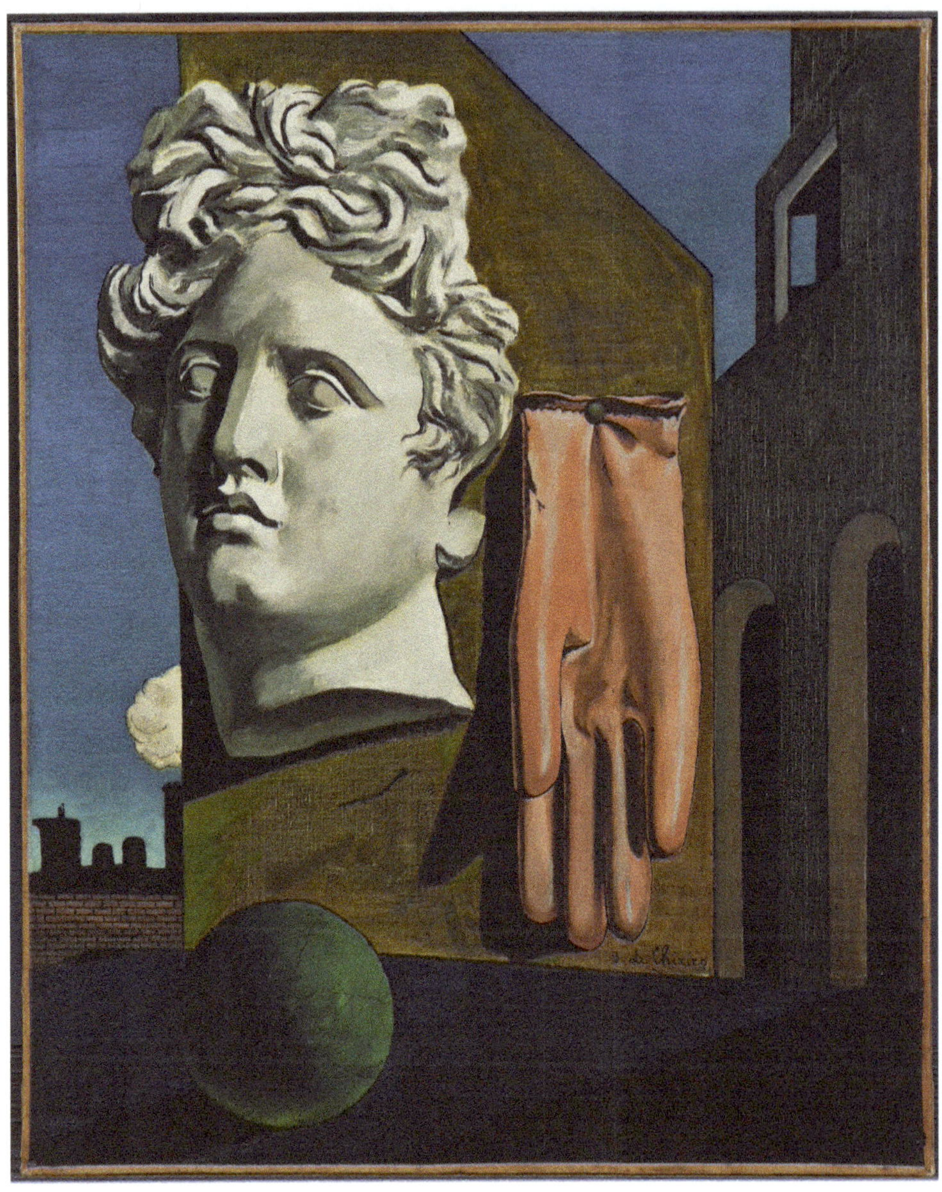

Figure 2.6. Giorgio de Chirico, *The Song of Love* (*Le chant d'amour*), 1914, oil on canvas, 73 × 59.1 cm, Museum of Modern Art, New York. © 2022 Artists Rights Society (ARS), New York/SIAE, Rome. Photograph © 1996 MoMA New York.

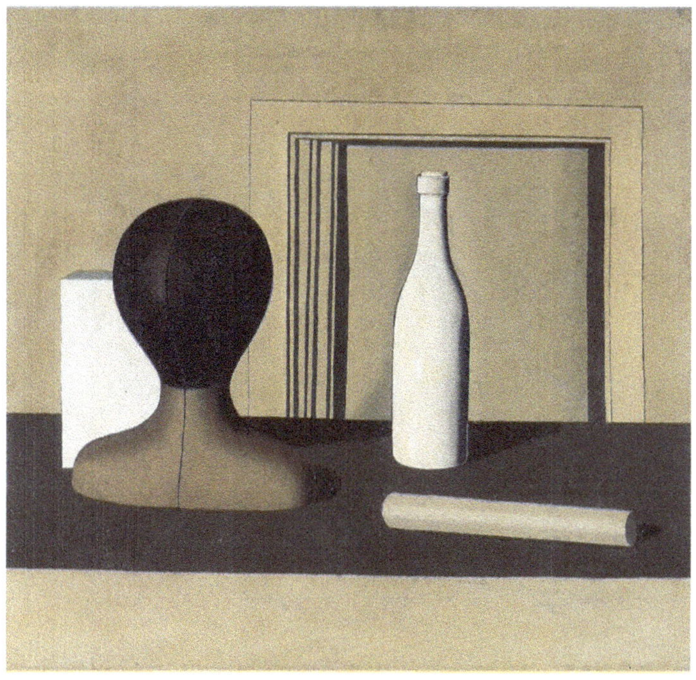

Figure 2.7. Giorgio Morandi, *Still Life* (*Natura morta*), 1918, oil on canvas, 68.5 × 72 cm, Pinacoteca di Brera, Milan. © 2022 Artists Rights Society (ARS), New York/SIAE, Rome. Photograph ©Pinacoteca di Brera, Milan.

between still life and portraiture that Giorgio Morandi, in his most Metaphysical phase, smashed in the Platonic purity of his 1918 exercises (figure 2.7). After the Ferrarese years, Metaphysical still lives interacted, as a pictorial genre, with landscape, drawing on the same kind of visual confusion between interior and exterior that Ariosto's *Satires* had inspired in Metaphysical interiors. When, in the mid-1920s, Savinio started painting in Paris, the manifestation of artefacts in natural settings became one of his most recurring themes. In some cases, like *La cité des promesses* (1928), the volumes and shapes of the objects themselves formed a landscape, in a blending of organic and inorganic, natural and artificial matter. In other works, like *Objets abandonnes dans la forêt* (1928), objects are abandoned in an otherwise pristine valley, like vestiges of a remote human presence. They recall the "confused jumble of ruins" (XXXIV, 79) that Astolfo sees while flying over the alien geography of the moon. In *Objets dans la forêt* (figure 2.8), a mound of recognizable and colourful toys

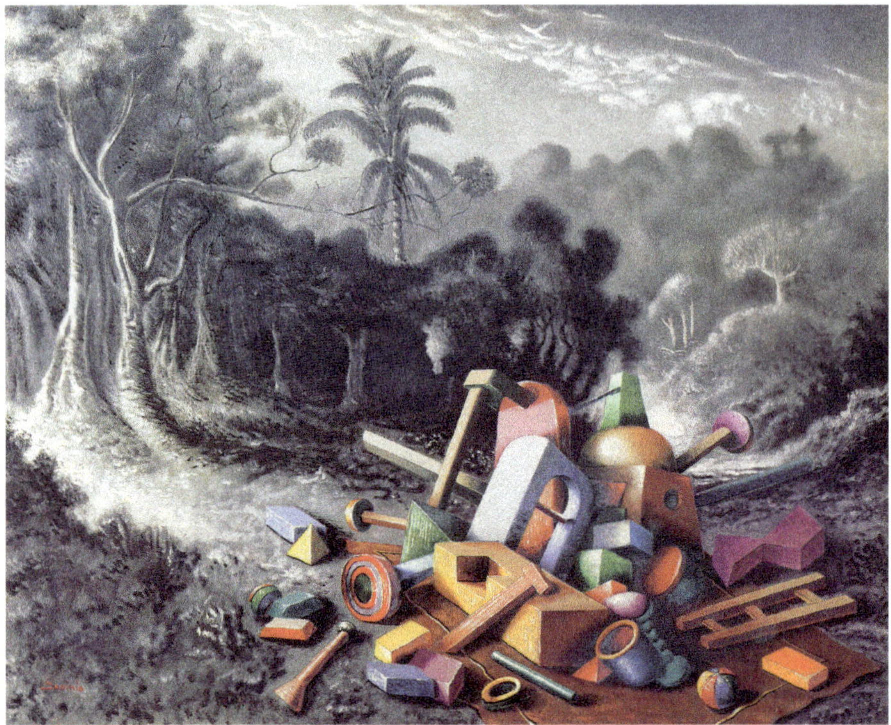

Figure 2.8. Alberto Savinio, *Objects in the Forest* (*Objets dans la forêt*), 1927–8, oil on canvas, 73 × 92 cm, Private Collection. © 2022 Artists Rights Society (ARS), New York/SIAE, Rome.

inhabits a valley enclosed by a monochrome, metal-like exotic forest. I believe that Ariosto and Bontempelli should be included in the genealogy that produced this imagery. And I would argue that their influence is even more evidently at play in one of de Chirico's coeval motifs: a series of paintings with pieces of furniture in a valley (figure 2.9).

This ultimate reversal of Metaphysical interiors is among the most estranging of de Chirico's visual ideas of the interwar period. He explained it by recalling the many times he saw pieces of furniture incongruously appear on the streets, when people were moving houses or were forced out by earthquakes. Jean Cocteau believed these paintings to be inspired by American comedy films.[89] However, Bontempelli's description of the

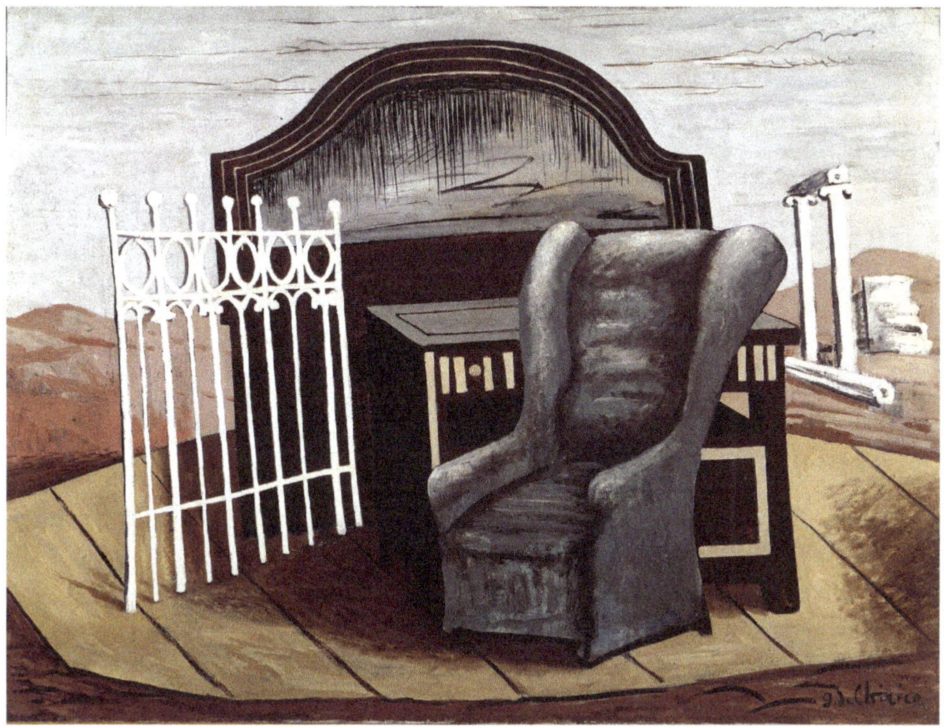

Figure 2.9. Giorgio de Chirico, *Furniture in the Valley* (*Mobili nella valle*), 1927, oil on canvas, 97 × 130 cm, Museo di Arte Moderna e Contemporanea di Trento e Rovereto, Rovereto. © 2022 Artists Rights Society (ARS), New York/ SIAE, Rome.

valley of objects in the mirror, inspired by the valley of lost things on Ariosto's moon, is a more compelling model for the absurd realism of de Chirico's furniture valleys.

> Let me explain: They weren't set down as if in a warehouse or a shop, where all the items of one kind are grouped together. Nor as if they were stacked in a storeroom where everything is put away in confusion and even new things seem old. Nor as though they were in a home, where everything is placed according to its use […]. No, in this world, as best [as] I can explain it, these objects were set out just the way trees and rocks are in the countryside. I don't know why, but it seemed perfectly clear that they were in their

> proper places – as though created exactly where one found them. They appeared almost to have become alive, and seen all together, they created a strange and pleasant harmony. It struck me that they formed a sort of landscape, one made of objects instead of plants and natural things.[90]

Stringless Puppets

The planet visited by Astolfo is not the only moon in Ariosto's poetry, and Bontempelli knew that. The third of Ariosto's *Satires* centres on the Horatian self-portrait as a "stay-at-home" that provided a model for the indoor voyages of Metaphysical art and literature. The same model was arguably at the root of *The Chess-Set in the Mirror*, which is ultimately an adventurous journey within the four walls of the narrator's room. At the end of the same *Satire*, Ariosto included a fable about the foolishness of insatiable ambitions. This fable tells the story of a group of boorish peasants who believed that they could get to the moon by reaching for it from the top of a mountain. When they finished climbing, the moon was of course still unreachable, and the peasants ended up exhausted and frustrated.

When Bontempelli published his edition of the *Satires*, in 1916, he was also writing a play that was destined to become his first theatrical success: *Guardia alla luna*.[91] The play is about a mother who goes insane, blames the moon for the death of her baby, and climbs a mountain in order to reach the moon and kill it. Critics later connected *Guardia alla luna* with the Stationendrama of coeval German Expressionist theatre,[92] with Pirandello's influence, and with Bontempelli's progressive detachment from Futurism.[93] Its structure and style are certainly in dialogue with Europe's avant-garde drama, and a parodic criticism of Marinetti's Futurist manifesto *Let's Kill the Moonlight!* is undeniable. However, the moral and thematic ancestor of *Guardia alla luna* is clearly Ariosto's satirical fable of the moon and the mountain.

In the passage from *Guardia alla luna* to *The Chess-Set in the Mirror*, Bontempelli's parallel move from the moon of the *Satires* to that of the *Furioso* encapsulated the evolution of his Ariostean poetics at the dawn of Magical Realism. His first works after the 1907 ode explored Ariosto's irony, his ability to harmonize imagination with reality, and his disenchanted modern elaboration of tradition. In the war years and immediately after, Bontempelli revived Ariosto's rhetorical strategies, his narratological innovations, and his oblique positioning in the face of aesthetic orthodoxy and the practical pressures of history and politics. After the experiments of *La vita intensa* and *La vita operosa*, another crucial feature of Ariosto's fiction became central for the development of Magical Realism:

the conception of permeable, parallel worlds of rational fantasy within reality (and in direct relation with it).

Right before inventing the mirror of *The Chess-Set in the Mirror*, Bontempelli had experimented with the concept in his second major success as a playwright, *Siepe a nordovest* (1921). In this play, the cast of human actors is joined on the stage by a group of puppets. The hedge of the title, just like Massimo's mirror, is a threshold between animate and inanimate characters. Both humans and puppets believe themselves to be each other's archetype. The distinction between the two worlds was built into the scenography when the play was produced. It is also eloquently visualized in the illustrations that de Chirico drew for the edition of the play in 1922, his first collaboration with Bontempelli. In one of these drawings, the world of puppets is demarcated by a barrier represented as a white canvas. In addition, the mannequin-like puppets, with their crowns and swords, recall the marionettes of knights and damsels used in Sicilian puppet theatre: an old and sophisticated traditional form of popular adaptation of the *Orlando Furioso* and other chivalric stories.[94] It is worth noting that, in the frontispiece of the play's edition, de Chirico portrayed Bontempelli as a painter: he looks up to an implicit canvas mounted on an easel rather than down to an escritoire, or directly to the viewer. In the drawing, Bontempelli is also subtly represented as a puppet. The hand of his muse reaches out from the background in a visual tribute to the three-dimensionality of Leonardo's and Antonello da Messina's fifteenth-century realism. While there are no visible strings, the Muse's fingers are raised and spread like those of a puppeteer.

In his study of Carlo Collodi's legacy, Harold Segel pointed out the importance of *Pinocchio* in Bontempelli's theatrical experiments.[95] Collodi's stringless puppet, arguably the most important cultural product of Italy's nineteenth century, is part of the literary genealogy of Metaphysical mannequins, and de Chirico had a special relationship with *Pinocchio.*[96] After all, in a 1916 writing, Savinio had compared Ferrara with the Pleasure Island where Pinocchio is transformed into a donkey: another remote place, separated from everyday reality, where adventurers encounter a kind of logical magic that does not apply to the rest of the world. When, in 1983, Calvino edited an anthology of nineteenth-century fantastical stories, he did not include any Italian work, arguing that the genre was simply absent in that segment of Italy's literary history. However, he closed his essay on fantastic literature with a quotation from *Pinocchio.*[97]

Stringless puppets and parallel worlds are at the centre of *Eva ultima*, the second of Bontempelli's "Metaphysical fables." The novel, published for the first time in 1923, synthesized many of the Ariostean techniques and tropes that Bontempelli had experimented with before. The plot, for once, was not autobiographical. The story revolves around a woman, Eva, seduced by a mysterious stranger, Evandro, who lures her into his villa. He is the king of the villa, a strange and secluded place surrounded by a forest, and wants Eva to become his queen. However, she falls in love with Bululù, the sentient puppet that he puts at her service, a talking marionette whose strings appear to be moved by no hand. The torments of this love triangle, as well as Eva's disquieting exploration of Bululù's impossible otherness, reach a peak when the woman manages to escape from the villa, which then immediately disappears. The villa itself is one of the most Ariostean inventions of Bontempelli's literature.

Merlin's Villa

In *Eva ultima* Bontempelli explored, as I mentioned before, some of the themes of Villiers de l'Isle Adam's *L'Ève future*: misogyny, automatons, agency. However, the similarities between the two novels, just like those between *The Chess-Set in the Mirror* and Carroll's *Through the Looking-Glass*, are evident and superficial. Rather than science, the novel is about magic, which is presented with Ariosto's ironic credibility.

In *Eva ultima*, as a narrator, Bontempelli needs to go out of his way to recount impossible events with the same level of credibility that he had achieved in *La vita intensa* or *The Chess-Set in the Mirror*. In those novels he could exploit his supposed status as a first-hand witness. In *Eva ultima* he could not. Thus, in the novel, he declares that he learned the story that he is telling from "direct sources," and that he even verified those sources by "sojourning for a while in the places where everything happened."[98] When, in the fiction, some of the most inexplicable and mysterious events take place, Bontempelli resorts to the "confessions" that he claims to have received from the protagonist herself. In doing so, he disrupts the narration to remind readers that he is just elaborating on the facts that Eva told him, which "served as a basis for writing the tale of her last adventure."[99]

A similar function is carried out, in the *Furioso*, by Turpin, a legendary witness of the deeds of Charlemagne's paladins. Since at least the *Chanson de Roland*, chivalric poems referred to the fictitious authority of Turpin as their ultimate source. Ariosto did the same, invoking the legendary Turpin to justify incredible elements of the plot. In his refined use of this old convention, he asked his readers to both believe and doubt Turpin's authority (and, ultimately, any form of storytelling) at the same time.

One example of this rhetoric is in Canto XXVI, when Ariosto described Marfisa's sorcery.

Turpin, relating marvels such as these,
Knows that he speaks the unvarnished truth and leaves
His hearers to accept whate'er they please.
He says (you may consider he deceives)
Almost as though Marfisa's enemies
Were ice, they melt as, like a torch, she weaves
Among their ranks, causing no less surprise
Than he on whom she turns astonished eyes. (XXVI, 91)

Similarly, in *Eva ultima* Bontempelli pretended to be relating "the unvarnished truth" to his readers. He worked scrupulously to prevent people from reading *Eva ultima* just as a fairytale or a symbolic fable. When he republished the novel, along with *The Chess-Set in the Mirror*, in the 1940 volume *Due favole metafisiche*, he added an appendix of notes. This appendix includes a detailed report of his meeting with Eva, explanatory comments on some vague details of the first edition, and even transcriptions of documents, such as Eva's letters or the original scores of the music played for her at Evandro's villa.[100] In the same text Bontempelli stated that it was Eva's idea to narrate the story as a novel with the "tone of a work of fiction."[101] He personally would have preferred to just report the bare facts, with neutral precision, as a journalist.

Bontempelli's efforts to construct a paradigm of authenticity for his patently invented story are evidently ironic and aware, like those in the *Orlando Furioso*. They are meant to avoid a trivialization of the novel through a clear moral, or a solvable allegory. In a particularly comedic passage of the appendix, Bontempelli stated that he regretted not having a photograph of Bululù, the animated puppet in Evandro's villa. If he had taken one, he could have published it in the new edition. A photo would have put at bay the rumour that Bululù had to be interpreted as a literary symbol of something rather than "just" a living puppet.[102] Albert Ascoli studied similar mechanisms of intentionally conspicuous deception in Ariosto's work. The narrative inventions of the *Furioso*, as he showed, resist the domestication of humanistic criticism, maintaining their autonomy from exempla and other forms of educational or symbolical readings.[103]

The Ariostean irony of *Eva ultima* is shared by the characters themselves, and in particular by Evandro, who frequently jokes about his own powers as a sorcerer. His magic, he tells Eva, "is too irreparably intelligent to conjure a parade of monsters,"[104] and when she tries to leave him on the way to the villa he teases her: "it's the second time you say farewell; if you want, I can take a magical attitude and foretell you that it won't be the last."[105] When Eva asks him how they will reach the villa, he mocks her chivalric expectations and reveals that they would use "the least magic, most modern, and most comfortable of transportations:"[106] a car. And when that car breaks down, in the middle of their trip, he comments: "a Hippogriff would never have conked out. Isn't this a perfect way to disenchant you?"[107]

The villa is the only site of truly fantastic events in the disenchanting reality of the story. Just as in the mirror of Bontempelli's previous novel, the magic qualities of the villa seem to respond to clear metaphysical rules that ultimately remain mysterious. Unlike the mirror, though, the villa is modelled after a combination of two different magical places in the *Furioso*: Merlin's tomb and Atlante's castle. The influence of Atlante's castle is the most evident.[108] The sorcerer Atlante, in the *Furioso,* builds this castle to save his protégé Ruggiero from the war and, ultimately, to prevent the risks of his marriage with Bradamante. Therefore, the castle is a major obstacle for the fulfilment of both the epic pillars of the plot: the beginning of the Estense dynasty through Bradamante and Ruggiero, and the war between Christians and Muslims. The castle's spell lures the best knights of the *Furioso*: it shows them the image of what they desire the most, and traps them in an eternal chase of that image. Unaware of the spell, they voluntarily remain in the castle, forgetting their military duties. The enchantment is finally broken by Astolfo in Canto XXII, and the castle vanishes.

Evandro's villa traps its guests, unaware that they are prisoners, in a similar way. In the novel, the modern sorcerer even explains to Eva: "it is crucial that you don't believe that you are forced to stay."[109] The magic, like that in the *Furioso,* is ultimately meta-literary: it prevents the story from ending. It also nourishes the romance storylines, forcing Eva to inexplicably go back to Evandro and Bululù despite her desire to leave. There is, in the villa, "a diabolical or divine force" that "attract[s] her back inside, almost as if she could sense that some inevitable event of her life had yet to happen there."[110] This magic ends when Eva finally escapes the villa's spell and turns back to look at it. Surrounded by Evandro's woods, "sinisterly smoky" and confused with the clouds in a "battle of sooty mists," the dark profile of the villa is finally "dissolved"[111] by the air ("l'aria la dissolse"). The villa vanishes like Atlante's castle when Astolfo breaks its spell and "The palace vanishes in mist and smoke" ("e si sciolse il palazzo, in fumo e in nebbia," XXII, 23).

As I mentioned, another sorcerer's sanctuary from the *Furioso* inspired Bontempelli's villa: Merlin's tomb. In Canto III, Bradamante falls into

Merlin's tomb and is trapped there. The enchantress Melissa comes to her help, and conjures a parade of ghosts. Bradamante, standing in a magic circle, witnesses the passage of these figures, which are not spirits of the dead but images of the future members of the Este house. The first is her son, whom she will conceive only at the end of the *Furioso*, and the last are Ariosto's patrons, the addressees of this encomiastic passage.

> Lo! from the outer chamber came straightway
> Spirits, to where the magic ring extended;
> But if they onward passed, they found their way
> Was barred, as though by moat and wall defended. (III, 22)

Here Ariosto imitated a passage from Virgil. In the sixth book of the *Aeneid*, Aeneas goes to the Underworld to meet his dead father. There, he sees all the future kings of Rome (his own progeny) up to Augustus, the emperor who commissioned the *Aeneid* itself to Virgil. However, there is an important difference. The future that both Bradamante and Aeneas see through their parades of ghosts is the present for Ariosto and Virgil, and it is the past for us later readers. However, in order to see this future, Bradamante never had to leave her own present. She remained within the flow of time, in the world of the living. Aeneas, on the other hand, had to go through katabasis to see the images of his future descendants. He exited time and space, like Dante, Orpheus, or Odysseus, and entered the realm of the dead.

Merlin's cave, like Atlante's castle and Astolfo's moon – like Massimo's mirror and Evandro's villa – does not suspend reality. Its magic does not evade realism, even if it advertises its own literary fictionality. The detail of the magical circle around Bradamante, impenetrable to the apparitions that gather in the cave, is reprised in very similar terms in *Eva ultima*. When Bululù brings Eva to the villa's woods and summons a legion of ghosts from her past, he walks in a circle around the trunk of a spruce tree. Like Melissa's demons, the ghosts cannot penetrate the circle that protects the protagonist, and gather around it at a safe distance.

> [...] from all the directions of the pale horizon, even the most far away points, fluid crowds of spectres rapidly came to her in silence [...]. Now all of them stopped around her, in a semicircle of which she was the centre; they pressed against one another and against that circle, as if it was an invisible barrier.[112]

In Bontempelli's fiction, the clarity of realistic fantasy is always enclosed in a magic circle: a membrane that, as in Ariosto's *Furioso*, can only be crossed by adventurers from our world. This screen can be an element of the fiction: the hedge or canvas in *Guardia alla Luna*, the surface of the mirror in *The Chess-Set in the Mirror*, Eva's circle in *Eva ultima*. But it can also be the point of view of the narrator's impossibly authentic testimony, as in *La vita intensa*. It can be a para-textual or structural element of the narration, or of the medium that carries it. It can be the filter of authorial irony. Whatever form it takes, this membrane or screen, this magic circle, establishes a controlled, transparent contact between realism and fantasy. It prevents these opposing forces from producing fairytales, evasive deceptions, or surreal dreams. It makes magic realistic, and reality miraculous.

The Duke and the Duce

In 1926 Bontempelli founded *"900"*, the journal in which he defined Magical Realism. In the same year, he took the position of president of the fascist writers' union, becoming a powerful figure in the cultural panorama of fascist Italy. These two intertwined events defined his legacy.

Bontempelli had entered the fascist party in 1924. In that year, Mussolini definitively took power over the parliament and was about to proclaim himself Duce, starting twenty years of dictatorship. Bontempelli's relationship with the regime was one of strange compromise. He benefited from his role as a fascist intellectual, confirmed, in 1929, with his election to the Accademia d'Italia, in the company of racist scientists and nationalist philosophers. On various occasions he praised Mussolini's criminal government, mythologizing the actions of the regime and the destiny of the nation under its rule. However, in 1938, when 896 professors were expelled from Italian universities because of the racial laws, Bontempelli refused to take one of the vacant positions. All positions were filled by other scholars who, like him, were considered "Aryan" and were involved with fascism to different degrees. Most of them were able to keep those positions, obtained through racial cleansing, after the fall of fascism. Bontempelli was the only one to be offered a position and reject it. In his case, it was the chair of Italian Literature at the University of Florence, held by Attilio Momigliano, a giant of Italian philology and, incidentally, one of the greatest connoisseurs of Ariosto – Borges chose his monograph on the *Orlando Furioso* as one of the one hundred books of his *Biblioteca Personal*.[113] At a commemoration of Gabriele D'Annunzio, held in the same year in which he rejected Momigliano's chair, Bontempelli expressed criticism towards the fascist regime. Because of these gestures, he was confined to Venice. The reprinting of his books was prohibited, and he was banished from any public event or new publication. During the war, under German occupation, he was sentenced to death by the Nazis, who failed to catch him.

Even in the years of his most clear involvement and collaboration with fascism, Bontempelli's advocacy for the autonomy of art from politics was a cause of friction with the regime. His Europeanism was a problem as well. His journal *"900"* was initially published in French, and then bilingually, until autarchic pressures imposed a monolingual Italian edition. Its initial subtitle was *Cahiers d'Italie et d'Europe*, and it had a prestigious international editorial board that included James Joyce and Ramón Gómez de la Serna. *"900"* brought to Italy the first translated excerpts of works by authors such as Woolf, Tolstoy, Rilke, and Max Jacob. It also hosted controversial texts, such as an illustrated essay on Georg Grosz's anti-nationalist Dadaism in Germany. Because of the exhibited internationalism and the political positions that it sponsored, the journal was boycotted by one of its co-founders. It was ultimately disrupted by the regime in 1929. Fascist culture favoured the localist and anti-Parisian agenda of the Strapaese (Ultra-Town, or Ultra-Country) writers and artists over the Stracittà (Ultra-City) movement that backed Bontempelli's vision.

The case of Bontempelli is anomalous and revealing within the history of fascist intellectuals. While Italophone scholarship mostly ignored or minimized his fascism, American scholars such as Keala Jewell recently studied the compromises and synergies that linked Bontempelli's public role with his aesthetic ideology.[114] I am interested, in particular, in showing that, in the interwar period, Bontempelli's negotiation of Magical Realism and political reality was indebted to Ariosto's influence. I will do so by using the editorials and essays that he penned for *"900"* from 1926 to 1929, when the journal was shut down. I will also look at his later interventions in national newspapers and other journals up until 1938, the year of his final rupture with fascism. In that same year, Bontempelli collected everything that he wrote for *"900"*, as well as later pieces on art and cultural politics, in a book titled *L'avventura novecentista.* In this book, he republished all the texts in their original form.[115] However, he added a rich apparatus of notes (all formulated in 1938) to justify some of his past positions, offer context, and correct what, in hindsight, was revealed to be wrong. The result was Bontempelli's most ambitious and substantial theoretical work, the crucial source for understanding Magical Realism and, in general, the Italian literature of the Return to Order. Ariosto is one of the most cited canonical authors in that book, second only to Dante. His model offered Bontempelli an authoritative paradigm for an aesthetic politics of ironic compromise and innovation through tradition, lucid evasion, and self-absolving individualism.

The title *L'avventura novecentista* refers to "Novecentismo," a label that Bontempelli adopted to describe his mature Magical Realism from the mid-1920s on.[116] He included in that label the coeval work of other Italian authors with similar styles and poetics, like Paola Masino, Anna Maria Ortese, Corrado Alvaro, and Cesare Zavattini. The term was modelled after the name of the journal *"900"* (which in Italian reads "Novecento" and means twentieth century). In the title of the book, it was accompanied by the keyword that Bontempelli had so often used to describe his stories: "avventura." The adventure, in this case, was not a fictional plot. It was an intellectual journey and, at the same time, a real battle of cultural politics. Both took place over the few exciting and complicated years in which Bontempelli directed *"900"*.

In the editorial that opened the second of those years, Bontempelli called the ideological and practical challenges encountered by the journal "Ariostean endeavours."[117] Ariosto offered Bontempelli a perfect model for criticizing his detractors' proudly provincial propositions. What Bontempelli was fighting was the idea (championed by Strapaese journals such as *Il Selvaggio* and *L'Italiano*) that art had to be be "adherent" to fascist nationalism and to the immediate reality of recent fascist history. According to Bontempelli's enemies, literature had to offer a direct, literal expression of the fundamental values of fascism, and of its material achievements. Here is what one of these fascist intellectuals, Mino Maccari, proposed in 1927:

> [...] a decisive repulsion of all the forms of civilization that do not conform to our own – or that, being indigestible, could spoil the classical qualities of Italians; then: a protection of the universal sense of the Country, which is, to put it clearly, the natural and immanent relationship between an individual and his land; lastly, the celebration of our own characteristics, in every aspect and activity of life, and specifically: our Catholic roots, religious sense of the world, fundamental simplicity and sobriety, adherence to reality, control of fantasy, balance between matter and spirit.[118]

Bontempelli, on the contrary, believed that modern artists (and in particular writers) should be "professionals, like the painters of the Renaissance."[119] As he explained in 1927 in *"900"*, writers have always needed to continuously negotiate the expectations of commissioning patrons and their personal vision. Already in 1924, in the book *La Donna del Nadir* (an essayistic prelude to the ideas of *L'avventura novecentista*), Bontempelli had written that "Art and Philosophy can admire [...] political power, but must make it realize that they cannot be subdued to any power of a practical and organized nature."[120] Later, in a 1936 page of *L'avventura novecentista*, he repeated this concept by modelling himself after Ariosto, the compromising "intellectual Sancho Panza" of his 1916 essay on the *Satires*. He updated his previous positions to address the reality of late fascism, and explained that the regime could not turn art into political propaganda without enslaving it.

> A wise regime (if it wants to take an interest in art) must know how to distinguish between help and protection. Help can be discreet, loving, brotherly (yet, always dangerous); protection is, in any case, heavy and awkward, and puts the protected subject in a condition of servitude. The most brilliant example is the way in which Cardinal Ippolito protected Ludovico Ariosto, and made him wait up for him, late in the night while full of sleep, so that the poet could take off his shoes when he got back home.[121]

Rather than opposing fascism itself, Bontempelli opposed the idea that, under fascism, fiction had to directly represent fascist Italy, its values and reality. At the same time, he did not want art to be entirely divorced from representation. He did not want it to become an obscure, solitary enigma, an exercise of intimate moral purity and resistance. From his point of view, that was happening to the coeval a-fascist poetry of Montale and the Hermeticists, and with the intransitive painting of bottles and landscapes that Giorgio Morandi was pursuing beyond his Metaphysical phase. Against the fascist aesthetics invoked by the writers of Strapaese, and against what he called "impoverished interiorism"[122] and "ultra-subjective lyricism,"[123] Bontempelli proposed the "cure of irony" of Magical Realism. He invoked "imagination, fantasy: but nothing like the fabulism of fairies: no *Arabian Nights*. More than for fairy-tales, we are thirsty for adventures."[124] The example of Ariosto became useful to explain how such fantasy could be, in fact, more authentically fascist than any overtly political fiction.

> Ariosto did not intend to do anything but to create a world of amusement and consolation: he couldn't even dream of the mechanics of criticism through which today his poem appears to be (if we believe in the historical theory of art) a representation of the spirit and even of the political history of his century. [...] Just to give an example and speak clearly: our contemporaries believe that a novel that speaks about fascist Italy is, *ipso*

> *facto*, more fascist (which means better at representing our time, O Italy) than a novel that only tells, for instance, of love and journeys through the sea. However, a hundred years from now a novel of pure fantasy could appear more adherent to the fascist spirit than one that describes the March on Rome.[125]

Bontempelli wrote these lines in 1929. He was clearly elaborating on ideas that Ariosto's *Satires* and the *Orlando Furioso* had already suggested to him before fascism. Later, in a 1934 article that I have referenced before, he articulated the same position by calling Ariosto "inaderentissimo" (the most unorthodox, non-adherent).[126] Then, in 1935, responding to Pirandello's idea that "one can either live life or write about it," he reminded his readers that "Ariosto's biography is a far cry from resembling a chivalric poem." He eventually included this response in a section of *L'avventura novecentista* titled "Adherence."

The concept of fascist adherence was Bontempelli's main polemical target, both in political and aesthetic terms. In another piece of the section "Adherence," originally written in 1936, he insisted on the fact that Ariosto's poetry was, at the same time, animated by "the most free of fantasies" and "continuously disrupted by references, divagations, exhortations, and frustrations linked to the political life of his time." He added that "even when he accompanied Astolfo to the moon, [Ariosto] did not miss a chance to drop a cutting remark about the supposed donation of Constantine."[127]

In sum, after decades of subtle revivals of Ariosto's ideas, techniques, and motifs, in the late 1920s and 1930s Bontempelli openly adopted Ariosto as a precursor of both literary modernism and modern literary politics. Let me show what this meant, specifically, for the development of Magical Realism.

Neither Tradition nor Avant-Garde

A major concern of *L'avventura novecentista* was the positioning of Magical Realism in the apparent dichotomy between classicism and avant-garde that polarized fascist Italian aesthetics. From Bontempelli's point of view, the tradition that Strapaese intellectuals claimed to protect was an arbitrary construct. The enthusiasm for technology and speed of the second wave of Futurism, on the other hand, was superficial and merely thematic. In contrast with such short-sighted interpretations of both sides of the debate, Bontempelli proposed a different approach to the revival of the past and the imagination of the future. He wanted to secure a patent of classicist untimeliness for his own work and, at the same time, to exalt its novelty and modernity. To achieve such goals, he repeatedly compared what he was doing with what Ariosto did at the threshold of modernity. Eventually, his rhetorical strategy was to make Ariosto join the ranks of his movement, the Novecentismo, in order to make Magical Realism evade chronology and directly link the sixteenth and the twentieth centuries. After all, already in his 1907 ode to Ariosto, he had made these two ages look at each other in a mirror.

In *L'avventura novecentista*, Bontempelli cited Ariosto as the quintessential example of creative freedom in service of political power. He mentioned his work as the emblem of a fictional fantasy able to represent historical reality. And, through his example, he theorized a form of literary innovation in direct dialogue with the classics. In addition to this, Bontempelli turned Ariosto's achievements into argumentative weapons (and shields) to reframe entirely the problem of origins and originality, responsibility and escapism, that characterized his polemic against other movements, inside and outside fascism. Through Ariosto, he wanted to demonstrate that what most artists and writers considered new and avant-garde was really classical and traditional, and vice versa.

An example of false novelty to be reconceived that recurs in *L'avventura novecentista* is that of aviation. In the 1920s, the second wave of Futurism was developing Aeropainting, a visual celebration of the ultimate technological expression of speed: flying airplanes. Since Mussolini's military propaganda was investing a lot in the spectacularization of Italian aviation, Aeropainting responded very well to the "adherence" demanded by Strapaese intellectuals, both in terms of realism and political opportunity. The exaggerated myth of Italy's air forces, controlled by the young and popular minister of the air, Italo Balbo, could engulf Marinetti's original techno-tropes, including Gazourmah, the aero-cyborg of his colonialist African novel *Mafarka le Futuriste.* At the same time, it could appropriate D'Annunzio's self-fashioning as a poet-pilot hero in the First War War.[128] Some Aeropainters, like Alfredo Ambrosi, directly tapped into this political myth, superimposing aerial visions of the new Italy with symbols of fascist imperialism. Others, like Tullio Crali, focused on a more literal depiction of aviation as modern heroism, indulging in elements of illustrative realism from the estranging perspective of the flight. Artists like Benedetta Cappa, faithful to the visual syntax of simultaneity of early Futurism, envisioned quasi-abstract analytical syntheses of flight itself as a multi-sensory event and technological achievement. For Bontempelli, these attempts at capturing the factual reality of a quintessentially modern experience were invariably regressive.

According to Bontempelli, Ariosto shows that a truly modern poet needs to imagine things that cannot yet be experienced at all. The best influence of science and technology on art, according to Bontempelli, is indirect and spiritual, not thematic. In three different pieces on this topic, originally published in 1931, 1932, and 1934, he insisted on the fact that "flying [...] is poetic only when it is imagined," before it can be actually experienced. Therefore, "the great poetry of aviation was made by the inventor of the myth of Icarus and by Ariosto, with the flights of the Hippogriff."[129] All three of Bontempelli's articles point to Ariosto's imagination to argue that the inventions of poetry always precede those of science. "Aeropoetry," in sum, "started with Icarus and continued with Ruggiero, four centuries before the invention of airplanes."[130] "Nobody," stated Bontempelli, "described flying, and the wonder of seeing someone flying, better than Ariosto, where he talks about the Hippogriff."[131]

By celebrating Ariosto's legacy, Bontempelli also deconstructed the concept of national tradition that anti-Futurist classicists were cultivating under Mussolini's autarchic and neo-Roman cultural agenda. In a list of suggestions to aspiring writers, originally published in 1927, he reminded his younger readers that "tradition is a path that takes many detours." "Ariosto," for instance, "was a great detour from Dante's tradition."[132] In a 1933 open letter to Ugo Ojetti, Bontempelli defended his sympathy towards the new architectural style of Rationalism by explaining that a revival of the past should not consist of imitative repetitions of the forms and techniques used in antiquity.

> [...] you say that we, the fanatics of new architecture, are *disgusted* to be of the same race as Alberti, or Bramante, or Palladio [...] that we want to *leave to the archaeologists* the Pantheon or Titus' Arch. [...] It would be like saying that, because I would find it ridiculous for someone to write sonnets or poems in tercets or octaves today, then I was *disgusted* to feel of the same race as Dante, Petrarch, and Ariosto, and that I *left to the literati* the *Commedia*, the *Canzoniere* and the *Orlando Furioso*.[133]

In *L'avventura novecentista*, Bontempelli's vision of Italy's aesthetic history emerges as a sequence of literary revolutions followed and preceded by irrelevant periods of unoriginal imitation. In a long 1934 explanation of this concept, he argued that Dante started Italian literature exactly because he burnt any direct bridge with classical tradition. His innovation was to write in vernacular rather than in Latin, as all his models had. Those who continued in his steps without adding anything new were forgotten by history.

Another example of revolutionaries are Boiardo and Ariosto, and another example of idiots are the post-Ariosteans, who believed the chivalric poem to be the new tradition to follow. They followed it, and ended up in a mass grave along with the Danteans and the Petrarchans.[134]

In order to follow Ariosto's lessons of modernity without joining the ranks of the "post-Ariosteans," Bontempelli treated him as his contemporary. The de Chirico brothers established a similar relationship with the "poet in marble," who was not a precursor of Metaphysical art but a Great Metaphysician, jumping off his pedestal to join their company. In the next chapter, I will discuss how a fascist revival of Ariosto, based on a distorted form of the philosophy of history proposed by Giovanni Gentile, presentified Ariosto's past in Ferrara through a number of cultural initiatives. The fascist festival for Ariosto was philosophically at odds with the way in which Metaphysical art and Magical Realism, through the de Chiricos and Bontempelli, dialogued with Ariosto. When he took part in those initiatives, attached to the celebration of the fourth centennial anniversary of Ariosto's death, Bontempelli had a chance to reflect systematically on his relationship with the *Orlando Furioso*, and clarified once and for all the many interconnected questions explored so far.

In the year of Ariosto's centenary, Bontempelli gave several lectures on the *Furioso*. None of them were collected in any of his books, but two were published right after he gave them. The first was part of a series of lectures organized by an Ariostean committee in Ferrara between 1928 and 1933. It appeared in the proceedings with the title "Ariosto as a Geographer" ("L'Ariosto geografo"). The second was published in the Argentinian-Italian newspaper *Il Mattino d'Italia*. Bontempelli had given it at the "Circolo Italiano" in Buenos Aires, at the end of a Latin American tour in which he was promoting Italy's Magical Realism in Argentina, Brazil, Chile, and Peru.[135]

In "Ariosto as a Geographer," Bontempelli gave a documented interpretation of Ariosto's geographical imagination. As has been recently noticed by Monica Farnetti[136] – and as the author himself admitted[137] – the lecture was largely based on the erudite work that Michele Vernero conducted on the same theme at the beginning of the twentieth century, starting a modern tradition of studies on Ariosto and geography that is still very active today.[138] However, I would argue that the main inspiration of Bontempelli's concern for the harmonization of fantasy and available geographical data in the *Furioso* was the scholarship of his university advisor, Arturo Graf, one of the four addressees of his 1907 odes. As a critic, Graf had worked extensively on the perceived reality of places that do not exist, like the Earthly Paradise, the land of Cockaigne, or Prester John's empire. He wrote on how the myth of such places was formed in the pre-modern European imagination. For Graf, geographical legends were not naive surrogates for unavailable geographical facts. He considered them to be syntheses of a different experience of the same reality that was later described by colonial cartographies and reports.[139]

Drawing on Graf's lesson, Bontempelli's lecture was not interested in verifying Ariosto's geographical beliefs on twentieth-century charts. On the contrary, Bontempelli asked how Ariosto could "believe in the island of Alcina as much as he believed in city of Ferrara."[140] He also reflected on why Ariosto based the routes of the Hippogriff's flight on the most updated maps and planispheres of his time, when those journeys were so obviously invented and impossible in the first place. Such questions allowed Bontempelli to explain once again his own poetics through Ariosto, who offered a synthesis of reality and fantasy, tradition and modernity:

> This is one of the most characteristic features of our poet; his fabulous imagination never allows itself to be unlimited and arbitrary like, for instance, that of the *Arabian Nights.* [...] Once he creates a fantastical element – the Hippogriff, or [Atlante's] shield, or [Angelica's] ring, etc. – he places this supernatural element in the middle of a world that remains natural, with all its laws: imagination only enriches nature, it does not stretch it, nor does it free or liberate it. One travels on a flying horse, but dismounts it to sleep at a good hotel. This sentiment, which is eminently Ariostean, is also eminently Western and profoundly Italian; this is the trend that reconciles and absorbs naturalism and fable: in this sense our art is quintessentially classical in the healthiest way.
>
> These are obvious things, and everyone accepts them to interpret the charms of a great poet who is no longer under our critical judgment. God forbid that we try to point to these same things as teachings of our future literature in a truly Italian sense! If we do so, they accuse us of sacrilege; we are the sacrilegious violators of two fetishes: reality and tradition. But reality is misunderstood, because they call "reality" the strict documentation of truth (either a photograph of facts and costume, or an analysis of the intimate movements of the soul). And tradition is misunderstood, because they call "tradition" the latest or penultimate trends, and they don't know that tradition must always drink from the source of its primordial fountainheads. One of these fountainheads is the Ariostean spirit.

> Indeed, when years ago I pointed at an artistic paradigm and I called it "Magical Realism," I made sure to cite Ariosto, and the whole literary "Novecentismo" is nothing but this: to rise up to the clouds on the back of the Hippogriff and then come down at night to eat and sleep at a decent inn, as our wise Ruggiero does.[141]

Three years later, in Buenos Aires, Bontempelli returned to the same points even more clearly. He started his lecture by saying that Ariosto was a poet of the twentieth century, and, therefore, there was no need to "commemorate" him. He called him "ours," and specified that, while it is generally true that all great poets belong to all the ages, Ariosto and the twentieth century are uniquely related. He repeated many arguments that he exploited in *L'avventura novecentista.* He insisted on the fact that Ariosto both followed and disrupted tradition: "he was such a revolutionary that he didn't even fear [...] to appear as an imitator [of Boiardo]."[142] He praised Ariosto's ability to "represent his times in a work of art exactly when he thought he was evading them."[143] In a passage that sounds like an indirect self-defence, he debunked the selfish individualism that critics traditionally attributed to Ariosto's fantasy: the idea that, "lost in his dreams, he sceptically and coldly witnessed the political ruin of Italy." Pointing to various passages in the *Furioso,* he showed that Ariosto was in fact hiding his political criticisms and denunciations in plain sight, harmonizing them in the perfect unity of his multifaceted poem. In the last section of the lecture he directly argued that Ariosto was a "poeta novecentista" and a representative of Magical Realism, categories that his listeners had learned to appreciate during his previous talks in Buenos Aires:

> This is the special modernity, the adherence to our time more than to any past, of the *Orlando Furioso.* Don't worry, I am not going to talk to you again about Novecentismo and Magical Realism: I have already sowed those theories enough in this city throughout the past weeks [...] but, since most of you remember them, [...] let me today present Ariosto to you as one of the most Novecentista poets that one can imagine.
>
> Our time [...] feels the need of breath, laughter, naturalness, freedom. We will try to give this new art of lighter and more profound breath to the young generation of the century. In the meanwhile, we offer to you the *Orlando Furioso.*[144]

It should be noted that the disquieting conclusion of Bontempelli's lecture was based on a parallel between Ariosto and Mussolini as magicians. The reason why Ariosto was able to create the most adventurous world with the sole force of his imagination, while being a sedentary stay-at-home, is that poetic reality must be first materialized in the mind in order to be experienced. Mussolini's political reality, according to Bontempelli, was born in the same way, through an effort of will, creative fantasy, and faith. In several passages of *L'avventura novecentista,* Bontempelli compared Mussolini's regime with that of the dukes whom Ariosto considered ungrateful and oppressive. In the Buenos Aires lecture of 1933, Mussolini became an Ariostean magician and, indeed, a modern political reflection of Ariosto himself.

Ariostean Fanfiction

Let me conclude this chapter with an analysis of the spinoff of the *Furioso* from which I started. That short story, *The Hippogriff's Wings,* represents Bontempelli's most complete and elegant tribute to Ariosto (figure 2.10). He wrote it in Venice, violating the creative silence that the regime had imposed upon him. It was published by the periodical *Il Tempo* as one of three instalments that formed Bontempelli's last book before the end of the war: *Giro del sole.* The other two episodes, published between 1939 and 1940,[145] consisted of renarrations of the myth of Zeus and Europa[146] and of Columbus' voyage. All three stories centred on the idea of a foundational European journey to the West. Europa swam, from Lebanon to Crete, on the back of the bull, Columbus navigated from Portugal to the American continent on the caravels, and Ruggiero flew from the Pyrenees to Japan on the wings of the Hippogriff. In Bontempelli's rewritings of their stories, these three travellers don't know where they are going. They are moved by imagination, and simply follow the route of the sun. The overall title of the book, which translates as "Around the Sun" or "Circle of the Sun," was evidently inspired by the last line of one of the octaves that, in the *Furioso,* summarize Ruggiero's world tour ("Now he decides his journey back again / He'll not to Aeolus's realm confine, / But of the global course he has begun / He will complete the circle like the sun," X, 70). The circle of the sun is also a central element of the plot of *The Wings of the Hippogriff.*

Unlike the other two stories, Ruggiero's adventure does not simply elaborate on an existing plot. Bontempelli invented an entire episode that is not narrated at all in the *Furioso.* He imagined an unexpected stop in Ruggiero's flight, a detour that could have simply been omitted by Ariosto. Bontempelli treated the universe of the *Furioso* as a

LE ALI DELL'IPPOGRIFO

Racconto di Massimo Bontempelli

(Tavole di Giorgio De Chirico)

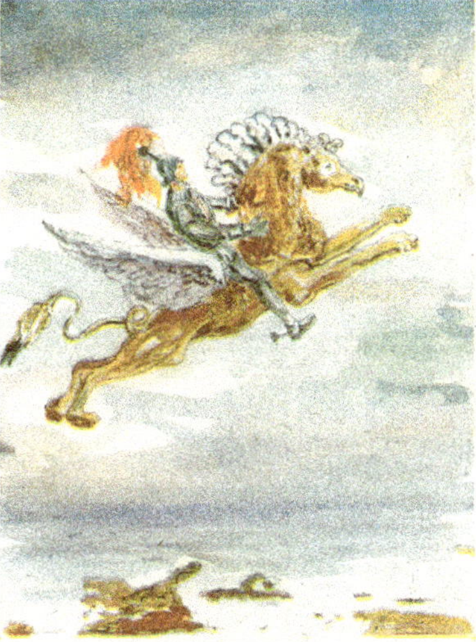

Il primo a traversarlo fu l'Ippogrifo quando portò Ruggero

1.

L'Oceano Pacifico ha un colore grigio di perla con lunghe venature rosee. Il primo a traversarlo fu l'Ippogrifo a volo quando portò Ruggero dai Pirenei a un'isola dell'Asia ove Alcina lo aspettava, ma lui non ne sapeva niente. Non gli avevano ancora dato la briglia per guidare l'Ippogrifo, e doveva lasciarsi portare. Da buon viaggiatore Ruggero non avrebbe avuto nessuna fretta d'arrivare nemmeno se avesse saputo dove andava; durante il viaggio guardava giù da una parte e dall'altra. Ma per parecchio tempo non scòrse che ogni tanto un isolotto roccioso con intorno i soliti gabbiani, o qualche zampillo di balena nel mare che non finiva mai.

Quando passarono sopra l'America non la potè scorgere perchè poco prima d'arrivare in vista della costa un ammasso di nuvole aveva costretto l'Ippogrifo a salire molto in alto; per qualche tempo navigò sopra a quella distesa che nascondeva la terra e pareva un altro mare un po' mosso. Ma alzando lo sguardo, c'era una luce straordinariamente vivida in tutta l'aria. Il cielo non era più azzurro ma colore dell'oro, quasi una cupola che in giro agli orizzonti s'appoggiava sulla pianura delle nuvole. Ruggero provò a dire all'Ippogrifo: — Un poco più adagio, ti prego — tanto gli piaceva guardare il polverio d'oro che pioveva dal cielo nell'aria. Si mise a ridere sentendo la propria voce in mezzo allo spazio. Non aveva mai parlato all'Ippogrifo e non pensava che lui capisse. Ma dicendo quelle parole gli aveva appoggiato e premuto un poco le due mani una di qua una di là sul collo: l'Ippogrifo intese certo non le parole ma il tocco, e rallentò l'andare. Ruggero non si stancava di guardare intorno, si domandò come poteva diventare quel cielo la notte quando vengono le stelle.

Tutto era silenzio. Ruggero udiva il rombo dolce delle ali dell'Ippogrifo, ma quel suono gli pareva facesse parte dell'essere suo, non rompeva il silenzio limpido dell'universo. Estatico non avvertiva trascorrere il tempo. Poi la luce cominciò a barcollare, egli allora sentì che l'Ippogrifo aveva ripreso velocità, ridiscendevano. Guardò in giù, c'era di nuovo oceano. Era il Pacifico colore di perla. Anche il cielo era tornato azzurro: solo d'un azzurro un poco più pallido dell'altro, perchè mare e cielo si mettono sempre d'accordo su questo.

L'Ippogrifo volava ora molto basso, Ruggero vedeva giocare la luce sulla pelle del mare, le vene rosate dell'acqua vanire. Non c'erano più balene nè rocce nè gabbiani. L'aria cominciò a farsi bruna: così venne rapidamente la notte, ma Ruggero non vide neppure una stella perchè s'addormentò subito sul collo dell'Ippogrifo.

Quando si svegliò la luce era poca e il silenzio s'era fatto triste in quel grigio stentato del mondo; Ruggero si sfregava gli occhi, stirava le braccia, s'accomodò sulla sella, mentre l'Ippogrifo continuava a volare diritto; a ognuno di quegli atti l'aria era più chiara. Il chiarore saliva dal mare, scendeva dal cielo, che erano bianchi come il latte.

Ruggero aveva ancora un po' sonno. Ma in mezzo al pallore diffuso, tutt'a un tratto scorse verso l'orizzonte senza alcun dubbio una terra. Il sonno subito gli scomparve, mentre la terra a ogni minuto si faceva più nitida. Era una costa lunga, e di qua e di là sfuggiva, forse un'isola dunque, questa volto non è uno scoglio, no, una vera isola grande, con alberi altissimi neri. Era felice. Gli pareva che anche il rumore delle ali fosse più allegro. Quando non furono più tanto lontani e l'isola si vedeva bene, l'Ippogrifo s'alzò alquanto, e là subito riprese il cammino orizzontale. Pareva un poco più lento; forse ricorda l'invito di ieri e la curiosità di Ruggero: è possibile che sia tanto intelligente? Erano quasi all'isola e Ruggero s'accorse che ancora correvano troppo per vederla bene. Fu preso d'impazienza. Ma non osava premere sul collo dell'Ippogrifo per farlo andar piano, come ha fatto ieri, ora che lo credeva intelligente. Ed è quasi certo che lui sta per scendere là; dev'essere quella la meta. Ora vedeva intera la forma dell'isola, che era grande, quasi tonda, con un largo orlo piano tutt'intorno, poi un circolo di piante basse tra folti cespugli che si movevano all'aria del mattino; e poco più in dentro un altro anello, di rocce alte e strette: quelle che al primo vedere gli erano parse alberi neri.

Da quando aveva lasciato la costa d'Europa, Ruggero non aveva più visto terra. Non sapeva calcolare il tempo. Forse era vicino ma gli pareva d'un giorno lontanissimo il minuto che dalla groppa dell'Ippogrifo volgendosi indietro vide sminuire e farsi un punto e in un tremolio scomparire l'ultimo segno. Quando v'era passato sopra c'era tanta gente a guardare. Ora gli pareva riconoscere che anche qui ci fosse sul lido gente adunata ma sulle prime non li aveva avvertiti perchè stava fissato a distinguere gli alberi dalle rocce.

L'Ippogrifo aveva trascorso il mezzo dell'isola. Ruggero temè forte che non volesse scendere, ma quello moderò molto la corsa e cominciò ad abbassarsi in una spirale ampia. E' intelligente davvero. Trepidando Ruggero guardava giù. Le forme delle piante, dei roccioni, del suolo, ingrandivano e a quel roteare si scomponevano alla sua vista in mescolanze buffe, l'aria più chiara vi generava sbandati sbattimenti d'ombre e di luce. Ruggero s'accorse che l'interno dell'isola era fatto di tante alture con praterie piane tra l'una e l'altra, anche i pendii erano invasi di verde fino alle cime. Qualche collina finiva tronca come un altipiano. Ruggero potè vedere nettamente queste cose perchè gli ultimi due giri l'Ippogrifo li fece in volo perfettamente orizzontale e lentissimo. Ruggero si domandava se sarebbero scesi in uno dei prati a valle, o in alto a una collina tronca. Ma con suo grande stupore l'Ippogrifo dopo quelle due ruote lente riprese la direzione di prima lasciandosi velocemente l'isola dietro le spalle.

La sorpresa fu tanta, che avevano corso un buon tratto avanti che Ruggero potesse fare un gesto o mettere una voce. Di colpo per il gran dispetto si mise a gridare: — Fèrmati maledetto animale — e insieme lo prese, ma non tanto forte, per il collo come per trattenerlo. L'Ippogrifo non si scosse ma accelerò l'andare e scoteva la testa come fosse un suo modo di ridere. Subito Ruggero si pentì e si disperava, gli carezzava le penne del collo, cercava di fargli compassione: — Scendiamo un momento nell'isola, ti prego, ho tanta fame — e con le mani tentava di volgergli dolcemente la testa, per fargli capire che non è comando ma preghiera. L'Ippogrifo alla fine cedette e con una elegante curva si rigirò verso l'isola. Ruggero vide l'altro orizzonte fatto colore di rosa. Già erano di nuovo sopra l'isola, ancora abbastanza alti per abbracciarla con lo sguardo in tutto il suo giro. Questa volta Ruggero distinse bene che sulla costa di levante c'erano molte persone. Volteggiando e di nuovo abbassandosi l'Ippogrifo si condusse là sopra; alcuni dal lido voltarono un momento il capo all'insù ma con gran maraviglia di Ruggero non mostrarono ammirazione e ognuno riprese a discorrere o camminare come prima. Erano vestiti di corte tuniche. Una sola di quelle persone s'allontanò dalle altre per correre a guardare l'Ippogrifo, anzi strappata una fronda delle piante basse la agitava verso lui in segno certamente di saluto. Ruggero si sporse con gran scotimento di braccia per ringraziare, ma già era fuori della vista della spiaggia; l'Ippogrifo stava calando in un bel prato dietro uno dei roccioni che prima a Ruggero erano sembrati alberi.

Ruggero smontò, palpò il collo dell'animale dicendogli — grazie. — Quello s'allontanò un poco e passeggiava per il prato fiorito come volesse rimettere in esercizio i muscoli delle gambe. L'erba era folta, i colori dei fiori pareva che cantassero.

Ruggero guardò in alto al roccione. Gli girò intorno, e fu somma la sua maraviglia quando s'accorse che era una statua. Scolpita nella pietra nera, rappresentava una lunga forma d'uomo, in piedi dritto, con in cima una faccia ovale che guardava all'orizzonte. Senza nessun rispetto Ruggero s'arrampicò su per la statua, alta come un cipresso, e andò a sederglisi sopra la testa.

Di là vedeva molto bene sotto sè la cortina dei cespugli e poi il lido con la gente. Scoprì pure che poco oltre, alla destra, c'era in mare una nave grande; non la aveva distinta la prima volta perchè stava attraccata stretta a una rupe in forma d'alta muraglia che poco sporgeva dal confine della terra. Della gente sul lido non si distinguevano sulle prime gli uomini dalle donne perchè tutti portavano una uguale tunica azzurra che dal collo arrivava al ginocchio, nudi i piedi e le gambe e le braccia. Tutti erano a capo scoperto, con chiome lunghe fino alle spalle. Ora s'erano messi in fila lungo la spiaggia, con i piedi appena sfiorati dall'orlo del mare, e in silenzio guardavano verso oriente. Là il colore di rosa s'era infiammato. Tutti vi stavano intenti, certo aspettavano il sole, di secondo in secondo i loro corpi s'inclinavano un poco più verso il mare, le braccia tese. A un tratto il filo dell'orizzonte in un punto si ruppe e ne scattò un raggio diritto che traversato lo spazio venne a ferire nel lido mentre quelli si piegavano e tuffavano nel mare le braccia, insieme levando un canto a note lunghe. Così stettero forse un minuto con le braccia nell'acqua: dietro quel raggio era sorto subito un piccolo fuoco, e saliva in arco, accese tutta l'aria. La gente continuando a cantare lentamente si rialzava, quando tutti furono ritti cessava il canto, la gente si sciolse; scoteva le brac-

Figure 2.10. Giorgio de Chirico, … *Il primo a traversarlo fu l'Ippogrifo quando portò Ruggero*, 1941, photoreproduction of watercolour on paper, from Massimo Bontempelli, "Le ali dell'ippogrifo," in *Tempo*, March 20, 1941. Biblioteca Nazionale Centrale di Roma (BNCR). No reproduction is permitted without authorization from the BNCR. © 2022 Artists Rights Society (ARS), New York/ SIAE, Rome.

permeable canon of events in which, if one respects its internal coherence, additional elements can be interpolated at any time. This narratological mechanism was actually the way in which the authorless expanded universe of chivalric fiction was built in the first place, with new poets continuing previous stories or, like Bontempelli, exploring an existing storyline that left room for additional details. Ariosto's success, along with the crystallization of a canon of authored books printed by publishers, eventually suffocated this fractal expansion. The sixteenth century effectively ended the proliferation of chivalric stories that the age of oral transmission and manuscripts had allowed and encouraged. Bontempelli, who had stated that "the supreme aspiration of all artists should be to become anonymous,"[147] restored this form of derivative creativity in the Machine Age. In doing so, he confirmed the idea that Ariosto was his contemporary.

As I mentioned, the "circle of the sun" is at the centre of the story's plot. On his way to Alcina's island (where, in the *Furioso,* he would arrive in Canto VI), Ruggiero lands on a Pacific island inhabited by a Utopian society. This is an involuntary stop: Ruggiero, as Bontempelli knew, would learn how to control the Hippogriff only later in the plot of the *Furioso.* The islanders that he accidentally finds gather every morning on the eastern shore, where they salute the rising sun with their song. Then, they spend the day on a boat, sailing west around the island. While constantly moving west, they replenish their supplies and get everything they need, completing their tasks and enjoying games and conversations. When they reach the western shore at sunset, they land to sing again and accompany the sun into the sea. They also immerse themselves in the water, to imitate the sun. Then, they sleep on the boat, which brings them back to the eastern shore. They arrive there on the following morning, and the cycle restarts. Everything, on the island, always happens the same way. However, the beautiful and young islanders, who stick to the day-long ritual without question, have forgotten why.

At the beginning of the narration, Bontempelli chronicles Ruggiero's arrival on the island. The knight meets an islander named Argentina (figure 2.11). In order to spend the day with Ruggiero, Argentina misses the boat. This disruption in the repetition of the islanders' ritual subverts the sterile serenity of the mysterious land. The ritual has always been occurring identically in living memory; no one has ever experienced the absence of an islander from the boat. The anomaly triggers a prodigy. Instead of setting into the sea, the sun calls the islanders into his light (figure 2.12), and only Argentina is left on the island. Alone on the shore when Ruggiero flies away, Argentina caresses her womb and smiles,

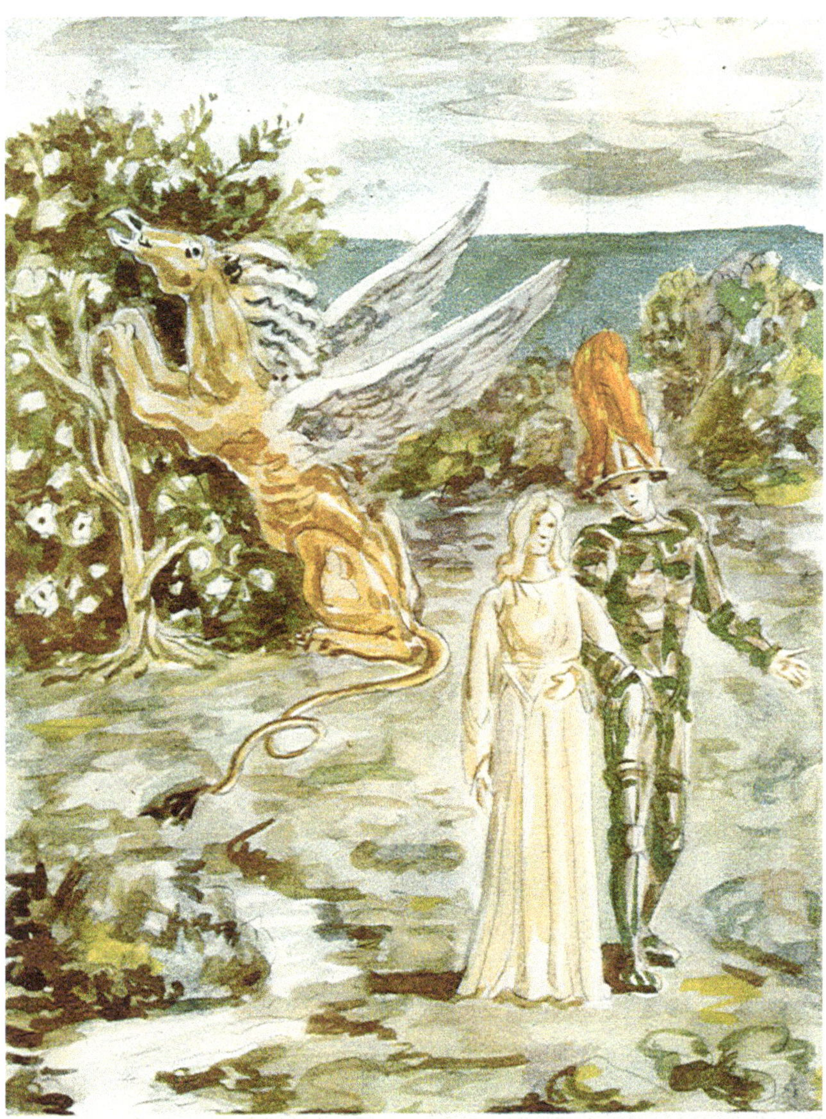

Figure 2.11. Giorgio de Chirico, … *la conduceva passo passo traverso il prato* …, 1941, photoreproduction of watercolour on paper, from Massimo Bontempelli, "Le ali dell'ippogrifo," in *Tempo*, March 20, 1941. Biblioteca Nazionale Centrale di Roma (BNCR). No reproduction is permitted without authorization from the BNCR. © 2022 Artists Rights Society (ARS), New York/SIAE, Rome.

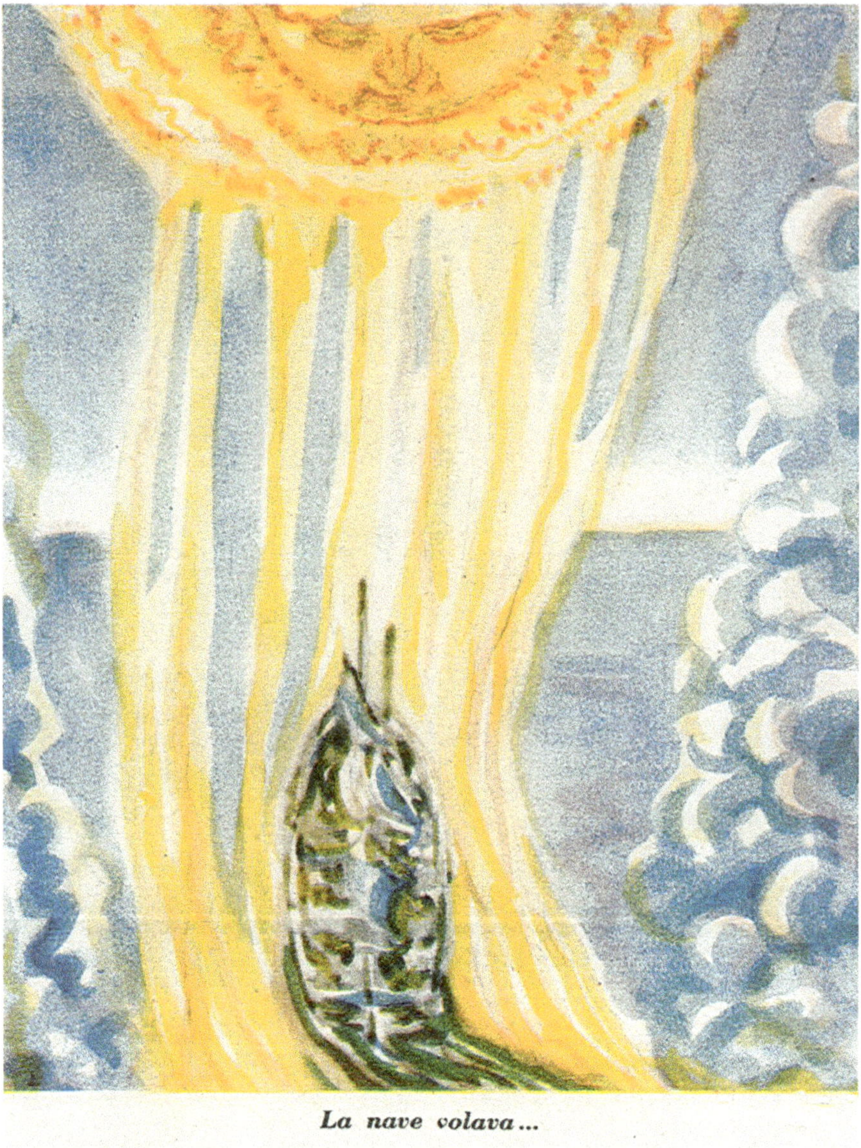

La nave volava ...

Figure 2.12. Giorgio de Chirico, *La nave volava ...*, 1941, photoreproduction of watercolour on paper, from Massimo Bontempelli, "Le ali dell'ippogrifo," in *Tempo*, March 20, 1941. Biblioteca Nazionale Centrale di Roma (BNCR). No reproduction is permitted without authorization from the BNCR.© 2022 Artists Rights Society (ARS), New York/SIAE, Rome.

clearly pregnant with the first new life of the island now that the cycle of blind adoration of the sun is broken.

While it might be too simplistic to read this story as an allegory of how fascist mysticism was progressively obnubilating Italian consciences, Bontempelli evidently played with the idea. The islanders, in the story, are surrounded by the vestiges of a great ancient civilization, like the titanic statue that surprises Ruggiero in de Chirico's illustration reproduced at the beginning of this chapter. However, they take these marvels for granted, and forget their origin. They wilfully live in autarchy, content in their way of life, but when they discuss why they stopped visiting other islands, or how else they could live, they are puzzled and awkward. The authority of the sun, who ends up devouring them in an ecstatic ascension, is absolute and unquestioned. They are completely unaware of the sterility and fragility of their automatic way of life, which so easily collapses when Argentina, the last person to be born on the island, does something different and mates with a foreigner. The other islanders cannot even remember how they used to make children until eighteen years before, when presumably their ritual (which they perceive as eternal) started. It may not be insignificant that eighteen years was also the chronological distance between the publication of *Giro del sole* and Bontempelli's adherence to fascism.

Bontempelli did not add any authorial comment to facilitate a political reading of the story. Unlike his earlier narrative experiments, *Giro del sole* flows without disruptions or divagations, like a collection of classical myths. The fantastic events in the stories, as a new seminal mythology, are presented as self-sufficient. What is certain is that Bontempelli presented the events with a masterful clarity, adopting the lessons of modernity offered by the *Furioso* with a new pathos. The depiction of the Hippogriff, for instance, is accurately chiselled. Reviving the magic of Ariosto's pre-aviation aerial imagination, Bontempelli made Ruggiero try things that would be impossible on a military airplane. In the story, while flying, Ruggiero speaks with his mount, and the strange sound of his own voice in mid-air makes him laugh. His biological aircraft produces natural sounds (the "sweet rumble of the wings")[148] and allows him to fall asleep during the trip. Argentina, seeing him from the island, believes that Ruggiero and the Hippogriff are one single flying creature.

De Chirico's calligraphic illustrations (figures 2.13, 2.14, and 2.15) mirror the elegant lightness of Bontempelli's storytelling, visually alluding to Fragonard's eighteenth-century drawings for the *Furioso.* De Chirico would later imitate the same sources in studies and sketches.[149] Both the story and the illustration, completed while de Chirico was playing with

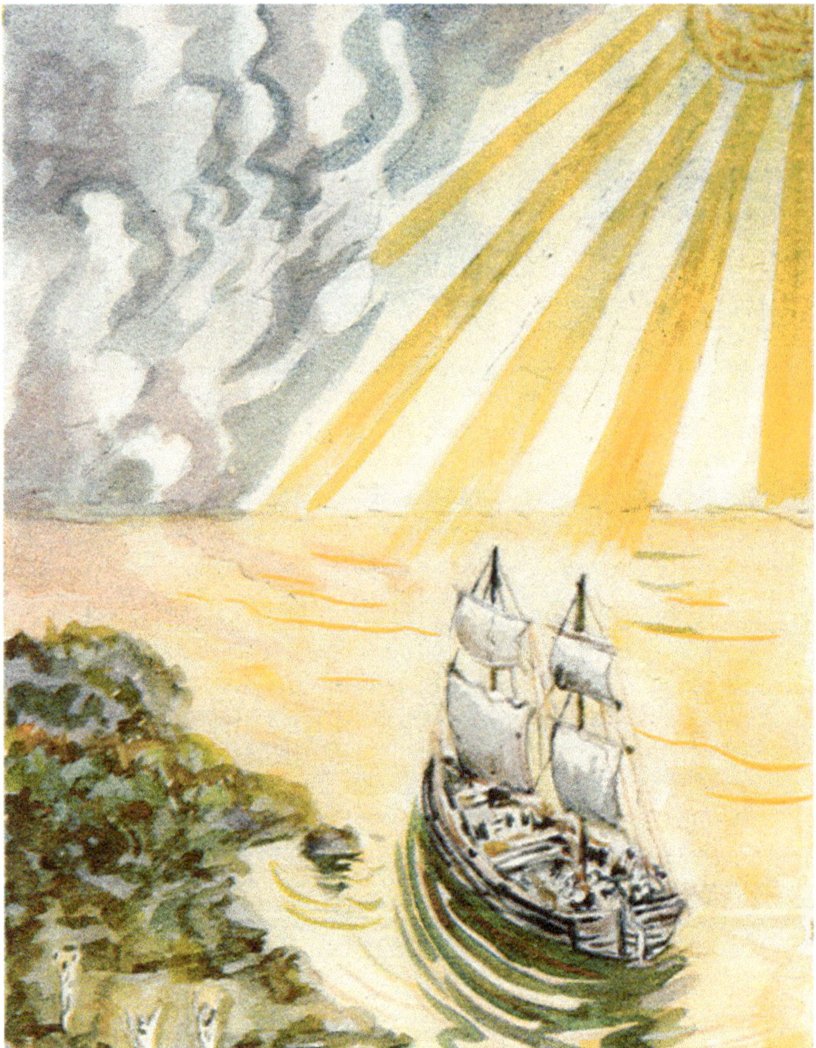

Intanto la nave andava...

Figure 2.13. Giorgio de Chirico, *Intanto la nave andava …*, 1941, photoreproduction of watercolour on paper, from Massimo Bontempelli, "Le ali dell'ippogrifo," in *Tempo,* March 20, 1941. Biblioteca Nazionale Centrale di Roma (BNCR). No reproduction is permitted without authorization from the BNCR.© 2022 Artists Rights Society (ARS), New York/SIAE, Rome.

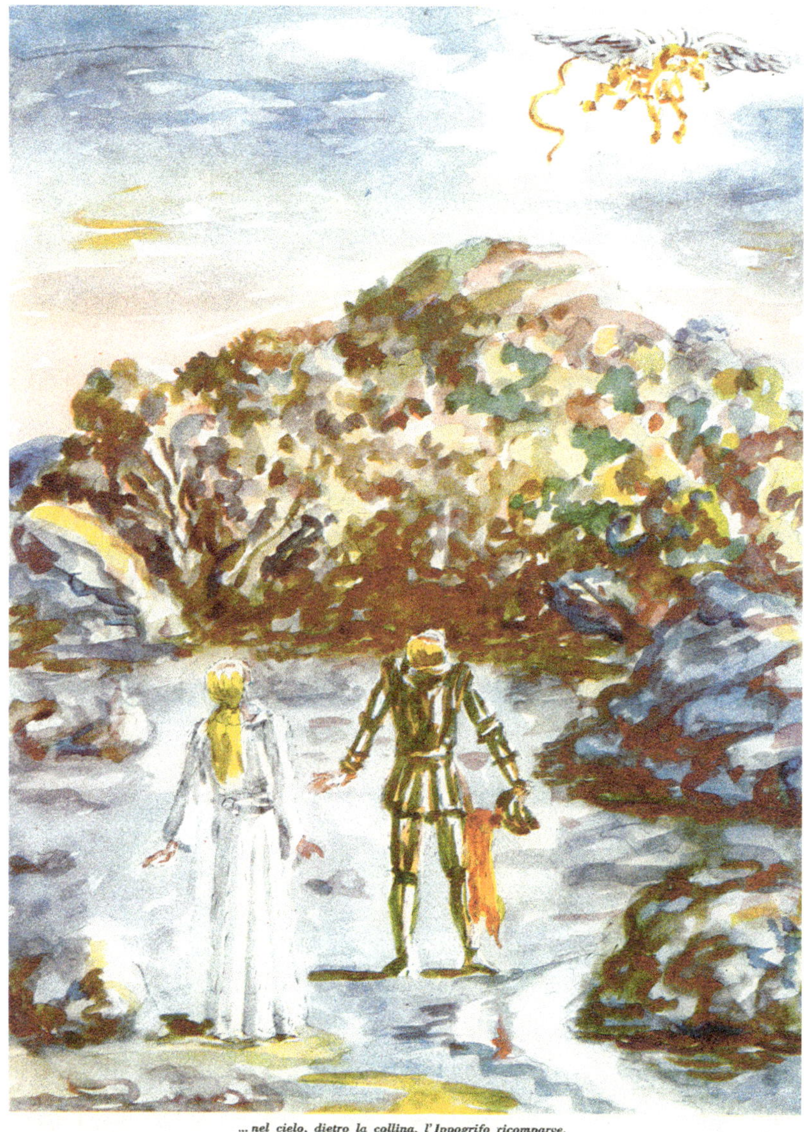

... nel cielo, dietro la collina, l'Ippogrifo ricomparve.

Figure 2.14. Giorgio de Chirico, ... *nel cielo, dietro la collina, l'Ippogrifo ricomparve*, 1941, photoreproduction of watercolour on paper, from Massimo Bontempelli, "Le ali dell'ippogrifo," in *Tempo*, March 20, 1941. Biblioteca Nazionale Centrale di Roma (BNCR). No reproduction is permitted without authorization from the BNCR. © 2022 Artists Rights Society (ARS), New York/SIAE, Rome.

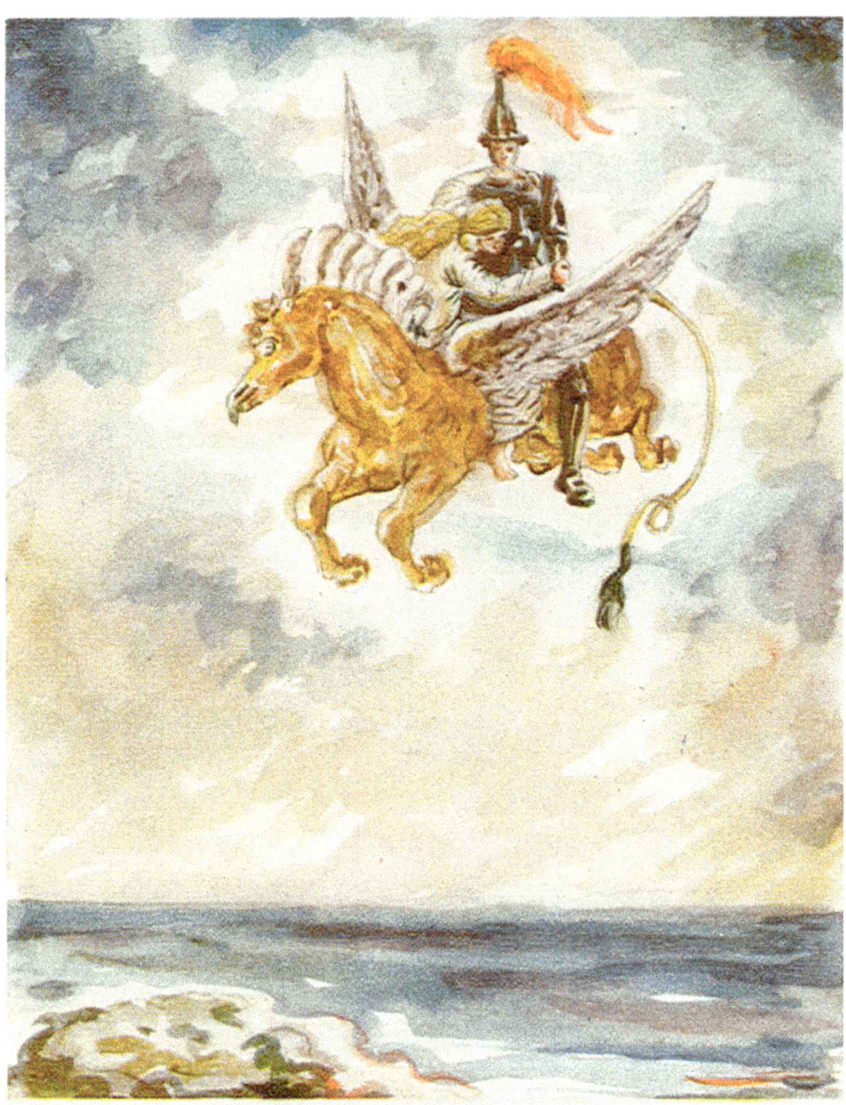

Figure 2.15. Giorgio de Chirico, ... *ma quasi in grembo a Ruggero,* 1941, photoreproduction of watercolour on paper, from Massimo Bontempelli, "Le ali dell'ippogrifo," in *Tempo,* March 20, 1941. Biblioteca Nazionale Centrale di Roma (BNCR). No reproduction is permitted without authorization from the BNCR.© 2022 Artists Rights Society (ARS), New York/SIAE, Rome.

the many echoes of the theme of Ruggiero and Angelica, are the latest, most obvious, and ultimately less significant symptoms of an Ariostean fever that affected visual and literary Metaphysics since their inception, defining their most important traits. It is worth pointing out that, just as in the scholarship about Metaphysical art, Ariosto's name is hardly mentioned in studies on Bontempelli.[150] Despite this fact, the story of uninterrupted and substantial trans-historical alliance reconstructed in this chapter leads to the conclusion that, without his continuous dialogue with Ariosto, Bontempelli would not have applied Magical Realism to literature.

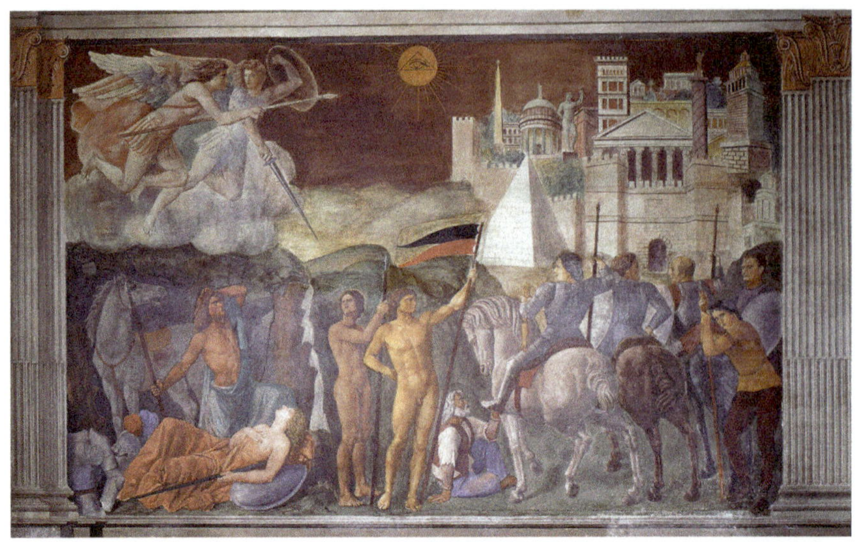

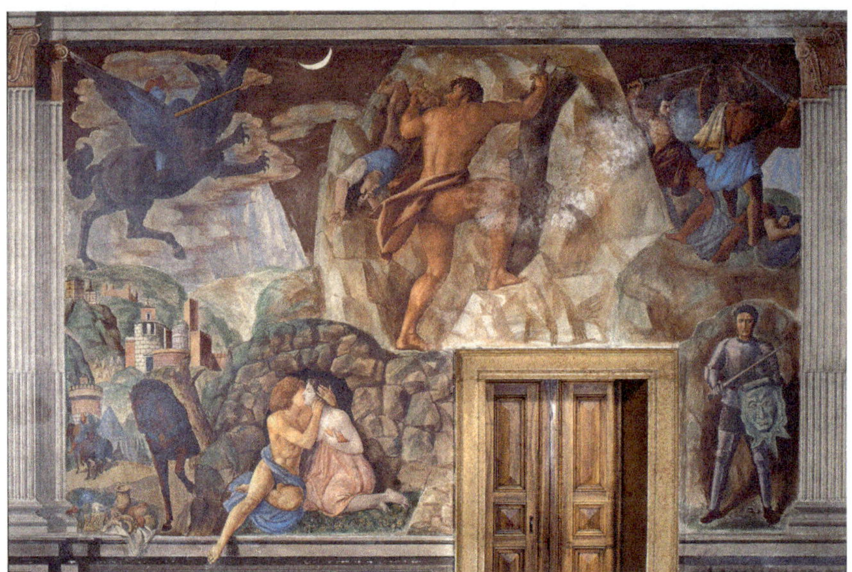

Figures 3.1 and 3.2. Achille Funi, *The Myth of Ferrara* (*Il mito di Ferrara*), details from the south wall: *Gerusalemme Liberata* (top, figure 3.1) and *Orlando Furioso* (bottom, figure 3.2), 1934–7, fresco, Town Hall, Sala dell'Arengo, Ferrara. Courtesy Archivio Achille Funi, Studio d'arte Nicoletta Colombo, Milan. Photograph Gallerie d'Arte Moderna e Contemporanea, Ferrara.

Chapter Three

Eternal Renaissance: Ariosto's Presence in Fascist Ferrara

Tell us some more, we have too little of you,
while we have blood in our veins, and roaring in our ears ...
Ferrara, you're a harsh town of lizards; there is no soul in you.
If only you would produce such men more often.

Osip Mandelstam, *Ariosto*, 1933

On the left, a single scene encompasses the entire epic tension of Tasso's *Gerusalemme Liberata* (figure 3.1). Led by Captain Goffredo, the crusaders are about to enter the conquered walls of Jerusalem while Saracen warrior Clorinda dies in the arms of Tancredi, Prince of Galilee. On the right, a myriad of episodes from Ariosto's *Orlando Furioso* share the visual space (figure 3.2). Astolfo flies towards the moon to recover the wits that Orlando (naked and furious, out of scale, in the centre) lost when he learned about Angelica and Medoro, who are kissing in a cave. Next to them, Agramante's Muslim encampment is on the background of a metaphysical still life, which includes a couple of loaves of Ferrarese bread. A door disrupts the fresco and, to the right of it, Ruggiero raises his sword and the magic shield of Atlante. Unlike the other Ariostean characters, whose faces are indiscernible, he looks directly at the observers.

Visitors can contemplate these modern depictions of Ferrara's chivalric masterpieces in the Hall of the Arengo of the Palazzo Ducale, which has been housing the City Hall since the nineteenth century. The grandiloquent style of the frescoes makes it easy to guess that they were commissioned under Mussolini's regime. Back then, the palace was the seat of a fascist administration. In the frescoes, the visual syntax didactically counterposes the Virgilian unity of the *Liberata*'s Christian mission with the harmonic but fractured chaos of the *Furioso*'s adventures. The two poems, for the fascists who commissioned the frescoes, represented the

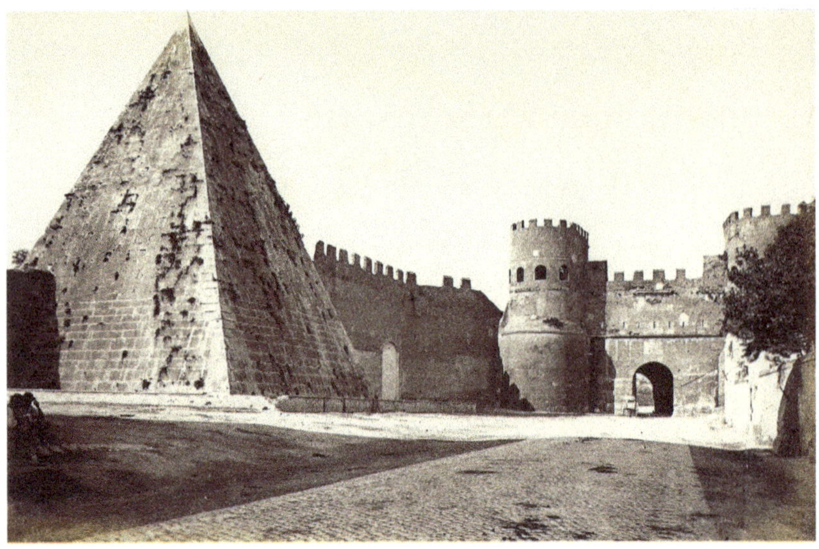

Figure 3.3. The pyramid of Caius Cestius in Rome, with Porta San Paolo in the background. Photograph Fratelli Alinari, 1880, albumen print, 9.5 × 15 cm, "Collezione Album." © Archivi Alinari, Florence.

literary souls of the city's remote golden age, finally revived in the new glory of the regime.

However, if one looks closer, some details are out of place. Why is the Cestia Pyramid (figure 3.3) right outside of the walls of Jerusalem? Why are those walls modelled after the Aurelian walls, and why does their gate look like Porta San Paolo? And what about all the other imperial landmarks (Trajan's column, Nero's colossus, the Lateranense obelisk, the façade of the Pantheon) that are visible beyond? Why are Tasso's knights marching on Rome, instead of Jerusalem?

The fact is that the crusaders themselves are not just literary characters. They bear the faces of local fascist notables. And so do all the recognizable figures in the frescoes, which cover the room up to its ceiling. The entire hall is a life-sized costumed portrait of the intelligentsia that controlled Ferrara's cultural self-fashioning under fascism. The crusaders, in particular, are modelled after engineers who oversaw the fascist renovation of Renaissance public buildings (Carlo Savonuzzi and Antonio Manfredini), painters and writers who animated the city's main magazine (Mimì Buzzacchi and Benso Becca), journalists of the local newspaper (Corrado Padovani and Nello Quilici), and politicians (the mayor, Renzo Ravenna, and lawyer Antonio Boari), along with members of their families.

These were, to borrow a term from Antonio Gramsci's political theory, the "organic intellectuals" of fascist Ferrara, those who contributed to the hegemony of fascist consensus in the city where Ariosto and Tasso had suffered under the Estense dominion. In the early 1930s, they carried out this function by organizing the largest public celebration of Ariosto's legacy that has ever been held. Unbeknownst to them, Ariosto himself mocked their efforts through the very iconography of the frescoes that they commissioned to immortalize themselves.

The Magic Shield

Completed in 1939, the chivalric frescoes in the Hall of the Arengo were the crowning achievement of a cultural program that Ferrara's administration had pursued throughout the fascist *ventennio.* The goal of this program was to revive a carefully selected (and conveniently rewritten) moment of the city's Renaissance past, the late reign of the Este dukes. The Estense Renaissance was to be revived by emphasizing its connections and parallels with the fascist present. The most visible and durable expression of this project was an ambitious campaign of renovation of Ferrara's sixteenth-century buildings and monuments[1] along the lines of fascist strategies of appropriating and integrating past displays of power in Italy's historic centres. Other efforts, such as public events, exhibitions, and the fabrication of folkloric traditions, were more ephemeral but highly impactful. They had the advantage of involving the general population of the city in the performance of the local élite's cultural agenda. In the vast historical landscape of the scholarship on fascist culture, the initiatives carried out in Ferrara have offered a case study to understand how peripheral fascist centres invented the local past beyond the direct identification of Mussolini's new empire with Augustus' Roman one. The frescoes in the Ducal Palace are an emblem of this fascist alternative to Neo-Roman imagery.

The Hall of the Arengo is a modern elaboration of the Hall of the Months in the Palace of Schifanoia, arguably the most important work of visual art of Renaissance Ferrara. The Schifanoia frescoes were, like the fascist ones, a grandiose tool of propaganda, as well as the self-portrait of an intellectual élite. Their top cycle represents the allegorical triumphal cart of each month's ancient deity, with the corresponding zodiac sign in the middle register. Under these two celestial levels, there are scenes of courtly and rural activities that relate to each moment of the year. The

Duke Borso d'Este and his courtiers appear in most scenes of this lower earthly register, which was meant to immortalize their good rulership.

Unlike those of Schifanoia, the fascist frescoes in the Arengo hall directly superimpose symbolic and historical registers. The foundational myths of the past overlap with the living agents of the present. Yes, allegories of the months, surmounted by zodiac signs, are painted above the scenes on the walls, but this is just an empty imitation of the Schifanoia iconography. No meaningful vertical reading is possible. On the walls of Schifanoia, the political present is in corresponding relation with (as well as hierarchically separated from) the archetypes of a revived classical tradition. In those of the Arengo, on the other hand, the past and the present coincide. The fascists are not heirs, interpreters, or modernizers of the myth that they are mobilizing. They are its protagonists.

Rather than unearthing or restoring the Renaissance – seen as repeating and surpassing the legacy of imperial Rome – fascist Ferrara intended to experience it again. Masquerading as Tasso's knights, the fascists represented themselves in the act of conquering classical antiquity (the Roman-like Jerusalem) just as they believed their compatriots did under the Este dukes. Their cultural program, in the frescoes, is depicted as a serene act of force. The tragic pathos of Tasso's poem, represented by Clorinda's death, is visually cut off from their dominant scene. The face of the crusaders' leader belongs to Nello Quilici, the influential director of a local fascist newspaper who worked for years on the iconography of the room, closely collaborating with Achille Funi, the artist chosen by the mayor to realize it. Funi was a Ferrarese painter who, after an early Futurist phase, embraced de Chirico's Metaphysical art and developed it into a classicist figurative rhetoric (figure 3.4). It is interesting that he chose to represent himself on the opposite end of the wall devoted to the chivalric poems, appearing as the only recognizable figure in the Ariostean portion. He lent his face to Ruggiero (figure 3.5), the ancestor of the Este dynasty. He armed his pictorial double with an instrument of defence that, ironically, is the most formidable weapon of the *Orlando Furioso*: an enchanted shield that astounds anyone who looks at it with its magic light.

In the *Furioso*, Ruggiero keeps the shield veiled, and never uses it against other knights (figure 3.6). Its magic is too powerful, and it would be unchivalrous of him to win a duel with it. In fact, when the veil accidentally falls during a battle and the magic instantly defeats Ruggiero's enemies (XXII, 84–7), he is so embarrassed that he throws the shield into a deep well, losing it forever (XXII, 90–3). He resorts, unenthusiastically, to the tremendous weapon only in two cases: when his opponent is not worthy of his sword, like a huntsman armed with a stick (VIII,

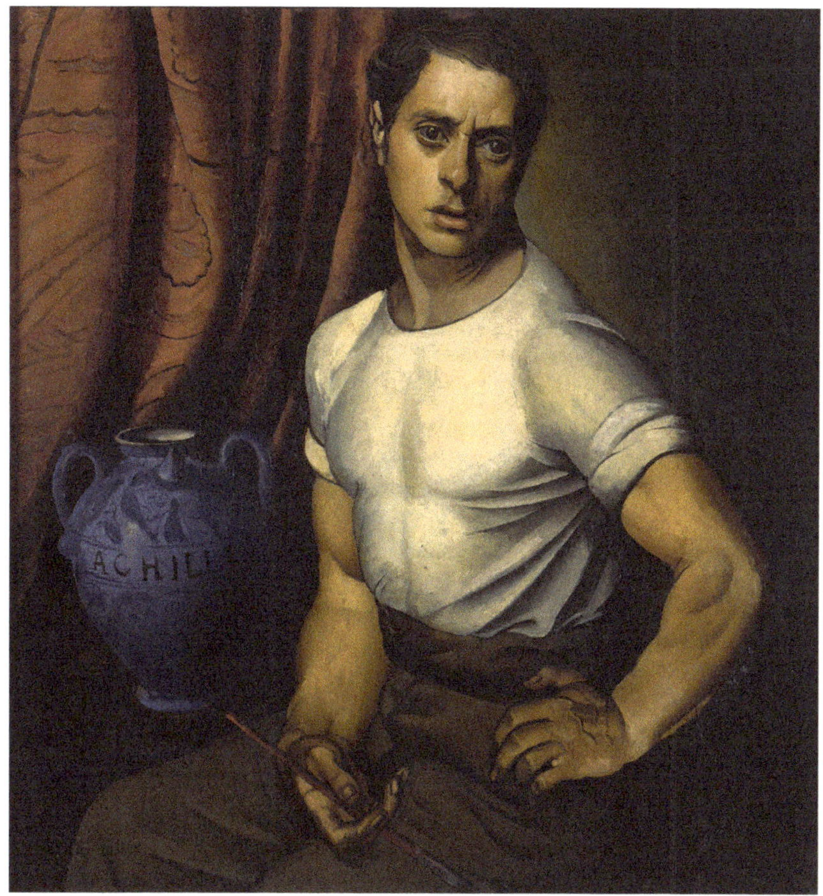

Figure 3.4. Achille Funi, *Self-Portrait with Blue Jar* (*Autoritratto con brocca blu*), 1920, oil on wood, 39.5 × 36.5 cm, private collection, Milan. © Archivio Achille Funi. Courtesy Archivio Achille Funi, Studio d'arte Nicoletta Colombo, Milan.

10), and when he needs to use magic to neutralize an equally powerful supernatural threat, like Alcina's army of monsters or the mighty Orca (X, 49–50, 110).

Did Funi read the poem that he painted? As I will show in this chapter, the answer is not obvious. But if he did, could he have decided that the audience of his fresco was either too unsophisticated or too monstrously potent to be faced with regular weapons? In any event, whether or not

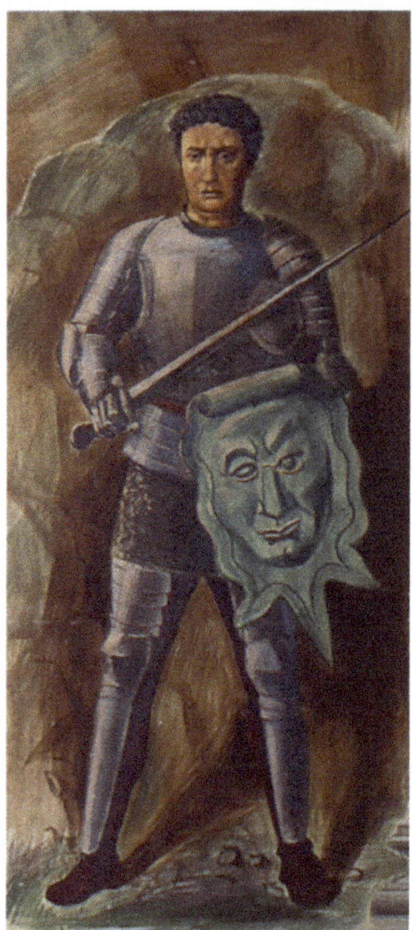

Figure 3.5. Achille Funi, *The Myth of Ferrara* (*Il mito di Ferrara*), detail from the south wall: Ruggiero with Atlante's shield, 1934–7, fresco, Town Hall, Sala dell'Arengo, Ferrara. Courtesy Archivio Achille Funi, Studio d'arte Nicoletta Colombo, Milan.

Funi intended to represent his work as a product of wizardry, a philological reading of this iconography makes the fresco's visual rhetoric either cravenly excessive or reluctantly inevitable. Ariosto, four hundred years after his death, challenged the fascist appropriation of his inventions. He still puts it into question today, from the Arengo's walls.

As I mentioned, the decoration of the Hall of the Arengo was the culmination of a long and articulate cultural program. Funi was hired to paint the fresco at the end of 1933, the year of the fourth centenary of Ariosto's death. The fascist personalities portrayed on the walls organized, in that year, the celebrations that I will discuss in this chapter. Many disparate initiatives (including the architectural renovation mentioned

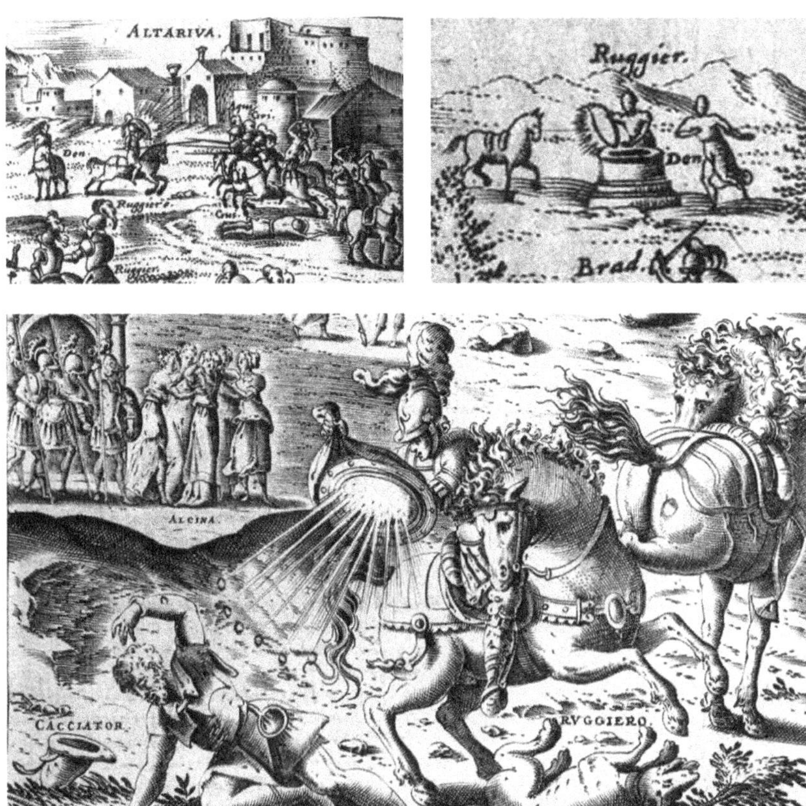

Figure 3.6. Girolamo Porro, details from copperplate illustrations of Ludovico Ariosto, *Orlando Furioso* (Venice: De Franceschi, 1584). Biblioteca Panizzi, Reggio Emilia. Canto XII (84–7 and 90–3): Ruggiero stuns the knights with Atlante's shield (left) and throws Atlante's shield into the well (right); Canto VIII (10): Ruggiero stuns the huntsman with Atlante's shield (below); copper engravings.

before, which started in the previous decade) were attached to Ariosto's anniversary. The anniversary offered a convenient formal opportunity to consolidate the city's cultural agenda around one symbolic occasion, and to display the administration's achievements to visitors (including the king) as well as to the local population. I do not intend to discuss Ferrara's fascist neo-Renaissance in general. This topic has been fruitfully explored by historians of art, architecture, and cultural politics. My aim is to look specifically at those initiatives that involved, or claimed to involve, Ariosto's legacy. As in the case of Funi's fresco, I am particularly interested in how that legacy reacted to fascist appropriations. I intend to spot the enchanted shields disseminated in various fascist revivals of the *Furioso* and its author in 1933, and to determine what kind of monster or swordless huntsman unleashed their magic.

As I mentioned in the previous chapter of this book, Ferrara could not be particularly proud of Tasso's myth. In the memory of artists and poets, from Byron to Carducci, Tasso's unjust imprisonment tarnished the legacy of the Este dukes, whose reign ended two years after Tasso's death. Ariosto had the potential to be a much better champion for the fascist administration, and that is why his anniversary easily became a flagship event. Yet, the rich and productive iconography generated by the *Orlando Furioso* (arguably the largest literary database of pictorial scenes in Europe since Ovid) did not offer a clear visual parallel for the aspirations of Quilici and his comrades. Therefore, they resorted to a distorted elaboration of the *Gerusalemme Liberata,* a poem that was otherwise largely ignored by the cultural politics of fascist Ferrara. Significantly, while Funi was portraying him as one of the crusaders in the fresco, engineer Carlo Savonuzzi was directing the works that dismantled most of Tasso's legendary madhouse in Sant'Anna.[2] That site of pilgrimage for Goethe, Shelley, and Stendhal had to make room for a Rationalist complex with a modern concert hall and a new museum of natural history. Quilici and Funi included Tasso's poem in the Hall of the Arengo only to provide the administration with its heroic self-portrait, which could not have been easily extracted from Ariosto or from the other great chivalric author of Ferrara, the forefather of all Italian romance epic: Matteo Maria Boiardo. Boiardo's *Orlando Innamorato* is nowhere to be found in the fascist frescoes.

Fascist intellectuals wanted to make Ferrara's Renaissance past directly respond to the symbolic needs of the present. Their partial, forceful conjuring of that past was certainly inspired by the modern revivals of tradition conceived by *La Voce,* Metaphysical art, de Pisis' and Savinio's literary experimentalism, and Magical Realism. However, while for instance de Chirico wanted to turn himself into a marble Ariosto and Bontempelli asked Ludovico for the gift of his modern lucidity, the dialogue with the past established by Ferrara's fascist administration was really a monologue in the present. Their Ariosto was not an interlocutor, a living monument to be encountered or a literary model to be imitated. He was, as I will show in the following pages, a relic, a trophy, a fetish, and a revenant.

What shall we do with our men in marble? Discussing fascist revivals of the past inspired by Giovanni Gentile's philosophy of history (known as actual idealism or actualism), Rik Peters showed that current theories of sublime historical experience risk repeating the fascist "presentification of the past"[3] enacted, for instance, in the 1932 exhibition of the fascist revolution – a defining paradigm whose echo shaped the Ariostean centenary in Ferrara. Gentile was the leading philosopher of Italian fascism, and the author of the manifesto of the fascist intellectuals. His influence over Italian culture was tremendous under the regime, and continued after.[4] He understood historical experience and aesthetic experience as one: a "creation without creator"[5] in which past and present, history and reality, coincide. He explained this in the foundational lecture of his doctrine, and used the experience of reading the *Orlando Furioso* as an example. When his ideas were put into practice, followers of Gentile's actualism limited the agency of the past, giving ontological priority to the present: Italy's past was not present as evidence, as an experienceable and interpretable body of monuments and documents, but rather as a self-fulfilling prophecy, a destiny.

In order to adopt the paradigm of presence without rewriting history (without becoming fascist), one must maintain a balance between the merging past and present. To use Peters' words, we need to remember that "true dialogue implies the real presence of the other," and that "when reading *Orlando Furioso*, Ariosto's thoughts have as much impact on my thoughts as I have on the reconstruction of his."[6]

Besides reconstructing the fascist presentification of Ariosto in Ferrara around 1933, this chapter intends to restore some balance between *Ferrara fascista* and *Ferrara estense*, giving Ariosto's legacy a chance to react to the colonization of the past attempted by the fascists.

Blackshirt Astolfo

I have already mentioned, in the previous chapter of this book, the earliest Ariostean initiative that germinated in fascist Ferrara. Bontempelli's lecture on Ariosto and geography was one of forty-one public lectures organized, from 1928 to 1933, to celebrate Ariosto in his city. This five-year conference, titled "L'Ottava d'oro," was imagined and championed by Antonio Baldini, a popular writer and essayist of the Neoclassicist group of *La Ronda*. Baldini's entire career revolved around a deep love and critical appreciation of the *Orlando Furioso*.[7] In order to turn his personal interest in Ariosto into a publicly sponsored initiative, Baldini involved Don Enrico Vanni, a journalist and priest who collaborated with Nello Quilici at the *Corriere Padano*, the fascist newspaper founded in

Ferrara by the most powerful local hierarch, Italo Balbo (figure 3.7). A protagonist of the March on Rome and an elected member of the Camera dei Deputati, in the late 1920s Balbo was becoming the face of Mussolini's aviation forces. A celebration of Ariosto's legacy could easily contribute to both his personal myth as a flying warrior and the prestige of Ferrara, his birthplace and political stronghold. Thus, he took an interest in Baldini's idea when the *Corriere Padano* group pitched it to him. In 1928, on May 6, he inaugurated the cycle of lectures himself, giving an immediate national resonance to the event.[8] The predictable topic of his oration was Astolfo's flight on the Hippogriff.

Besides recounting the paladin's adventures, Balbo used his lecture to launch the "Ariostean day" as a popular event,[9] and to rhetorically frame the initiative so that it could be supported by fascist propaganda through a clear message: "we will read Ariosto to exalt the epic Ferrara."[10] This exaltation, as in Funi's frescoes, took the shape of a masquerade, mixing reality and fiction, the sixteenth and the twentieth century. Balbo invited his audience to let Ariosto's stories overlap with the Estense past and the fascist present of Ferrara. He directly asked Ferrara's people to see themselves as fictional paladins and Saracens, the city as a sixteenth-century town, and himself as a flying Astolfo. He opened the lecture by pretending to have just landed his plane in the Renaissance halls of the Palazzo dei Diamanti,[11] and immediately coopted Ariosto in the architectural renovations realized and planned by the administration. He explained that the city only needed a little polishing to shine again as it did under the Estensi: "Ferrara is still the same as it was then. The splendour of ancient times never really vanishes from the great bronzes of the golden age."[12] According to him, however, the glory of Ariosto's age was to be found not only under the patina that four centuries of negligence had let accumulate on buildings and monuments (and that the fascist mayor now had the task of removing), but also in the bodies and minds of contemporary Ferrarese citizens.

Imagining a flight to the moon on "some modern white Hippogriff with silk wings and a heart of steel,"[13] Balbo directly addressed the fascist notables in the audience as if he was talking to them from the lunar skies. Instead of using their names, though, he called each of them by the name of one of Ariosto's characters. He promised to recover their wits from the moon's valley, and renamed them "new Rinaldos and Ruggieros, Fieramontes and Fulgosos, Leonettos and Mandricardos, born again, after many centuries, as judges or journalists, politicians or businessmen."[14] Only a handful of the Ariostean aliases that he chose are recognizable today: "Sacripante" (as we learn from a later article in *Corriere Padano*)[15] was the mayor, Renzo Ravenna, "Mandricardo" was the

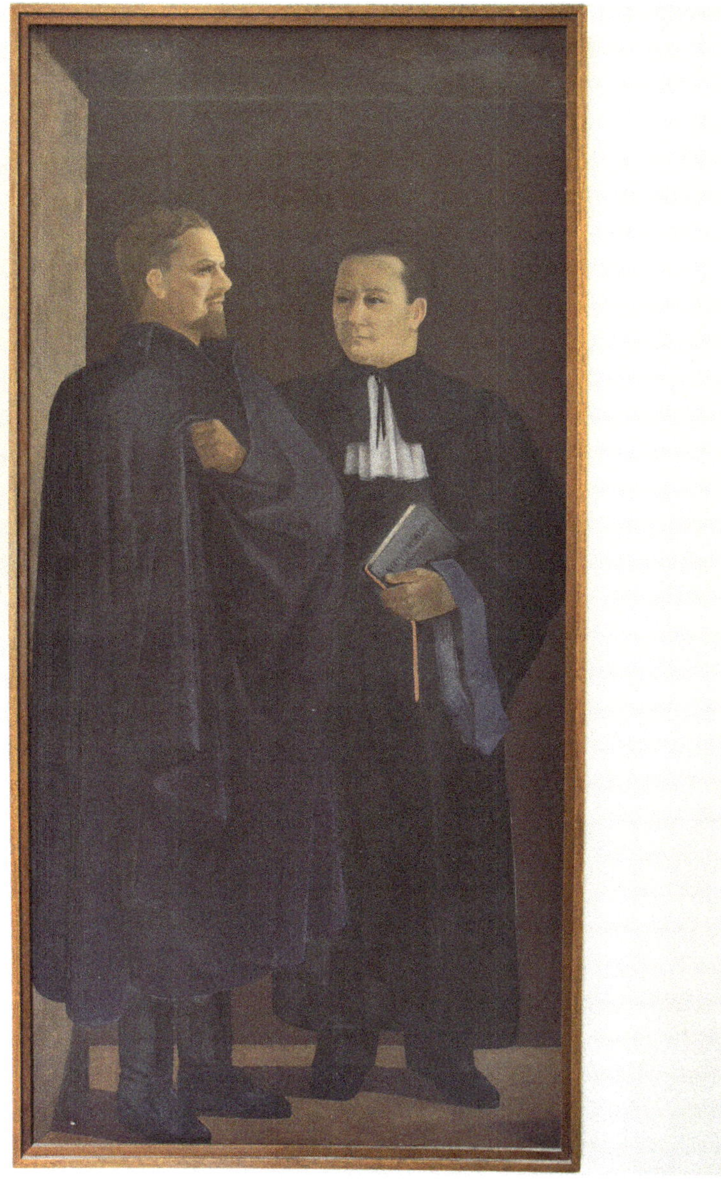

Figure 3.7. Mimì Quilici Buzzacchi, *Portrait of Italo Balbo and Nello Quilici* (*Ritratto di Italo Balbo e Nello Quilici*), 1942–3, oil on wood, 181 × 91 cm, Università degli Studi di Padova, Padua. © Archivio Mimì Quilici Buzzacchi. Courtesy patrimonio storico-artistico diffuso dell'Università degli Studi di Padova.

founder of the local section of the fascist party, Olao Gaggioli,[16] and "Sansonetto" (Astolfo's sidekick in the poem) was likely Quilici. What counts, anyway, is the strategy that Balbo followed to make Ariosto's legacy present, popular, and familiar to the bourgeois audience.

The eagle eye perspective that Balbo adopted to look at Ferrara and its modern citizens from the moon "under an Ariostean filter"[17] is at the same time entertaining and disciplining. The lecture's undeniable "charm and humour"[18] were delivered from a position of invigilating aerial control. This imagined flight fulfilled the same two criteria that Diane Ghirardo, using Ferrara as an example, proposed as the defining features of fascist strategies of urban propaganda in the 1930s: "surveillance and spectacle."[19] Simultaneously, Balbo's continuous references to reality and the present, invariably based on details of Ariosto's text taken too literally, informed a distorted interpretation of Gentile's actualism mixed with local pride. The poem had to be directly experienced, rather than read, by its legitimate owners (i.e., Ferrara's people), who needed to believe that it was literally about them and their current reality. The impossible task of being, at the same time, faithful to the letter of Ariosto's text and part of it (of validating the most unmediated and anti-intellectual reading of the *Furioso* while claiming its absolute actuality) produced irresolvable paradoxes. Balbo, for instance, identified with Astolfo, choosing him as the emblem of the modern Italian flying warrior who disdained the Earth and was eager to leave it on his airplane/Hippogriff. But when he noted that Astolfo, in the fiction of the poem, comes from England, he immediately cut off historical and philological distances and stated that Ariosto described him as a "modern Englishman": an unperturbed dandy who only needs a few "whiskeys and cups of tea" to become "a perfect tipperary of modern times."[20]

This form of extreme and pedestrian actualization of Ariosto's fiction became a defining aspect of the 1933 anniversary. As we will see in a moment, the scope and budget of the celebrations were negotiated with Mussolini's central government only in 1932, but the program of the conference L'Ottava d'oro, inaugurated by Balbo in 1928, already observed the cultural strategies that would later inform the 1933 initiatives.

Baldini stated that the idea of the Ottava d'oro lectures came to him in his sleep. In the dream, he and Vanni, along with other "old friends," went to a "trattoria in Ferrara called 'All'Ottava d'oro'" where they all ate, drank, and commented, "very freely, [on] the raunchiest of Ariosto's cantos."[21] To underline the lowbrow, convivial vocation to popularization allegorized in this vision, Baldini chose a meaningful passage from the *Furioso* as the epigraph of the conference proceedings (VIII, 29):

My lord, like the good instrumentalist
Who plays on many different strings at will,
And tunes and modulates as he thinks best,
Moving from bass to treble, soft to shrill
So, as I tell you of Rinaldo's quest,
Thoughts of Angelica I harp on still.

Different Strings

An original list of the speakers invited to the Ottava d'oro conference – including those who were excluded from the final proceedings[22] – is available in the municipal archives of Ferrara (figure 3.8). Its composition reflects Baldini's intention to provide variety as well as the cultural strategy established by Balbo's opening lecture. The program mixes high and low registers, juxtaposing prestigious names from disparate contexts. It includes at least two proper academic speakers for each year: most were prominent Italianists, some were Ariosto specialists (such as Michele Catalano and Giuseppe Fatini), and others were brilliant orators borrowed from other disciplines (like the Germanist Arturo Farinelli, the archaeologist Filippo Tambroni, or the Latinist Giuseppe Albini). Many of the speakers who were not scholars worked as public intellectuals and journalists, and a few were writers of great fame, such as Bontempelli, Alfredo Panzini, and the founder of Futurism, Filippo Tommaso Marinetti. But the most curious and meaningful lectures in the list are those given by professionals, scientists, and technical experts who were invited to comment on the intersection between their non-literary field of expertise and Ariosto's poem.

In 1930, as I mentioned in the first chapter of this book, the experimental filmmaker and photographer Anton Giulio Bragaglia gave a lecture titled "L'Ariosto cineasta." His reading of the *Furioso* as a cinematic production went beyond the acute comparison between *entrelacement* and modern montage that influenced Savinio. Bragaglia analysed Ariosto's use of lights as an "electrician," commented on the special effects that the poet could have achieved using a "Schufstein machine," and fantasized about the best possible casting for the resulting film (swashbuckler star Douglas Fairbanks as Orlando, "Latin lover" Rudolph Valentino as Zerbino, Wallace Beery as Rodomonte, and so on).[23]

In 1932, Dr. Gaetano Boschi, head of the psychiatry department at Ferrara's public hospital, was invited to scientifically discuss the "Diagnostics

CELEBRAZIONI ARIOSTESCHE

LETTURE TENUTE NELL'ANNO 1928

Balbo	Il volo d'Astolfo
Baldini	La difesa d'Angelica
Malaparte	La pazzia d'Orlando
Lipparini	Angelica e Medoro
Quilici	Fiordiligi e Brandimarte
Farinelli	L'estremo canto del Furioso
Campanile	L'umorismo dell'Ariosto

LETTURE TENUTE NELL'ANNO 1929

Turati	Ruggero e Brandimarte
Bacchelli	Una difesa di Messer Ludovico
Agnelli	Il Furioso nell'età nostra
Borgese	Il sovrumano nel Furioso
Marinetti	Una lezione di futurismo tratta dall'Orlando Furioso
Momigliano	Nell'Isola di Alcina
Ravegnani	Vita, morte e miracoli di Rodomonte
Albini	Riflessi Virgiliani dell'Ariosto
Tumiati	Come si legge l'Ariosto
Ferretti	Le artiglierie nell'Orlando Furioso

LETTURE TENUTE NELL'ANNO 1930

Bragaglia	L'Ariosto cineasta
Maccari	Orlando e strapaese
Titta	l'Ariosto misogino
Di Marzio	L'Ariosto diplomatico
Rocca	Elementi di teatro nell'Orlando Furioso
Torri	La musica alla corte Estense
Galletti	L'epos medioevale nell'Orlando Furioso
Bontempelli	L'Ariosto geografo
Catalano	Gli amori dell'Ariosto

LETTURE TENUTE NELL'ANNO 1931

Bodrero	La vita prodigiosa di L. Ariosto
Bertoni	Il linguaggio poetico di L. Ariosto
Tambroni	Riflessi artistici della poesia ariostesca
Arcari	Medoro
Fancini	Angelica nell'Ariosto e nel Boiardo
Toffanin	L'amore sacro e l'amore profano nel Furioso
Fumagalli	Paesaggi ariostei
Fatini	La genesi del " Furioso "

LETTURE TENUTE NELL'ANNO 1932

[illegible]	L'Italia ai tempi dell'Ariosto
[illegible]	Il mare nell'O.F.
[illegible]	Di messer Ludovico [illegible]
Bianchi	Eterno femminino ariosteo
Boschi	Diagnostica della pazzia d'Orlando
Tumiati C.	Il castello magico
[illegible]	L'ultimo canto

Figure 3.8. List of invited lecturers for the Ottava d'oro conference (1928–33), Archivio Storico Comunale di Ferrara.

of Orlando's Madness." The neurologist treated the octaves of Canto XXIV as a medical report, using Freud's theories and technical terminology to take the symptoms of his "patient" seriously and address them as a modern practitioner. He also explained some of the poem's magical events and objects through contemporary pseudo-scientific theories. According to his lecture, Angelica's ring works like X-rays, Astolfo's transformation into a tree alludes to Moleschott's pseudo-physiology, the wits in the vials on the moon anticipate the principles of opotherapy, and so on.[24] In 1930, Cornelio Di Marzio, who had worked at the Italian embassy in Istanbul and directed the network of foreign *fasci italiani*, lectured on "Ariosto as a diplomat," while in 1929 war veteran Lando Ferretti, the theorist of the fascist permanent militia, intervened on bombs and firearms in the *Orlando Furioso*.

As a matter of fact, none of these visibly spurious speakers was a complete stranger to the world of arts and letters. Bragaglia was part of the Futurist movement and collaborated with Pirandello and Savinio, Boschi had had de Chirico and Carrà under his care, Di Marzio and Ferretti were journalists and essayists, and the latter had even studied philology at Scuola Normale Superiore. However, what matters in their contribution to the polyphony of the conference is the mixture of literary culture and practical expertise that they could offer: a demonstration that Ariosto's legacy did not belong only to scholars and bookworms, but also (and foremost) to the varied and industrious new white-collar Italy that fascist culture wanted to involve beyond the coercive rituals of rallies and parades.[25] The conference was evidently modelled after the *Lecturae Dantis* of Florence, Rome, and Ravenna, a tradition that is still active today in many cultural institutes and universities all over the world. However, while those public readings and interpretations of the *Divine Comedy* always maintained an ultimately academic frame, Baldini's Ferrarese version intended to make Ariosto's relevance tangible and immediate in modern everyday life: to force parallels between the *Furioso* and the cultural horizon of a wider, mainstream audience of occasional readers (or even non-readers). Promoting an interpretation of Ariosto's actual texts was not the point. In fact, most non-academic speakers claimed that their unsubstantiated speculations were more genuinely connected to Ariosto's mind than any historical reconstruction or close reading of what he wrote.

This perspective predictably produced a number of hermeneutic monstrosities. Ferretti, for instance, tried to use the *Orlando Furioso* to glorify modern weapons such as "toxic gases, aerial bombings of open cities, and submarines,"[26] and pulled Ariosto into a twentieth-century polemic of military ethics about remotely controlled torpedoes and missiles.[27] Ariosto, who backdated the invention of guns in his poem just to be able to depict them as the most un-chivalric and abominable of human creations,[28] would have certainly opposed Ferretti's position, and was hardly naive (as the fascist speaker described him) when he criticized the new technological wars of his time by adding ironic invectives against firearms to the latest edition of the *Furioso*.[29] Marinetti's lecture in 1929 was probably the most blatant (and somewhat awkward) distortion of Ariosto's poetry resulting from a similar attempt to make it directly speak to the present. His title was "A Lesson of Futurism Drawn from the *Orlando Furioso*," but the text of the lecture shows a complete reversal of roles. Rather than learning anything from it, Marinetti claimed that the sixteenth-century poem "strives" to be futurist, and he welcomed such efforts. According to him, "the *Orlando Furioso* strives to conjure the future synthetic, dynamic, and simultaneous joys of our futurist words in freedom" and "strives to become a rich film of adventures for our screens of swift worldwideness."[30]

This bombastic rhetoric recycled, after twenty years, the usual formulas of the original futurist manifestoes. When Marinetti tried to apply such formulas to Ariosto's life and poetry, the result was probably enticing for the audience, but laughably wrong for any reader of Ariosto's *Furioso* and *Satires*. Not an ounce of irony smoothed Marinetti's counterfactual statements about the idea that Ariosto "had fun when he was given the task of fighting the bandits of Garfagnana, even if he didn't put this into writing," or that his poem "is really a profusion that was not planned or restrained, but instinctive."[31] Basically, an absolute lack of interpretation[32] leaves room, in Marinetti's lecture, for an assertive invention of the past, which did not spare the very recent past of Futurism itself. In his 1909 manifesto, Marinetti had declared "We want to destroy museums and libraries." In the 1929 lecture he conveniently alleged: "We wouldn't have brutally condemned libraries and museums if we had found there Italians that were lively, in rebellion against the past, and eager to use it to powerfully help the present and prepare the future."[33] In many ways, the Ariostean tirade of this middle-aged Marinetti is a self-parody, and ultimately a tombstone on Italy's once pioneering avant-garde. Mussolini had elected the inventor of Futurism as a founding member of the newborn Accademia d'Italia less than four months before the lecture, domesticating his fading brazenness and securing, at the same time, a paradoxical anti-academic flair for the new fascist institution.

Tin Can Heroism

It is interesting to note that, among fascist celebrities like Marinetti and prominent members of the party like Ferretti, the varied program of L'Ottava d'oro included non-compliant intellectuals who were later persecuted by the regime. Alfredo Galletti, who was invited to speak in 1930 about Ariosto and medieval epic, had signed, five years before, Benedetto Croce's Manifesto of the Anti-Fascist Intellectuals. Giuseppe Antonio Borgese, who lectured in 1929 about supernatural elements in the *Furioso*, refused, in 1931, to take the oath of loyalty that Mussolini required of all university professors, and remained in exile in the United States, where he was teaching as a visiting professor at Berkeley. Attilio

Momigliano, the philologist whom Bontempelli refused to replace when he lost tenure because of the racial laws, was invited to speak about Alcina's island, and gave the most refined and cogent scholarly lecture of the series in 1929. He too was a known supporter of the Anti-Fascist Manifesto.

When these kinds of speakers established a more interpretative dialogue with Ariosto's past, their lectures subtly subverted the rhetoric of the entire conference, exposing the contradictions of the fascist initiatives from within. For instance, novelist Riccardo Bacchelli gave an extremely well documented lecture about Ariosto's role in one of the most horrific episodes of courtly politics in Renaissance Ferrara: the failed conspiracy that Giulio and Ferrante d'Este organized in 1506 to assassinate and replace Duke Alfonso and his brother Ippolito. Bacchelli's relationship with both fascism and Ariosto was complex and evolving in the late 1920s. He structured his lecture as a public defence of Ariosto, who was blamed by modern literary critics for supporting the gruesome vengeance of his patrons against the conspirators. He used letters, the *Satires*, the *Furioso*, and other texts by Ariosto (including the eclogue with which he had defended the dukes)[34] to prove that the poet was a lucid politician, able to read the Machiavellian "effectual truth"[35] of his times and to act, with practical responsibility, for the greater good. Bacchelli concluded that twentieth-century critics cannot separate Ariosto from the political reality in which he operated, and that such a political reality cannot be measured by ethical standards developed after the Enlightenment.[36]

From a methodological point of view, Bacchelli's lecture challenged the outlook taken by most of the other speakers. Rather than dragging Ariosto's life and works into the present, he deemed it necessary to adopt the perspective of the past in order to understand them. At the same time, his insistence on the darkest page of Ferrara's sixteenth century (a violent story of betrayal and ruthless vendetta among brothers) stained the cheerful portrait of the local Renaissance hero with blood. More subtly, Bacchelli showed that Ariosto was not afraid to appear like a sycophantic coward to protect himself and his city. When the stability of the state and his own safety and independence were at stake, Ariosto wrote an eclogue that reads like propaganda: he exonerated the dukes even if, from our posthumous perspective, they were acting as tyrants. In Bacchelli's words, "Ariosto was not a hero, and he knew what were the consequences of being a saint."[37] This profile was very distant from the smiling and adventurous images of the poet fabricated by many fascist speakers throughout the five years of L'Ottava d'oro. Bacchelli's interpretation of Ariosto was close to the one reclaimed by Bontempelli in the same years, and provided a model of bitter compromise for intellectuals who did not identify as fascists but did not openly criticize the regime.

To be sure, less compromising options were available. A popular self-proclaimed apolitical poet and satirist like Trilussa, for instance, simply declined the invitation to speak at L'Ottava d'oro, avoiding Ferrara's Ariostean celebrations just as he avoided most contexts in which he could be forced to take a clear position about the regime. Benedetto Croce, arguably the most prominent anti-fascist in Italy's cultural landscape, declined as well. And Achille Campanile, the famous humorist who would become a favourite of Umberto Eco's after the war, used his role as a comedian to mock the chivalric ambitions of Ferrara's fascists from the very podium of their conference. Invited to speak on Christmas Day in 1928, he filled his lecture with jokes, but he also acutely rejected the idea (repeated many times in the previous lectures, from Balbo to Quilici) of an absolute and idyllic Renaissance in Ferrara's sixteenth century. In fact, he argued that the *Furioso* "closes the Renaissance and opens the door to modern times,"[38] and drew on Ariosto's own disenchantment to reveal how ridiculous are, in hindsight, the values of chivalry that were seriously embraced up until Boiardo. His parallel between Ariosto's age and the fascist present is not a superimposition but rather a trans-historical contact, mediated by a metaphorical fire: the fire of Agramante's Saracen city, which closes the epic mission of the *Furioso* and mirrors the dissolution of the independent Italian states witnessed by Ariosto at the end of the Renaissance.

> Well, that fire with which Ariosto almost concludes the thousand adventures of his heroes [...] that gigantic fire that devours a kingdom, is a great bonfire in which an entire literary world of cardboard crackles, burns, and vanishes: a world that loudly collapses; the world of fake and useless heroism, with its warriors made out of tin cans. [...] And so it goes today: in an age that is, like that of Ariosto, superficial, sceptical, arid, more concerned with appearances than substance: an age, like that of Ariosto, of great inventions that change the face of the world, the age of the radio, of the cinematograph, of the great journeys towards unknown places, of the solid construction of some states, of the dissolution of others, of revolutions, of discoveries.[39]

Campanile reminded his Ferrarese audience that Ariosto, in 1533, could not believe in the chivalric values of feudalism anymore. The *Furioso* is, paradoxically, the greatest poem about knights and, at the same time, an ironic envoi to the rapidly disappearing world of chivalry itself. With philological acumen, protected by his role as a comedian,

Campanile ridiculed the fascists' gross misuse of the poem's legacy. It is hard not to see, in his words, a parody of the "fake and useless heroism" of hierarchs such as Balbo, the new "warriors made out of tin cans" destined to be soon portrayed in Funi's fresco.

High Art, Fascist Festival

The success of the Ottava d'oro lectures, concluded in January 1933 after five years, generated anticipation for the actual centenary. Baldini and Vanni formed an official Ariostean Committee under Balbo's honorary direction, involving all the major political figures of fascist Ferrara along with local intellectuals, librarians, journalists, and industrialists. In 1932, while the last lectures were being scheduled, Mayor Ravenna reoriented the efforts of this group towards the planning of the celebrations to be held the following year. Both an executive and a cultural sub-committee were formed to manage the bureaucracy and the content of the festival.

The initial project was sent to Mussolini in July 1932. It revolved around an official commemoration of Ariosto on the day of the fourth centennial anniversary of his death, and included three kinds of initiatives: exhibitions and editorial projects about the poet, his work, and his time; showings of the hydraulic and agricultural achievements accomplished in the region by the fascist administration (a sort of local and technical version of the exhibition of the fascist revolution, which opened in Rome in October);[40] and manifestations of a folkloric and popular nature (sport competitions, gatherings, and the revival of traditional parades). Mussolini immediately involved the newborn Accademia d'Italia and forwarded the Ferrarese program to the director, who at the time was Guglielmo Marconi. Before doing so, he personally crossed out all the initiatives related to fascist achievements.[41] On November 10 the mayor sent a revised program to Marconi, which was approved, and on November 25 he called the first official meeting of the executive sub-committee.[42]

The program detailed in the 1932 meeting continued to slightly change for the following six months, until its definitive version was printed in an illustrated brochure titled *Bollettino d'informazioni per il forestiero* (Bulletin of informations for visitors). However, its substance remained the same, mirroring the cultural ideology and strategies tested with the lectures. Meaningfully, the day of the actual anniversary of Ariosto's death, originally at the centre of the festival, appeared to be forgotten in the sub-committee's tentative version of the program. Eventually, it was officially filled with one of the minor planned events whose date had yet to be determined in the 1932 draft (specifically, a national convention of librarians). The initiatives that took centre-stage (and the most significant portions of the budget) were three exhibitions and a revival of the local Palio, a medieval festive tradition that the Committee reinvented as a sort of re-enactment in costume that involved the entire city. I will return to the Palio towards the end of this chapter. For now, I would like to focus on the other events, starting from the three main exhibitions: the grandiose Mostra della pittura ferrarese del Rinascimento at Palazzo dei Diamanti and the so-called "bibliographical" and "iconographic" exhibitions in the library of Palazzo Paradiso and Ariosto's house.[43] The different coverage that these events received in the local press, controlled by the administration through the Ariostean Committee, allows us to understand the priorities and the cultural ideology of the festival's propaganda.

In terms of scope, scale, and expense, the exhibition of Renaissance painting at Palazzo dei Diamanti was incomparable to any other initiative. A milestone in the history of Italian art, this comprehensive gathering of fifteenth-century masterpieces from all over the world generated some of the most important studies in the field, including Roberto Longhi's seminal monograph *Officina ferrarese.* A special curatorial team, coordinated by Nino Barbantini, worked on the event with a significant degree of independence from the Committee for Ariosto's centenary.[44] This group, not particularly invested in the revival of Ariosto's legacy per se, was largely composed of eminent scholars such as Adolfo Venturi and Igino Benvenuto Supino. The exhibition, inaugurated on May 7, had international resonance and was widely publicized. Foreign papers that advertised the manifestations for the centenary, such as the *Christian Science Monitor* in Boston, emphasized the exhibition as the flagship event (figure 3.9). Taking advantage of nationally mandated discounts on train tickets, thousands of visitors from all over Italy came to Ferrara specifically to see the Renaissance paintings, which were by far the main tourist attraction[45] during the six months of the celebrations – and beyond, since the exhibition was prolonged until the end of the year.[46] Yet, the high art event hardly contributed to the cultural strategy of the Ariostean Committee. It certainly allowed Ferrarese citizens to immerse themselves, along with out-of-town visitors, in the imagery of Ariosto's time, and it is rather telling that Dosso Dossi's disquieting depiction of Melissa, the sorceress who protects Bradamante in the *Furioso,* was the painting most often used to advertise it (figure 3.10). However, its connection with the rest of festival was evidently not a priority for the curators, many of whom had no particular affiliation with Ferrara and its administration. The propaganda machine of the Ariostean Committee,

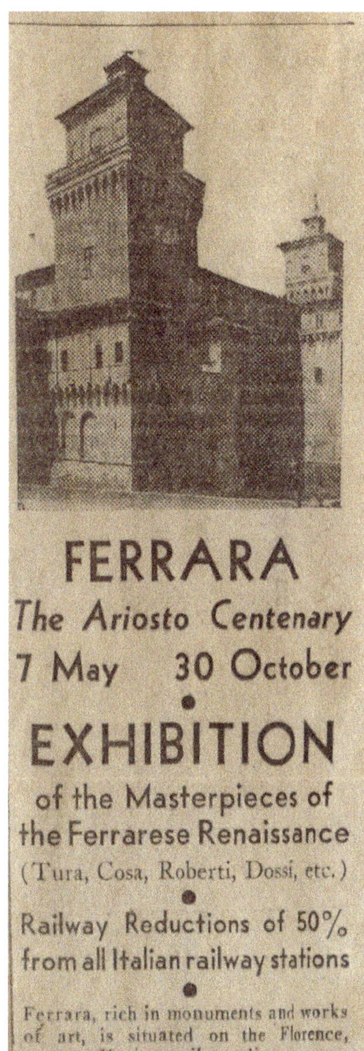

Figure 3.9. Clipping from *Christian Science Monitor*, Boston, February 3, 1933. Courtesy Archivio Storico Comunale di Ferrara.

for its part, celebrated the most superficial aspects of the exhibition (its site, its scale, its organizational success), and exploited its credibility and resonance. However, the local press invested more in the experience of the past offered by the other two exhibitions, which were directly related to Ariosto's fascist myth. In sum, the most important and fruitful exploration of Ferrara's past related to the centenary was a foreign body in

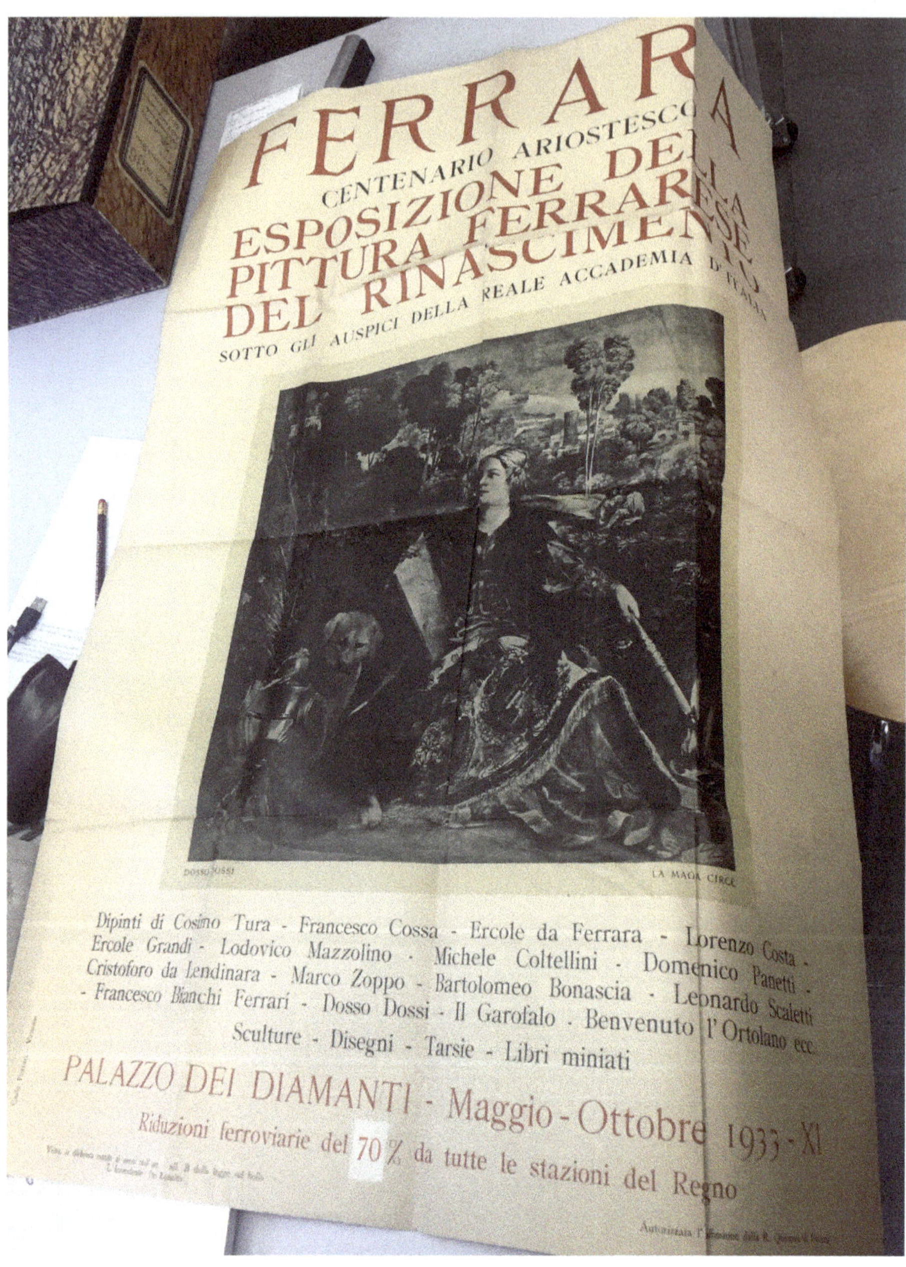

Figure 3.10. Original poster of the Esposizione della pittura ferrarese del Rinascimento (1933). Courtesy Archivio Storico Comunale di Ferrara.

the organizational physiology of the festival. As a matter of fact, it was ideologically at odds with it.

Venturi, arguably the most famous Italian art historian at the time, had very clear scholarly and didactic priorities when he agreed to be involved in the curatorial committee led by Barbantini. In a 1932 letter to Mayor Ravenna, he expressed scepticism about the generic and grandiose goals of the local authorities, mentioning that the National Gallery, for instance, was unlikely to lend its prestigious Ferrarese collection, since it denied loans even to nearby institutions in London.[47] "The idea however," he added, "is excellent, but it should be developed so that the exhibition will serve a purpose: not just to gather beautiful and historically important works, but rather works that would make it possible to shed light on, and solve, problems."[48] He followed up with unresolved research questions about lesser-known fifteenth-century masters, such as Galasso di Matteo Piva and Lorenzo Costa, and advocated for the inclusion of miniatures, drawings, medals, and manuscripts in the exhibition – a curatorial idea that was eventually put into practice. He saw the initiative as a philological opportunity to investigate the "historical landscape of Ferrara's artistic life"[49] in its own pictorial terms, along a teleological trajectory that did not lead straight to the fascist present, but rather to what he considered to be the "crowning of all the efforts in the genius of Emilia's art." According to Venturi, the peak of Northern Italian painting was Antonio da Correggio's High Renaissance work, which had to be included in the exhibition as the end point of a parable concluded in the past.[50] Ariosto's name is nowhere to be found in Venturi's letter.

In a book about Ferrara's culture in the interwar period, Giorgio Bàrberi Squarotti compared the 1933 Renaissance art exhibition (which he called, adopting the title of Longhi's influential study of it, *Officina ferrarese*) with the Ottava d'oro conference that formed the cultural and rhetorical bedrock of the centenary initiatives – as well as the main published product of the event. His intention was to show how the same cultural milieu could generate, under fascism, two opposite approaches to the revival of the local Renaissance. Venturi and the other curators of the exhibition were able to collect the scattered vestiges of Ferrara's rich art history and to display them in an iconographic program of unprecedented coherence. Their goal was to make it possible, for scholars and visitors, to contemplate the development of Ferrara's various pictorial schools at once, in one single curated space. Contrarily, the Ariostean Committee forced the past into the fantasies of the present. In Bàrberi Squarotti's words, the conference made the *Furioso* "float in the void of a Renaissance that appeared to be summarized and concluded in the poem itself,"[51] pretending that Ariosto's harmony was insulated from the complex and contradictory tensions of early modern Italy. This evaluation, as will be apparent in the following pages, applies to all the other initiatives of the fascist Committee.

Metaphysical artists gave life to Ariosto's monument, Bontempelli asked for his technical help and ideological protection, as a literary ancestor, to forge Magical Realism, and the exhibition in Palazzo dei Diamanti reconstructed the art of his time through curatorship. The Ariostean Committee, on the other hand, intended to forcibly eradicate Ariosto from his century, to co-opt his afterlife. That is why an anti-fascist luminary such as Longhi could root his most important work in the 1933 painting exhibition, while no critic has ever used the material produced in the same time and place by the Ariostean Committee (from the proceedings of the Ottava d'oro to the various published lectures held during the celebrations) to further understand Ariosto. The greatest mass celebration of Ariosto ever held, after four centuries of euphoric reception across media and critical fortune, distorted the modern image of the poet, his work, and his age rather than disclosing it to a larger public. Ariosto, as we will further see, was popularized and glorified, but grossly misunderstood (and hardly read at all) by Ferrara's fascists.

Marble and Paper

While the valuable content and rigorous structure of the Renaissance art exhibition remained relatively extraneous to the Ariostean Committee's vision, its resonance and its material site drew in the administration's self-fashioning efforts. The event was held in Biagio Rossetti's Palazzo dei Diamanti (figure 3.11), a jewel of local Renaissance architecture whose modernization was accelerated to meet the deadline of inauguration day. This too was an initiative of presentification rather than restoration.

The police were ordered to offer a special service of vigilance in the area,[52] and the vestibule of the palazzo was equipped with state-of-the-art machines for the automatic distribution of tickets. These "Automatickets" devices, produced in Milan, were the same used for the exhibition of the fascist revolution in Rome – the Ariostean executive Committee contacted the curators to ask for the exact brand.[53] To match the modern accessibility of Mussolini's Palazzo delle Esposizioni, they also commissioned the electrical illumination of the entire building, which was connected to telephone lines for the first time.

Palazzo dei Diamanti had to be quickly adapted to public use. It already housed the city's municipal art collection, as well as part of the university, but many of its spaces had been closed for decades and needed to be refurbished. Engineer Savonuzzi directed these speedy works, which

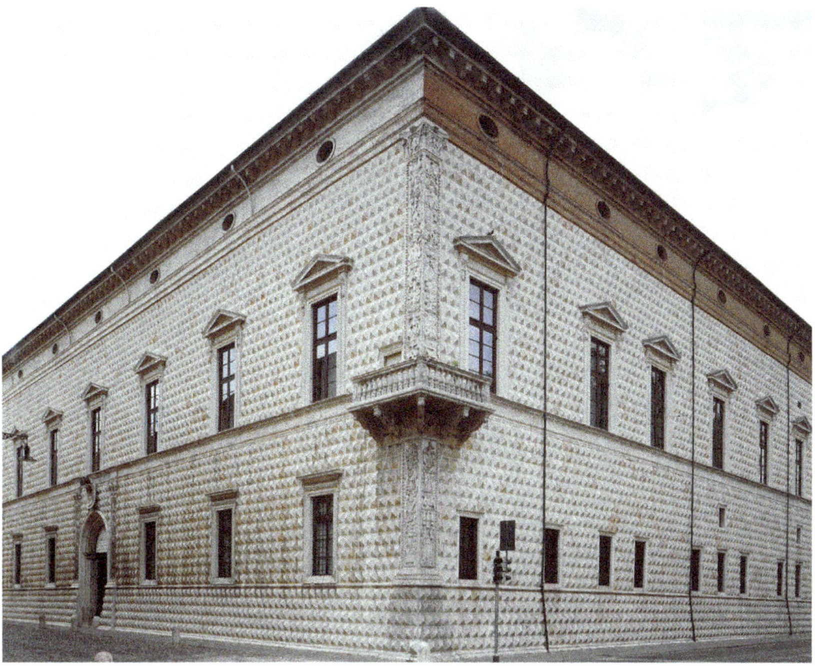

Figure 3.11. Palazzo dei Diamanti in Ferrara, exterior. Photo credit: Scala/Luciano Romano/Art Resource, NY.

included the cleaning of the iconic façade. Turning the familiar old palazzo into a credible asset for the modern city was a sudden and violent act of maquillage, an occupation that saw itself as a reclamation. Most of the building's west wing was still rented by a local farmer, who tended to a vegetable garden in the Renaissance courtyard. The relocation of this picturesque "ortolano," whose name was Ferrari, was a curious early conundrum for Savonuzzi, who had to design and commission a new cottage for the evicted tenant in January.[54]

In April, on the eve of the opening, the revamped landmark was featured on the cover of *Rivista di Ferrara* (figure 3.12), a new local magazine that became the official platform of the Ariostean propaganda. The magazine, which reinvented the city's image between 1933 and 1935, was launched in January 1933 under Quilici's direction. It was the immediate heir of a mostly statistical periodical that had been published by the township since 1925, reporting agronomic and demographic data about fascist Ferrara and

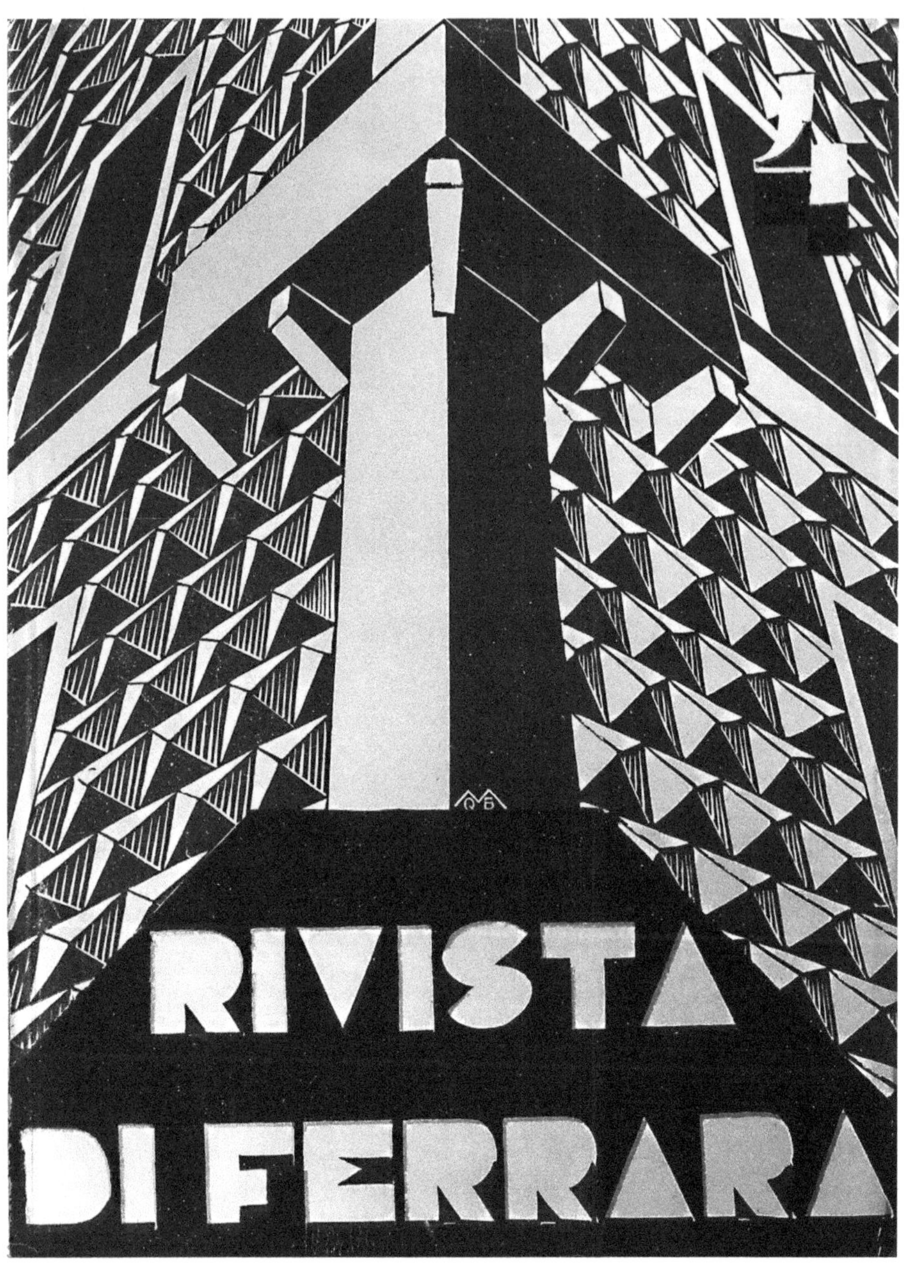

Figure 3.12. Mimì Quilici Buzzacchi, "Palazzo dei Diamanti," cover of *Rivista di Ferrara* 1.4 (April 1933). © Archivio Mimì Quilici Buzzacchi. Photograph © Giuseppe Tassinari.

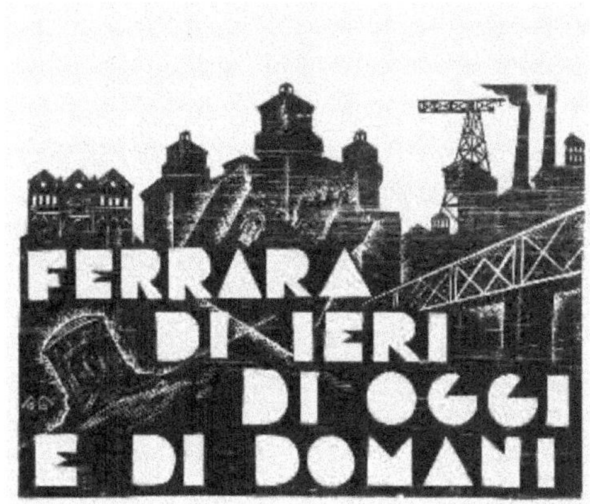

Figure 3.13. Mimì Quilici Buzzacchi, illustration for Nello Quilici, "Ferrara di ieri di oggi e di domani," *Rivista di Ferrara* 1.1 (January 1933): 6.

its province under the masthead *Bollettino statistico*. Using funds allocated for the Ariostean celebrations, the revamped *Rivista* focused its glossy pages on art and culture instead, significantly increasing its circulation. Heavily illustrated, throughout its first year of life it primarily amplified the initiatives related to Ariosto's anniversary, spreading the vision of the Ariostean Committee through entertaining reports and comments. However, in line with its predecessor, the new magazine also maintained a section exclusively devoted to the tabulation of vital statistics, printed on matte paper. True to the dual fascist paradigm of "surveillance and spectacle" with which Ghirardo described other cultural initiatives in Ferrara, the monthly periodical juxtaposed demographic surveillance and propaganda, detailed biopolitical records and cultivated leisurely content

In this new format, the *Rivista di Ferrara* had opened the Ariostean year, in the inaugural issue, with a declared aspiration to catalyse the presentification of the old city. In his first editorial, titled "The Ferrara of Yesterday, of Today, and of Tomorrow," Quilici stated that the past was Ferrara's greatest asset, but also its main burden: "Ferrara has resonance all over the world. Not for the present though: for the past. We have said how burdensome legacy is. Here is the problem: how to adapt that past to the present."[55] The illustration that accompanied these lines (figure 3.13) combined medieval and Renaissance landmarks with new industrial shapes in a single monochrome skyline. Thematically reminiscent of de Chirico's Ferrarese cityscapes, but formally in line with the more recent, fascistized second wave of Futurism, the image was composed by avant-garde painter Mimì Buzzacchi (figure 3.14). She was Quilici's wife, as well as a friend and collaborator of fellow Ferrarese artists de Pisis and Funi – the latter portrayed her, in the fresco of the Sala dell'Arengo, as a pensive androgynous foot-soldier (figure 3.15).

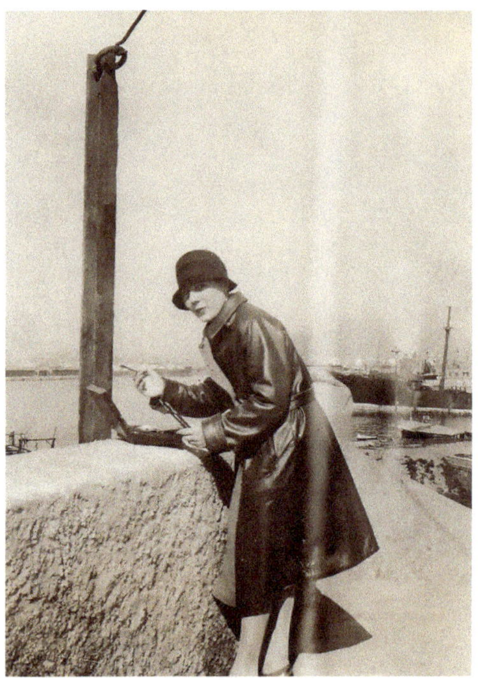

Figure 3.14. Mimì Quilici Buzzacchi in Cadice, 1929, photograph. Courtesy Archivio Mimì Quilici Buzzacchi.

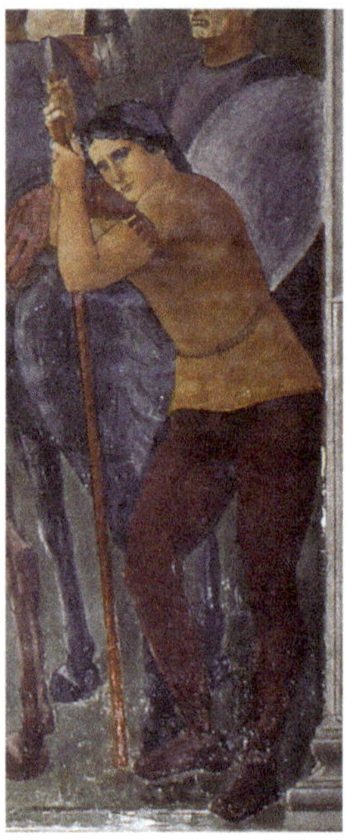

Figure 3.15. Achille Funi, *The Myth of Ferrara* (*Il mito di Ferrara*), detail from the south wall: foot-soldier in the Christian army, 1934–7, fresco, Town Hall, Sala dell'Arengo, Ferrara. Courtesy Archivio Achille Funi, Studio d'arte Nicoletta Colombo, Milan.

An active member of the Ariostean Committee, Buzzacchi created most of the covers of *Rivista di Ferrara* in 1933. Her distinctive style was a perfect visual expression of the Committee's actualist projects of presentification. Palazzo dei Diamanti was her third architectural subject, after the Estense castle on the *Rivista*'s first issue (figure 3.16) and the eighteenth-century arch of the Prospettiva di Corso Giovecca, which appeared on the third (figure 3.17).[56] In all three covers, Buzzacchi adopted the dramatic cavalier perspective typical of early modern representations of military fortresses and Antonio Sant'Elia's legendary sketches of futurist architecture (figure 3.18). In Buzzacchi's etchings, this monumentalizing optical angle turned familiar urban objects into uncanny polyhedrons, iconizing the illustrious but "burdensome" vestiges of the past into a new, aggressive plastic grammar. The monochrome regularity of Palazzo dei Diamanti, with its absolute volumes and smooth surfaces, offered the ideal material for such an exercise of "adaptation," to use Quilici's terms. Buzzacchi reimagined and simplified the classical marble bugnato of the façade in a futurist key, visualizing the sixteenth-century geometrical decoration as an imposing orthogonal projection seen from an unnaturally low, wide-angled, and cropped point of view. The resulting image, appearing on all the newsstands of the city in April, adapted the new trends of Piacentini's coeval rational buildings to the local architectural heritage of Ariosto's age. It completed the fascist reclamation of the recognizable Renaissance structure.

It is interesting to compare this cover of the *Rivista di Ferrara* (figure 3.12) with the cover of the catalogue of the exhibition, which was designed by Buzzacchi as well (figure 3.19). The artist, the subject, even the technique, are the same. And yet, the different perspectives and lines make the two etchings antithetical. Two diverging approaches to the Renaissance revival of 1933 are represented by the same hand: one championed by Quilici and the Ariostean Committee, the other by Brabantini, who edited the catalogue, and his curatorial team. The *Rivista* cover focuses on a corner: the sharp edge of a fortifying buttress. The catalogue's one shows instead an arch, which welcomes the eye on two more levels of open thresholds. The compositional centre is a lamp; the central escape point organizes the space in the traditional linear perspective for which Italy's Renaissance painting is famous. The façade of Palazzo dei Diamanti is the elegant crust of an ideal residence, architecturally pierced and ready to be accessed, not the armoured surface of a stronghold.

While this literal façade was featured on the *Rivista di Ferrara*, the *Corriere Padano* insisted, as I mentioned, on the organizational façade of the exhibition that took place in Palazzo dei Diamanti, glossing over the cultural

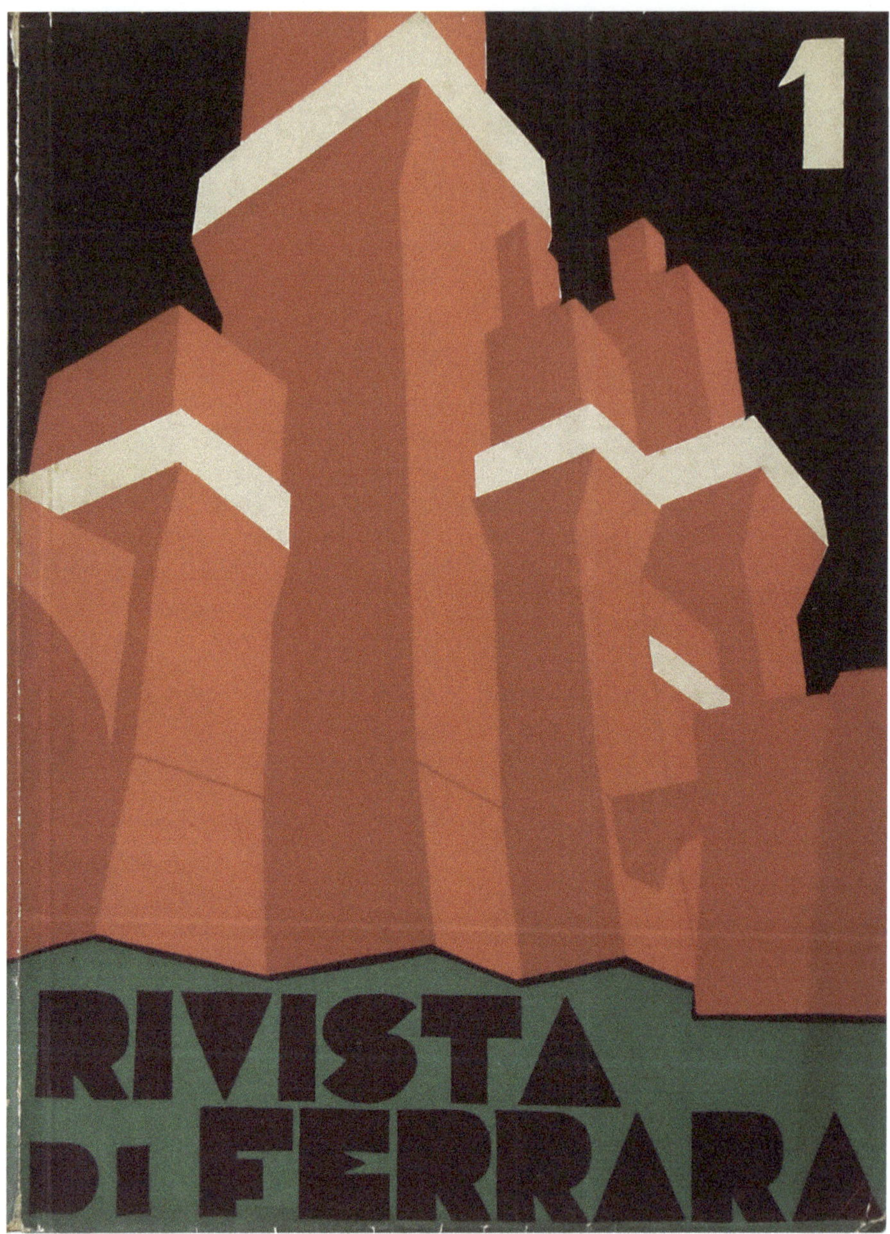

Figure 3.16. Mimì Quilici Buzzacchi, "Castello Estense," cover of *Rivista di Ferrara* 1.1 (January 1933). © Archivio Mimì Quilici Buzzacchi. Photograph © Giuseppe Tassinari.

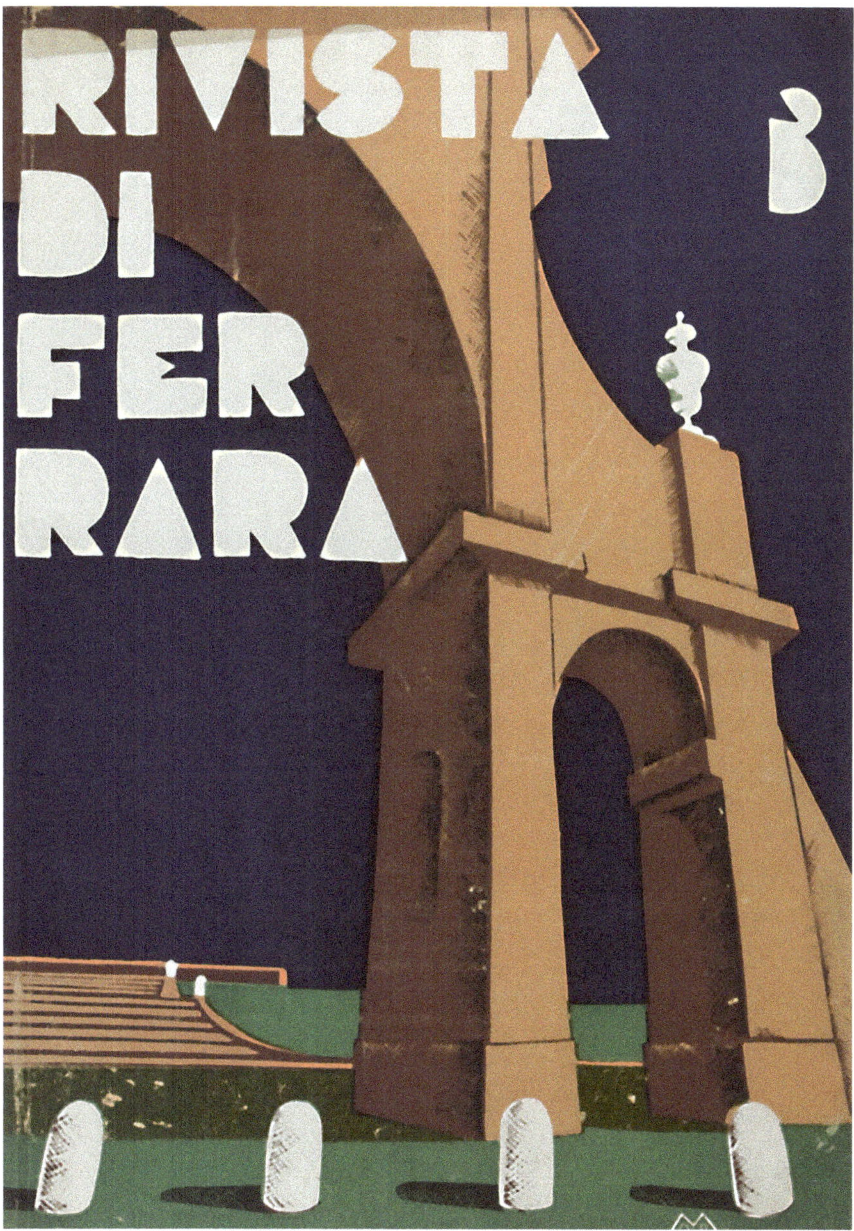

Figure 3.17. Mimì Quilici Buzzacchi, "Prospettiva di Corso Giovecca," cover of *Rivista di Ferrara* 1.3 (March 1933). © Archivio Mimì Quilici Buzzacchi. Photograph © Giuseppe Tassinari.

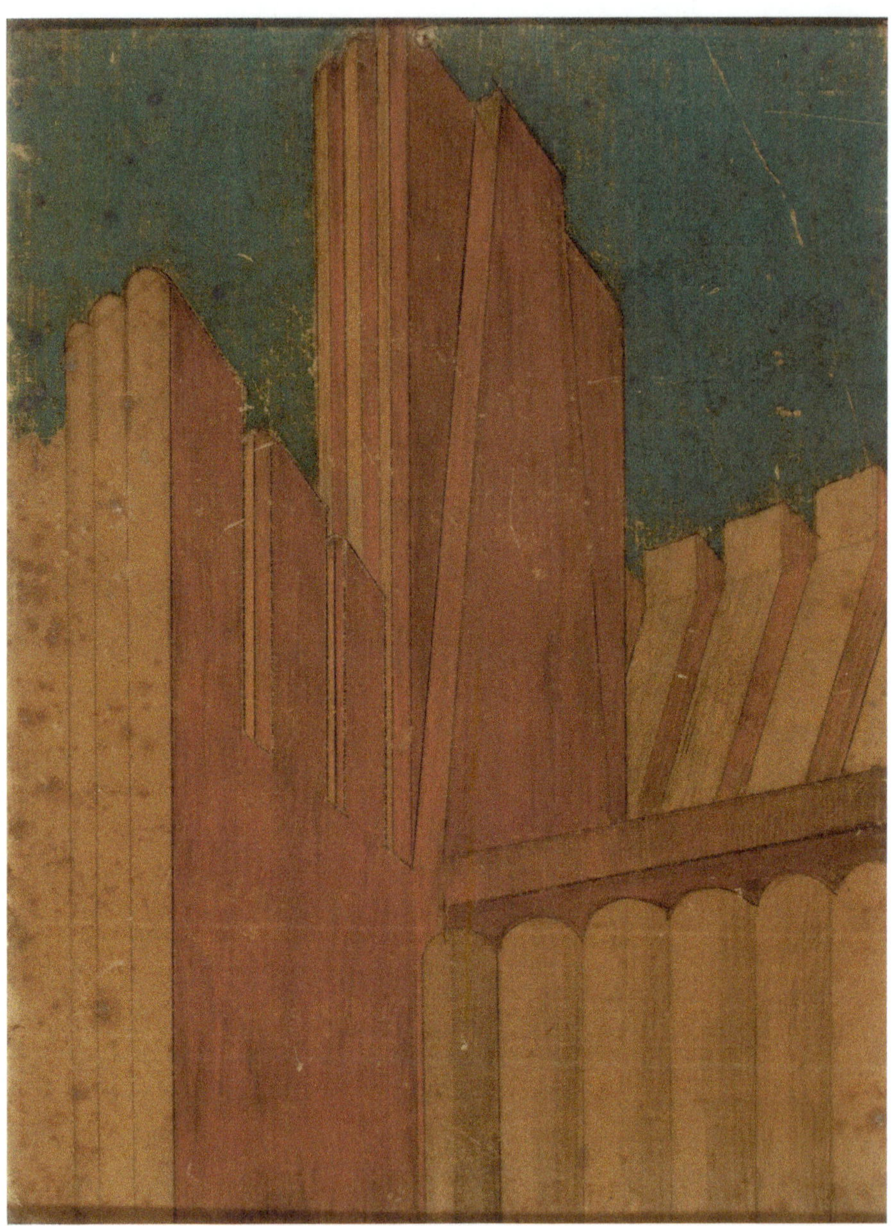

Figure 3.18. Antonio Sant'Elia, *Plastic-Architectural Study for an Industrial Building* (*Studio plastico-architettonico per edificio industriale*), 1913, pencil and pastel on paper, 39.5 × 29.8 cm, Pinacoteca Civica di Palazzo Volpi, Como. © Comune di Como.

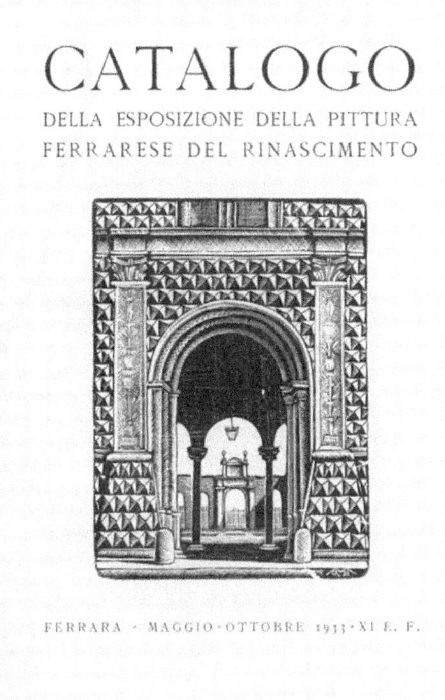

Figure 3.19. Mimì Quilici Buzzacchi, engraving on the cover of *Catalogo della esposizione della pittura ferrarese del rinascimento* (Ferrara, 1933). Bilioteca Comunale Ariostea, Ferrara.

and scholarly significance of its content. The rhetoric of the articles[57] presented it to the local population as a political accomplishment, focusing on the effectiveness of the municipal committee rather than on the art. The gathering of the paintings, actually based on scholarly curatorial criteria, was described as a brave repatriation of Ferrara's treasures from illegitimate overseas possessors. On inauguration day, the first page of the newspaper was titled "Una battaglia vinta" (the battle was won). Rather than discussing the curators' historical vision and choices, the paper commended their diplomatic skills, lauding their ability to convince foreign owners to loan their paintings. Because most of Ercole de' Roberti's works came from museums and collections outside of Italy, the main editorial article defined the room devoted to the artist as a small League of Nations ("una piccola Società delle Nazioni").[58] Actual descriptions of works and rooms did appear in the paper, but adopted a condescendingly didactic tone, reinforcing the paradoxical anti-intellectualism endorsed by the Ariostean Committee.[59] Readers' ignorance and fundamental lack of interest in the curators' work were appeasingly taken for granted in the press releases of the Committee.

In contrast with the rigour and connoisseurship of the exhibition, anti-intellectual and even anti-literary local pride was, in general, the defining feature of the administration's narrative. The fascist festival in honour of Ariosto intended to restore a glorious past through the legacy of a literary idol, and yet its organizers represented themselves (along with their fellow Ferrarese) as allergic to dusty books and old stories. Their presentification of Ariosto aimed to bypass literature and history. This anti-intellectualism was part of a larger strategy in fascist cultural politics. As Ghirardo noted in her study of fascist Ferrara, the spies of Mussolini's Ministry of Interior consistently reported that the working class was the most sceptical about fascism, while scholars and bourgeois professionals hardly ever appeared in lists of subversives and political enemies of the regime. Though envisioned and promoted by intellectuals, the initiatives for Ariosto's centenary had to involve and directly appease common and unlearned people, to the point of openly rejecting and mocking readers and historians. Despite being a revival of the past, the Ariostean festival had to speak directly to the everyday experience of Ferrara's least cultivated citizens.

The organization of the *Mostra bibliografica* at Palazzo Paradiso is emblematic of this actualist contradiction. The Committee did sponsor the gathering of the most complete collection of original prints, manuscript fragments, and modern editions of the *Furioso*, allowing the librarians of the Biblioteca Ariostea to compile a monumental Ariostean bibliography. Such a work, published right before the inauguration of the exhibition, was presented to the princes of Piedmont as a gift from the Committee, and is still a useful repertoire for scholars today. However, the exhibition itself was intended to be experienced as a reliquary, not a tool: a display of antique literary amulets and fetishes able to make visitors travel through time without ever reading a page of the exhibited books. Rather than didactic, its conception was touristic. It turned Ariosto's texts into material attractions: material landmarks able to conjure the presence of the author as an idol, instead of convening his ideas and stories.

Bones and Books

The *Corriere Padano* article that presented the bibliographic exhibition, based on a press release directly diffused by the Committee, invited the Ferrarese people to relish the "true pleasure" of "recognizing a century

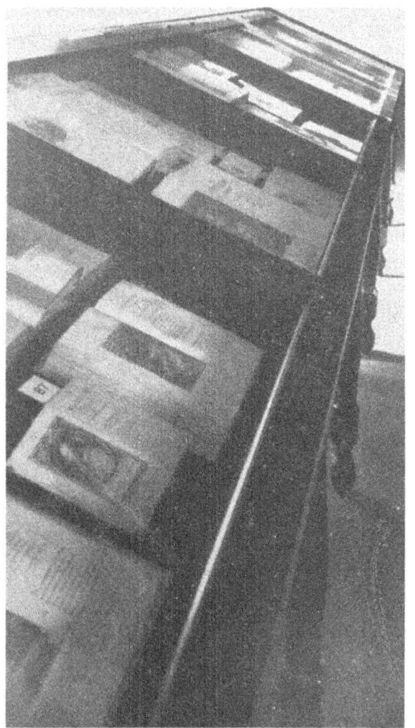

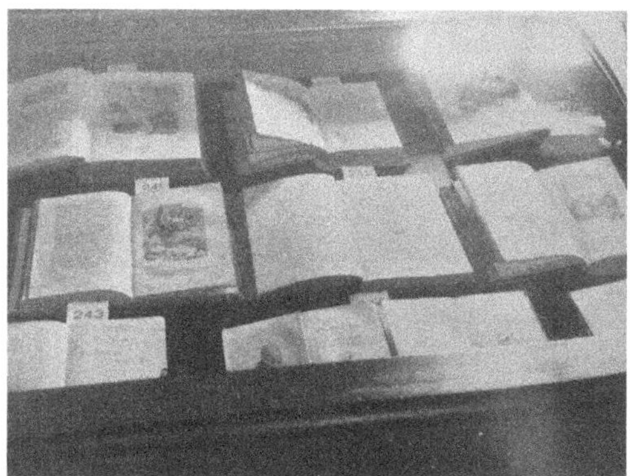

Figure 3.20. Exhibited documents at the Bibliographic Exhibition in Palazzo Paradiso, anonymous photographs from *Rivista di Ferrara* 1.6 (June 1933).

from the open pages of a book, from the typesets, the paper, and the etchings used by artisanal printers" (figure 3.20).[60] What the propaganda promised to visitors was not textual documents but heirlooms: not old literature but "the allure that history itself is able to cast."[61] Bibliography was not the point. The very concept of a bibliographic exhibition was even mocked by the anonymous author of the article (likely Quilici himself), who opened the piece with the question "Can you imagine the face of the public (even the so-called intellectual public) when they hear about an Ariostean Bibliographic Exhibition?" The answer is unmerciful:

> Noses wrinkling, eyebrows furrowing, lips sketching an ironic smile: An exhibition of books? [... M]any will imagine a rather uniform series of lifeless and meaningless volumes: they were dusted and cleaned, and yet one can still smell, even from afar, the stale stink of centuries of imprisonment in library showcases. Many will imagine some sort of bald professor, with his

> gold-rimmed spectacles and his skin turned into parchment like the yellow papers in which he basks: he wanders around the books with a complacent smile and a greedy eye.[62]

The grotesque description of the stereotypical egghead professor – someone who could actually be excited about the "uniform series of lifeless and meaningless volumes" by Ariosto – ridicules (and warns off) the kind of visitors that the Ariostean propaganda did not care for. These unwelcome visitors were directly identified, in the article, as "a very modest number of experts, of scholars who look a bit crazed and monomaniacal in their enthusiasm for their beloved books." Their ability to "find reasons for pleasure and joy in things that are known by few, appreciated by fewer, and admired by even fewer people – and that most consider useless"[63] is sarcastically framed as peculiar, and extraneous to the real aims of the exhibition. While the Committee sought the sponsorship of the Accademia d'Italia, organized a national "congresso dei bibliotecari," and counted, among its founding members, local bibliophiles and historians such as Giuseppe Agnelli and Guido Angelo Facchini, its public narrative was one of anti-academism and youthful scorn for books. Bookish professors, the most obvious and natural audience for an exhibition of Ariostean manuscripts and rare prints, were not welcome in Palazzo Paradiso – which, it should be noted, was in fact a university library. Arguably, a psychology of self-hatred pervaded the economy of hospitality in the spaces occupied by the Committee for its initiatives: designed and set up, like the other events, by people who identified themselves as intellectual leaders, the bibliographic exhibition was propagandized as anti-intellectual.

This rhetoric also reveals the image that the Committee had of its own local audience, and of the ideal modern and fascist reader (?) of Ariosto in general. This pseudo-reader, whose nose wrinkles at the very idea of smelly, dusty books, does not really read, but rather "recognizes history" through paper and parchment. He is part of a majority of non-experts and non-scholars, ready to reclaim cultural territories and artefacts from the shrivelled minority of professors who appreciate them. He is interested in the allure of "history itself," in the material presence of the past as it survives in the evidence of authentic objects. He will fruitfully visit a mausoleum, not a book collection.

It is meaningful that the bibliographic exhibition was indeed held in Ariosto's tomb. The poet's funerary monument, designed by Giovan Battista Aleotti in 1612, was moved to the library of Palazzo Paradiso in 1801 along with Ariosto's remains. The exhibition path led directly to it (figure 3.21). Visitors were, at the same time, in the presence of

Figure 3.21. The path of the Bibliographic Exhibition leading to Ariosto's tomb. Anonymous photograph from *Rivista di Ferrara* 1.6 (June 1933).

Ariosto's bones and of his books. And the books, exactly like biological relics, were to be read (or rather "recognized") as proof of an enduring mystical presence. Ariosto's manuscript notebooks and letters, in particular, were exhibited to conjure the poet's body and mind, not his words. His tired hand and quick fantasy, his smile, his paternal care for the peasants whom he administered: all this, according to the article, shone not through the literary style or linguistic choices in the documents, but through their very physical appearance and holographic aura. The visual evidence of the many corrections in the exhibited manuscript fragments of the *Furioso* was supposed to evoke, in a trivialization of Croce's influential essay on Ariosto, the frantic hesitations of a scrupulous and obsessive harmonizer, whose pen could not keep the pace of his genius.

It goes without saying that actual philological examinations of the same documents directly debunk the generic claims of the propaganda article.

Four years after the centenary, Gianfranco Contini redefined Ariosto's profile as a writer by studying the handwritten variants mentioned in the article, whose analysis and classification finally opened the way for a post-Croce appreciation of the historical and literary workshop in which the *Furioso* took shape. Contini's seminal 1937 essay on "How Ariosto Worked"[64] was triggered by Santorre Debenedetti's edition of the very manuscript fragments exhibited as intransitive relics by the Ariostean Committee, and inaugurated modern textual criticism. It distinguished between two possible conceptions of literary texts: a "static" one (in line with Croce's purist ideas) that considers poetry as "an object or achievement," and a "dynamic one, that sees it as a human artefact or work in progress." While the first is "absolute," the second is, "in the highest sense, pedagogical."[65] The approach of the Committee to the material remains of Ariosto's work expected to take both these directions at once, fetishizing variants and handwriting not as data to be interpreted but as sublime, tangible sites of pure poetry. This is what the article meant by "history itself," "la storia stessa" – a history without historians, a past immediately accessible through a pilgrimage to the objects and places in which it is present. A ritual of voodoo.

As a fascist zombie,[66] Ariosto was deprived of the agency granted by the letter of his literary voice. His personal impresa, which appeared as a xylography in the first edition of the *Furioso* (reproduced in the Introduction of this book), was an emblem of ingratitude, with the bitter motto "Pro bono malum" (evil for, or in exchange for, good) and the image of bees smoked out of a log. His late, unfinished *Five Cantos* were tragic and pessimistic, lucidly aware of the political and ethical crises of the late Renaissance. Both the impresa and the surviving fragments of the *Cantos* were included in the exhibition, and clearly described in the *Corriere Padano* article. And yet, their meaning was ignored. On the same front page of the newspaper, in an editorial titled "The Lord of Harmony," the 1933 celebrations were described as a rebellion against the false image of an ironic, sceptical Ariosto. The enemies of such a rebellion, those responsible for the invention of this fake Ariosto, are of course literary scholars. Instead of "arbitrary interpretations," the poet had to be appreciated through a "popular apotheosis":

> We have reclaimed for Ludovico Ariosto this rich, and lively, and marvellous humanity of his [...] and we have rebelled against the arbitrary interpretations that, by exaggerating some general aspects of his times, turned him into a sceptical caricaturist or a frigid aesthete. As such we reinvent him today, in the light of popular apotheosis. Only the disgraceful pedantry of literary scholars, or the insidious obsessions of third-rate historians,

> propagandized the image of a different Ariosto. The living Ariosto is this, and no other: a stupendous specimen of the gentile Latin race [...]: the lord and singer of harmony.[67]

In sum, the propaganda of the Ariostean Committee saw itself as fighting against an opposite propaganda: that of qualified readers and historiographers. In this battle between fascist optimism and the complex contradictions unearthed by Renaissance philology, Ariosto himself was conjured as an ally to fight against his own literary legacy: "the poet returns among us, magical and familiar, whimsical and wise, master of serene living; he returns when an industrious optimism pushes men to joyfully work in his favourite land, after the vanquishing of centuries-old lethargies."[68] But of course, this "living Ariosto" was really a cadaver.[69]

Body and Blood

What could a poet's body offer this fascist battle? How could a mere cadaver catalyse a city's aspiration to modernize, and its illusions of past glories? Catholic rituals and retraced ancestries, grief and genealogy, were important weapons in the administration's arsenal, especially in its interactions with the local population. These aspects of the 1933 Ariostean celebrations did not appear much in the propaganda, but archival documents still bear their traces, as we will see in a moment. In fascist Ferrara, Ariosto's biological and spiritual presence "among us" ("fra noi," to use the formula of the article cited before) was not just boasted at a national and international level, but also experienced within the dimension of the municipal community: a matter of surviving bloodlines and communal mourning. The event, after all, was the anniversary of a death. And, since Ariosto was actually born and raised in Reggio Emilia, death was the main card to play: the last rites were the only sacrament that he received in Ferrara. In order to appropriate the "living Ariosto," local fascists had to invest in the immanence of his dead body. They had to reclaim and ostend it as a civic trophy.

The tension between Ariosto's bones and Ariosto's books (between the "actual" Ariosto of the centenary's propaganda and the "arbitrary" Ariosto of critical readers) was patent in the bibliographic exhibition held in his tomb, and played out on the day of the anniversary. As I mentioned before, that day (the sixth of July) progressively lost relevance in the drafts of the program. It was then filled with a national convention of librarians. But while these experts on bibliography and textual studies from all over Italy gathered in the Biblioteca Ariostea, on the other side of the old town the fascist authorities sponsored a requiem Mass for Ludovico Ariosto's "salma" (literally, his "corpse").[70] This competing event was actually initiated by the Church of San Benedetto in Contrada Mirasole. This Benedictine monastery was the site of a Salesian boarding school at the time, but it had been, four hundred years before, Ariosto's local parish – the place where his funeral was celebrated and his body was originally buried. On June 27, with a letter to the mayor, the head priest informed the Ariostean Committee of the "centuries-old relationship" between the church and the Ariosto family, and of the intention of commemorating the poet "with a Solemn Mass, sung and officiated [...] in the morning of July the 6th."[71]

The Committee did not just approve the religious event: it actively promoted it. The program of the celebrations had already been printed and diffused in May, and the official event of the day was still the librarians' convention. However, true to the anti-intellectualism with which they imbued their propaganda, the Committee members quickly prepared and printed two hundred copies of an invitation to the Mass, shifting the community's attention to this alternative event. The draft of the card, in fact, reads more like an order than an invitation:

> On Thursday July 6, 1933-XI, the centennial anniversary of the death of LUDOVICO ARIOSTO, a SOLEMN MASS will be celebrated, at 11, in memory of the Great Poet, whose Corpse [Salma] was entombed in the Temple of S. Benedetto and given, for three Centuries, to the custody of the Monastic Order, which honoured It with constant requiems.
>
> The Function will be officiated by Benedictine Monks of the Praglia Abbey. The Authorities and the Representatives of the Institutions and Corporations [Enti e Sodalizi] of the City will be present.

The closing, peremptory sentence is the most edited in the document, with at least two strata of typed and manuscript corrections. The original formula was limited to generic "Authorities," which were then joined by "Representatives of the Districts [Rioni] of the City." This crossed-out addendum was corrected into "Representatives of the Institutions and Districts [Enti e Rioni] of the City," which was turned into the final version by hand. It was not empty language. To be certain that all the relevant administrative authorities, public institutions, and social, cultural, and industrial corporations received the message, the Committee typed a scrupulous list of invitees. Single-spaced and annotated in pencil, this list included two pages of institutions (schools, universities, sports clubs, Jewish and Catholic cultural circles, charities, and of course fascist groups)[72] and two of specific people.[73] Such widespread and surgical coverage was remarkable for a relatively improvised, last-minute addition to the official program. The only comparable lists of attendees preserved in Ferrara's municipal archives are those for the inauguration of the Ariostean celebrations on May 7 (an event attended by the heir to the throne, with simultaneous openings of all the exhibitions, a marching band, and discounts on train tickets to reach the city). No such effort was made to ensure the success of the librarians' convention, held at the same time. Once again, the collection and study of Ariosto's books was put in direct rivalry with the veneration of his dead body.

Blood, as I mentioned, played a role in the celebrations as well. At the end of June, Mayor Ravenna received a curious personal letter from a former mayor of Ferrara, Ettore Magni, who had been contacted by a woman who claimed to be the last living member of Ludovico Ariosto's bloodline. "Because of such qualification," the letter explained, "she should be entitled to be officially invited to the current centenary celebrations, and, in addition, she would like the city to pay for the transportation of her mother's body [from Turin] to a special site [in Ferrara], with an epitaph composed by the Township."[74] This woman, Ida Pochintesta Negri degli Ariosti, was indeed a direct descendant of the Ariosto family. At least, she was identified as such in the bulletin of the main Italian institute of heraldry, which published her obituary when she died two years later. The obituary confirms that her requests were promptly satisfied by the fascist administration, which apparently invited her to visit the city during the Ariostean celebration "as a representative of the family of the Poet." Her own body, in 1935, was "transported to Ferrara under the supervision of the Mayor [Ravenna], in order to be buried in the same Tomb that already contained the mortal remains of her ancestress and mother."[75]

No other trace of Pochintesta Negri's participation in the celebrations appears in coeval publications or in Ferrara's archives, but the Committee's interest in Ariosto's bloodline did not end with her mother's burial. The visit of another descendant of Ariosto, directly sought after by the administration, was mentioned in the chronicles of the closing celebrations of the Ariostean year, on October 15. The day was widely covered by the *Corriere Padano*, which, the following morning, opened with two full pages entirely dedicated to a meticulous account of the many events. The king himself had agreed to visit Ferrara for the occasion, so the report followed his movements throughout the various ceremonies, lectures, receptions, and public appearances. It was in Ariosto's house, in Contrada Mirasole, that Mayor Ravenna introduced him to "Daria Malaguzzi Valeri, descendant of the family of Ariosto's mother,"[76] while presenting him, at the same time, with the published proceedings of the Ottava d'oro lectures.

Except for members of the Ariostean Committee and regional authorities, Malaguzzi Valeri was the only person to be privately introduced to the king. Her function as a walking relic, as a vessel for the genetic presence of her ancestor in 1933 Ferrara, is obvious. Ironically, she might very well have been the least fascist person in the city on that day. As shown by Victoria de Grazia in her work on women under fascism, Malaguzzi Valeri was one of the most cultured and progressive feminist intellectuals of interwar Italy.[77] Born in Reggio Emilia, like Ariosto, and named after Ariosto's mother, she had moved to Milan to study in 1904. There, she became a successful writer and journalist, and married (refusing the Catholic rites) a socialist historian and philosopher, Antonio Banfi. With Banfi, she promoted underground partisan activism at the University of Milan,[78] and eventually took part in the Resistance – as she documented in a late book.[79] After the war, she became a prominent figure in literary circles related to the Italian Communist Party.

While she was not openly against the regime, unlike her husband, and received literary prizes from fascist institutions,[80] Malaguzzi Valeri promoted censored authors like Paola Masino and criticized fascist heroic novels such as Lorenza Arghito's *Combattenti*.[81] In the late 1920s and early 1930s, her salon was animated by liberal scholars and writers such as Ludovico Geymonat and Sibilla Aleramo, and formed the left-wing counterpart to the other main anti-fascist salon in Milan – the right-wing one of Lella Gallarati Scotti, often visited by Benedetto Croce himself.[82] It is unlikely that the Ariostean Committee did not know her political inclinations, since her husband had signed Croce's Manifesto of the Anti-Fascist Intellectuals in 1925. But while this kind of oblique position was clearly acceptable within the "different strings" policy discussed before, the Committee must not have realized that Malaguzzi Valeri actually disdained the Ariosto family, as well as the sixteenth-century court of the Este dukes and Ferrara's urban Renaissance in general.

During the summer of the centennial anniversary, the prestigious Milanese magazine *L'illustrazione italiana* had published a special issue on Ariosto, and asked Malaguzzi Valeri to contribute an essay on "The Ariostean Family Tradition." She did so, and the essay came out on July 2. The very first sentence clarifies that she was really going to talk about the "maternal" side of the "family tradition" of the title, glossing over the Ariosti bloodline. "We have never spoken much of the paternal family [...] and the few things we know are neither pleasant nor good."[83] She spent the following two paragraphs elegantly (but sharply) badmouthing Ariosto's father: "an intractable character [...] violent [...] unscrupulous [...] it is impossible to explain why the Malaguzzis [...] gave their daughter Daria to such a man."[84] And the rest of the article insists on how

Ludovico "abhorred" the vulgar city of Ferrara, with its corrupted court, and actually preferred his native Reggio Emilia, a rural retreat where he could study and write in the company of his maternal cousins.[85] On top of this anti-Estense sentiment, Malaguzzi Valeri connected her family's blazon with that of the poet erased by Ferrara's fascist celebrations, Matteo Maria Boiardo – whose family from Scandiano, in the essay, is described as more illustrious and genteel than that of Ariosto's father. She also alluded to the fact that the known manuscript fragments of the *Furioso* had probably been stolen from the Malaguzzi family in the eighteenth century. Of course, she was talking about the documents that, in 1933, were proudly showcased in the Ariostean bibliographic exhibition, a few feet from her ancestor's bones.

Despite her lack of sympathy for both Renaissance Ferrara and its fascist 1933 imitation, this unruly carrier of Ariosto's blood served her purpose in the necromantic economy of the Ariostean celebrations: that of showing the whole country, embodied by the king, that Ariosto was indeed "living" in the city where he died, both in the minds of his readers and in the flesh of his descendants. And who cares if most of the Ottava d'oro lecturers had not read him at all? Who cares if his mother's progeny scoffed at his name and his relationship with Ferrara?

Ariosto's Face

Ariosto's tomb, Ariosto's parish, his manuscripts and his prints, his patrons' ducal palaces and the art produced under their rule, his descendants' living bodies, and his dead one. Beyond these, two more physical relics were available to the fascists, and we encountered them in previous chapters: Ariosto's house, and his statue in Piazza Ariostea. From the viewpoint on its pedestal, in 1933 the statue bore witness to the Palio's costumed parades, for which Piazza Ariostea was turned into a racetrack. Ariosto's house, on the other hand, beheld an unusual exhibition, one which the Ariostean Committee called an "iconographic exhibition." In truth, it had more to do with spirit photography than iconography. Much like the Palio, this exhibition interpreted the centenary's actualist mission of presentification in the most literal sense.

"Poor house of Ariosto, how they had abandoned you!"[86] With this cry, in February, an editor of the *Rivista di Ferrara* opened his celebratory article about the restoration of Ariosto's house for the 1933 celebrations. In fairness, Ferrara's modern administrations had not invested much in the preservation of the building since it was purchased by the township in 1811. Before the fascist renovation, according to the article, windows were broken, humidity had damaged the walls, and both the interiors

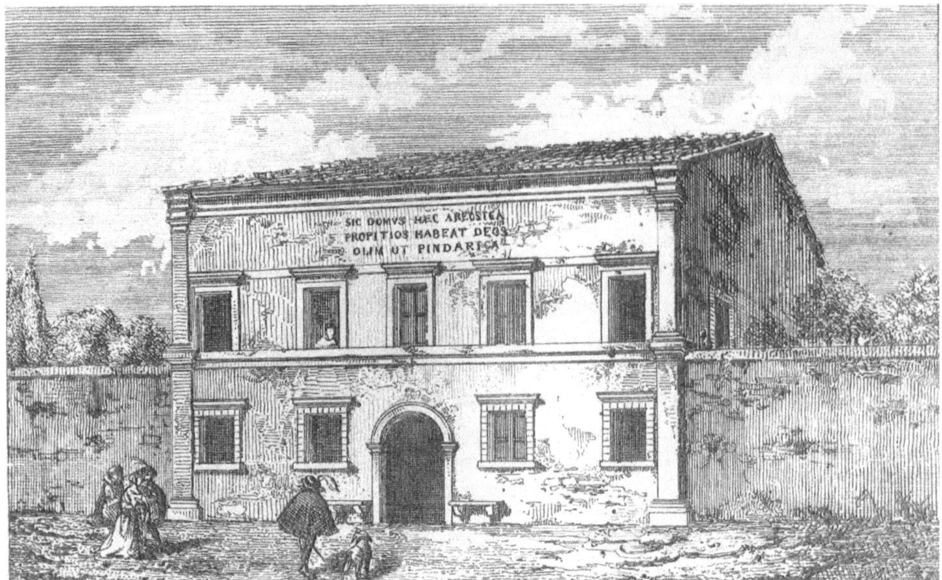

Figure 3.22. Engraved illustration of Ludovico Ariosto's house in *L'Omnibus Pittoresco* 19 (July 26, 1838).

and the garden were unkempt. Despite this negligence, as we know from the chronicle of Agnoletti and Govoni's nostalgic visit in 1915, nineteenth-century and early twentieth-century tourists could walk through the house (figure 3.22) and see a variety of historical objects and relics: some of Ariosto's furniture, including his legendary chair, manuscripts of the *Satires* and editions of the *Furioso*, medals, and even the bone of Ariosto's index finger.[87] Visitors could sign a register at the entrance, and many illustrious ones did, from Lord Byron to William Dean Howells. Byron, as we know, was hardly impressed, and preferred Tasso's prison to Ariosto's house. Howells, at the turn of the century, insisted on the provincial anonymity of Ariosto's house, then "inhabited by living people" (the private owners) who "reserved certain rooms to visitors" and had modernized the rest for their own comfort. His visit was dominated by a ghostly sentiment inspired by the relic of the finger, which was proudly shown to him by the local librarian before they walked together to the house, "as if the melancholy fragment of mortality had marshalled us the way."[88]

This Romantic aura of decay around Ariosto's house would not do for the propaganda of the Ariostean Committee. Thus, the house was not just refurbished and cleaned, with new windows, a new register to sign, and a fresh coat of paint. It was also repurposed. Rather than a monument crystallized in time – a messy haunted house filled with cursed trinkets, as the *Rivista di Ferrara* article described it[89] – it had to become the home of Ariosto's living, tangible human presence. Rather than a historic house museum, it had to become a medium to get directly in contact with Ariosto as a man: yet another act of presentification of Ferrara's sixteenth-century spaces. And this time, the main ingredient was Ariosto's face.

As it was presented in the *Corriere Padano*, the iconographic exhibition was designed to satisfy a specific curiosity: "what did Lodovico Ariosto look like?"[90] To answer this question, the walls of the little house (figure 3.23) were filled with etchings, drawings, and paintings; mostly minor originals and copies of famous ones. Busts of various qualities, from marble sculptures to chalk casts, populated the rooms. Most of these objects had little or no value, but all shared the same subject: Ludovico Ariosto. "Among the many portraits," asked the *Corriere Padano* presentation, "which one is the actual Lodovico?"[91]

The idea of looking for "il vero Lodovico" among Ariosto's early modern portraits is emblematic of the philosophy of history (and art history) embraced by the Committee. By looking at Renaissance painting as if it was some sort of defective proto-photography – an attempt, limited by the technology of the times, to record optical reality and to document, in this case, the facial features of "the *actual* Lodovico" – the fascists were distorting the very concept of iconography. To be sure, the iconography of Ludovico Ariosto was certainly the theme of the exhibition, and the variety of visual sources included in the catalogue (more than fifty) allowed for an exploration of this theme. Yet, any iconography of a notable early modern figure (especially a famous poet) is more about the visual translation of inner qualities and literary achievements than the "actual" physical features of their face. This is especially true for a courtly figure like Ariosto, who carefully fashioned his own image – not only in his autobiographical writings, like the *Satires*, but also in the visual apparatus of his early editions.

While the fascist administration of Ferrara was turning Renaissance portraiture into a tool to resurrect the facial physiognomy of the dead, Erwin Panofsky was developing a theory of iconography that opened the way for the modern interpretation of Renaissance art. He was doing so in exile, because he had to escape fascist persecutions. In 1933, in particular, he was working on a portrait of Giovanni Arnolfini and his wife, painted by Jan Van Eyck in 1434. A masterpiece of

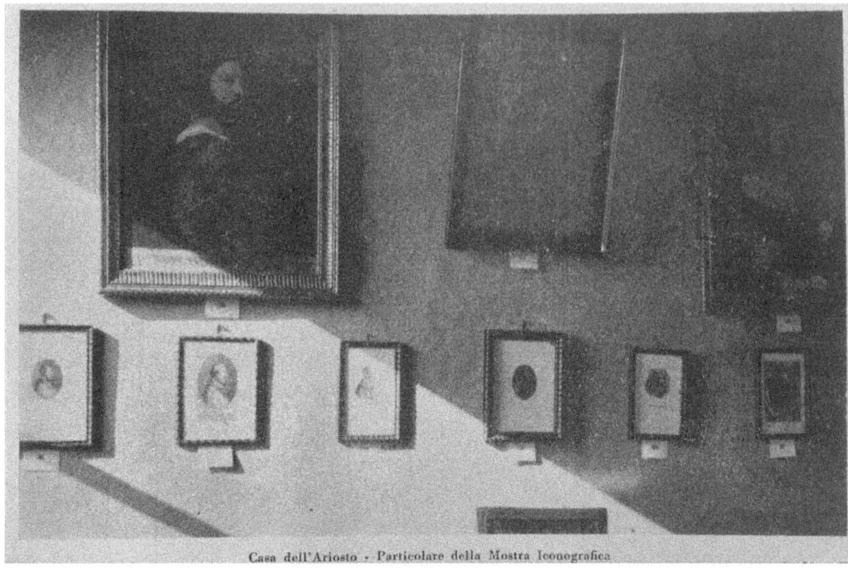
Casa dell'Ariosto - Particolare della Mostra Iconografica

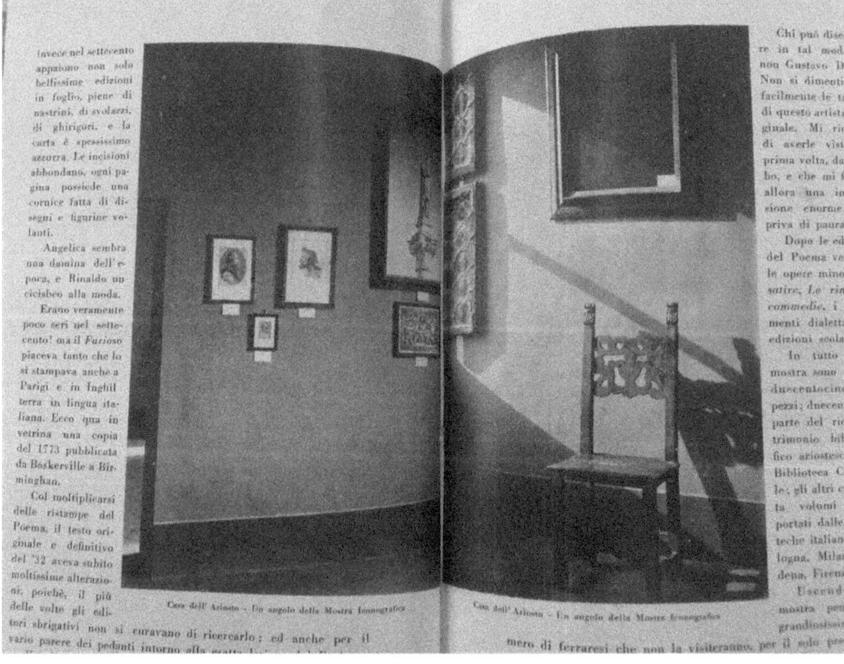
invece nel settecento appaiono non solo bellissime edizioni in foglio, piene di nastrini, di svolazzi, di ghirigori, e la carta è spessissimo azzurra. Le incisioni abbondano, ogni pagina possiede una cornice fatta di disegni e figurine volanti.

Angelica sembra una damina dell'epoca, e Rinaldo un cicisbeo alla moda.

Erano veramente poco seri nel settecento! ma il *Furioso* piaceva tanto che lo si stampava anche a Parigi e in Inghilterra in lingua italiana. Ecco qua in vetrina una copia del 1773 pubblicata da Baskerville a Birminghan.

Col moltiplicarsi delle ristampe del Poema, il testo originale e definitivo del '32 aveva subito moltissime alterazioni, poichè, il più delle volte gli editori sbrigativi non si curavano di ricercarlo; ed anche per il vario parere dei pedanti intorno alla ...

Casa dell'Ariosto - Un angolo della Mostra Iconografica

Casa dell'Ariosto - Un angolo della Mostra Iconografica

Figure 3.23. The Iconographic Exhibition, anonymous photographs from *Rivista di Ferrara* 1.6 (June 1933).

Northern realism, this painting offered Panofsky a prime example of what he called "transfigured reality": a blending of naturalism and allegorical meaning that is typical of early modern European art ("medieval symbolism and modern realism are so perfectly reconciled that the former has become inherent in the latter").[92] The Renaissance and early modern portraits of Ariosto exhibited in his house in 1933 could only render this kind of reality, but the fascist propaganda was looking for something else. The article about the exhibition in *Corriere Padano* insisted on details such as Ariosto's "crossed eye," or the length of his "goatee," or the progress of his "baldness," or the "pallor" of his skin.[93] Lips, forehead, ears, the distance between the eyes and the shape of the nose: these measurable details, as in a phrenology report by Cesare Lombroso (or a racial profile in *Difesa della razza*), were the focus of the article.[94] The questions from which it started were neither rhetorical nor metaphorical.

Before the inauguration of the iconographic exhibition, curator Giuseppe Ravegnani wrote an open letter to Ariosto. Ravegnani was also the director of the cultural pages of *Corriere Padano*, and his letter was published on the front page of the newspaper. In the letter he apologized to "Messer Ludovico" because his house lacked the two famous Titian portraits, blaming "the strict rules of the National Gallery in London [that] prevented their transportation." "However," he added, "two perfect soft reproductions match the charming beauty of the originals."[95] The point was not to show visitors actual paintings, but rather the "actual Ariosto." Ravegnani's curatorial justification was that the most famous of Titian's paintings (the one that had appeared in Bontempelli's edition of the *Satires* in 1916 and then inspired de Chirico's self-identification with Ariosto's monument in the 1920s) was a portrait of an anonymous merchant, not Ariosto. Elsewhere in the letter, the curator listed the "actual" features of Ariosto. These he took from detailed descriptions given by Giovan Battista Pigna, the courtly historian of Ferrara under Duke Alfonso II d'Este, in a 1556 edition of the *Furioso*.[96]

Pigna played a crucial role in the canonization of the *Orlando Furioso*, and his writings on Ariosto's life and work were extremely influential. His literary assessment of Ariosto's poetics has indeed been considered the first example of modern criticism. But when it comes to a biographical description of Ariosto, the "actual" Ariosto, Pigna is hardly a reliable source for modern historiographical standards.[97] And this is especially true on the matter of Ariosto's face. After all, how could he be expected to describe it faithfully? Pigna was only three years old when Ariosto died. Thus, Pigna's 1556 description was not based on any direct experience, but rather on some of the same images that would be gathered for the 1933 exhibition – including the engraved copy of Titian's portrait of Ariosto, which Pigna refers to directly. As a result, Pigna's description was of an idealized Ariosto, not what we would today call a "true to life" Ariosto. Yet, in May 1933, Pigna's representations were taken for the article that advertised the iconographic exhibition in Ferrara. The authenticity and actualism of the exhibition were, therefore, illusions, predicated on a textbook misuse of documents from the past. To quote Panofsky, "the case should be a lesson to us not to attempt to use literary sources for the interpretation of pictures, before we have interpreted the literary sources themselves."[98]

It was no coincidence that Ariosto's house was where Daria Malaguzzi Valeri was introduced to the king. In the Ariostean Committee's distorted conception of iconography, the face of Malaguzzi Valeri was the last piece of the puzzle which truly completed the exhibition. Deputizing for the "actual" Ariosto, she was a living and breathing bearer of the somatic data that the curator was searching for in reproduced portraits and sixteenth-century texts. She was the most indubitably authentic of relics. Fascist Ferrara now had a living face to showcase for Ariosto's centenary. Much better than a dead finger.

The propaganda's preoccupation with Ariosto's "actual" face extended beyond the iconographic exhibition. The main image in the official poster of the centenary (figure 3.24) is a photographic reproduction of a sixteenth-century portrait of Ariosto. The portrait comes from the frontispiece of the 1532 edition of the *Orlando Furioso* (figure 3.25): a xylography approved by the poet himself and very much in line with Pigna's description. Hardly a flattering or inspiring image, it represents Ariosto's gravitas and stoicism as an old, authoritative, and frugal master. The story behind the design of the poster sheds light on the reason why this specific image was chosen to represent the celebrations.

One of the earliest initiatives taken by the executive commission of the Ariostean Committee was to announce a competition for the design of a "mural poster." "The purpose of this poster," read the announcement, "is to propagandize the celebrations with which the Estense City intends to pay homage to her greatest Poet."[99] The competition was limited to artists from Ferrara and its province, and started on August 15, 1932. By September 30, the Committee had received twenty-three proposals, but none of them was deemed acceptable. Thus, in November, the Committee asked the fascist national artists' union to supervise a new, larger competition,[100] and

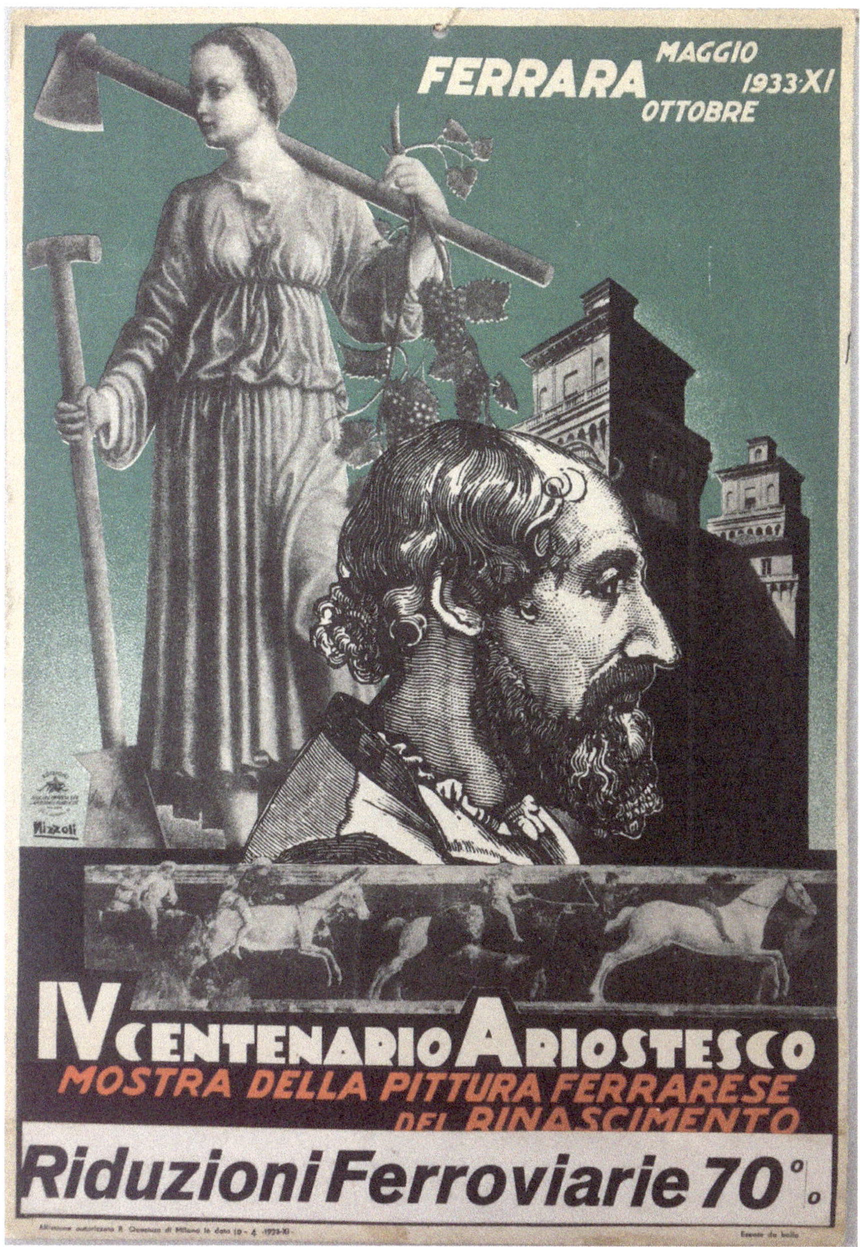

Figure 3.24. Marcello Nizzoli, poster for the IV Centennial Anniversary of Ariosto's death, print, 1933. Archivio Storico Comunale di Ferrara.

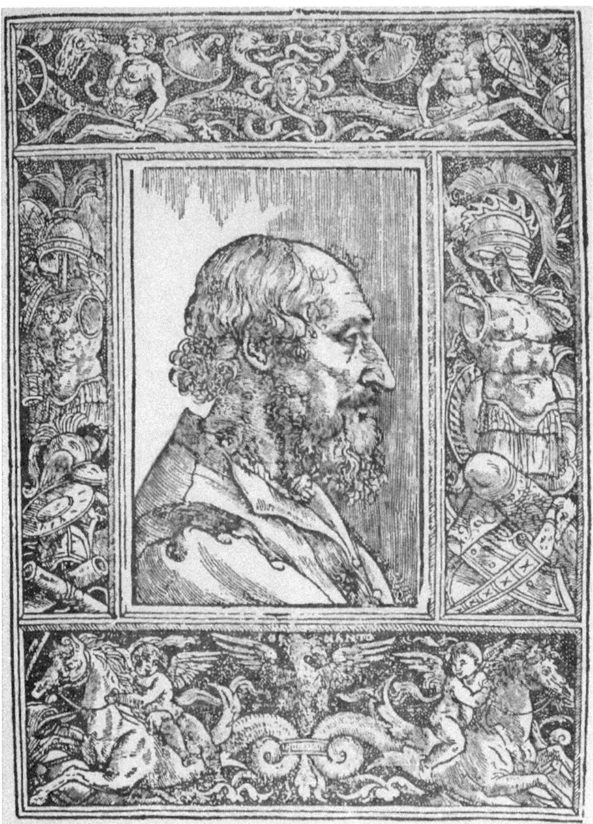

Figure 3.25. Francesco Marcolini, portrait of Ludovico Ariosto after a drawing by Titian, with a decorative frame by Francesco de Nanto, xylography on the frontispiece of Ludovico Ariosto, *Orlando Furioso* (Ferrara: Francesco Rosso, 1532). Biblioteca Comunale Ariostea, Ferrara.

a second announcement was released – raising the prize from three thousand to ten thousand lire.[101] This time the Committee received seventy-seven proposals, which were exhibited in Ferrara for a public evaluation.[102] However, although "some proposals presented considerable artistic qualities, [...] the Committee had to conclude that not even among those was there a work that fully responded to the goals and needs required by the theme."[103] At that point, in January 1933, it was too late to start a third competition, so the Committee contacted a renowned graphic designer, Marcello Nizzoli, and commissioned the poster from him. The instructions given to Nizzoli were clear. Instead of an original drawing, the Committee requested a photomontage of four existing images: the Estense castle, Francesco del Cossa's *Allegory of Autumn* (figure 3.26), the representation of the Palio di San Giorgio from the Schifanoia frescoes, and, of course, Ariosto's face.[104] Nizzoli merely juxtaposed four printing stereotypes (still preserved in Ferrara's municipal archives)[105] and added the text suggested by the Committee.

Nizzoli's clunky assemblage is a far cry from the inventive glamour of his coeval hand-drawn works. Could the one hundred proposals received by the Committee have all been much worse than the photomontage? In February 1933, in *Rivista di Ferrara*, Aroldo Canella published a small selection of the posters that were sent in 1932 for the two competitions (figure 3.27). While some of them look unclear or old-style, many are elegant and imaginative. What did they lack, in the eyes of the Committee? The problem was probably that most of the proposed posters represented elements from the *Orlando Furioso*: Astolfo's magic horn, the flight on the Hippogriff, Orlando's formidable lance impaling multiple enemies, and so on. Evidently, the "theme" that the Committee was looking for was not to be found in Ariosto's poem, which was not even mentioned in Nizzoli's instructions. Some rejected posters did focus on Ariosto's face, but, as Canella's comment underlined, they were not based on the "actual" Ariosto, and took too many liberties in representing him ("with the beard, without the beard, old, young").[106]

If he was to be actually present in Ferrara, and familiar to the people celebrating him, Ariosto could only have one face: a real, human face, unencumbered by the medieval imagery of his poetry and unadulterated by the idealizing filter of his Renaissance portraitists. The 1532 profile that appeared on the poster, pasted on every corner of the old city (figure 3.28), was faithful enough to Titian's portrait and Pigna's description to conjure his presence. And it was, unlike the images produced by the rejected contestants, a photographic reproduction of a sixteenth-century etching, not the invention of a modern artist. The only other image of Ariosto authorized by the propaganda was essentially traced over the same etching. It appeared on the cover of *Rivista di Ferrara* in October, at the end of the celebrations (figure 3.29). Among Buzzacchi's graphic presentifications of Ferrara's sixteenth-century legacy, it is the simplest, least colourful, and closest to the original.

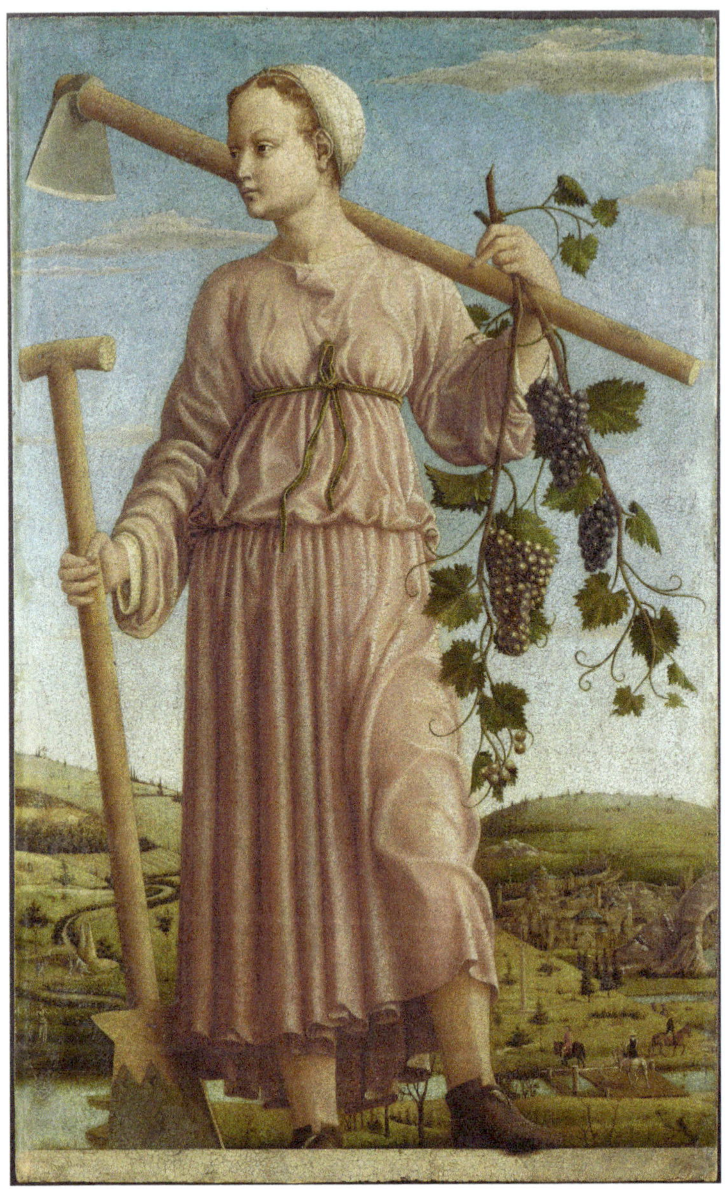

Figure 3.26. Francesco del Cossa, *The Muse Polyhymnia or Allegory of Autumn*, 1455–60, oil on canvas, 117 × 73.2 cm, Gemäldegalerie der Staatlichen Museen, Berlin. Photo Credit: bpk Bildagentur/Gemäldegalerie/Christoph Schmidt/ Art Resource, NY.

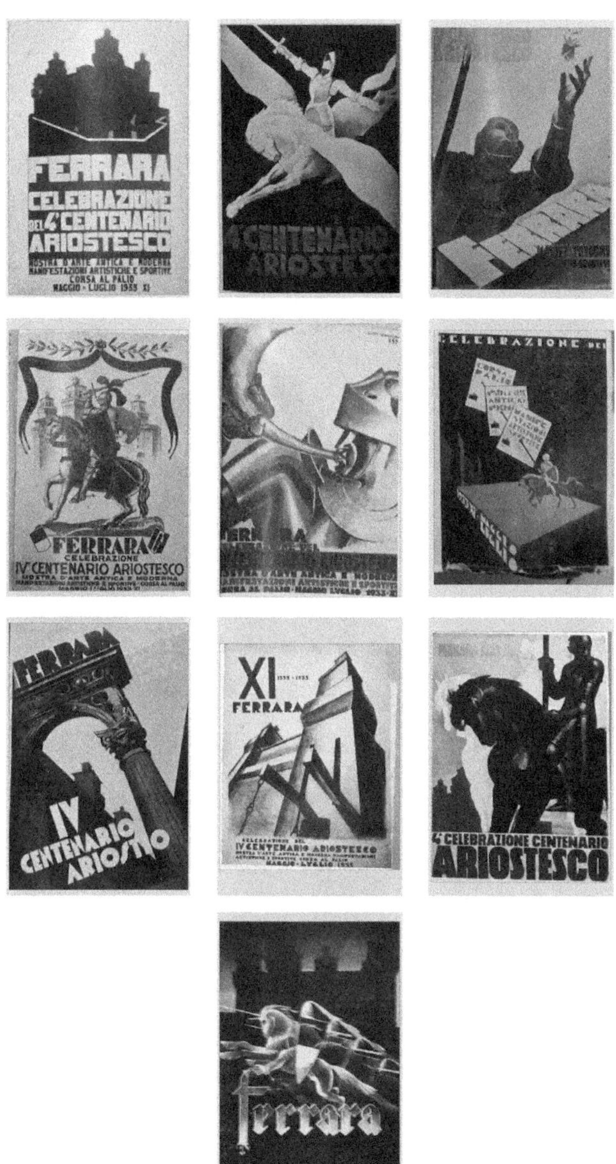

Figure 3.27. Ten rejected submissions, from various artists, for the poster of the IV Centennial Anniversary of Ariosto's death, from *Rivista di Ferrara* 1.2 (February 1933).

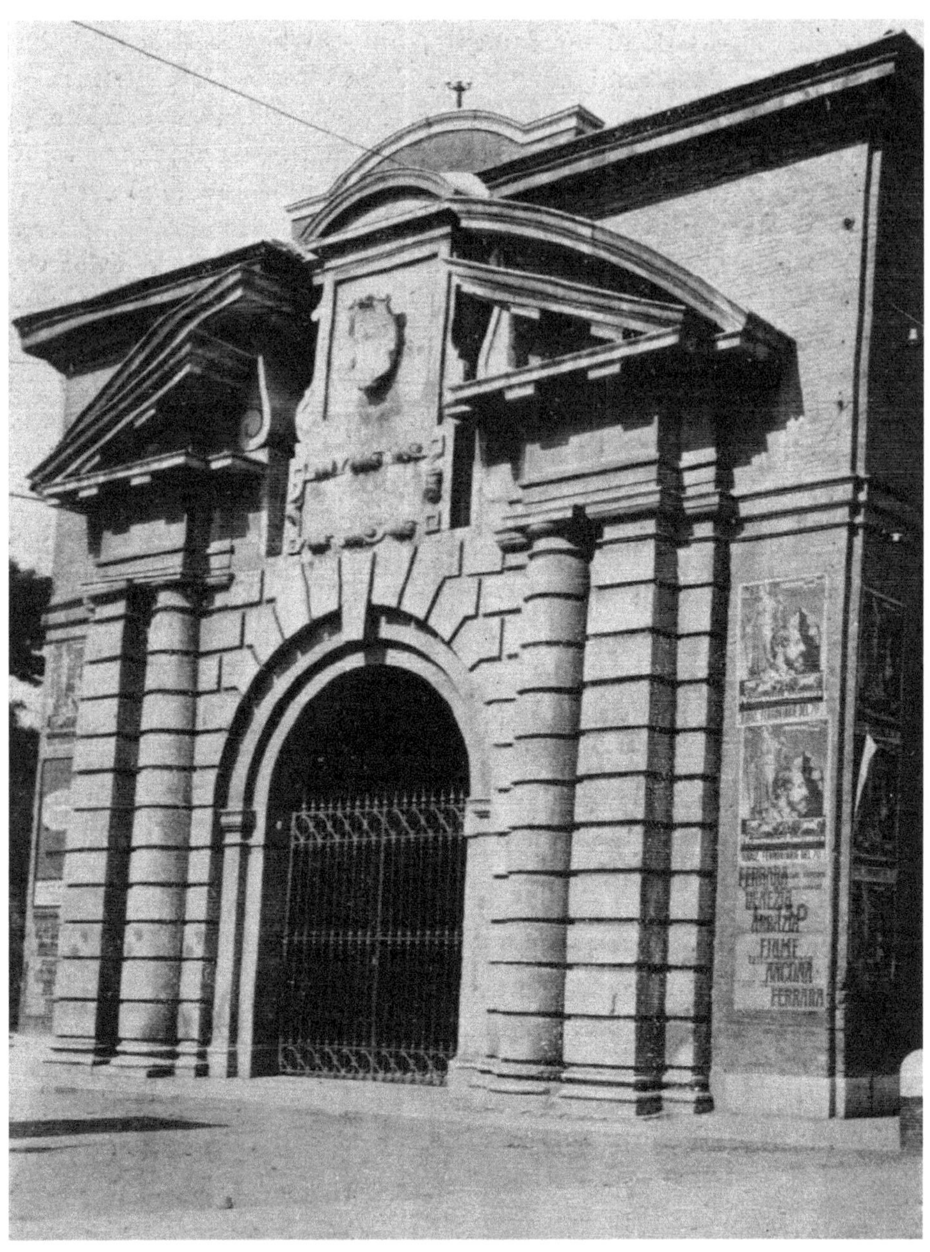

Figure 3.28. The official poster of the centenary pasted on the corners of Porta San Paolo in Ferrara, anonymous photograph from *Rivista di Ferrara* 1.7 (July 1933).

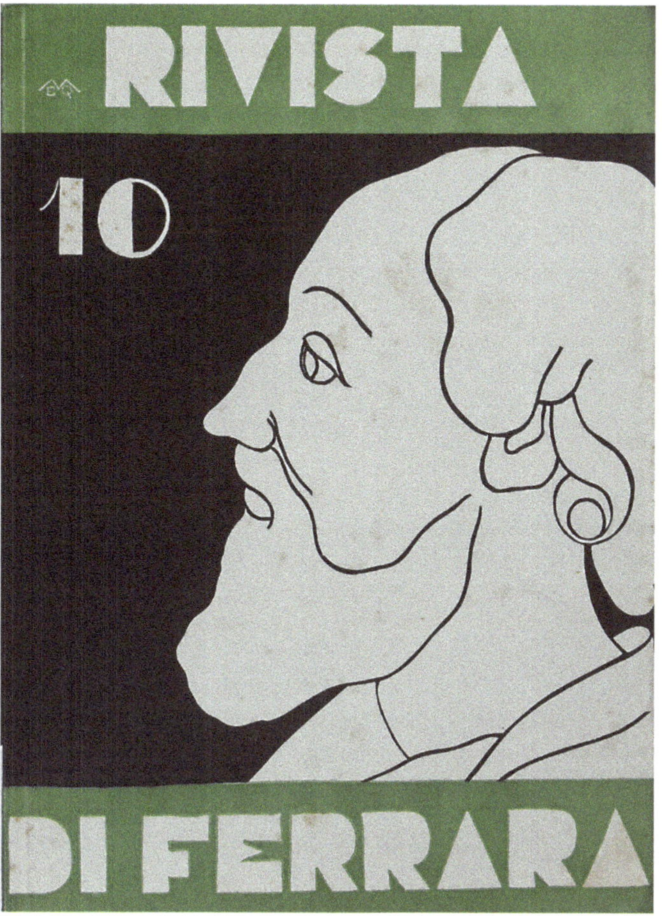

Figure 3.29. Mimì Quilici Buzzacchi, "Ludovico Ariosto," cover of *Rivista di Ferrara* 1.10 (October 1933). © Archivio Mimì Quilici Buzzacchi. Photograph © Giuseppe Tassinari.

Eternal Presence

To be sure, the fetishization of Ariosto in Ferrara was not a fascist invention. Centennial anniversaries of Ariosto's birth and death were celebrated in Ferrara before 1933 (and after). Ariosto's house and tomb have been destinations of literary pilgrimages throughout early modernity, at least since Gregorio da Montagna's visit in 1572.[107] Artists and writers have consistently paid homage to Ariosto by visiting his adoptive city. The poet Vittorio Alfieri signed the margin of Ariosto's autographs to express his veneration. In the first chapter of this book I quoted extensively what vanguardists such as Govoni, Agnoletti, and de Pisis wrote about touring Ariosto's house. Furthermore, throughout Romanticism, Ariostean landmarks in Ferrara were well integrated in the Southern European networks of the Grand Tour. This kind of tourism was no stranger to the fetishistic allure of immanent authenticity.

In 1818, Percy Bysshe Shelley was fascinated by the armchair in Ariosto's house, and entertained the "willing delusion" of seeing the poet sitting in it. Suspiciously, he noticed that, in the same room, the brass inkstand had "an antique rather than an ancient appearance."[108] He was onto something there: another, less illustrious British tourist had purchased the original (?) inkstand from the tenants of Ariosto's house, who had discreetly replaced it with a painted cast in the eighteenth century. Later in the nineteenth century, in her journal notes from Ferrara, a third British tourist wrote: "some of our countrymen have carried their veneration for the poet's residence so far, that they have actually taken away a considerable piece of the wooden door of the apartment in which he used to pass his days." The splinters of Ariosto's door, she added, "might justly be termed protestant relics."[109]

The preservation and public exhibition of writers' remains, belongings, inhabited spaces, and effects is a well-documented historical phenomenon. As Nicola Watson argued in her study of writers' house-museums in modern Europe, the aim of these practices is "to evoke the simultaneous materiality and immateriality of the author."[110] However, the 1933 Ferrarese initiatives for Ariosto's centenary were different from traditional forms of tourism and commemoration. Their use of Ariosto's "protestant relics" was imbued with a rather catholic belief, the same that made the Committee's "willing delusions" real in the propagandized initiatives. Rather than evoking Ariosto's material and immaterial legacy, the fascist administration convoked his presence in Ferrara.

As an act of both surveillance and spectacle, the 1933 centenary forced the entire city into a collective performance of misbelief. Ariosto was *actually* back, Ferrara was *actually* experiencing the Renaissance again. In this unaware – rather than willing – delusion, Ariosto's Ferrarese relics comprised him entirely (his mind, his life, the meaning and power of his work), more than any of his writings. This fantasy had consistently informed the Ariostean propaganda since Balbo's inaugural lecture for the Ottava d'oro in 1928. It had little to do with literature or history. Or better, like any form of propaganda under totalitarianism, it effectively blurred the margin between the interpretation of historical or literary evidence and magical thinking; complex facts and convenient fictions. And, along the same lines, the delusions of this Ariostean propaganda affected both its producers and its consumers during the 1933 centenary. While the administration certainly exploited the occasion to display the city's wealth and importance at a national and international level, the main target of the propaganda was Ferrara herself. Ferrara, where Ariosto had to dismiss his authorial aura and become a friendly idol of the masses, was both the stage and the parterre; the citizens were co-performers and spectators of the initiatives. Rather than an abstract revival of Ariosto, the presentification of the Renaissance was framed as Ariosto's literal return.

The concept underlying all the initiatives of the 1933 anniversary was clear: the "actual" Ariosto was not to be found in academic essays or old books – not even his own poem. To know Ariosto (or rather, to meet him) one had to leave the library and walk the revamped streets of Ferrara. That is where he "came back," according to the rhetoric of the propaganda. That is where Nello Quilici said to have personally encountered him in the most important Ariostean piece that he wrote in 1933:

> Sir Ludovico walked towards me from Contrada Mirasole with an enigmatic smile: "Young man, he told me, poetry is in the living life that flows and reflects the lights of reality along with the clouds of fantasy [...]
>
> What you consider absolute and certain, O young man, is really precarious; the century is renewing itself [...] but the fire is born again under the ashes; intangible and incorruptible, the mirror of the heart reflects the game of life defeating death."
>
> That is when I understood why Ariosto was the most modern of Italy's poets: and how his return coincided with the third resurrection of the city of Ferrara from its ashes.[111]

It is important to underline that this text is not excerpted from a work of fiction or literary prose. It is part of an essay with scholarly pretences. Quilici gave it as a public lecture in Palermo, in April 1933, and then he published the script in *Corriere Padano*, with the title "The Poet of the Eternal Renaissance," in October. In both cases, the text served as a closing reflection on Ariosto's centenary. In 1934, Quilici included it in his first book of essays, published by a press specializing in history and social sciences. For this last editorial passage, he added numerous bibliographic footnotes. Tellingly, most of the names of foreign scholars that he cited are misspelled or misgendered.[112] But what matters here is that he considered the text to be not just a propaganda piece, but a legitimate essay on Ariosto. Before chronicling his conversation with him in Contrada Mirasole, Quilici argued that Ariosto inaugurated modern times, building a new world with his poetry. Establishing a direct parallel between Ariosto and Mussolini (who, like Ariosto, "sculpts human matter with an artist's thumb"),[113] he stated that, in 1933, Ferrara was experiencing again what had happened in Ariosto's age. Back then, the city had suddenly dismissed its centuries-old medieval decadence; under fascism, it was finally freeing itself from the gothic lugubriousness of Romanticism: "no more Romantic nightmares of decadent poetry, but rather a push to the new greatness."[114] As the title suggests, for Quilici Ariosto was the ever-present herald of an "Eternal Renaissance," destined to cyclically re-emerge from its ashes.

Within the discourse generated by Ariosto's centenary, a similar achronological theory of the Renaissance pervaded even the most sophisticated rhetorical products. In October 1933, under the auspices of the Accademia d'Italia, Giulio Bertoni was invited to give the closing lecture of the Ariostean celebrations in Ferrara's public theatre. A philologist trained in the historical method, for the most part Bertoni echoed traditional positions on Ariosto – those of Carducci and de Sanctis, and those that he had adopted himself in his monograph on the *Furioso*. However, when he moved to the question of Ariosto's modernity, his speech converged on the actualism of Quilici's "Eternal Renaissance." "The secret of Ariosto's modernity," concluded Bertoni, is in "the intimate quality of the poetry that he liberally gave to us." By virtue of this poetry, Ariosto "ascended to an enchanted sphere, where there are no chronological distinctions and where past and future coincide in an eternal present."[115]

According to Giovanni Gentile, "the past that enters into history is the past that survives in the present: it is the present itself." The "actual" present (unlike the "false" relative present conceived as a mid-point between past and future) "is extra-temporal, eternal," and the "process of experience, in its actuality, is an eternal process."[116] Both Quilici's and Bertoni's speeches are clearly based on Gentile's doctrine, which, after all, was a crucial touchstone for fascist intellectuals. But, as we saw at the beginning of this chapter, putting actualism into practice for cultural initiatives of commemoration and didactical experiences of history leads to what I have been calling, using Rik Peters' term, a "presentification of the past." In Ferrara, it led to the misbelief that Ariosto was truly back in the streets of his city: that his legacy was a birthright of the Ferrarese people, that his poetry was living in fascist policies and initiatives.

The actualist delusion interlaces all the examples of cultural propaganda that we have encountered so far. And, as in the emblematic case of Atlante's shield in the fresco at the beginning of this chapter, the past (through the muted voice of literary interpretation, historical evidence, philology, iconography, and even "protestant relics") resisted the fascists' presentification.

When Ravegnani, the curator of the iconographic exhibition, wrote his open letter to Ariosto in *Corriere Padano*, he didn't do so metaphorically. As I mentioned, Ravegnani was also the director of the *Padano*'s cultural section. His rhetorical strategies were organic to the Ariostean propaganda, and his letter appeared to be really addressed to a person, a "You" (the "actual," returning Ariosto) who, of course, could not directly answer. This unwilling addressee was not, as in the case of Bontempelli's ode to Ariosto, a literary master who could teach something to those who read his writings. Nor was he the animated monument encountered by de Chirico and his fellow metaphysicians. He was a man, a returning living man, treated for too long as if he was an immaterial author or a ghost. Yes, Ariosto was dead, and the curator even discussed the circumstances of his death in the letter. But then he invited him for a stroll in Ferrara's streets and, switching to the present tense, he started to chronicle this stroll. He invited Ariosto to knock on the door of his house, and told him: "a tidy old lady comes to open and, as she sees You, she marvels and pays homage to You."[117] Then, he proceeded to give Ariosto a tour of the iconographic exhibition. It is directly to Ariosto that Ravegnani cited Pigna's description, almost as if he needed to impose the features of the "actual" Ariosto on Ariosto himself, resuscitating Ariosto as a recognizable golem through the prescriptive iconography of his exhibition.

The head of the press office of the Ariostean Committee, Alberto Brizio, represented Ariosto's comeback in even more literal terms. In an article that appeared in *Illustrazione del Popolo* (figure 3.30), illustrated by a reproduction of the xylography of Ariosto's "actual" face, Brizio described the return of a revenant. His account of Ariosto's awakening even echoes the Gospels.

> Sir Ludovico returns. He returns simple, smiling, benevolent, a bit stooped under the weight of many centuries of glory, a bit slow because he hasn't moved for a long time. He was awakened from the eternal sleep by the noises that arise, in adoration, around his name, and he left the marmoreal sepulchre of the Palazzo delle Scienze to walk towards the modest house in Contrada Mirasole.[118]

Of course, both Ravegnani and Brizio seemed to intentionally ignore that the "marmoreal sepulchre" was a late honour (with a wrong date of death inscribed on it), and that Ariosto wanted to be buried humbly in his local parish, where his body remained for forty years. More importantly, their new mythology of Ariosto's return is at odds with the fact

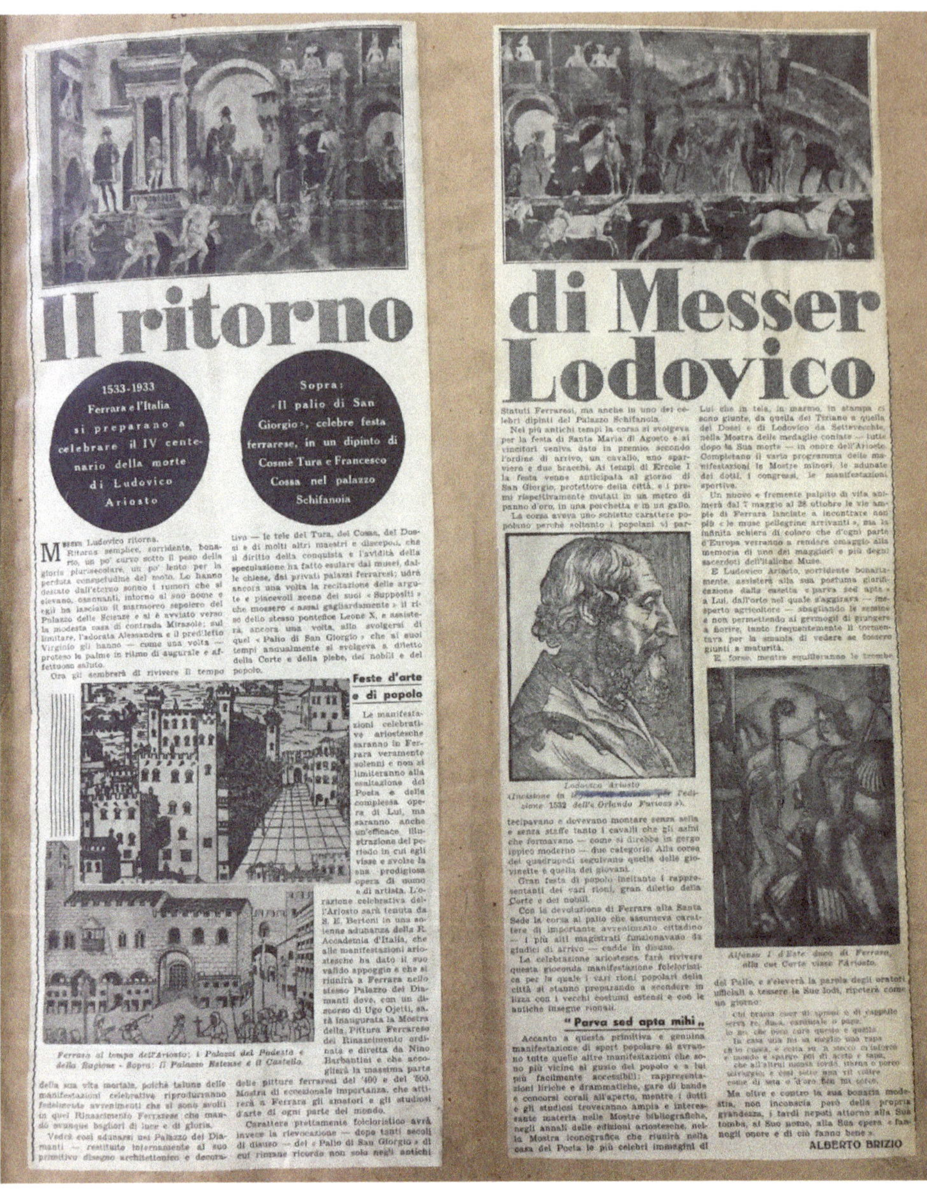

Il ritorno di Messer Lodovico

1533-1933
Ferrara e l'Italia si preparano a celebrare il IV centenario della morte di Ludovico Ariosto

Sopra: «Il palio di San Giorgio», celebre festa ferrarese, in un dipinto di Cosmè Tura e Francesco Cossa nel palazzo Schifanoia

Messer Ludovico ritorna.

Ritorna semplice, sorridente, bonario, un po' curvo sotto il peso della gloria plurisecolare, un po' lento per la perduta consuetudine del moto. Lo hanno destato dall'eterno sonno i rumori che si elevano, osannanti, intorno al suo nome e egli ha lasciato il marmoreo sepolcro del Palazzo delle Scienze e si è avviato verso la modesta casa di contrada Mirasole; sul limitare, l'adorata Alessandra e il prediletto Virginio gli hanno — come una volta — proteso le palme in ritmo di augurale e affettuoso saluto.

Ora gli sembrerà di rivivere il tempo della sua vita mortale, poichè talune delle manifestazioni celebrative riprodurranno fedelmente avvenimenti che si sono svolti in quel Rinascimento Ferrarese che mandò ovunque bagliori di luce e di gloria.

Vedrà così adunarsi nel Palazzo dei Diamanti — restituito internamente al suo primitivo disegno architettonico e decorativo — le tele del Tura, del Cossa, del Dossi e di molti altri maestri e discepoli, che il diritto della conquista e l'avidità della speculazione ha fatto esulare dai musei, dalle chiese, dai privati palazzi ferraresi; udrà ancora una volta la recitazione delle argute e piacevoli scene dei suoi «Suppositi» che mossero «assai gagliardamente» il riso dello stesso pontefice Leone X, e assisterà, ancora una volta, allo svolgersi di quel «Palio di San Giorgio» che ai suoi tempi annualmente si svolgeva a diletto della Corte e della plebe, dei nobili e del popolo.

Ferrara al tempo dell'Ariosto: i Palazzi del Podestà e della Ragione - Sopra: Il Palazzo Estense e il Castello.

Feste d'arte e di popolo

Le manifestazioni celebrative ariostesche saranno in Ferrara veramente solenni e non si limiteranno alla esaltazione del Poeta e della complessa opera di Lui, ma saranno anche un'efficace illustrazione del periodo in cui egli visse e svolse la sua prodigiosa opera di uomo e di artista. L'orazione celebrativa dell'Ariosto sarà tenuta da S. E. Bertoni in una solenne adunanza della R. Accademia d'Italia, che alle manifestazioni ariostesche ha dato il suo valido appoggio e che si riunirà a Ferrara nello stesso Palazzo dei Diamanti dove, con un discorso di Ugo Ojetti, sarà inaugurata la Mostra della Pittura Ferrarese del Rinascimento ordinata e diretta da Nino Barbantini e che accoglierà la massima parte delle pitture ferraresi del '400 e del '500. Mostra di eccezionale importanza, che attirerà a Ferrara gli amatori e gli studiosi d'arte di ogni parte del mondo.

Carattere prettamente folcloristico avrà invece la rievocazione — dopo tanti secoli di disuso — del «Palio di San Giorgio» di cui rimane ricordo non solo negli antichi Statuti Ferraresi, ma anche in uno dei celebri dipinti del Palazzo Schifanoia.

Nei più antichi tempi la corsa si svolgeva per la festa di Santa Maria di Agosto e ai vincitori veniva dato in premio, secondo l'ordine di arrivo, un cavallo, uno sparviero e due bracchi. Ai tempi di Ercole I la festa venne anticipata al giorno di San Giorgio, protettore della città, e i premi rispettivamente mutati in un metro di panno d'oro, in una porchetta e in un gallo.

La corsa aveva uno schietto carattere popolano perchè soltanto i popolani vi partecipavano e dovevano montare senza sella e senza staffe tanto i cavalli che gli asini che formavano — come si direbbe in gergo ippico moderno — due categorie. Alla corsa dei quadrupedi seguivano quella delle giovinette e quella dei giovani.

Lodovico Ariosto (Incisione in [illegible] per l'edizione 1532 dell'«Orlando Furioso»).

Gran festa di popolo incitante i rappresentanti dei vari rioni, gran diletto della Corte e dei nobili.

Con la devoluzione di Ferrara alla Santa Sede la corsa al palio che assumeva carattere di importante avvenimento cittadino — i più alti magistrati funzionavano da giudici di arrivo — cadde in disuso.

La celebrazione ariostesca farà rivivere questa gioconda manifestazione folcloristica per la quale i vari rioni popolari della città si stanno preparando a scendere in lizza con i vecchi costumi estensi e con le antiche insegne rionali.

«Parva sed apta mihi»

Accanto a questa primitiva e genuina manifestazione di sport popolare si avranno tutte quelle altre manifestazioni che sono più vicine al gusto del popolo e a lui più facilmente accessibili: rappresentazioni liriche e drammatiche, gare di bande e concorsi corali all'aperto, mentre i dotti e gli studiosi troveranno ampia e interessante materia nelle Mostre bibliografiche, negli annali delle edizioni ariostesche, nella Mostra iconografica che riunirà nella casa del Poeta le più celebri immagini di Lui che in tela, in marmo, in stampa ci sono giunte, da quella del Tiziano a quella del Dossi e di Lodovico da Settevecchie, nella Mostra delle medaglie coniate — tutte dopo la Sua morte — in onore dell'Ariosto. Completano il vario programma delle manifestazioni le Mostre minori, le adunate dei dotti, i congressi, le manifestazioni sportive.

Un nuovo e fremente palpito di vita animerà dal 7 maggio al 28 ottobre le vie ampie di Ferrara lanciate a incontrare non più «le muse pellegrine arrivanti», ma la infinita schiera di coloro che d'ogni parte d'Europa verranno a rendere omaggio alla memoria di uno dei maggiori e più degni sacerdoti dell'italiche Muse.

E Ludovico Ariosto, sorridente bonariamente, assisterà alla sua postuma glorificazione dalla casetta «parva sed apta» a Lui, dall'orto nel quale s'aggirava — inesperto agricoltore — sbagliando le semine e non permettendo ai germogli di giungere a fiorire, tanto frequentemente li tormentava per la smania di vedere se fossero giunti a maturità.

E forse, mentre squilleranno le trombe

Alfonso I d'Este duca di Ferrara, alla cui Corte visse l'Ariosto.

del Palio, e s'eleverà la parola degli oratori ufficiali a tessere le Sue lodi, ripeterà come un giorno:

Chi brama onor di sprone o di cappello
serva re, duca, cardinale o papa;
io no, che poco curo questo e quello.
In casa mia mi sa meglio una rapa
ch'io cuoca, e cotta su un stecco mi inforco
e mondo e spargo poi di aceto e sapa,
che all'altrui mensa tordo, starna o porco
selvaggio; e così sotto una vil coltre
come di seta o d'oro ben mi corco.

Ma oltre e contro la sua bonaria modestia, non inconscia però della propria grandezza, i tardi nepoti attorno alla Sua tomba, al Suo nome, alla Sua opera «fannogli onore e di ciò fanno bene».

ALBERTO BRIZIO

Figure 3.30. Clipping of Alberto Brizio, "Il ritorno di Messer Lodovico," in *L'illustrazione del popolo*, April 23, 1933. Courtesy Archivio Storico Comunale di Ferrara.

that the modest house in Contrada Mirasole was actually an emblem of Ariosto's bitterness towards Ferrara's ingratitude. It was modest because the Estense dukes did not provide Ariosto with the means that he hoped for. Rather than a warm ancestral home, it was the alcove of an acclimated stranger, the refuge where Ariosto could finally rest after years of unpleasant political service in Garfagnana. It represented Ariosto's last spell of independence from a city whose court disappointed him. He lived there for less than four years.

When William Dean Howells visited Ferrara in 1862, he was disappointed to see that Ariosto's house had just been repainted and modernized by its tenants, who were happy to exploit the tourist attraction but did not care much about preserving its authenticity. When he complained about the sacrilege, the Ferrarese doorman shrugged his shoulders. It is unlikely that this nineteenth-century local commoner had read the *Satires*, or studied the oblique references to Renaissance history and personal troubles in Ariosto's *Furioso*. The American visitor probably knew more about Ariosto's life and works than he did. Nonetheless, the doorman knew that Ferrara's relationship with its most famous poet was much more troubled than readers and tourists could think. His answer to Howells' consternation was simple: "Yes, it is true. But then, you must know, the Ariosti were not one of the noble families of Ferrara."[119] Two generations later, the main mission of the fascist propaganda was to rewrite the past and to erase this secular memory from the minds of Ferrarese people: to turn them into tourists in their own hometown.

Reenacting Frescoes

One of the ways in which the Committee popularized the idea of Ariosto literally coming back to Ferrara for the anniversary of his own death was to produce a musical revue on the topic. The show, titled *Lodovico*, debuted on the stage of Teatro Nuovo at the beginning of 1933. The premiere went so well that the following five performances (all sold out) were moved to the larger and more prestigious Teatro Verdi. The only surviving document of the show is a photograph of the cast in costume, which includes the disquieting detail of an actor wearing blackface (figure 3.31). Despite the lack of the original libretto, the very simple plot can be inferred from the enthusiastic local reviews. It consisted of a didactic pantomime of the message propagandized by the Ariostean Committee. I am going to summarize it.

Ariosto, who has been living on Mount Parnassus for four centuries, finds out that his beloved Ferrara is preparing to celebrate him for the 1933 anniversary of his death. He decides to return to the city in modern

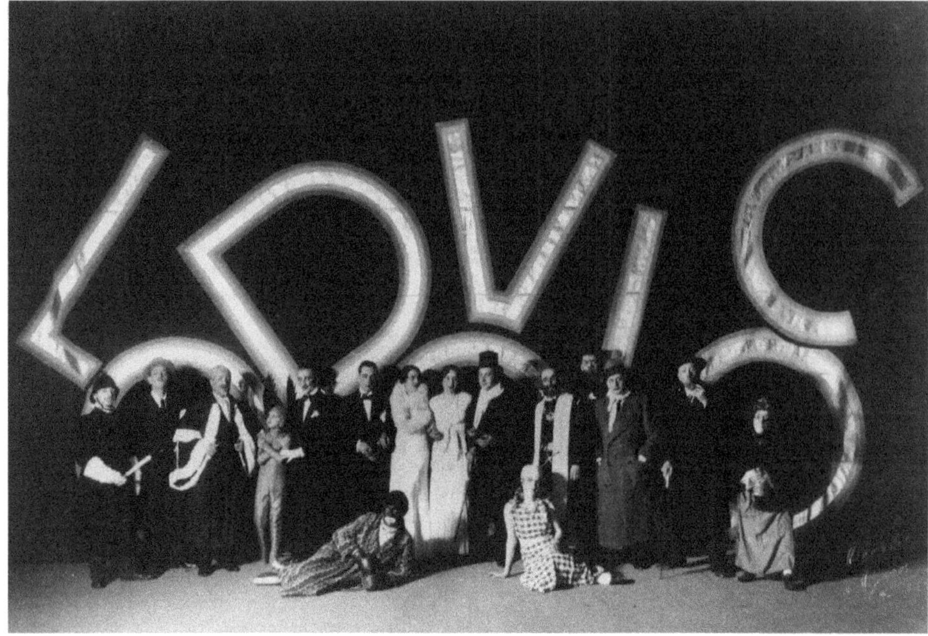

Figure 3.31. The cast of *Lodovico*, photograph, 1933. Archivio Storico Comunale di Ferrara.

clothes to attend the celebrations, and so he travels to a theatre in Ferrara. There, one of the scholars invited for the Ottava d'oro conference is giving his lecture on the *Furioso*. Ariosto, disguised as a modern man in the audience, finds the lecture unbearably boring and pedantic. Therefore, he decides to reveal his identity and stop the academic oration. The local authorities immediately recognize him, and invite him for a walk in the city. They show him how modernity has changed Ferrara, with traffic lights, automobiles, and industrial buildings. However, the architectural restorations carried on by the fascist administration allow Ariosto to recognize the Ferrara of his times, and to reminisce nostalgically about the Estense court, the chivalric deeds, and the Palio races of the Renaissance.

Clearly, the show was a simplified, accessible epitome of the main themes of the Ariostean propaganda – from the disdain for scholarly readings of Ariosto to the fantasy of walking with him along the streets of the Renaissance city, while taking pride in the achievements of fascist modernity. Since the reviews praised the humour related to present-day

Ferrara and the satirical depictions of Ferrarese notables of the time, it is safe to assume that the show was designed specifically for a local audience that could understand and enjoy the inside jokes. *Lodovico* was a tool to definitively frame the centenary as a Carnival spectacle, aimed at policing the literary imagination and cultural self-perception of Ferrara's middle and lower classes.

The inception of the delusion of Ariosto's physical return to Ferrara was so successful that, at the end of the centenary, a second revue was written and staged at Teatro Verdi. This time, the goal was to represent Ariosto's farewell: to show the audience that Ariosto, after visiting the city for the anniversary, was going to leave it again. Part exorcism, part paradoxical funeral, part closing party of the Ariostean year, this second musical revue, titled *Lodovico se ne va* (Lodovico Goes Away) was performed in December 1933.

Ten stage photographs from the premiere were published in *Rivista di Ferrara* (figure 3.32), along with a report of the show's success. This time, the Committee printed[120] and distributed a libretto with the lyrics of the musical numbers. By collating these documents it is possible to appreciate just how literal was the comedic popularization of the initiatives of the centenary. The poster designed by Nizzoli, for instance, was the protagonist of one of the scenes, performed by a choir composed of the elements of the photomontage. The Allegory of Autumn by Del Cossa was played by a local actress in the same costume and pose of the painting, who sang, "Io son giunto prima d'apparir / sul calendario" (I appeared on the poster before I appeared on the calendar). Another member of the choir – or maybe some element of the scenography animated by performers[121] – played Ariosto's face (called "il testone," the big head, in the libretto), who mocked the photomontage technique by singing that he was hard to recognize "poiché a pezzi ed a boccon / Nizzoli ha creato questo cartellon / del centenario" (because Nizzoli created this poster of the centenary by combining bits and pieces). The third element of the poster, the representation of the Palio in Schifanoia, was played by a group of women dressed as horses, "i cavallini," whose song praised local historian Guido Angelo Facchini for his reconstruction of the old races.

Throughout the two acts of *Lodovico se ne va*, various characters staged uncomplicated versions of the cultural shifts and tensions that Ariosto's centenary animated in fascist Ferrara. A competition between modernist and traditionalist aesthetics was championed by opposite groups of dancers, called "Le Quattrocento girls" and "Le Novecento girls." Many caricatures and personifications of the common people and urban features appeared on the stage. Their variety showed the all-embracing

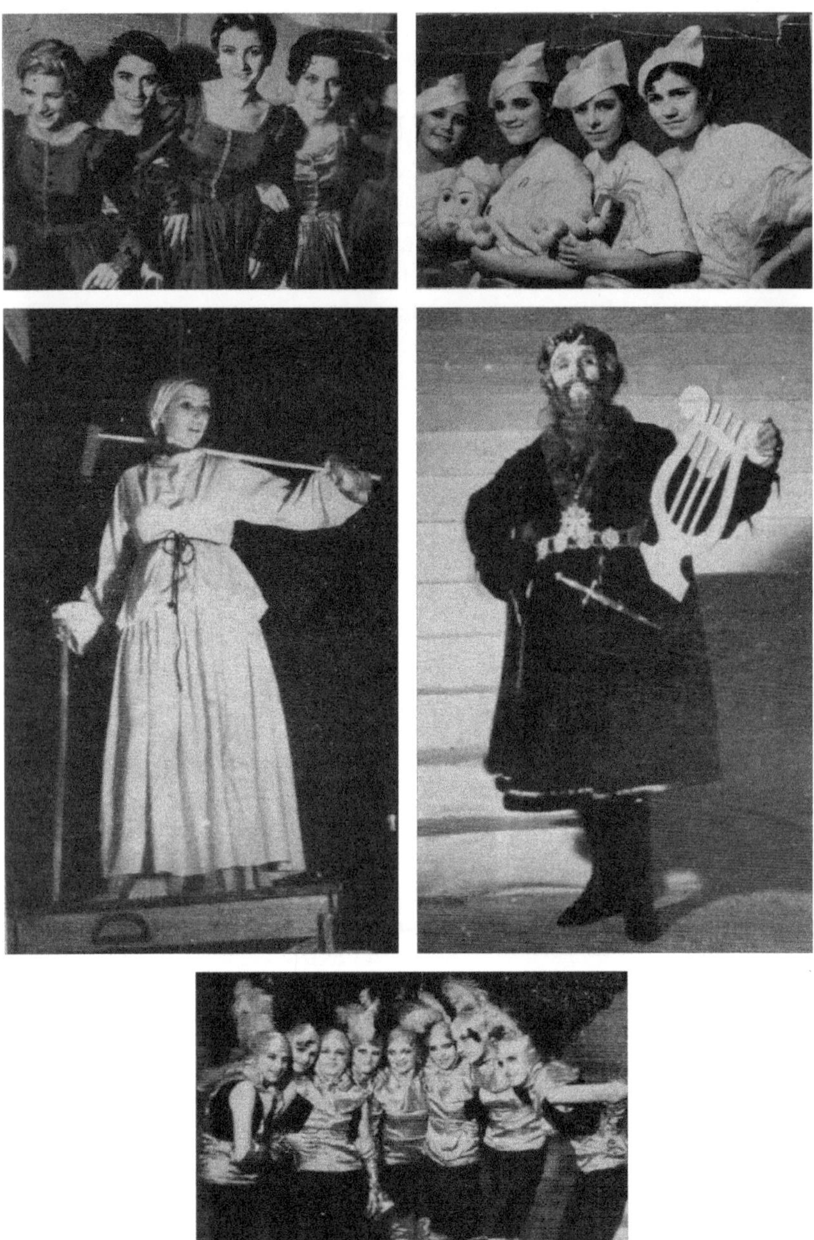

Figure 3.32. E. Leziroli, photographs from the premiere of the musical review *Lodovico se ne va*, from *Rivista di Ferrara* 1.12 (December 1933).

involvement of Ferrara in the celebrations: hotel managers and tourist guides, traffic lights ("Le semaforo's girls") and church bells, a bill sticker, a drunkard, an old lady, a garbageman, and so on. Some metaphorical, literary, or historical figures joined these more mundane characters in the eternal present of the show. In a scene, the previous three centenaries ("Il Seicento," "Il Settecento," and "L'Ottocento") came to the theatre to congratulate their fellow 1933 centenary for its success. A group of eight actresses, all dressed in gold, offered a literal personification of the metre of Ariosto's epic poetry, which had inspired the title of the Ferrarese lectures on the *Furioso*: L'Ottava d'oro – the golden octave. During the second act, Tasso barged into the comedy to express his jealousy. And of course Ariosto, with the familiar bearded face of the poster and the same lyre held by his monument in Piazza Ariostea, was the protagonist.

The libretto of *Lodovico se ne va* opens with Ferrara's lament for Ariosto's departure, a song that explains the revue's title: "Lodovico se ne va / lascia ormai questa città / si è annoiato già" (Ludovico goes away, he leaves this city, he is bored already). The city, however, is not resigned to letting him go, and wants to keep him at least until the end of the show: "Lodovico non andrà / lo teniamo qua: / senza lui non si fa / rappresentazion" (Ludovico won't go, we will keep him here: there won't be any show without him). Two acts and many musical numbers later, the revue concludes with an absurd, second death of Ariosto, which is certified by three Ferrarese doctors. A notary signs his testament, which officially assigns to Ferrara the sole ownership of Ariosto's legacy. The final scene is, again, a funerary lament, but this time the choir adds that Ariosto may resurrect and come back again, and that he only remained in the modern world for Ferrara's people ("Lodovico se ne va [...] e ritornerà / se rinascerà. / Ma solo per noi / ei qui restò"). With this last act of appropriation, the fascist celebrations for Ariosto came to an end.

The most active promoter of the two musical revues, at the beginning and at the end of the Ariostean year, was Nives Comas Casati, who served as stage director, designed all the costumes, and acted in both shows. Casati was a young, energetic member of Balbo's cultural entourage, and followed him to Tripoli when, in 1934, he was appointed governor of colonial Libya. A journalist and artist, during the centenary Casati collaborated with Quilici and assisted Funi when he painted the frescoes in the Sala dell'Arengo. However, her main contribution to the Ariostean celebrations was certainly the curatorship of all the aesthetic and choreographic aspects of the Palio di San Giorgio. As the artistic director of the whole initiative, she designed hundreds of costumes, banners, and props, as well as the emblems on the shields of the competing Rioni and Borghi (the supposedly old neighbourhoods of Ferrara). She planned and choreographed the mass spectacles related to the races, which involved the entire city in a costumed reenactment of the Palio inspired by the Schifanoia frescoes.

In her seminal work on fascist urban rhetoric, Diane Ghirardo studied the 1933 Palio in detail as part of Ferrara's strategies of surveillance and spectacle under totalitarianism. Ghirardo worked on the history of the Palio and of its fascist revival. Her study shows how the fascist administration, through the Palio, was able to refashion Ferrara without altering its secular architectural stratigraphy: a propaganda strategy that "entailed the projection of fascism into the city fabric."[122] The main purpose of this ephemeral but spectacular transformation of the city was to foster the support of working masses while surveilling their life at the local, folkloric scale that Stefano Cavazza, more recently, identified under the category of "piccola patria" (little homeland).[123] According to Ghirardo, the superimposition of *Ferrara fascista* and *Ferrara estense* typified a fascist strategy employed, through the collaboration of organic intellectuals, in many Italian cities and towns characterized by strong medieval and early modern urban legacies.

> The point was not just the spectacle itself, but the attempts to domesticate fascism and to emphasize its local character, to affirm it as a political movement as forward looking as local lore claimed the Este family to have been in the fifteenth century, but as rooted in the past as the Este likewise claimed to be, and in both cases by means of public display.[124]

To conclude this chapter, I am going to look at the 1933 Palio mostly from the point of view of "the spectacle itself," asking how its gigantic aesthetic apparatus contributed to the specific myth that it was supposed to pay homage to: Ariosto's return in fascist Ferrara. My goal is to show how the Palio was an exercise of presentification of the past, but also, once again, how the past resisted it. To investigate this aspect of the event, the nature and the results of Casati's work are particularly revealing. Casati's costumes and choreographies were at the base of the suspension of disbelief that allowed Ferrara to see itself as truly experiencing an eternal Renaissance. At the same time, they constructed a Palio that never existed historically, cherry picking from the convenient iconographic source of Schifanoia and sparse chronicles of medieval and early modern events. In any event, these para-historical spectacular elements constituted the material core and the dominating imagery of what Ferrarese people experienced in 1933 while invoking Ariosto's presence.

As Ghirardo noticed, what made the Palio more effective than typical fascist mass rallies was its interactive aspect. The masses were more than passive spectators and participated in the event by parading in the city, performing group movements, and competing in the races. They did all this while wearing sixteenth-century garments, waving embroidered flags, and following choreographed scripts (figure 3.33).

The paradigm of reenactment, with its concern for authenticity and performative approach to presentification, seems a good one to frame the Ferrarese Palio. However, as I mentioned, the pageants, rituals, and races held in 1933 were not a reconstruction of any historical event. As Ghirardo showed in her study of the correspondence between Mayor Ravenna and Mussolini's central government in 1932, Ferrara intentionally pretended that the Palio was an Estense tradition of Ariosto's times, albeit never practised again since the end of the dukedom. In truth, there are records of Ferrarese Palio races as late as the nineteenth century, and, like most analogous folkloric events in other Italian cities and towns, the race had really a medieval, not Renaissance, origin. The philological reenactment of an "original" (so to speak) Palio would have had to look at thirteenth-century imagery, from before the Este were proclaimed dukes. But, besides clashing with the occasion of Ariosto's centenary, a neo-medieval Ferrarese Palio would have probably been perceived just as a mere copy of Siena's more famous tradition. As a matter of fact, the Sienese people were particularly offended by the news that Ferrara had organized its own costumed Palio in June, knowing that the Palio di Siena had been celebrated every year on July 2 for almost four centuries. Mayor Ravenna received a threatening letter, signed "The Offended People of Siena," that invited him to visit Tuscany to see the real Palio: "your skin will undeservedly remain intact, but your brain will be messed up [...] by the awareness of the unjustified insult that you made to a sister Italian city by robbing her of this tradition with impunity."[125]

Historians and librarians involved with the Committee (Ravegnani, Agnelli, and, most of all, Facchini) did research Ferrara's archive to determine the best names and symbols for the Rioni, the rules of the races under the Este dukes, the elements of the ritual parade, and other details. However, it was Casati who, through the visual design of the spectacular mass events, envisioned a Palio that was, as much as possible, different from that of Siena, related to Ariosto, and in line with the idea of an eternal Renaissance.

Her inspiration was not much in archival documents and philological reconstructions of actual Palios of the past. She looked instead at the frescoes in Schifanoia – though mostly not, as I will show, at the depictions of the Palio in the wall of April. As we saw at the beginning of this chapter,

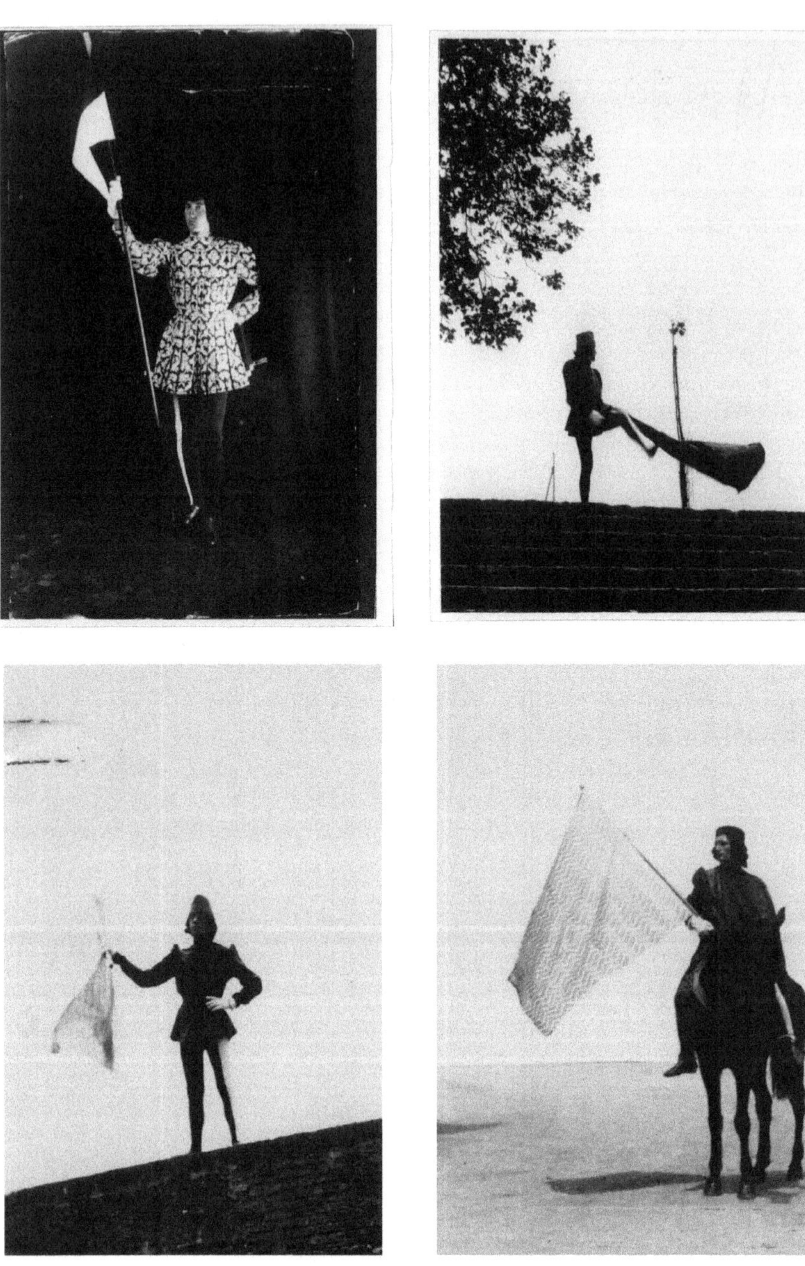

Figure 3.33. Propaganda photographs of Ferrara's people practising and performing for the Palio events in 1933. Archivio Storico Comunale di Ferrara.

Achille Funi, in the following years, had the task of transporting Ferrara's fascist intellectuals into the sixteenth-century epic of Tasso and Ariosto by painting them in a neo-Renaissance fresco. By contrast, in 1933, Casati reenacted the Renaissance frescoes of Schifanoia in the fascist city.

Renaissance Masquerade

The Palio races were held in Piazza Ariostea. Some of the most significant expenses for the event[126] were related to the transformation of the Piazza into a sort of urban stadium, with a lower oval conformation and movable raised seating areas around the loop of the racetrack. Ariosto's monument, in the centre of the Piazza, was kept at its original height by adding a large horizontal plinth under the vertical column that had fascinated the de Chirico brothers. During the structural alteration, Ariosto's statue was temporarily put on the ground and cleaned. A cartoonist captured this moment by imagining the envy of two prominent poets of fascist Italy, Giuseppe Ungaretti and Ugo Betti, at the attention reserved to Ariosto by Ferrara (figure 3.34). Soon enough, the marmoreal Ariosto got back on his pedestal. The statue's aerial perspective was the protagonist of the June cover of *Rivista di Ferrara*, one of Buzzacchi's most synthetic and estranging works (figure 3.35). Looking down at the Piazza from Ariosto's invigilating point of view, the image represented the column as a white beam, almost the vertical contrail of an airplane that either took off or landed in the middle of the square's walkways. The stylized architecture and the Paolo Veronese green of the grass evoke de Chirico's Ferrarese cityscapes. Buzzacchi's etching could be seen as an aero-futurist version of *The Great Metaphysician*, framed from above. Interestingly, Buzzacchi did not represent the piazza as it looked after the adjustments for the Palio (figure 3.36), but used instead the familiar rectangular simplicity of its original design, which had appeared on countless maps for centuries.

For the setting of Piazza Ariostea, Casati produced a series of choreographic schemes that integrated Ariosto into the display of the various costumed figures of the Palio (figure 3.37). At the centre of the choreographic formations, Ariosto provided a focal point for the visual balance of the performance. Because of its twirling posture, the statue's face was oriented towards the tribune and the judges of the races. After parading the city and completing a loop around the piazza, the figures of the Palio were instructed to orient themselves the same way. These figures, called *rappresentanze* (delegations), were fourteen for each of the eight neighbourhoods, for a total of 112 different costumes with special props – including wigs, headgear, swords, trumpets, drums, torches, flags, and

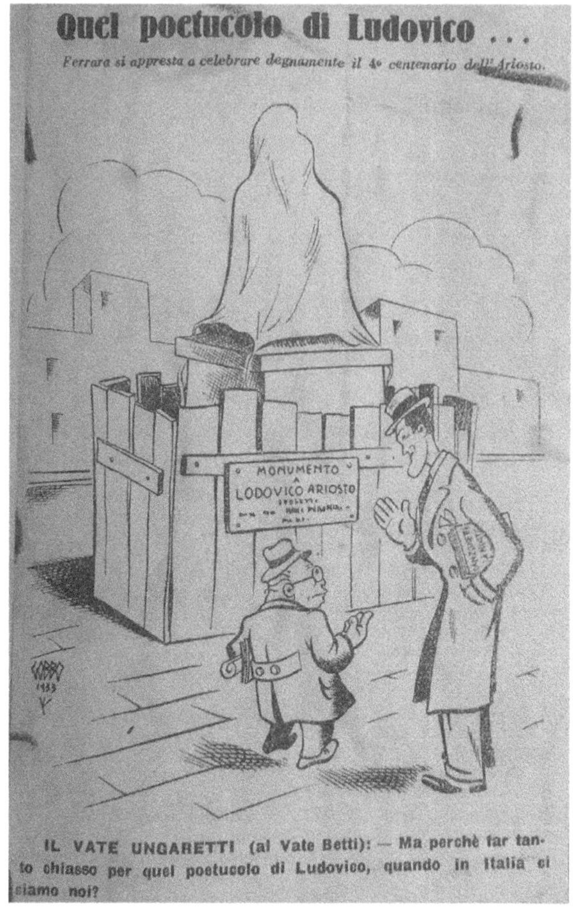

Figure 3.34. Gobbo, cartoon in *Il Settebello*, February 4, 1933.

banners. The Ariostean Committee supervised the purchase of precious textiles, used to realize Casati's designs.[127] To obtain the props, they reached out to theatrical companies and to the organizers of the neo-medieval "Calcio Fiorentino" tradition in Florence.[128] Each neighbourhood established its own local committee, which elected local people for the fourteen roles of the Palio, from the leading consul (a coveted position, reserved for fascist notables such as the daughter of Colonel Vanzi) to simple standard bearers. The local committees also came up with additional choreographic schemes for parades and flag-waving numbers specific to each neighbourhood.

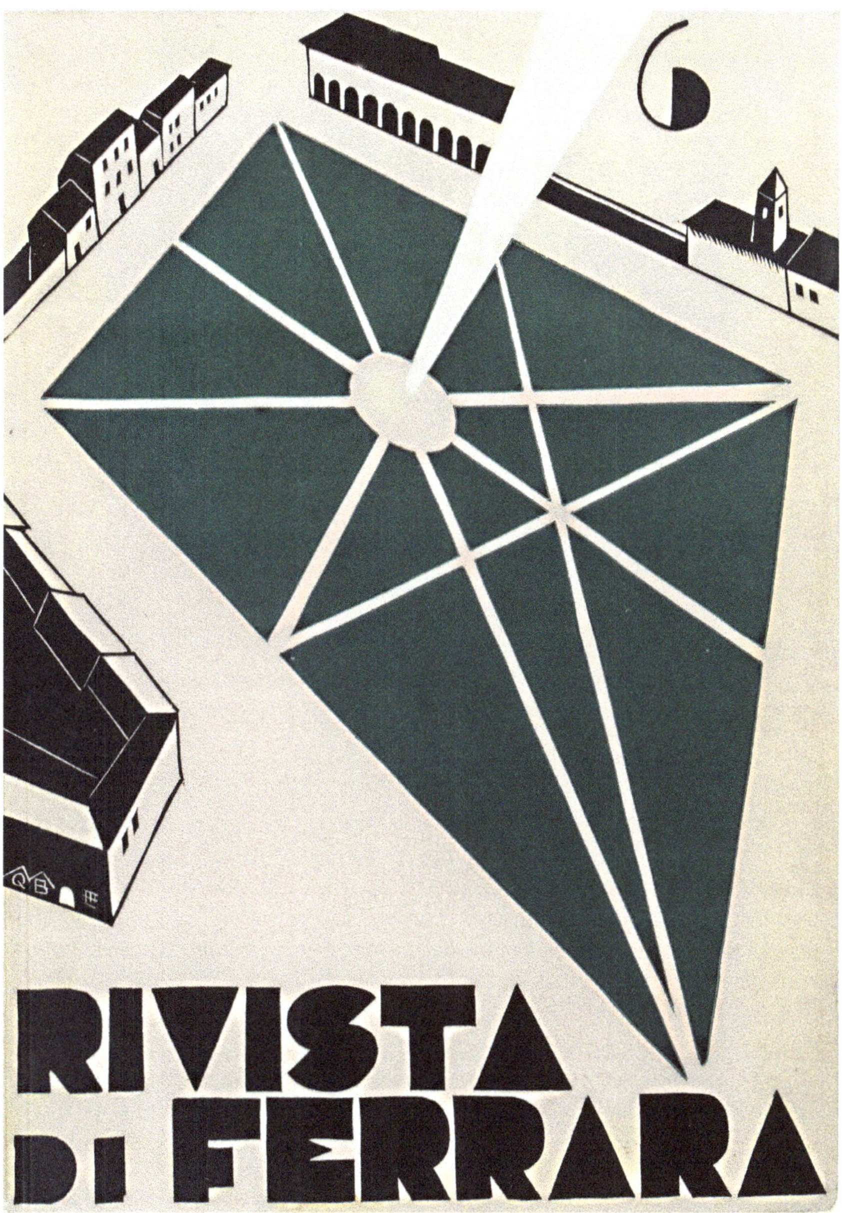

Figure 3.35. Mimì Quilici Buzzacchi, "Piazza Ariostea," cover of *Rivista di Ferrara* 1.6 (June 1933). © Archivio Mimì Quilici Buzzacchi. Photograph © Giuseppe Tassinari.

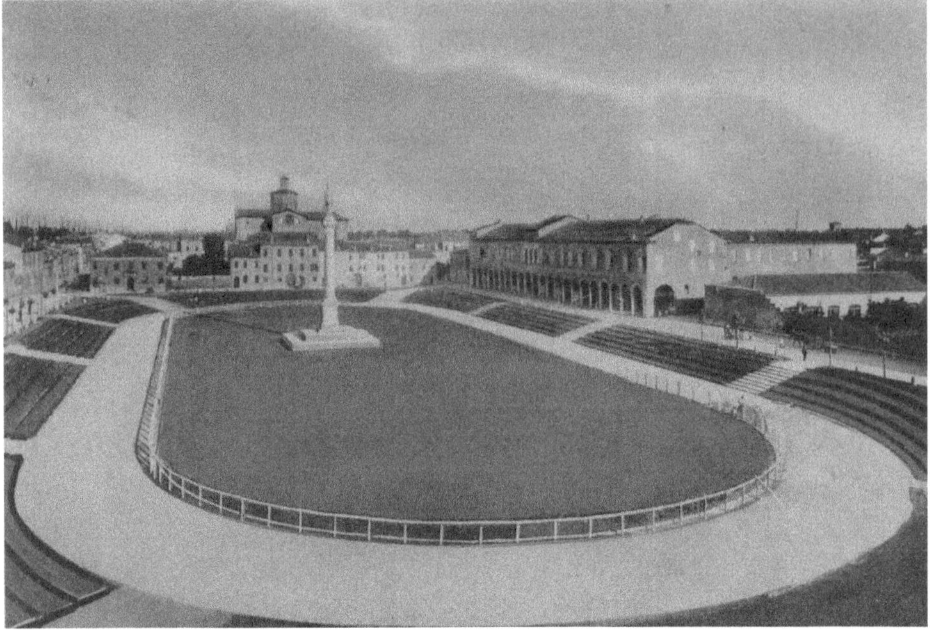

Figure 3.36. Piazza Ariostea in 1939, after the adjustments for the Palio. Postcard owned by the author, image in the public domain.

The involvement of common citizens in the Palio was pervasive and well organized. The system of competing neighbourhoods was actually a faux-Renaissance veil laid down on the pre-existing network of fascist recreational groups established in Ferrara in the previous decade.[129] Neighbourhood chapters of the National Fascist Party were masquerading as centuries-old Contrade, each with its visual identity. The stationery of these neo-Renaissance communities shows the widespread diffusion of the reenactment aesthetics coordinated by Casati.

To officially confirm to the Ariostean Committee the names of the citizens selected for each role in their delegations, the neighbourhoods used their new letterheads with the Palio shields (figure 3.38). As I mentioned, each of these supposedly historical communities organized its own portion of the choreographed rituals that preceded the actual races. In order to take part in these rituals and parades, people of all ages and social extractions were trained for weeks, using various municipal resources and spaces. Mayor Ravenna interceded personally with the army and the local police so that neighbourhoods could use military barracks to

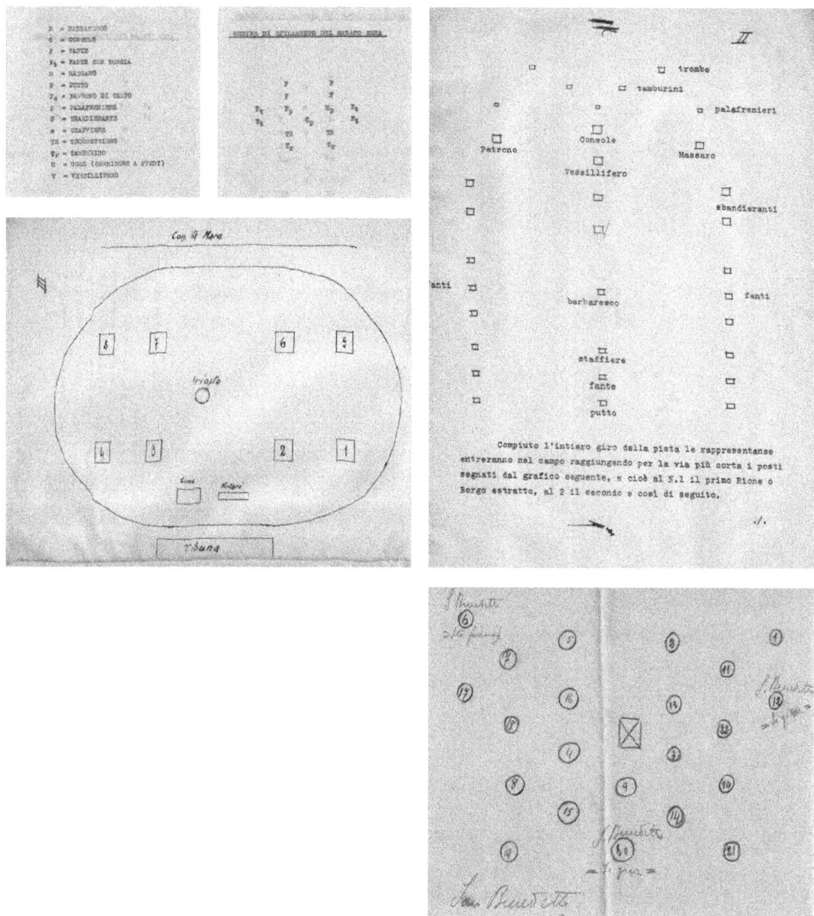

Figure 3.37. Nives Casati's choreographic instructions and schemes for the Palio parades sent to the neighbourhood delegations from the Ariostean Committee, 1933. Archivio Storico Comunale di Ferrara.

rehearse.[130] Neighbourhood leaders directed their people to the shops of seamstresses and shoemakers tasked with the adjustments of their costumes. The local leaders also enforced the administration's orders about the decor of streets and balconies. Locally elected to the neo-Renaissance fictitious offices of Consul, Notary, or Judge of the Massaria, these leaders signed their letters and communiqués with their Palio titles, adding their real names in brackets.[131] With Ravenna's help, they administered

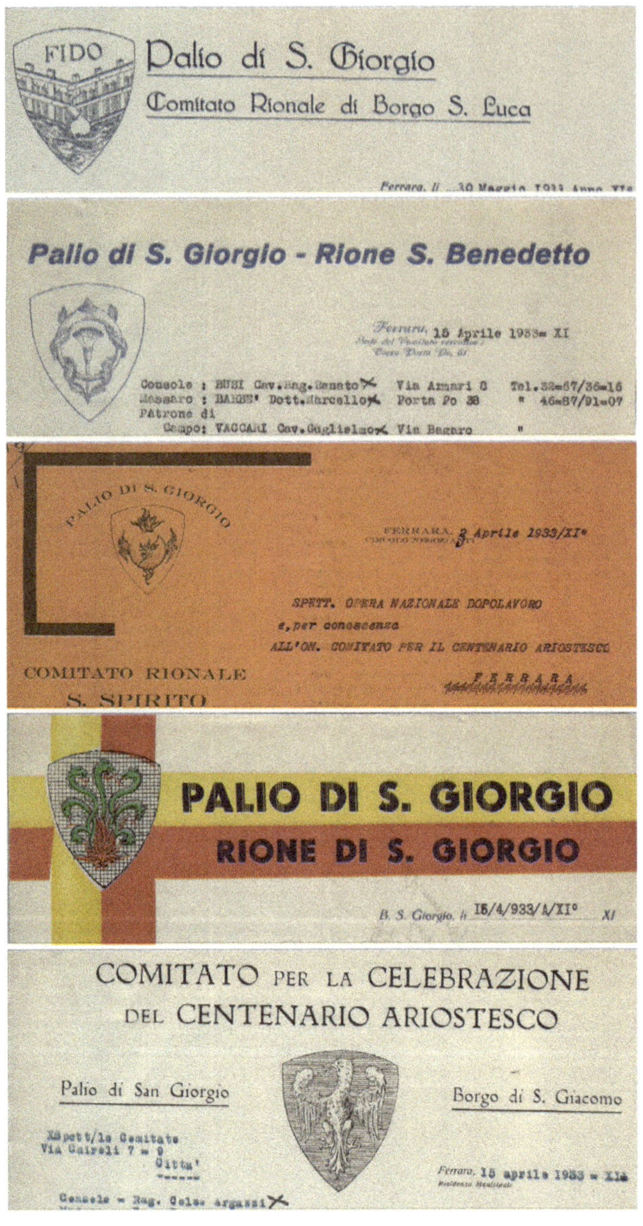

Figure 3.38. Insignia of the neighbourhoods in their respective official letterheads, used for correspondence about the Palio, 1933. Courtesy Archivio Storico Comunale di Ferrara.

training sessions for trumpet and drum players, racers, and flag wavers. The hierarchic control of these mandatory activities reached the entire population. Those who did not take part in parades, rituals, and races, like most women and children, were still expected to wear a costume on the day of the Palio, so that they could wave neighbourhood banners from their homes' windows and greet their delegation's cortège.

To characterize the collective willing delusion at the base of this performance of a fictitious past, I used the term "suspension of disbelief" before. "Secondary belief" may be a better formula to capture the diligence undertaken by fascist Ferrara to revive the Palio during Ariosto's centenary. Coined by J.R.R. Tolkien to talk about world building in fantasy literature, the term "secondary belief" acquired currency in the analysis of narrative role-playing games, some of which are not set in entirely fictional secondary worlds (like Tolkien's Middle Earth) but in partially fictional versions of the past. In fact, even "reenactment" might be fruitfully replaced by the terms "cosplay," or "live action role-playing," to describe the city-wide masquerade, set in an imaginary eternal Renaissance, that the Ariostean Committee envisioned. Rather than impersonating historical figures from the city's Renaissance, the Ferrarese were creating their own characters, pretending to be Renaissance men and women themselves. Costumes and props, based on famous local public art rather than historical reconstructions, corroborated their secondary belief – Ariosto was back, Ferrara was again a chivalric dukedom, and the Ferrarese people were direct protagonists of this fascist resurgence of the Renaissance glory. The promotion of the event, again based on the technique of photomontage (figure 3.39), playfully projected local pride.

Some of Casati's models for the costumes were published in *Rivista di Ferrara* (figure 3.40). The literal imitation of the clothes depicted in the Schifanoia frescoes is immediately evident. The surviving staged photos of the delegations in costume are often spectacular quotations of Francesco del Cossa's iconography (figures 3.41 and 3.42), while others were later used by Funi for his fascist fresco (figures 3.43 and 3.44). The aesthetic of the Palio was immersive in the propaganda, and exploited the background of Ferrara's renovated monuments to give the impression of an uninterrupted tableau vivant encompassing the entire city. This impression reached its full extent in the most striking effort of costumed self-representation ever produced by modern Ferrara: a film, directed by Casati, that represented the Ariostean Committee's vision of the Palio.

Reporters from Mussolini's Istituto LUCE were invited to document the Palio, and shot two films destined for fascist newsreels. These films, still available in the LUCE's archives, were classic products of the visual rhetoric of the regime's cinematic propaganda: static documentaries,

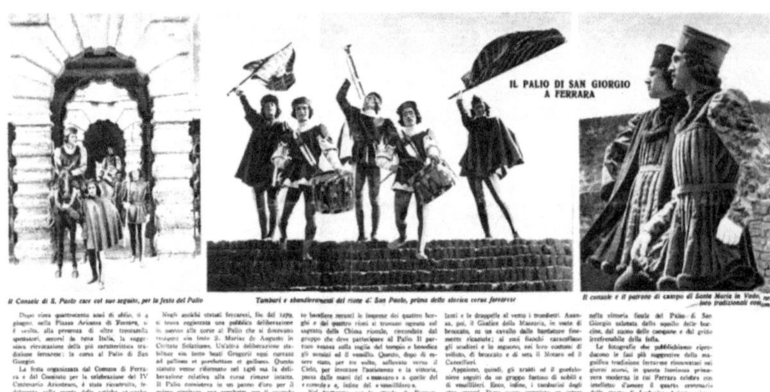

IL PALIO DI SAN GIORGIO A FERRARA

Il Console di S. Paolo esce col suo seguito, per la festa del Palio

Tamburi e sbandieratori del rione di San Paolo, prima della storica corsa ferrarese

Il console e il patrono di campo di Santa Maria in Vado, nei loro tradizionali costumi

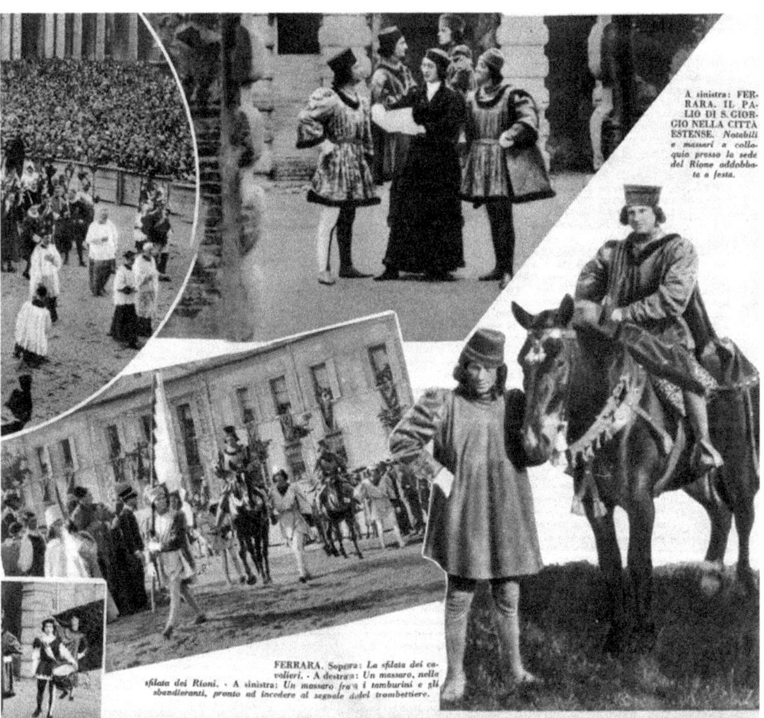

A sinistra: FERRARA. IL PALIO DI S. GIORGIO NELLA CITTÀ ESTENSE. *Notabili e massari a colloquio presso la sede del Rione addobbata a festa.*

FERRARA. Sopra: *La sfilata dei cavalieri.* - A destra: *Un massaro, nella sfilata dei Rioni.* - A sinistra: *Un massaro fra i tamburini e gli sbandieranti, pronto ad incedere al segnale del trombettiere.*

Figure 3.39. Promotional photo-compositions in *Rivista di Ferrara* 1.5 (May 1933) and in booklets distributed in the region by the Ariostean Committee. Archivio Storico Comunale di Ferrara.

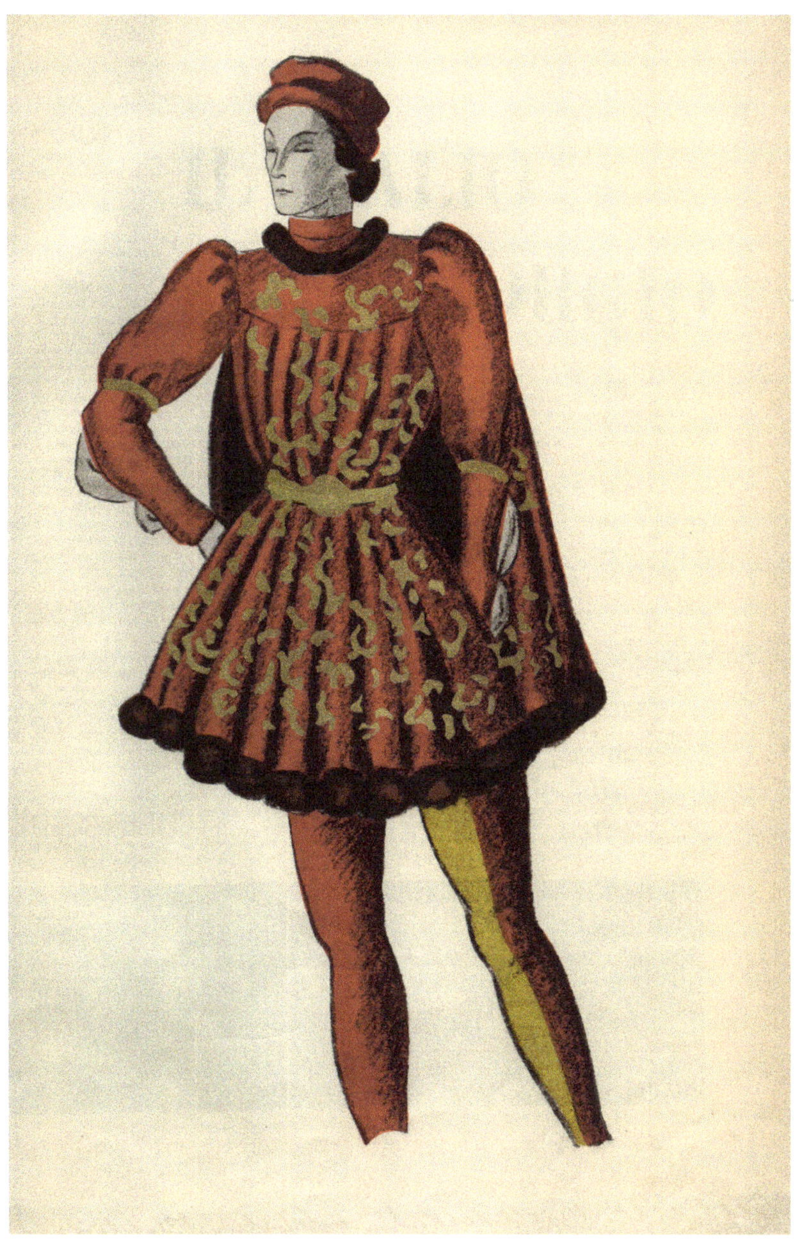

Figure 3.40. Nives Casati, sketch for the Palio Costumes in *Rivista di Ferrara* 1.5 (May 1933).

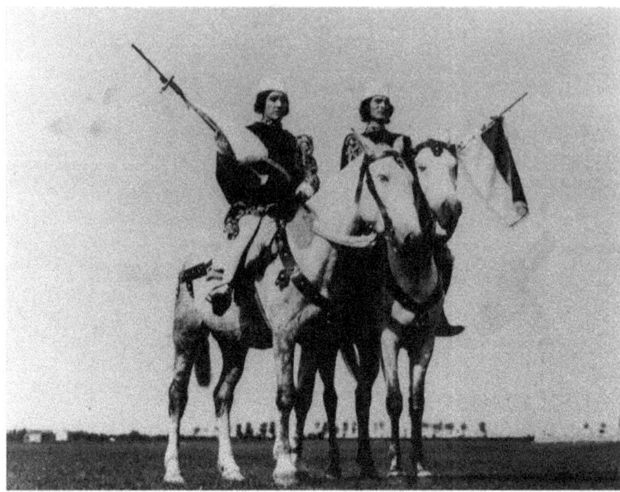

Figure 3.41. Ferrarese youth in their Palio costumes, 1933, photograph. Archivio Storico Comunale di Ferrara.

with a voice-over commentary, meant to inform and educate rather than narrate. The Ariostean Committee had something different in mind, and combined Casati's inventive vision with the technical mastery of a local photographer, Antonio Sturla. Sturla had already proved his technical ability in a 1926 short titled *Ferrara Epica e Cortese*: an aerial portrait of the city entirely shot from a flying airplane. A shy but prolific pioneer of what was then called "tecnica fotocinematografica," Sturla was an experimenter: Carlo Rambaldi, one of the greatest special effects artists of all time, started his career by creating animatronics for Sturla's documentaries. Sturla's perfectionist, fast-paced cinematography distanced Ferrara's film on the Palio from the didactic plainness of newsreels. Casati's narrative, which encompassed the entire ritual of the Palio in less than four hundred seconds of screen time, was staged and montaged as a sequence of pictorial frames.

The first image of the film is, predictably, a detail of the Schifanoia frescoes (figure 3.45). It is not, however, from the allegory of the month of April, which includes the depiction of the Palio. Casati chose a detail from the lower register of the month of March, dominated by the triumph of Minerva and the zodiacal sign of Aries. The detail frames a small portion of a scene of Borso d'Este's government. The duke, with other noble men (and maybe, in the middle, a woman), is

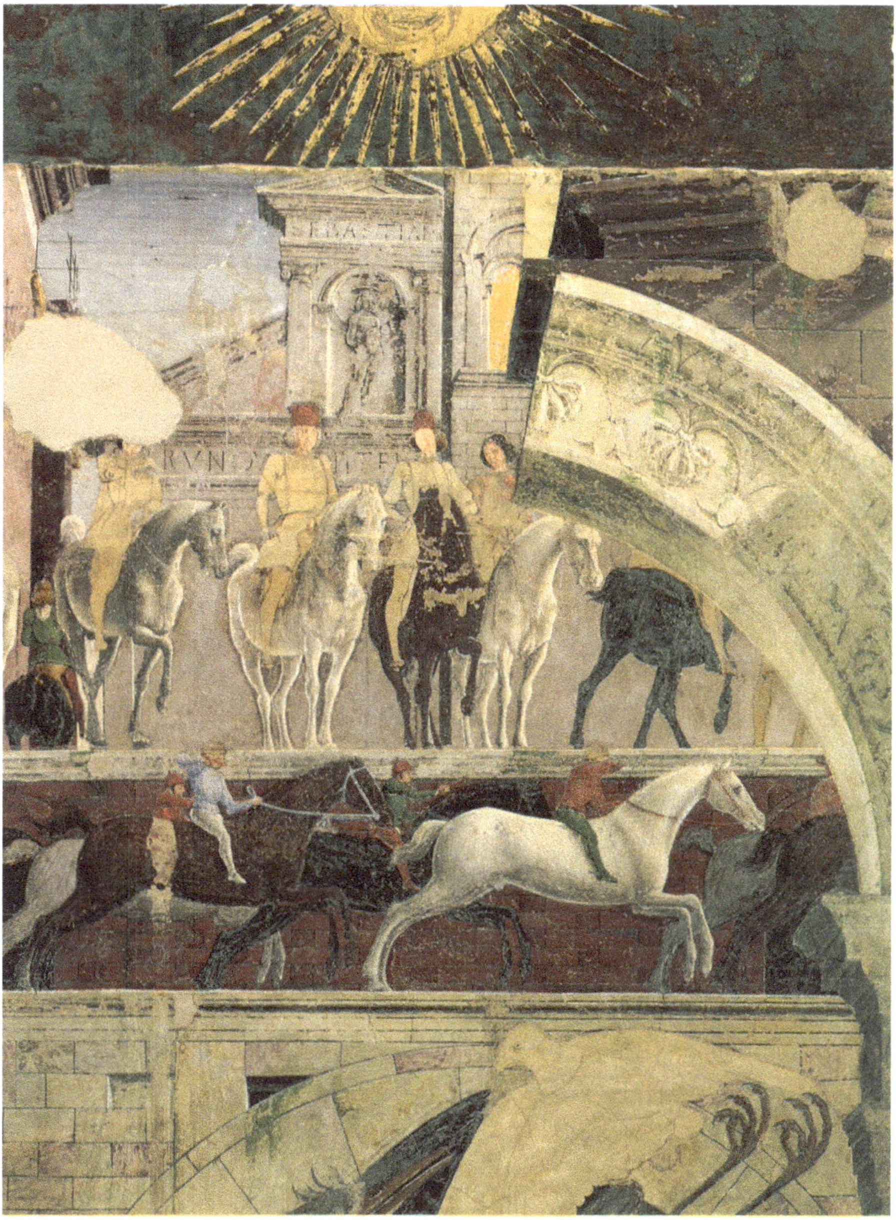

Figure 3.42. Francesco del Cossa, *Horse Race*, detail from the month of April, ca. 1470, fresco (post-restoration), Palazzo Schifanoia, Ferrara. Su concessione dei Musei di Arte Antica del Comune di Ferrara. Photo Credit: Scala/Art Resource, NY.

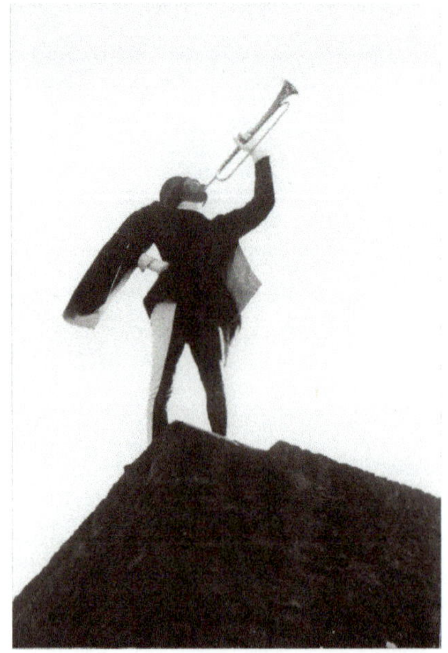

Figure 3.43. Ferrarese youth in his Palio costume playing the trumpet, 1933, photograph. Courtesy Archivio Storico Comunale di Ferrara.

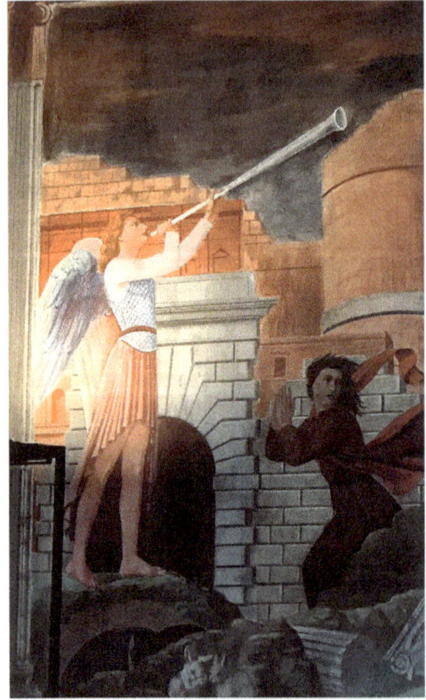

Figure 3.44. Achille Funi, *The Myth of Ferrara* (*Il mito di Ferrara*), detail from the north wall: Saint George slaying the dragon, 1934–7, fresco, Town Hall, Sala dell'Arengo, Ferrara. Courtesy Archivio Achille Funi, Studio d'arte Nicoletta Colombo, Milan.

departing for a hunt after having administered justice. Perhaps this portion of the fresco was chosen because the figures are all on horseback. In any event, the frame is so narrow that only the heads of the group are visible in the film, with their characteristic headgear imitated in Casati's costumes. Likely, Casati did not want to insist on the iconography of the Palio employed for the poster of the Ariostean celebrations. A close inspection of that smaller portion of the fresco reveals the obscenity of the old races, with the naked putti and racing prostitutes – which were conveniently cut off in Nizzoli's poster. The film started instead with a quintessential image of Ferrarese good government, glorifying the Estense élite in which the fascist intellectuals of the Ariostean Committee mirrored themselves. The second image is the Palio di San Giorgio, the banner given to the winner of the horse race. The Palio banner was embroidered with another pictorial masterpiece of Renaissance Ferrara: Cosmè Tura's depiction of Saint George, from the organ case of the city's Cathedral.

Embroidery and the allegory of March from Schifanoia are the protagonists of the following scene, introduced by the title card "And in the closed cloisters, the women embroider again the Estense emblems." The montage of the segment juxtaposes the private and the public dimensions of the preparation for the Palio, dividing them by gender. A trio of Ferrarese women placidly work on hand-made flags that, in a sudden cut, are festively waved in the sky by flag throwers. The image of the three sewing women, so reminiscent of the myth of the three Parcae, is a visual quotation from the triumph of Minerva (figure 3.46). There, Francesco del Cossa divided the goddess's cortège by gender: male doctors and scholars on the left, and female weavers and sewers on the right. Casati and Sturla cinematically reproduced the three weavers in the foreground, separated from the rest of the group. The alternating scene of flag wavers, on the other hand, visually alludes to a frescoed portion of the north wall of Schifanoia: a group of knights with banners that has been attributed to Borso's brother, Baldassarre d'Este, who was a painter. The flags in the film are those of the competing neighbourhoods. They were designed by Casati (figure 3.47) and synthetically represented by Buzzacchi on the May cover of *Rivista di Ferrara* (figure 3.48).

The next segment of the film is introduced by the title card "On the night of the eve [of the Palio], the neighbourhoods' delegations go to the Ducal Palace for the enrollment." The costumed parade towards the Palace is illuminated only by torches, showing Sturla's photographic mastery. Right afterwards, the Judge of the Massaria is introduced. He receives the delegations' parchments, while a higher

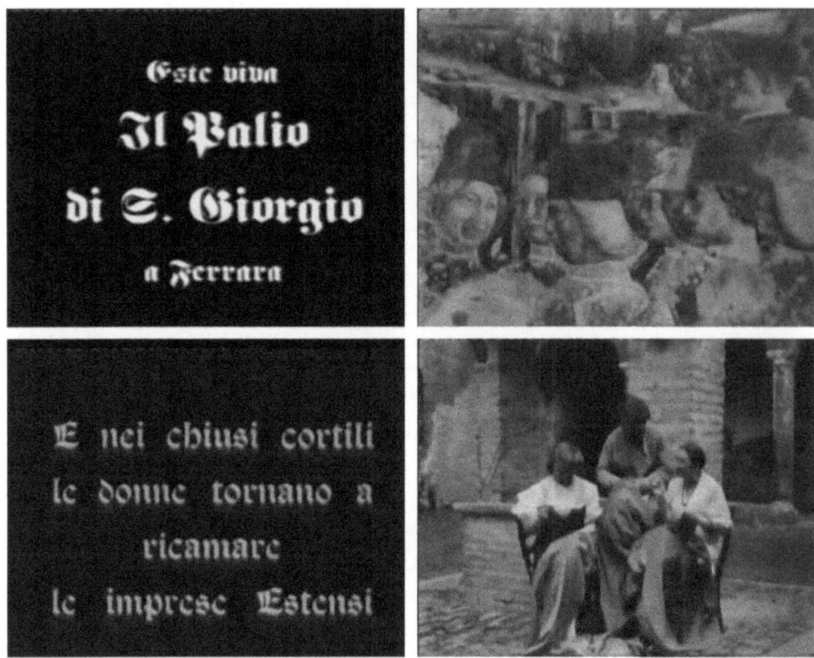

Figure 3.45. Stills from *Este Viva, Il Palio di San Giorgio*, 1933 film directed by Nives Casati and shot by Antonio Sturla. Courtesy Paolo Sturla Avogadri.

figure, shown in a brief cut, surveys the reception from a balcony. Then, as the title card states, "The Herald reads the Ducal edict to the Consuls and the Vassals." I am going to translate this speech, which is imbued with the secondary belief of an eternal Renaissance to the point of erasing the four hundred years that separated Ferrara Estense and fascist Ferrara.

> People of Ferrara! For the glory and honour of the blessed George, patron saint of our most beloved city, we, the Lords of Ferrara, have established that, on the fourth day of the current month of June, the races for the Palio that were instituted by order of our Dukes, the princes of Este, will be reinstated! Whether the Eagle or the Diamond, the Unicorn or the Wheel, the Lynch or the Grenade, the Hydra or the Fence, will grab the victory, it will always be for the glory of Este and the glory of Ferrara. We greet you, Consuls and Vassals, Knights and Foot-soldiers, we greet the whole people, who came from every land in exultation so that we may renew the cry: "Este Viva!"[132]

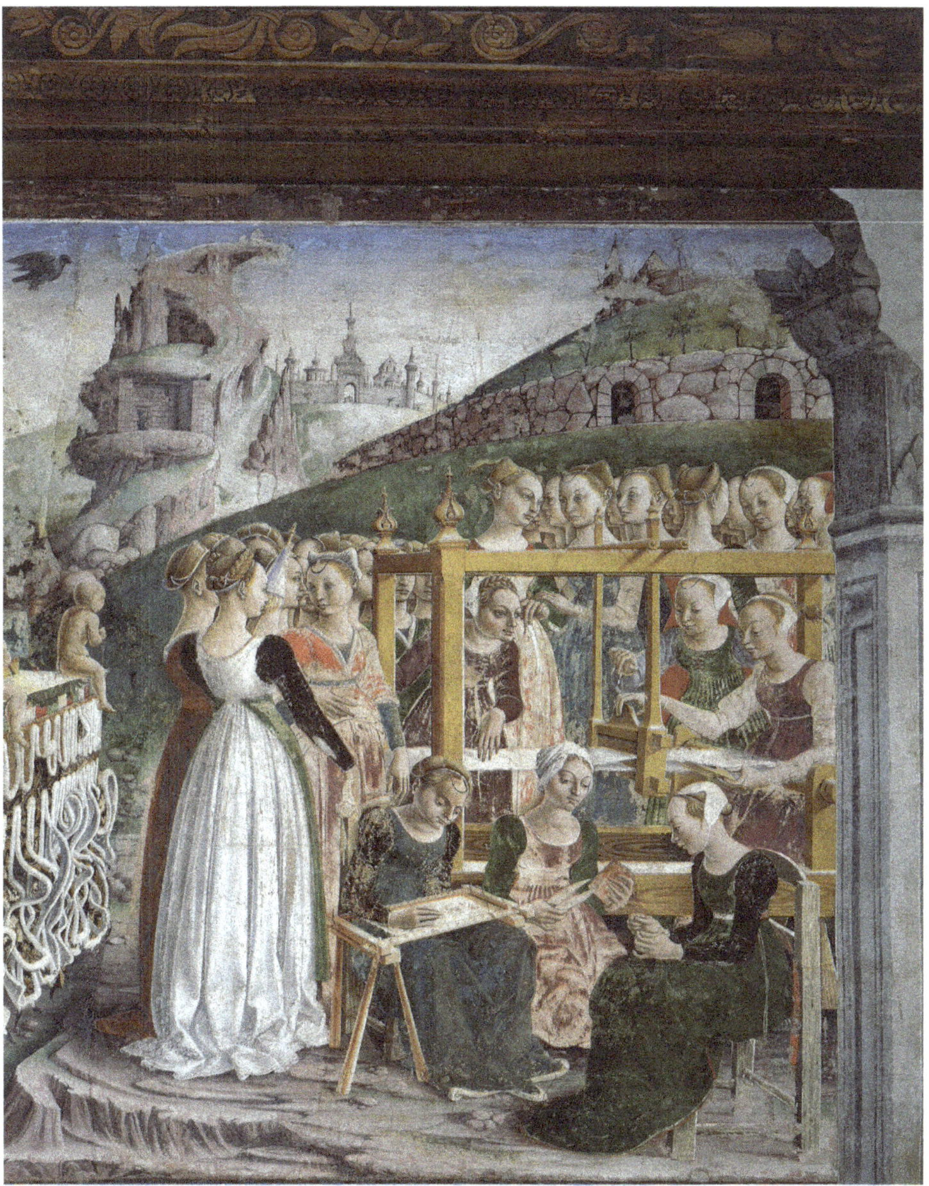

Figure 3.46. Francesco del Cossa, *Women Weaving and Embroidering*, detail from the month of March, ca. 1470, fresco (post-restoration), Palazzo Schifanoia, Ferrara. Su concessione dei Musei di Arte Antica del Comune di Ferrara. © Alinari Archives/Art Resource, NY.

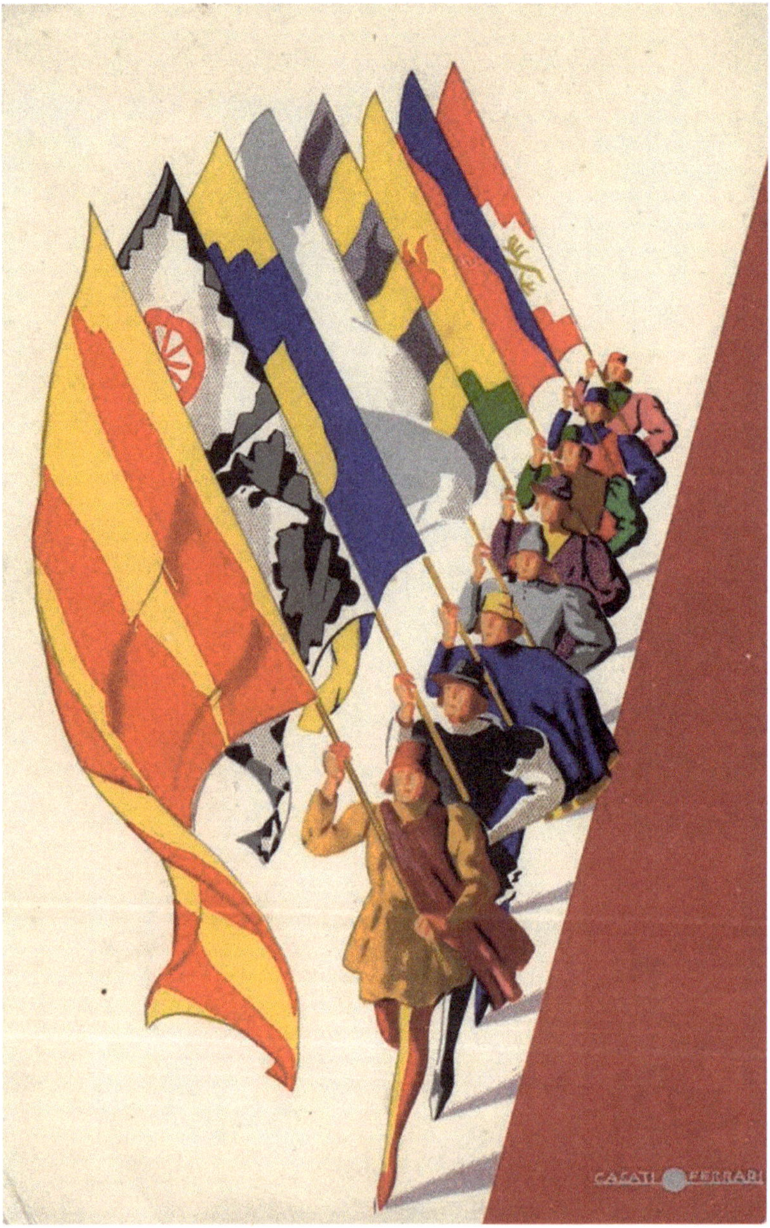

Figure 3.47. Nives Casati and Amerigo Ferrari, poster for the Palio di San Giorgio, 1933. Courtesy Archivio Storico Comunale di Ferrara.

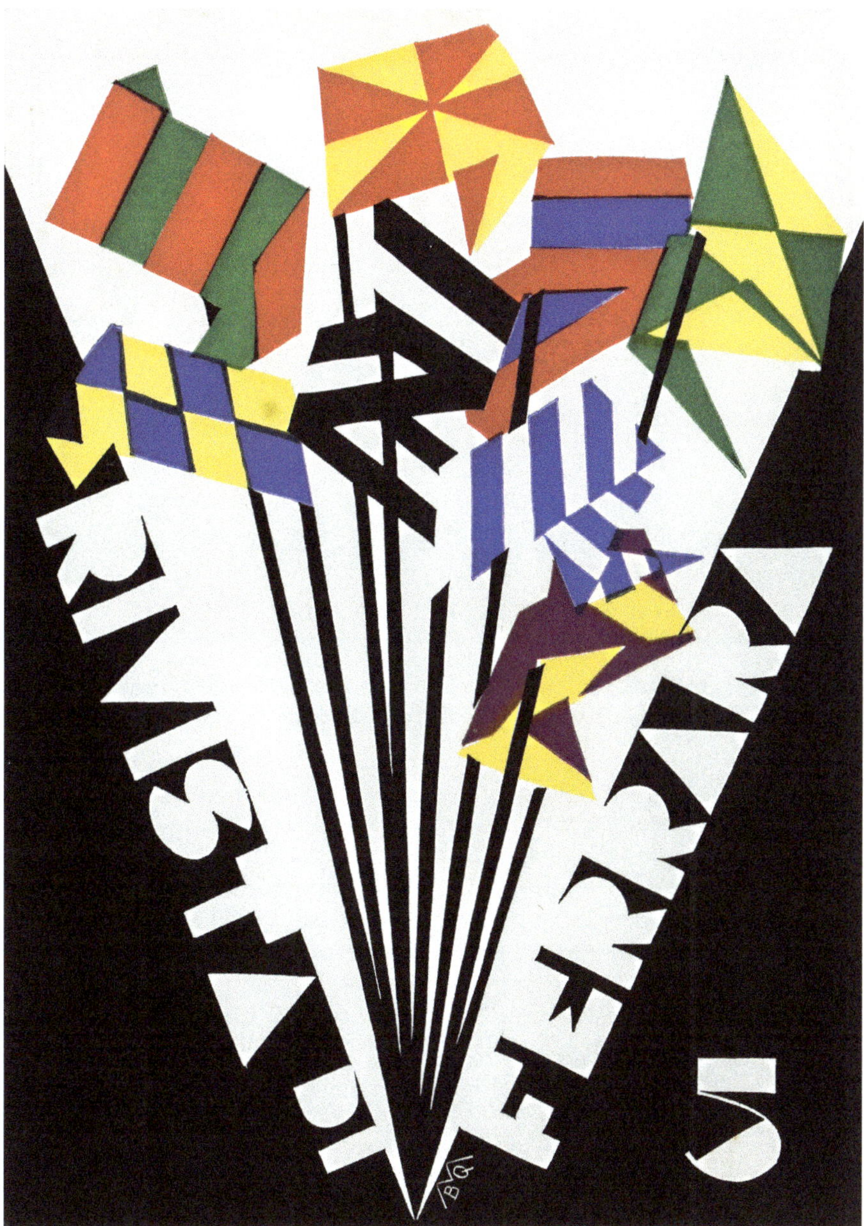

Figure 3.48. Mimì Quilici Buzzacchi, "Palio di San Giorgio," cover of *Rivista di Ferrara* 1.5 (May 1933). © Archivio Mimì Quilici Buzzacchi. Photograph © Giuseppe Tassinari.

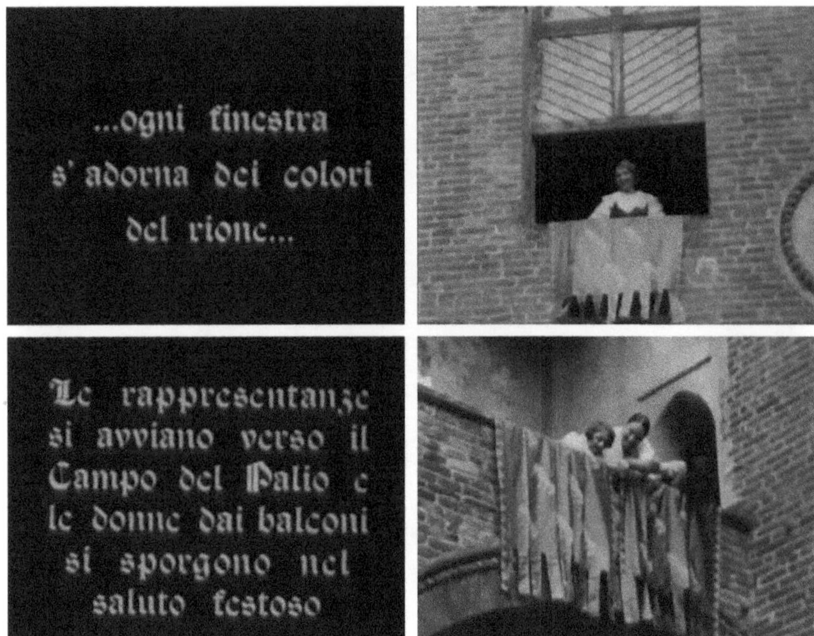

Figure 3.49. Stills from *Este Viva, Il Palio di San Giorgio,* 1933 film directed by Nives Casati and shot by Antonio Sturla. Courtesy Paolo Sturla Avogadri.

The Herald brought to the eight neighbourhoods, to their local leaders, and to the common people the message of the Ariostean Committee, led by Mayor Ravenna and his entourage of organic intellectuals. They identified themselves as "i Signori di Ferrara" and launched a motto that was perfectly in line with the necromantic propaganda that they had promoted through the exploitation of Ariosto's bones, body, blood, and relics. "Este Viva" may be translated as "Hurray for Este," but also "May Este live," or, more literally, "Living Este," "Este is alive." The following scene of the film ("... every window is decorated with the colours of the neighbourhood ...") shows how the Estense legacy, like Ariosto himself, is alive in the very streets of Ferrara, among its common people. It shows a woman hanging a neighbourhood banner out of her window, and then greeting the passing parade of flag wavers (figure 3.49). Then, as the title card explains, "... the champions invoke the blessing of the Patron Saint of their neighbourhood." Once again, the gendered division between the domestic and the public space is based on a shared loyalty to the local community, represented by the cloth of flags and banners. In the

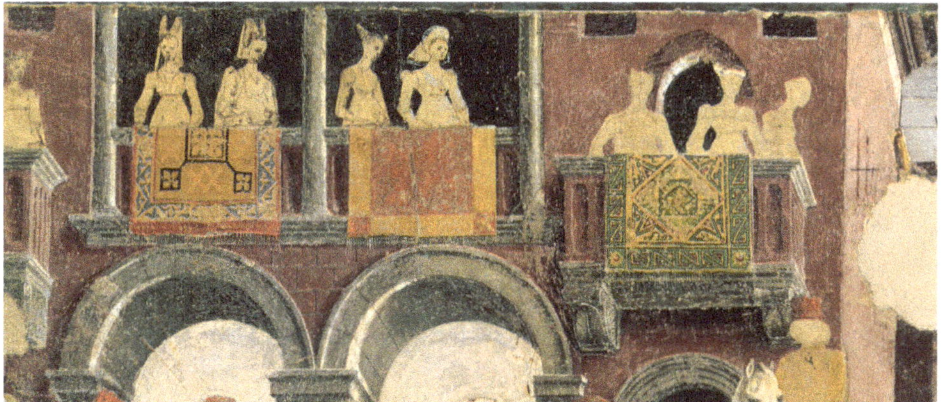

Figure 3.50. Francesco del Cossa, *Women Cheering the Horse Race*, detail from the month of April, ca. 1470, fresco (post-restoration), Palazzo Schifanoia, Ferrara. Su concessione dei Musei di Arte Antica del Comune di Ferrara. Photo Credit: Scala/Art Resource, NY.

following scene, "the delegations go towards the field of the Palio and the women, from their balconies, hang out their festive salute." Like the previous feminine scene, this image is actually the first direct quotation from the depiction of the Palio in the allegory of April at Schifanoia (figure 3.50). This time, however, the greeting women are joined by children, who help them wave the banners. From their elevated point of view, the camera watches the parade of Palio delegations: flag wavers, drummers, knights with their squires, standard bearers. In the following cut, a different balcony is now seen from below: it is on the corner of Palazzo dei Diamanti. The subsequent sections of the film show the entry of the delegations into Piazza Ariostea and the parade of the cart with the prizes. The cart imitates the one on which Aphrodite, in the allegory of April at Schifanoia, enjoys her triumph, pulled by majestic swans. The four races (of the young men or putti, of the foot-soldiers, of the donkeys, and of the horses) are quickly shown in a fast-paced montage, with interspersed longer pictorial shots of perfectly costumed knights and judges.

The final scene, before one last festive waving of flags while victory bells ring, is a shot of Ariosto's monument. On the left of the column, higher than the statue, a long pole is erected. Slowly, the standard with the colours of the winning neighbourhood is hoisted. Meaningfully, victorious and invigilating, it rises higher than Ariosto, above the fascist city masquerading as a Renaissance dukedom.

Chapter Four

Theatrical Ghosts: Not Adapting the *Orlando Furioso* in Late Modernity

Don't tell me you had a scene on the stage of Orlando stripped naked, crossing all of France and Spain with his balls hanging out before he swam the Mediterranean Sea and went to the Moon, just like that, like nothing at all.

Alejo Carpentier, *Baroque Concerto,* 1974

In an Italian villa, a German director, a French screenwriter, and an American producer are discussing, each in his own language, their project to make a film about the *Odyssey.* The continuous interjection of the interpreter's translations raises the level of frustration, which is rooted in radically opposite views on Homer, on cinema, and, ultimately, on what literature is for. A subtle, claustrophobic tension is underlined by the camera, dollying between two gigantic windows. The stunning landscape of Capri looms beyond the glass. The characters remain trapped in their unresolvable conflict. The only resolution that the dialogue can reach is a puzzling platitude: "either we do Homer's *Odyssey* or we don't." They won't.

Ironically, this scene is from a film that was adapted from a work of literature. In 1963, Jean-Luc Godard adapted it from Alberto Moravia's *Il disprezzo* – a novel, among other things, about adapting literature into cinema. When he wrote this novel, in the early 1950s, Moravia was inspired by his own frustration as a writer for cinema, and in particular as an adapter of literary works for the screen. While he loved cinema as a medium for narration, Moravia found the process of adaptation[1] enervating and seldom successful. His character Riccardo (Paul in the film) has to face the humiliation that the film industry invariably exerts on self-important intellectuals, especially when it lures them with apparently prestigious literary projects.

None of the many essays on Moravia's rapport with cinema reports that, roughly ten years before writing *Il disprezzo,* he was involved in the most ambitious attempt to write a screenplay for an adaptation of the *Orlando Furioso.* In fact, that unrealized film has never been studied, like all the adaptation projects that preceded it in the twentieth century. This is probably because none of them were successful. If one looks for the *Orlando Furioso* in the national archives of Rome's Cineteca Nazionale, the only result is an eight-minute-long homemade video. It was shot in the 1940s in someone's vacation residence, and it stars children. A similar search for other Italian classics of the so-called canon (the *Gerusalemme Liberata,* the *Decameron,* the *Divine Comedy, I Promessi Sposi*) yields much more impressive results, including some of the best works by masters such as Enrico Guazzoni and Pier Paolo Pasolini.

In the following pages, I am going to fill this gap in the story of Ariosto's afterlife, asking why cinema was so keen to try to adapt the *Furioso* but, at the same time, so ineffective at doing so. This is the only chapter of this book that focuses entirely on the *Orlando Furioso* rather than on Ariosto's multifaceted legacy. It is the poem itself, in its idiosyncratic structure and anomalous scale, that challenged the technical imagination of filmmakers. Among the figures that I will analyse, maybe only Moravia was interested in Ariosto's intellectual and political model the way Bontempelli or de Chirico was, as we saw in previous chapters. The rest of the filmmakers, screenwriters, and film critics featured in this chapter were in direct dialogue with Ariosto's most famous poem, and with the multimedia legacy that it had produced in Europe throughout the centuries.

The film project that involved Moravia is the last production that I will discuss, after reconstructing attempts to film Ariosto in the silent era and Federico Fellini's fantasies of adaptation. I will start, however, from a very particular case: that of a failed adaptation of the *Furioso* for the stage. It involved one of Italy's most famous film directors of all time, Luchino Visconti, and challenged the very definition of theatre as a medium. It also helps to connect my research on Ariosto and adaptation with one of the most successful episodes of trans-codification of the *Furioso*: Luca Ronconi's theatrical and cinematic spectacles of 1969 and 1975.

Ariosto in the Park

As one of the founders of Italian neorealism, Luchino Visconti was among the most prominent filmmakers of the twentieth century. He was born into one of Milan's oldest noble families but, thanks to his friendship with Coco Chanel and Jean Renoir, he was soon introduced to the leftist circles of the Front Populaire in Paris. Therefore, he embraced socialist and internationalist ideas as a young man. Towards the end of Mussolini's regime, under the alias Alfredo Guidi, he actively took part in the anti-fascist Resistance in Rome. An openly bisexual Marxist aristocrat, after the war Visconti became one of the leading intellectuals affiliated with Italy's Communist Party. His first film as a director, *Ossessione* (1942), was an unauthorized adaptation of the 1934 novel *The Postman Always Rings Twice* by James M. Cain. Instead of setting the film in the United States, like the novel that inspired it, Visconti used Cain's plot to build a realistic cinematic portrait of Italy's socio-sexual struggles under fascism. *Ossessione*'s petit bourgeois and proletarian characters inhabit the provincial landscape of the Po valley, the port of Ancona, and, in the second half of the film, Ferrara. The estranging presence of majestic Estense monuments in the background turned the Ferrarese scenes into emblems of Italy's decay during the last years of fascism.

After pioneering neorealist settings and storytelling with *Ossessione*, in 1948 Visconti wrote and directed *La terra trema*, a seminal masterpiece inspired by Giovanni Verga's nineteenth-century novel *I Malavoglia*. Famous for its use of non-professional actors speaking in dialect, *La terra trema* received a special international prize at the Venice film festival, where it debuted on September 2, 1948. During the same summer, Visconti was approached by the Florentine festival Maggio Musicale with the idea of writing and directing an adaptation of the *Orlando Furioso* for the stage.

The Maggio Musicale was founded in Florence in the same year as Ariosto's centenary, 1933. It quickly became one of the most popular musical events in Italy, and still attracts an international crowd of opera lovers to Florence every May. When the executive secretary of the Maggio, Pariso Votto, contacted Visconti in 1948, the Florentine festival was already an established institution. Open-air productions were – and still are – held in the Boboli Gardens, a historical park originally designed for the Medici family in the Renaissance. The festival traditionally combined a series of opera productions (called Maggio Lirico) with a program of theatre shows mostly staged in Boboli (the Maggio Prosa, or Maggio Teatrante). Votto, who had been the secretary of the Maggio since its foundation,[2] invited Visconti to participate in this second branch of the festival with an original piece based on Ariosto.

Votto and Visconti were from the same generation and had both taken part in the Resistance. They met in Rome, where they discussed possible collaborations. Visconti was mostly interested in bringing to Florence a production of Alfred de Musset's *Lorenzaccio*, a complex Romantic closet drama about the conspiracy that led to Alessandro de' Medici's assassination in 1537. Votto, on the other hand, was more excited about a modern adaptation of the *Furioso*. In August 1948, he wrote a letter to Visconti from Venice inviting him to begin this project.

Illustrious Maestro,
A few months ago, we spoke in Rome about the possibility of staging the *Orlando Furioso* in the Green Lawn of the Meridiana in the Boboli Gardens for the 1949 Maggio Musicale. The idea found the enthusiastic approval of Florence's intellectual society, and still entices me today. My only concern is about the text of the adaptation. I believe that we should have it ready in the next couple of months, so that we can consider all the necessary elements for the formation of the cast and the production. I believe that the elaboration of the text must absolutely be done under your personal direction, so that the resulting work will have not only literary qualities, but also positive theatrical aspects. [...] I would like to meet you soon, so that we can discuss the project thoroughly and be ready for a production worthy of both the tradition of the festival that I have the honour to represent and your great name as a director.[3]

The "Green Lawn" ("Prato Verde") mentioned by Votto is a grassy terraced garden in front of the Palazzina della Meridiana in Boboli. A large, open green space, geometrically designed on rising slopes, this quintessentially Italian garden is organized around the statue of a flying winged horse. This Pegasus, based on a 1537 medal attributed to Benvenuto Cellini, was sculpted by Aristodemo Costoli in the nineteenth century. Since 1983, the statue has been positioned in the centre of the first level of the garden. However, at the time of Visconti's project, it was mounted on a cart that could move along steel tracks and was used as a scenographic element in the theatre productions of the Maggio set in the Meridiana lawn. Both the location and the statue were perfect for an outdoor adaptation of Ariosto's poem, with its perilous gardens, enchanted palaces, and flying Hippogriffs.

Visconti's *Furioso*, however, never actually reached the grass of Boboli, and was likely abandoned by the director before the end of the summer. I will come back to the reason why it failed, and to the shape that it probably took in Visconti's mind before he decided that it was unfeasible. What is immediately fascinating, in the context of Ariosto's modern reception, is that Visconti's unrealized project seems to be a direct genealogical antecedent of the most popular and studied theatrical adaptation of the *Orlando Furioso*: Luca Ronconi's environmental spectacle of the same title, which debuted in 1969 in Spoleto.

The Origins of Originality

Ronconi's *Furioso* was adapted from Ariosto's text by the leader of Italy's neo-avant-garde, Edoardo Sanguineti. This influential, legendary adaptation of the *Orlando Furioso* was both radically experimental and popular. It revolutionized Italian theatre after a long period of stagnation and, thanks to a cinematic version that was broadcast on national television, it colonized the imagination of a generation of Italians. Ronconi's spatial investigation of the *Furioso* disentangled the poem's narrative, staging simultaneous scenes along a labyrinthine path that was to be freely explored by the audience. The film version tried to maintain the same deconstruction of Ariosto's original text, employing montage to recreate the disorienting superimpositions of the theatrical experience. This famous production and its cinematic iterations were considered for a long time to be a completely original interpretation of Ariosto's titanic text, a novelty "without models that preceded it."[4] However, Visconti's vision, twenty years before, was similarly to turn the poem into an interactive spectacle played in an open space without a central stage: a remarkable anticipation of what made Ronconi's *Furioso* revolutionary.

Visconti's imaginative plans for the direction of the *Orlando Furioso* were consistently described by scholars who curated his archives and interviewed him to reconstruct his artistic biography. The descriptions echo each other since before Ronconi's 1969 production. Already in 1955, for instance, Giulio Cesare Castello characterized Visconti's unrealized project as "a series of scenographic stations meant to evoke the tableaux of folkloric troubadours."[5] Later, in a heavily documented monograph on Visconti and theatre, Caterina D'Amico De Carvalho explained that Visconti's intention was "to stage the *Orlando Furioso* at Boboli by dismembering it into a number of scenes that would be acted in different locations, the way troubadours recited chivalric poems."[6] According to Cristina Gastel Chiarelli, Visconti had a "grand and spectacular, revolutionary vision: a path through the spheres of fantasy and dream that would have materialized in different acting areas on the hills of the Boboli gardens." In her reconstruction, "various scenes of [Visconti's] theatrical adaptation of Ariosto's work would have crossed each other and multiplied on various levels."[7]

The most recent analysis of Visconti's unrealized *Furioso* was conducted by Federica Mazzocchi in her comprehensive study of Visconti's theatre directions. Mazzocchi showed that Visconti's unrealized projects of the late 1940s (and the *Furioso* in particular) represented the missing link between the traditional theatre of post-fascist Italy and later avant-garde movements that sought to "call into question theatre as a closed form, either by exploring non-dramaturgical texts [...] or through a work on space that made theatre evade the frame of the stage and take over the audience."[8] Mazzocchi's conclusion is that Visconti's 1949 *Furioso* would have been "extremely advanced" for the times, and that it provided early evidence of "the director's interest in an expansion of the theatrical medium." Mazzocchi also established a direct parallel with Ronconi's 1969 experiment, stating that "Visconti was conceiving an extension of the notion of dramaturgical text, anticipating forms and practices that would find a full concretization in the experimental theatre of the 1960s."[9]

In a recent archival study of the New York production of Ronconi's *Furioso*, staged in Bryant Park in 1970, Stefano Tomassini mentioned Visconti's earlier project as a similar idea, but invited caution. It is tempting to imagine Visconti's *Furioso* as the lost progenitor of Italy's avant-garde theatre, but one cannot forget that the 1949 project was, indeed, just a project, and that Visconti's aristocratic Communism was ideologically different from that of younger, more aggressive reformers of artistic codes such as Ronconi and Sanguineti. In any event, Tomassini still admitted that Visconti's unrealized *Furioso* "is indubitably an incredible antecedent."[10]

I am not interested in establishing whether or not Visconti's *Furioso* should be definitively included among the sources of Ronconi's. Nonetheless, these two adaptations of Ariosto by Marxist intellectuals (one never completed and mostly forgotten, the other a defining and widely studied chapter in the story of Ariosto's reception in the twentieth century) ultimately represent similar attempts to answer some of my book's central questions. How should one read Ariosto right after the age of active colonialism, fascism, and world wars? Can an early modern poem like the *Orlando Furioso* remain itself while also becoming a catalyst for (neo-)avant-garde projects? Can an influential Renaissance text be trans-coded into a new, modern text, rather than just offering a pretext for modern inventions? I am interested in Visconti's project because it already tried to address these questions in 1949, before the rise of postmodern interpretations of the *Furioso.* Ronconi's deconstructive and, ultimately, mannerist answers to my questions emerged right when humanity reached the moon on board of propelled machines instead of an imaginary Hippogriff. Visconti, on the other hand, tried (and failed) to adapt the *Furioso* before the hegemony of Structuralism and Deconstruction, when Idealism and textual criticism were, essentially, the only ways to read the classics, even from a Materialist perspective. The fact that both adaptations contemplated similar solutions for the same problem suggests something about Ariosto's text in itself. Visconti's failure represents, per se, a statement on the *Orlando Furioso.*

What I intend to do is to look at Visconti's project in its own context and through the original unpublished documents that bear its traces. I am interested in the relationship between Visconti's innovative dramaturgic ideas and the text of Ariosto's poem. I also ask why he did not finish it. While we know, from Visconti's correspondence with Votto, that the project was abandoned because there was not enough time for the completion of the text, an analysis of the working papers of the adaptation allows us to understand why and how time ran out.

Courtly Islands

Before I turn to the surviving papers that document Visconti's work on the *Furioso*, let me consider what were the available tools, in the summer of 1948, to imagine a theatrical adaptation of Ariosto's poem in the open space of Boboli.

While original adaptations have seldom appeared in the program of the Maggio Musicale, the staging of Renaissance plays in Florence's Renaissance park was not uncommon in the twentieth century. The sixth version of the Maggio for instance, in 1939, ended with a representation of Tasso's pastoral play *Aminta* in the Boboli gardens.[11] Back in the sixteenth century, *Aminta* had been written especially for a garden party of the Estense court in Ferrara. Its first representation, in 1573, took place in the Belvedere, an idyllic garden on a natural island in the Po River. Between 1513 and 1520, Alfonso d'Este had turned the river islet into an architectural marvel: a space to entertain (and, of course, surveil) his court. A decade later, Ariosto used three octaves of the last edition of the *Furioso* to praise the beauty of this "isle / which near the city lies," filled by the dukes with exotic plants and animals, waterworks, elegant structures, and frequent spectacles: "Its beauty being held beyond compare, / no one who saw it would thereafter praise / Nausicaa's island, as in olden days" (XLIII, 56–9). The 1939 production of *Aminta* for the Maggio Musicale in Florence mirrored its Ferrarese Renaissance counterpart in many ways. It took advantage of the Isolotto, a small island in one of the two artificial lakes of Boboli, surrounded by tall hedges that separated it from the rest of the gardens. On the island, as during Tasso's 1573 premiere in Ferrara, actors and spectators shared a space with no strong demarcation between stage and audience, fiction and reality. Both were immersed in a curated natural landscape that served as the scenography for the pastoral fable.

After the end of the Maggio, a few weeks into the summer of 1939, the Royal Princess of Piedmont hosted a second recital of *Aminta* on the Boboli island to celebrate the wedding of the Duke of Savoia-Aosta to

Irene of Greece. This private iteration of the Maggio production, on the eve of the conflagration of the Second World War, reenacted even more closely Tasso's original project. In 1573, Ferrara had just experienced a catastrophic earthquake, from which the economy of the once powerful dukedom never fully recovered. Indeed, the duke who attended the performance of *Aminta* on the Belvedere islet was the last ruler of the Estense family. When he died, Ferrara's independent territory dissolved into the Papal State. In 1939, fascist Italy had just promulgated the Racial Laws and was about to enter, on Nazi Germany's side, the global conflict that ended the Savoias' kingdom. The aristocratic invitees, on the Isolotto of Boboli, were the last representatives of a crumbling world, like the Ferrarese courtiers on the islet of Belvedere. Their Arcadian spectacles, literally and figuratively secluded, were evasions from history, escapist courtly dreams in the face of ineluctability. They were engineered to allow the audience to enter the theatre (or, rather, the Renaissance island) not just as spectators but also as part of the spectacle: to cross, with their bodies, the boundary between reality and fiction, history and idyll, the garden of the Belvedere, or Boboli, and that of the pastoral fable.

When Votto, who had administered the Maggio since its foundation, invited Visconti to work on an adaptation of Ariosto in 1948, he immediately underlined the enthusiasm of "Florence's intellectual society" for the project. The *Furioso* in the Boboli garden was evidently meant for this new bourgeois court of writers and artists, journalists and academics: a sophisticated audience like that of Tasso's *Aminta* in 1939 (and 1573). The cultural leadership of Italy's newborn Republic was ready to appropriate the spaces and reform the rituals that were once occupied and performed by the dismantled hierarchies of fascism and the monarchy, which in turn had adopted those of early modern feudal aristocracies. Such intellectual elitism did not really clash with Votto's and Visconti's Marxist ideas. After all, the founder of Italian Communism, Antonio Gramsci, was a keen analyst of Renaissance courtly politics. A significant part of his political thought was rooted in Machiavelli's *Prince*.[12] From a Gramscian perspective, highbrow entertainment was a crucial tool to spread antagonistic visions of the world, undermining the hegemony of dominant classes. The political potential of high culture lay precisely in the fact that it was addressed to intellectuals, whose cooptation was the key to any revolutionary project based on Gramsci's philosophy. And of course, unlike Tasso's *Aminta*, Ariosto's text had intrinsic revolutionary potential. With its radical contradictions, ironic subtexts, and amused subversion of Aristotelian traditions, the *Orlando Furioso* offered the ideal raw matter for an original Marxist interpretation, as Ronconi's successful adaptation demonstrated twenty years later.

However, how did Visconti's dramaturgic interpretation come about in technical terms? In the late 1960s, Ronconi could be inspired by famous experiments of theatrical simultaneity and collage like Charles Marowitz's 1966 production of *Hamlet*, in which an eminently classic text was deprived of its unity on a fractured and permeable stage. Visconti, on the other hand, could not draw on similar anti-traditional reconceptions of space and time in theatre. His innovative solutions for the *Furioso* had to be inspired by the *Furioso*'s own irreducible entanglement, and, as his critics and biographers pointed out, by the performative origins of chivalric epic in the oral tradition of troubadours. Indeed, it is unlikely that the roots of Visconti's idea of articulating a spectacle in dislocated tableaux or "scenographic stations" went beyond the specific textual qualities of the *Orlando Furioso* itself. If they had, then it would be hard to explain why he never put the same idea into practice with other texts in his long career as a theatre director. After all, the *Furioso* was the only narrative text that he tried to adapt for theatre: all his other productions, staged or planned, were of texts either written for theatre or already adapted by others. The play that Visconti ended up staging for the 1949 Maggio had nothing to do with the experimental plans of the abandoned *Furioso* project. It was a lavish production of Shakespeare's *Troilus and Cressida*. The set, designed by Franco Zeffirelli, was still in the Boboli garden. However, it was not erected in the open lawn of the Meridiana, but in the more traditionally theatrical Anfiteatro in front of Palazzo Pitti, with bleachers for the audience. While grandiose and operatic, it was a relatively conventional production, like that of Visconti's 1948 *As You Like It* in Rome with Salvador Dalì's scenography.

Magic within Magic

Instead of reducing the boundless and unresolvable plot of the *Furioso* to the linear progression of a series of acts divided into scenes, Visconti planned to bring to the stage the inherent theatricality of the poem, its spectacular nature. The most logical theoretical interlocutor for this project was the greatest Italian playwright of the century, Luigi Pirandello. Pirandello, who had died in 1936 as a world-famous Nobel Laureate, was a keen reader of the *Orlando Furioso*.[13] In the fundamental text of his poetics, *L'umorismo* (On Humour), he analysed the interplay of illusion and reality, spectacle and narration, both within and outside the diegesis of the *Furioso*. When Pirandello insisted, in particular, on the episode of the enchanted castle, he described the magical mechanics of Ariosto's irony in theatrical terms.

In the *Furioso,* the sorcerer Atlante conjured the enchanted castle to keep his protégé, Ruggiero, away from the war. The wizardry is simple: everyone, in the castle, sees the person or thing that they desire the most. These visions, however, can never be reached, and the castle compels its unwilling and unaware inhabitants to ceaselessly chase the object of their desire in a labyrinthine architecture that has no exit. By luring and trapping all the most valiant knights of the poem, the castle represents a sudden knot that unexpectedly ties together the main storylines of the poem, deferring the progression of the plot. It is also a dead end: it effectively interrupts the action of the *Furioso* by entertaining its protagonists in a potentially eternal looping spectacle. Readers enter the castle in Canto XII by following Orlando, who is lured into it by a vision of Angelica. In the castle, the image of a fleeing Angelica, produced by the spell, is chased by three different characters: Orlando, the Saracen knight Ferraù, and the king of Circassia, Sacripante. All three are ultimately freed by the real Angelica, who enters the castle wearing a magic ring that makes its bearer invisible and immune to any spell. Once the three knights and Angelica are out of the castle, she mocks them and uses the ring again to disappear, leaving their desires unfulfilled. At the end of the canto, the three resume their pursuit, this time in the real world.

In order to explain "the true magic of Ariosto's style,"[14] Pirandello reflected on the fictional nature of the castle within the fiction of the poem. The knights who enter the castle are entering a stage. On this stage, Atlante's spell creates the fiction of Angelica's presence for them, stopping their action and turning them into spectators. When the real Angelica enters the stage, she pretends not to be there by wearing the magic ring of invisibility. While the magic of the stage itself plays the part of Angelica, the magic of the ring allows the real Angelica to walk the stage unseen, as a spectator. In Pirandello's words, "it is a magic that enters another magic."[15]

To Angelica's eyes, the knights are not spectators, but part of a spectacle that she can (and does) tamper with from outside the fiction. She is on the stage, but not in the spectacle. She is both present and absent in the castle, fictional and real, in the know and unaware. She is invisible to the knights just as the audience is invisible to the characters of a play. The Angelica that the knights are chasing is not really in the castle, while the one that they don't see is – and is looking at them. As spectators of the fake Angelica, the knights don't know that they are trapped in a spectacle with its own spectator. And of course this spectator, the real Angelica, does not know that she is herself part of the ultimate fictional spectacle: Ariosto's poem itself.

Pirandello's interpretation of this emblematic canto as "magic within magic" turns Ariosto's irony into a form of theatrical incantation, a competition with Atlante's wizardry. Like Atlante, who set the stage in the first place, the narrator of Canto XII is a sorcerer. His audience (we readers, who believe ourselves to be on the outside of any magic castle or layer of fiction) is involved in the same game that disorients the characters in the poem. The boundary between the space of representation and that of supposed reality is a mirror: the rapport between the castle and the poem is equivalent to that between the poem and the world of us readers. While the episode of Atlante's castle reveals this most clearly, Pirandello applies the same principle to the entire poem.

> [Ariosto's] style has the virtues of magic from the beginning. The whole first canto is, in its representation, phantasmagoric: crossed by lightnings, by fleeing apparitions. And these lightnings do not flash to dazzle only the readers, but also the actors on the stage [...]. The poet performs this magic of his in full awareness [...] he is astonished, and smiles at both his own astonishment and that of his readers and his characters.[16]

I believe that Visconti's 1948 project was more a consequence of Pirandello's reading of the *Furioso* than an origin of Ronconi's adaptation. I also believe that it could not have been conceived without the precedents (and revivals) of Renaissance courtly spectacles, held in non-traditional spaces that challenged the division between reality and play. The "radical expansion of fictional space" recognized by Pirandello, with "fiction invading the extra-fictional space,"[17] was sufficient to suggest a theatrical adaptation of Ariosto's text in which stage and audience share the same physical space. Especially if that space was to be the lawn of the Meridiana in Boboli: a Renaissance garden with a moving Pegasus in it, next to a Medicean palace; the site of a recent revival of Tasso's courtly play suspended between fable and reality.

Typewriter Tricks

Let me now get closer to what Visconti had concretely planned before abandoning the project. The most important document of Visconti's work on Ariosto is stored in the Visconti archive at Rome's Istituto Gramsci. It is a typed manuscript of six pages with autograph corrections, titled *Orlando Furioso.* The text summarizes most of the events of the poem, divided into scenes by Visconti. It stops after thirteen scenes that cover the first three cantos.

Part personal memo and part tentative plan for the staging, these working notes represent genetic material for the production in the Boboli gardens. An analysis of the text and of the material condition of the document suggests a simple scenario for its composition. Visconti must have started working on the reduction personally in the summer of 1948, as Votto recommended. Rather than typing a previously handwritten draft, he likely worked directly on the typewriter's keys.[18] He then lightly revised the typed draft with a pencil, paying attention to clarity rather than elegance or precision.[19] Ariosto's original text was clearly on his desk while he worked. The document represents an intermediate stage between a systematic close reading of Ariosto's *Furioso* and a script for its adaptation; a sort of annotated outline. Its content and format are the result of many early decisions. In particular, it shows a selection of episodes and characters for the script, lines for the actors' dialogues, and some dramaturgic choices. However, inconsistencies and personal notes show that Visconti's ideas were changing while he was writing, and that the outlining exercise itself was part of his adaptation process. Once completed, this initial sketch would have been used (either by Visconti himself or under his direct supervision) to write the actual play. In sum, this preliminary document offers a glimpse into Visconti's mental workshop. It lays out his theatrical interpretation of the *Orlando Furioso.*

Since epic poems start, by definition, *in medias res,* the first canto is introduced, in Visconti's document, by an *antefatto*: a summary of the events that precede the plot. Visconti took note that, when the action starts, Orlando and Rinaldo are already in love with Angelica, and that Charlemagne wants to avoid a fight between his strongest paladins. Thus, the king promises to betroth Angelica to the knight who kills the most infidels in battle. The battle, however, favours the Saracen army, and, in the confusion, Angelica jumps on a horse and flees.

Already in these first lines, Visconti started using a typographical code that is typical of scripts and characterizes the entire document. He highlighted some of the characters' names (here Orlando, Rinaldo, and Angelica) by typing them in all caps. These, presumably, were the characters destined to appear on the stage. The names that Visconti did not highlight, like that of Charlemagne in the *antefatto*, mostly belong to characters who are mentioned in order to make the story understandable but have no important actions in the selected scenes summarized for the script. I believe that Visconti decided not to feature these characters in the play as roles. Some of them are actually primary characters in the poem, and I will discuss them in a moment. For now, I would like to reflect on why the minor characters were still mentioned in the document, and on how Visconti could feature them in the adaptation without having actors play their roles on the stage.

Since all of Ariosto's storylines are entangled, Visconti had two choices. He could radically rewrite the plot, extracting from the *Furioso* a linear epic (like that at the core of Tasso's *Gerusalemme Liberata*) or a series of self-concluded quests (like the adventures of Arthurian poems). Or, he could keep marginal and inactive characters in the narrative of his adaptation, pointing at a wider fictional world beyond the events represented on the stage. His decision is already evident in the notes for the first canto, after the first three scenes. He chose the second option, and realized that the only way to turn the stage into a selective portion of a wider fictional reality was to incorporate a narrating voice in the play. A narrator's (or multiple narrators') ability to mention the names, or describe the actions, of the dozens and dozens of characters and settings of the poem that could not directly appear on the stage was a crucial solution to avoid turning the adaptation into a banal anthology of episodes or a betrayal of Ariosto's anti-Aristotelian experimentalism. Thus, the fourth scene of Visconti's document reads: "Angelica, 'through dark and terrifying woods, flees' (The narrator, whatever form he may take, is necessary to adapt this poem)."[20]

Besides mentioning the necessity of a narrator, the unusually brief summary of the scene directly incorporates a line from the poem: the first hendecasyllable ("fugge tra selve spaventose e scure" I.33) of the long description of Angelica's flight. It is likely that Visconti planned to leave room for Ariosto's original text here, narrating rather than representing Angelica's flight on the stage. He clearly did not want to cut this iconic trope of the *Furioso* from the adaptation. Thus, instead of having it happen off-stage, or asking an actress to pretend to ride through a dark wood, he planned to have the narrator ("whatever form he may take") declaim the passage. This way, Ariosto's original text could glue together the more theatrically feasible scenes that precede and follow Angelica's flight in the first canto.

This is probably how the model of folkloric troubadours helped Visconti envision an experimental mise en scène of the *Orlando Furioso*. The echo of Pirandello's lesson is also important to understand the necessity of an on-stage narrator for such a goal, especially when Visconti, as I will show in the rest of this section, planned to make the audience enter Ariosto's dramatized fiction not just as spectators of what is on the stage but as silent interlocutors of the characters: as the recipients of the stories narrated, rather than played, on the stage. My hypothesis is that the reason why not only the names of minor characters but also those of some primary figures of the poem are not highlighted in Visconti's document is that the roles of these protagonists were to be entirely narrated by other characters or "played," so to speak, by the audience. The case of Bradamante is emblematic, and I will use it to explain what I mean.

When he mentioned Bradamante for the first time, in the fifth scene of the first canto, Visconti typed her name in the same style used for inactive and minor characters. Even the name of Rinaldo's horse, Baiardo, is highlighted, but Bradamante's is not. This is disorienting, not only because Bradamante appears prominently in the summarized episode, but also because she is very active in it. The scene is about Sacripante, one of Angelica's suitors. His goofy but relatively successful erotic chase is soon disrupted by a mysterious knight in white armour, who beats and humiliates Sacripante. Unbeknownst to him, the white knight is none other than Bradamante, who is thus introduced as a strong fighter and primary character by Ariosto. After being unseated and left on the ground by Bradamante, Sacripante resumes his pursuit of Angelica, but encounters a wandering messenger who is looking for a white knight. Sacripante tells him about his misadventure, and learns from him that the knight that defeated him was, in fact, Bradamante, a woman.

Now, since the central action of this episode is the duel between Sacripante and Bradamante, why is Sacripante's name highlighted in Visconti's document and Bradamante's is not? One explanation would be that Bradamante's character is not needed for a theatrical representation of the scene. In fact, to maintain the mystery and the ironic game of indirect narrations of the original, it is best not to have her on the stage. If Sacripante is given the role of an intra-diegetic narrator, the duel with Bradamante can be entirely narrated by him to the messenger, so that the audience, rather than seeing it happen on the stage, can imagine it. Sacripante would be alone on that stage, or rather on one of the "scenographic stations" that Castello, in 1955, mentioned when describing Visconti's innovative project for the lawn in Boboli. The audience would reach that station in the garden as the messenger, in the poem, reached Sacripante in the wood. There, the audience would learn of Bradamante from Sacripante's version of the story. Spectators would have to decide whether or not they believe this internal narrator, without seeing the duel. By becoming the messenger, the theatrical audience would have less objective information than the readers of the poem, but would be directly immersed in it.

A similar but more complex version of this dramaturgic solution is suggested by the summary of Bradamante's second appearance, in the third scene of the following canto. Once again, her name is not highlighted, while those of other characters in the scene (Gradasso, Ruggiero, and

Pinabello) are. Instead of directly narrating, as in the previous scenes in the document, this time Visconti introduces the events through an intermediary troubadour-like narrator,[21] external to the diegesis:

> The Narrator starts talking about Bradamante, the sister of Rinaldo. She is in love with RUGGIERO. They met only once and now Bradamante is looking for him. After unseating Sacripante (scene 5 of Canto I), she reaches a wood where she meets a pensive, sorrowful, and exhausted knight: PINABELLO. Urged by the damsel's questions about his pain, he narrates his extraordinary adventure. [...][22]

Pinabello, like Sacripante in the previous canto (but unlike Bradamante), is a role to be played by an actor. Not only is his name highlighted in the document but Visconti also sketches a description of his characteristics and mood: a stub of stage directions. The narrator hands over the narration to him, and he starts telling his adventure. To whom, though? Bradamante, if my interpretation is correct, is not on the stage. It is the audience, I believe, that is supposed to take her role, and listen to Pinabello's story. But the story, in Visconti's document, is suddenly disrupted by the dramatic interference of two characters with highlighted names, who come to the scene just when Pinabello is telling about the "winged horse" on which a strange flying knight kidnapped his beloved and brought her to his palace of steel.

> And here come two knights, RUGGIERO and GRADASSO, guided by a dwarf. They come to challenge the strange knight. Gradasso blows the horn. The knight appears on his winged horse and, from above, fights the two knights, who are powerless against this sort of anachronistic airplane. Then the knight [...] unveils his shield. [...] Pinabello passes out. When he wakes up he is alone, in front of the palace of steel. And here he is, crying.[23]

This episode shows how Visconti could base his tableaux on internal and external narrators without reducing the play to a series of recitations from the poem. The narrator introduces Bradamante, and then leaves the stage to Pinabello. Pinabello's narration on the stage is disrupted by a dramatic action (the fight between Ruggiero, Gradasso, and the flying knight) that is actually part of the tale that he is recounting to the audience/Bradamante. His storytelling (essentially a prolepsis) comes to life in the scene, and the audience can see a portion of it in real time. While, in the poem, the readers (and Bradamante) learn about the fight only from Pinabello's flashback, in the play they can see it. This is the opposite of what happened, in the previous canto, with Sacripante, whose duel with the white knight was directly narrated by Ariosto in the poem but became the character's narration in Visconti's adaptation hypothesis.

In both Sacripante's and Pinabello's scenes, Bradamante is dematerialized. Rather than an active character, she becomes the protagonist of a narration, or the recipient of one, within the play. While not on the stage, Bradamante is still part of the adaptation. It is as if she is wearing Angelica's ring in Atlante's enchanted castle: she is both there and not there. Ruggiero and Gradasso, on the other hand, are conjured on the stage by Pinabello's narration, and start acting in front of the audience. They don't know they are part of a narration within the play, just as they don't know that the flying knight that they are fighting is in fact Atlante on the Hippogriff.

The competition between Atlante's fictional magic and Ariosto's authorial magic described by Pirandello in his reading of the *Furioso* is joined, in Visconti's adaptation project, by a third competitor: Visconti himself. Visconti approached his theatrical *Orlando Furioso* as a third level of magic, making characters disappear while they enter the story, or turning them into the audience of his spectacle. And, by adopting Ariosto's own narration as a tangible voice in the adaptation, he trapped the author himself in the enchanted castle of his fictional world. The garden of Boboli, which had hosted the modern remake of Tasso's *Aminta* a decade before, was the ideal battleground for this competition between fiction and reality, poetry and theatre.

Lost in the Labyrinth

As the case of Pinabello's episode shows, Visconti's division of the original cantos into numbered scenes did not simply follow Ariosto's frequent transitions from one storyline to another in the poem. Sometimes, the scenes that Visconti chose to focus on were individual actions of one character, like Angelica's flight. In other cases, he planned to use a single theatrical unit to represent some of Ariosto's most complex narrative superimpositions of places, timelines, and points of view. In any event, the content and order of the scenes in the document respond to Visconti's vision, allowing him to play tricks like Bradamante's disappearance from the stage (but not from the story). If he had planned to feature Bradamante as a character at the beginning of his play, his outline of Sacripante's and Pinabello's episodes in the first two cantos would have been different. This is why I believe that the preliminary document that Visconti started in the summer of 1948 was not a mere summary of the poem, but a concrete step towards adaptation. This adaptation relied on the unique literary features of Ariosto's text, as they were revealed by modern commentators such as Pirandello. And it took advantage of the opportunities offered by the set in a Renaissance garden, drawing on the hybridization of fictional and non-fictional space experienced by precedents such as Tasso's *Aminta* in 1573 and 1939.

What made this enchanted house of cards collapse was the very material of its foundations: Ariosto's text. One of the simplest reasons why Visconti needed to start from a systematic sketch of the *Furioso*, canto by canto, is that it is virtually impossible to remember Ariosto's plot in its intricate structure. What Pirandello called the "magic of Ariosto's style" is truly akin to Atlante's disorienting spell. Taking consistent notes is the only magic ring available to a reader, especially one who aspires to use the text as a high-resolution blueprint for a new text, animated by the same magic. If my interpretation of his typewritten reading is correct, Visconti intended to challenge the main distinctive feature of Ariosto's poem: its paradoxical unrepresentability – what I called, in the Introduction, its vastness. The meticulous outlining was not only the stub of a stage plan but also a map to avoid getting lost in the labyrinth of the poem while rebuilding it as a play. Drawing a reliable, detailed map of such a labyrinth, however, is hardly the work of a summer. As I mentioned before and will discuss below, publishers, artists, and commentators have tried for centuries to make the *Furioso* more manageable through a parallel universe of derivative art, but the result was mostly a diffraction of its entangled narrative: a system of satellite objects, autonomous or para-textual, that inspired an aura of familiarity for the labyrinthine poem. This domestication of Ariosto's fictional universe is both the reason for and the consequence of its popular success and critical canonization. It makes it more accessible and memorable but also less thoroughly known and hard to remember as a whole.

The *Furioso*'s resistance to synthesis, along with its immediate popularity, turned the poem into one of the most illustrated and visualized texts in the history of Western literature. Since early editions, images offered an orienting tool to approach the absorbing but frustrating chaos of Ariosto's gargantuan narrative structure. Rather than decorating the poem, illustrations made it easier to follow its plot without getting lost in temporal or geographical jumps, disrupted and resumed storylines, and sudden changes of protagonists, goals, and contexts. Soon, textual recaps and moralizing summaries started accompanying the iconographic apparatus of the *Furioso*, making one of the longest popular books of Renaissance Italy even more massive. This progressive expansion of para-textual material changed the way in which readers experienced texts in Europe. Indeed, recent projects in Digital Humanities, such as Lina Bolzoni's *Galassia Ariosto*,[24] show that the mnemonic challenges presented by the

Furioso's structural acrobatics made the very format of early modern illustrated books evolve. This evolution took place at a critical juncture in the history of European print. It is hard not to suspect that Ariosto himself, with his practical understanding of the potential of his own medium of expression, intentionally sought such a legacy. His poem was conceived as a book to be printed, to inspire artists, to entertain occasional readers, and to mesmerize systematic analysts.

The anti-Aristotelian maze of alternating subplots that forms the narrative tapestry of the *Furioso* tested the limits of an entire medium, the printed book, just as it was starting to inform a global market. Book making had to improve and adapt in order to meet the challenges of a poem that is too long, too entangled, and too varied to be visualized or summarized into a progression of main scenes. Market demand incentivized such a process of technological adaptation, which in turn inspired a vertiginous number of objects outside of the book medium: paintings, ceramics, frescoed palaces, anthological selections – and, later, comic books, board games, and radio shows. Some iconic tropes, like the episodes of Ruggiero liberating Angelica or Orlando's madness, have been particularly popular in the trans-historical visualization and retelling of the *Furioso*, in and outside of books. However, the available material from the text is so diverse and so wide that even the most densely illustrated and annotated editions cannot cover it all.

Cover to Cover

In 1969 Ronconi was able to exploit this long and productive history of representation by dismembering the poem into truly autonomous scenes, actively connected by the audience walking among them. Rather than challenging Ariosto's narrative game as a second-degree author, Ronconi translated into theatre the experience of playing that game as a reader. Not a systematic reader though, like Visconti with his dense notes. Ronconi famously considered plots irrelevant for theatre. Interviewed by Franco Quadri in 1973, he said that "it is not necessary to read the *Orlando Furioso* from beginning to end to grasp its spirit. The important thing is to have an idea of the *Orlando*, to know what it can be." He added that "it is not even true that, because we read a text, we know it well."[25] It is meaningful that Sanguineti, the author of Ronconi's script, used the term *travestimento* (disguise, travesty, masquerade), rather than adaptation, for his text.

If one approaches the *Furioso* as a re-combinable puzzle of potential disguises, then adaptation through deconstruction and rewriting becomes a radical but manageable exercise of mannerism and tarot reading, in the highest sense of the terms. A new, mercurial arrangement of old and stable material. Or even "a critical essay," as Sanguineti defined his experiment with Ronconi.[26] Calvino's re-use of Ariosto's characters and scenes in *The Nonexistent Knight* (1959) and, more clearly, in the combinatory novel *The Castle of Crossed Destinies* (1973) is based on a similar approach. The original text becomes a source of mythology rather than a story to be disentangled and transposed into a new text. What counts is to "grasp its spirit," not to retrace its gigantic structural arabesque.

This modern use of Ariosto (and of his para-textual and extra-textual afterlife) was different from the appropriation and presentification attempted by fascist Ferrara in 1933. It was based on a reading experience of the poem and, at the same time, on the awareness of its ultimate intransitivity. It was more akin to Massimo Bontempelli's spin-off of the *Furioso* that I analysed in Chapter 2: an expression, both experimental and traditional, of literary influence, modern but in open dialogue with the past: an encounter. Visconti, on the other hand, tried to faithfully adapt the *Orlando Furioso* rather than rewrite it or adopt it as a source and a model. While he did, I believe, "grasp its spirit," he also tried "to read the *Orlando Furioso* from beginning to end." He had the ambition to translate its text, rather than its spirit, into theatre, episode by episode, without banalizing the complexities that readers such as Pirandello had highlighted in the twentieth century. The task was simply too monumental.

As I mentioned, the fact that the *Furioso*'s ungovernableness produced so many images and interpretative summaries in the past five centuries increased the familiarity of the poem among occasional readers, especially in late modernity. The poem counts three or four times the number of lines of comparably famous classics of the epic genre, from the *Aeneid* to the *Gerusalemme Liberata*, and is even longer than Boiardo's and Pulci's fifteenth-century chivalric poems. Reading it from cover to cover takes weeks, and it is almost impossible to keep in mind who is where, or what are the causes of most events. Reading the *Furioso* as a whole is very different from reading a novel, or a narrative poem centred on an epic mission, or even a series of interrelated but auto-conclusive adventures. Yet, anyone who went through the Italian school system – at least in the past two centuries – has the impression of knowing the text, whose episodes and heroes (from Astolfo on the moon to Ruggiero on Alcina's island) are ubiquitous in art and music, puppet theatre, school anthologies, and popular illustrated editions. I suspect that Visconti's project was a victim of this insidious sense of familiarity. It had an original and promising premise, but would have required months, if not years, to be completed.

Visconti's 1948 document invariably uses two pages for the outline of each canto. The space is rather generous, considering that, once finished, the notes would have amounted to ninety-two pages – and probably between 175 and 200 scenes. We know for a fact that Visconti did not intend to spare expenses. The production of *Troilus and Cressida* that he staged instead of the *Furioso* in 1949 was unusually long, and so rich in scenographic art, props, costumes, animals, and actors (many stars, as well as countless extras) that it almost bankrupted the Maggio festival. Resources were not a problem and, as I showed, Visconti had a strong and ambitious vision. However, the labour required to fulfil that vision for the entire poem could not meet the deadline of the Maggio. The real problem was time. Indeed, the correspondence between Visconti and Votto confirms that the project was abandoned because Visconti realized that he could not write the text in time for the scheduled production.[27] At least not by himself.

The manpower of a cinematic production (by definition, a team effort) would have made Visconti's process more likely to succeed. However, as I will discuss in the rest of this chapter, attempts to adapt Ariosto for cinema were no more successful than Visconti's dramaturgic project. After Vivaldi's 1727 opera, and before Ronconi's 1969 play, the *Orlando Furioso* consistently resisted time-based adaptations.

Attempted Ariosto vs. Telegenic Tasso

The story of Visconti's unmade *Furioso* shows both the appeal and the difficulty of imagining the poem as script. It makes it easier to understand why several major filmmakers planned to adapt Ariosto for cinema, but none of them was able to finish a screenplay. And not, as I will show in the next two sections, for a lack of trying. Still today, the only completed film that can be considered as an adaptation of the *Furioso* is the cinematic version of Ronconi's play.[28] It was shot in 1974, using monumental interiors with theatrical painted scenery and stage machines. In 1975, as I mentioned, it was broadcast in five weekly episodes on Italy's national television.

A surreal, five-hour tour de force, Ronconi's film is highly experimental but paradoxically more linear than the original version for the stage. The very nature of the time-based optical medium made it impossible for Ronconi to directly transpose the core features of his play. The intermediary lens of the camera abolished the simultaneity of the scenes, the suppression of a central stage, and the direct involvement of spectators. At the same time, Ronconi's alienating choices resisted cinema as a medium and, in particular, any form of cinematic realism. The settings, the costumes, and the acting style of the cast members (who mostly came from stage careers and classical training) consistently reminded the audience that they were not watching a film, but rather a filmed play. In sum, the only existing film adaptation of the *Orlando Furioso* was really the adaptation of a 1969 avant-garde play that deconstructed it.

After Ronconi, there was one finished attempt to turn some of Ariosto's stories into Hollywood-style entertainment. In 1983, Giacomo Battiato debuted as a director with a glossy sword-and-sorcery film titled *I Paladini: Storia d'armi e d'amori.* This visually beautiful fable, filmed in Italy with an international cast, was a successful attempt to put together a commercially viable Italian production in the popular genre of fantasy. It was distributed internationally in multiple languages, including the Anglophone version, *Hearts and Armours.*

Battiato's plot, for the most part, is a radical simplification of major storylines from the *Furioso.* In particular, it centres on the forbidden love between Bradamante and Ruggiero, with the interferences of Atlante, Marfisa, and Melissa. However, the straightforward screenplay skipped most of the narrative material that is at the core of Ariosto's originality. As a matter of fact, much of its treatment of the paladins' stories is closer to that of Ariosto's hypo-texts, from the *Chanson de Roland* to Boiardo's *Orlando Innamorato.* Suffice it to say that there is no Hippogriff, and that the conflict between Christians and Saracens (often called "infidels") is devoid of any irony and rather solemn. Angelica and Isabella are merged and simplified into the character of a Saracen princess, almost a female Ruggiero, while Orlando (named Rolando) does not get furious at all, and replaces Rodomonte as Ruggiero's final adversary in the climax. In addition, Battiato's direction is obsessed with stylized duels and stunning natural settings, which seem to distract him from the supposedly epic plot. This excursive narrative style is actually the strength of the film, and even gives it an involuntary Ariostean aura of charmed digression. However, it is clear that *Hearts and Armours* is only superficially inspired by Ariosto's poem, and did not have the ambition to adapt it. It is not surprising that it was saluted by critics as a "medieval romp," "silly but a visual wow."[29]

Ronconi's and Battiato's films represent two opposite extremes: a prodigiously self-aware experiment across media and a pop-culture exploitation with no literary ambition. Everything in between, in the history of the *Orlando Furioso* and cinema, invariably failed before filming. I believe that this happened for the same reasons that prevented Visconti from completing his stage adaptation. Before I move to reconstructing some of the failed attempts to adapt Ariosto for cinema, it is revealing to consider that Tasso's *Gerusalemme Liberata*, on the other hand, was successfully adapted more than once.

Strongly influenced by the *Furioso*, the *Liberata* was nonetheless a critical response to the same Ariostean features that attracted Visconti while making his project unfeasible. Tasso rejected Ariosto's style and structure, and arguably that is why his text offered an ideal platform for several productions since the silent era of cinema.

A colossal production of the *Liberata* was one of the first movies written and directed by Enrico Guazzoni in 1911.[30] A pioneer of feature-length films, Guazzoni directed some of the earliest global blockbusters of cinema's history, including the adaptation of *Quo Vadis?* in 1913. In 1918, he directed a second and more grandiose version of the *Liberata*, partly filmed in Palestinian locations. In 1935, this film was reissued in a third extended edition, adding sound and voicing. The three versions had a strong international success. Along with similar productions, such as the 1911 adaptation of Dante's *L'Inferno*, they established Italian production houses as a global force at the dawn of commercial cinema. After the war, when Italian films regained the attention of a wide international market, a fourth successful adaptation of Tasso was directed by Carlo Ludovico Bragaglia. He was the brother of Anton Giulio Bragaglia, the Futurist photographer who, as I mentioned in the previous chapter of this book, spoke at the Ottava d'oro about the *Furioso* as a proto-film. Carlo Ludovico Bragaglia's *Gerusalemme Liberata* was written by prolific screenwriter Sandro Continenza and was distributed globally in 1957 with the title *The Mighty Crusaders.* It joined a fortunate trend of heroic costumed films initiated by Mario Camerini's 1954 adaptation of the *Odyssey*, starring Kirk Douglas.

Why were adaptations of Tasso so successful, like those of Homer's or Dante's epics, while Ariosto's poem never had a traditional cinematic treatment? In the preface to one of the most popular Italian paperback editions of the *Gerusalemme Liberata*, critic Ezio Raimondi insisted on the intrinsic cinematic qualities of Tasso's narrative and structure. He praised Tasso's ability to transition organically from the wide angle of massive battle scenes to emotional close-ups of heroic individuals, portrayed in their intimate pathos. He found the cinematicity of the poem to be rooted in the structure of the highest form of Aristotelian aesthetics, tragedy, and discussed it through Eisenstein's theory of montage.[31] Tasso's technical agility as a narrator, applied to solid epic material of Virgilian solemnity, follows the classical laws of dramatic composition. This allowed Raimondi to present the *Liberata* in universally familiar modern filmic terms (zoom, wide angle, close up, and so on). However, what makes it easy to read Tasso's poem as a compelling realistic film is not only the way in which the plot is delivered but also the plot itself, with its strong unity of space and action based on historical events. In a little over fifteen thousand lines, divided into twenty cantos, Tasso built an arc sustained by an ultimately inescapable tension towards a single possible solution. The poem is, after all, the story of a successful siege.

In addition, the *Liberata*'s cohesiveness and Ariostotelian unity invites us to project political sentiments over its epic mythology rooted in medieval history. It is significant, I believe, that the first two versions of Guazzoni's adaptation were screened during two major international conflicts: the colonial Italo-Turkish war in Libya and the First World War. In 1911, an Italian review of the first *Gerusalemme Liberata* welcomed the film as a representation of "the eternal war of the cross and the crescent moon," at a time in which "our brothers fight and win, and the Italian flag waves over the mosques."[32] In 1919, in the magazine *Bioscope*, a British reviewer reported that English screenings of the second version of the *Liberata* had an alternative finale, in which "the last scene, of the Crusaders marching triumphantly into Jerusalem, dissolves, with a striking effect, into a parallel picture of representative troops of the Allies repeating the victorious entry eight hundred years later."[33] And I should mention again, here, that Achille Funi, in the 1930s, chose the *Liberata* to represent Ferrara's fascists in his fresco, despite the fact that those same fascists had adopted Ariosto as their literary idol.

Unfinished Business

As I mentioned, the lack of traditional adaptations of the *Furioso* in twentieth-century cinema is not due to a lack of interest in the poem among filmmakers. Cinema, especially in Italy, has fantasized about Ariosto's poem since before Visconti planned and abandoned his theatrical adaptation. I am not just alluding to the influence that Ariosto cast on auteurs such as Silvio Soldini, Jim Jarmusch, or Visconti himself.[34] Nor am I referring to those films that, in the vein of Battiato's *Hearts and Armours*, concocted a chivalric fantasy and picked some ingredients from the *Orlando Furioso*, like Pietro Francisci's *Roland the Mighty* (1956). I am talking about concrete projects of cinematic adaptation that never saw the light of day: productions of the *Furioso* that were announced, brainstormed, or even partially scripted, before being abandoned.

The first film project on the *Orlando Furioso* that we know about dates back to the years of the first adaptations of Tasso. According to film scholar Cristina Bragaglia, the success of Guazzoni's *Gerusalemme Liberata* pushed the Roman production house Cines to explore the possibility of a similar film based on Ariosto's poem. Bragaglia traced this project back to 1918, and attributed its failure to the "audaciousness of the scenes and situations of Ariosto's poem," which would have proved much less adaptable than the realistic battles and duels of Tasso's *Liberata.*[35] One could argue that, in the same years and in the same country, equally "audacious" literary scenes and situations were adapted for cinema by Giuseppe De Liguoro, Giuseppe Bertolini, and Adolfo Padovan. Their 1911 adaptation of Dante's *Inferno* required, of course, innovative special effects, including flying creatures and gigantic monsters. As I stated before, I believe that the obstacle was not in the *Furioso*'s visual demands or fantastical elements, but rather in the tricks of Ariosto's narrative style, in his labyrinthine structure, and in the sheer scale of his poem. Guazzoni's *Liberata* was one of the first pictures ever to break the limit of four hundred metres of film, reaching a length of one thousand metres. The *Furioso* would have required either an unfeasible length or a monumental work of reduction in the writing phase, which would have made pre-production intellectually complex and extraordinarily laborious for the time.

Another unrealized adaptation of Ariosto might have been conceived by one of the directors of *L'Inferno.* Some lists and chronologies credit Giuseppe De Liguoro with a film project titled *Orlando Furioso* in either 1918 or 1919. This information seems to originate from the entry on De Liguoro in an authoritative encyclopedia of performing arts, published in Italy between 1946 and 1966.[36] The encyclopedia includes an *Orlando Furioso* among De Liguoro's films of 1918, the same year as Guazzoni's second *Liberata.* Since there is no trace of such a film in the Cineteca Nazionale, nor was it reviewed in periodicals or newspapers at the time, this *Furioso* was either lost or never filmed. In fact, it was probably announced but never completed, like the Ariostean projects that I will discuss in the rest of this section.[37]

The most striking ghost of the *Orlando Furioso* in the history of cinema made its appearance, in 1966, in the pages of the weekly American magazine *Motion Picture Herald.* In exactly 160 words, an unnamed journalist reported a press conference held in Rome by famed producer Dino De Laurentiis. The title of the short article was "L'Orlando Furioso," and it announced that one of the most celebrated filmmakers in the world, Federico Fellini, had signed a two-picture agreement with De Laurentiis. As the title suggested, one of these two films was to be an adaptation of Ariosto's poem.

In the previous decade, De Laurentiis had already produced two important films by Fellini: *La Strada* (1953) and *Nights of Cabiria* (1956).

Both received the Academy Award for best international feature film. At the beginning of the 1960s, De Laurentiis was committed to financing and promoting two more projects by Fellini. However, Fellini and De Laurentiis had a disagreement about casting, and the production rights for the two scheduled films were sold to Angelo Rizzoli. This was probably the greatest faux pas in De Laurentiis' career. Both the films that he ceded to Rizzoli, *La Dolce Vita* and *8 ½*, were difficult to produce, but the efforts were rewarded with immense success. They turned Rizzoli into a global player, and are now considered among the greatest achievements in cinema history. Therefore, in 1965, De Laurentiis offered Fellini a strong degree of freedom to attract him back to his production house. Fellini proposed to start with an original project that obsessed him, titled *The Journey of G. Mastorna* and loosely based on a novella by Dino Buzzati. The follow-up, which would have begun production in 1967, was the *Orlando Furioso* announced in the 1966 *Motion Picture Herald* article.

According to the article, De Laurentiis announced a *Furioso* "on a similar scale to his production of the Bible," which was indeed a majestic adaptation of the Book of Genesis directed by John Huston. The idea of Fellini envisioning a similarly grand film "from the Italian classic by Lodovico Ariosto" was enticing. It would have been the first film by Fellini based on a classical literary source. The scale promised by De Laurentiis matched the visionary grandeur that Fellini had just demonstrated in his first colour film, *Juliet of the Spirits* (1965), a phantasmagoric visual dream awarded the 1966 Golden Globe for best foreign-language picture. In sum, Fellini's *Furioso* was particularly promising, and that is probably why the article focused on it instead of *The Journey of G. Mastorna.* The reporter added: "no cast has been chosen as yet to portray the mythic and fabulous characters of Orlando, his lady-love Angelica, knights Rinaldo, Astolfo, and many others, but these roles will be filled by international stars."[38] In passing, they also specified that the first Fellini film announced by De Laurentiis, *The Journey*, would "commence production on August 29," and that therefore the *Furioso* was to be released a couple of years later.

Despite De Laurentiis' announcements, Fellini never made another film with his production house. Neither *The Journey* nor the *Furioso* was ever filmed. Yet, throughout the rest of his career, Fellini pitched both projects several times to various producers. He also incorporated elements of both in his subsequent films, mining his own mental workshop for ideas, characters, and quotes.

Interestingly, while the project for *The Journey of G. Mastorna* has been widely studied and was even described as "the most famous unrealized film in the history of cinema,"[39] the project for the *Orlando Furioso* is seldom discussed by Fellini scholars. The main reason for this unbalanced attention is that *The Journey* was a much more developed project. At the time of the *Motion Picture Herald* article, Marcello Mastroianni was committed to play its lead role and, more importantly, Fellini had already developed a script. The script survived, and a critical edition of it was published fifteen years after Fellini's death. During Fellini's life, it was read by several collaborators and producers, and was adapted into a comic strip by Milo Manara. As I mentioned, it also inspired many of Fellini's own films: an operation of self-scavenging that Fellini commented upon several times.[40] Unlike this obsessive passion project, the *Orlando Furioso* was never actually written. Critics mostly described the Ariostean project as a bait that Fellini used to persuade producers to back other films that he wanted to pursue but were harder to pitch.

It is hard to speculate about the seriousness of Fellini's commitment to Ariosto, especially considering the many ideas for adaptations that he explored and never actually made.[41] However, it is worth remembering that, after the 1965 announcement, Fellini did use Ariostean ideas more than once in his movies, just as he exploited his ideas for *The Journey* in later masterpieces such as *Roma* (1972) and *Amarcord* (1973). After all, as John Baxter noted in his official biography of Fellini, "the *Satyricon* of Petronius and Ariosto's *Orlando Furioso* were, aside from Kafka's fragmentary, uncompleted *Amerika* and Giacomo Casanova's plotless memoirs, almost the only literary works he ever contemplated adapting to film."[42]

Among the literary texts listed by Baxter, the *Furioso* is the only one that Fellini never adapted at all.[43] Yet, Fellini often mentioned the poem in interviews, declaring that he wanted to make a film on it.[44] He told Costanzo Costantini that the experience of watching Kurosawa and Drayer "is like reading Ariosto,"[45] and speculated with Aldo Tassone about how well Giacomo Casanova could have known the *Orlando Furioso*.[46] In his film about Casanova (1976), the protagonist recites two octaves from a crucial episode in Ariosto's poem: Orlando's madness (XXIII, 135–7).[47] And Fellini's last film, *The Voice of the Moon* (1990), is deeply connected with Ariosto's poetry.

The Voice of the Moon revolves around two mentally ill men, played by comedic actors Paolo Villaggio and Roberto Benigni, who manage to capture the moon. This plot combines both of Ariosto's moons: the one of the *Furioso*, which stores the wits of men who lost their minds, and the one that foolish peasants try to capture in the third of the *Satires*. The inspiration for the script was Ermanno Cavazzoni's book *Il poema dei lunatici* (*The Poem of the Lunatics*, 1987), an openly Ariostean novel of quotidian magic about madness and delusion. Cavazzoni, who was a young and relatively unknown scholar and writer at the time, co-wrote the film with Fellini.

Among Italy's living authors in the twenty-first century, Cavazzoni is the most passionately Ariostean. His poetics of ironic enchantment, his exhibited localism centred in the valley of the Po River, and his sardonic nostalgia for pre-modern simplicity made him the clearest Italian heir of Ariosto's literary legacy after Calvino. Born in Reggio Emilia, like Ariosto, he wrote the preface to one of the most popular contemporary editions of the *Orlando Furioso*, and discussed his literary debt to the poem in many occasions. The moon of his novel, and of Fellini's film, recalls that of Bontempelli's *Guardia alla luna*, adding a postmodern branch in the satirical lunar genealogy, established by Ariosto's model, that I discussed in Chapter 2.[48] His collaboration with Fellini cast an Ariostean aura on the production of *The Voice of the Moon*, "one of the most serenely uninhibited of Fellini's sets," according to Tullio Kezich. At the end of filming, Benigni recited a poem in ottava rima to the crew and cast, recounting the experience of working on the film in the metre of Ariosto's *Furioso*.[49]

When exploring texts for adaptation with collaborator Bernardino Zapponi, Fellini looked for literary works that, like the *Furioso*, "continue to grow within the imagination of their adapters."[50] Besides Ariosto's *Furioso*, other Italian classics that he considered with Zapponi were Dante's *Divine Comedy* and Giovanni Boccaccio's *Decameron*.[51] With its otherworldly plot and autobiographical elements, the project of *The Journey of G. Mastorna* can be considered as Fellini's attempt to adapt Dante. The Boccaccio hypothesis was made redundant, in 1971, by Pier Paolo Pasolini's successful adaptation of the *Decameron*. I believe that an important reason why Fellini never really worked on Ariosto, despite announcing the film in 1965, was the success of Ronconi's 1969 play and its 1974 cinematic adaptation. Timing, as in Visconti's case, kept Fellini's *Furioso* in the embryonic state of a recurring idea, never fulfilled but relevant for understanding his later works, from *Casanova* to *The Voice of the Moon*.

There is only one project of adaptation of the *Orlando Furioso* that, like Fellini's *The Journey of G. Mastorna* or Visconti's unfinished play, is documented by significant archival material. It was pursued before Fellini's announced *Furioso* and after the failed projects of the silent era. It involved the most prominent filmmaker of fascist Italy, Alessandro Blasetti, and would have been one of the most expensive European productions of its age. In the rest of this chapter, I am going to reconstruct this ambitious attempt to be faithful to Ariosto's text while truly translating it for the cinematic medium.

A Cinematic Reading Group

Alessandro Blasetti started his career as a filmmaker when Italian cinema was experiencing a profound crisis under Mussolini's regime. His first film as a director, *Sun* (1929), was a realist drama set during the fascist draining of the Pontine marshes, between Rome and Naples. Despite its modest commercial performance, *Sun* was saluted by critics as the beginning of a Renaissance of Italian cinema. After watching it, Mussolini proclaimed "the dawn of the fascist film."[52] Indeed, throughout the 1930s, Blasetti spearheaded a renewal of the industry in fascist Italy, championing, in particular, the development of the Cinecittà studios in Rome.[53] Through his influence in artists' unions, he successfully lobbied for generous state investments in technology and propaganda related to cinema, benefiting from the renewed attention to the medium. He was the first Italian director to shoot a sound film and to experiment with colour.

Thanks to the support of fascist producers and the government, Blasetti was able to explore many genres in his early career. However, at the end of the 1930s, he developed a particular affinity for cloak-and-dagger adventures, based on either early modern history or fantastic scripts. His idea of adapting the *Orlando Furioso* was rooted in the success of these chivalric films, such as *Ettore Fieramosca* (1938), *Un'avventura di Salvator Rosa* (1940), and especially the fantasy fable *The Iron Crown* (1941). While still alluding to themes of honour and virile heroism that were favourably welcomed by fascism, such costume dramas offered a chance to evade the inevitably political content of scripts based on recent history or contemporary society. An adaptation of Ariosto's poem would have been the crowning achievement of this politically safe series of escapist films.

At the beginning of the 1940s, Blasetti proposed the *Furioso* to the brothers Carlo and Renato Bassoli, who directed a production house in Rome. On October 30, 1941, the three signed an agreement for a very ambitious production. The initial budget was twenty million lire, equivalent to more than half of what Metro-Goldwyn-Mayer had set to spend, two years before, for *The Wizard of Oz*. Promotional posters and official stationery of the film were printed in 1942.

Despite its promising origins, Blasetti's *Orlando Furioso* was never filmed because of the producers' financial preoccupations and second thoughts. The Bassoli brothers had initially asked Blasetti to shoot in 1942, then postponed the project to 1943, then wanted to shelve it because of the uncertainties generated by the war. As his correspondence shows, Blasetti was frustrated by the Bassolis' hesitations.[54] Their motivations seemed unreasonable, considering that, when the initial agreement for the film was signed, Italy was already involved in the Second World War on multiple fronts. Therefore, towards the end of 1942, Blasetti decided to sue the Bassoli studios, and in January 1943, he obtained a settlement.[55] At that point, however, his career was taking a different turn. His *Four Steps in the Clouds* (1942) made him one of the founders, with Visconti and De Sica, of Italian neorealism. After the war, with the acclaimed *A Day in the Life* (1946), Blasetti definitively reinvented himself as a post-fascist neorealist. The unfinished Ariostean project kept haunting him, and he tried to resume it a decade later, in 1953.[56] However, this second attempt was quickly abandoned, and he never went back to the chivalric adventures of his pre-war cinema.

Besides its litigious production history, what makes this episode of Ariosto's cinematic reception unique among the many unfinished and failed projects is its pre-production – in particular, the nature and the amount of preparatory material that this pre-production generated. Many papers related to Blasetti's *Furioso* survived, and today they read like a polyphonic seminar on Ariosto and screen narration, held during a crucial transitional moment for Italian cinema. These documents have never been studied, but they offer a unique perspective on both the poem and the cinematic imagination of Italy's intellectuals during the Second World War, on the eve of the birth of neorealism and the subsequent success of Rome as an international capital of cinema. The curators of the Blasetti archives at the Cineteca di Bologna have catalogued this rich and entirely unpublished material, which constitutes by far the largest corpus in the section dedicated to Blasetti's unmade projects. These papers represent a collective reading exercise on the *Orlando Furioso*, conducted by some of the best minds of Italy's film culture under fascism.

The main reason why Blasetti's unrealized *Furioso* produced such vital documentation is that, unlike Visconti with his play, Blasetti did not work alone on the challenges of Ariosto's text. More an artisan than an auteur, Blasetti approached filmmaking as a collegial and synergistic activity. To use a political expression, he directed by consensus, listening to different voices in the diverse spectrum of intellectuals who were involved in the entertainment business. While this was arguably a symptom of the political ambiguity that, despite his many pro-fascist films, allowed him to remain relevant after the war, Blasetti's "big tent" process was artistically and commercially productive. With the subject of the *Orlando Furioso*, both prestigious and popular, he expected to make a film that could be enjoyed by different kinds of moviegoers. Most of all, as the list of his consultants shows, he sought the approval and advice of film professionals and members of the specialized press in Rome, Turin, and Milan. Through their expertise (and thanks to their sympathy towards the project), he could hope to reach both a lowbrow and a highbrow audience, like the poem that he was adapting.[57]

It should also be noted that, unlike the other failed adaptations of Ariosto, Blasetti's *Orlando Furioso* was funded, and initially green-lit. Thus, the director was able to do substantial work, assembling a real pre-production workshop – though mainly through correspondence. This collective enterprise, which remained active for more than two years, is going to be the object of my analysis. Through it, Blasetti and his collaborators pioneered practices that were later very effective for the development of complex and expensive films, and they did so in order to solve the same problems that Ariosto posed to Visconti and to the other aspiring adaptors discussed so far. For once, neither time nor resources were an obstacle, at least until the sudden disruption of the project.

Let me start from Blasetti's first initiative, which can be described as a preliminary survey. Between 1941 and 1942, he personally invited the most accomplished or promising writers of Italy's film industry into his workshop, asking them to respond to a questionnaire on the *Orlando Furioso*. These consultants were film critics, entertainment reporters, screenwriters, and directors. Some of them, like Filippo Sacchi and Giovanni Mosca, were anti-fascists. Others were organic to the regime, like Ferdinando Palmieri and Alessandro De Stefani. Most were young, and destined to shape Italian cinema after the war: director Stefano Vanzina, for instance, and legendary screenwriter Sergio Amidei. A few, like Alberto Moravia, Giacomo Debenedetti, and Ercole Patti, were about to become bestselling authors, and champions of Italian literature.

All of the intellectuals whom Blasetti contacted received the same five questions, and responded with their technical and poetic advice on how to successfully adapt the poem. This initial exchange ignited an epistolary network that generated outlined scripts, marketing analyses, and guidelines for direction. Most of the correspondents had the impression that the film would have a global resonance and artistic significance. Many expressed their desire to contribute to Blasetti's achievement because of its cultural ambition, and some, like film critic Mario Gromo, even forfeited compensation for their service. The questions that they received are the following:

1. What should be the main motif of a cinematic translation of the "Orlando"? And what are the themes that, in any event, should not be omitted?
2. On which of the main characters, as a consequence, should the spectacular appeal of the film be based? And which characters should be at least mentioned?

3. Which of the magical elements, fantastic features, and choreographic actions of the "Orlando" would be most interesting to include in the film?
4. What are the elements and the characters that, as a consequence, could be omitted without the risk of betraying the spirit of the poem?
5. For obvious reasons of length, it is inevitable that most of the narrative material of the "Orlando" will have to be omitted. What is the best approach? To focus the attention on a single group of episodes, as Ariosto recounts them, and therefore exclude all the plot elements and characters that are not part of it? Or rather to synthetically interpret the whole poem by preserving the largest possible amount of main elements, and therefore rearrange and use events and characters differently?[58]

The way the questionnaire was formulated shows that Blasetti had a clear idea of the specific challenges that the *Furioso*, more than any other Italian classic, presented to cinema – and, in general, to time-based trans-codifications. Any Italian high school student knew who the most important figures of Dante's *Inferno* were supposed to be, or what episodes of Tasso's *Liberata* were not absolutely necessary to understand the Christian epic of the plot. With Ariosto, the hierarchy of characters and situations was less established in the reading tradition, and less deducible from the mere mechanics of the narration. That is why brainstorming was the most promising tool for the project.

The responses that Blasetti received outlined equally viable but very different perspectives on the *Orlando Furioso*. Many potential films emerged from them: a war drama, a metaphor for racial conflict, a mixture of adventures from Boiardo's and Ariosto's poems, the story of Orlando's love for Angelica or Bradamante's for Ruggiero, and so on. By reimagining it as a film, the writers and filmmakers in Blasetti's epistolary workshop tried to uncover the secret of the *Orlando Furioso*'s popular success and structural inaccessibility. Familiar and unknown, apparently epic but really romantic (or vice versa), the classic appeared both a precursor of cinematic imagination and an intransitive literary monolith, impossible to adapt.

Spirit, Script Skeletons, and Style

Blasetti's concern for "the spirit of the poem," for its elusive "main motif" ("motivo principale") and inalienable "themes" ("temi"), reveals a technical anxiety. It is meaningful that, in his questionnaire, he used such musical terms, as if he was trying to orchestrate a symphony. Maybe the influence of Croce's concept of Ariostean harmony, along with the meta-literary musical metaphors in the *Furioso*, influenced his approach to adaptation. Certainly, he expected to fulfil his task through logic and craftsmanship, with a practicality that was very different from the later interpretative experimentalism of Visconti or Ronconi.

As his last question shows, Blasetti started from the assumption that, in order to be feasible, a film on the *Furioso* had two rhetorical options. The first was synecdoche: a faithful representation of a portion of the poem, leaving the structure of Ariosto's narration intact but sacrificing most of his narrative inventions. The second was paraphrase: a deconstruction and reorganization of the poem's architecture, aimed at preserving the storylines that cross its fabric at the expense of diversions, internal echoes, and subplots. Both ways would have forced the film to renounce a defining aspect of the *Orlando Furioso*: either its worldness[59] or its interlacing narrative style. To borrow two terms from Russian formalism, Blasetti asked his consultants to choose between Ariosto's *fabula* and his *sujet*: to either cut off most of the *Furioso*'s plot or turn the poem into an Aristotelian drama. The real question was about which of the two elements, mutually exclusive from a cinematic perspective, was the true vessel of "the spirit of the poem."

The apparent goal of Blasetti's questions (which characters, which episodes, which magical elements) was to compile an inventory and reverse-engineer "the spirit of the poem," so that it could be replicated in a different medium. Rather than representing the unrepresentability of the *Furioso* by "grasping" this "spirit" and "disguising" the poem as a script, as Ronconi and Sanguineti did with their *travestimento*, Blasetti approached his task as an analytical problem of conversion and framing, to be solved through competence rather than artistry. The word that he used in his questionnaire was "translation," "traduzione." To him, adaptation was a complex narrative equation across the technical idioms of two texts based on different media. It could be balanced through a systematic study of the original text, "cover to cover."

In this, Blasetti's mentality was similar to that adopted by Visconti a few years later. Indeed, like Visconti, Blasetti started by interposing an intermediate layer between himself and the poem. Thanks to the resources and time at his disposal, he was able to complete a full outline of the *Orlando Furioso*, canto by canto. This manuscript, which counts almost two hundred typed pages,[60] organizes the progression of storylines by dividing the plot into sequences. The names of characters that appear in each sequence are typed in the margin. They are also colour coded, so that Ariosto's disorienting *entrelacement* is neatly visualized in the document, and can be followed by flipping through its pages. Blasetti shared this resource with the people who received the questionnaire. Two of them, Mario Gromo and Achille Vesce, used it to develop complete preliminary treatments of the poem. Before I illustrate these proposals for script outlines, let me discuss the theoretical ideas on which they were based.

Gromo was the film critic of Turin's historic newspaper, *La Stampa.* Before and after his collaboration with Blasetti on the *Furioso,* he was invited several times to be part of the jury of the Venice Film Festival, four times as its president. His take on Blasetti's project was that the main goal of the film was to be "worthy of the poem." In order to achieve this, as he wrote in his response to the questionnaire, "the first quality that one must expect from this film is that of being a film."[61] By "being a film," Gromo meant that Blasetti's adaptation had to avoid turning into "an illustration," "a popular 'divulgation' (a very convenient term that usually does not divulgate anything at all)," or an "obsequious or school-like paraphrase."[62]

Despite rejecting paraphrase, Gromo's technical approach ultimately tended towards the second option envisioned in the questionnaire. He suggested a selection of episodes that would cover the entire arc of the poem, disentangling Ariosto's *entrelacement* for purposes of clarity and the linear progression of the film. In a letter that he sent to Blasetti a few weeks after responding to the questionnaire, he clarified that, while observing "the most cautious form of discretion," the screenplay could make use of two "audacious options": "incastro" (interlock, puzzle) and "sviluppo" (development). He explained that by "incastro" he meant "the practice of attributing an episode to one character instead of another," and by "sviluppo" he "contemplated even the option of ... adding something to what is already in Ariosto: an addition produced by the fantasy of the screenwriters [...] for reasons of rhythm or clarity."[63] In sum, Gromo encouraged Blasetti to subordinate Ariosto's authority to the specific technical needs of cinema: to allow himself, as a translator between media, the creativity demanded by the specific grammar and syntax of film.

Not that the poem itself, according to Gromo, lacked elements of inherent cinematic quality. In fact, a central point of his response was that "this film will be an important and memorable opportunity for cinema to remember one of its most authentic possibilities: the ability to concretely express fantasy." This opportunity, "as difficult as it is wonderful," was presented by "superb passages of real cinema, of 'pure' cinema" already there in Ariosto's text.[64] According to Gromo, the "main motif" of the film had not much to do with episodes, characters, and narrative order – the "skeleton of the script," as he called it. Ariosto's spirit was to be found in the "tone"[65] dictated by the magic and ironic atmosphere of the poem.

> This is why one cannot be faithful enough to the *spirit* of Ariosto. Thus, fantasy and fable will have to be strongly interlaced with adventure and heroism, in turn enveloped in a veil of light irony, which represents the most authentic "modernity" of Ariosto: as when one enjoys their own game, knowing perfectly that it is just a game.
>
> Let us banish, then, any realistic element, even when Charlemagne's endeavour may seem to require them; let us never indulge, not even occasionally, not even for a moment, in the so-called historical reconstruction [...] This will be the best way to be faithful not to the letter, but to the spirit of the poem.[66]

A general lack of fantasy, as a genre, in Italian cinema has been studied by scholars in its political and sociological aspects.[67] In 1942, Gromo, an authority on the young but rich history of Italian films, saw Ariosto and Blasetti as the right subject and executor to bring Italy's industry back to the visionary origins of the medium. Blasetti, after all, had just directed the most fable-like production of the fascist era, *The Iron Crown*. However, Gromo warned him about the stylistic inconsistency of that film, apparently similar to the *Furioso* project but designed with too much anachronism in the visual grammar.

Both in his response and in a subsequent letter, Gromo insisted that the new film had to adopt a "unity of style" in all its aspects: landscapes, costumes, architecture, objects, creatures, and scenography in general. While with *The Iron Crown* Blasetti had let his scenographers juxtapose Romanic and Gothic structures, medieval and Renaissance armour, and scenery that could have appeared in a Tarzan film or in a sword-and-sandal drama, the *Furioso* had to respond to a strong visual coherence. Creativity was to be exercised in the structure and content of the script, not in the visual reconstruction of Ariosto's world.

> By achieving a unity of style this film will triumph. It is through such a unity, and only through it, that the film will obtain its full and unmistakable atmosphere, its credibility, its effectiveness, even if it will only represent a portion of the episodes of the poem. And it will be this unity of style that will impress both learned and unsophisticated audiences.[68]

To reinforce the importance of tone and stylistic unity, Gromo argued that the adaptation of *Don Quixote* directed by Georg Pabst in 1933 was entirely based on style. According to him, Cervantes' literary work was barely a pretext for that film, and yet it was a successful adaptation. A fantastic, ironic tone, delivered with a coherent style, was the failsafe recipe to be faithful to both Ariosto and cinema. The "skeleton of the script" that Gromo offered to Blasetti in his response was based on this program. Episodes and narrative structures had to be simplified and clarified, trusting in the unifying force of a stylistic affinity with Ariosto's tone. This tone had to be transported from literature into the visual grammar of cinema, with a liberal attitude towards the letter of the original text.

Achille Vesce, on the other hand, believed that, in order to successfully adapt the *Furioso*, certain propelling epicentres of the plot had to be preserved and highlighted. These narrative nodes were to be imported into the film by observing Ariosto's own structure, which could be excerpted, but not strongly altered, in the screenplay. The "spirit" of Ariosto's poem, according to Vesce, was in the gravitational pull of Ruggiero and Bradamante's story, which organizes and determines the entire system of romance and epic tensions of the *Furioso.* For his proposed script, therefore, Vesce selected eleven crucial sequences of events from the poem, choosing only seven storylines that involved ten main characters. From Vesce's perspective, the task of screenwriters was to extract a careful selection of intact narratives from the original text. They were not to exercise their own creativity, as in Gromo's game of "incastro" and "sviluppo," to summarize the whole mass of the *Furioso* into a couple of hours of cinematic action. Less concerned with pure cinema, Vesce invested more than Gromo in the dramaturgy of the project and in Ariosto's unique ability to give new life to the popular characters and situations of the tradition that preceded him. His storytelling and narrative architecture, more than the style of his poem, were to be adapted on the screen.

In 1942, Vesce used to write, like Gromo, a weekly column on cinema in a major Italian newspaper: Naples' *Il Mattino.* However, he was also a prominent theatre critic, remembered in particular for his relationship with Pirandello and his influence on Eduardo De Filippo's groundbreaking Neapolitan work. His approach to cinema was more textual than visual. The premise to his response was essentially an exercise of literary criticism, influenced by the overall moral readings of the *Furioso* given by canonical readers such as Carducci and de Sanctis.

> Two motifs should dominate the film. One is the humanity of Orlando, whose madness is God's punishment but also the tool that the Lord uses to call his champion back on a straight path. The other is the love of Bradamante for Ruggiero, the recurring motif of the whole poem.

> In addition, I would not omit the following themes: the love of the beautiful Angelica for the humble Medoro, and the triumphant entry of the Woman in the normal life of knights, whether they may be Christians or pagans.[69]

A passionate argument about the centrality of Ruggiero and Bradamante followed this general analysis. Blasetti underlined most of it with a red pencil. Vesce believed that the best way to give a cinematic unity to the *Furioso* was to make all the characters and episodes of the script either contribute to or mirror the development of Ruggiero and Bradmante's love story. The risks, otherwise, would have been confusion and distraction.

Vesce believed that every single part of the *Furioso,* including its smallest and most peripheral figures, was essential to the poem and autonomously representative of it. He also found all minor characters to be artistically relevant and beautifully developed by Ariosto. Precisely because of this, he invited Blasetti to cut most of the narrative material of the poem from the film, rather than simplify any of it. Besides Orlando and Angelica, Ruggiero and Bradamante, Medoro, Rinaldo, and Astolfo, the only characters to be kept were those necessary to make the central actions "coherent and organic."[70] Wizards and sorceresses, the two competing kings, and their armies would have provided the entire context for the few essential protagonists. Vesce's reasoning was based on what he called "the economics of cinema." A film simply does not have the time and narrative resources to transpose Ariosto's grandiose world building, or his chiselled character development. And even if it did, Vesce argued, "a crowd of characters would eventually appear as a shapeless and faceless mass, from which any protagonist would hardly emerge."[71] He concluded that "a synthetic interpretation of the poem would be very interesting" but would ultimately turn the film into "a sort of moving album of untied episodes, not always easy to understand."[72]

In sum, Gromo and Vesce proposed two opposite approaches to the adaptation of the poem. A comparison of their "script skeletons" shows the potential of Blasetti's pre-production workshop. The unrealized film could have been a philological rendition of some of Ariosto's central stories or an attempt to imitate his modern approach to fantasy.

A Popular Classic

Vesce's and Gromo's responses represent the two main orientations taken by most of Blasetti's consultants in the virtual typewritten debate generated by the questionnaire. However, some interlocutors recommended more radical approaches to Ariosto's narrative. For instance,

Sergio Amidei and Giacomo Debenedetti proposed to reduce the whole poem to the two essential elements highlighted in its first octave, love and war. As a consequence, they imagined a script focused entirely on Orlando's love for Angelica and Charlemagne's war with Agramante, with substantial alterations of the original plot.

Amidei and Debenedetti wrote their response to Blasetti's questionnaire together. While they were both film critics and interested in the aesthetics of cinema, their collaboration was of a technical and practical nature: they co-wrote screenplays. In 1941, they were on the writing teams of three different films: *Jealousy* (an adaptation of Luigi Capuana's realist novel *Il marchese di Roccaverdina*), *The Taming of the Shrew* by Shakespeare, and the costumed adventure *Don Cesare di Bazan*. Because of the racial laws, Debenedetti was not credited for his contribution to any of these films. In fact, since 1939, he had been able to work in cinema only by using pseudonyms, or as a ghostwriter for Amidei.[73] The two had met as students at the University of Turin, in the years of consolidation of Mussolini's regime, and were both anti-fascists. After the war, Debenedetti's relationship with cinema loosened in favour of his vocation to literary criticism, which lead him to a politically ostracized but highly influential academic career. Amidei, on the other hand, quickly became a prominent voice of Europe's postwar film industry. His screenplays for Roberto Rossellini's and Vittorio De Sica's films brought him four Academy Award nominations between 1946 and 1961.

According to Amidei and Debenedetti, Orlando's love for Angelica was "the only 'motif' that a popular audience, used to the 'poetics' of cinema, would be able to understand."[74] As a consequence, the two screenwriters suggested a complete reconception of Ariosto's plot. In their hypothetical script, after Orlando's madness, Angelica would change her mind and fall in love with him. The two would marry at the end of the film, becoming the ancestors of the Este dynasty instead of Bradamante and Ruggiero. As a "counterpoint" to this erotic main "motif," Amidei and Debenedetti proposed to highlight the "epic fabric" of the poem, making the war more central, serious, and easy to follow. Unlike Vesce and Gromo, they believed that Ariosto's ironic and fantastic spirit was not something that a cinematic production could really pursue. Indeed, they urged Blasetti to "disregard the most authentic literary identity of Ariosto's poem," which, they admitted, "is not epic, but of a different, more varied, and more elusive nature." Such a nature, they argued, "would be inherently in contradiction with the axioms of cinema."[75]

Amidei and Debenedetti believed that adapting the poem "in its specific narrative quality" would have meant accepting "that its *becoming* is substantiated by a continuing sense of flight [...] an endless change of *accents.*" This style, so fruitful and original in Renaissance literature, "would only create confusion in a cinematic narration." Amidei and Debenedetti were concerned about the effect that Ariosto's irony and *entrelacement* intentionally produce in readers: frustration, impatience, stupefied disorientation. A film, according to them, could not afford such reactions. Unlike readers, who can come back to the same book many times or flip through its pages to reread or skip passages, a film's audience "is accustomed, from a certain point on, to have a clear sense of the arc of the story, and to root for one small group of characters against another."[76] Therefore, they concluded, Blasetti had to "violate [violentare] the spirit of the *Furioso* in order to simplify the poem and make it accessible to the needs of the screen."[77]

Alberto Moravia had the opposite opinion. His lucid response to the questionnaire took the form of an eighteen-page essay, written with the authority and clarity that would later make him one of the leading intellectuals of postwar Italy. In this unpublished proof of his early intuitions about what is a classic and how new media can echo vital literary traditions, Moravia tried to redefine, from an anti-fascist perspective, the true meaning of abused terms like "popolare" (popular) and "folla" (mass).

According to Moravia, any adaptation of a great work of literature for cinema can serve either the original text or the supposed simple tastes of the masses. Screenwriters, he argued, usually choose the second option, because the first requires deep love for literature and a deep understanding of its spirit. However, stated Moravia, they are wrong, not only because masses are much less vulgar and simple than intellectuals think, but also because there is a reason why a classic became a classic in the first place. History shows that a book like the *Orlando Furioso* is already popular in itself, and does not need simplifications to meet the enthusiasm of its audience. The job of a filmmaker is not to make literature less complex or more polarizing, but to project on the screen those parts of literature that are suitable for cinema's narrative tools.

> To make an example: it would be easy to place the conflict between Christians and infidels at the centre of this work, in order to please the supposed popular taste: to give Christians and their paladins a halo of sanctity and mysticism, while blaming infidels for any sort of cruelty and barbarity; to represent the first as noble defenders of a threatened homeland and the second as invaders and destroyers, so that the mass [la folla] can "root" for the Christians and take the bait of a simple emotion and interest. All these elements may well be human, poetic, charming, and also historically true. However, they are not in the *Orlando*.[78]

Unlike Amidei and Debenedetti, Moravia thought that there was no reason to turn Ariosto's poem into an epic film about a clash of civilizations. If that was the goal, why adapt the *Orlando Furioso* at all? Why, asked Moravia, not the *Gerusalemme Liberata*? Or simply an entirely new story, with an invented title, that "took mere cues and spectacular or fantastic elements from the ancient poems"?[79] Admittedly, one could not "ask the director to become a reincarnation of Ludovico Ariosto [...] able to rewrite the *Orlando* in cinematic images instead of octaves." And yet, "a film titled *Orlando Furioso* should be the *Orlando Furioso*, and not something else."[80]

To root his position in textual evidence, Moravia showed how blurred the distinction between Christians and pagans is in the poem. He insisted on how Ariosto essentially represented their encounter, the similarities between their respective chivalric values, and even their fascination for each other, rather than their conflict. He concluded that "at the core of the *Orlando Furioso* there is no political or religious idea, least of all a polemic. [The poem] is what it is, namely a fable, a marvellous game of free fantasy."[81] Rather than thematizing fantasy in general, as Gromo proposed to do, Moravia wanted to honour Ariosto's unique kind of ironic fantasy, his ability to evade the contingencies of politics and religion while remaining in the world – while appearing to represent, in fact, the world's political and religious conflicts. To do so, he proposed to stick to the *Furioso*'s narrative anomalies and amusing games of irony, trusting the audience's ability to enjoy such features as much as generations of readers had done for centuries.

For those who know Moravia's most famous literary works, such a position may appear out of character. Moravia's fame as a writer is mostly related to realistic novels, which analyse pettinesses and perversions of the bourgeois and intellectual classes. However, one has to consider two facts while reading his notes on Ariosto and cinema. The first is that, while writing those notes, Moravia was experiencing the dangers and frustrations of fascist censorship. Some of his greatest accomplishments, such as the coming-of-age novel *Agostino*, had been banned, and his allegory of totalitarianism *La Mascherata* was seized right after publication. Ariosto's ability to criticize power from behind a translucent screen of ironic fantasy, with "that air of amusement and adventure, light and gratuitous, delightfully free and unreal,"[82] was an aspiration for him in the early 1940s. Indeed – and here is the second fact to consider – Moravia had pursued, in the first phase of his career, a magical realism akin to that of Massimo Bontempelli, who promoted his early writings and published him in *"900"*. As I showed in the second chapter of this book, Bontempelli's poetics was inspired by Ariosto's model, and his spinoff of the *Furioso* was published precisely when Moravia was working on the response for Blasetti. Some surreal and apparently apolitical tales that Moravia wrote in the same years, such as *Il sogno del pigro*, should be inscribed in a modern literary genealogy originated by Bontempelli's encounter with Ariosto.

Critics like Gromo and Vesce, as well as screenwriters like Amidei and Debenedetti, ultimately expected that Blasetti would use cinema to bring Ariosto to common people. Moravia, on the other hand, believed that cinema could bring common people to Ariosto, just as editions, public recitations, and folkloric adaptations had been doing for centuries. It is hard to speculate about the film that would have resulted from this debate. But, along with the struggles of other aspiring adaptors such as Visconti and Fellini, Blasetti's workshop on the *Orlando Furioso* confirms the uniqueness of the poem among the other classics of what we call the Western tradition.

In the Machine Age, on the eve of the end of modernity, Ariosto's unreadable and yet enticing poem, as popular as it is impossible to popularize, was one with its own centuries-old afterlife. As a cultural object, destined since its conception to mass consumption, one could not adapt it without renouncing its most authentic powers. Its "spirit," to use Blasetti's keyword, was as much in its text as it was in the many other texts, images, puppet shows, and operas that generations of readers produced in order to capture and transmit its entangled stories.

Notes

Introduction: Peeking from Parnassus – Ariosto the Amphibian

1 In the sixteenth century, Vasari initially identified him with another Ferrarese poet, Antonio Tebaldi; see Giorgio Vasari, *Le vite de' più eccellenti pittori scultori e architettori, nelle redazioni del 1550 e 1568*, ed. Paola Barocchi and Rosanna Bettarini (Florence: Sansoni, 1966–87), 4:171. For a recent discussion of identifications in the fresco (and their political consequences), see Alberto Casadei and Vincenzo Farinella, "Il *Parnaso* di Raffaello: criptoritratti di poeti moderni e ideologia pontificia," *Ricerche di storia dell'arte* 123 (2017): 59–73 – which identifies the bearded poet with sixteenth-century humanist Jacopo Sadoleto.

2 Michele Catalano, *Vita di Ariosto ricostruita su nuovi documenti* (Florence: Olschki, 1930), 333.

3 For a historical panorama of interpretations of *Parnassus* that identify the bearded poet with Ariosto, see Arnold Nesselrath, *Raphaël et Pinturicchio. Les grands décors des appatements du pape au Vatican* (Paris: Louvre éditions, 2012), 135–41.

4 This is what two of the most authoritative twentieth-century critics of the *Furioso*, Eduardo Saccone and Robert Durling, meant when they associated the poem's effect of *straniamento* with the poetics of alienation of Bertold Brecht's theatre. See Saccone, *Il soggetto del Furioso e altri saggi tra quattro e cinquecento* (Naples: Liguori, 1974), 225; Durling, *The Figure of the Poet in Renaissance Epic* (Cambridge, MA: Harvard University Press, 1965), 254, 273. See also Jane Tylus, "The Curse of Babel: The *Orlando Furioso* and Epic (Mis) Appropriation," *Modern Language Notes* 103, no. 1 (1988): 154–71: 169–71.

5 Jorge Luis Borges, *Dreamtigers*, trans. Mildred Boyer and Harold Morland (Austin: University of Texas Press, 2004), 83.

6 See Daniel Javitch, "The Emergence of Poetic Genre Theory in the Sixteenth Century," *Modern Language Quarterly* 59, no. 2 (1998): 139–69;

Stefano Jossa, *La fondazione di un genere* (Rome: Carocci, 2002); and Valeria Finucci, ed., *Renaissance Transactions: Ariosto and Tasso* (Durham, NC: Duke University Press, 1999).

7 For the latest developments of this debate, see Alberto Casadei, "Il Pro Bono Malum Ariostesco e la bibbia," *Giornale Storico della Letteratura Italiana* 173 (1996): 566–8; and Ita Mac Carthy, *The Grace of the Italian Renaissance* (Princeton: Princeton University Press, 2020), 139–41.

8 Georg Wilhelm Friedrich Hegel, *Aesthetics* (Oxford: Clarendon, 1975), 1:591–2, 605; 2:1107–8.

9 Benedetto Croce, *Ariosto*, ed. Giuseppe Galasso (Milan: Adelphi, 1991). Croce's foundational essay, which appeared for the first time in 1917, dominated Ariosto studies for half a century.

10 Gianfranco Contini, with his seminal study "Come lavorava l'Ariosto," opened the way for the philological appreciation of the *Furioso* as a work in progress, deeply affected by the author's life. See Contini, *Esercizî di Lettura* (Florence: Parenti, 1939). Riccardo Bacchelli, in a 1933 lecture that evolved into a very long treatise (discussed in the third chapter of this book), was among the first to read Ariosto also as a politician. The historicism of Italian critics of the following generation, such as Carlo Dionisotti and Walter Binni, continued in important studies based on philology such as Rosanna Alahique Pettinelli, *L'immaginario cavalleresco nel Rinascimento ferrarese* (Roma: Bonacci, 1983); Maria Cristina Cabani, *Costanti ariostesche* (Pisa: Edizioni della Scuola Normale Superiore, 1990); and Alberto Casadei, *Il percorso del Furioso* (Bologna: il Mulino, 1993).

11 I am referring in particular to Italo Calvino's essays, on which see Lucia Re, "Ariosto and Calvino: The Adventures of a Reader," in *Ariosto Today*, ed. Donald Beecher, Massimo Ciavolella, and Roberto Fedi (Toronto: University of Toronto Press, 2016), 211–34. Calvino's vital relationship with Ariosto is emblematized in his rewriting *L'Orlando furioso di Ludovico Ariosto raccontato da Italo Calvino* (Turin: Einaudi, 1970).

12 I am referring to a series of studies that culminated in Albert Ascoli, *Ariosto's Bitter Harmony* (Princeton: Princeton University Press, 1987).

13 Along the lines of Calvino's influential reading of Ariosto, see Corrado Bologna, *La macchina del Furioso* (Turin: Einaudi, 1998).

14 Contradiction (in a fruitful, generative sense) is the keyword that Giulio Ferroni, since at least his popular history of Italian literature, adopted to define Ariosto's poetry. See in particular Ferroni, *Ariosto* (Rome: Salerno, 2008).

15 See for instance Gianluca Genovese, *Le vie del "Furioso"* (Naples: Guida, 2017); Stefano Jossa, "Sentieri interrotti e coincidenze casuali: Ariosto oggi," *Versants* 59, no. 2 (2012): 189–211; Christian Rivoletti, "Ironia,

distanza e contrasto tra il poeta e il mondo: Ariosto e Tasso alle soglie della modernità," in *The Italian Renaissance in the 19th Century: Revision, Revival, and Return*, ed. Lina Bolzoni and Alina Payne (Cambridge, MA: Harvard University Press, 2018); and Sonia Trovato, *A chi nel mar per tanta via m'ha scorto* (Rome: Carocci, 2018).

16 This introduction is inspired by bisexual theory, which adopted the metaphor of the fence (as opposed to that of the closet) with the ambition of queering queer theory. See Jonathan Alexander and Serena Anderlini-D'Onofrio, eds, *Bisexuality and Queer Theory: Intersections, Connections and Challenges* (New York: Routledge, 2012) – in particular pages 105–23. On my own take on bisexual theory within trans-historical Italian Studies, see Alessandro Giammei, "(It)Aliens on the Fence," *Forum Italicum* 57, no. 3 (2023), 70–82.

17 See Patricia Parker, *Inescapable Romance: Studies in the Poetics of a Mode* (Princeton: Princeton University Press, 1979), 16–52; and Jo Ann Cavallo, *The Romance Epics of Boiardo, Ariosto, and Tasso: From Public Duty to Private Pleasure* (Toronto: University of Toronto Press, 2004), 3–152.

18 Sergio Zatti, *The Quest for Epic: From Ariosto to Tasso* (Toronto: University of Toronto Press, 2006), 13–58.

19 I would like to thank Geoff Klock for helping me clarify the parallel between chivalric romance and superhero comic books at the conference Chivalric Imageries, which I organized at Princeton University in 2017. On superheroes, see Klock, *How to Read Superhero Comics and Why* (New York: Continuum, 2002).

20 Osip Mandelstam, *The Moscow Notebooks*, trans. Richard McKane and Elizabeth McKane (Hexham: Bloodaxe Books, 1991), 106. Thanks to Michael Wachtel for helping me understand Mandelstam's poems on Ariosto with some philological depth.

21 See Jo Ann Cavallo, *The World beyond Europe in the Romance Epics of Boiardo and Ariosto* (Toronto: University of Toronto Press, 2013); and Ita Mac Carthy, "Ariosto the Traveler," *Modern Language Review* 102, no. 2 (2007): 397–408.

22 See Mary-Michelle DeCoste, *Hopeless Love: Boiardo, Ariosto, and Narratives of Queer Female Desire* (Toronto: University of Toronto Press, 2009); and Eleonora Stoppino, *Genealogies of Fiction: Women Warriors and the Dynastic Imagination in the Orlando Furioso* (New York: Fordham University Press, 2012).

23 I am borrowing the key terms "double-edged pen" and "knots" respectively from Ita Mac Carthy, *Women and the Making of Poetry in Ariosto's Orlando Furioso* (Leicester: Troubador, 2007); and Mary-Michelle DeCoste, "Knots of Desire: Female Homoeroticism in *Orlando Furioso* 25," in *Queer Italia: Same-Sex Desire in Italian Literature and Film*, ed. Gary Cestaro (London: Routledge, 2004), 55–69.

24 In the twenty-fifth chapter of the first part of *Don Quixote*, the protagonist performs a direct parody of the brutal deeds that characterize Orlando's

madness in the *Furioso*, electing him as the chivalric model of the most unchivalrous of behaviours.

25 See Brian Richardson, *Printing, Writers and Readers in Renaissance Italy* (Cambridge: Cambridge University Press, 1999), 85–91.

26 Ariosto's *Satires* is probably the first literary work to use the word "umanisti." In the sixth satire, Ariosto writes to his friend Pietro Bembo, a leading humanist, to ask for recommendations: he intends for his son Virginio to get a proper humanist education. The very line in which he uses the term (VI, 25) is about a "vizio" (vice) that most humanists are supposedly prone to: pederasty. The whole text illustrates the virtues and new canons of *humanae letterae* as a paradigm for education while openly mocking its practitioners.

27 Although Torquato Tasso, who is considered the main Italian epic poet after Ariosto, did write a continuation of romance epic (the *Rinaldo*, published in 1562), it is not by chance that he then moved to other content and devoted his mature work to the mythologized history of the first crusade.

28 In *The Goose and the Swan*, a swan taken for a goose is almost killed by a man, who stops when he hears the swan's song. See Laura Gibbs, *Aesop's Fables* (Oxford: Oxford University Press, 2002), 303.

29 In his seminal study, David Quint underlies Ariosto's veiled mockery of his patron, directly compared to Nero. Robert Durling instead insisted on the absurdity of debasing a dynasty in the very poem supposed to celebrate its legacy. See Quint, "Astolfo's Voyage to the Moon," *Yale Italian Studies* 1 (1977): 398–408; and Durling, *The Figure of the Poet in Renaissance Epic*, 148–9.

30 Jorge Luis Borges, *The Book of Imaginary Beings*, trans. Andrew Hurley (London: Penguin, 1974), 79–81.

31 Alberto Manguel, *Fabulous Monsters* (New Haven: Yale University Press, 2019), 145.

32 On the role of epic in world making during the age of humanism and colonialism, see Ayesha Ramachandran, *The Worldmakers: Global Imagining in Early Modern Europe* (Chicago: University of Chicago Press, 2015), 106–45.

33 See David Foster Wallace, *A Supposedly Fun Thing I'll Never Do Again: Essays and Arguments* (New York: Back Bay Books, 1997), 96–107.

34 Stefano Ercolino explained the fragmentary cohesion of Wallace's narrative with the term *entrelacement*, a narrative technique typical of the oral tradition of chivalric romances that Ariosto adopted and perfected in his book. See Ercolino, *The Maximalist Novel* (New York: Bloomsbury, 2014), 54.

35 In the central episode of Jarmusch's 1989 film *Mystery Train*, an Italian woman is stranded in Memphis and carries around, in every single scene in which she appears, a paperback edition of the *Orlando Furioso*. She is often interrupted while trying to read it. On Jarmusch and Ariosto, see Stefano

Jossa, "Entertainment and Irony: The Orlando Furioso from Modern to Postmodern," in *Ariosto, the Orlando Furioso and English Culture*, ed. Stefano Jossa, Jane Everson, and Andrew Hiscock (Oxford: Oxford University Press, 2019), 286–307.

36 On the process of canonization of the *Furioso*, see Daniel Javitch, *Proclaiming a Classic: The Canonization of Orlando Furioso* (Princeton: Princeton University Press, 1991).

37 See the translator's preface in Ludovico Ariosto, *Orlando Furioso: A New Verse Translation*, trans. David R. Slavitt (Cambridge, MA: Harvard University Press, 2009), viii.

38 See *Galassia Ariosto: Il modello editoriale dell'Orlando Furioso dal libro illustrato al web*, ed. Lina Bolzoni (Rome: Donzelli, 2017).

39 There are many studies of the vast iconographic legacy of the *Furioso*, and I cite a number of them elsewhere in this Introduction and in the book. I will mention here the recent monumental volume *L'Orlando furioso nello specchio delle immagini*, ed. Lina Bolzoni (Rome: Treccani, 2014); the illustrated catalogue *L'Arioste et les arts*, ed. Monica Preti-Hamard and Michel Paoli (Paris: Louvre éditions, 2012); and, for the specific case of modern visualizations of the *Furioso*, the virtual gallery "Il poema immaginato: 'Visioni' dell'Orlando furioso tra XX e XXI secolo," ed. Alessandro Giammei, Fabrizio Bondi, Giovanna Rizzarelli, and Andrea Torre, *Arabeschi* 1, no. 2 (2013): 191–227.

40 See Fredric Jameson, "Magical Narratives: Romance as a Genre," *New Literary History* 7 (1976): 135–63: 158.

41 See in particular Margaret Adams Groesbeck, "'Tra noi non restò più differenza': Men, Transvestites, and Power in *Orlando Furioso*," *Annali d'Italianistica* 16 (1998): 65–83.

42 On the problematic historical category of Italian Surrealism, and on its relationship with Surrealism in general, see Alessandro Giammei, "Surrealismo italiano," in *Il contributo italiano alla storia del pensiero – Letteratura*, ed. Giulio Ferroni (Rome: Treccani, 2018), 661–6.

43 I would like to thank Susan Stewart for helping me think of ruins and spolia as trans-historical agents of simultaneity. See in particular Stewart, *The Ruins Lesson* (Chicago: University of Chicago Press, 2020). Another strong influence on the trans-historical perspective adopted in this book comes from *Anachronic Renaissance*, ed. Alexander Nagel and Christopher S. Wood (New York: Zone Books, 2010).

44 See Giorgio de Chirico, *Il meccanismo del pensiero*, ed. Maurizio Fagiolo (Turin: Einaudi, 1985), 463.

45 "Noi abbiamo tutto intorno e vicino a noi, – soleva dire il signor Dudron – le cose più inverosimili. I mostri più favolosi stanno qui, a due passi; guardate per esempio quella lucertola [...] quella lucertola è il drago dei

miti, delle religioni e delle leggende. È il drago atterrato da S. Giorgio, vincitore dello spirito del male, è il drago trafitto dalla lancia di Perseo per salvare Andromeda, decapitato dal brando di Ruggiero per salvare Angelica." Giorgio de Chirico, "Il signor Dudron (dal romanzo di prossima pubblicazione)," *Prospettive* 43, no. 5 (1940): 7–11.

1. The Great Metaphysician: Ariosto's Encounters with Ferrara's Avant-Garde

1 Charles Stuckey, "La scultura immaginaria del primo de Chirico e *Il grande metafisico* nel contesto delle avanguardie postbelliche," in *De Chirico a Ferrara: Metafisica e avanguardie*, ed. Paolo Baldacci and Gerd Roos (Ferrara: Fondazione Ferrara arte, 2015), 91–5.

2 I am using here the title that the essay took when de Chirico re-elaborated it in the so-called Paulhan Manuscripts. The reference to Ariosto was in the original 1911 manuscript owned by Paul Eluard. I will discuss it in detail later in this chapter.

3 Fernando Agnoletti, *Dal giardino all'Isonzo* (Florence: Libreria della Voce, 1917), 37–42. Giuseppe Prezzolini included this book in the canon of "i più bei libri, alcuni dei rari libri che sopravviveranno del tempo della guerra." However, Agnoletti was largely forgotten after the 1920s. Giuseppe Prezzolini, *La coltura italiana* (Florence: Libreria della Voce, 1923), 160.

4 "Sul colmo delle mura larghe, tutte verdi e vestite, c'è la pista dei cavalieri e agli orli il sentiero erboso. Un cavallo passò col passo smorzato." Fernando Agnoletti, "I poeti di Ferrara," *La Voce* 7, no. 11 (May 1915): 672.

5 "Sopra le mura, le case e gli orti mi accennò una figura confusa sospesa in cielo.
– È l'Ariosto, disse.
– Dove l'hanno messo?
– Sotto c'è una piazza. Gli orti di Ferrara sono così grandi e tanti che di qui non si conoscono le piazze. La città è tutta radure ariose, piene d'alberi fioriti. Vedesse com'era grande il suo! Ora non più.
– Andiamo a vederlo.
– Andiamo. L'Ariosto mi piace.
– E a me!
– Ci sono stanze soleggiate, melodiose, piene di respiro.
– C'è quella gioia di galoppare sui prati intatti portando in groppa la meraviglia." Ibid., 673.

6 The same photo had been used by Art Nouveau illustrator Adolfo de Carolis as a model for the woodcut portrait in the first edition of Govoni's *Fuochi d'artifizio*, a 1905 experimental book of poems that preceded his Futurist phase.

7 Filippo Tommaso Marinetti, "The Founding and Manifesto of Futurism," in *Futurism: An Anthology*, ed. Lawrence Rainey, Christine Poggi, and Laura Wittman (New Haven: Yale University Press, 2009), 51.

8 "– Che direbbe Soffici? [...] – Che direbbe Papini?" Agnoletti, "I poeti di Ferrara," 674.

9 "Chi negherà che in un tale impeto abbondante di voracità amorosa sia come presentito e preannunziato il linguaggio e il ritmo della passione contemporanea?" Ardengo Soffici, "Prefazione," in Ludovico Ariosto, *Elegie, sonetti e canzoni*, ed. Soffici (Lanciano: Carabba, 1911), 9.

10 "Io dove l'ho veduto? Hanno tagliato il lauro di Astolfo! [...] Marmi, sepolcri, vergini bianche sulla navata d'oro. [...] Mi tornava Ravenna nel cuore." Agnoletti, "I poeti di Ferrara," 674.

11 A myrtle though, not a laurel, just like Astolfo and Pier delle Vigne. The change of tree might be related to the most famous vegetal transformation of Greco-Roman mythology: that of Daphne becoming a laurel in Ovid's *Metamorphoses* (I, 452–567). Ariosto, following Boiardo's invention of the fountain of hate and the river of love as chivalric tropes in *Orlando Innamorato*, draws on Daphne's myth for the premise of the *Furioso* – Daphne and Apollo, in the *Metamorphoses* (I, 466) are hit by arrows of lead and gold respectively, developing opposing feelings towards each other like Rinaldo and Angelica, who drank the two magical waters (I, 78). In the *Furioso*, before reaching the moon, Astolfo meets Daphne in hell, where she regrets her ingratitude for Apollo's love along with other metamorphic women (XXXIV, 12). On the myth of Daphne in the *Orlando Furioso*, see Chiara Cassiani, "Il mito di Dafne nell' 'Orlando Furioso,'" in *Nello specchio del mito. Riflessi di una tradizione*, ed. Giuseppe Izzi, Luca Marcozzi, and Concetta Ranieri (Florence: Cesati, 2012), 273–94.

12 The superimposition of Ferrara and Ravenna in Agnoletti's recollection could also be read as a literary tribute to Ariosto's ability to intersect fantasy and historical reality. In the *Furioso*, Ariosto associated the siege of Paris with his own experience of the battle of Ravenna, where the Estensi prevailed, thanks to the French allies, over the papal army supported by the Spaniards – but at a great cost ("Anguished Ravenna! Better had it been / By far, if no resistance you had made," XIV, 9: 1–2).

13 "Tendevo l'orecchio invano all'usignolo che mi parlava le sere fresche dal lauro d'Astolfo. Avevo abitato quelle stanze e gli orti, ma in un'altra città, in un'altra età. Siamo saliti allo studio. L'uomo buono ci cercò la pace mite. A questa tavola aveva ravviato le rime, conchiuso il gran ciclo giocondo, ospitato i paladini faticosi fra i colonnati dell'ultimo grande cantare. Qui! questa tavola! lui! Gli uomini vivi sono quelli che amano i morti. Segnai sull'albo l'ultima firma. Mandai col cuore il bacio di chi ama e parte." Agnoletti, "I poeti di Ferrara," 675.

14 Jacob Burckhardt, *The Civilization of the Renaissance in Italy* (London: Phaidon, 1995), 33.

15 “Scorro la *Voce* da Govoni,” wrote Savinio, on September 18, 1915, to Ardengo Soffici. The letter, preserved in Florence’s State Archives, was published in Maurzio Fagiolo dall’Arco, ed., *Alberto Savinio* (Ferrara: Galleria Civica d’Arte Moderna, 1980), 21.

16 Giorgio de Chirico, *Geometry of Shadows,* trans. Stefania Heim (New York: A Public Space Books, 2019), 31. Here and elsewhere, I am using Heim’s translations of de Chirico’s poems. However, in this case, I corrected a slight imprecision. Heim translates “la fante” as “the foot soldier.” Unless de Chirico’s foot-soldier was a woman (highly unlikely, considering the times and the context), he probably meant “fantesca,” which means “maid.” This old-style term, which has the same root of the English word “infant,” originates from the word for young person and evolved to mean two different things according to gender: foot-soldier in the masculine, servant woman in the feminine. The first gendered meaning is still widely circulating. In the second sense, the term is used consistently in Italian classical literature, for instance by Boccaccio, in the *Decameron* (V, 5): “aveva Giacomino in casa una fante attempata.”

17 On de Chirico and Nietzsche, see Ara Merjian, *Giorgio de Chirico and the Metaphysical City: Nietzsche, Modernism, Paris* (New Haven: Yale University Press, 2014).

18 The epiphany in Santa Croce is a foundation in the mythology of Metaphysical art. The earliest recollection by de Chirico himself appears in the Paulhan manuscripts of the early 1910s, to which I will return. A transcription of the passage in the original French is available in Giorgio de Chirico, “Manuscrits Paulhan,” *Metaphysical Art* no. 17/18 (2018): 34–5.

19 On this series of paintings, see Michael Taylor, ed., *Giorgio de Chirico and the Myth of Ariadne* (London: Merrell, in association with the Philadelphia Museum of Art, 2002).

20 “Vidi morir le statue dei politici: / curvarono le teste e dissero / l’ultimo canto, poi, / rotte su’ fianchi, caddero / come le Arianne abbandonate … […] Vidi una donna calva / salir come lucertola di latta / su per lo zoccolo / d’Emanuele Filiberto nella pura Torino.” Alberto Savinio, *Hermaphrodito e altri romanzi,* ed. Alessandro Tinterri (Milan: Adelphi, 1995), 10.

21 Arthur Schopenhauer, *Parerga and Paralipomena: Short Philosophical Essays,* trans. Eric F.J. Payne (Oxford: Oxford University Press, 2000), 450.

22 “Schopenhauer, che la sapeva lunga in tali faccende, consigliava ai suoi conterranei di non porre le statue dei loro uomini illustri sopra colonne o piedistalli troppo alti ma di posarle invece su zoccoli bassi, ‘come si usa in Italia, diceva, ove alcuni uomini di marmo sembrano trovarsi al livello dei passanti e camminare con essi.’” Giorgio de Chirico, “Sull’arte metafisica,” *Valori Plastici* 1, nos. 4–5 (1919): 15–18. Rpt. in de Chirico, *Scritti,* ed. Andrea Cortellessa (Milan: Bompiani, 2008), 291. My translation here is largely

based on the one provided in James Thrall Soby, *Giorgio de Chirico* (New York: Museum of Modern Art, 1955), 35. Soby's version, which made this passage known to Anglophone scholars, is completely satisfying but cuts parts of the text.

23 "D'être mêlés à la vie des hommes, les dieux n'en devenaient que plus divins. J'ai senti cela à Olympie par une nuit de clair de lune en apercevant du dehors, à travers les fenêtres du musée bâti parmi les pins et les ruines, sur les bords de l'Alphée à l'eau boueuse, la statue d'Hermès, chef-d'œuvre de Praxitèle. Cette statue repose sur un socle très bas, ce qui fait que quand il y a des visiteurs elle paraît vivre elle aussi. On dirait qu'elle va bouger, parler et même se mettre à marcher, sortir, disparaître. C'est en effet une grave erreur esthétique et, dirais-je, métaphysique, de poser les statues sur des socles trop hauts et surtout de les jucher sur des colonnes. Schopenhauer a stigmatisé cette hérésie, répandue particulièrement en Allemagne." Giorgio de Chirico, "Quelques perspectives sur mon art," in *Il meccanismo del pensiero*, ed. Maurizio Fagiolo (Turin: Einaudi, 1985), 320.

24 "Ferrara è una città quanto mai metafisica." Giorgio de Chirico, "Gaetano Previati," in ibid., 177.

25 "Riguardai come a fenomeno consueto: su quella piazza tagliata nell'ordine del quadrante solare, vidi nel mezzo la colonna altissima di marmo; in cima al gambo il poeta avventuroso, vissuto e morto in odor di borghesia." Alberto Savinio, *Hermaphrodito e altri romanzi*, 69.

26 "Come ad un vento sapeur, che pur non arieggiava, guardai l'enorme fusto tubolare: scivolava ... lava ... lava e si piegò. Scrisse sul cielo la quarta parte di un cerchio ideale. Scese, come un dito benigno e bianco che volesse segnare, all'orizzonte: via libera, en avant, route! Con molta mollezza, senza rumore, s'adagiò mansueto sull'erba ove si ruppe e si snodò in tanti tamburi che piano rotolarono. Attesero un po'; poscia si sciolsero come residui nevosi nelle conche di piccole vallate." Ibid., 69.

27 "Il poeta di marmo era balzato dallo zoccolo ove troppa la noia dei secoli lo ratteneva, con la leggiadra pirouette d'un fattorino telegrafico che schizza da un tram tutto in corsa. ('la patria,' scritta in nero, rimase lì, per l'ordine dei popoli). Prima si grattò la natica mancina; poi si buttò a tergo la teorba appesa al collo mediante una cordicella con nodi, e s'allontanò con passi saccadés e malsicuri verso il palazzo Massari, tirandosi sugli occhi un po' della sua toga per schermirsi dal gran sole." Ibid., 69–70.

28 To be precise, Ariosto is named once in the Epilogue of *La partenza dell'Argonauta*, the longest section of *Hermaphrodito*. I will return to this modernist, autobiographical rewriting of Jason's mythical travels. For now, let me just say that, in its last few pages, Savinio makes an Ariostean pun on the name of Vittorio Emanuele Orlando, who was prime minister of Italy after Paolo Boselli, between 1917 and 1919.

29 The tram, younger and more modest urban brother of the train that so emblematically pervaded Giorgio's early painting, appears outside the window in de Chirico's 1916 Ferrarese drawing *The Melancholy of the Room* (fig. 1.16). In Savinio's *Drame de l'après-midi entre deux saisons,* it greeted Soffici as the only friend remaining in a deserted Ferrara. Savinio, *Hermaphrodito e altri romanzi,* 42.
30 "Funi racconta sovente i suoi sogni. [...] Egli sogna che si trova a Ferrara, nella casa paterna [...] apre una porta ed entra in una camera, ed in quella camera, immersa nella luce crepuscolare dei sogni, vede in un angolo una statua [...]. La statua comincia a muoversi un po', indi lentamente s'avanza verso lui." De Chirico, *Il meccanismo del pensiero,* 370.
31 "È a Firenze che s'è svolto il dramma di Gerolamo Savonarola [...] ma è a Ferrara che la psiche tenebrosa e corrosa dalla bile del frate dal profilo di montone, si rivela più chiaramente." Ibid., 177.
32 The monument was dismantled in 1954, and both the statues are now preserved in the Museo del Risorgimento di Ferrara.
33 The "cielo aspiratore" in these lines verses is paralleled by the "cielo prosciugatore" in *Ferrara ... Partenza.* Also the "strane iscrizioni" that "sorgono a ogni quadrivio" in de Chirico's poem seem to allude to the cryptic messages appearing in the cityscape of Savinio's prose – not only the monument's inscription, but also the author's date of birth and the fragment of the Greek national anthem written in the sky right after the statue walks away. Like de Chirico's "piazze," Savinio's "città" is "deserta," and the dramatic endings of both texts insist on the same nostalgia and are addressed to a woman.
34 De Chirico, *Geometry of Shadows,* 49.
35 "Per conto mio credo che ci sia molto più mistero in una piazza fossilizzata nel chiarore del meriggio che non in una camera buja, nel cuore della notte, durante una seduta di spiritismo." De Chirico, *Il meccanismo del pensiero,* 62.
36 "un bel sogno profetico sognato a occhi aperti e in pieno meriggio in faccia all'inesorabile realtà." Ibid., 63.
37 "Il cielo deve essere serrato tra i rettangoli delle finestre e le arcate dei portici cittadini perché lo si possa mungere sapientemente alle vaste mammelle della sua cupola traditrice. La stessa terra, dura e soda che sentiamo sotto la suola dei nostri stivali, è vinta oggi dalla metafisicità delle umane costruzioni, malgrado le catene delle sue granitiche montagne, la notte delle sue selve secolari e l'inquietudine dei suoi mari tormentatori ed infecondi. E oggi tu vedi un'opificio [*sic*] suburbano vegliato dalla scolta solenne dei comignoli; tu vedi una stazione ferroviaria, una piazza circondata da cubi di pietra colorata ed adorna di squares e di statue in paletot, far zampillare getti altissimi, veri *geyser* di lirismo metafisico, che

chiederesti invano a tutti i paesaggi ridenti o tetri del nostro pianeta." Ibid., 63.

38 "quella gioia, quella serenità che ci procura in arte l'apparizione di un'immagine metafisica." Ibid., 64.

39 "Ieri, nel pomeriggio passando per una via che s'allunga lenta e stretta fiancheggiata da case alte e scure vidi apparire in fondo una colonna sormontata da una statua che seppi poi essere quella dell'Ariosto. Visto così, tra quelle due pareti di pietra annerata – che parevano muri d'un santuario antico – il monumento assumeva un ché di misterioso e di solenne, e il passante tampoco metafisicizzante si sarebbe aspettato di udire la voce d'un nume vaticinare." Ibid.

40 I primi popoli sfruttarono incoscientemente la potenza metafisica delle cose, isolandole, tracciando intorno a loro magiche e insormontabili barriere [...] Tutto dipende da un certo *modo* d'inquadramento e d'isolamento. Il primitivo lo fa incoscientemente seguendo un vago istinto mistico; l'artefice moderno, invece, lo fa coscientemente." Ibid.

41 "[...] guidando, anzi aumentando, truccando o sfruttando scaltramente la metafisicità scoperta negli oggetti. Tale stato metafisico viene rappresentato negli oggetti che lo possiedono da un distintivo che ne determina il grado. S'intende che intrinsecamente l'oggetto graduato vale quanto quello non graduato. Gli oggetti fregiati e gallonati in tal modo acquistano tra la folla dei volumi polimorfi o monomorfi che ingombrano il nostro pianeta, un valore e un significato speciale." Ibid.

42 "Ferrara è una città quantomai metafisica [...] Ferrara è la città delle sorprese; oltre che l'offrire in alcuni punti, come in quella ineffabile piazza ariostea, splendide apparizioni di spettralità e bellezza sottile, che fermano e stupiscono il passante astuto ed educato nei misteri della intelligenza, quella città offre pure il vantaggio di conservare in modo affatto particolare lembi della grande notte medievale." Ibid., 177.

43 "Bisognerebbe che voi vi foste fermati un giorno nell'alta quiete meriggiale di Piazza Ariostea a Ferrara, dove il quadro è stato dipinto per sentire la grande suggestione che a me produce lo sfondo della tela. '*Il grande metafisico* del De Chirico.' Deserta è la piazza, il fondo, a destra, la casa rossa cubica come un castello medianico in uno scritto di Alberto Savinio; davanti, più giù, la casa giallina con il timpano e le chiare finestre verdi *Paolo Veronese* in fila, vuote. In fondo un uomo alto rinchiuso tutto in una toga nera, aspetta. Le ombre lunghe si delineano silenziosissime mentre l'intricato groviglio degli oggetti triangolari, lucidi geometrizzanti del centro, che s'erge come una ingente colonna sembra ricantare *assurde declinazioni, e problemi insoliti al nostro spirito.* Ecco che il piano quadro della piazza nel tremolio dei raggi solari, sembra agli stanchi occhi che si metta a girare lentamente 'come la *roulette* quando sta per fermarsi.'" Filippo de

Pisis, *La città dalle cento meraviglie e altri scritti*, ed. Sandro Zanotto and Bona de Pisis (Florence: Vallecchi, 1965), 139.

44 "Io somministravo idee e materiale al compagno [de Chirico], egli a me. Di questo periodo è un mio roseo libretto intitolato Futuristicamente *Mercoledì 14 Novembre 1917* e che fu preso per furutismo, ma che con esso nulla o ben poco aveva a che fare. In esso gettavo la base di una nuova prosa, che potremmo chiamare per intenderci Prosa metafisica." Filippo de Pisis, *Futurismo dadaismo metafisica*, ed. Bona de Pisis and Sandro Zanotto (Milan: Scheiwiller, 1981), 146.

45 "Una notte, *il sepolto vivo* si rizzò come un fachiro dal sonno e si divinizzò." De Pisis, *La città dalle cento meraviglie*, 109.

46 "Io ora risorgo, mi divinizzo." Ibid., 114.

47 "… Sulla terra, sperduti ma anche per noi *l'ora fatale* venne! Erano spezzate le barriere! Vedevo lucido finalmente! O la mia vigliaccheria, la mia miseria fin'ora! La piazza quadrata, dopo il molto peregrinare fu il teatro della nostra gioia e della nostra elevazione. Quasi tutto scomparve nell'istante divino! La trepidazione è ancora in me e la pena indicibile, per il timore che l'attimo svanisca, senza lasciare traccia, come tanti altri." Ibid., 113.

48 See Filippo de Pisis, *Opere su Carta*, ed. Giorgio Bombi (Milan: Electa, 1985), 15.

49 "La piazza quadrata con la colonna alta nel mezzo! Noi l'abbiamo girata attorno precisamente e poi ci siamo fermati sotto la colonna a guardare in su. Le impronte delle nostre orme non restarono sul terreno, l'aria non solidificò le nostre forme in tanti stampi, nulla si mutò, ma noi eravamo due potentissimi dominatori della materia che passava, che stava." De Pisis, *La città dalle cento meraviglie*, 114.

50 "Io ad un tratto avrei voluto levare le braccia e restare così immobilizzato nel *sogno attimo, visione prepotente* di un'essenza primordiale. E richiamai disperatamente, senza lagrime, senza neppure sospirare (dio mio, dio mio! …) altre notti! Noi fermi sotto la colonna, il piedistallo, bianco parallelepipedo con gli spigoli acuti, gli angoli retti, le labbra dello sguscio taglienti come rasoi, e poi il cilindro bianco della colonna che si piega pian piano un po' indietro, si svinca, e la statua fatua, vedetta eroica, muta-gessosa, olimpiaca, occhi cieca, marmorea, ferma, *mannequin* che sta lì lì per cadere come un birillo rigido, fissato a una cerniera, come il romano bianco, magnetizzato dall'istriona con la faccia infrarinata o un clown da CIRCO." Ibid., 115.

51 "Rievochiamo, rievochiamo ancora le altre notti in questa piazza quadrata!" Ibid., 116.

52 "Quella notte, eravamo di nuovo nella piazza quadrata: la girammo tutt'attorno. I portici ci videro, godemmo della loro areosità, non numerammo le colonne." Ibid., 117.

53 "Ecco, io ti vedevo il costruttore sullo spiano libero, (la sfericità del globo era vinta, il tuo spazio era davvero *essere* nel *non essere!*) ti vedevo costruttore del tuo mondo architettonico del piacere e tu non eri più il creatore felice, ma il mondo eri tu e lui te. Sui più alti pinnacoli sventolavano allegre, fremebonde le tue bandierine! Forsennato avrei voluto attaccarmi coi denti agli stipiti di marmo per divorarli. […] La colonna sembrava un dado. Sollevandola, il marciapiede, leggermente piramidoide, sarebbe restato attaccato, come uno stampino, i portici erano ben costruiti, il soffitto del cielo quasi angusto (solo una strana nebulosa, come un aborto di luna, su su, molto alta, imprigionava ancora lo spirito che andava avanti ora con piedi di mamut). Eppure lo spirito si tese, si liberò, ebbe la gioia rapida della invenzione. Ecco fatto! …" Ibid., 118.

54 "Il quadro piazza non era più, sabato 22 dicembre 1917; era stato, era, e sarebbe stato." Ibid., 119.

55 "Alla mia destra Lodovico Ariosto, che fuma un toscano: uniforme da sottotenente, mostrine nere, stellette d'argento." Ibid., 124.

56 "La solitudine era immensa: sulla lavagna le semirette e i segmenti delle indeterminabilità più indeterminate. Grande giostra dei valori ultrasensori. Le *camere metafisiche* ormai o CARRÁ stavano per animarsi e De Chirico (l'amico comune!) trasfigurato in *fantomas* bianco, statua romanica, pieghe accannellate, testa ogivale-liscia, retino del tennis, palla quadrata in mano, assisteva alla *mirabilia delle mirabilie*." Ibid., 124.

57 See Ara Merjian, *Giorgio de Chirico and the Metaphysical City*, 142–3.

58 The pose is also rooted in a famous ancient statue, the so-called Lateran Sophocles, which appeared in the Reninach repertoire that I mentioned before.

59 "La piazza desolata del *Ritornante* (uno dei più bei quadri del De Chirico) è piazza Ariostea." De Pisis, *Futurismo dadaismo metafisica*, 147.

60 "In una piazza quadrata […] c'era una bianca colonna alta assai nel mezzo." De Pisis, *La città dalle cento meraviglie*, 186.

61 "Staccato da tutto il resto, sotto la colonna bianca, fatua nella notte, ascoltavo, dopo avere attraversata la piazza." Ibid., 197.

62 "Angelica e Medoro, sotto il boschetto di alloro, e fra le siepi di mirto, bellissimi, semignudi; lui, forte pastore, dai riccioli d'oro e dalle carni bianco alabastro, lei perfetta e delirante di passione; si sfibravano in abbracciamenti lunghi e reiterati." Ibid., 207.

63 "Il terreno, dove ha attinto succhi vitali il mio *essere*, è piuttosto fecondo di poeti e poetastri, fra essi però io pochi sento degni di me. […] al caro messer Lodovico mi inchino e posso anzi considerarlo mio antenato. (I miei vecchi forse gli furono amici, e lo vedevano passare per le oneste strade della città di allora)." Ibid., 420.

64 De Pisis probably quoted by heart. There are quite a few imprecisions in his quotation. Some of these imprecisions, however, are useful to bend Ariosto's

text to the needs of de Pisis' narration. For instance, the first line of the octave, "Lontan si vide una muraglia lunga" is switched, in *La città dalle cento meraviglie,* to the present tense ("Lontan si vede"), so that de Pisis can use Ariosto's words to describe what one sees, while walking, from Ferrara's walls.

65 "per virtù di quei versi pensi a una ciclopica città tutta cinta intorno da una muraglia lunga, rosa, con finestre paurose, una città alta fino al cielo e tutta d'oro, una città forse sorta per un sortilegio d'alchimia (come dice Messer Ludovico 'benedetto lui dalla Madonna') una città, dove tutti gli uomini camminan leggeri e sono invasati dal demone del mistero e non si curan che della contemplazione degli 'Eterni Veri.'" De Pisis, *La città dalle cento meraviglie,* 461–2.

66 "O per quei versi ti ricordi di aver visto un salone, nelle pareti tutte frescate del quale erano davvero 'giovani e donne qual presso a fonte ... qual d'un arbore all'ombra' ecc. ecc. [...] e continui così a vagabondare sentendo che è dolce aver perduta l'aderenza con questo 'basso loco' e vivere tutto in balia degli antichi fantasmi e degli eterni veri." Ibid., 462.

67 Ita Mac Carthy, "Ariosto the Traveler," *Modern Language Review* 102, no. 2 (April 2007): 397–409.

68 The ironically credible description of the Hippogriff was particularly admired by Borges, who included the beast in his 1957 *Book of Imaginary Beings.*

69 See Jo Ann Cavallo, *The World beyond Europe in the Romance Epics of Boiardo and Ariosto* (Toronto: University of Toronto Press, 2013).

70 For a detailed analysis of these passages, see Giammei, "(Quick)Silver Masks: Modern and Postmodern Revivals of Quattrocento Chivalric Poems," *Italian Studies* 74, no. 2 (2020): 208–18.

71 "Una fraterna dimestichezza con i cavalieri erranti." Savinio, *Hermaphrodito e altri romanzi,* 179.

72 "Quel Boselli non mi andava [...] Orlando è per me una luce nuova e più viva che sorge nel punto ove s'è spento il lucignolo del vecchiardo. Riguardo all'Ariosto: Orlando sarà furioso. Ecco che l'idea della Furia mi nasce dall'immagine imbambolata e calva del nuovo ministro. La Furia ci vuole: e quindi – Orlando!" Ibid., 182.

73 "Questa pezzuola è istoriata con una bellissima raffigurazione dell'Italia. Il fatidico stivale, appoggiato saldamente con le larghe staffe al cuore dell'Europa, si slancia, esile e fremente, nel bagno dei tre mari. [...] Porto quindi la mia attenzione alla parte geografica della pezzuola ove la figura dello stivale è rotta dalle ondosità delle pieghe. Sulle gobbe della tela trovo il Lazio e Roma segnata con un disco cerchiato di nero. Più in alto, il Tirreno bagna le sponde del golfo ligure. A destra scopro Ferrara, marcata con un asterisco piccino, e seguo la traccia del mio viaggio sulla linea rossa che indica la rete ferroviaria." Ibid., 110–11.

74 Giorgio de Chirico, *Hebdomeros with Monsieur Dudron's Adventure, and Other Metaphysical Writings,* trans. John Ashbery (Cambridge: Exact Change, 1992), 37.
75 Ibid., 25.
76 Ara Merjian, "Giorgio de Chirico's Willful Claustrophilia: The Ferrara Interiors, 1915–18," *Art Bulletin* 101, no. 2 (2019): 54–82.
77 de Chirico, *Geometry of Shadows,* 27.
78 Ibid., 39.
79 Ibid., 43.
80 Ibid., 29.
81 On maps in the sixteenth-century illustrations of the *Furioso,* see Alessandro Benassi and Serena Pezzini, "Mappe ed ecfrasi nell'edizione Valgrisi del 1556," in *L'Orlando Furioso. Lo specchio delle immagini,* ed. Lina Bolzoni (Rome: Istituto dell'Enciclopedia Italiana Treccani, 2014), 183–226; and Alexandre Doroszlaï, "Les sources cartographiques et le Roland Furieux: quelques hypotèses autour de l''espace réel' chez l'Arioste," in *Espaces réels et espaces imaginaires dans le Roland Furieux,* ed. Alecandre Doroszlaï, José Guidi, Marie-Françoise Piéjus, and André Rochon (Paris: Université de la Sorbonne Nouvelle, 1991), 11–46.
82 As de Chirico himself recalled in a 1928 letter, now preserved in the Archivio Antonio Vastano and partially transcribed in Gerd Roos, *Giorgio de Chirico e Alberto Savinio: Ricordi e documenti: Monaco, Milano, Firenze, 1906–1911* (Bologna: Bora, 1999), 265.
83 Mario Ursino, *Giorgio de Chirico e l'antico* (Rome: Nuova Cultura, 2006), 60–1.
84 See for instance Maurizio Fagiolo, *L'opera completa di De Chirico 1908–1924* (Milan: Rizzoli, 1984), 106–7.
85 Ibid., 101.
86 "L'œuvre de Chirico se divise en deux périodes: la première et la mauvaise." Raymond Queneau, "A propos de l'exposition Giorgio de Chirico à la galerie Surréaliste (15 février–1ere Mars 1928)," *La Révolution Surréaliste* 4, no. 11 (March 15, 1928): 42.
87 "quel periodo di pittura a tempera che gli storici dell'arte moderna chiamano, ma senza insistere troppo, il periodo romantico." Giorgio de Chirico, *Memorie della mia vita* (Milan: Bompiani, 2016), 138.
88 "un passage d'Homère me captive – Ulysse dans l'isle de Calypso." De Chirico, *Il meccanismo del pensiero,* 17.
89 On this lost drawing, the earliest known by Savinio, see Roos, *Giorgio de Chirico e Alberto Savinio,* 274–7; and Nicole Mocchi, "The Enigma of the Double: Sources and Symbols in Alberto Savinio's Poetics," *Italian Modern Art* 2 (July 2019) italianmodernart.org/journal/articles/the-enigma-of-the-double-sources-and-symbols-in-alberto-savinios-poetics.

90 "ou bien en lisant Arioste, Roger, ce type de Chevalier errant se repose sous un arbre, il s'endort, le cheval broute l'herbe autour de lui; tout est solitaire et silencieux, on s'attendrait à voir passer un dragon dans les airs; la scène me captive, je me figure le chevalier, le cheval, le paysage tout d'un coup, c'est presque une révélation mais cela ne me suffit pas encore." De Chirico, *Il meccanismo del pensiero*, 17.
91 "Dall'Ariosto Böcklin trasse l'ispirazione di alcuni suoi quadri più belli." Alberto Savinio, *Narrate uomini la vostra storia* (Milan: Adelphi, 1984), 45.
92 Roos, *Giorgio de Chirico e Alberto Savinio*, 277–8.
93 For a survey of the theme of chivalry in de Chirico's work in general, see Jole de Sanna, "Il cavaliere errante (crasi del tempo)," in *Giorgio de Chirico dalla Metafisica alla "Metafisica,"* ed. Vittorio Sgarbi (Venice: Marsilio, 2002), 25–43.
94 Pia Vivarelli, *Alberto Savinio: Catalogo generale* (Milan: Electa, 1996), 131.
95 Alberto Savinio, *La nascita di venere: scritti sull'arte* (Milan: Adelphi, 2007), 58–9.
96 Ibid., 62–3.
97 "pienezza spirituale." Ibid., 59.
98 "Se Ludovico Ariosto ha potuto senza danno montare in groppa agli ippogrifi e mandare in giro i suoi paladini per gli spazi interplanetari, è perché messer Ludovico non si è mai lasciato sfuggir di mano questo utilissimo filo d'Arianna: l'ironia. Il tipo contrario di Ariosto, si chiama Flammarion." Alberto Savinio, *Torre di guardia*, ed. Leonardo Sciascia (Palermo: Sellerio, 1993), 54.
99 Alberto Savinio, "Ottobrata," *Rivista di Firenze* 1, no. 7 (1924): 16–19.
100 See for instance Carolina Pernigo, "Angelica, la forma del desiderio nella letteratura contemporanea," *Between* 3, no. 5 (2013): 1–22.
101 Savinio, *Hermaphrodito e altri romanzi*, 411.
102 Ibid., 363–5.
103 Sonia Cavicchioli, *"L'Aquila e l'Pardo." Rinaldo I e il mecenatismo di casa d'Este nel Seicento* (Modena: Franco Cosimo Panini, 2015), 59.
104 On the development of the narrative techniques that were fully expressed in the *Furioso*, see Marco Praloran, *"Maraviglioso artificio": Tecniche narrative e rappresentative nell'"Orlando innamorato"* (Pisa: Pacini Fazzi, 1990); and *Tempo e azione nell'"Orlando furioso"* (Florence: Olschki, 1999).
105 Sergio Zatti, *The Quest for Epic: From Ariosto to Tasso* (Toronto: University of Toronto Press, 2006), 19.
106 These two interlaced storylines establish a connection between *Angelica o la notte di maggio* and the myth of Eros and Psyche, which was repeatedly explored by Savinio – most prominently, in the 1944 novella *La nostra anima*. This intertextual parallel suggests an ulterior layer in Savinio's stratigraphy of sources: Boiardo's *Orlando Innamorato*. Angelica is a central character in Boiardo's poem as well, and it is Boiardo who established her as an erotic engine of narration. He built her character in direct

intertextual relation with Apuleius's Psyche in *The Golden Ass*, which was translated into Italian by Massimo Bontempelli in 1929. I thank Jo Ann Cavallo for suggesting this alternative intertextual chain that links Savinio's Angelica to Psyche through Boiardo's Angelica.

107 "Aggiungo che *Angelica o la notte di maggio* è un libro ispirato dal cinematografo: dallo spirito e dalla tecnica del cinematografo." Savinio, *Hermaphrodito e altri romanzi*, 934.

108 "una complessa catena d'originali e compiuti quadri. Quadri pittorici in movimento [...] ciò che si dice nel gergo dei *films* arte di montaggio." Anton Giulio Bragaglia, "L'Ariosto come cineasta," in *L'Ottava d'Oro*, ed. Antonio Baldini (Milan: Mondadori, 1933), 652.

109 "un poeta costretto a usar la parola solo per la mancanza di una macchina da presa." Ibid., 641.

110 Daniel Javitch, "Cantus Interruptus in the Orlando Furioso," *Modern Language Notes* 95, no. 1 (January 1980): 66–80.

111 For a thorough discussion of this painting within both the de Chiricos' post-war poetics, see Alessandro Giammei, "Stratigraphy of Andromeda: Giorgio de Chirico, Alberto Savinio, Origins, and Originality," *Modernism/modernity* 25, no. 1 (2018): 21–43. See also Flavio Fergonzi, "Episodi della fortuna del Furioso nella pittura del Novecento in Italia," in *L'Orlando furioso nello specchio delle immagini*, ed. Lina Bolzoni (Rome: Istituto dell'Enciclopedia Italiana Treccani, 2015), 525–43. I would like to thank Flavio Fergonzi for referencing this research of mine (at the time still in progress) in his essay.

112 On which, see Alessandro Giammei and Taylor Yoonji Kang, "Staging (or Not Staging) Ovid for Modern(ist) Self-Fashioning," *Modern Language Notes* 135, no. 1 (2020): 203–30.

113 "L'arte che edifica non una civiltà, ma un mondo. Che perfeziona la vita, che perfeziona l'uomo. Che umanizza i mostri, che dà una personalità agli oggetti, un'anima alle cose, *che fa scendere le statue dagli zoccoli e le aggrega alla nostra compagnia*. Che esclude a poco a poco quanto c'è di bestiale, di duro, di settario, di ottuso, di ostile, di incomprensibile nelle cose, nella natura, nell'uomo. Che perfeziona la biologia, che mette tregua alla lotta feroce dei sessi [...]. Questo l'arte moderna, l'arte italiana ha il fine nonchè di rappresentare ma di attuare." Alberto Savinio, "Pittori italiani del '900 in Francia," in *Italiani nel mondo* (Florence: Sansoni, 1942), 566. My emphasis.

114 "Presentiva che un giorno avrebbe raggiunta questa forma di libertà suprema. Già mirava al modello dell'Uomo Solitario e Durissimo, dell'Uomo Diamante, di Achille fuso con Orlando, dell'Uomo di Marmo che Cammina. [...] dalla speranza che l'Uomo di Carne, l'Uomo Marsupiale, l'Incurabile Plebeo sparisca un giorno dalla faccia del mondo." Savinio, *Hermaphrodito e altri romanzi*, 606.

115 de Chirico, *Geometry of Shadows*, 33.

2. Ludovico's Gifts: The Ariostean Spirit of Magical Realism

1 On the basis of Ariosto's clues, most sixteenth-century commentators, such as Simone Fornari, placed Alcina's realm in Japan (the island that Marco Polo called "Zipangri"). Current criticism generally confirms the location, with some divergent hypotheses – see for instance Alice Spinelli, "Intorno al 'lato destro de la terra.' Nuove proposte esegetiche sull'immaginario cosmografico e geoculturale di Ariosto," *Babel* 32 (2015): 65–92.

2 Italo Calvino, *Italo Calvino: Letters, 1941–1985*, ed. Michael Wood, trans. Martin McLaughlin (Princeton: Princeton University Press, 2013), 336 and 342. The two statements come from two letters that Calvino sent to critics Michael David (December 13, 1967) and Luigi Baldacci (January 15, 1968) after receiving their comments on his *Cosmicomics*, which was published in 1965 in Italian and in 1968 in English. Both Baldacci and David believed Bontempelli to be a direct influence on Calvino's fantastic narrative, and so do I.

3 Alejo Carpentier, "The Baroque and the Marvelous Real" (1975), in *Magical Realism: Theory, History, Community*, ed. Lois Parkinson Zamora and Wendy Faris (Durham, NC: Duke University Press, 1995), 96. Carpentier's lecture on "The Baroque and the Marvelous Real" was given in Caracas in 1975 and published for the first time in Alejo Carpentier, *La novela latinoamericana en vísperas de un nuevo siglo* (Mexico City: Siglo XXI, 1981), 111–32.

4 "quando, anni fa, ho additato una legge artistica e l'ho chiamata 'realismo magico,' ho avuto cura di citare per l'appunto Ariosto; e tutto il 'novecentismo' letterario non è appunto che questo: salire alle nubi in groppa all'Ippogrifo, e scenderne la sera per andare a dormire in una buona osteria." Massimo Bontempelli, "L'Ariosto geografo" (1930), in *L'ottava d'oro, La vita e l'opera di Ludovico Ariosto*, ed. Antonio Baldini (Milan: Mondadori, 1933), 554.

5 Once he became an established author, Bontempelli minimized the importance of his literary activity before 1912. However, his eagerness to gain literary fame and to express his poetics in the first years of the twentieth century is clear from his letters. In particular, he soon secured an editorship at the regional journal *Piemonte* and collaborated with many other local literary groups, trying hard to get his first tragedy, *Costanza* (1905), reviewed "su un buon giornale"; see his letter to Emilio Bordero in Silvana Cigliana, "Due epistolari e un carteggio inediti: A Emilio Bordero (1903–1939)," *L'Illuminista* 5, nos. 13/14/15 (2005): 25–6. Getting reviews was his main preoccupation, as he confessed to publisher Angelo Fortunato Formiggini, and he mailed, at his own expense, all the copies of his first book of poems to potential reviewers; see his letter to Formiggini in François Bouchard, "Les Années d'apprentissage de

l'écrivain: Massimo Bontempelli et Angelo Fortunato Formiggini," *Rassegna Europea di Letteratura Italiana* 32 (2008): 111–23. For more information on Bontempelli's relationship with the publishing industry in the first years of his activity, see François Bouchard, "Dalla tragedia al dramma: gli esordi teatrali di Massimo Bontempelli," *Bollettino 900* 1/2 (2010), www.boll900.it/numeri/2010-i/Bouchard.html.

6 See Massimo Bontempelli, *Giosue Carducci* (Genoa: Carlini, 1907). A minor but well-received event within the national celebrations for Carducci, the eulogy (delivered in L'Aquila on March 16) was Bontempelli's first public lecture and made him visible as a "carducciano" in the dispute between the supporters of Benedetto Croce's philosophical approach to literature and the historicism that characterized Carducci's school of criticism.

7 Appearing in an obscure periodical from the Abruzzi region and penned by a southern teacher who was an admirer of Carducci, the only critical reaction to the four poems comments on them within the small book in which Bontempelli collected them three years later – Bontempelli, *Odi* (Milan: Formiggini,1910). While the reviewer finds the poem for Ariosto weaker than the one for Tasso, he praises the former for its powerful trans-historical bridge between the sixteenth and twentieth centuries: "questa seconda ode non è povera di poesia [...] specialmente nel raffronto del secolo dell'Ariosto con il nostro." Giuseppe Checchia, "Un nuovo poeta: Massimo Bontempelli," *Aprutium* 1, no. 3/4 (1912): 1–19, 17.

8 Two initiatives centring on Bontempelli's literary prehistory are the special issues of *Il caffè illustrato* (edited by Silvana Cigliana in 2004) and of *Bollettino 900* (edited by Eleonora Conti in 2010).

9 Already in 1919, Bontempelli considered his poems and novellas published before 1912 to be "rifiutate." See Baldacci's reconstruction in Massimo Bontempelli, *Opere scelte*, ed. Luigi Baldacci (Milan: Mondadori, 1978), 967. Bontempelli officially organized his own bibliography when he was elected by the fascist regime to the Accademia d'Italia, publishing a list of rejected and acknowledged works in the institution's bulletin: Bontempelli, "Bibliografia delle opere," in *Annuario della Reale Accademia d'Italia, v. II, a. VIII, 1929–1930* (Rome: Tipografia del Senato G. Bardi, 1931), 83–6. In it, the only poems acknowledged are the Futurist experiments of *Il Purosangue – l'Ubriaco.*

10 "Sfacciatamente ultraclassicistica," as Bontempelli defined his lyric season in the Introduction to his recognized Futurist poems: Bontempelli, *Il Purosangue* (Milan: La Prora, 1933), 3.

11 In *Per Giosue Carducci*, Bontempelli recovers the topos of the poetic silent witness (established by Manzoni in his famous posthumous portrait of Napoleon, *Il cinque maggio*) and includes himself among those who stayed silenced while Carducci lived and then, after his death, were able to forget

the man and uphold his ideas: "tacquer, mentr' Ei vivea, / fisi nel gran concento; / sepper, quand' Ei fu spento, / obliar l'uomo e sublimar l'idea." Bontempelli, "Versi," *Nuova Antologia* 132, no. 864 (1907): 595–601, 599.

12 The ode *Ad Arturo Graf* mostly revolves around the metaphor of writing as navigation, looking for a safe and happy port. Bontempelli represents himself as having only a modest ship and his master's approval ("con barca piccola, anima gioconda / e il vostro auspicio"). He recounts to Graf the many difficulties of his literary career, venting about the hardships of any literary life and the specific obstacles presented by late modernity.

13 "Amo, Torquato, più che le tue rime / te." Bontempelli, "Versi," 598.

14 On Tasso's biographical myth, see Maria Luisa Doglio, *Origini e icone del mito di Torquato Tasso* (Rome: Bulzoni, 2002). On the specific Romantic strand of this tradition, see Hugh Honour, *Romanticism* (London: Harper and Row, 1979), 179; Arnaldo Di Benedetto, "'La sua vita stessa è una poesia': sul mito romantico di Torquato Tasso," *Esperienze letterarie* 22 (1997): 7–34; Jason Lawrence, "'When Despotism Kept Genius in Chains': Imagining Tasso's Madness and Imprisonment, 1748–1849," *Studies in Romanticism* 50, no. 3 (2011): 475–503; and Kari Lokke, "Weimar Classicism and Romantic Madness: Tasso in Goethe, Byron, and Shelley," *European Romantic Review* 2 (1992): 202–22. On the Italian side, see Umberto Bosco, "Il Tasso come tema letterario nell'800 italiano," *Giornale storico della letteratura italiana* 46 (1928): 1–66.

15 George Gordon, Lord Byron, *The Works of Lord Byron Complete in One Volume* (Frankfurt: Broenner, 1826), 762.

16 "ingiurïare in impeto sublime / tutta una Corte." Bontempelli, "Versi," 597.

17 "Alfonso sposa una Gonzaga; male / teme da Roma; ha i calvinisti attorno." Ibid. The duke needed a male heir to secure his succession, but his marriage didn't produce any, and the feared annexation of Ferrara to the Papal State eventually happened two years after Tasso's death, in 1597.

18 "maledetta da Dante, maledetta pe 'l Tasso." Bontempelli, "Versi," v. 164.

19 "Ma il Genio tuo, quel tuo Demone mesto, / fola ai volgari, a te sì dolce e vero." Ibid., 598.

20 "Il poeta si farà maestro all'artigiano." Ibid.

21 A typographical treatment reserved to the poet ("Poeta"), the poet's genius ("Genio"), and Platonic universal law ("Legge").

22 "Uomo nel cuore e negli affetti, ei va / mite con gli altri e appare un nume in terra. / Egli è la calma, e il riso, e l'ubertà / dopo la guerra –" Bontempelli, "Versi," 599.

23 "Dammi la gioia, o Ludovico, il dono / di riguardar serenamente il mondo / e delle cose disfiorando il buono / trarne un succo giocondo. / Quel secol tuo d'oro e di sangue intriso / così intendensti amandolo; e un tal frutto / n'hai colto, che ove sian lacrime e lutto / esser non può che tu non levi un riso." Ibid., 598.

24 The rhymes scheme, however, is different, and follows the rispetto form of the strambotto genre. The fourth line of each stanza is a septenary.
25 "di cento crudeltà dentro cattivo / di bell'ingegno lucido ai fastigi [...] più denso e grande / dell'êre scorse" Bontempelli, "Versi," 598.
26 "Anch'io, Poeta, amo il mio tempo." Ibid.
27 "Libertà da immagine / cerca farsi energia [...] divien sangue, intelletto, / ideal norma dell'umana gara. / Ribellione, istinto bruto, impara / leggi e s'impone un corso ed un concetto. / E curïosa la scïenza investe / tutto il dominio delle forze attive. / Più non l'appaga sollevar la veste / alle inerti e alle vive / nature, e né più tenta arcana porta." Ibid.
28 Benedetto Croce, *A Croce Reader: Aesthetics, Philosophy, History, and Literary Criticism*, ed. and trans. Massimo Verdicchio (Toronto: University of Toronto Press, 2017), 68.
29 "il riso precursore della scienza." Francesco De Sanctis, *Storia della letteratura italiana* (1871), ed. Niccolò Gallo (Turin: Einaudi, 1981), 530.
30 "Sesto io no, ma postremo [...]." Giosuè Carducci, *Rime Nuove* III.12, in Giosuè Carducci, *Tutte le poesie*, ed. Pietro Gibellini (Rome: Newton Compton, 2011), 333.
31 For Carducci, each of the five masters of the sonnet provides modernity with a specific poetic feature, from Dante's ecstatic transcendence to Alfieri's political ire and Foscolo's Hellenic art. Tasso's classical perfume is represented by the honey that "gl'impetrò da le tiburti muse" (a reference to Horace's Tivoli) and the "mantuana ambrosia" (a reference to Virgil's Mantua).
32 The intertextuality is pointed out by the editors in Giosuè Carducci, *Opere, tomo ii, Poesie*, ed. Emma Giammattei (Milan and Naples: Ricciardi, 2011), 123.
33 Carducci worked on an academic essay about Ariosto's youth. In addition, he wrote an essay on Ariosto and Tasso in which he framed Ariosto as a poet of his time: a lucid artist who should not be reduced, as simplistic criticism does, to the freedom of fantasy and the entertainment of chivalric stories. See Giosuè Carducci, "Su Ludovico Ariosto e Torquato Tasso," in *Opere*, vol. 14 (Bologna: Zanichelli, 1954), 90–1.
34 The advertisement appeared in *"900"* without a signature, but it was clearly penned by Bontempelli as director and editor in chief. The mention of the episode of Ruggiero dismounting the Hippogriff to have breakfast at a good inn is a recurring leitmotif of Bontempelli's; see Bontempelli, "L'Ariosto geografo," 554.
35 The narrative section of *Nuova Antologia* remained under Bontempelli's direction until the Great War. He then published anticipations of his novels and entire short stories in the journal throughout the 1930s and the beginning of the 1940s (from his election in the Accademia d'Italia to his definitive expulsion from the fascist party). A complete bibliography

of Bontempelli's works is not available, but it is possible to follow his relationship with *Nuova Antologia* through the journal indexes at the Fondazione Spadolini in Florence.

36 "chiamano tradizione le ultime e penultime mode, e non sanno che la tradizione deve riabbeverarsi alle fonti primigenie. Una di queste fonti è lo spirito ariosteo." Bontempelli, "L'Ariosto geografo," 553–4.

37 He started a soldiers' journal, *Montebello*, and completed the Futurist poems of *L'Ubriaco*, later collected in Bontempelli, *Il Purosangue*.

38 A recurring trope is Marinetti's idea of war as hygiene. See, for instance, Bontempelli, *Dallo Stelvio al mare* (1915), ed. Ugo Piscopo (Naples: Guida, 2002), 36: "Com'è igienico vedere tutte le lotte elettorali d'ieri affratellate nel grande fatto nazionale che le ha improvvisamente scompigliate e sommerse!"

39 "Si affidano le piante alla tutela del pubblico." Ibid., 219.

40 "In questa desolazione può fiorire l'ironia." Ibid., 218.

41 "Prima di entrare si pregano gli austriaci di farsi annunciare." Ibid., 51.

42 "Potrebb'essere nell'Orlando Furioso." Ibid.

43 "è un modo di allontanarci dal contingente, di liberarci da un'aderenza troppo minuta con la superficie delle cose […] l'avviamento a una lucidità superiore." Bontempelli, *Opere scelte*, 757.

44 "il gusto e la cultura classica s'imponevano e si diffondevano traverso lo snobismo – diremmo oggi – delle classi migliori, che pagano, s'annoiano e mostran di divertirsi e di esaltarsi; com'è avvenuto ai nostri tempi, per esempio, del wagnerismo." Ludovico Ariosto, *Commedie e Satire*, ed. Massimo Bontempelli (Milan: Istituto Editoriale Italiano, 1916), 12–13.

45 "le maggiori propagande di novità artistiche o pratiche vanno affidate allo snobismo: il wagnerismo che dominò l'Europa nel trentennio ultimo […] è il più grande esempio di tale verità." Bontempelli, *Opere scelte*, 86.

46 "I cortigiani che si sentivan leggere dall'Ariosto le ottave dell'Orlando, non sognavano certo che le fantasticherie di quell'inaderentissimo sarebbero riuscite per noi la più vera e profonda interpretazione del Cinquecento italiano." Bontempelli, *L'avventura novecentista* (1938), ed. Ruggiero Jacobi (Florence: Vallecchi, 1974), 204.

47 In addition to Albert Ascoli, *Ariosto's Bitter Harmony* (Princeton: Princeton University Press, 1987), I am thinking of Alberto Casadei, *La fine degli incanti: vicende del poema epico-cavalleresco nel Rinascimento* (Milan: Franco Angeli, 1997) and Ida Campeggiani, *L'ultimo Ariosto: dalle Satire ai frammenti autografi* (Pisa: Edizioni della Normale, 2017).

48 See Bontempelli's preface in Ariosto, *Commedie*, 23–4.

49 "accostarsi alquanto alla vita reale del suo tempo" "veramente ariostesche." Ibid., 22.

50 Bontempelli, *Opere scelte*, 571.

51 As Elena Pontiggia concluded in the most recent systematic chronological study of the use of the term Magical Realism: "la sua concezione del realismo magico l'aveva già formulata fin dal 1919–1920, sia pure senza formule, nei romanzi." Pontiggia, "Bontempelli e gli artisti," in *Realismo magico e altri scritti sull'arte*, ed. Pontiggia (Milan: Abscondita, 2006), 134.

52 "rinnovare il romanzo europeo." Bontempelli, *Opere scelte*, 7.

53 "uno che scrive un romanzo, e ci mette la prefazione, non può assolutamente dichiarare di meno." Ibid., 8.

54 I agree with Luigi Baldacci, who detects "un filo conduttore unitario" among the adventures, linked together "sotto l'apparenza di aggregazione aperta di capitoli." Baldacci, *Massimo Bontempelli* (Turin: Borla, 1967), 35. Other critics, such as Mariella Mascia Galateria, read the book as an open work composed of self-sufficient units; see Mascia Galateria, *Tattica della sorpresa e romanzo comico di Massimo Bontempelli* (Rome: Bulzoni, 1977), 21.

55 "alla signorina *Ardita*." Bontempelli, *Opere scelte*, 16.

56 "(Il seguito [...] sarà narrato nel prossimo fascicolo: così in questa mia serie romantica, in cui non deve mancare nessuno degli effetti trovati dall'arte narrativa lungo i secoli, abbiamo anche quello magnificamente sospensivo d'un 'continua' proprio nel punto più ansiosamente vibrato dell'intrico.)" Ibid., 77.

57 He used it only three other times, as a technical term, in literary essays on Leopardi and D'Annunzio and in a footnote: see ibid., 834 and 893; Bontempelli, *Teatro* (Milan: Mondadori, 1947), 7–16.

58 "Lo scrivo per i posteri," he stated in the preface: Bontempelli, *Opere scelte*, 7.

59 See Marco Villoresi, *La letteratura cavalleresca* (Rome: Carocci, 2000), and Alessandro Giammei, "L'Immaginario cavalleresco," in *Il contributo italiano alla storia del pensiero: Letteratura*, ed. Giulio Ferroni (Rome: Treccani, 2015), 78–83.

60 See Maria Cristina Cabani, *Le forme del cantare epico-cavalleresco* (Lucca: Pacini Fazzi, 1988).

61 Daniel Javitch, "Cantus Interruptus in the Orlando Furioso," *Modern Language Notes* 95, no. 1 (1980): 66–80.

62 See Javitch, "Narrative Discontinuity in the Orlando Furioso and Its Sixteenth Century Critics," *Modern Language Notes* 103, no. 1 (1988): 50–74.

63 "la cosa più caratteristica del mondo moderno." Bontempelli, *Opere scelte*, 17.

64 "un dovere categorico, serio, fatale." Ibid., 24.

65 "invece di un romanzo d'avventure io potessi oggi scrivere una perturbante storia d'amore." Ibid.

66 "Aristotele, che dovrò talvolta citare, dice che quando uno è andato troppo avanti bisogna che torni un po' indietro." Ibid., 26.

67 "Il seguire una diritta e predisposta linea d'azione, è ciò che distingue l'uomo dalle bestie." Ibid., 24.

68 "la mia missione sacrosanta." Ibid. 40.
69 "vuole aiutarmi in quest'opera di giustizia?" Ibid., 38.
70 "Racconto fatti veri, accaduti a me." Ibid., 7.
71 "solo anni dopo"; "le constatazioni di legge." Ibid., 91.
72 Jorge Luis Borges, *The Book of Imaginary Beings*, trans. Andrew Hurley (London: Penguin, 1974), 79–81.
73 See in particular Robert Durling, *The Figure of the Poet in Renaissance Epic* (Cambridge, MA: Harvard University Press, 1965), 112–35.
74 Daniel Javitch, "The Advertising of Fictionality in Orlando Furioso," in *Ariosto Today*, ed. Donald Beecher, Massimo Ciavolella, and Roberto Fedi (Toronto: University of Toronto Press, 2003), 106–25.
75 "E facile sarà a chiunque spingere la tesi alle sue conseguenze estreme. – O l'Orlando Furioso? – L'Orlando è un vero e proprio 'romanzo d'appendice,' che l'Ariosto leggeva a puntate (ogni puntata un canto, con tutte le sospensioni proprie al romanzo d'appendice) ai signori e alle signore della corte." Bontempelli, *L'avventura novecentista*, ed. Ruggiero Jacobi (Florence: Vallecchi, 1974), 51.
76 Bontempelli, *Due favole metafisiche* (Milan: Mondadori, 1940).
77 The most recent American edition appeared in a series for young adults, and the prestigious Italian publisher Sellerio republished it both in its classics series, formerly curated by Leonardo Sciascia, and in its collection of books for school-children. The novel is, in any case, included in the "Meridiani" volume dedicated to the author.
78 Lewis Carroll, *Alice nel paese delle meraviglie*, trans. Silvio Spaventa Filippi (Milan: Istituto Editoriale Italiano, 1913).
79 See Alessandro Giammei, *Nell'officina del nonsense di Toti Scialoja. Topi, toponimi, tropi, cronotopi* (Milan: edizioni del verri, 2014), 19–36.
80 The Italian edition of the Istituto Editoriale included both *Alice in Wonderland* and (for the first time) *Through the Looking-Glass*, for a total of twenty-four chapters.
81 Untranslatable examples of these mechanisms are the fact that if one is intelligent enough to "diventare un aquila," she can also fly, or the fact that a "carta topografica" is full of "topolini." See Maria Truglio, "Annie in Wonderland: Vivanti's Sua Altezza! and Children's Literature during Fascism," *Quaderni d'Italianistica* 1 (2004): 121–43. On both *Sua Altezza!* and *The Chess Set in the Mirror* in the landscape of children's literature during fascism, see Mariella Colin, *I bambini di Mussolini* (Brescia: Editrice La Scuola, 2012).
82 Calvino, "Definizione di territorio: il fantastico," in *Una pietra sopra* (Turin: Einaudi, 1980).
83 Bontempelli, *The Chess Set in the Mirror*, trans. Estelle Gilson (Philadelphia: Paul Dry Books, 2007), 31.
84 Ibid., 50.
85 Ibid., 60.

86 Ibid., 64.
87 Ibid.
88 I am borrowing a thematic terminology from Francesco Orlando, *Obsolete Objects in the Literary Imagination: Ruins, Relics, Rarities, Rubbish, Uninhabited Places, and Hidden Treasures* (New Haven: Yale University Press, 2006).
89 Jean Cocteau, *Le Mystère Laïc. Essay d'étude indirecte* (Paris: Editions des Quatre Chemins, 1928), 50.
90 Bontempelli, *The Chess Set*, 65.
91 Written in 1916 for the actress Maria Melato, the play premiered only in 1920, when it was also published in the journal *Comeodia.*
92 See Stefano Cracolici, "La luna che uccide: l'espressionismo di La guardia alla luna di Massimo Bontempelli," *Forum Italicum* 2 (2004): 400–17.
93 See Gigi Livio, *Il teatro in rivolta. Futurismo, grottesco, Pirandello e pirandellismo* (Milan: Mursia, 1976), 120–5.
94 Jo Ann Cavallo, "Boiardo and Ariosto in Contemporary Sicilian Puppet Theatre and the Tuscan-Emilian Epic *Maggio*," *Modern Language Notes* 133 (2018): 48–63.
95 Harold Segel, *Pinocchio's Progeny: Puppets, Marionettes, Automatons, and Robots in Modernist and Avant-Garde Drama* (Baltimore: Johns Hopkins University Press, 1995), 280–97.
96 See Ara Merjian, *Giorgio de Chirico and the Metaphysical City* (New Haven: Yale University Press, 2014), 261.
97 Italo Calvino, *Saggi 1945–1985*, ed. Mario Biraghi (Milan: Mondadori, 1995), vol. 1, 1682.
98 "da fonti dirette e in certo qual modo riscontrati dimorando qualche tempo nei luoghi ove si svolsero." Bontempelli, *Opere scelte*, 343.
99 "confessioni [...] che hanno servito di fondo nello stendere [il] racconto della sua ultima avventura." Ibid., 408.
100 Bontempelli, *Due favole metafisiche*, 233–84. The scores, which were written by Bontempelli for this purpose, are at pages 96–100.
101 "l'intonazione del romanzo inventato." Ibid., 236.
102 Ibid., 238.
103 See Ascoli, *Ariosto's Bitter Harmony*, 224–46.
104 "la mia magia è troppo irrimediabilmente intelligente per evocarti un corteo di mostri." Bontempelli, *Opere scelte*, 390.
105 "è la seconda volta che mi dici addio. Se vuoi posso assumere un atteggiamento magico per profetarti che non sarà l'ultima." Ibid., 356.
106 "col mezzo meno magico, più moderno, più comodo." Ibid., 358.
107 "certamente un ippogrifo non sarebbe rimasto in panne. Non è questo un mezzo ottimo per disincantarti?" Ibid., 365.
108 It was intuited by Vita Giordano in a footnote of her monograph on Bontempelli; see Giordano, *Dalle avventure ai miracoli: Massimo Bontempelli fra narrativa e metanarrativa* (Leicester: Troubador, 2009), 142n.

109 "È necessario che tu non creda di rimanere per forza." Bontempelli, *Opere scelte*, 387.

110 "una diabolica o divina forza l'attirava colà, come parendole che qualcosa di inevitabile della sua vita ancora vi si dovesse compiere." Ibid., 386.

111 "torbidamente fumoso" "combattimento di fumi fuligginosi" "l'aria [...] la dissolse." Ibid., 444.

112 "da tutti i punti del pallido orizzonte, fin dalle estreme lontananze, fluide folle di larve silenziosamente vennero rapide sino a lei [...] Ora tutti si fermarono intorno intorno in un mezzo giro di cui ella era il centro; e l'uno all'altro si stringevano, e contro quel cerchio come contro un invisibile ostacolo." Ibid., 404.

113 Jorge Luis Borges, *Biblioteca Personal* (Buenos Aires: Emecé, 1998), 198–200.

114 Keala Jewell, "Magic Realism and Real Politics: Massimo Bontempelli's Literary Compromise," *Modernism/modernity* 15, no. 4 (2008): 725–44.

115 Except for those that he had originally written in French, which he translated into Italian for the book.

116 On Bontempelli's poetics and its rapports with coeval Italian and French trends, see Beatrice Sica's work and, in particular, "Aux Pays de la Magie: art et littérature 'magiques' en France et en Italie dans l'entre-deux-guerres," *Revue des Études Italiennes* 59, nos. 1–4 (2013): 219–30; "Dai miti del Neosofista al realismo magico di '900': identità, senso del sacro e impegno in Massimo Bontempelli," *Revue des Études Italiennes* 58, nos. 1–2 (2012): 93–108; and "Massimo Bontempelli au miroir d'André Breton: l'aventure de 900 et le surréalisme français," *Revue des Études Italiennes* 57, nos. 1–2 (2011): 43–63.

117 Bontempelli, "Ripresa," *"900": Cahiers d'Italie et d'Europe* 2, no. 5 (1927): 9: "prove ariostesche."

118 "avversione decisa a tutte quelle forme di civiltà che non si confacciano alla nostra o che guastino, non essendo digeribili, le doti classiche degli Italiani; poi: tutela del senso universale del paese, che è, per dirla alla spiccia, il rapporto naturale e immanente fra l'individuo e la sua terra; infine, esaltazione delle caratteristiche nostrane, in ogni campo e attività della vita, e cioè: fondamento cattolico, senso religioso del mondo, semplicità e sobrietà fondamentali, aderenza alla realtà, dominio della fantasia, equilibrio fra spirito e materia." Mino Maccari, "Gazzettino ufficiale di Strapaese," *Il Selvaggio* 15, no. 23 (1927), 125.

119 "occorre che lo scrittore diventi un mestierante, com'erano i pittori del Rinascimento." Bontempelli, *Opere scelte*, 761.

120 Ibid., 211.

121 "Un saggio regime deve saper distinguere (se vuole interessarsi dell'arte) tra l'aiutare e il proteggere. L'aiuto può anche essere discreto, amorevole, fraterno (pericoloso sempre); la protezione è in ogni modo una cosa

pesante e ingombrante, che pone il protetto in condizioni di servitù. Il più bell'esempio è il cardinale Ippolito che proteggeva Ludovico Ariosto, e lo faceva star alzato ad aspettarlo, tardi la sera e pieno di sonno, per farsi da lui cavare gli stivali quando rincasava." Ibid., 772.

122 "interiorismo impoverito." Ibid., 757.

123 "lirismo ultrasoggettivo." Ibid., 768.

124 "una cura d'ironia […] Immaginazione, fantasia: ma niente di simile al favolismo delle fate: niente milleunanotte. Piuttosto che di fiaba, abbiamo sete di avventura." Ibid., 750.

125 "L'Ariosto non intese se non creare un mondo di divertimento e di consolazione, non avrebbe mai potuto sognare i meccanismi critici mediante i quali quel poema ci può apparire oggi (se crediamo alla teoria storica dell'arte) una rappresentazione dello spirito e perfino della storia politica del suo secolo. […] Il contemporaneo crede, per fare un esempio e parlar chiaro, che un romanzo dove si parli di Italia fascista sia *ipso facto* più fascista (cioè rappresenti meglio il nostro tempo, Italia) che un romanzo ove non si parli, per esempio, che d'amore o di viaggi per mare." Ibid., 775–6.

126 Bontempelli, *L'avventura novecentista,* 204.

127 "liberissima fantasia […] continuamente trascinato a richiami, divagazioni, esortazioni, rassegnazioni tutte riferite alla vita politica del suo tempo; perfino quando accompagna Astolfo nella Luna, non perde l'occasione di tirare una frecciata alla presunta donazione di Costantino." Ibid., 206.

128 Following the formula of the "Mostra della rivoluzione fascista," a "Mostra areonautica" was organized in Milan in 1934. It included an entire room for D'Annunzio. See Fernando Esposito, "In the 'Shadow of the Winged Machine …': The Esposizione dell'areonautica italiana and the Ascension of Myth in the Slipstream of Modernity," *Modernism/modernity* 19, no. 1 (2012): 139–54.

129 "La grande poesia dell'aviazione l'hanno fatta l'inventore della favola di Icaro e Ariosto con i voli dell'Ippogrifo." Bontempelli, *Opere scelte,* 203.

130 "il volare […] è poetico solo in quanto è immaginato; e la scienza non farà mai niente che la poesia non abbia già saputo immaginare. La aeropoesia comincia con Icaro, continua con Ruggiero, quattro secoli prima che s'inventi l'aeroplano." Bontempelli, *L'avventura novecentista,* 73.

131 "nessuno ha descritto il volo, e la meraviglia del vedere volare, meglio che l'Ariosto ove parla dell'Ippogrifo." Ibid., 72.

132 "La tradizione è una strada che fa qualunque giro […] l'Ariosto era una grossa scappata alla tradizione Dante." Bontempelli, *Opere scelte,* 763.

133 "dici che noi fanatici dell'architettura nuova abbiamo *orrore* a essere della stessa razza dell'Alberti o del Bramante o del Palladio […] Sarebbe come dire che, trovando io ridicolissimo chi oggi si mettesse a scrivere sonetti o

poemi in terza e in ottava rima, ho l'*orrore* di sentirmi della razza di Dante del Petrarca e dell'Ariosto, *abbandono agli eruditi* la *Commedia* e il *Canzoniere* e l'*Orlando Furioso*." Ibid., 794.

134 "Altri rivoluzionari sono il Boiardo e l'Ariosto; e altra fila di fessi sono i postariosteschi, che credono di riconoscere nel romanzo alla cavalleresca la nuova tradizione da seguire, e la seguono e vanno a finire, con i danteschi e con i petrarchisti, nella fossa comune." Bontempelli, *L'avventura novecentista*, 40.

135 See Cecilia de Aldama Ordóñez, "Romper el cerco. Massimo Bontempelli en América del Sur," *Cuadernos de Filología Italiana* 25 (2018): 181–96.

136 Monica Farnetti, "Ariosto: Landscape Artist," in *Ariosto Today*, 96.

137 Bontempelli, "L'Ariosto geografo," 568.

138 See for instance Ita Mac Carthy, "Ariosto the Traveler," *Modern Language Review* 102, no. 2 (2007): 397–409.

139 Arturo Graf, *Miti, leggende e superstizioni del medioevo* (Milan: Bruno Mondadori, 2002), 1–155.

140 "Ariosto credeva all'isola di Alcina quanto alla città di Ferrara." Bontempelli, "L'Ariosto geografo," 564.

141 "Questo è uno dei tratti più caratteristici del nostro poeta; la sua inventiva fiabesca non si permette mai d'essere illimitata e arbitraria, quale è per esempio quella delle *Mille e una notte*. [...] Creato un elemento fantastico – l'Ippogrifo, o lo scudo, o l'anello, o altro – egli fa vivere questo elemento soprannaturale in mezzo a un mondo che rimane naturale con tutte le sue leggi: l'immaginazione non fa che arricchire la natura, non la forza, né la libera o sfrena. Si viaggia sopra un cavallo alato, ma si scende a dormire a un buon albergo. Questo carattere, eminentemente ariostesco, è anche eminentemente occidentale e profondamente italiano; questa è la tendenza che concilia e assorbe verismo e favolismo, in questo senso l'arte nostra è classica per eccellenza e nel modo più sano. Cose facili; e tutti le accettano se si tratta d'interpretare per mezzo di esse il fascino di un grande poeta che non è più sotto giudizio. Guai invece se tentassimo di additare queste cose come insegnamento della nostra letteratura di domani in un senso validamente italiano: allora ci accusano di sacrilegio; siamo i sacrileghi violatori di due feticci: la realtà e la tradizione: una realtà male interpretata, perché chiamano realtà la stretta documentazione dal vero (sia fotografia di fatti e di costumi, sia analisi di movimenti intimi dell'animo); tradizione male intesa, perché chiamano tradizione le ultime e penultime mode, e non sanno che la tradizione deve sempre riabbeverarsi alle fonti primigenie. Una di queste fonti è lo spirito ariosteo; quando, anni fa, ho additato una legge artistica e l'ho chiamata 'realismo magico,' ho anche avuto cura di citare per l'appunto l'Ariosto; e tutto il 'novecentismo' letterario non è appunto che questo: salire alle nubi in groppa all'Ippogrifo, e scenderne la sera per andare a

mangiare e dormire all'osteria, come fa il nostro savio Ruggiero." Ibid., 553–4.

142 "Tanto rivoluzionario era [...] che non ebbe paura di apparire imitatore." Bontempelli, "S.E. Massimo Bontempelli commemora Ludovico Ariosto," *Il Mattino di Buenos Aires*, October 11, 1933.

143 "rappresenta in un'opera d'arte il suo tempo nel momento stesso in cui crede di straniarsene, di liberarsene e svagare nei campi della più libera fantasia." Ibid.

144 "Questa è la modernità particolarissima, l'aderenza al nostro tempo più che a ogni altro dei passati, dell'*Orlando Furioso.* Non abbiate paura che mi rimetta a parlarvi di novecentismo e di realismo magico; ne ho abbastanza seminato in tutte le scorse settimane per questa città [...] ma insomma, poiché molti di voi ricordano quelle teorie, [...] permettetemi oggi di presentarvi nell'Ariosto uno dei poeti più novecentisti che si possano immaginare. Il nostro tempo [...] sente il bisogno di respiro, di sorriso, di naturalezza, di libertà. Noi tenteremo di darla alla generazione giovane del secolo quest'arte di nuovo e più leggero e insieme profondo respiro; intanto, vi offriamo l'*Orlando Furioso.*" Ibid.

145 "Toro primo" appeared in *Tempo* from November 1939 to January 1940. It was then published in an autonomous edition illustrated by Arturo Martini (Milan: La Chimera, 1943) with the title "Viaggio d'Europa," which remained in the collection *Giro del sole.* "La via di Colombo" appeared in *Tempo* on December 12, 1940.

146 On this story, and in general on Bontempelli's rapport with Ovid, see Alessandro Giammei, "Massimo Bontempelli's Re-Inventions: Magism, Metaphysics, and Modern(ist) Mythology," in *Ovid's Metamorphoses in Twentieth Century Italian Literature,* ed. Alberto Comparini (Heidelberg: Winter Verlag, 2018), 129–41.

147 "L'ideale supremo di tutti gli artisti dovrebbe essere: *diventare anonimi.*" Bontempelli, *Opere scelte,* 762.

148 "il rombo dolce delle ali." Ibid., 538.

149 See, for instance, the "tema ariostesco da Fragonard" reproduced in Fergonzi, "Episodi della fortuna del Furioso nella pittura del Novecento in Italia," in *L'Orlando furioso nello specchio delle immagini,* ed. Lina Bolzoni (Rome: Istituto dell'Enciclopedia Italiana Treccani, 2015), 525–43.

150 The only analysis, if brief, of Bontempelli's long loyalty to the model of Ariosto is in Mara Boccaccio, "Massimo Bontempelli. Un esempio di contaminazione dei generi," *Italianistica* 39, no. 1 (2010): 113–16. Generic parallels between the rational fantasy of Magical Realism and that of Ariosto are mentioned in Luigi Baldacci, *Massimo Bontempelli* (Turin: Borla, 1967), 91 and Walter Pedullà, "L'infinito presente di Ludovico Ariosto," *L'Illuminista* 16 (2006), 55. Renzo Cremante considers Bontempelli's relationship with Ariosto occasional and superficial. Cremante, *Archivi del nuovo. Tradizione e Novecento* (Milan and Naples: Ricciardi, 1984), 50.

3. Eternal Renaissance: Ariosto's Presence in Fascist Ferrara

1 See Diane Ghirardo, "Inventing the Palazzo del Corte in Ferrara," in *Donatello among the Blackshirts: History and Modernity in the Visual Culture of Fascist Italy*, ed. Claudia Lazzaro and Roger Crum (Ithaca: Cornell University Press, 2005), 97–112.

2 On this Romantic landmark, see Stefano Jossa, "Il luogo della poesia: la prigione del Tasso a Sant'Anna," in *Spazi, geografie, testi*, ed. Siriana Sgavicchia (Rome: Bulzoni, 2003), 45–57.

3 Rik Peters, "Actes de présence: Presence in Fascist Political Culture," *History and Theory* 45, no. 3 (2006): 362.

4 Not only through his philosophical works, but also through the policies and reforms that he established as Mussolini's minister of public education and the director of Scuola Normale Superiore. See Gabriele Turi "Giovanni Gentile: Oblivion, Remembrance, and Criticism," *Journal of Modern History* 70, no. 4 (1998): 913–33.

5 "creazione senza creatore." Giovanni Gentile, "L'esperienza pura e la realtà storica," in *La riforma della dialettica hegeliana* (Florence: Sansoni, 1975), 260.

6 Peters, "Actes de présence," 373.

7 Baldini wrote his *Laurea* on Ariosto's late years, curated the first modern edition of the *Cinque canti*, in 1915, and returned to the *Orlando Furioso* in many occasions. On Baldini and Ariosto, see Renzo Cremante, *Archivi del nuovo. Tradizione e Novecento* (Milan and Naples, Ricciardi, 1984), 49–94.

8 His lecture was advertised and integrally published not only in the local *Corriere Padano* but also in other newspapers throughout Italy – including *Corriere della Sera*, which promoted the event a month in advance (April 6, 1928, 3) and printed a report by Baldini the following day ("Italo Balbo sull'Ippogrifo," May 7, 1928, 7). Gabriele D'Annunzio sent two messages to Balbo himself to bless the initiative, and both were printed in the conference proceedings, *L'Ottava d'oro*, ed. Antonio Baldini (Milan: Mondadori, 1933), xxi–xxiii. In the notes, D'Annunzio played with the theme of Ariosto and aviation, embodied by Balbo, with a riddle based on a Renaissance emblem: see Alessandro Giammei, "D'Annunzio emblematista," in *Il dialogo creativo*, ed. Matteo Residori, Maria Pia Ellero, Massimiliano Rossi, and Andrea Torre (Pisa: Pacini Fazzi, 2017), 41–56.

9 "tanto consenso di popolo, un così vivo movimento di curiosità, una aspettazione così gioiosa, accompagna la nostra giornata ariostesca, da un capo all'altro della penisola." Italo Balbo, "Il volo di Astolfo," in *L'Ottava d'oro*, 3.

10 "leggeremo l'Ariosto per esaltare Ferrara l'epica." Ibid., 7.

11 "Piombo tra voi con così tranquilla disinvoltura." Ibid., 3.

12 "Ferrara è pur sempre quella d'allora. Non svanisce mai del tutto sui grandi bronzi dell'età dell'oro lo splendore degli antichi tempi." Ibid., 7.

13 "qualche bianco Ippogrifo moderno dalle ali di seta e dal cuore di acciaio." Ibid., 28.

14 "Rinaldi e Ruggieri, Fieramonti e Fulgosi, Leonetti e Mandricardi novelli, rinati, dopo tanti secoli, in veste di consoli o giornalisti, di uomini politici o di capitani d'industria." Ibid.

15 Nello Quilici, "Bilancio di un centenario," *Corriere Padano*, October 15, 1933, 2. This article, written at the end of the Ariostean celebrations, shows that the nickname assigned by Balbo remained popular. Quilici explains that Ravenna is Sacripante because of his "ricca barba nera" and because he is "travagliato d'amore: d'amore per la sua città."

16 Gaggioli was a rival of Balbo. See Claudio Segré, *Italo Balbo: A Fascist Life* (Berkeley: University of California Press, 1987), 38–43. In the lecture he is addressed as "Olao Mandricardo, nobile generoso paladino di cause sballate" (28).

17 "sotto l'aspetto ariostesco." Balbo, "Il volo di Astolfo," 27.

18 Segré, *Italo Balbo*, 125.

19 Diane Ghirardo, "Città Fascista: Surveillance and Spectacle," *Journal of Contemporary History* 31, no. 2 (1996): 347–72.

20 "un inglese moderno [...] cosa gli manca per essere un perfetto *tipperary* dei tempi moderni? Appena qualche bottiglia di *wisky* e qualche tazza di tè." Balbo, "Il volo di Astolfo," 10.

21 "un sogno nel quale m'era come parso di trovarmi con lui e con altri vecchi amici in una trattoria di Ferrara chiamata all'Ottava d'oro [...] dove si commentava molto liberamente il più scabroso canto dell'Ariosto." Baldini, "Introduzione," in *L'Ottava d'oro*, xv.

22 The 1933 book edited by Baldini and printed by Mondadori includes thirty-nine lectures, but forty-one were given (or at least scheduled) in Ferrara. One essay was added even though there is no record of a corresponding lecture (Arturo Pompeati on Ariosto's melancholy). Mino Maccari, the enemy of Bontempelli's Stracittà (see the previous chapter of this book), gave a lecture titled "L'Orlando e Strapaese" in 1930, but it is not in the volume. Both a 1934 review of *L'Ottava d'oro* and a 1959 bibliographical survey on Ariosto (the first appeared in *Leonardo*, the second in *Nuova Antologia*) report a slightly different title ("L'Orlando a Strapaese") and claim that it was Maccari's decision not to publish his lecture (Alfredo Grilli, "L'Ariosto e la critica," *Nuova Antologia* 475, no. 1897 (1959): 110–14). Luigi Torri, a musicologist who directed the National Library in Turin, was invited to give a lecture about music at the Estense court, scheduled for 1930. It is not clear why his contribution is not included in the final volume. Alfredo Panzini offers a more interesting case: he gave a lecture, in 1931, about

Angelica in Ariosto and Boiardo, but spent most of his time speaking about Boiardo and his prominence over Ariosto. Baldini, whose lecture was about Angelica as well (but only in Ariosto), probably decided to leave Panzini's lecture out in order to avoid a Boiardesque highjacking of Ariosto's celebrations. Panzini, who was single-handedly reviving Boiardo's legacy against the Ariostean trend, responded with a number of editorial initiatives (including the publication of his lecture in a prominent magazine). On this episode and on Panzini and Boiardo in general, see Alessandro Giammei, "Quoting the 'Orlando Innamorato' to Mussolini: Alfredo Panzini and Fascist Reuses of Boiardo," *Purloined Letters* 23 (June 2021): 165–88.

23 "Il poeta è un bell'elettricista [...] costretto a usar la parola solo per la mancanza di una macchina da presa e d'un apparecchio Schufstein." Bragaglia, "L'Ariosto come cineasta," in *L'Ottava d'oro,* 639–66.

24 Gaetano Boschi, "Diagnosi della pazzia di Orlando," in *L'Ottava d'oro,* 195.

25 On this turning point in fascist culture, see Ghirardo, "Città Fascista," 350–1, and Marla Stone, *The Patron State: Culture and Politics in Fascist Italy* (Princeton: Princeton University Press, 1998). Stone's seminal work also helps us to understand the relationship between fascist institutions (such as Ferrara's administration) and the arts in cultural initiatives as one of patronage.

26 Lando Ferretti, "Le armi nell'Orlando Furioso," in *L'Ottava d'oro,* 586: "i gas tossici, i bombardamenti aerei di città aperte, i sottomarini."

27 Ferretti referred to a dilemma, proposed in 1904 by Alfredo Orlandi, about whether or not it was ethical for a defence employee to be able to destroy an entire ship by pressing a button in a safe room many miles away (see ibid., 587).

28 On firearms and war in general in the *Furioso,* see Lina Bolzoni, "O maledetto, o abominoso ordigno: la rappresentazione della guerra nel poema epico-cavalleresco," in *Storia d'Italia,* Annali 18, *Guerra e Pace,* ed. Walter Barberis (Turin: Einaudi, 2002), 201–47.

29 On the anti-gun rhetoric and motives in the late additions to the *Furioso,* see Wiley Feinstein, "The Strategic Rhetoric of Ariosto's Invective against Firearms," *Italian Culture* 8 (1990): 63–73.

30 "Così il poema dell'*Orlando Furioso* si sforza di evocare le future gioie sintetiche dinamiche e simultanee delle nostre parole in libertà futuriste. Così il poema dell'*Orlando Furioso* si sforza di diventare un ricchissimo film di avventure per i nostri schermi di veloce mondialità." Filippo Tommaso Marinetti, "Una lezione di futurismo tratta dall'Orlando furioso," in *L'Ottava d'oro,* 623.

31 "si divertì, anche se non lo scrisse, quando ebbe l'incarico di combattere i briganti della Garfagnana [...]. In realtà il poema è una profusione non meditata né frenata, ma istintiva." Ibid., 619–20.

32 According to Enrico Ghidetti, the "rigida applicazione della precettistica futurista" prevents Marinetti from any "spiraglio interpretativo originale." Ghidetti, *Marinetti futurista* (Naples: Guida, 1977), 219. Sandro Bernardi, on the other hand, argued that Marinetti's "electric or mechanical Ariosto" paved the way for the neo-avant-garde recuperation of the *Furioso* by Sanguineti and Ronconi. Bernardi, "From Poem to Theatre to Cinema: Luca Ronconi's *Orlando Furioso*," in *Ariosto Today*, 204.

33 "Noi futuristi non avremmo mai condannato con brutalità le biblioteche e i musei se vi avessimo trovato degli italiani vivi, ribelli al passato, e ansiosi di utilizzarlo per aiutare potentemente il presente e preparare il futuro." Marinetti, "Una lezione di futurismo," 615.

34 Ariosto's *Egloga* has been traditionally read as an allegory of the conspiracy and an unfair piece of ducal propaganda. Besides Bacchelli's work, see Giorgio Masi, "The Nightingale in the Cage: Ariosto and the Este Court," in *Ariosto Today*, 73–4.

35 Riccardo Bacchelli cited Machiavelli in the concluding remarks of a volume entirely devoted to Ariostean essays (including the lecture) that he published in 1958, stating that Ariosto was "una delle cime del Rinascimento" because, while remaining the greatest inventor of fables, he didn't reject "'la verità effettuale della cosa' […] ossia la realtà del 'mondo.'" Bacchelli, *La congiura di Don Giulio d'Este e altri scritti ariosteschi* (Milan: Mondadori, 1958), 13.

36 The lecture's topic obsessed Bacchelli for years, and eventually developed into the aforementioned volume *La congiura di Don Giulio d'Este.*

37 "L'Ariosto non era un eroe e sapeva che cosa sia esser santi." Bacchelli, "Una difesa di Messer Ludovico," in *L'Ottava d'oro*, 684.

38 "chiude il Rinascimento e apre la porta ai tempi moderni." Achille Campanile, "L'umorismo dell'Ariosto," in *L'Ottava d'oro*, 614.

39 "Ebbene, quell'incendio, con cui l'Ariosto quasi conclude le mille peripezie dei suoi eroi, che s'è divertito a far muovere pazzamente nel gran poema, quell'incendio gigantesco che divora un regno, è un gran falò, in cui crepita, si consuma e si distrugge tutto un mondo letterario di cartapesta, che crolla con fracasso: il mondo dei falsi eroismi inutili, coi suoi guerrieri di latta […] Così oggi: epoca come quella dell'Ariosto, superficiale, scettica, arida, più nell'aspetto che nella sostanza: epoca, come quella dell'Ariosto, delle grandi invenzioni, che mutano la faccia al mondo, epoca della radio, del cinematografo, dei grandi viaggi verso luoghi ignoti, della costruzione solida di alcuni Stati, del crollo di altri, delle rivoluzioni, delle scoperte." Ibid., 612–13.

40 On the Mostra della rivoluzione fascista, which was held from 1932 to 1934 and was a touchstone for fascist events like the Ariostean celebrations, see, in addition to Peters, "Actes de présence," and Stone, *The Patron State*,

Jeffrey Schnapp, *Anno X – La mostra della Rivoluzione fascista del 1932* (Pisa: Istituti Editoriali e Poligrafici Internazionali, 2003).

41 Diane Ghirardo argues that the technical and agricultural exhibitions were redundant in the vicinity of the exhibition of the fascist revolution, and that Mussolini was probably worried about the appeal that such events could have for the general population. She concludes that "the celebration of a history that could now be seen through the light of fascism was itself a sufficient accomplishment in no need of further embellishment" (Ghirardo, "Città Fascista," 360).

42 Seduta della commissione esecutiva, November 25, 1932. Archivio Storico Comunale di Ferrara (ASCFe): Carteggio Amministrativo Sec. XX (XXC), Istruzione Pubblica – Celebrazioni del Centenario Ariostesco (CCA), Busta 36, sottofascicolo 1, "Commissioni e calendario delle manifestazioni."

43 An exhibition of bronze statuettes was also inaugurated at Schifanoia. By mixing classical and early modern sculptures, the organizers mirrored the encounter of ancient Greek deities and Renaissance rulers depicted on the walls of the Hall of the Months in Schifanoia. A fifth exhibition, devoted to modern painting and sculpture, was sponsored by the regional artists' union. Curiously, it was held in Sant'Anna, the quintessential Tasso landmark. The Ariostean Committee did not include it in any of its official programs and propaganda ephemera, but mentioned it in one of the many press communiqués released to local, national, and international agencies: "Né l'arte moderna è stata trascurata: un'esposizione di pittura e scultura moderna, organizzata dal Sindacato Regionale Artisti, è stata aperta al Palazzo Sant'Anna caro alla tradizione tassesca" ("Per celebrare il IV Centenario ..." ASCFe, CCA, b. 36, s. 4 "Comunicati alla stampa"). Many years after his peregrinations with the de Chirico brothers around Ariosto's totemic statue, Filippo de Pisis was one of the main artists featured in this exhibition.

44 The "Sottocommissione per la Esposizione della pittura Ferrarese del '400" was established on November 25, 1932 during the meeting of the executive Committee of the centenary. Seduta della commissione esecutiva, November 25, 1932, ASCFe, CCA, b. 36, s. 1 "Commissioni e calendario delle manifestazioni."

45 A press release issued by the Ariostean Committee on June 7, 1933 stated that 15,751 people visited the exhibition during its first month, calculating that 7,000 additional visitors reached Ferrara on six discounted trains on the first Sunday of the month. "Il I mese della mostra ferrarese del Rinascimento," ASCFe, CCA, b. 36, s. 4, "Comunicati alla stampa."

46 The official communiqué released by the curatorial Committee about this extension states that Mussolini authorized it in response to "richieste formulate dalla stampa italiana e da numerose personalità artistiche,"

adding that the Ministry of Communications prolonged the special train fares. The exhibition eventually closed on December 24. It is interesting to note that the line "Centenario Ariostesco," which opened the official letterhead of the exhibition's administration, was crossed out in this and future documents. By surviving the Ariostean festival, the exhibition, in the end, completely detached from it. "La Proroga della esposizione della pittura ferrarese del Rinascimento," October 31, 1933, ASCFe, CCA, b. 37, s. 3, "Mostra della pittura del Rinascimento."

47 "La Galleria Nazionale di Londra, ad esempio, non manda neppure alle esposizioni che si tengono all'*Academy* e al *Burlinghton Fire* [sic] *Arts Club* in Londra stessa, i quadri che dovrebbero soltanto passare dalla porta di quella Galleria per entrare in un'altra porta prossima." Venturi to Ravenna, April 27, 1932, ASCFe, CCA, b. 37, s. 3, "Mostra della pittura del Rinascimento."

48 "L'idea però è eccellente, ma conviene svilupparla in modo che l'esposizione serva, non solo a raccogliere opere belle e storicamente importanti ma anche tali da permettere di chiarire e risolvere problemi." Ibid.

49 "un quadro storico della vita artistica ferrarese." Ibid.

50 "[...] finché si vedrà il coronamento di tanti sforzi nel genio dell'arta [*sic*] emiliana: il Correggio." Ibid.

51 "Il poema ariostesco [...] galleggia nel vuoto di un rinascimento che pare in esso compendiarsi e concludersi." Giorgio Bàrberi Squarotti, "L'Ottava d'oro e l'Officina ferrarese," in *La cultura ferrarese fra le due guerre mondiali. Dalla scuola metafisica a Ossessione*, ed. Walter Moretti (Bologna: Cappelli, 1980), 146.

52 The archives of the centenary in Ferrara include a number of communications between the administration and the local police forces about how to protect the renewed Palazzo dei Diamanti and the priceless works of art that arrived there. On April 17, 1933, Mayor Ravenna directly contacted the Regio Prefetto della Provincia di Ferrara to alert him about the arrival of the paintings and ask for a personal visit to assess the best way to surveil the building. Ravenna to Andreani, ASCFe, CCA, b. 37, s. 3, "Mostra della pittura del Rinascimento." The following day, the Questore alerted the State Police and the Carabinieri and instructed them to coordinate with the staff of the exhibition. A. Andreani, "Palazzo dei Diamanti – Esposizione della Pittura Ferrarese Vigilanza," April 18, 1933. ASCFe, CCA, b. 37, s. 3.

53 Stanchi to the Amministrazione della Mostra della Rivoluzione fascista, February 16, 1933; Stanchi to Gandolfi at the Italiana Automaticket Coinometer in Rome, February 23, 1932. ASCFe, CCA, b. 37, s. 3, "Mostra della pittura del Rinascimento."

54 See the exchange between the mayor, the president of the Ente Autonomo Case Popolari, and Savonuzzi (January 5–7, 1933) in ASCFe, CCA, b. 37, s. 3, "Mostra della pittura del Rinascimento."

55 "Ferrara ha risonanza mondiale, non per il presente però: per il passato. Abbiamo detto quanto l'eredità sia pesante. Adeguare quel passato al presente, ecco il problema." Nello Quilici, "Ferrara di ieri di oggi di domani," *Rivista di Ferrara* 1, no. 1 (January 1933): 6.

56 The cover of the February issue was designed by Guglielmo Sansoni, an aero-painter who went by the futurist pseudonym Tato. The only other cover of the *Rivista di Ferrara* not signed by Buzzacchi in 1933 was the one of the November issue, a drawing by local painter Donato Santini.

57 "Una battaglia vinta," *Corriere Padano*, May 9, 1933, and "Attraverso le sale della Mostra del Rinascimento," *Corriere Padano*, May 7, 1933.

58 See "Una battaglia vinta," 1.

59 See, for instance, "Attraverso le sale della Mostra del Rinascimento," 3.

60 "procura un vero compiacimento riconoscere un secolo dalle pagine aperte di un libro, dai caratteri, dalla carta, dalle incisioni che hanno adoperato gli stampatori." "La mostra bibliografica," *Corriere Padano*, May 7, 1933, 1.

61 "l'attrattiva che la storia stessa suole suscitare." Ibid.

62 "V'immaginate il viso del gran pubblico anche di quello cosiddetto intellettuale quando sente parlare di Mostra Bibliografica Ariostea? Si arriccia il naso, si corrugano le ciglia e si abbozza un sorriso ironico sulle labbra. Una mostra di libri? Ed ecco che molti immaginano una teoria pressoché uniforme, senza vita e senza significato, di libri, spolverati e puliti di fresco, ma che lasciano sentire anche da lontano l'odor di chiuso e di stantio che si sono accumulati nella secolare prigionia delle biblioteche; e immaginano su questi libri vagare con occhio avido e con sorriso compiacente qualche tipo di professore, calvo e con gli occhiali cerchiati d'oro e colla pelle fatta pergamena come le carte ingiallite di cui si bea, il quale a ogni volger d'occhi dà in escandescenze ammirative." Ibid.

63 "un numero assai ristretto di competenti, di studiosi i quali nell'entusiasmo e nell'amore per i loro libri sembrano un po' degli invasati, dei monomaniaci che trovano ragioni di compiacimento e di gioia in cose che pochi conoscono, pochissimi apprezzano, e ancor più pochi ammirano, e che i più ritengono senza utilità." Ibid.

64 Published in *Il meridiano di Roma* and then collected in Gianfranco Contini, *Esercizî di Lettura. Sopra Autori Contemporanei con un Appendice Su Testi non Contemporanei* (Florence: Parenti, 1939).

65 "un modo, per dir così, statico, che vi ragiona attorno come su un oggetto o risultato, e [...] un modo dinamico, che la vede quale opera umana o lavoro in fieri [...]. Il primo stima l'opera poetica un 'valore'; il secondo,

una perenne approssimazione al 'valore'; e potrebbe definirsi, rispetto a quel primo e assoluto, un modo, in senso altissimo, 'pedagogico.'" Ibid., 36.

66 Using the term "zombie" here, in line with what I theorized in the Introduction of this book, I am also thinking of the critical proposals in *Zombie Theory*, ed. Sarah Juliet Lauro (Minneapolis: University of Minnesota Press, 2017).

67 "Noi abbiamo rivendicato a Ludovico Ariosto questa sua umanità ricca e viva e stupenda [...] e ci siamo ribellati alle interpretazioni arbitrarie che facevano di lui, esagerando certe generiche qualità dei tempi, uno scettico caricaturista o un frigido esteta. Tale lo ripensiamo oggi, nella luce dell'apoteosi popolare. Soltanto la sciagurata pedanteria dei letterati o l'infida manìa dei catoni da strapazzo hanno propagandato l'immagine di un Ariosto diverso, l'Ariosto vivo è questo e non altro: un esemplare stupendo della gentil stirpe latina [...]: il signore e il cantore dell'armonia." "Il signore dell'armonia," *Corriere Padano*, May 7, 1933, 1.

68 "Il poeta ritorna fra noi, magico e familiare, estroso e saggio, maestro di vita serena; ritorna quando nella sua terra prediletta fugate le secolari accidie, un operoso ottimismo spinge gli uomini al lavoro in letizia." Ibid.

69 Fascist abuses of the bodies (and physical features) of historical figures perceived as quintessentially Italian, and in particular of icons from the national literary canon, extended well beyond Ariosto's case. Dante, of course, represents a paradigm of this practice, as demonstrated in a book that deeply inspired the present study: Guy P. Raffa, *Dante's Bones* (Cambridge, MA: Harvard University Press, 2020). I would also like to mention Martina Piperno's paper "Giacomo Leopardi's Zibaldone in the Pages of 'La difesa della razza' (1938–1940)," which she gave at the Columbia Seminar in Modern Italian Studies on March 5, 2021, along with the lecture "Dante's Nose" that she would have given at Bryn Mawr College if it hadn't been for the Covid-19 pandemic.

70 Draft of the invitation for the solemn Mass in commemoration of Ariosto, July 6, 1933, ASCFe, CCA, b. 37, s. 1, "Pubblicazioni Commemorative."

71 "Il Tempio di S. Benedetto, memore delle relazioni secolari con la Famiglia Ariosto, che gli aveva anzi assegnato un piccolo legato per un '*honorato Ufficio*' funebre annuale alla memoria del Poeta – si propone di commemorarlo religiosamente nella mattinata del 6 luglio prossimo con una *Messa Solenne* celebrata e cantata, con ogni probabilità, dai Monaci Benedettini dell'Abbazia di Praglia." Umberto Caramaschi to Renzo Ravenna, June 27, 1933, ASCFe, CCA, b. 37, s. 1, "Pubblicazioni Commemorative."

72 Elenco degli enti da invitare alla messa solenne nell'anniversario della morte di Ludovico Ariosto, 1933, ASCFe, CCA, b. 37, s. 2, "Inviti alle manifestazioni."

73 Elenco delle personalità da invitare alla messa solenne nel giorno della morte di Ludovico Ariosto, 1933, ASCFe, CCA, b. 37, s. 2, "Inviti alle manifestazioni."

74 "in tal sua qualifica, avrebbe diritto ad essere ufficialmente invitata alle attuali celebrazioni centenarie e di più vorrebbe che la salma della madre sua fosse collocata, a spese del Comune, in uno speciale posto e con epigrafe dettata dal Municipio." Ettore Magni to Renzo Ravenna, June 28, 1933, ASCFe, CCA, b. 39, s. 3, "Corrispondenza."

75 "Nel 1933 in occasione del centenario ariostesco a Ferrara la Sig.ra Pochintesta fu invitata a partecipare alle cerimonie commemorative quale rappresentante della famiglia del Poeta; ed ora a cura di quel Podestà la salma venne trasportata a Ferrara per esservi deposta nella Tomba che già racchiude le spoglie mortali dell'ava e della madre sua." "Necrologio," *Rivista Araldica* 34, no. 11 (1936): 430.

76 "Uscito dal Palazzo dei Diamanti, S.M. si è recato alla Casa dell'Ariosto. Il Podestà ha presentato i membri del Comitato Ariostesco di Ferrara e di Reggio Emilia, prof. Borrettini, e la Contessa Daria Malaguzzi Valeri discendente della famiglia della madre dell'Ariosto." "Alla casa di Ariosto," *Corriere Padano*, May 7, 1933, 2.

77 Victoria de Grazia, *How Fascism Ruled Women: Italy, 1922–1945* (Berkeley: University of California Press, 1992), 267–8. Both de Grazia and Ruth Ben-Ghiat, *Fascist Modernities: Italy, 1922–1945* (Berkeley: University of California Press, 2001), 104–5, erroneously identify her as a "Bolognese writer," maybe because she won the Premio Bologna for children's literature in 1939. In any event, her presence in both de Grazia's and Ben-Ghiat's seminal books about fascist culture shows Malaguzzi's prominence in the *ventennio.*

78 Pietro Secchia, *Enciclopedia dell'antifascismo e della Resistenza* (Milan: La Pietra, 1971), 233.

79 Daria Malaguzzi Valeri, *A Milano nella Resistenza* (Rome: Editori Riuniti, 1958).

80 In particular, the Premio Bologna, which she erased from her biographies and curricula after the war. See Renata Lollo, "La letteratura per l'infanzia tra questioni epistemologiche e istanze educative," in *La letteratura per l'infanzia oggi*, ed. Anna Ascenzi (Milan: Vita e Pensiero, 2002), 51.

81 Maria Enrica Balestra, "Writing Women in 1930s Italy," *Italianist* 21, no. 1 (2001): 60–81.

82 Angela Amoroso, "I gruppi di difesa della donna a Milano," in *Donna Lombarda 1860–1945*, ed. Ada Gigli Marchetti and Nanda Torcellan (Milan: Franco Angeli, 1991), 93–111: 99.

83 "Della famiglia paterna e, più precisamente, del padre di Ludovico, non si è mai parlato volentieri, e ciò che se ne conosce non è né lieto né buono." Daria Malaguzzi Valeri, "Tradizione familiare ariostesca," *L'illustrazione italiana* 27 (July 2, 1933): 15–16.

84 “Perché i Malaguzzi e più precisamente Gabriele e Taddea dessero ad un così fatto uomo la loro figlia Daria non è spiegabile.” Ibid., 15–16.
85 “Lontano dalla corte fastosa, ma grossolana e corrotta, libero dagli obblighi della vita di corte che egli, come i cugini, aborriva, Ludovico poteva studiar le antiche storie di cavalieri e di paladini [...]” Ibid., 16.
86 “Come ti avevano abbandonata povera casa d’Ariosto!” “La casa dell’Ariosto,” *Rivista di Ferrara* 1, no. 2 (February 1933): 47.
87 These objects, which are still exhibited in Ariosto’s house today (including the finger), are listed in an 1875 commemorative publication of the Università di Ferrara, which chronicles the hereditary prince’s visit to the house for the anniversary of Ariosto’s birth in 1874. The booklet, which counts seven pages, is titled *Nel IV centenario di Ludovico Ariosto.*
88 William Dean Howells, *Italian Journeys: From Venice to Naples and Beyond,* ed. Matthew Stevenson (New York: Bloomsbury, 2011), 14–15.
89 “quasi ci fossero stati dentro gli spettri e la maledizione per colui che ne toccava una pietra sia pure per metterla a posto.” “La casa dell’Ariosto,” 47.
90 “quali erano le fattezze di Lodovico Ariosto?” “La Mostra iconografica,” *Corriere Padano,* May 7, 1933, 2.
91 “quale sarà, fra i tanti ritratti, il vero Lodovico?” Ibid.
92 Erwin Panofsky, “Jan Van Eyck’s Arnolfini Portrait,” *Burlington Magazine* 64, no. 372 (March 1934): 117–27: 126–7.
93 “un notevole strabismo [...] gli hanno accorciato il pizzo, accomodato la calvizie, soffuso di un pallore inquieto e agitato il volto.” “La Mostra iconografica,” 2.
94 “Di fronte invece vi è un ritratto in cui la capigliatura è polita, lunga fino a farne una zazzera che copre l’orecchio. Lo sguardo aperto e, si direbbe, orizzontale [...]. Un altro invece attribuisce al poeta una fronte alta, con due occhi aperti e gravi, labbra volitive [...], facile è poi riuscito con un paio di baffi spioventi, con un naso greco, una capellatura armoniosa [...]. C’è chi invece ha dato all’Ariosto un’attitudine pensosa, due occhiaie incavate, un naso aquilino dalle narici capaci [...]. Invece c’è stato un artista che gli ha attribuito una fronte fuggente che fa tutt’uno con un naso curvilineo [...].” The physiognomical descriptions continue. The conclusion is “Si dovrà fare la media statistica a mo’ dei gravi scienziati per rifarne un ‘Ariosto medio.’ Non v’è affatto bisogno. Lodovico è caro al cuore di ogni ferrarese anche se la poca abilità, la mancanza d’estro, o la fantasia degli artisti hanno congiurato nei secoli a confondere le vere sembianze del poeta.” Ibid.
95 “Di codesti due celebri dipinti del Tiziano mancano gli originali, ché il ferreo regolamento della National Gallery di Londra ne vieta la rimozione; tuttavia due perfette morbide riproduzioni ne uguagliano la fascinosa bellezza.” Giuseppe Ravegnani, “Giustificazione e lettera a Messer Ludovico Ariosto,” *Corriere Padano,* April 17, 1933, 2.

96 On the 1556 Valgrisi edition, see Ilaria Andreoli, "L'Orlando Furioso 'tutto ricorretto et di nuove figure adornato.' L'edizione Valgrisi (1556) nel contesto della storia editoriale ed illustrativa del poema fra Italia e Francia nel '500," in *Autour du livre italien ancien en Normandie*, ed. Silvia Fabrizio-Costa (Bern: Peter Lang, 2011), 41–132.

97 The headstone of Ariosto's funerary monument still bears the wrong date of death because of a mistake in Pigna's *I Romanzi*. See Michele Catalano, *Vita di Ludovico Ariosto ricostruita su nuovi documenti* (Geneva: Olschki, 1931), 632–3.

98 Panofsky, "Jan Van Eyck's Arnolfini Portrait," 123.

99 "Scopo del cartello è quello di propagandare le feste colle quali la Città Estense intende onorare il suo maggior Poeta." Concorso per un cartello murale, August 15, 1932, ASCFe, CCA, b. 36, s. 3, "Concorso per il cartellone pubblicitario e manifestazioni pubbliche."

100 Renzo Ravenna to the president of the fascist artists' union, November 7, 1932, ASCFe, CCA, b. 36, s. 3, "Concorso per il cartellone pubblicitario e manifestazioni pubbliche."

101 Bando di concorso per un cartello murale, 1932, ASCFe, CCA, b. 36, s. 3, "Concorso per il cartellone pubblicitario e manifestazioni pubbliche."

102 "Una mostra eccezionale: Il cartellone per il Centenario Ariostesco," *Corriere Padano*, January 17, 1933.

103 "Mentre alcuni bozzetti mostravano qualche considerevole pregio artistico [...] la Commissione ha dovuto constatare che neppure tra questi si è presentato il lavoro che rispondesse in pieno agli scopi ed alle esigenze che il tema richiedeva." Renzo Ravenna to the president of the fascist artists' union, November 7, 1932.

104 The four requested subjects were: "1) Il castello estense 2) L'allegoria dell'autunno di Francesco Cossa 3) Il ritratto dell'Ariosto di Tiziano 4) L'affresco del palio di Palazzo Schifanoja." The requested technique ("in photomontage") was underlined in the letter to Nizzoli. Renzo Ravenna to Marcello Nizzoli, February 8, 1933, ASCFe, CCA, b. 36, s. 3, "Concorso per il cartellone pubblicitario e manifestazioni pubbliche." The committee called Ariosto's supposedly "actual" portrait "di Tiziano" because, at the time, the 1556 engraving was considered to be a copy of a lost drawing by Titian. See Roger Fry, "Titian's Ariosto," *Burlington Magazine for Connoisseurs* 63, no. 368 (November 1933): 194–5.

105 ASCFe, CCA, b. 41, "Clichés usati per il centenario Ariostesco."

106 "i ritrattisti dell'Ariosto lo pittarono con o senza barba, giovane o vecchio." Aroldo Canella, "La mostra iconografica," *Rivista di Ferrara* 1, no. 2 (February 1933).

107 Cesare Cavara, *Sulla prima sepoltura di L. Ariosto e su Gregorio da Montagnana* (Vicenza: Burato, 1872).

108 Percy Bysshe Shelley, *Letters*, ed. Nathan Haskell Dole (London: Virtue and Company, 1906), 58.
109 Marianne Colston, *Journal of a Tour in France, Switzerland, and Italy, during the Years 1819, 20, and 21* (London: Whittaker, 1823), 248.
110 Nicola Watson, *The Author's Effects: On Writer's House Museums* (Oxford: Oxford University Press, 2020), 4.
111 "Dalla contrada del Mirasole mi veniva incontro messer Ludovico, con un sorriso enigmatico: giovane, mi diceva, la poesia è nella vita vivente che scorre e riflette, insieme con le nuvole della fantasia, le luci della realtà [...] Tutto è precario, o giovane, quel che tu giudichi assoluto e certo; il secol si rinnova [...] ma il fuoco rinasce sotto la cenere: intangibile e incorruttibile, lo specchio del cuore riflette il giuoco della vita che vince la morte. Compresi allora perché l'Ariosto fosse il più moderno tra i poeti italiani: e come il suo ritorno coincidesse con la terza risurrezione dalle ceneri della città di Ferrara." Nello Quilici, "Il poeta dell'eterno rinascimento" (1933), in *Otto Saggi* (Ferrara: Nuovi problemi, 1934), 43.
112 For instance, Ida Wyss became "J. Wyss," Edmund Gardner turned into "L.G. Gardner," and masculine agreements are used to speak about Ella Noyes.
113 "lavora la materia umana col pollice dell'artista." Quilici, "Il poeta dell'eterno rinascimento," 44.
114 "Questo non era più l'incubo romantico della poesia decadente, ma lo stimolo alla nuova grandezza." Ibid.
115 "il segreto della modernità dell'Ariosto va ricercato nell'intimo pregio della poesia di cui ci ha fatto liberalmente dono e per la quale si è sollevato in una sfera incantata, ove non esistono distinzioni cronologiche e ove passato e futuro coincidono in un presente eterno." Giulio Bertoni, *Ludovico Ariosto. Discorso pronunciato a Ferrara nel teatro comunale il 15 ottobre 1933 – XI* (Rome: Reale Accademia d'Italia, 1933), 5.
116 "il passato che entra nella storia è il passato che sopravvive nel presente: è lo stesso presente [...] il vero presente è estratemporale, eterno [...] sicché il processo dell'esperienza nell'attualità sua è un processo eterno." Giovanni Gentile, *La riforma della dialettica hegeliana* (Florence: Sansoni, 1942), 254.
117 "Ma battiamo alla porta, Messere. Al picchio, una linda vecchietta viene ad aprire, e, nel vederTi, meravigliata Ti fa onore." Ravegnani, "Giustificazione e lettera a Messer Ludovico Ariosto," 2.
118 "Messer Ludovico ritorna. Ritorna semplice, sorridente, bonario, un po' curvo sotto il peso della gloria plurisecolare, un po' lento per la perduta consuetudine del moto. Lo hanno destato dall'eterno sonno i rumori che si elevano, osannanti, intorno al suo nome e egli ha lasciato il marmoreo sepolcro del Palazzo delle Scienze e si è avviato verso la modesta casa

di contrada Mirasole." Alberto Brizio, "Il ritorno di Messer Lodovico," *Illustrazione del Popolo* (April 23, 1933).

119 Howells, *Italian Journeys*, 16.

120 The booklet is sometimes indexed in libraries as a publication of the "Nègar d'Ungia" editions. The name of this fictitious press is a pun: it is Ferrarese dialect for "nero d'unghia," literally "black of the nail," or "nail dirt," an expression that means "a little bit."

121 The review in *Rivista di Ferrara* ambiguously reports that the poster was "miraculously" animated on the stage, probably alluding to some form of special effect ("il 'fotomontaggio' di Nizzoli che, quasi per miracolo, prendeva vita e movimento)." Boarino and Boarone, "Attualità del mese," *Rivista di Ferrara* 1, no. 12 (December 1933): 47.

122 Ghirardo, "Città fascista," 349.

123 Stefano Cavazza, *Piccole patrie. Feste popolari tra regione e nazione durante il fascismo* (Bologna: il Mulino, 1997).

124 Ghirardo, "Città fascista," 366.

125 "La Sua pelle immeritatamente rimarrà intatta, solo il cervello rimarrà scombussolato e l'animo pienamente conscio dell'ingiustificato affronto compiuto verso una consorella città italiana nel rubarle impunemente questa tradizione." The Sienese people to Renzo Ravenna, 1933, ASCFe, CCA, b. 39, s.1, "Manifestazioni popolari e riunioni sportive."

126 Bilancio del Centenario Ariostesco, 1934, ASCFe, CCA, b. 40, "Bilanci. Personale. Contabilità e finanziamenti."

127 The Committee was in touch with various institutions, including Andrea Torres of Rome's ICSA (February 8, 1933), for recommendations about companies who could create sixteenth-century costumes for mass spectacles. They ended up choosing the Ditta Egisto Peruzzi in Florence, which, on February 25, 1933, sent a seven-page invoice. The most important costumes, however (those of notable figures, part of the choreographies), were made entirely in Ferrara under Casati's supervision, using material imported from all over northern Italy. The correspondence with artisans (including hairdressers and embroiderers) is in ASCFe, CCA, b. 38, s. 2, "Palio (1933 e 1934)."

128 Raffaele Bacci (Società Storica per il Gioco del Calcio Fiorentino) to the Ariostean Committee, January 18, 1933, ASCFe, CCA, b. 38, s. 2, "Palio (1933 e 1934)."

129 Ilaria Pavan, for instance, noted that the "Borgo San Luca" was in fact based on the "Gruppo Rionale Fascista 'Arturo Breviglieri,'" and that the eponymous "Rione San Giorgio" of the Palio was really the "P.N.F. Fascio di Borgo San Giorgio." Pavan, *Il podestà ebreo* (Bologna: il Mulino, 2006), 88.

130 Ravenna to Giuseppe Malinverni, May 29, 1933, ASCFe, CCA, b. 38, s. 2, "Palio (1933 e 1934)."

131 Giudice della Massaria (Luigi Andreis) to Ravenna, May 11, 1933, ASCFe, CCA, b. 38, s. 2, "Palio (1933 e 1934)."

132 "Popolo di Ferrara! A gloria e onore del beato Giorgio, santo patrono della dilettissima nostra città, noi signori di Ferrara abbiamo stabilito che il giorno quattro del corrente mese di giugno siano ripristinate le corse al palio istituite con ordinanza dei nostri duchi, i principi d'Este. Sia l'aquila o il diamante, l'unicorno o la ruota, la lince o la granata, l'idra o lo steccato che afferri la vittoria, è sempre gloria d'Este e gloria di Ferrara. Salute a voi consoli e massari, cavalieri e fanti, salute a te popolo tutto accorso in esultanza da ogni terra perché si rinnovelli il grido: 'Este Viva!'"

4. Theatrical Ghosts: Not Adapting the *Orlando Furioso* in Late Modernity

1 As it revolves on this particular modern process of trans-mediation, this chapter is indebted to the pioneering work, in the field of Italian studies, of Millicent Marcus, *Filmmaking by the Book: Italian Cinema and Literary Adaptation* (Baltimore: Johns Hopkins University Press, 1993).

2 On the history of the Maggio and on Votto's role, see Leonardo Pinzauti, *Il Maggio Musicale Fiorentino dalla prima alla trentesima edizione* (Florence: Vallecchi, 1967).

3 "Illustre Maestro, alcuni mesi fa parlammo a Roma della possibilità di realizzare al Prato Verde della Meridiana nel Giardino di Boboli per il Maggio Musicale 1949 l'Orlando Furioso. L'idea, che ha incontrato la entusiastica approvazione del ceto intellettuale fiorentino, mi alletta anche oggi: sono perplesso soltanto per quanto riguarda il testo della riduzione. Penso che bisognerebbe, al massimo entro due mesi, esserne già in possesso per averne tutti gli elementi per la formazione della compagnia e la messinscena. Penso anche che la elaborazione del testo debba assolutamente venir fatta sotto le Sue direttive per ottenere un lavoro oltre che di pregio letterario, che abbia positivi aspetti teatrali. [...] Desidererei incontrarmi con Lei per trattare esaurientemente il progetto in tempo utile per una realizzazione degna in tutto delle tradizione dell'Ente che ho l'onore dio rappresentare e del Suo grande nome di Regista." Pariso Votto to Luchino Visconti, August 23, 1948. Fondazione Gramsci Roma (FGR), Luchino Visconti 1906–76 Papers (LV), CR.337.1, "Teatro di Prosa (1936–1973)."

4 "un evento che non ha modelli che lo precedono." Cesare Milanese, *Luca Ronconi e la realtà del teatro* (Milan: Feltrinelli, 1973), 11.

5 "da rappresentarsi per mezzo di una serie di 'stazioni' scenografiche, le quali volevano richiamare i quadri dei cantastorie popolari." Giulio Cesare Castello, "Ritratti critici di contemporanei. Luchino Visconti," *Belfagor* 31, 10, no. 2 (March 31, 1955): 166.

6 "mettere in scena l'Orlando furioso a Boboli, smembrandolo in un certo numero di scene da recitare in luoghi diversi, alla maniera dei cantastorie." Caterina D'Amico De Carvalho, *Luchino Visconti: Il mio teatro (1936–1953)* (Bologna: Cappelli, 1979), 160. The same idea had already been expressed in D'Amico De Carvalho, *Visconti: Il Teatro* (Reggio Emilia: Edizioni del Teatro Municipale, 1977), 205: "doveva essere realizzato in diverse azioni spezzate e dislocate in diversi punti di Boboli."

7 "una visione grandiosa e spettacolare quanto rivoluzionaria, un percorso nella sfera del fantastico e del sogno, da realizzare su diverse aree di recitazione nei digradanti giardini di Boboli. Le varie scene della riduzione teatrale dall'opera ariostesca si sarebbero incrociate e moltiplicate su vari piani." Cristina Gastel Chiarelli, *Musica e memoria nell'arte di Luchino Visconti* (Milan: Archinto, 1997), 11.

8 "la messa in discussione del teatro come forma chiusa, sia attraverso il ricorso a testi non drammaturgici [...] sia attraverso un lavoro sullo spazio che può uscire dalla cornice scenica e dilagare in sala." Federica Mazzocchi, *Le regie teatrali di Luchino Visconti: Dagli esordi a Morte di un commesso viaggiatore* (Rome: Bulzoni, 2010), 168.

9 "I progetti non realizzati appaiono oggi estremamente avanzati e testimoniano l'interesse del regista per la dilatazione della forma-teatro. [...] Visconti pensava così a un allargamento della nozione di testo drammaturgico, intuendo forme e modalità che troveranno piena realizzazione nel teatro di ricerca degli anni Sessanta." Ibid., 228.

10 "È senz'altro un incredibile antecedente." Stefano Tomassini, *New York Furioso: Luca Ronconi e "quelli dell'Orlando" a Bryant Park (1970)* (Venice: Marsilio, 2018), 28.

11 On this production, in the context of the twentieth-century reception of *Aminta,* see Alessandro Giammei, "L'Aminta dell'Officina Bodoni: un libro rinascimentale alle soglie della seconda guerra mondiale," *Nuova Informazione Bibliografica* 14, no. 1 (2014): 185–91.

12 See Antonio Gramsci, *The Modern Prince and Other Writings* (New York: International Publishers, 1957).

13 On Pirandello as a reader of Ariosto, see Antonio Saccone, "Ariosto letto da Pirandello," *Studi Rinascimentali* 2 (2004): 143–9; and Stefano Jossa, "Pazzia e finzione. Appunti sul modello ariostesco nella letteratura del XX secolo," *Anticomoderno* 4 (1999) 349–81.

14 "la vera magia dello stile ariostesco." Luigi Pirandello, *L'umorismo e altri saggi,* ed. Enrico Ghidetti (Florence: Giunti, 1994), 73.

15 "è una magia che entra in un'altra." Ibid., 74.

16 "E fin da principio lo stile [di Ariosto] ha virtù magica. Tutto il primo canto è, nella rappresentazione, fantasmagorico, corso da lampi, d'apparizioni fugaci. E questi lampi non sprazzano per abbagliar soltanto i lettori, ma

anche gli attori della scena [...]. Il poeta esercita, cosciente, questa sua magia [...], sbalordisce e sorride dello sbalordimento altrui e de' suoi stessi personaggi." Ibid.

17 I am citing from Walter Geerts' analysis of Pirandello's theoretical work on the *Furioso*: "radicale espansione dello spazio fittizio [...] la finzione invade lo spazio estrafittizio." Geerts, "La magia dello stile: le glosse pirandelliane sull'Orlando Furioso," in *Pirandello saggista*, ed. Gösta Andersson and Paola Daniela Giovannelli (Palermo: Palumbo, 1982), 73.

18 It is unlikely that the typescript is a transcription of a pre-existing manuscript draft. A number of minor corrections that are not mere typos (two on the first page, seven on the fourth, another one on the fifth) are directly typed (covering the deleted words with "x") without superscript or interlinear additions. This shows that Visconti was composing on the keys rather than copying a definitive draft.

19 A number of formal imprecisions are not corrected, while potentially confusing typos are. For instance, in the first paragraph of the first page, the verb "dà" is typed without an accent and remains uncorrected, while the typo "icristiani" for "i cristiani" is fixed with a pencil stroke between article and noun. The third paragraph in the same page is very convoluted, with sentences like "Siccome non ha mantenuto la promessa, ora egli si tiene l'elmo caduto dicendogli che se ne vuole un altro prezioso, si acquisti col suo suo valore o quello di Orlando o quello di Rinaldo." However, the only handwritten interventions in the whole paragraph are to correct the typo "ricerrare" into "ricercare" and to change the generic adjective "suo" (which could mean his, hers, or its) into "di lui," which clarifies who the sentence is talking about.

20 "Angelica 'fugge tra selve spaventose e scure' (Il narratore, sotto una forma qualsiasi, è necessario alla realizzazione del poema)." Luchino Visconti, *Orlando Furioso*, 1948, FGR, LV, CR.337.1 "Teatro di Prosa (1936–1973)."

21 This choice mirrors the original text, in which Ariosto's authorial voice introduces Bradamante before starting to narrate the episode (II.31).

22 "Il Narratore prende a parlare di Bradamante, sorella di Rinaldo. Essa è innamorata di ruggiero. Essi si sono visti una volta sola, e ora Bradamante va in cerca di lui. Dopo aver atterrato Sacripante (v scena del canto i), ella giunge in un boschetto dove incontra seduto pensoso, addolorato e lasso un cavaliere: PINABELLO. sollecitato dalle domande della donzella sulla ragione del suo dolore, egli narra la sua straordinaria avventura." Visconti, *Orlando Furioso*.

23 "Ecco però giungere due cavalieri GRADASSO e RUGGIERO guidati da un Nano, che vengono a sfidare lo strano cavaliere. Gradasso dà fiato al corno. Il cavaliere appare sul suo cavallo alato e combatte dall'alto i due cavalieri impotenti di fronte a questa specie di aeroplano ante-litteram. Poi il

cavaliere, che aveva lo scudo coperto da un drappo di seta celeste, scopre lo scudo, che manda un tale bagliore da abbacinare e tramortire. Pinabello perde i sensi. Quando si riprende non c'è più nessuno. Solo il castello d'acciaio innanzi a lui. Ed ora eccolo a lamentarsi." Ibid.

24 www.galassiaariosto.sns.it.

25 "Non è necessario leggere tutto l'*Orlando furioso* da cima a fondo per afferrarne lo spirito. L'importante è percepire un'idea dell'*Orlando*, sapere che cosa può essere. Non è poi neanche vero che quando leggiamo un testo sappiamo benissimo cos'è." Franco Quadri, *Il rito perduto* (Turin: Einaudi, 1973), 82.

26 "questo *Orlando* risulta un vero e proprio saggio critico sull'*Orlando* ariostesco." Ibid., 87.

27 "Purtroppo il progetto non viene realizzato, per mancanza di tempo per la riduzione del testo." D'Amico De Cervalho, *Luchino Visconti: Il mio teatro*, 160.

28 On which see Sandro Bernardi, "From Poem to Theatre to Cinema: Luca Ronconi's *Orlando Furioso*," in *Ariosto Today* (Toronto: University of Toronto Press, 2003), 195–210.

29 Susie Eisenhuth, "Medieval Romp Silly, but a Visual Wow," in *Sydney Morning Herald*, November 27, 1983.

30 There are no surviving copies of this film. For an analysis that includes the following two versions of the *Liberata* by Guazzoni, see Antonio Costa, "Fedelmente infedele. La Gerusalemme Liberata di Enrico Guazzoni dalla versione muta del '18 alla versione sonorizzata e parlata del '35," *Chaiers d'études romanes* 13 (2005): 131–41.

31 Ezio Raimondi, "Introduzione," in Torquato Tasso, *Gerusalemme liberata*, ed. Bruno Maier (Milan: Rizzoli 1982): vii–viii.

32 "I nostri fratelli combattono e vincono, e sulle moschee sventola il tricolore. È la guerra eterna della croce contro la mezzaluna." Aldo Bernardini and Vittorio Martinelli, *Il cinema muto italiano: I film degli anni d'oro, 1911* (Turin: ERI, 1991), 209.

33 "The Crusaders," *Bioscope* (March 6, 1919): 66. Such a final scene is not present in the copy of the film stored in the George Eastman Museum. In his essay on Guazzoni's versions of the *Liberata*, Costa reports that it is not in the copy stored at the Cineteca Nazionale in Rome either. It is likely that it was added in Britain for nationalist and pro-Israel propaganda.

34 I would like to thank Jane Tylus for pointing out to me the Ariostean features of Soldini's *Bread and Tulips* (2000), in which the Icelandic co-protagonist learned Italian by reading and reciting the *Furioso*. On this linguistic aspect, see Matteo Milani, "L'italiano aulico del 'prode Fernando' in Pane e tulipani (Soldini 1999)," *Italianistica* 45, no. 1 (2016): 167–78. On Ariosto and Jarmusch, see Stefano Jossa, "Laboratorio d'intrecci ed eros

in agguato: Ariosto oggi," in *L'Orlando furioso: incantamenti, passioni e follie*, ed. Stefano Parmiggiani (Reggio Emilia: Silvana Editoriale, 2016), 339–95; and Jossa, "Entertainment and Irony: The Orlando Furioso from Modern to Postmodern," in *Ariosto, the Orlando Furioso and English Culture*, ed. Jane Everson, Andrew Hiscock, and Stefano Jossa (Oxford: Oxford University Press, 2019), 286–307.

35 "Forse spaventa il cinema di allora l'arditezza delle scene e delle situazioni del poema di Ariosto." Cristina Bragaglia, "L'Orlando furioso e il cinema: il ricalco e l'allusione," in *Boiardo, Ariosto e i libri di battaglia*, ed. Andrea Canova and Paola Vecchi Galli (Novara: Interlinea, 2007), 424.

36 See Silvio D'Amico, *Enciclopedia dello Spettacolo* (Rome: Unedi, 1954–66), 4:395. Other mentions of De Liguoro's *Orlando Furioso* either reference D'Amico or draw on its information. See John Stewart, *Italian Film: A Who's Who* (Jefferson, NC: McFarland, 1994), 130; Gian Piero Brunetta, *Cent'anni di cinema italiano* (Rome and Bari: Laterza, 1991), 94; Renato Tomasino, "Ariosto Barocco e Neo-Barocco," *Rope* 4–5 (2011): 126.

37 In any event, it is unlikely that De Liguoro's *Orlando Furioso* is the same early unrealized project mentioned in Cristina Bragaglia's essay: De Liguoro did not work in Rome at the Cines studios, but in Milan at Milano Film.

38 "Orlando Furioso," *Motion Picture Herald*, July 1, 1966.

39 "Il film non realizzato più famoso della storia del cinema." This often quoted statement was made by Italy's most famous entertainment journalist, Vincenzo Mollica, in the preface to the edition of the script of *The Journey*. See Federico Fellini, *Il viaggio di G. Mastorna*, ed. Ermanno Cavazzoni (Macerata: Quodlibet, 2008), i.

40 See Marcus Perryman's introduction in Fellini, *The Journey of G. Mastorna: The Film Fellini Didn't Make*, ed. Dino Buzzati, Brunello Rondi, and Bernardino Zapponi (New York: Berghahn Books, 2013), 9–11.

41 On this topic, see Alessandro Casanova, *Scritti e immaginati: I film mai realizzati di Federico Fellini* (Rimini: Guaraldi, 2005).

42 John Baxter, *Fellini: The Authorised Biography* (London: Fourth Estate, 1993), 56.

43 The *Satyricon* was Fellini's first adaptation of a literary work, in 1969. He adapted Casanova's memoirs in 1976 (*Fellini's Casanova*). He never completed his adaptation of Kafka, but the unfinished project is prominently featured in *Intervista* (1987).

44 Tullio Kezich, *Federico Fellini: His Life and Work* (New York: Faber and Faber, 2006), 25.

45 Federico Fellini, *Raccontando di me: Conversazioni con Costanzo Costantini* (Rome: Editori riuniti, 1996), 224.

46 Fellini, "Intervista di Aldo Tassone a Federico Fellini," in *Casanova: rendez-vous con Federico Fellini*, ed. Laura Betti (Milan: Bompiani, 1975), 140.

47 The most recent and thorough analysis of Fellini's use of Ariosto in *Casanova* is Francesco Brenna, "Fellini's Negative Art: Petrarch and Ariosto in Il Casanova," *Forum Italicum* 54, no. 2 (2020).

48 This intertextual genealogy is rooted in classical literature. For an updated intertextual reading of Ariosto's third satire, see Ida Campeggiani's commentary in Ludovico Ariosto, "Satira III," in Ariosto, *Satire*, ed. Emilio Russo (Rome: Edizioni di Storia e Letteratura, 2019), 95–130. An intermediate link between Bontempelli and Cavazzoni could be in Tommaso Landolfi's short story *Il racconto del lupo mannaro*. This story of brutish men catching the moon through a chimney was included by Gianfranco Contini in his anthology *Italie Magique* in 1946 along with writings by Bontempelli and other "magical" Italian writers. It also opened Italo Calvino's selection of Landolfi's best writings in 1982.

49 Kezich, *Federico Fellini*, 385.

50 Olivier Curchod, "Un monde impassible et souriant: Entretien avec Bernardino Zapponi," *Positif* 413–14 (1995): 69.

51 On Fellini's literary influences, see Federico Pacchioni, *Inspiring Fellini: Literary Collaborations behind the Scenes* (Toronto: University of Toronto Press, 2014).

52 Mira Liehm, *Passion and Defiance: Italian Film from 1942 to the Present* (Berkeley: University of California Press, 1986), 25.

53 On Blasetti's role in the revival of the film industry, see Stephen Gundle and Michela Zegna, "Art, Entertainment and Politics: Alessandro Blasetti and the Rise of the Italian Film Industry, 1929–1959," *Historical Journal of Film, Radio and Television* 40, no. 1 (2020): 6–28.

54 At the end of a long and tense exchange, on August 23, 1942, Blasetti wrote a letter to Bassoli detailing all their wrongdoings and concluding "non mi resta che dichiarare decaduti tutti i termini delle mie offerte di conciliazione e delle mie rinuncie [sic] incondizionate […] passerò tutto l'incartamento che ci riguarda all'Avv. Ercole Graziadei." Cineteca di Bologna (CdB), Archivio Alessandro Blasetti (AAB), busta CRS 17, CP 49, 0185, "Corrispondenza con Renato Bassoli e Sergio Amidei, 1941–1943."

55 Verbale di Conciliazione di Controversia Individuale del Lavoro, January 11, 1943, CdB, AAB, CRS 17, CP 049, 0185, "Corrispondenza con Renato Bassoli e Sergio Amidei, 1941–1943."

56 See Stefano Masi, *A. Blasetti: 1900–2000* (Rome: Comitato Alessandro Blasetti per il centenario della nascita, 2001), 362; and Luca Verdone, *I film di Alessandro Blasetti* (Rome: Gremese, 1989), 54.

57 On the commercial landscape of Italian cinema under fascism and Blasetti's position, see Stephen Gundle, "We Have Everything to Learn from the Americans: Film Promotion, Product Placement and Consumer Culture in Italy, 1945–1965," *Historical Journal of Film, Radio and Television* 40, no. 1 (2020): 55–83.

58 “1. Quale dovrebbe essere il motivo principale di una traduzione cinematografica dell' ‘Orlando’? E quali i temi che, comunque, non si dovrebbero omettere?

2. Su quali dei personaggi principali dovrebbe quindi essere impostato l'interesse spettacolare del film? E di quali dovrebbe per lo meno esser fatto cenno?

3. Quali degli elementi magici, dei fattori favolosi, dei complessi coreografici dell'‘Orlando’ sarebbe più interessante includere nel film?

4. Quali in ogni modo gli elementi e i personaggi che potrebbero essere omessi senza preoccupazione di tradire lo spirito del poema?

5. Poiché inevitabilmente la maggior parte della materia dell'‘Orlando’ dovrà essere omessa per ovvie esigenze di durata della pellicola, quale via sarà consigliabile: concentrare l'attenzione su un solo gruppo di episodi tali e quali li racconta l'Ariosto, con esclusione quindi di tutta la materia e i personaggi che non li riguardano; oppure una interpretazione sintetica del poema che comprenda la massima parte dei suoi elementi principali, ciò che comporterebbe naturalmente lo spostamento e la diversa utilizzazione di fatti e personaggi?”

I am transcribing the questions, in the original order, from various response reports preserved in CdB, AAB, CRS 17, CP 049, 0186, “Relazioni ‘Orlando furioso’ 1937, 1942.”

59 I am borrowing this terminology from recent developments of Narratology that consider the cohesiveness of fictional universes across media. See *Possible Worlds Theory and Contemporary Narratology*, ed. Alice Bell and Marie Laure Ryan (Lincoln: University of Nebraska Press, 2019).

60 The Blasetti archive at the Cineteca di Bologna includes two versions of this document, which was likely circulated, in different copies, among Blasetti's correspondents. One counts 183 pages, the other 193. They are preserved, along with the correspondence and the questionnaire responses here cited, in the “Progetti non realizzati” subsection of the “Copioni 1928–1981; 1995” section of the fondo Blasetti. Their segnatura numbers are CP 49, 0187 and CP 50, 0188.

61 “Il film ‘L'Orlando furioso’ non dovrà essere indegno del poema; e, per esserne degno, la prima dote che gli si chiederà sarà quella di essere un film.” Relazione di Mario Gromo [1942], CdB, AAB, CRS 17, CP 049, 0186, “Relazioni ‘Orlando furioso’ 1937, 1942.”

62 “Non quindi un'illustrazione più o meno colorita, non una parafrasi più o meno scolastica e ossequente, non una ‘divulgazione’ più o meno popolare (termine molto di comodo, e che di solito non divulga un bel nulla).” Ibid.

63 “Con la parola incastro intendevo per l'appunto di definire l'attribuzione di un episodio a questo anziché a quel personaggio; e con la parola sviluppo

arrivavo persino ad ammettere un'eventualità di … aggiunta a ciò che nell'Ariosto c'è, un'aggiunta di fantasia degli sceneggiatori, un'aggiunta, naturalmente, dovuta soprattutto a esigenze di ritmo o di chiarimento." Gromo to Blasetti, May 31, 1942, CdB, AAB, CRS 17, CP 049, 0185, "Orlando. Corrispondenza 1941–1943."

64 "Questo film potrà essere un'occasione tanto importante quanto memorabile perché il cinema ritrovi alcune delle sue possibilità più vere: quelle di poter concretamente esprimere il fantastico. Brani superbi di vero cinema, di cinema 'puro,' subito si offrono a chi abbia anche soltanto una superficiale conoscenza del poema [...] Un'occasione tanto difficile quanto stupenda." Relazione di Mario Gromo [1942].

65 "Non credo perciò che il 'motivo' principale del film [...] possa essere confuso con lo 'scheletro del soggetto' da trarsi dal poema; ma debba, quel 'motivo,' intendersi come l'inconfondibile e necessario 'tono' da dare al film." Ibid.

66 "Per questo, non si sarà mai abbastanza fedeli allo *spirito* dell'Ariosto. E saranno allora il fantastico e il favoloso cuciti a filo doppio nell'avventura e nella [*sic*] gesta, e ancora avvolti come in un velo di lieve ironia, che è la più vera 'modernità' dell'Ariosto: come di chi gode del suo gioco, che ben sa essere un gioco.

Bandire quindi ogni elemento realistico, anche quando l'impresa di Carlo Magno potrebbe apparentemente pretenderlo; non cadere mai, nemmeno a tratti, nemmeno per un istante, nella cosiddetta ricostruzione storica [...]. Sarà questo il modo migliore per essere fedeli, non alla lettera, ma allo spirito del poema; e per contemporaneamente conquistarsi la più assoluta aotonomia di espressione cinematografica." Ibid.

67 In particular, see Cristina Bragaglia, *Lo specchio dei mondi impossibili: Il fantastico nella letteratura e nel cinema* (Florence: Aletheia, 2001), 173–94.

68 "Una raggiunta unità di stile vorrà dire il trionfo del film. È da questa unità, e da questa soltanto, che il film potrà infatti avere la sua compiuta e inconfondibile atmosfera, la sua persuasione, la sua efficacia, anche se rivolto ad esprimere soltanto alcuni episodi del poema; e sarà questa unità di stile a imporsi tanto allo spettatore provveduto quanto all'ignaro." Relazione di Mario Gromo [1942].

69 "Due motivi dovrebbero prevalere nel film: la umanità di Orlando, la cui pazzia è una punizione di Dio ma è anche il mezzo di cui si serve l'Onnipotente per richiamare sulla retta via il suo campione; e l'amore di Bradamante per Ruggero [*sic*], motivo ricorrente per tutto il poema. Non ometterei inoltre i seguenti temi: l'amore della bellissima Angelica per l'umile Medoro, e l'ingresso trionfale della Donna nella vita normale dei cavalieri, siano essi cristiani o pagani." Relazione di Achille Vesce [1942], CdB, AAB, CRS 17, CP 049, 0186, "Relazioni 'Orlando furioso' 1937, 1942."

70 "quel tanto che possa rendere coerente ed organica l'azione." Ibid.
71 "Tengano conto gli sceneggiatori che una folla di personaggi finirebbe per apparire una massa amorfa e senza volti, sulla quale le figure protagonistiche si staglierebbero a fatica." Ibid.
72 "Una interpretazione sintetica del poema sarebbe molto interessante. Ma [...] non sarebbe, in definitiva, una specie di album vivente di episodii slegati e non sempre comprensibili?" Ibid.
73 On Giacomo Debenedetti and cinema, see Paola Frandini, "Giacomo Debenedetti cinecritico, sceneggiatore e altro," *Studi Novecenteschi* 33, no. 2 (2006): 263–81.
74 "quello solo che un pubblico semplice ed avvezzo alla 'poetica' del cinema è in grado di afferrare." Relazione di Sergio Amidei e Giacomo De Benedetti [*sic*] [1942], CdB, AAB, CRS 17, CP 049, 0186, "Relazioni 'Orlando furioso' 1937, 1942."
75 "bisognerebbe prescindere dal carattere letterariamente più vero del poema ariostesco [...] che non è epico, ma di tutt'altra e più varia e sfuggente natura. La quale natura [...] sarebbe di per sé contraddittoria con l'assunto cinematografico." Ibid.
76 "sarebbe di per sé contraddittoria con l'assunto cinematografico. Anche a volere affrontare il poema nella sua specifica qualità narrativa (accettando che il suo *divenire* sia materiato [*sic*] da un continuo senso di fuga) si rischierebbe di trovarsi di fronte ad un incessante mutar di *accenti*; che, se costituisce – in questo suo stesso mutare – una riconoscibile e plausibile ragione di unità stilistico-letteraria; non potrebbe che ingenerare confusione e scarsa attendibilità in un racconto cinematografico (In una parola, si rischierebbe di eccitare l'impazienza di un pubblico avvezzo, da un certo punto in poi di un film, ad afferrare con chiarezza le fila della storia, a parteggiare per pochi personaggi contro pochi altri)." Ibid.
77 "violentare a volte lo spirito del Furioso per renderlo poi semplificato e accessibile alle esigenze dello schermo." Ibid.
78 "Per esprimerci con un esempio: sarebbe facile per compiacere ai creduti gusti popolari mettere alla base dell'opera la lotta tra cristiani ed infedeli, rivestendo i primi e i loro paladini e soldati di un'aura di santità e di misticismo; attribuendo invece ai secondi ogni empietà e barbarie. Mostrando i primi quali nobili difensori della patria minacciata e i secondi quali invasori e distruttori, così che la folla 'facesse il tifo' per i primi e avesse subito una facile esca all'emozione e all'interesse. Tutti gli elementi suddetti non mancano affatto di umanità, di poeticità, di bellezza e sono anche storicamente veri; ma non ci sono nell'Orlando." Relazione di Alberto Moravia [1942], CdB, AAB, CRS 17, CP 049, 0186, "Relazioni 'Orlando furioso' 1937, 1942."

79 "non si capirebbe allora perché si dovrebbe fare un film sull'Orlando e non, poniamo, sulla Gerusalemme Liberata [...] se non addirittura fare un nuovo soggetto intitolato 'il Segno della Croce' o qualcosa di simile che dagli antichi poemi [...] prendesse puramente lo spunto e gli elementi spettacolari e fantastici." Ibid.

80 "non si chiede al regista di essere un Ludovico Ariosto redivivo, il quale, se veramente il cinema è la nuova arte, riscriva l'Orlando in immagini cinematografiche anziché in ottave. Soltanto, a nostro parere, un film intitolato Orlando Furioso deve essere l'Orlando Furioso e non un'altra cosa." Ibid.

81 "Insomma alla base dell'Orlando Furioso non c'è un'idea politica o religiosa e tanto meno una polemica. Esso è quello che è, ossia una fiaba, un gioco meraviglioso della libera fantasia." Ibid.

82 "quell'aria svagata e avventurosa, leggera a gratuita, deliziosamente libera e irreale." Ibid.

Index

Page numbers in italics refer to figures.

Milton Keynes UK
Ingram Content Group UK Ltd.
UKHW051827040324
438897UK00021B/127/J